The New Testament and the Theology of Trust

The New Testament and the Theology of Trust

'This Rich Trust'

TERESA MORGAN

Great Clarendon Street, Oxford, OX2 6DP,
United Kingdom

Oxford University Press is a department of the University of Oxford.
It furthers the University's objective of excellence in research, scholarship,
and education by publishing worldwide. Oxford is a registered trade mark of
Oxford University Press in the UK and in certain other countries

© Teresa Morgan 2022

The moral rights of the author have been asserted

First Edition published in 2022

All rights reserved. No part of this publication may be reproduced, stored in
a retrieval system, or transmitted, in any form or by any means, without the
prior permission in writing of Oxford University Press, or as expressly permitted
by law, by licence or under terms agreed with the appropriate reprographics
rights organization. Enquiries concerning reproduction outside the scope of the
above should be sent to the Rights Department, Oxford University Press, at the
address above

You must not circulate this work in any other form
and you must impose this same condition on any acquirer

Published in the United States of America by Oxford University Press
198 Madison Avenue, New York, NY 10016, United States of America

British Library Cataloguing in Publication Data

Data available

Library of Congress Control Number: 2022930035

ISBN 978–0–19–285958–7

DOI: 10.1093/oso/9780192859587.001.0001

Links to third party websites are provided by Oxford in good faith and
for information only. Oxford disclaims any responsibility for the materials
contained in any third party website referenced in this work.

To the memory of Judith L. Kovacs
amica docta humana

Acknowledgments

This book was written partly under the auspices of the John Templeton Foundation-funded project 'The philosophy, theology, and psychology of Christian trust in God', and I am grateful to the Foundation for making the project possible. The core members of the research group, fellow-PIs Daniel McKaughan and Michael Pace, together with Don Davis, Peter Hill, Joshua Hook, Daniel Howard-Snyder, and Daryl van Tongeren, formed a remarkable group of interlocutors, and I have been greatly enriched by their range of expertise, diverse perspectives, generous help, and good conversation. Other members of the project came from an even wider range of disciplines, and particular thanks are due to Lara Buchak, Matthew Bates, Andrew Chignall, Oliver Crisp, Katherine Dormandy, Lindsay Driediger-Murphy, Judy Exline, Paul Faulkner, Judith Gundry Volf, and Benjamin Schliesser for their written and oral contributions.

Much of the book was prepared under various 'lockdowns' in 2020–1 during the Covid-19 pandemic, when there were fewer opportunities than usual to share work in progress at conferences and seminars. I am therefore especially grateful to Boston College, Cambridge University's CRASSH, Emory University, Leicester Theological Society, The Logos Institute of St Andrews University, Oxford University, and the Trustees of the Prideaux Lectures of the University and Diocese of Exeter, for invitations to give lectures and papers. Various chapters were generously read by Robert Audi, Helen Bond, Katherine Dormandy, Susan Hylen, Daniel McKaughan, Robert Morgan, George Newlands, Michael Pace, Joseph Spooner, Benjamin Schliesser, and Keith Ward, and I profited immensely from their stringent and stimulating comments and suggestions. Mak Sue Ann kindly suspended work on her D.Phil. to create the index of biblical passages.

During the writing of this book a dear friend and colleague, Professor Judith L. Kovacs, died. A distinguished New Testament scholar and patrologist, she was also, intellectually and personally, one of the most generous, engaging, and hospitable people it has been my privilege to know. In her last illness she corresponded with a number of colleagues about the relationship between scholarship and faith, and how the shadow of death affects one's thinking about it. She was concerned that life in the academy, in an increasingly secular culture, risks fostering unreflective scepticism more than reflective faith. She was not able to read this book, but she knew that I was concerned with what New Testament exegesis, and theological reflection on it, might have to contribute to contemporary Christian faith, and she gave permission for the book to be dedicated to her.

Contents

1. 'Trust is the foundation of things hoped for': The New Testament
   and the Study of Trust ... 1
   Trust at the Origins of Christian Faith ... 3
   Approaches to Trust in the Social Sciences and Philosophy ... 8
   The Psychology of Trust ... 18
   Trust in this Study: A Definition and Some Questions ... 22
   History, Theology, and the New Testament ... 26
   Outline of Chapters ... 31

2. 'The one who calls you is trustworthy': The *Pistis* of God ... 39
   Paul on the Trust, Trustworthiness, and Faithfulness of God ... 40
   Trust, Covenant, and Promise ... 50
   Foundations of Divine–Human Trust ... 64
   The Trustworthiness of God in Other New Testament Writings ... 67
   Trust and Risk ... 68
   Is God Reliable? ... 72
   An Unusual Form of Three-Place Trust? ... 75
   Trust, Trustworthiness, and Exemplarity ... 75
   Trust before Trust: God, Christ, and Creation ... 80
   Conclusion ... 90

3. 'So we preach and so you believed': *Pistis* between God, the Risen
   and Exalted Christ, and the Faithful ... 97
   The Role of Resurrection Belief in Trust ... 99
   Trust in Christ and Christ's Future Coming ... 109
   Trust in Cosmic Conflict ... 118
   The Exalted Christ as Mediator ... 122
   Further Activities of the Exalted Christ ... 127
   Living 'in Christ's Hands' ... 131
   Imitation of the Exalted Christ ... 135
   Trust and the Pre-existent Christ ... 136
   Conclusion ... 137

4. 'The righteousness of God has been revealed... through the *pistis* of
   Jesus Christ, for all who trust': Trust and Atonement ... 142
   Sin, Suffering, and *Apistia* ... 143
   Pistis and Reconciliation ... 153
   Why do Participants in the Nexus of Trust Trust One Another? ... 162
   Trust and Revelation in Christ's Death and Resurrection ... 164
   Did Christ Need to Die, and if so, Why? ... 167

Jesus' Suffering and Death as Exemplary	174
Trust, Suffering, and Sin	180
The Absence of Trust in the Passion Narratives	188
Pistis in Healings, Exorcisms, and Resurrections: Christ as Mediator and Imitating Christ	190
Conclusion	191

5. 'Because you have seen me, you have trusted': The Trustworthiness of Jesus Christ in his Earthly Life — 196
   Contexts and Consequences of Trust — 199
   The (Un)trustworthiness of Signs, Miracles, Prophecy, and Teaching — 202
   Finding *Pistis* in the Scriptures — 212
   Trustworthy Encounters — 214
   The *Pistis* of Jesus as a Model for Others — 219
   Jesus with God as Creator and Carer — 224
   Who is the Jesus in whom Trust is placed? — 229
   Trust and Revelation — 237
   Conclusion — 241

6. 'Your trust has saved you': Coming to Trust — 247
   Coming to Trust: Healing Stories — 247
   Coming to Trust: Challenge and Openness — 255
   The Adequacy of Imperfect Trust — 258
   The Failure to Trust — 263
   The Gospel Narratives and the Creation of Trust — 268
   Conclusion — 277

7. 'Guard this rich trust': The Entrustedness of the Faithful — 282
   Entrustedness and Trustworthiness in the Pauline Corpus — 283
   Entrustedness in the Synoptic Gospels and Acts — 291
   Entrustedness and the Scriptures — 297
   Trust, Power, and the Gift(s) of the Spirit — 298
   Towards an Ethic of Entrustedness — 312
   Conclusion — 319

8. 'This saying is trustworthy': Propositional Trust in the Divine–Human Relationship — 324
   Propositional Trust — 325
   Trust and the Challenge of Believing or Knowing — 328
   The Challenge of Knowing or Believing in Other Humanities Disciplines — 334
   Propositional Trust in the Face of Uncertainty — 343
   Four Test Cases for Propositional Trust — 346
   Propositional Trust and Metaphysical Choices — 351
   Propositional Doubt and Scepticism? — 353

    Propositional Trust in the Dialogue between History and Theology
        in New Testament Studies   354
    Conclusion   356

9. 'I trusted, therefore I spoke': Concluding Reflections   361

Bibliography   369
Index of Biblical Passages Cited   437
Index of Subjects   463

1

'Trust is the foundation of things hoped for'

The New Testament and the Study of Trust

This study argues for the recovery of trust as a central theme in Christian theology.[1]

In broad terms, trust can play either or both of two roles in theological thinking. It can constitute an aspect of the relationship between the human and the divine, or—in conjunction, for instance, with belief or knowledge, or in contrast to them—it can act as one of the foundations of the relationship.[2] What follows will explore both possibilities.

If we can make a case for either possibility, let alone both, it may seem surprising that trust has not played a larger role in theology hitherto. Since the late second century, however, when trust has been discussed at all, it has been seen as part of the broader attitude and practice of faith, which can also include, for instance, belief, knowledge, confidence, hope, fideism, prayer, and worship.[3] Some theologians and some churches have seen trust as a more significant aspect of faith than others. Clement of Alexandria and Augustine are both interested in the role of trust at the beginnings of faith, though both see belief and knowledge as more important when faith is more developed.[4] Martin Luther distinguishes two kinds of faith: acceptance of what God says as true, and trust in God as able and willing to bring about what God has promised.[5] The Heidelberg Catechism of 1563 affirms that '[t]rue faith is not only a sure knowledge whereby I hold for truth all that God has revealed to us in his Word, but also a hearty trust, which

---

[1] The chapter title quotation is from Heb. 11.1; see pp. 113–14.
[2] On the relationship between trust and the spirit, see pp. 298–312.
[3] I use 'fideism' throughout to refer to the idea of faith as independent of, or even adversarial to, reason (cf. Plantinga (1983), 87, Amesbury (2017)). Religions as systems, including 'the faith' of Christianity, as distinct from the attitude and practice of faith, can have further dimensions (Smart (1996)). On the Greek and Latin roots of 'faith', 'trust', and related terms see below, p. 4.
[4] E.g. Clem. Al., *Str.* 1.6.27, 2.3.13, 2.9.45, 2.12.55, cf. 2.2, 2.9–12, 2.4.14–15, 5.1; Aug., *Ver. rel.* 8.14, 24.45, *F. invis.* 1.2–3.4; cf. Or., *Cels.* 1.19–11, 2.3–4, 6.13.
[5] Luther, WA 7:215. In the *Preface to the Letter of Paul to the Romans*, Luther identifies faith with 'a living, bold trust in God's grace', but goes on to identify trust with both confidence in and knowledge of God's grace, two concepts which most modern commentators would distinguish from each other and from trust (Irmischer (1854), 63:125).

the Holy Spirit works in me by the gospel....'.[6] The Council of Trent (1545-63) includes trust among the steps by which human beings are justified before God.[7] In recent years some philosophers of religion have begun to suggest that trust is a more significant aspect of Christian faith than is usually recognized, though they have not explored it at length.[8] But most philosophers and theologians have preferred to write about faith, in all its complexity, rather than specifically about trust.[9] Two notable exceptions are Pierangelo Sequeri, who, in *Il Dio affidabile, L'idea della fede*, and elsewhere, has explored in depth the trustworthiness of God and the relationship between trust, reason, and truth, and Ingolf Dalferth and Simon Peng-Keller, who, in a trilogy of interdisciplinary volumes, have sought to characterize trust in God in the context both of Christian faith and of human trust.[10]

There are, though, good reasons for theology to take more interest in trust. One is simply that prima facie it deserves as much attention as belief, knowledge, hope, the 'leap of faith', the 'eye of faith', or other aspects of faith which attract more discussion. Another, as noted, is that philosophers of religion are increasingly interested in the importance of trust between God and humanity, and their arguments invite more engagement by theologians than they have yet received.[11] A third is that it has become clearer, in recent years, that trust (with related concepts such as trustworthiness and faithfulness) is important to writers of New

---

[6] 'Trust' translates *fiducia/Vertrauen* from the parallel text (Gerhart et al. (1863), 153). The catechism was controversial in seeking to modify Aquinas' view of faith as intellectual assent (e.g. *Summa* 2.2 ii a9).

[7] Denzinger et al. (2012), 798. These steps also include grace, hope, love, personal renewal, and faith (Mackey (1975), 208). In his entry on *pistis* in TDNT 6:203-15, Bultmann recognizes that New Testament writers sometimes use *pistis* language in a way that reflects mainstream Greek usage, to refer to trust or faithfulness, though he argues that they use it mainly to mean acceptance of the kerygma, saving faith in Christ, and the content of Christian faith (cf. Florkowski (1971), von Sass (2011)).

[8] Below, pp. 13-16.

[9] This study, since it focuses on trust, will not discuss theologies of the more complex concept faith, but see e.g. in the modern era McKenna (1914), Ebeling (1955, 1963), Tillich (1957), Mouroux (1959), Vallotton (1963), Hick (1967), Schreiber (1967), Coventry (1968), Malevez (1969), Congar (1969), Surlis (1972), Rousselot (1990), Dulles (1994), Gaziaux (1995), Sequeri (1996, 2002, 2007), Funda (2012), Beckermann (2013), Tirres (2014), Kirkpatrick (2016), Horn (2018). Mackey (1975) offers a survey of the theology of faith to date, observing that it is a relatively neglected field (so also Surlis (1972), ix). Dulles (1994) draws out the theological thinking about faith which, in many instances, is scattered throughout the works of a wide range of modern theologians.

[10] Sequeri (1993, 1996, 2002), Dalferth (1992, 2006, 2010, 2016), Hunziker and Peng-Keller (2009, 2010), Dalferth and Peng-Keller (2012a, 2012b, 2013), Peng-Keller and Hunziker (2011). Küng (1980), 442-78 discusses 'fundamental trust' as the 'Yes to the uncertain reality of himself and the world' which opens a person to reality, including the reality of God. Küng anticipates more recent studies in drawing on both philosophy and psychology for his models of trust. See also Brown (1969), Bourgeois (2000) (arguing that trust, rather than the content of belief, is fundamental to Christian faith), Lassak (2010, 2015) (arguing for the parallels between human and divine–human trust), Holtzen (2019). Bühler (2010) discusses Ebeling's view of trust as a response to grace. Schreiber (1967) focuses on the 'theology of trust' in Mark but does not clearly distinguish *Vertrauen* and *Glaube*.

[11] E.g. Cantwell Smith (1979), Jordan and Howard-Snyder (1996), Swinburne (2005), 147-58, Schellenberg (2005), 106-26, Davis (2006), Audi (2011a), 71-85, Crisp et al. (2012), McKaughan (2013, 2016, 2018a, 2018b), Rice, McKaughan, and Howard-Snyder (2017), and below, pp. 13-16.

Testament and other very early Christian writings.[12] Yet another is that trust in God plays a significant part in the thinking of modern Christians beyond the academy. A brief search reveals a wealth of recently published books with titles such as *Trusting God, Trust God's Plan, Voll Vertrauen, Vertrauen kann man nur auf Gott, Accroître sa foie en Dieu,* and *En los brazos del Padre: Confianza en Dios*.[13] In a 2017 study, Francesca Montemaggi found that relational trust in God was even more important to British evangelicals than the content of what they were taught to believe.[14] Social psychologists and psychologists of religion have long recognized the importance of trust in God to Jews, Muslims, and Christians, but theologians have yet to respond to them to any great extent.[15]

More study of trust by theologians, and even systematic theologies of trust, would therefore be welcome. This volume, however, has a more limited agenda. It aims to draw out some of the theological implications of 'trust' language in New Testament writings, recognizing that this language is not fully consistent, let alone exhaustive or systematic, but arguing that it forms one vital strand in Christian thinking with which it is worth entering into dialogue if one is interested in the nature of faith. In reflecting on the ways in which trust between God and humanity is characterized in these writings, this volume builds on the findings of my 2015 monograph *Roman Faith and Christian Faith*.[16]

Trust at the Origins of Christian Faith

Roman Faith and Christian Faith was a historical investigation into the meaning and operation of *pistis, fides,* and related concepts in the world of the early Roman principate. Using all the surviving literary and documentary sources from the first century BCE to the second century CE, it sought to map the historically distinctive shape of the cluster of ideas and practices represented by these lexica in this period, and to explore the role they played in the social and political life of the Roman empire (including in Hellenistic Judaism). Within this project, early Christianity formed an extended case study, exploring how one micro-society within the empire adopted a lexicon in common use to describe what it understood

---

[12] Below, pp. 3–5; cf. Hooker (1989), Hays (2002), Schliesser (2007), Morgan (2015a), with p. 270 n. 39 discussing recent interpretations, Frey, Schliesser, and Ueberschaer (2017), Oakes (2018), Bates (2020). On this cluster of meanings see below, pp. 7–8.

[13] Bridges (2016), Härry (2011), Drewermann (2020), Deville (2017), Martin (2020), Trigo (2013).

[14] Montemaggi (2017). 'Trust' has increasingly been written into contemporary liturgies and forms of worship: e.g. the Anglican *Common Worship: Services and Prayers for the Church of England* ((2000), 144) offers a version of the Creed which begins: 'Do you believe and trust in God the Father, source of all being and life, the one for whom we were made? *We believe and trust in him.*' Rowan Williams ((2007), viii) begins his 'introduction to Christian belief', *Tokens of Trust*, by saying, 'Basic to everything here is the idea that Christian belief is really about knowing who and what to trust.'

[15] Below, p. 8 n.107.   [16] Morgan (2015a).

as a (re)new(ed) relationship between human beings and the divine, and gradually, over time, adapted that lexicon to its increasingly distinctive understanding of that relationship. In other words, the book sought to show the beginnings of the process by which Greek and Roman *pistis* and *fides* became Christian faith. It argued, however, that this process was slower than is usually assumed. Most New Testament writings, for instance, use *pistis* language in ways which fall well within contemporary usage, and it is not until the late fourth century that we find *pistis* and *fides* used to describe Christian faith in what is almost its modern complexity.[17]

Pistis, *fides*, and their relatives, as they are used by Greek and Latin speakers in general, have very wide ranges of meaning, which are not absolutely identical in the two languages but are extremely similar.[18] Both *pistis* and *fides* (confining ourselves to the noun for the sake of simplicity) can mean 'trust', 'trustworthiness', 'faithfulness', 'loyalty', 'good faith', 'honesty', 'credibility', 'confidence', 'assurance', 'pledge', 'guarantee', financial 'credit', legal 'proof', 'credence', 'belief', a 'position of trust/trusteeship', a 'trust' in the sense of something with which one is entrusted, 'protection', or 'security'. The commonest meanings across the range of surviving literature and documents, which are almost certainly also the foundational meanings of both terms, are relational 'trust', 'trustworthiness', and 'faithfulness'.[19]

Roman Faith approached the use of this language in New Testament, and some other early Christian texts, as elsewhere, inductively, analysing it passage by passage, and found that early Christian texts are well in line with contemporary norms, almost always using *pistis*, *pisteuein*, *pistos*, and so on, to refer to relationships of trust, trustworthiness, and faithfulness—mostly, though not always, between God and/or Christ and human beings.[20] Relational *pistis* language can refer to an attitude, an action which helps to form and maintain a certain type of relationship, or both. Normatively, users of this language seem to assume that attitude, action, and

---

[17] Morgan (2021a, forthcoming).
[18] There are arguably more shades of legal meaning attested in Latin, while in Greek rhetoric and philosophy *pistis* may mean 'argument' as well as 'proof', but this may reflect the fact that more legal material survives in Latin and more philosophy in Greek. In general, '[t]he semantic correspondence... could not be fuller' (Calderone (1968), 92).
[19] Bates (2017, 2018) argues for translating *pistis* primarily as 'loyalty' or allegiance, which works well in some passages, but I take loyalty to be part of faithfulness, which has a wider application. On loyalty as part of *pistis* or trust see also Niebuhr (1989), 99, Fletcher (1993), Pace and McKaughan (2020) (who also argue that good sense can be made of traditions of exemplars of faith like Job, who protest to God within their relationship of trust and loyalty). I will take 'belief' to refer to the cognitive attitude which takes something to be the case or regards it as true (Schwitzgebel (2019)). Greek tends to use 'thinking' language (*nomizein*, *phronein*, *dokein*), together with *peithesthai*, rather than *pistis* language to refer to belief. English can use 'believing in' a person in a sense that seems to encompass both trust or confidence and belief, but, with most philosophers currently writing about trust, I think it preferable to distinguish between trust and belief, so I will try to avoid this potentially ambiguous phrase. There is little doubt that trust is the foundational meaning of *pistis* and *fides* language: Fraenkel (1916) tried to overturn this consensus, but a series of studies culminating in Freyburger (2007) has re-established it.
[20] This study will not argue at length whether the *pistis* language of every passage cited refers to trust, belief, or another meaning, but will sometimes refer to the analysis in *Roman Faith*.

relationship go together, but they also recognize, for instance, that sometimes people hold an attitude of *pistis* without acting, or act with *pistis* without holding the attitude.[21]

We have noted that *pistis* can mean 'belief', though it is not one of the commonest meanings of the word in the early principate, and the relationship between belief and trust will be one of the themes of this study. The dominance of belief over trust in most Christian thinking since late antiquity has led to a regular choice, in modern English translations of the New Testament, to render *pistis* with 'belief' language.[22] The fact that, as *Roman Faith* argued, very early Christian *pistis* language is usually better rendered as relational trust, faithfulness, and so on, does not, of course, mean that early Christians did not hold beliefs, nor that that New Testament writings, for instance, do not articulate beliefs or attribute them to characters within their narratives. They do, and on occasion they use *pistis* language in this, and also in other meanings. But *pistis*, for these writers, is above all an identity-defining, life-changing commitment to God and Christ which makes possible right-standing with God, salvation, new life and hope, an ongoing relationship with God and Christ, participation in a community, and certain types of activity. There are good reasons, both within the texts and in the social context in which they were written, to think that this kind of commitment demands more than belief.[23]

Jews and Jewish Christians of the early principate could identify a great leader as Messiah, Son of God, Son of Man, or Son of David; they could believe that a person had been raised from the dead or taken up to heaven like Abraham or Enoch, or that he would return from heaven like Elijah, without making a life-changing commitment to him, worshipping him, or thinking of him as God. For gentiles, the gap between belief and what they would have thought of, in broad terms, as worship (*therapeia, latreia, timē, eusebeia*), was even greater. Ancient

---

[21] It is less clear whether *pistis* is also an emotion, but it is, at least, often associated with other emotions (Morgan (2015a), 447–50). Barr (1961), 161–205 emphasizes the relationality of Hebrew *'emunah* and related terms, which, directly or via translation in the Septuagint and other writings, form one root of Christian thinking, and shows that their meanings of trust, belief, and truth are all grounded in God's stability and steadfastness.

[22] Though some more recent translations, notably the New American Bible, sometimes render *pistis* language with 'trust'.

[23] Most explicitly at Jas 2.19. We are concerned here with qualifying attitudes, not with identifying practices or rituals such as baptism and participation in the eucharist. 'Christ-confessor' (cf. Rom. 10.9) and 'faithful' are used throughout as reflecting contemporary insider language; I avoid 'believer' on the basis that it is not belief per se that leads to righteousness or salvation, and 'Christ-worshipper' because it remains debatable whether very early Christians worshipped Christ (below, p. 6 n.26, pp. 97–8 n.5). Belief is not only not enough to identify a Christ-confessor in this period: some Christians seem to have continued to frequent Greek and Roman temples, suggesting that even if they were interested enough in the possibility that there was one 'true and living God' (cf. 1 Thess. 1.9) to be baptized, they did not believe it in a sense which would have made it nonsensical to continue to cultivate other gods. In addition, community members are not recorded as being excluded for holding wrong beliefs until at least the mid-second century (Tert., *Praes. Her.* 30.2, of Marcion; Lieu (2015), 396 thinks even mid-second-century references to excommunication are probably anachronistic).

polytheists believed in the existence and qualities of many divinities whom they did not themselves worship: not least because many were divinities of a particular tribe, city, or locality which was not the worshipper's own, or because the divinity offered something, such as healing or oracular advice, which the worshipper happened not to need.[24] To believe that a certain divine or heavenly being existed and to believe certain things about him or her was distinct from committing to a relationship with that being: putting one's trust in, relying on, confessing, or worshipping him or her.[25] Whether or not we think that the relationship of the earliest Christians to Jesus Christ amounted to worship of Christ, it is beyond doubt that they were called to make a life-changing commitment to Christ, and so to take a decisive step beyond believing propositions about him.[26] The language early Christians use for that step is *pistis*, in what must therefore be not just a propositional, but a relational sense.[27]

The importance of *pistis* language to early Christ-confessors is evident everywhere in the writings of the New Testament and beyond.[28] It is present in every New Testament text apart from 2 John. It appears fourteen times in the five chapters of 1 Thessalonians, probably the earliest surviving Christian writing in its present form, and is integral to some of the most creative and influential thinking in Paul's letters. Every layer of tradition in the synoptic gospels puts it in the mouth of Jesus, and it is used a hundred times in the gospel of John, usually by Jesus.[29] Within books of all genres, *pistis* is widely distributed, and is used of God and human beings, individuals and groups, of conversion and of life in communities of the faithful. Occurrences of *pistis* language far outnumber those of other key concepts such as love, righteousness, salvation, and hope; no contemporary or

---

[24] Polytheists sometimes offer cult to divinities whom they regard as ill-disposed towards human beings (such as the Erinyes), to encourage good relations. Though most, if not all Jews and Christians in this period probably believe in the existence of demons or evil or unclean spirits, there is no sign that they worship them, marking that for them, the gap between belief and trust, confession, or worship is even greater than for polytheists.

[25] Cf. Moser (2010), 110: 'belief becomes faith when...the one who has these beliefs actually entrusts himself, relying upon the one the evidential beliefs identify and characterize, and engages in trust for the goods in question'.

[26] The vigour of recent debate about whether or not very early Christians worshipped the risen Christ suggests that if they did not, what they did came close to worship (cf. e.g. Segal (1977), Bauckham (1981), France (1982), Hurtado (1988, 2003), *contra* Stuhlmacher (1965), 211, Roetzel (1972), 113, Aune (2002), 81–3), and see also Newman et al. (1999). Gentile former polytheists surely found the idea of worshipping Christ easier than did Jewish Christians.

[27] On the involvement of beliefs and/or other attitudes in trust see also pp. 218–19.

[28] Though with a few exceptions (including some apostolic letters, arguably *The Shepherd of Hermas*, and the gnostic *Pistis Sophia*), it is not nearly as common in non-canonical early writings, and this is one reason why *Roman Faith* focused mainly on New Testament writings. In light of Christians' persistent interest in *pistis/fides*, their wealth of *pistis* language may have contributed to certain writings' becoming canonical, but that process is beyond our purview.

[29] This points to the significant possibility that the historical Jesus called people to trust: probably in God, though conceivably also in himself. The synoptic gospels often leave open whether Jesus is telling the disciples to trust in God or in him; John's Jesus explicitly tells them to do both (Morgan (2015a), 350–1, 354–9, 400–1, 424).

earlier corpus of texts, Jewish or gentile, makes such extensive use of it. *Pistis* language therefore forms the single most dominant cluster of terms and concepts in very early Christian writings, and one distinctive to Christian discourse.[30]

The findings of *Roman Faith*, however, raise questions which that book did not consider. If relational *pistis* plays a leading role in the earliest Christian accounts of the relationship between God, Christ, and humanity, how should we understand it, not only historically but theologically?[31] And how might that understanding affect our understanding of Christian faith or Christian life more broadly? These are the basic questions of this study.

The findings of *Roman Faith* also help to define the scope of 'trust' (*Vertrauen, confiance, fiducia, confianza*) for our purposes. 'Trust' will serve as an umbrella term under which we will also discuss faithfulness, trustworthiness, and entrustedness: the cluster of relationships which stand at the heart of early Christian *pistis*.[32] Trust, faithfulness, trustworthiness, and entrustedness hang together in Greek both conceptually and linguistically. *Pistis* (and *fides*) is an 'action nominal', one of the class of nouns (relatively common in both Greek and Latin) derived from verbs which abandon distinctions of transitivity to encompass both active and passive meanings of the verb.[33] *Pistis* therefore means both the trust I put in you and the trustworthiness I attribute to you and which (ideally) you display; it means both my faithfulness to you (say, as your slave) and yours to me (as my mistress). *Pistis* is a social virtue (unlike, for instance, wisdom or self-control,

---

[30] The findings of *Roman Faith* have been discussed e.g. by Frey, Schliesser, and Ueberschaer (2017), Howard-Snyder (2017, 2018), Pace (2017), Alexander (2018), Driediger-Murphy (2018), Konstan (2018), Lieu (2018), McKaughan (2018a), Oakes (2018), Seifrid (2018), Watson (2018), Bates (2018), Downs and Lappenga (2019), Gupta (2020), Pace and McKaughan (2020).

[31] Morgan (2015a) offers a number of reasons why *pistis* may have become so important to Christians so early, including that Jesus may be remembered as teaching people to trust in God; it is prominent in the Exodus narrative; it is widely treated in the early principate as a paradigmatic virtue of times of crisis and opportunity and a building block of new societies; and both the Jewish scripture and gentile writings can speak of God or gods as trustworthy. Here, we will propose some other reasons based on the way trust is represented in New Testament writings, but we will not suggest that trust is a consequence of e.g. the Thomist desire for good, Newman's illative sense, or Rousselot's 'natural knowledge', see also p. 347 n.103.

[32] Trustworthiness and faithfulness are not always easy to distinguish, but where either is possible or both are involved I will normally use 'faithfulness' where the emphasis is on a long-term relationship, and 'trustworthiness' where the emphasis is on a particular moment or action: e.g. God is faithful to Israel through time (and, of course, by that token trustworthy), but trustworthy in (the new act of) the Christ event; the slaves of Mt. 25.14–30 are no doubt consistently faithful to their master, but when they are given the talents the immediate issue is that they should be trustworthy in carrying out their commission. NB it is possible to be faithful without being trustworthy (if, for instance, one were not very capable), and trustworthy on a particular occasion without being faithful in the longer term.

[33] Comrie and Thompson (2007), 334–76. A classic example is the *pistis* or *fides* of a Roman magistrate, which is usually taken to be his trustworthiness: the quality which reassures those over whom he has power that he will fulfil his office with integrity (Freyburger (2007), 206–8). This trustworthiness, however, is not self-sufficient, but is founded on the magistrate's trust in (or loyalty to) the laws of his city or state, his trust in (or devotion to) the gods, sometimes on his virtue (which itself is probably understood as founded on his relationship with the divine), and on his trust in the people to allow him to govern. The magistrate's *fides* is therefore two-sided: he is both trusting and trustworthy, and *qua* magistrate he would not be trustworthy unless he were simultaneously understood as trusting.

which one can practise equally well in isolation). I cannot trust if there is no one to trust,[34] be entrusted if there is no one to entrust me with something, or be trustworthy if there is no one to whom to be trustworthy, so my trustworthiness is linked with your trust, and so on. At various points we will discuss the connections between relational *pistis* and other meanings of *pistis* language in New Testament writings, but these will not be our main focus.[35]

It is worth repeating that what follows will not claim that trust, trustworthiness, faithfulness, and entrustedness constitute all the possible, or interesting, meanings of *pistis* language, in Greek in general or even in New Testament texts: only that they are, for these writers, the most significant meanings of that language. Nor is the idea of trust invariably couched in *pistis* language. From time to time we will also discuss *paradidonai* and *paratithenai*, terms for entrusting and for something which is entrusted, and the language of confidence, hope, and obedience, not to mention fear, doubt, and scepticism, which are sometimes so closely associated with trust as to be almost inseparable from it.[36] Above all, what follows will not claim that Christian faith, as it has been understood at any time, is synonymous with trust: only that trust is an important and under-discussed aspect of it. (It will reserve the term 'faith' for the complex concept, and avoid using it as an alternative to trust, faithfulness etc.) What follows will, however, argue that the operation of trust in the relationship between God, Christ, and humanity is, for Christians, historically and theologically foundational, and that by exploring it we do better justice to our understanding of Christian faith.[37]

Approaches to Trust in the Social Sciences and Philosophy

If trust has been relatively neglected within theology, it has, for the past half-century, been a topic of sustained interest elsewhere: notably in political and social theory, economics, anthropology, history, philosophy (including the philosophy of religion), and psychology (including the psychology of religion).[38] *Roman Faith* drew on research on the social sciences and history: disciplines which focus on how trust works to form, shape, and maintain communities and relationships between people. It investigated why *pistis* was so important to early Christians by asking how, in early texts, it helps to create a relationship between God, Christ, and humanity; how it gives that relationship, and the communities

---

[34] Though that person may only be myself.
[35] On the history of interpretation of New Testament *pistis* language see Morgan (2015a), 7–15.
[36] Throughout Christian history and across cultures: e.g. Wiles (1975), Weber (1998), Pelkmans (2013). Fear refers here to negative fear, not appropriate fear of God.
[37] On the relationship between history and theology see pp. 26–31, 354–6.
[38] Morgan (2015a), 15–21 surveys key developments in the social sciences and history.

that embody it, a distinctive shape; and how the relationship is understood as enduring and evolving between the resurrection and the end time.[39]

This historical approach and its findings were appropriate in their own terms, but there is more to be said from a different perspective.[40] *Roman Faith* focused more on how *pistis* between God, Christ, and humanity works than on what it is; more on the way it shapes communities than on what it means to community members; on its significance for early writers but not its significance today. This study draws on the rich and fast-growing scholarship on trust in moral philosophy, the philosophy of religion, and psychology, to help it frame some new questions and reframe old questions in new terms. When and why do New Testament writers affirm that God is trustworthy, and in what sense? Is their account satisfying? Do New Testament writings encourage listeners or readers to trust equally in Jesus of Nazareth in his earthly life and death and in the risen and exalted Christ? Must life-changing trust be predicated on belief (for instance, in the resurrection), and, if so, on what understanding of belief? What does it mean for an apostle, or any Christian, to be entrusted by God and Christ with the gospel or the gifts of the spirit?

Behind these questions, and behind the difference between *Roman Faith* and this study, lies a long-standing and complex debate about the relationship between history and theology in general, and in the study of the New Testament in particular. We will have a little more to say about this below, but first it is worth outlining some of the work in related disciplines which is particularly relevant to this volume.

If the social sciences and history see trust primarily as a practice which creates and maintains communities, psychology and philosophy see it primarily as a cognitive attitude held by an individual in regard to another individual. For many early studies the starting-point was what is going on in the mind of a person who trusts. The social psychologist Roy Lewicki, for example, defines the person who trusts as holding 'confident positive expectations regarding another's conduct'.[41] Interest in the attitude of the 'truster', however, quickly led to interest in what the

---

[39] Morgan (2015a), 222–3, cf. Morgan (2020), 209–10.
[40] Occasionally I will note a change of mind about a particular point.
[41] Lewicki et al. (1998), 439, cf. Lewicki et al. (2006), 1002, which also offers a helpful discussion of approaches to trust in psychology to date. Denise Rousseau's team, which is also influential in the psychological study of trust, characterizes trust as 'a psychological state comprising the intention to accept vulnerability based on positive expectations of the intentions or behaviour of another' (Rousseau et al. (1998), 400; cf. Bhattacharya et al. (1998), 481, McKnight et al. (1998)). Dictionaries struggle to formulate definitions which range widely enough without becoming vague or tautologous: e.g. the *OED* offers a series of definitions limited in some directions and vague in others: 'confidence in or reliance on some quality or attribute of a person or thing or the truth of a statement', 'confident expectation', 'confidence in the ability and intention of a buyer to pay at a future time for goods supplied', 'the quality of being trustworthy', 'the condition of having confidence reposed in one', and 'the confidence reposed in a person in whom the legal ownership of property is vested to hold or use for the benefit of another'.

truster believes (or hopes, assumes, or speculates) about the attitude of the 'trustee'. The political theorist Russell Hardin, in a series of monographs on trust, trustworthiness, and distrust which has been influential across disciplines, argues that one person is more likely to trust another when at least one of the following is true:

- the truster thinks the trustee will be able to respond to his trust,
- the truster thinks it is in the trustee's interest to maintain a relationship with him,
- the trustee has a perceived moral commitment to trustworthiness,
- the trustee has a perceived psychological disposition to trustworthiness,[42]
- the truster thinks the trustee is (e.g. professionally) competent,
- the trustee has a perceived commitment to professional integrity.[43]

A recurring question in the chapters that follow will be how far trust between human beings is analogous to trust between human beings, God, and Christ, in at least some of these respects.

Hardin shares with most scholars in the social sciences and psychology the view that trust is typically 'three-place'. One person does not normally trust another independently of circumstances (which would be 'two-place' trust), but trusts the other for something, or to do something.[44] This could be something small and discrete, like buying a carton of milk, or something large and ongoing, like being faithful within a life partnership.[45] Another question of this study will be whether trust between human beings, God, and Christ is two-place or three-place.

Among philosophers, whether trust between human beings is typically two- or three-place is one of a series of debates which trace their origins to a

---

[42] Hardin (2006), 16–18, cf. (2002), ch. 2. See Mayer, Davis, and Schoorman (1995) for a very similar analysis; cf. Brownlow (1992), Jones (1996), Sheppard and Sherman (1998), 425–31, Ben-Ner and Halldorsson (2010).

[43] Within these broad outlines, every aspect of what trust is and does has generated further questions, some of which will appear in later chapters: what kind of state of mind is trust (rational or emotional)? On what basis does one person judge the trustworthiness of another (evidence-based belief, reason, hope, a wager, or something else)? Does someone who trusts choose to make a positive assessment about another or is she compelled to do so (by evidence, temperament, or force of circumstances)? What difference does it make whether the trustee is a human being, an organization, a process, or an inanimate object (or, we might add, a divine being)? Are fear, doubt, or scepticism compatible with trust?

[44] Some philosophers also recognize 'one-place' trust: on one-, two- and three-place trust see Faulkner (2015); cf. Simpson (2013), debating Hardin's 'instrumental' account of trust. For a recent account of trust drawing eclectically on the sciences and social sciences see Mercier (2020).

[45] Trusting another person for something can be either 'predictive'—if, for instance, I trust that you will wash the car this weekend, as you promised—or 'normative'—if I trust you, in general, to fulfil your promises (see the discussion of Dormandy (2020b), 2–7). Since it is axiomatic for early Christians that God fulfils what God promises and that for which they trust appropriately in God, and they hope that they will be able to fulfil what God entrusts to them, between God, Christ, and humanity predictive and normative trust, for practical purposes, hold together.

groundbreaking essay by Annette Baier.[46] Observing that philosophers had had surprisingly little to say about trust, and recognizing that trust between people can have both positive and negative consequences, Baier sought to establish the features of morally proper trust.[47] She argues that trust is related to, and often involves, reliance, but they are not the same thing because, though you can be let down by something or someone you rely on, you can only be betrayed by someone you trust.[48] My trusting a person involves depending on her goodwill towards me, which means that I am vulnerable to her, so '[t]rust...is accepted vulnerability to another's possible but not expected ill will (or lack of good will) toward one'.[49]

We trust people, Baier holds, even though it makes us vulnerable, because human beings are not self-sufficient on any level, from the practical to the emotional.[50] This basic observation, she observes, has not been sufficiently taken into account in western moral philosophy. The theorists who dominate the field have tended to see trust as a form of contract, established voluntarily, on the basis of reason and self-interest, by equal, autonomous adults.[51] Such relationships, Baier points out, may be the norm for 'adult males whose dealings with others are mainly business or restrained social dealings with similarly placed males',[52] but they not the norm for human beings in general. We should look for paradigms of trust among family members, lovers, friends, the very young or very old and their carers, and those of unequal power and status. Among these, trust looks very different.[53] The trust between infants and their parents, for instance, involves trust, or self-entrusting, by one who is effectively powerless and has little or no control over the other. It is not earned or won by the other person, but is given a priori, unless and until it is destroyed, and it is not specifically contractual because it is not given with a view to a specific return.[54] One of its features (though Baier makes this observation without discussing it in detail) is that it is liable to be 'two-place' rather than 'three-place'. In a relationship, one trusts someone before one trusts them for something, and one may go on trusting them even when one does not need anything from them.[55]

None of Baier's claims has been uncontroversial, but all have attracted strong support and much discussion and further development.[56] Richard Holton develops one of them to argue that although, in his view, trust is commonly three-place, it can also be two-place.[57] Suppose, for example, a rock climber needs help at a

---

[46] Baier (1986). For overviews of recent debates in the philosophy of trust see Hawley (2012). Further sources of interest in trust include interest in the relationship between trust and belief in the philosophy of religion (below, pp. 13–16), and concern with the role of trust in contemporary public life (e.g. O'Neill (2002)).
[47] pp. 231–2. [48] pp. 234–5. [49] p. 235. [50] p. 236.
[51] pp. 244–53. She identifies this form of thinking especially with Kant. [52] p. 248.
[53] pp. 249–50. Baier draws here on the work of Carol Gilligan (1982): see p. 16.
[54] pp. 240–3. [55] pp. 258–9.
[56] For a discussion of Baier's argument see Faulkner and Simpson (2017), 1–3, cf. Faulkner (2007).
[57] Holton (1994), 69–70; cf. Gratton (1982), distinguishing interpersonal trust from 'doxic confidence' and contractual trust in socio-economic contexts.

certain point in a climb. He can grasp a nearby rope, or take the offered hand of a fellow-climber. He believes that both are reliable, but when he takes the hand, he acknowledges that his fellow-climber wants to help him, affirms the relationship of trust between them, and strengthens it. This relationship can persist even when the climb is over, so trust can be more than three-place. Victoria McGeer and Philip Pettit take one aspect of this view further, arguing that, by trusting another person and offering him (what we think or hope he will see as) a positive vision of himself as trustworthy, we may boost his sense of his own trustworthiness and his self-confidence, and inspire him to become more trustworthy.[58]

The idea that trusting someone can inspire them to become more trustworthy is known as 'therapeutic trust'.[59] It is further developed by Michael Pace in an article which argues that trusting someone means 'being confident enough to take certain kinds of risk on someone's proving trustworthy'.[60] In some circumstances, it is reasonable to do this even if one is not, at this point, confident that it will work.[61] This kind of trust, however, Pace argues, only makes sense in the short term, because it relies on the idea that trusting the other person encourages or inspires them, and this is typically an immediate or short-term type of response.[62] Pace is discussing relationships between human beings, but his analysis raises the question whether, for instance, we can imagine God offering human beings therapeutic trust, and if so, whether this too must be short-term, or whether it may also be long-term.

Stephen Darwall builds on the work of Richard Holton, together with that of Karen Jones and Peter Strawson, to argue that trust is a 'participant attitude' which belongs to a participant in a relationship, rather than an 'objective attitude' which is held by a person towards a (human or non-human) object.[63] When we trust we lay ourselves open to another person, hoping that our trust will be accepted and returned. In the process, we do not so much recognize a vulnerability and find a way to mitigate it, as a contractual account of trust might claim, as create a vulnerability by offering our trust to another person. The result is not the creation of a relationship which lessens vulnerability, but the creation of a relationship in which we continue to be vulnerable, but which is worthwhile for its own sake.[64]

---

[58] McGeer and Pettit (2017). Jones (2017) offers an explanation for our typical expectation that someone who is trusted will respond positively to our trust, on the basis that we all have an interest in living cooperative social lives.

[59] Horsburgh (1960), Frost-Arnold (2014a, 2014b).   [60] Pace (2020), 4.

[61] pp. 11–4. One can also trust without being sure that trust will be justified without therapeutic intent: e.g. if the trust is worth the risk. Some argue that therapeutic trust is not true trust because it does not involve belief, but I follow the increasing number of scholars who argue that trust need not always involve belief (e.g. Holton (1994), Hieronymi (2008)).

[62] pp. 22–5.   [63] Darwall (2017).   [64] pp. 46–8.

Some of those who emphasize the relationality of trust, some of whom also argue for the primacy of two-place over three-place trust, are indebted not only to Baier but also to a 1956 monograph by the philosopher and theologian Knud Eijer Løgstrup.[65] *The Ethical Demand* is an account of those ethical foundations of human life which, Løgstrup argues, are prior to any other social or ethical norms. It begins with an extended discussion of the love command in the gospels, which, for Løgstrup, rests on Jesus' recognition of the fundamental fact and value of human interdependence. Jesus exhorts human beings to recognize and embrace their interdependence by coming to depend on each other so deeply that what they say or do to each other becomes of decisive importance for their lives. To understand the nature of this interdependence, Løgstrup holds, they must understand and recognize the importance of trust. Trust is fundamental to all human lives: 'It is a characteristic of human life that we normally encounter one another with natural trust.'[66]

To trust, in Løgstrup's view, is 'to lay oneself open'.[67] Trust is a form of self-surrender: when we trust, we 'dare[d] to come forward in the hope of being accepted...Through the trust which a person either shows or asks of another person he or she surrenders something of his or her life to that person.'[68] We offer ourselves and ask someone to give himself in return. When another person trusts himself to us in this way, we have a choice whether to harm him or take care of him. This, for Løgstrup, is, ethically, no choice: '[o]ut of this basic dependence and direct power arises the demand that we take care of that in the other person's life which is dependent upon us and which we have in our power'.[69] Care, however, does not involve objectifying or disempowering the other person. 'Responsibility for the other person never consists in our assuming the responsibility which is his or hers.'[70]

Many of Løgstrup's arguments run parallel to those of Baier and her successors. Many of the themes they explore are also central to this study, including the roles of vulnerability, reliance, and care in divine–human trust; the roles of self-entrusting, entrusting of the other, and therapeutic trust; and who benefits from the relationship and how.

Another study indebted to Baier's work, which also draws extensively on recent philosophy of belief and studies of trust in other disciplines, is Joseph J. Godfrey's *Trust of People, Words and God: A Route for Philosophy of Religion*.[71] Godfrey argues (against what he thinks many Christians take for granted) that belief is not enough for salvation. The divine–human relationship also depends on trust,

---

[65] Notably Domenicucci and Holton (2017), who also describe some of the ways (relatively little considered in the literature) that trust can be unwelcome or difficult, sometimes putting relationships under tension rather than strengthening them.
[66] Løgstrup (1997), 8.   [67] p. 9.   [68] pp. 10, 17.   [69] p. 28.   [70] p. 28.
[71] Godfrey (2012) (he does not seem to know Løgstrup).

which Godfrey understands as both an attitude and an action.[72] Trust, moreover, is not only an interpersonal relationship: we also trust propositions which, Godfrey suggests, form some of the bases of interpersonal trust.[73] Godfrey identifies four main types of trust, which have in common that they make us 'receptive to enhancement', changing and enlarging us in positive ways.[74] Among the themes which emerge from Godfrey's wide-ranging discussion and rich engagement with other philosophers is that interpersonal trust does not arise in a 'Cartesian subject in isolation' but through mutual human awareness;[75] that trust can appropriately coexist with doubt and scepticism, which keep us from naïve credulity;[76] that it is reasonable to understand trust in God as analogous to trust between human beings;[77] and that trust can be a foundation of knowledge 'insofar as knowledge can be supported by taking well the reliable word of another person'.[78] Godfrey makes clear that his book is a study in the philosophy of religion, not in Christian theology, but he rightly suggests that it offers much food for theological thought.[79]

While Godfrey was writing, I. U. Dalferth and Simon Peng-Keller were editing three collections of essays on trust in the secular and sacred spheres. *Kommunikation des Vertrauens* brings together scholars of trust in a range of therapeutic disciplines, economics, and education, to examine the nature of trust and trustworthiness between human beings.[80] The editors draw from these contributions a definition of trust as a 'practical attitude' (encompassing cognition and action) which also involves emotion, and argue that, since the trustworthiness of another person can never be established beyond doubt, trust always involves some kind of 'leap of faith'.[81] *Gottvertrauen: die ökumeische Diskussion um die Fiducia*, as its title suggests, focuses on the relationship between trust and faith, considered historically, exegetically, and theologically.[82] The editors conclude that trust is essential to the divine–human, as to human relationships.[83] Trust in God is distinctive, however, in that, when God reaches out to us in grace,

---

[72] pp. ix, 87, 89. He sees trust as central to all religions, but sometimes falls into using markedly Christian language when discussing religions in general.

[73] p. xi; though he does not explore propositional trust far. Godfrey is sceptical of the functional approach to trust in the social sciences (p. 57). His four types of (mutually compatible) trust are reliance trust (which relies on someone to help us in a specific way), I–thou trust (which entrusts another person with ourselves, because of the person they are, for the sake of our relationship), security trust (in which we have a sense of being secure, at home), and openness trust (which is a disposition of openness and receptivity towards the world and all it offers) (pp. 28–56).

[74] p. 89. [75] p. 220. [76] p. 168. [77] pp. 396–9. [78] p. 198 and ch 6, *passim*.
[79] Ch. 11, *passim*.
[80] Dalferth and Peng-Keller (2012a), with discussion of the trilogy by Schmiedel (2014).
[81] p. 20.
[82] Dalferth and Peng-Keller (2012b). The editors see faith as a way of life and trust as part of it, and aim to establish a 'hermeneutics of religious trust' under which Christian trust can be considered (pp. 8, 431). Contributions include studies of *'emunah* and *pistis* in the Hebrew Bible and New Testament, of mediaeval debates about faith, and of the writings of Zwingli and Melanchthon on trust in God.

[83] They also think it always involves belief (pp. 410–1).

we trust God 'all or nothing'.[84] *Grundvertrauen: Hermeneutik eines Grenzphänoms* seeks to connect the previous two volumes by establishing a working definition of trust that can be used in both human and divine–human contexts.[85] The editors compare models of 'basic trust' in developmental psychology and the social sciences, and propose an inter-disciplinary definition of trust as 'accepted vulnerability'.[86] Many of the themes of these studies parallel those we have seen elsewhere, but Dalferth and Peng-Keller are unusual in seeking not only to use the insights of one discipline or more to illuminate another, but to establish an account of trust which is equally defensible in multiple disciplines. Their questions about the relationship between human and divine–human trust will recur here.

A number of philosophers of religion have become interested in trust via an interest in the nature of faith or belief. In recent years, some of the most influential voices in the field, including William Alston, Robert Audi, Richard Swinburne, and Nicholas Wolterstorff, have recognized or explored the role of trust in faith in the course of investigating the nature and foundations of belief in God.[87] Meanwhile, a growing group of 'pistologists' is interested in the extent to which faith (Christian or secular) may not require belief, or not belief alone, but instead, or additionally, acceptance, reliance, hope, imaginative assent, credence, 'belief-less assuming', loyalty, faithfulness, self-entrustment, or propositional or relational trust.[88] Not all of those who think that faith need not be doxastic (that is, have belief content) think that its non-doxastic aspect is, or includes, trust or faithfulness, but for many trust and faithfulness are central to Christian faith.

Daniel McKaughan has argued in a series of articles that Christian faith is centrally relational, rather than centrally cognitive, and has shown that his model of

---

[84] pp. 425–6.   [85] Dalferth and Peng-Keller (2013).
[86] p. 212. They distinguish this both from reliance and from mistrust and doubt. They also suggest that it may be possible to see basic trust between human beings as a kind of secularized trust in God (pp. 11, 201).
[87] Below, pp. 326, 328, 331–2: see e.g. Swinburne (2005), 147–58, Wolterstorff (1983), 398, cf. (1964), Alston (1996), Schellenberg (2005), 106–26, (2013), Audi (2008, 2011a), Zagzebski (2012); cf. Chignell (2013), Pawar (2016), Michon (2017); cf. Schreiber (1967), Hart (1994), who also note that trust deserves more attention. McCraw (2015), 141 claims that it is now a platitude that faith in God involves trust; if so, it is still surprisingly little explored. Among those who argue that trust is not part of belief of faith are Muyskens (1979), Pojman (1986), Tennant (1989), Sessions (1994); Dougherty's (2014) argument that faith and trust are the same thing does not do justice either to the complexity of Christian faith or to other recent discussions of faith and trust.
[88] E.g. Pojman (1986), McKaughan (2013) (propositional hope); Golding (1990), Buckareff (2005), Howard-Snyder (2013, 2016, 2017) (assuming, cf.; Alston (1996, 2007), McKaughan (2013) (acceptance); Schellenberg (2005, 2013) (imaginative assent); Moser (2010) (self-entrustment); Buchak (2012, 2017a, 2017b, 2018) (credence); McKaughan (2013, 2016, 2017) (propositional trust); Rath (2017) (propositional reliance); Niebuhr (1989), Pace and McKaughan (2020) (trust and loyalty); Kvanvig (2016, 2018) (loyalty) with McKaughan and Howard-Snyder (2021); Helm (2000), Stump (2018) (relational trust). Eklund (2018, cf. 2014) outlines the main lines of the argument that faith need not involve belief, though he concludes (probably, I think, in line with New Testament writings) that their alternatives fail to show that non-doxastic attitudes can fulfil the cognitive requirements of Christian faith; cf. the similar conclusions of Collier (2003), Malcolm (2018).

faith fits well with the way in which New Testament writings portray trust in God and Christ.[89] He also shows that people of faith can be said to have faith in God, and be faithful or trusting, even when they undergo significant periods of doubt or feel they do not believe.[90] He takes St Teresa of Calcutta as an example of someone whom Christians readily identify as a person of faith and trust in God, but who, for much of her life, suffered profound doubts about God's love for her.[91] Her doubts coexisted with an extraordinarily resilient faithfulness which kept her in her vows and her vocation. Michael Pace has shown how relational faith and trust can vary in strength in two dimensions: in how far they motivate a person to take risks, and in how resilient they make a person to counterevidence. He concludes that his analysis fits well with what we hear in the gospels, for instance, about the possibility of Jesus' followers having little faith or being encouraged to have more.[92]

Baier's approach to trust was developed in part out of Carol Gilligan's seminal monograph on the moral development of male and female children, *In a Different Voice*.[93] Gilligan's work was also foundational for the development of the ethics of care. Care ethicists recognize human beings as by their nature interdependent, and as created and nurtured in and by relationships.[94] Like Baier and other feminist philosophers, they resist models of ethical agency in which agents are primarily independent, autonomous individuals acting in the public sphere.[95] Care, which is understood as both an attitude and a practice, is seen as fundamental to human flourishing, even the fundamental human good, and some care ethicists also recognize explicitly that care involves trust.[96] Care ethics is increasingly engaging theologians, for whom it is axiomatic that human beings exist aboriginally in a relationship with God the Creator which is often characterized as one of care,[97] and the relationship between care and trust will also interest us in the chapters that follow.[98]

This brief survey of a sizeable cluster of approaches to trust, many of which, at the time of writing, are developing in dialogue with one another, but by no means

---

[89] McKaughan (2013, 2016, 2017, 2018a, 2018b). He observes that the relative lack of interest in New Testament writings in the interiority of *pistis* makes it hard to claim [or, at least, to be certain] that their view of trust or faith requires belief in the sense of an interior attitude, and this opens to question not only the importance of belief to early Christians, but its central place in Christian faith today.
[90] McKaughan (2016, 2018a).   [91] (2017), 23–7, cf. McKaughan (2016), 73–4.
[92] Pace (2017), developing an idea of Howard-Snyder (2013).
[93] Gilligan (1982).   [94] Held (2006), 46.   [95] Ruddick (2002), Slote (2007), 1.
[96] Koehn (1998), ch. 3, Held (2006), 30, 37, Noddings (1984), 7–8, Kittay (2020), 34–5.
[97] E.g. Sang (2007), de Lange (2014), Mannering (2020).
[98] Some care ethicists also argue for a distinctive and much discussed view of justice, seeing it as intrinsic to relationships of care, but not as involving the 'blind', even-handed application of the same principles in the same way to everyone (e.g. Bubeck (1995), Held (1995), Engster (2007), Wolterstorff (2008, 2011). A fast-growing body of scholarship now discusses the relationship between justice and care in specific contexts, especially education, medicine and other 'caring professions', the aid sector, and business).

all of which agree, cannot do justice to all the directions of travel or debates in progress. In broad terms, however, the increasing interest of moral philosophers in trust, together with the increasing interest of philosophers of religion in trust among other non-doxastic aspects of faith, offers food for thought for anyone interested in investigating the nature of trust at the roots of Christianity.

Pierangelo Sequeri is a theologian, not a philosopher of religion, but since he is one of very few theologians now working who have a significant interest in trust and the trustworthiness of God, we can say a little more here about his thought. As noted above, his theory of faith is central to much of his writing.[99] The introduction to *Il Dio affidabile* outlines his project to explore faith as 'a particular form of knowing truth and justice'.[100] He argues that truth and justice should be understood not as static objects of evidence, argument, and knowledge, but as rooted in human beings' relationship with God and witness to that relationship: *In effetti è proprio così: la verità e la giustizia sono accessibili soltanto attraverso la mediazione della fede. La ragione argomentativa, che conduce alla esplicitazione della struttura dell'evidenza, deve riconoscere e articolare tematicamente le modalità secondo le quali l'istanza della verità e della giustizia si rendono persuasive alla conscienza.*[101] Even more is Godself not the object of knowledge: the reality of God is discernible in an encounter of trust with the God who is *affidabile*: reliable, trustworthy, and dependable.[102] Sequeri grounds this argument in an anthropology which affirms the centrality of trust in human knowing of all kinds.[103] We have a basic tendency to trust, and when we trust, one of our most basic needs is fulfilled: we see each other and are seen; we recognize and are recognized.[104] In a relationship of trust and faithfulness, we know and are known, and this personal orientation is also an ethical orientation. We experience the truth we encounter in our relationship with God as beautiful, attractive, and right; it fulfils both our ethical and our aesthetic desires.[105] Furthermore, Sequeri argues, Christian 'faith' both fulfils and transforms everyday human 'faith'. Sequeri's work, which has not been translated into English and is notoriously dense and challenging even to native Italian readers, has had few points of contact with anglophone moral philosophy and philosophy of religion, but it shares some of the same concerns. Trust is central to the divine–human relationship and to knowing God. Human beings have a basic need to trust, and not only good relationships, but also much of our sense of self, depends on our ability and opportunity to trust.

---

[99] Ricotta (2007), 51–70.   [100] (1996), 15.
[101] 'In point of fact, the situation is precisely as follows: truth and justice can only be accessed through the mediation of faith. Argument by reason, which leads us to an explanation of the structure of the evidence, must recognise and articulate thematically the means whereby the appeals of truth and justice are rendered persuasive to the conscience.' Transl. Joseph Spooner.
[102] (2002), 64.   [103] (1996), 354–5, (2002), 194.
[104] (1996), 135; Gallagher (2008), 11–13.   [105] (1996), 378–88.

The Psychology of Trust

The study of trust also has a substantial history in social psychology and the psychology of religion.[106] One influential research group, led by David H. Rosmarin, has developed an account of what it means to trust in God which involves both believing and feeling that God is taking care of one's best interests.[107] Another, led by Neal Krause, has shown that, in the Christian groups studied, a strong sense of trust in God tends to be positively correlated with confidence in divine justice.[108]

Especially interesting for this study has been some well-known work on trust in experimental psychology and psychotherapy. Experimental psychologists have long emphasized the importance for infants and very young children of the people around them interacting with them and responding to them, and being recognized by the infant as responding to them. This finding is particularly associated with the 'Still Face experiment' conducted by Edward Tronick in 1975. Tronick found that an infant, after three minutes of exposure to a non-responsive expressionless mother, 'rapidly sobers and grows wary. He makes repeated attempts to get the interaction into its usual reciprocal pattern. When these attempts fail, the infant withdraws [and] orients his face and body away from his mother with a withdrawn, hopeless facial expression.'[109] Wariness suggests a loss of trust, and Tronick explicitly suggests that the infant experiences a loss of hope. Subsequent iterations of the experiment have concluded that the child experiences not only a loss of attachment but also a loss of agency. He can come to feel that he can no longer have an effect on the world, and the effect is a degradation of both happiness and trust.[110]

---

[106] Studies of trust in God have been driven largely by interest in its correlation with physical and psychological wellbeing (Harris and Koenig (2006), Miller and Thoresen (2003), Rosmarin et al. (2009, 2011), Krumrei et al. (2013), Krause and Hayward (2015); for a cognitive developmental perspective see Atran (2002). From early studies which measured what were seen as relatively accessible global indices of trust in God, such as church attendance or prayer, the field has moved increasingly towards measuring attitudes of individuals. Trust in God has often been found to be important to individuals who are invested in 'initiating, maintaining, and repairing a relationship with God' (Hook et al. (2021), 2, cf. Godfrey (2012)). Almost all studies hitherto, however, assume that trust in God is cognitive, and constitutes a set of beliefs held by individuals about the nature and role of God in human life: see the critique of Hook et al. (2021), 1–5.

[107] E.g. Rosmarin, Krumrei et al. (2009), drawing on Ibn Pekuda (1996), Hafizi et al. (2014), Pirutinsky and Rosmarin (2020). They identify six 'core domains' which identify subjects as trusting in God: God has constant regard for all worldly affairs; God has absolute knowledge of what is in people's best interests; no power is greater than God; God must be involved for anything to occur; God is merciful and generous; God is righteous in judgment; on this basis, Rosmarin and co. have developed several scales of trust or mistrust in God, which have been used to measure trust in God among Jews, Christians, and Muslims.

[108] Krause (2015a). They also argue that people who trust in God tend to acknowledge that their own understanding of their needs is limited, and they need to trust God's better judgment (Krause et al. (2000), Krause (2004)).

[109] Tronick et al. (1975), quoted by Adamson and Frick (2003), 452; cf. Tronick (1978, 2003).

[110] Weinberg and Tronick (1996), Fuertes et al. (2006, 2009), Mattson et al. (2012). Eastman (2013, 2017, 2018) notably puts biblical and theological thinking in dialogue with experimental psychology

The psychologist and psychotherapist Doris Brothers has explored the effects of trauma on the ability of people of all ages to trust. Her influential study *Falling Backwards: An Exploration of Trust and Self-Experience* argues that trust is universally prized by human beings because a positive experience of the self is impossible in its absence.[111] Trust is fundamental to a functioning personality, 'the glue of self-experience'.[112] When we learn to trust, it is equally important to be able to trust those around us and to trust ourselves. If those around us do not acknowledge us or our trustworthiness and reliability, then we cannot develop trust in the reliability of our own thoughts, feelings, or actions.

Brothers distinguishes between the 'world of subjective reality', which she describes as the 'objective world' as we perceive it, and 'the realm of selfobject relations', in which external things and beings are experienced as to some degree part of ourselves or as serving the maintenance and restoration of ourselves.[113] 'Selfobjects' can be described as external objects which are not part of ourselves but which we experience as indivisible from ourselves. As infants, our prime selfobjects are likely to be our parents, and our relationship with them is likely to be indivisible from any sense of self. As we grow older, our life partner, our profession, or groups we belong to may all act as selfobjects. My understanding of myself, for example, might be inextricably involved with my being a violinist, or a classicist, or my mother's daughter. The language which we use to describe these selfobjects is revealing. I do not simply play the violin: I *am* a violinist. I do not simply get paid to teach classics: I am a classicist. Brothers describes the ways in which we relate to selfobjects (without any pejorative connotation) as 'selfobject fantasies'. Selfobject fantasies, which typically operate below the level of consciousness, organize our experience of ourselves through our relationships with our selfobjects.

Trust, Brothers argues, operates in the 'shadowy region between the world of subjective reality and the world of selfobject fantasies'.[114] We trust (or do not trust) in the people and the world around us as we perceive them, but who and what we trust, and how, is also intrinsic to the way we perceive ourselves, and our inner and outer lives interact constantly to reinforce or modify our sense of self. Brothers calls the trust which operates in this region 'self-trust' (in a technical

---

and neuroscience to explore how personhood is realized in relationship with God and Christ, including through *pistis*, and how sin and living in a state of sin can be seen as damaging and destroying the self.

[111] Brothers (1995) with a critical review of thinking about trust in psychotherapy, pp. 5–30; cf. (2008). The link between trauma and the erosion of trust, and its effects on the ability of trauma victims to make successful relationships and engage effectively with the world around them, is much discussed in social psychology and psychiatry: see e.g. Horney (1950), Ebert et al. (2013), Guasto (2014), Ratcliffe et al. (2014). Hanckel (2015). Daniel Paul Schreber describes traumatic childhood abuse as 'soul murder' (Schreber (1973), 65).

[112] p. 31. Rizzuto (2001) makes a similar argument, and argues further (pp. 203–4) that religious faith requires the same social conditions as interpersonal trust to develop well.

[113] pp. 31–2.   [114] pp. 32–3.

sense distinct from the trust in oneself which we will discuss at various points). She defines it as 'the hope or wishful expectation of obtaining and providing the selfobject experiences necessary for the development, maintenance, and restoration of cohesive selfhood'.[115] She sees the betrayal of self-trust as standing at the heart of trauma and, combining theory with clinical experience, develops a model of how and why trust is central to our positive sense of ourselves, and how to restore trust after trauma.

Brothers identifies four dimensions of self-trust:

1) trust-in-others, which sees others as trustworthy providers of experiences which for us are part of ourselves (selfobject experiences). [For example, I might trust others to affirm my sense of myself as a musician];
2) trust-in-self, which sees oneself as capable of eliciting selfobject experiences from others. [For example, I might trust myself to present myself to the world in such a way that it sees me as a musician];
3) self-as-trustworthy, which sees oneself as able to provide trustworthy selfobject experiences for others. [For example, I might trust myself to provide my colleagues with the confirmation they need that they are intellectuals];
4) others-as-self-trusting, which sees others as trusting of their ability to provide trustworthy selfobject experiences. [For example, I might trust my colleagues to be able to show me that they are intellectuals.]

Everyone operates with these dimensions of self-trust to some degree, but those who have not been traumatized tend to make use of them all roughly equally, while those who have been traumatized tend to show dramatic variations in use. (A person, for example, might be able to trust his friends to be able to show him that they are good people, but have little confidence in his ability to show himself to his friends as a good person.) Trauma damages not only our ability to trust other people, but our ability to trust ourselves and our relationship with the world and the people around us.[116] It degrades our empathy with others and tends to foster feelings of shame or anger.[117] An important aspect of Brothers' model is that it emphasizes how significant it is for people not only to be able to trust, but to be trusted: to feel that they are seen as trustworthy.[118] We will see, especially in Chapters 6 and 7, the importance for followers of Christ not only of trusting, but of being, in various ways, trustworthy.

Those who do not trust their ability to show themselves to the world as they feel they are and be seen, or the ability of others to show themselves to them and

---

[115] p. 33. [116] pp. 55–7.
[117] pp. 57–60. Brothers notes that the betrayal of trust does not typically destroy self-trust in adults, but does in infants and children.
[118] pp. 209–30.

be seen, can cease to feel that they are real in the world that others are living in, or that others are real in the world they are living in. They may seek refuge in—or find themselves trapped in—dreams, fantasies, or delusions which seem more real than the world around them.[119] The world in which we are able to trust and feel trusted, Brothers demonstrates, is the world which we experience as real, and the world in which we experience ourselves as real. The questions, who do we trust? By whom do we feel trusted? are also the questions, who is real for us? In what relationships do we experience ourselves as most real? In what world are we material; in what world do we matter?[120]

Brothers' quadripartite analysis of self-trust explains why the Still Face experiment is so powerful. Trust in others and in ourselves cannot be separated, and both are integral to our wellbeing and that of those around us. When we lose either, we begin to lose our ability to interact with others; to make and receive impressions. Our selves or our surroundings, or both, begin to seem less real. We become prey to anger and depression, shame and insecurity, and our dysfunction has unpredictable consequences for those around us. As Harold Kelman puts it, describing the loss of trust which follows trauma, 'In saying nobody was there for me, that person is also saying I didn't exist for anybody, they acted as if I didn't exist. What is implied is, that since I didn't exist for anybody, how was I to feel I had an existence, that I existed for myself and that existence had a meaning for me?'[121]

When people cannot develop trust, or lose trust, they are also liable to lose hope. The relationship between trust and hope is less well studied in psychology than that between trust and other forms of wellbeing, but it is well explored in an article by Matthew Ratcliffe, Mark Ruddell, and Benedict Smith.[122] Taking their cue from a passage in the 1999 UN Istanbul Protocol, which states that victims of torture often have 'a sense of foreshortened future without expectation of a career, marriage, children, or normal lifespan',[123] Ratcliffe, Ruddell, and Smith investigate how torture and other forms of trauma 'can lead to a loss of "trust" or "confidence" in the world. This undermines the intelligibility of one's projects, cares, and commitments, in a way that amounts to a change in the structure of temporal experience...' (p. 1). The loss of trust makes it difficult or impossible to look forward, to have any confidence in the future, or to hope. The connection between trust and

---

[119] pp. 64–8, 70–3, 114–8.
[120] Cf. Craffert (2011), who argues from a neuroanthropological perspective that human experiences of both physical and metaphysical phenomena can be so different that they can properly be said to be living in different worlds. Härle and Preul (1992), 1–2 note the need to think further about the relationship between divine–human *pistis/fides* and the fulfilment of human personhood from a theological perspective.
[121] Kelman (1971), 9:105.   [122] Ratcliffe et al. (2014).
[123] United Nations (1999), 47.

hope is another that will recur in our discussions of the trust between God, Christ, and human beings.

Like the increasing interest in trust in moral philosophy and philosophy of religion, the increasing interest in trust in psychology offers food for thought for those investigating trust at the roots of Christianity. We cannot take for granted that any of their approaches, or conclusions, map neatly onto the ways in which New Testament writers characterize *pistis*, but bringing them into dialogue offers new and potentially fruitful ways of thinking about *pistis*.

Trust in this Study: A Definition and Some Questions

Many of these developments in the study of trust are not well known outside their own discipline, and many are likely to be unfamiliar to biblical scholars and theologians. We have passed over others which are valuable in their own right, but those we have discussed have all contributed to the approach of this study. Drawing on some of their widely shared elements, we can offer a working definition of the relational trust which will be our main concern in all but the last chapter:[124]

> Trust is the action of putting something (which might include an object, an outcome, or oneself), or the attitude of willingness to put something, in someone else's hands[125] (i.e. in their power, responsibility, and/or care), on the basis (which might be e.g. a belief, hope, wager, or assumption) that the other will respond positively (for instance, because she is willing and/or able to do so, and/or because she is encouraged to do so by one's trust).[126]

One can have an attitude of trust without acting, while the action of trust normally involves an attitude of trust, but need not always do so.[127] Opinions vary as to whether an attitude of trust can coexist with mistrust, fear, doubt, and scepticism, but we will assume, as a starting-point, that they are all compatible, at least, with the practice of trust.

We will assume that relational (and sometimes also propositional[128]) trust seeks to create, accept, maintain, and/or inflect relationships, either on the basis

---

[124] For a definition of propositional trust see pp. 325–6.

[125] This phrase is not meant to suggest that the truster resigns *all* responsibility or care for himself, any more than does the Greek preposition *en* with the dative, which is often translated 'in the hands of' (see pp. 131–2).

[126] This definition encompasses both two- and three-place trust, though not one-place trust, which plays only a marginal role in current philosophical thinking about trust, and which I do not detect in New Testament writings, where trust is always in relation to God, Christ, or someone, such as an apostle, entrusted with a role by God and Christ. I assume that, in a case of three-place trust, when we trust someone to respond positively, we cannot necessarily be sure that they will succeed in doing what we trust them for.

[127] See also pp. 23 n.129, 70–1, 111–12, 163–4, 260, 316–17, 348–9.

[128] Propositional trust can be reducible to personal trust (e.g. trusting that you will buy me a pint of milk, as I have asked you to, is tantamount to trusting you to do so), but not always: p. 325.

that the relationship is worthwhile in itself, or in the expectation or hope that something positive will emerge from it, or both.[129] Trust is always risky, with no guarantees, but, at a minimum, when we trust we believe (or accept, hope, assume, or wager) that (for instance) the person we trust is trustworthy in some particular respect or, more broadly, as the person she is.[130] Normally, we also believe (or accept, and so on) that the benefits of trust outweigh the risks.

Sometimes trust is contractual and specific: if, for example, I decide to pay you for a loaf of bread and trust you to give it to me. If you then tell me that you have run out of bread and refuse to give my money back, I may feel disappointed and annoyed, even betrayed, but my sense of betrayal is specific to this context. But often trust is much broader and more open-ended than this. As your friend, I may trust you and invite you to trust me for the indefinite future, through life events we cannot yet predict. In this relationship, I accept my vulnerability and yours. As a trustworthy friend, I engage not to exploit your vulnerability or betray it, and trust (or assume, hope, and so on) that you will reciprocate. If we both fulfil this trust, our relationship will also be one of care. Our trust may last for many years, and be part of many and varied situations; it may persist when we are trusting each other for something specific and when we are not; and if it fails, either of us may feel betrayed in a way that affects significantly our sense of our self, of the other, and of the world we are living in.

Following Brothers, we will take trust to be essential to our sense of ourselves in relation to those around us. When we trust interpersonally, we trust ourselves to be able to make ourselves seen and recognized as we understand ourselves to be, and to be able to see and recognize others as they understand themselves to be, and we trust others to be able to do the same.[131] If this trust fails, then we are liable to become angry or depressed, ashamed and insecure; detached from our own reality and that of others. The world may become a painfully lonely, inexplicable, and unnerving place.

Sometimes we risk trusting another person 'therapeutically', treating them as more trustworthy than we think they really are, in the hope (or belief, and so on) that this will change their sense of themselves and inspire them to become more trustworthy in the future. In some relationships, however, we do not so much trust despite the risks, as because we have no other option that is not self-destructive.

---

[129] Attitude and action (and emotion, if it is present), as noted above, are normatively envisaged as operating together in Greek *pistis* (and other qualities). They are well described by the concept of a script (Berne (1961)), which is increasingly used in historical and literary studies but as yet relatively little in the study of the New Testament (cf. Morgan (2020), 206–7) to describe how an attitude of mind leads people to speak and act in certain ways.

[130] O'Neill (2002), 4–7.

[131] Occasionally, in later chapters, we will point to contexts in which self-trust is a mistake: above all, when people trust themselves to be able to assess, objectively, what God wants of them or who Christ is (e.g. pp. 148–51, 211–2, 241–2, 264–5, 359–60). I take self-trust as trustworthy and appropriate when it is interactive and intersubjective, and so is formed and informed in part by openness to others (cf. pp. 261–3, 359–60).

Sometimes we cannot survive (if, say, we are very young or very elderly) without trusting others to look after us. In these cases, trust may be practically indistinguishable from reliance.

Both philosophers and psychologists are interested in the relationship between trust and reliance, and this is also an important question in divine–human relations. Katherine Hawley sets out the issues, arguing that we often speak of 'trusting' objects such as the chair we sit on or the car we drive, but that 'trusting' an object to perform as it is designed to do is better characterized as reliance.[132] There may also be contexts in which we rely on human beings in this functional sense. For instance, if I am very ill, I may rely on qualified doctors and nurses to treat me, whether or not I trust them.[133] Most philosophers, psychologists, and social scientists assume that trust involves reliance, but that trust is a richer concept, characteristic of personal relationships. When we trust another person, we have 'heightened expectations' of them.[134] We rely on them to meet their commitments and, if, they let us down, we can feel not just disappointed but betrayed.

Some philosophers, however, have pointed to various ways in which trust is distinct from reliance and does not necessarily involve it.[135] A person who is trustworthy, as opposed to reliable, does not simply do what she has been trusted to do, but sees the truster's dependence, his self-entrusting, as a reason to respond.[136] People sometimes trust one another in situations in which they cannot be certain whether they can rely on one another (for instance, because they do not know each other, or because the trustee has no 'form' in a relevant context).[137] In the case of therapeutic trust, moreover, one person may choose to trust another to do something which they are fairly sure they cannot currently rely on them to do. If an act of trust can involve one or more of several different attitudes of mind (either positive or negative), these need not include reliance. Conversely, we can rely on someone, not just functionally, as above, but relationally, without trusting them. I can rely on my competitor, for instance to look for an advantage over me, or my enemy to be hostile to me, without trusting them. These examples suggest that rather than treating trust as 'reliance plus', we should assume that trust and reliance are separate attitudes and actions which may, but need not operate together. This will be important as we explore the relationship between humanity, God, and Christ, because it opens up the possibility, in principle, that we could rely on God or Christ without trust, or trust God or Christ without reliance, as well as, sometimes, doing both.

---

[132] Hawley (2012), 3–6, cf. Jones (1996).
[133] Holtzen (2019), 39 is an outlier in arguing that we rely only on objects.
[134] p. 5.
[135] Discussed by Thompson (2017).
[136] E.g. Darwall (2017), Hinchman (2017), Jones (2017).
[137] Faulkner (2017); on the relationship between knowledge and trust more broadly see Faulkner (2011).

This picture of trust is inevitably an image of trust between human beings. The possibility of trust between humanity, God, and Christ, however, raises further questions. Should we assume that trust between God, Christ, and human beings is analogous to trust between human beings, or should we expect to find significant differences? Does it make sense to view trust in God or Christ as risky? Is it appropriate to trust God or Christ for something, or should we simply trust them, period? When (if ever) is it appropriate for God or Christ to trust human beings? Is trust in God or Christ compatible with fear, doubt, or scepticism?[138]

We have already, implicitly, begun to answer the first of these, and it is worth saying a little more about it here. New Testament writers inherit both Jewish and gentile traditions of speaking of the divine in personal terms. They also affirm, in various terms, the closeness of Christ to God, and that the relationship of the faithful with Christ is, in most respects, analogous to their relationship with God.[139] Jesus Christ, who lived and died as a human being, was undoubtedly a person, and all New Testament writers assert the continuity of Christ's personhood and identity in his earthly, risen, and exalted (and sometimes his pre-existent) life.[140] It follows that if the relationship of the faithful with the exalted Christ, for instance, is personal, then so is their relationship with God. When our sources, or we, speak of God as a person and use, for instance, trust language about our relationship with God, moreover, we assume, at least as a starting-point, that we are using this language approximately as we use it of human persons. If that is not our starting-point, then it is hard to know what we mean by such language at all. At the same time, to say what we might want to say about the divine–human relationship, we inevitably recognize that we may sometimes need to stretch or limit our language. (For example, we might want to claim that trust in another human being always involves a degree of risk, but trust in God is uniquely risk-free because we cannot conceive of God as other than perfectly reliable.[141]) It is possible, in principle, that our understanding of the divine–human relationship might emerge, at some point, as so distinctive that it ceases to be describable in human terms, but in practice I do not think what follows drives us in that direction.

The questions in the last paragraph but one are what we might call supporting questions: they help us to think about divine–human trust by drawing on ideas about trust between human beings, without making too-easy assumptions about the parallels. With their aid, we can frame the bigger questions of this study. Why

---

[138] There is no semantic difference in English between 'trusting in' e.g. God and 'trusting' e.g. God (see *OED, ad loc.*); I will use both interchangeably.

[139] Though e.g. they can trust Christ distinctively as mediator or as human teacher or healer.

[140] I am not raising here the spectre of the mid-twentieth-century debate as to whether the origins of Christianity lie in the kerygma, the resurrection experience, the 'Christ-idea', or the life of the historical Jesus (see notably Käsemann (1969), 23–65), but observing that almost all New Testament writing explicitly connect Jesus of Nazareth with the risen and coming Christ.

[141] So e.g. Helm (2002); below, pp. 72–4.

do New Testament writers think anyone should or does trust in God or in Jesus Christ? What happens when human beings put their trust in God? What is it like to live in a relationship of trust with God and/or Christ? What happens if and when God and/or Christ put their trust in human beings? What understanding of trust do New Testament writings offer as a possibility for modern Christian trust?[142]

History, Theology, and the New Testament

We have noted that this study builds on the findings of the historical monograph *Roman Faith and Christian Faith*.[143] Since the relationship between historical and theological study of the New Testament is much debated, we should say a little more about how this study understands itself in that context.[144] In principle, theology can be written from a confessional or non-confessional standpoint, but since the debate between historical and theological study of the New Testament has taken place largely among scholars who are Christians, often explicitly with a confessional agenda, and since this study, by focusing on New Testament rather than all early Christian texts, also locates itself in a confessional context, we will take theology as confessional for the purposes of this section.

It is worth beginning with a few negatives. What follows does not aim to construct a 'New Testament theology', or even a New Testament theology of trust, in any comprehensive or systematic sense. It does not address all the traditional themes of systematic theology (though most will feature, in some form). It does not seek to do equal justice to every writer or book (though almost all will appear at some point), and it does not argue that the findings of each chapter add up to a coherent whole. Rather, it follows New Testament writers' own use of *pistis* and related language to develop a series of sketches of the nature of trust between God, Christ, and humanity, where it is most significant, how it works and to what

---

[142] Paraphrasing Via's summary ((2002), 60) of the two key questions of Bultmann's New Testament theology: 'What does the text tell me about the past?...What understanding of existence does it offer as a possibility for my existence?'.

[143] Some reviewers described *Roman Faith* as a work of historical theology, in the sense that it describes the theological thinking of New Testament writings, but for clarity I would call it a history of ideas.

[144] The nature of New Testament theology, and in particular the relationship between theological and historical study, is the subject of sustained debate. On the history and taxonomy of scholarship see Boers (1979), Räisänen (2000), Via (2002), with Bauer (2016). Among key contributions since c.1950 see Bultmann (1952, 1955, cf. 1997), Cullmann (1967), Conzelmann (1969), Jeremias (1971), Käsemann (1972), Morgan (1973, 2003, 2008, 2016, 2018), Dunn (1977, 2008), Goppelt (1981), Stendahl (1962, 1984), Strecker (1975, 2010), Donahue (1989, 1996), Wright (1992, 1996), Caird (1994), Gnilka (1994), Riches (1994), Adam (1995), Stuhlmacher (1995), De Lubac (1996), Watson (1997, 2008), Schnelle (1998, 2009a), Schüssler Fiorenza (1999), Moberly (2000), Esler (2005), Matera (2005), Luz (2014); recently see notably Perdue, Morgan, and Sommer (2009), Frei (2013), Hatina (2013), Heringer (2014), Longenecker and Parsons (2014), Reynolds et al. (2014), Walsh and Elliott (2016), Martin (2017); cf. (from a philosophical perspective) Dalferth (2010).

purpose, and why it matters. To do this, it seeks to give a sustained reading of a number of writers' understanding of trust that makes sense within their writings as a whole. (The exception is Chapter 4, which, like many models of atonement, begins with an idea found, in this case, in Paul, but develops it well beyond what Paul himself says.) In this process, what follows keeps in mind that these writers have different perspectives and agenda, that the texts were written for very varied occasions, in diverse communities, and that none of them sets out to define *pistis* or give a complete account of Christian trust.[145] With this caveat, it will argue that there are some significant overlaps and coherences in their visions of divine–human trust, as well as some differences.

This may therefore be best characterized as a work of theological reflection on New Testament writings, or what Heikki Räisänen calls 'theologizing about the sources' as a way of reflecting on their significance in the present.[146] As such, it will begin from (what it argues are) historically defensible readings of the texts, on the basis that *Roman Faith* showed that these offered food for thought, but sometimes it will explicitly draw further readings or implications from them which it does not claim their writers intended or their first audiences are likely to have heard. It will, however, leave open the question whether everything modern Christians need to understand or help them to think about trust between God, Christ, and humanity can be found in these texts in some form.[147]

The most striking absence, for many readers, resulting from this approach, will be that of the holy spirit, which plays a role in Chapter 7 but appears only occasionally elsewhere. Direct connections between the spirit and trust in New Testament writings are rare: though two aspects of *pistis* are a gift and fruit of the spirit at 1 Corinthians 12.9 and Galatians 5.22, and at 2 Corinthians 4.13 Paul refers to the 'spirit of trust', human beings are not invited to trust in the spirit as they trust in God and Christ; the spirit is not said to be faithful or trustworthy towards humanity as God and Christ are, and the spirit is not described as entrusting the faithful with the tradition or with their roles in the present time.[148]

---

[145] The closest thing to a definition of *pistis* in ancient literature is at Heb. 11.1, but this (*pace* Attridge (1989), *ad loc.*) may be better read as a description of what *pistis* does than a definition of what it is; moreover, we should not assume that it would have been recognizable or acceptable to all Christ-confessors.

[146] Räisänen (2000), 203 (though Räisänen is more optimistic than I am that this exercise can take historical criticism as its foundation); cf. Ebeling (1963), 94, 96.

[147] E.g. the tradition of loyal protest (cf. Pace and McKaughan (2020)) which can be identified in the Hebrew scriptures is at most embryonic in New Testament writings (though it is pointed to e.g. at Rom. 9.14, 11.1).

[148] Though the trustworthiness of the spirit is implicit at 1 Jn 4.1, and, more obliquely, at 1 Thess. 5.20–1. At 2 Cor. 4.13, Ἔχοντες δὲ τὸ αὐτὸ πνεῦμα τῆς πίστεως is not likely to refer to 'the spirit that is trust' (cf. Rom. 1.5), since the spirit is not elsewhere identified with trust and the *pistis* in question, in the rest of the verse, is the speaker's own; grammatically we would not expect it to mean 'the trust that comes from the spirit' but it could mean 'the spirit that comes from trust', which would be grammatically straightforward and fits well both with what Paul says elsewhere about trust and the spirit, and with the implication of the quotation: the speaker trusted, and so was inspired to speak.

Rather than insisting, for example, that theological reflection on the New Testament ought to take Trinitarian form, and creating a connection between the spirit and trust to give it that form, what follows prefers to draw out the implications of divine–human *pistis* as these writings present it.

This study 'builds on' *Roman Faith* in the sense that it takes as its starting-point that book's finding that *pistis* language, for New Testament writers, is more relational (focusing on trust etc.) than propositional (focusing on belief). This does not mean that this study assumes, in a tradition that goes back to Johann Philipp Gabler and was memorably articulated by Krister Stendahl, that the 'descriptive task' necessarily precedes the 'theological task' in the study of the New Testament.[149] It simply means that a historical study, in this case, generated a conclusion which the author thought deserved consideration from a theological perspective too. On another day, or for another reader, an idea for theological exploration might equally well arise from a rhetorical, political, allegorical, or aesthetic reading of the texts.

As a historian, I am sceptical in general of the idea that historical study of the New Testament should precede theological study. Aside from the truism that study of the material world cannot prove or disprove claims about the metaphysical, Stendahl's model of the 'descriptive task' is typical of many in invoking a view of history-writing as the impartial search for objective truths that correspond to the reality of the past.[150] As we will see in Chapter 8, however, for almost all historians, the study of the past is more complex and less objective than this.[151] For one thing, our evidence is always fragmentary, and is framed by the context in which it was created and the attitudes and agenda of those who created it, so making arguments about it is always a tricky and contestable balance between excavation and construction.[152] For another, every investigation is shaped in part by the historian's own interests, questions, and assumptions about everything from the nature of argument to the nature of the world—and it must be, because without these one could not frame a question at all, or make any kind of argument.[153] For another—especially when we are looking beyond the heavily documented past century or so—it is often uncertain whether the past we think we are looking at even existed: that the words on the papyrus mean what we think they mean, or

---

[149] Stendahl (1962), 418–19; Ollenburger (1986). Barr (1999), 202–4, equally influentially, goes further and argues that the meaning the Bible *had* remains its only meaning, though he also recognizes (pp. 204–5) that even historical 'description' makes use of modern categories of thought, so no reading is free of interpretation.

[150] 'The past' here might include the meaning of the texts as we have them, the history of their composition, or what they represent, e.g. about the historical Jesus.

[151] pp. 334–9.

[152] Recognized and explored by Schlatter and Bultmann (discussed by Morgan (1973), 21, 36–52), Räisänen (2000), 189–202.

[153] Cf. pp. 343–6, 351.

that an event occurred or had precisely the causes or consequences we suppose.[154] We will never know enough, or certainly enough, about most of the past to use it unproblematically as a descriptive basis for other arguments, and arguably even the quest for objective historical truths is misconceived.[155] It is preferable to see history and theology (together with literary, and other approaches) as working in parallel and in dialogue, each periodically offering the other questions and ideas, as *Roman Faith* prompted questions and ideas which led to the present study.[156]

Two of the ways in which history and theology work in parallel and in dialogue deserve outlining a little further. Historians value historical-critical readings not least for their ambition to take us out of ourselves and our view of the world and show us something of the material, social, and cognitive worlds of others: people who, in some ways, perhaps, were very like us, and, in some ways, were unpredictably and amazingly different. Granted that we always approach the past with our own agenda and assumptions, we also aspire to be open to being surprised, challenged, and informed by others and by the Other. We listen as carefully as we can to the evidence to give the Other the best chance of communicating itself, and ourselves the best chance of being surprised and challenged. Studying history is therefore an exercise in intersubjectivity, in which we bring to our subject-matter our assumptions and interests, but stay to listen to the assumptions of our subjects and what interests them.[157] In this exercise, we not only look at the remains of the past, but allow ourselves to be looked at by them. We not only decide what we think about them, but allow them to question the way we think about them, and by implication about ourselves.[158]

The idea that our subject-matter, as we look at it, is also looking at and challenging us, is equally central to the confessional study of theology. Paradigmatically, the God whom human beings seek to know, knows humanity, and to seek to know God is to open oneself to being known, challenged, and changed.[159]

New Testament writings, studied historically, act like any other historical subject in responding to our agenda and assumptions, while at the same time

---

[154] Cf. pp. 337–8.

[155] Whether there are objective or timeless theological truths is beyond the scope of this study, but what follows does not assume that there are, or that, if there are, human intelligence can access them in this world. It would, however, be compatible with this study's focus on relational trust and knowledge to argue that, in the divine–human relationship, seeking objective truths about the divine (or the human), even if they exist, is not of the first importance in religious life, any more than seeking objective truths about one's sibling or partner is of primary importance in family life.

[156] We can go further and see dialogue as the model for all our interaction with the divine, and with texts and traditions: see notably Luz (2014), Theissen (2014).

[157] On intersubjectivity in the study of history see e.g. Holden (2016); on the relationship between objectivity and intersubjectivity in the sciences, with implications for the humanities too, see Nordmann (2012). Ricoeur (1965), 37 observes that in the practice of historical intersubjectivity the past does not talk back to the historian, and calls history-writing 'a kind of unilateral friendship, like unrequited love'.

[158] Morales et al. (2020).

[159] E.g. Louth (1983), Rosner (2017), Schnabel (2017).

subjecting us to question and challenge. If the historian is a Christian, then the questions and challenges are all the sharper, since what she is studying represents (and stands tantalizingly close to the origins of) a world-view, community, and way of life which she also understands as her own. Since she is also likely to understand this world-view, community, and way of life as the way to salvation and eternal life, then her historical studies cannot help raising theological as well as historical questions, and history and theology come into dialogue. If she changes discipline and seeks to reflect on these writings theologically, then she opens herself to being questioned and challenged by what is being said through them by God.[160] If what she hears with a theologian's ears challenges her view of the world or of the past (if, for instance, she reads that God is just, and also that those who worship God can suffer brutal oppression and persecution), then theology and history come into dialogue on a different front.

One aim of this study, by reflecting theologically on texts which *Roman Faith* read historically, is to bring the intersubjectivity of history-writing (and, more generally, of our interactions with the material world) into dialogue with the intersubjectivity of theology (and, more generally, of our interactions with the metaphysical). How does New Testament writers' understanding of trust in God and Christ relate to ours? If, for these writers, trust stands at the heart of the divine–human relationship, how might we understand the role of trust in atonement, for instance, which no New Testament writer explores at length?[161] If Christians believe that human beings are called to order their lives around trust in God and Christ, what implications might that have for their ethics? Can the call to trust challenge contemporary antipathy or indifference to religion?

Some readers may be thinking at this point that the preceding paragraphs gloss over one respect in which we do tend to assume that history is (logically, if not necessarily diachronically) prior to theology, and to metaphysics in general. A person who takes seriously the challenges that history can pose to our world-view might find his metaphysical assumptions or convictions challenged by his account of the past (for example, his belief in divine justice might be challenged by historical persecutions of Christians), but it is harder to imagine that his view of the past might be challenged by his metaphysical commitments. This assumption has some intuitive appeal, but in fact, I think, it is mistaken. Leaving aside, for instance, the strand of pre-modern historiography which sees the divine as working through human agents and institutions, or the determination of some contemporary conspiracy theories to interpret all information that bears on the theory, however plausibly or implausibly, in support of it, we have noted that all historians bring to their work their assumptions and intuitions about the ways in

---

[160] This holds whether we take a 'high' view of the scriptures as the divine Word or a 'lower' view of them as human responses to the experience of the divine.

[161] Though see pp. 153–62.

which people, societies, and the world work. These can be very varied in kind: they might include, for example, that all power tends to corrupt; that social groups generally favour stability over change; that some leaders have mysterious qualities of charisma or luck; or that the market has a mind of its own.[162] Historians' readings of their evidence and arguments about it are constantly informed, and can be challenged, by such broad, abstract ideas, which may be drawn from tradition, the surrounding culture, or personal experience, are often widely shared and unconsciously held, and are effectively metaphysical commitments.[163]

A further way in which history and theology work in parallel and in dialogue, therefore, is by recognizing that both make metaphysical assumptions and claims, bringing those claims into conversation with each other, and letting them challenge one another. Accordingly, another aim of this study is to explore whether theologizing about *pistis* in New Testament writings offers a vision of the world which offers a conversation partner, or a challenge, to the material or metaphysical landscape of contemporary society.

Outline of Chapters

Chapter 2 begins with God, and with the Pauline corpus, where most of the New Testament's explicit language of God's *pistis* is found. Paul and his followers take for granted that God is faithful to God's people, keeping God's covenant with Israel and fulfilling God's promises. This faithfulness, among much else, is a reason to trust God when God does what Isaiah calls a 'new thing'. For Paul, God has revealed God's trustworthiness anew in the Christ event, which fulfils all God's promises. Paul recognizes that the Christ event is not how Israel would have expected God to fulfil God's promises, but God is the God who has done radically unexpected things in the past, and Paul affirms that a person can be trustworthy in doing the unexpected. The gospel is an invitation to Israel to renew her trust in God in new circumstances by putting her trust in Jesus Christ. To gentiles, it is an invitation not only to put their trust in the God of Israel and in Christ—a new and relatively untried heavenly being—but to relinquish their other gods.

The trust relationship therefore involves risk for all involved: for God and Christ, who must trust human beings to respond to the Christ event, and for human beings, who must trust that God has taken a new initiative and trust in Christ as God's son. Israel remains beloved by God and entrusted with God's prophecies, and Paul expects all Israel to be saved, but the revealing of

---

[162] On the personification of markets see e.g. Caginalp (2002), where the market not only has a mind of its own, but can 'get carried away' by its own concerns.

[163] Theissen (1999), 39 notes in similar terms that 'the historical Jesus already lived a myth' in a world shaped by mythical thinking.

God's righteousness and salvation no longer depends on Israel's faithfulness or unfaithfulness, and salvation, for Israel as for the gentiles, depends on putting one's trust in both God and Christ. The trust relationship 'surpasses' (2 Cor. 3.10) the covenant and the law, creating a new and holy community of trust which Paul envisions as living, as in God's kingdom or in a new golden age, with minimal institutions and laws, by love, peace, and shared hope. Modern readers, however, may recognize, as Paul does not, that Paul's assumption that right-standing with God not only now comes through Christ, but always will, is inconsistent with his own view of God. Humanity cannot rule out that God might choose—or already has chosen—to do another 'new thing', and call human beings into another new and different relationship with God.

Though the trust relationship to which God calls human beings is, in some ways, risky on both sides, the risks are also limited. Paul does not envisage the possibility that God will fail humanity, and, though he recognizes that human beings may fail in trust and faithfulness, he does not think God's demands are beyond what the faithful are capable of fulfilling. The risk God takes on humanity, meanwhile, is an example of therapeutic trust, which trusts someone with something, knowing that they will probably not prove trustworthy at this time (or not fully), but trusting that they will become more trustworthy in the future. This idea challenges the later doctrine that God is omniscient in the sense of having foreknowledge of everything that will happen. It makes good sense, however, if, with some modern commentators, we think of God's omniscience as relational rather than propositional. God deeply knows God's creation, and so can confidently trust that human beings will, ultimately, respond to God's trust. In this vision, however, the faithful cannot rely on God in the sense of relying on God to do what they want or ask for. God can be relied on always and only to be God and to enact God's will.

Paul's focus on righteousness, salvation, and the *parousia* means that his picture of divine–human trust can look strongly 'three-place', but it also has a 'two-place' aspect. The faithful trust God and Christ not only for eventual salvation, but also as part of the right-standing with God which trust itself makes possible. Two-place trust is a powerful, but open-ended bond, allowing both partners to contemplate a future which human beings cannot predict, which may change them and which they may change in unexpected ways, but towards which they can move with confidence together.

The final section of Chapter 2 shows how a number of New Testament writers draw on a scriptural vision of God as creator which puts care, and the trust intrinsic to it, at the heart of the divine–human relationship. In several passages, the creation of the world is invoked to affirm that Christ, as the one who pre-exists with God and participates in creation, is trustworthy as God is trustworthy, and exists in the same relationship of trust and care with the faithful as does Godself.

In this relationship, the faithful are far from passive: as Chapter 7 shows, they have their own role in caring for one another and for creation. The identification of Christ with God the creator is another way in which these writings affirm that, though trusting in Jesus Christ is risky, its risks are limited. These passages also tend to have eschatological connections, affirming that trust in God and Christ will ultimately restore humanity to the divine–human relationship for which it was created. The restoration of this relationship is not only humanity's best hope for itself, but also the best hope of creation as a whole for the relief of its present suffering.

Chapter 3 turns to the newly ascended being, the exalted Christ, and to the idea that people are called to trust in Christ as they trust in God. The call to trust in the exalted Christ may be the earliest form of the call to trust in Christ, but it is striking how strongly and explicitly New Testament writings affirm the continuity of Christ's identity in his earthly life, death, resurrection, and exalted life. Across New Testament writings, a key basis for trust in the exalted Christ is belief in the resurrection. Resurrection belief, however, is complex, involving resurrection experiences (one's own and/or others'), preaching, the interpretation of scripture, and the coherence of all these things with one's existing commitment to the God of Israel or willingness to put one's trust in God. Although, therefore, there is no real doubt that Christ-confessors believe that the resurrection occurred, resurrection *pistis* also has an aspect of propositional trust. The faithful trust that they can trust their experience and their ability to interpret it, the experience of others, the community's interpretation of scripture, and their past experience of God, and that all these things fit together.

The exalted Christ is unusual among exalted human beings of the early principate in being active in oversight and support of the faithful. He does battle with hostile powers to save those who trust. For Paul, especially, he mediates between God and the faithful, lays the foundations of communities and welcomes people into them, and directs the travels of apostles. The faithful are often said to be 'in Christ's hands', emphasizing both Christ's authority over them and his care for them. The faithful, for their part, remain faithful to God and Christ, seek to become more faithful, and try to imitate the exalted Christ in living for God until the end time. The ongoing relationship of the exalted Christ with the faithful in the present, turbulent and uncertain time, is another aspect of divine–human trust that mitigates its risk.

Chapter 4 offers a model of atonement centred on Christ's restoration of trust between God and humanity. It begins once more with Paul, who uses *pistis* language in all the key passages in which he writes about the death of Christ, but, like all models of atonement, it moves beyond the texts in seeking to explicate the role and significance of saving trust. It begins by arguing that sin is everywhere entwined with the suffering which it is liable to cause both the guilty and the innocent: including in the scriptures, in messianic traditions, in stories of Christ as saviour, and in everyday experience. Ideally, a model of atonement should therefore show how the death and resurrection of Christ make possible the release of humanity both from sin and from the suffering caused by sin.

For Paul, especially in Romans, both suffering and sin are closely connected with the failure of trust. All three are very difficult, if not impossible, for human beings to extricate themselves from, even if they long to be free of them. Christ, however, trusts and is trustworthy to God, and trusts and is trustworthy to human beings, who are invited to trust in him. Through this double nexus of trust Christ offers mediation between God and humanity to enable their reconciliation. To recognize that Christ's trust in God is vindicated, however, and that they can trust in both God and Christ, human beings also need the revelation of the resurrection. Since the trust of the faithful in God and Christ is partly trust for the future, and will not be vindicated and fulfilled until the end time when the faithful hope to be saved, trust in the atonement can be seen not only as a discrete act of saving trust, but as a long-term relationship in which the faithful respond incrementally to the trust of God and Christ and continue, and even grow in it until the *parousia*.

The idea that Christ mediates between God and humanity through trust does not, in itself, explain why Christ needed to die. This chapter argues that Christ had to allow himself to be arrested, because to try to avoid arrest or execution would have been a failure of trust in God, and not to trust in God would have been to deny the person he was. It draws on Paul's language of dying with Christ and being raised with him, to propose that Christ also allows himself to be crucified as an act of grace, because he understands that human beings must die to the power of sin and suffering in order to be restored to right-standing with God. Using the image of a child who is accompanied by her mother so that she will not get lost on a new and intimidating journey to a longed-for destination, it argues that the exalted Christ accompanies human beings on their death to the power of sin and suffering, so that they experience that death as dying 'with' Christ, and are able to go through it in trust and confidence. In addition, it suggests that Christ's suffering and death change human beings' sense of what is possible for humanity, and so encourage them to put their own trust in God. Drawing on contemporary psychology, and on accounts of the rehabilitation of ex-offenders through initiatives that focus on the creation or restoration of trust, it seeks to show how this model of atonement might work, in practice, to release people from the power of both suffering and sin. In these examples, trust emerges as a powerful tool of restoration, reconciliation, and rehabilitation. Finally, this chapter argues that trust in God and Christ also makes possible propositional trust that one will be saved. It considers why there is little trust language in the gospels' passion narratives, and shows how, in the gospel narratives, Jesus acts as a mediator in his earthly ministry, and how other people can also act, Christ-like, as mediators between the suffering and Jesus himself.

Chapters 5 and 6 turn to Jesus in his earthly life, focusing first on the gospels' portrait of the Jesus in whom people trust, and then on how and why people trust, or fail to trust, in Jesus, and with what consequences. Trust language in all four gospels (which are often, though not always, closer in their portrayal of trust than we often assume) is nearly always put in the mouth of Jesus. It appears in multiple literary forms and layers of tradition, and is soteriological, Christological, eschatological, charismatic, caring, and kerygmatic. Chapter 5 begins by arguing that, for all four evangelists, signs, miracles, prophecies and teaching, though they are all reliable indicators of Jesus' identity for those who trust, cannot prove who he is, and do not create trust, or not lasting trust. Those who seek signs, moreover, or trust their ability to assess who Jesus is rather than responding to him with trust, are fundamentally *apistos*. The gospels sometimes invoke the scriptures to testify, for their listeners, to the trustworthiness of Jesus by association with the God of Israel, and to affirm that Jesus cares for God's creation as does Godself, but even the appeal to scripture cannot prove Jesus' trustworthiness. Trust arises from personal encounters with the Jesus who is present or near, sees and is seen, calls and is followed. Jesus' own trust in God is everywhere a model for those who trust in him, and the trust that responds to Jesus brings new or renewed life.

For the final redactor of John, those who have eternal life must recognize and trust in Jesus as Son of God, and only those who have been pre-elected can do so. The synoptic gospels and Acts, in contrast, suggest that, in Jesus' lifetime, no new or special revelation or pre-election should have been needed for people to put their trust in him. Jesus should have been recognizable, to both Jews and gentiles, as a prophet, healer, and exorcist by the power of God, a man of God, and a man through whom God acted, and this should have been sufficient for the beginnings of trust. This, it is suggested, makes better sense of the theme, especially in Mark, that Jesus went unacknowledged by many, than the now widely shared but, in the world of the first century, counterintuitive idea that a divine revelation went unrecognized. Finally, this chapter considers the possibility that the gospels' portrait of Jesus in his earthly life and death also acts, for the faithful, as an image of the exalted Christ. If so, it considers whether, even after Jesus' ascension, trust in him may acceptably be based on a more partial and imperfect understanding of his identity than we sometimes assume.

Chapter 6 turns to those who put their trust in Jesus in his earthly life, and to the paradoxical adequacy of fragile and imperfect human trust. Through an anti-ableist reading of Jesus' healings and other stories, it argues that no one who encounters Jesus in his earthly life fully or adequately understands who he is. Multiple stories about the disciples, moreover, show that even Jesus' closest followers regularly fail in understanding and trust. There is, though, no sign that, for the gospel writers, the inadequacy of human trust is a deal-breaker at any time before the end. The gospels offer a compassionate vision of human trust, in which any response to Jesus is an acceptable starting-point, bringing human beings into a life-giving relationship with God.

The story of the last night of Jesus' life raises the possibility that even Jesus' trust in God is not unshakeable. This chapter argues that Jesus' trust in God does not waver in Gethsemane, but that his trust in himself to be faithful may. If so, he responds by submitting to God's will, replacing any self-trust with trust and obedience to God. Finally, this chapter considers whether the gospels as narratives seek to foster trust, and reflects on the ways in which the birth narratives highlight the significance of human beings as collaborators in the new divine–human relationship.

Chapter 7 explores the theme of human entrustedness by God and Christ, arguing that there is more language of entrustedness, especially in the Pauline corpus, than has been recognized, and that divine trust in humanity plays a vital role in the divine–human relationship. Paul describes himself as entrusted with the gospel and, more broadly, with stewardship of his communities, and entrusts others with acting on his behalf. Other community members are entrusted with various gifts, while communities as a whole are entrusted with teachings and traditions, with being faithful, and with being examples for one another. Being entrusted is both a gift and an obligation, and is strongly eschatological in focus. In the gospels and Acts, Jesus' followers are entrusted by him with their own mission, while, in parables of the end time, the master's slaves are entrusted with his wealth until his return. These parables envisage the faithful as entrusted with care for the material world and those who live in it until the end time, and with an obligation to help it grow and flourish.

This chapter explores the relationship between trust and the spirit and between entrustedness and power, arguing that trust precedes the reception and gifts of the spirit, and that power also depends on trust. Finally, it offers an outline of an 'ethic of entrustedness', exploring how faithful individuals and communities might understand themselves as entrusted today, and with what implications for their behaviour and relationships.

Chapter 8 turns from relational trust, which is the focus of most of this study, to propositional trust: trust that something is the case. Propositional trust is neglected even in the philosophical literature, and is almost absent from discussions of divine–human trust. It is argued, though, that propositional trust has a role to play both as one of the foundations of divine–human trust, and when people commit themselves and their future to their trust in God and Christ. 'Trusting that' means entrusting oneself, or being willing to entrust oneself, and the future, to a proposition about which one accepts that one is not certain. It is not common in New Testament writings, but we have seen that it is implicit in the process of belief formation. In addition, it occurs in the Johannine corpus where Jesus' followers are invited to trust (i.e. to commit themselves to the proposition) that Jesus is the Son of God. In Paul's letters it occurs where the faithful are called to trust that God will raise the dead, and that they will live with Christ in the eschatological future; in the Pastorals, it occurs where the faithful are invited to trust that the teachings they have inherited are true. In addition, it is implicit wherever we can see God and Christ as acting with therapeutic trust towards humanity.

Though philosophy and theology have not taken much explicit interest in propositional trust, all humanities disciplines (and others) implicitly make use of it in constructing arguments and making claims. Taking the study of history and music as examples, this chapter argues that humanities subjects have in common that they are in dialogue with subjects that 'are not': not beyond doubt, not literally true, not here and how, not univalent, or not material. There is always more than one appropriate, interesting, and constructive way to discuss their subject-matter, and never only one right view of it, not least because the observer's viewpoint is always implicated in her view. When we make arguments about the subjects, we therefore do so knowing that taking a view of them is necessary (because not taking any view leads to paralysis of thought and action) but risky, and involves making choices about which the only certainty is that they will affect the future. In this intellectual and ethical sequence propositional trust plays both a discursive and protreptic role.

In the context of this study, propositional trust is important when we are considering whether our account of divine–human trust is trustworthy, whether it has the capacity to engage us and illuminate our experience, and whether, on that basis, we are willing to commit ourselves and entrust the future to it. Four test cases are proposed, to see whether propositional trust might, for people in different situations, offer a route to trust in God and Christ, and consider the relationship between propositional trust, fear, doubt, and scepticism. Finally, this chapter reflects on the role of propositional trust in the dialogue between history and theology in the study of the New Testament.

Roman Faith discussed at length the differences between representations of *pistis* in different writers and books. We have noted that this study, too, aims to outline not a single, systematic account of New Testament trust, but a series of sketches of aspects of divine–human trust. We should not automatically expect these to cohere, both because different writings focus on different facets and instantiations of the divine–human relationship (in God's past, present, and hoped-for actions; in Christ's pre-existence, earthly life, death, resurrection, and exalted life), and because different writers have different perspectives and agenda. It comes as no surprise to find, for instance, that Paul's interest in the relationship between trust, the covenant, and the law is not widely shared, while Chapter 4's model of atonement through trust and dying with Christ is rooted in distinctively Pauline language (though its themes of mediation, shared suffering, and imitation have parallels elsewhere).

That said, some significant coherences do emerge in these writings' vision of divine–human trust. The assumption that God is faithful and trustworthy and can be relied on to enact God's will, which is affirmed strongly in Jewish scripture and tradition, and rather more patchily in polytheistic religiosity, is implicit everywhere. The conviction that Jesus Christ is trustworthy as God is trustworthy is also universally accepted, and widely linked with the theme of divine care for creation, though it is expressed differently by different writers. Multiple writings envisage the exalted Christ as overseeing and acting for the faithful. Entering a relationship of trust with God and Christ is widely understood as a kind of rebirth: a death to the power of sin and suffering, leading to new life and new relationships under God's rule and in Christ's hands. New Testament writings share with modern psychology a conviction that where you trust is your reality: the place where you are seen and known; the place that matters to you and where you matter.

Trust is widely portrayed as both three-place and two-place: trust for salvation which shares God's hope for the world, and trust that lives for God and shares God's care for the world. Most writers recognize both that trust and faithfulness are important, and that they can be fragile; different books emphasize one more than the other but most, in some form, affirm the adequacy of imperfect human trust. By extension, though usually implicitly, they recognize that the trust God and Christ invest in human beings is risky. Multiple writers, however, by their interest in entrustedness, imply that God's risky trust is therapeutic: rooted in God's deep knowledge of God's creation and confidence that human beings will, ultimately, prove trustworthy. Last, but not least, propositional trust, implicit if not explicit, is widespread in these writings. If, in this life, objective truths elude us, whether about the nature of God, the end time, or the life, death, or resurrection of Christ, nevertheless, we can hope to develop reasoned convictions to which we are prepared to entrust ourselves and the future. Though it would be an exaggeration to claim that there is a New Testament theology of trust, therefore, there are signs that New Testament writings share much of their theological understanding of this most central and characteristic of Christian concepts.

Pistis, in these writings, is never only the attitude and act of saving trust. It is ongoing, sometimes progressive, and involves the faithful in entrustedness and in all kinds of this-worldly action. It is therefore not only soteriological and eschatological but ethical and ecclesial. It enters into partnership with God and Christ: God and Christ entrust human beings with all kinds of work in the present time and care for the world, and human beings accept their trust. *Pistis* is therefore, anthropologically, a strikingly optimistic concept. It affirms that most people, or everyone, however imperfect, can trust, persist in trust, be entrusted, and, through trust, come eventually to salvation and eternal life. On this basis, this study will conclude by offering some suggestions as to why trust was so important to early Christ-confessors, and why it matters to Christians today.

2
'The one who calls you is trustworthy'
The *Pistis* of God

Most of the New Testament's explicit *pistis* language relates to Jesus Christ:[1] the newly ascended being with whom people are invited to make a relationship of trust.[2] Occasionally we encounter a reference to trust in God in traditional terms.[3] The Paul of Acts, for example, facing shipwreck in the Adriatic, assures the ship's crew that they will survive because he trusts in God that he will, as he has been told in a dream, face trial before the emperor.[4] Any Jew or gentile could have said something similar. In Mark's gospel, Jesus once tells his disciples explicitly to 'have trust in God':[5] any Jew or gentile could have given the same advice.[6] John's Jesus, who often emphasizes his closeness to his father, tells the disciples, 'Trust in God, trust also in me.'[7]

If it is not often explicit, however, the idea that one can trust God, and God is faithful or trustworthy, is implicit everywhere.[8] It must have fulfilled slightly different functions for Jewish and gentile audiences. The faithfulness (*pistis*) of God to Israel and the assurance that God keeps God's promises are themes of the Jewish scriptures and other writings, so, when preaching to Jews and God-fearers,

---

[1] The chapter title quotation is from 1 Thess. 5.24.
[2] Much *pistis* language in the gospels has no direct object, leaving open whether it refers to God, Christ, or both, but see pp. 197–9. In Acts, people often come to *pisteuein* where the implied object is what they have heard preached.
[3] By the standards of contemporary Greek and Roman stories about the gods and divine men, and with the exception of Revelation, God and his messengers are rarely envisaged in New Testament writings as intervening directly in the material world, and in none of the relevant passages are people called explicitly to trust (though see, pp. 275–6). Outside Revelation, the invitation to trust comes to human beings through human beings.
[4] πιστεύω γὰρ τῷ θεῷ ὅτι οὕτως ἔσται, 27.25.
[5] Ἔχετε πίστιν θεοῦ, 11.22. Whether or not this saying was used by Jesus, the idea that faithfulness, righteousness, wisdom, *vel sim.* enables one to do great deeds also appears in the rabbis (Ebeling (1963), 228–9, Evans (2001), *ad loc.*).
[6] Parallels at Mt. 21.21–2 and (less close) Lk. 14.13, 16.23 omit trust in God. Heb. 11.6 could also have been affirmed by Jews or gentiles.
[7] πιστεύετε εἰς τὸν θεόν, καὶ εἰς ἐμὲ πιστεύετε, 14.1. Cf. e.g. 5.24 (Brown (1966), Beasley-Murray (1999), *ad loc.*).
[8] Trustworthiness and faithfulness, as already noted, are closely related and often difficult to distinguish. For clarity, I will tend to use 'trustworthiness' to refer to God's fulfilment of promises and to the basis on which people are invited into a new trust relationship or a specific act of trust, and 'faithfulness' of God's commitment, particularly to Israel and within covenants, over time. The Pauline corpus which is the focus of this chapter is not tolerant of doubt (cf. Jas 1.6–8, 4.8), but for a nuanced exploration of doubt across New Testament writings see Schliesser (2012, 2021).

Christ-confessors needed to convince them to trust in Jesus Christ in addition to trusting in God.[9] When preaching to gentiles, they must also have sought to convince them that the promise of salvation through Jesus Christ was so trustworthy that they could afford to stop trusting any god other than the God of Israel.[10]

Given that most of the New Testament's explicit *pistis* language relates to Christ, it is not self-evident that we should begin this study with God.[11] We do so for two reasons: in these writings the call to trust in Christ is rooted, implicitly or explicitly, in the assumption of God's trustworthiness, and New Testament writers' picture of the Christ in whom people can trust is framed partly by scriptural depictions of God or those who act on God's behalf as trustworthy. The relationship of trust between God and humanity (and Christ and humanity) is not all one way: we will see that not only do human beings put their trust in God and Christ, but God and Christ trust in human beings. Divine trust in humanity will be explored further in Chapter 7; this chapter will touch on God's trust in humanity as enacted in the Christ event, but its main focus is on humanity's trust in God and God's trustworthiness.[12]

Paul on the Trust, Trustworthiness, and Faithfulness of God

Some of the most striking instances of New Testament trust language in relation to God refer to the trust (*pistis*) God invests in humanity or to the idea that God is trustworthy or faithful (*pistos*) to humanity. Most of these are in the Pauline corpus,[13] so the vision of God's *pistis* in the first part of this chapter is largely that of Paul and his followers.[14]

---

[9] I use 'scriptures' throughout as early Christians use the term, to refer to the Jewish scriptures, while 'the Bible' refers to the modern Christian Bible. Appeal to the scriptures may have been attractive to gentiles too, for whom the antiquity of a cult, the wisdom of those who over time have attested to its validity, and stories of what a particular divine–human relationship has achieved, contribute to its authority (e.g. Plu., fr. 157.16–25 Sandbach. Tert., *Apol.* 19, Or., *Cels.* 1.14).

[10] In the early principate, surviving sources generally avoid accusing Greek and Roman gods of being unfaithful or untrustworthy, though there are stories of individuals wanting to test the trustworthiness of gods and debate about the reliability of oracles (Morgan (2015a), 136–7). The exception is discourse about Tyche/Fortuna, who is notorious for changing her allegiance and breaking faith even with those who have not offended her. According to Dio (65.7), people trust Tyche even while calling her *apistos*, because she is so powerful that the temptation to trust her is overwhelming.

[11] Systematic theologies, of course, regularly do so, but the aim of these chapters is to follow the shape of New Testament writers' thinking about God and Christ rather than to create a systematic theology in a modern form.

[12] These twin themes create an implicitly circular argument: that God can be trusted because of what has been done through Christ, and Christ can be trusted because God has acted through him. Logic is not these writers' main concern, but we can also note that both claims have further, mutually independent bases in the existing assumption among Jews that God is trustworthy, and in experiences of the earthly and risen Christ.

[13] On God's reliability see below, pp. 72–4. On trust in teachings see p. 125.

[14] pp. 125, 290–1. D-Pauline texts treat God's trustworthiness very similarly to Paul (Morgan (2015a), 313–14).

Paul takes for granted that the God of Israel is the one 'living and true God' (1 Thess. 1.9) who created and oversees the world.[15] As creator and God of Israel God has a history of trustworthiness and faithfulness, especially in keeping God's covenants, fulfilling God's promises, and saving Israel from her enemies.[16] All these are reasons for Paul, and Israel as a whole, to envisage God as trustworthy. Now, however, God has been revealed as trustworthy anew, through the earthly life, death, resurrection, and exaltation of Jesus Christ and the experiences of those who have encountered Christ. Accepting that God can be trusted in and for the Christ event is a new challenge for Jews as much as gentiles, and therefore risky.[17] What it is about the Christ event that, for Paul and others, makes it worthy of trust, and Christ trustworthy in it, is one of the themes of the next four chapters. Much of this chapter, however, considers how, in Paul's view, God's actions through Christ change what most Jews took for granted about God's relationship with Israel and Israel's relationship with the nations, and how God can be affirmed as trustworthy in these actions.

At 2 Corinthians 1.18, Paul invokes the trustworthiness of God to emphasize his own trustworthiness as one set apart by God to be Christ's apostle (cf. Gal. 1.15).[18] 'Do I plan what I plan according to the flesh [i.e. as human beings plan], so that with me it is "yes, yes" and "no, no"? As God is trustworthy ($\pi\iota\sigma\tau\dot{o}s$ δὲ ὁ θεός), our word to you is not "yes" and "no".'[19] The reference to 'yes' and 'no' may hint that Paul, like Godself, is truthful, but Paul's main point is that he himself is trustworthy or faithful to the Corinthians: when he has said that he will do something, he does not change his mind capriciously.[20] Even if Paul has not 'acted lightly' (cf. 1.17), however, he has, in fact, changed his plan to travel to Corinth (cf. 1.15). He has done so, he says, to spare the Corinthians, because he does not want to return only to be angry with them (cf. 2.1–3). Evidently, for Paul, one can be trustworthy while not doing what other people, with some reason, expected one to do.[21]

From justifying his own trustworthiness, Paul shifts to the trustworthiness of Godself, whose 'yes' 'in' Jesus Christ (1.19) is the foundation of Paul's apostolic trustworthiness (v. 19): 'For however many are the promises of God, their Yes is

---

[15] On the trustworthiness of God as creator see pp. 80–5.
[16] pp. 43–4, 50–3.   [17] On the nature of the risk see pp. 68–72.
[18] So Hooker (2003), though she does not distinguish God's or Christ's trustworthiness from reliability.
[19] Lietzmann-Kümmel (1949), 103, cf. e.g. Deut. 7.9 LXX, Isa. 49.7, Ps. 89.38, Prov. 14.5, 25. Translations are my own unless otherwise noted. On Paul's unusual emphasis on all God's promises being fulfilled in Christ see Furnish (1984), Martin (1986), Thrall (1994), ad loc.
[20] In the Septuagint, *alētheia* is often used instead of *pistis* to translate Hebrew *'emet*, capturing the sense of God's faithfulness as 'active, efficacious reality, the reality of God in covenant-relationship' (Barr (1961), 187), but Paul also uses it in its more usual sense of propositional truth, and can move between the two (see also below, p. 45). On trust and trust language in the Old Testament see Ziegert (2019).
[21] See further below, pp. 61–2, 72–4.

in him; which is why the Amen from us to God also goes through him for glory' (1.20). The 'yes' of God is 'in' Christ both in the sense that God's promises to Israel are fulfilled through the death of Christ (cf. 5.15, 18–19, 21), and in the sense that they are seen to be fulfilled through Christ: because of the Christ event human beings have a new assurance and conviction of God's trustworthiness. Paul affirms, moreover, that all God's promises, 'however many', are fulfilled through Christ. This could simply be a way of saying that the Christ event is the culmination of God's relationship with Israel, but it implies rather more: that the times in the past when God is remembered as having fulfilled God's promises to Israel may now, in light of the Christ event, be seen as provisional or interim fulfilments.

At Romans 1.16–17 Paul proclaims,

> So I am not ashamed of the gospel, for it is the power of God for salvation for everyone who trusts: first for the Jew, and then for the Greek. For the righteousness of God is revealed in it from *pistis* to *pistis*; as it is written [Hab. 2.4], 'The one who is righteous by *pistis* will live'.[22]

Whose *pistis* is at issue in the three appearances of the term in verse 17—God's, Christ's, or that of faithful human beings—is debated, and I have argued that this ambiguity is productive and likely to be intentional.[23] The Hebrew Bible's (MT) version of Habakkuk 2.4 says that the righteous man lives by his own faithfulness to God, while the Septuagint's says that he lives by God's faithfulness (towards Israel) but, both here and when he cites the verse at Galatians 3.11, Paul omits any pronoun.[24] He could be referring to the trust, trustworthiness, or faithfulness of God which reaches out to enable an answering trust[25] in human beings (cf. Rom. 3.21-2), the trust of Christ to God (and arguably also to human beings) which reveals the righteousness of God and enables trust in human beings (cf. 3.22, 24), the trust of Christ-confessors toward God and Christ (cf. 2.10), or even the trust of the preacher towards God and Christ which reveals the righteousness of God for the enabling of trust in others (cf. 1 Cor. 4.1-2)—or all four. Since Paul speaks of all these patterns of *pistis* activity elsewhere, any of them would fit his thinking in general, and all are possible in this context. Assuming, however, that 1.17 refers, at least in part, to the *pistis* of God, it affirms this in relation first to the

---

[22] I use variously 'righteousness', 'right-standing', and 'justice' to translate *dikaiosynē*, to reflect differences of emphasis in different contexts.

[23] Morgan (2015a), 286–7.

[24] The LXX textual tradition is secure, but Heb. 10.38 has another variant again: 'my just one shall live by faith', where it is clear that the *pistis* is that of the faithful person. At Gal. 3.11 it is also the *pistis* of the faithful person that is at issue, but Paul is making a different argument here from that of Rom. 1: that righteousness comes through *pistis* not the law.

[25] Or trustworthiness or faithfulness, which we will take as included in 'trust' throughout this paragraph.

Jews and then to the 'Greeks' (1.16). In this context, in which Paul is speaking of the gospel as the power of God for salvation through Christ, God has enacted *pistis* first to the Jews, in the sense that the first post-resurrection preaching was to Jews.[26] Implicit in this affirmation may be another: that the Jews hear the preaching first because of their existing relationship with God, to which God is faithful.[27] Now, however, God's righteousness is decisively revealed, and God's power for salvation enacted, in what God has done through Christ and in the preaching about it, so the gospel constitutes at least an invitation to Jews to renew their trust in new circumstances, and possibly an invitation to a new relationship of trust through Christ.[28]

In chapter 3 Paul has more to say about God's *pistis*, as he seeks to explain further God's (re)new(ed) relationship with Israel.[29] Interpretation of this passage tends, understandably, to focus on God's justice and the value (*ōpheleia*) of the Mosaic covenant, but it also speaks to the nature of God's trustworthiness and faithfulness.[30] Paul first insists (3.1-3) that it is still an advantage to be Jewish, even if God's impartiality offers 'glory, honour, and peace' to gentiles too (cf. 2.10-11).[31] In the first place, the Jews have been 'entrusted with the oracles [or 'sayings'] of God (ἐπιστεύθησαν τὰ λόγια τοῦ θεοῦ)', (3.2). This is a slightly less ringing statement of the advantage of being Jewish than we might have expected at this point: all the more since there turns out to be no second place.[32] To be entrusted with something, in any sphere of life from politics to law, commerce, or cult, is an honourable and responsible position (as Paul affirms when he describes himself as entrusted with the gospel), but it is normally a means to an end, not an end in itself.[33]

---

[26] See the discussions of Cranfield (1975), Fitzmyer (1993a), *ad loc*. This is not to claim that preaching first to Jews was necessarily Paul's own missionary strategy, though, as Dunn (1988), *ad loc*. points out, 'the synagogue provided the most obvious platform for his message'.

[27] Cf. Barker (2004) on God's faithfulness (focusing on Deuteronomy), Rayburn (2019) (focusing on Psalms and Hebrews).

[28] Cf. pp. 73-4.

[29] The configuration (re)new(ed) is used here and elsewhere to signal that Israel's relationship with God is, in some sense, both renewed and new in Christ; that if Israel's relationship with God is renewed, that of the gentiles is new; and sometimes to suggest that the relationship of Jews and gentiles alike with God is both new in Christ and a renewal of the relationship for which humanity is created.

[30] On the covenant see below, pp. 50-4.

[31] On the tight relationship between ch. 2 and 3.1-9 see Flebbe (2008), 22-57.

[32] Noted by Williams (2002), 98-9. The *logia* may be the promises to Abraham and the patriarchs, the law, the scriptures as a whole, or the messianic promises: see the discussions of Käsemann (1980), Fitzmyer (1993a), Jewett (2007), *ad loc*., with Doeve (1953).

[33] Cf. 1 Cor. 9.17, Gal. 2.7, 1 Thess. 2.4, though Rom. 9.4-5 describes the advantages of being Jewish as more than a trust. If God's *logia* here are oracles, we should note that there is more than one kind of oracle: some refer to one event and, once fulfilled, are not used again; others, especially in authoritative books, can be referred to repeatedly. The reference to both law and prophets at 3.21 indicates that Paul thinks of the 'oracles of God' as the second kind, and the use of the phrase outside Paul strengthens this view: e.g. at Acts 7.38 *logia* of God refer to the law handed down on Sinai; at Heb. 5.12 and 1 Pet. 4.11 they refer to teachings from unspecified sources.

'What', Paul continues, echoing Psalm 88.31–8 LXX, 'if some were unfaithful?[34] Will their faithlessness nullify the *pistis* of God? Heaven forbid!'[35] God has been faithful to Israel despite Israelite unfaithfulness before. This time, however, God has fulfilled God's promises neither, as in the past, because Israel has been faithful (as, in part, he implies, she has been), nor because she has been unfaithful, has been punished, and/or has repented (as those who have been unfaithful apparently have not).[36] Rather, the grace of God manifested through the redemption in Christ (3.24, cf. 21) is a response to the fact that 'all have sinned and fallen short of the glory of God' (3.23, cf. 3.9, 3.10–12). In these verses Paul makes three claims. The advantage of being Jewish lies not in God's unique care for Israel and promises to Israel, but in Israel's having been entrusted with God's utterances (implicitly, in the context of his preaching, on behalf of both herself and the gentiles). Salvation has not come specifically for Israel. And salvation has not come, as might traditionally have been expected, as a result of Israel's attitude or behaviour towards God, whether good or bad. The *pistis* of God consists in God's entrusting Israel with God's *logia*, and in God's faithfulness to God's *logia* in God's action through Christ on behalf of all humanity.

It is tempting to see Israel's entrustedness with God's *logia* as drawing on Deutero-Isaiah's image of Israel as a 'covenant for the people' and a 'light to the nations' (42.6, cf. 49.6),[37] but the context in chapters 2–3 as a whole, which emphasize Israel's failings along with those of gentiles, makes this unlikely. It may be closer to the mark to think of the relationship of Israel to the rest of humanity here as more like that of the priests and teachers of Israel to Israel as a whole. Israel has been tasked with a particular service to God which involves knowing (even) better than others, and doing more punctiliously than others, what God requires. The fact that some Israelites have been faithful is no doubt praiseworthy; the fact that some have not is deplorable; but neither is the main reason for God's action on behalf of humanity as a whole.[38]

---

[34] Following Jewett's punctuation ((2007), *ad loc.*). 'Good faith' is another possible translation of God's *pistis* here, which fits well with the idea that God has acted with regard to God's relationship with Israel, but in a new way. Jewish *apistia* here may refer to non-confession of Christ (so e.g. Jewett (2007), *ad loc.*; cf. 11.17), but τί γάρ; εἰ ἠπίστησάν τινες would be an odd way to describe the fact that almost all Jews have not confessed Christ, so it may be preferable to see this as a more general reference to past failures to understand the spirit, as opposed to the letter of the law (cf. 2.29, 9.32) (the aorist does not necessarily imply a single point of unfaithfulness: cf. e.g. 2.12).

[35] τί γάρ; εἰ ἠπίστησάν τινες, μὴ ἡ ἀπιστία αὐτῶν τὴν πίστιν τοῦ θεοῦ καταργήσει; μὴ γένοιτο, 3.3–4.

[36] Acts 15.10, possibly influenced by Paul, goes further than Paul here, suggesting not only that Israel has failed to keep the law but that it has proved a yoke she was not strong enough to bear (and hence it would be unreasonable to ask gentile Christ-confessors to bear it). The possibility of being saved (v. 11) by trust (vv. 7, 9) is therefore a grace (v. 11) not only in the sense that it is a new gift, but in the sense that it renders law-keeping no longer necessary.

[37] As Acts 13.47 has Paul saying, quoting Isa. 42.6.

[38] Paul may be drawing here on his own experience as a Pharisee who, while he was persecuting Christians, was, by his own later lights, unknowingly sinful, but to whom God and Christ reached out despite both his faithfulness and his sinfulness (cf. Gal. 1.13–16).

Paul follows up the rhetorical question of 3.3 with the pious wish, 'let God be true, though every human being is a liar' (3.4). We have noted that, in the Septuagint, 'truth' is often used of what James Barr calls 'the reality of God in covenant relationship',[39] so at the beginning of the verse Paul's Jewish and god-fearing listeners may hear God's being 'true' as another reference to God's trustworthiness or faithfulness. Paul, however, pivots to contrast God's truth not with human faithlessness, but with lies.[40] The truth, in this sense, that is attested by God's words must be that God's righteousness has been manifested through the death of Jesus Christ. God's truth, moreover, Paul goes on to proclaim, will abound to God's glory, even through human falsehood (3.7).[41] This 'truth' is resoundingly described towards the end of the chapter:

(21) But now the righteousness of God has been revealed apart from the law, though witnessed to by the law and the prophets, (22) the righteousness of God through the trust(worthiness) of Jesus Christ for all who trust/believe (διὰ πίστεως Ἰησοῦ Χριστοῦ, εἰς πάντας τοὺς πιστεύοντας), for there is no distinction. (23) For all have sinned and fall short of the glory of God. (24) They are righteoused as a gift by his grace through the redemption in Christ Jesus, (25) whom God put forward as a supplicatory offering, through trust, by his blood, to show his righteousness because of the forgiveness of sins previously committed, (26) through the forbearance of God—to prove his righteousness in the present time, that he might be righteous and righteous the one who [is righteoused by] the trust(worthiness) of Jesus (εἰς τὸ εἶναι αὐτὸν δίκαιον καὶ δικαιοῦντα τὸν ἐκ πίστεως Ἰησοῦ).[42]   (Rom. 3.21-6)

Most of the complexities of this passage need not concern us here, but Paul again highlights that God's righteousness has been manifested for everyone, despite universal sinfulness; that it fulfils the testimony of the law and the prophets; and that both God's relational commitment to humanity and the truth of the gospel are 'shown' by the forgiveness of sins (vv. 25, 26). Paul also underlines not only the trust and trustworthiness of Christ in this event, to which we will return,[43] but that the appropriate human response to it is *pisteuein*: probably a combination of believing (that Christ died for the forgiveness of sins) and trusting (in God and Christ).[44] In this passage, the outcome of God's grace (v. 24) is said to be not the renewal of the covenant, nor a new covenant, but a new relationship of

---

[39] Above, p. 45.   [40] Quoting Ps. 116.11, 51.6 LXX.   [41] Dunn (1988), *ad loc.*
[42] On *hilastērion* as 'supplicatory offering' see Collins (2019), 278, following Higbie (2003), 24-5. Collins notes (p. 275) that even if 25-6a is not Pauline, it is preferable, if we can, to find an interpretation of *hilastērion* that fits with his own language, as this does better than e.g. 'sacrifice of atonement' NRSV, NIV, 'propitiation' KJV, NASB, 'expiation' NAB.
[43] pp. 153-9.   [44] Below, pp. 64-6, 99-109.

trust (v. 26). The novelty of this development is emphasized: '[b]ut now...apart from the law' (v. 21).[45]

Paul does not need to remind either a Jewish or a gentile audience that the manifestation of God's grace and righteousness through the death of Christ constitutes the fulfilment of prophecy in a thoroughly unexpected way. Nobody foresaw the kind of messiah that Christ-confessors recognized Jesus as being in his earthly life or death. God, Paul therefore affirms, is both truthful and trustworthy, but not in the way that anyone expected or that Israel hoped. To the claims he made at the beginning of this chapter, therefore, we can add another, already adumbrated at 2 Corinthians 1.18: a trustworthy God fulfils God's promises, but not necessarily in the way that human beings hope or expect.

Though Paul's, and all Christians' application of the claim that God has fulfilled God's promises in an unexpected manner to Jesus Christ is radical in itself, the idea that God fulfils God's promises in unexpected ways is not. Identifying Cyrus the Great as Israel's saviour, to take one well-known example, might have taken as great a shift in Israelite expectations as identifying Jesus as the Christ.[46] In imagining God's *pistis* Paul has a wide range of scriptural affirmations, as well as contemporary writings and debates, to draw on, especially in some passages of Genesis and Exodus, the psalms, the books of wisdom, and some of the prophets.[47] Most of these refer either to God's trustworthiness or good faith as creator, or to God as faithful to Israel within the Mosaic covenant. Although they regularly affirm that God is trustworthy and faithful to creation in general, and in particular to Israel, they tend to avoid specifying exactly how God is, or will be faithful, or whether the specific form of God's faithfulness in the past surprised its beneficiaries.[48] That said, the idea that God is faithful to the covenant with Israel

---

[45] Paul insists this does not 'annul' (*katargein*) the law. He may mean 'law' here in the sense of scripture (so Byrne (1996), *ad* 3.31); alternatively, he may be affirming that where people trust in God and Christ (cf. 3.28, 30, 10.4), they are doing everything that the law, as a reification of deferred trust, is designed to help them do, which would fit well with modern understandings of the relationship between trust and law.

[46] Assuming that he is treated as a messianic figure at some point in the evolution of D-Isaiah, on which see Fried (2002), Sawyer (2018), *ad* Isa. 45.

[47] The LXX contains *c.*150 references to divine–human *pistis*.

[48] E.g. Ps. 32.4 LXX. Psalm 110.7 LXX praises God for keeping his covenant, and calls his commandments *pistos* (cf. Ps. 88.28 LXX (God's covenant is *pistos*), 18.8 LXX (God's law is *pistos*, cf. 110.7, 118.66). At Ps. 77.22 Israel lacked trust in God's saving power, with negative consequences, while at Micah 7.20 God is faithful to God's covenant with Moses and the patriarchs, and Isaiah's God is faithful to his promises to Abraham (Oswalt (1998), especially 334, cf. Greenberg (2004)). The wisdom books refer regularly to the importance of trusting God and God's commandments and not being afraid, or seeking to test God's covenant faithfulness (Morgan (2015a), 200–4: e.g. Prov. 12.22, cf. 15.27–8, 15.27a). In the scriptures trust between God and human beings is also foundational for intra-human trust, which is rarely the case in early Christian texts (Morgan (2015a), 204–10). By the later Hellenistic period, the covenant faithfulness of God has become axiomatic, as has the importance of trusting in God and trusting that God will vindicate the righteous: if not in this life, then in the next: e.g. *Wis. Sol.* 1.2, 3.8, cf. 12.2. On the importance of trust in God in the Hymn of the Maskil (1QS IX, 25b–XI, 15a see Gayer (2015). Philo (who makes little use of covenant ideas) speaks of God's trustworthiness at e.g. *Fug.* 152, *Mut. Nom.* 182, 201. Trust in God is not easy (*Her.* 90–4), but it is within a

(e.g. Ps. 88.38 LXX) and fulfils his promises to his chosen people (e.g. Isa. 25.1, 49.7, cf. 42.6, 42.21, 45.8) must always have opened the door, if only a crack, to the idea that God can be trusted to do what God's faithful people expect or want. The writer of Ben Sira more than once comes close to saying as much: 'Who has ever trusted in the Lord (*pisteuein*) and been disappointed (τίς ἐνεπίστευσεν κυρίῳ καὶ κατῃσχύνθη)? (2.10)'. 'Trust in him, and he will support you (πίστευσον αὐτῷ, καὶ ἀντιλήμψεταί σου)' (2.6). We will return to this theme.[49]

Paul is evidently not wholly satisfied with what he has said about the *pistis* of God in relation to Israel in Romans 3, because he returns to it in chapters 9–11, seeking again to harmonize his convictions that a faithful God has a unique and unbroken relationship with Israel; that his own preaching is in continuity with that relationship; that right-standing with God now rests entirely on human beings' new *pistis*-response to Christ and the preaching about Christ; and that the 'redemption in Christ Jesus' (3.24) is offered on equal terms to everyone. The word of God, Paul insists at 9.6, has not failed.[50] God has kept God's promise to Abraham (9.7–8). It is the definition of Abraham's children that is revealed as not what it was thought to be, but as including the gentiles (v. 8). It behoves the Jews to recognize and accept this because it is God's prerogative to 'show mercy to whom I will show mercy' (vv. 14–15, cf. 18).[51] Divine mercy depends not on human will or action (v. 16), but only on God, and God acts through whom he chooses, good or bad (v. 17, cf. 22–3).[52] It is part of God's 'elective plan' (9.11) that, in the words of Genesis 11.5–6, 'the older shall serve the younger': as at Romans 3.2, Israel has been entrusted with a word or promise (cf. 9.6–9) which, it turns out, is not just for her but for the whole of humanity. Paul acknowledges (e.g. 9.6, 9.14, 11.1) that this is not the way Jews had understood God's plan, but, quoting Exodus 33.19, he repeats that the trustworthiness (and, at 9.14, the justice)

---

relationship of trust in God that human beings can begin to understand the truth of God (*Post. Cain.* 13, *Conf.* 31, *Abr.* 270, 273, *Somn.* 2.68); see Morgan (2015a), 152–5).). In the absence of *pistis* language, references to God's promises to the patriarchs and to the covenant(s), also speak implicitly to God's trustworthiness and faithfulness, notably in the psalms: e.g. Ps. 14.7; 20.1; 22.23; 24.6; 44.4; 46.7, 11; 47.4; 53.6; 59.13; 75.9; 76.6; 77.15; 78.5, 21, 71; 79.7; 81.1, 4; 84.8; 85.1; 87.2; 94.7; 99.4; 105.6, 10, 23; 114.1, 7; 132.2, 5; 135.4; 146.5; 147.19.

[49] pp. 72–4. On this idea in modern psychological studies of trust in God see e.g. Rosmarin et al. (2009), Pirutinsky and Rosmarin (2020).

[50] Οὐχ οἷον δὲ ὅτι ἐκπέπτωκεν ὁ λόγος τοῦ θεοῦ.

[51] Even if God continues faithful to Israel 'because of the patriarchs', the trust relationship now on offer to both Jews and gentiles (9.8, 10.12, 11.11) is essentially new (cf. 10.9). At 9.4–5 all the things that distinguish Israel could be read as historical and connected with her role as entrusted with God's *logia* (especially if, with Byrne (1996), *ad loc.* we take the reference to 'glory' to refer to past manifestations of the glory of God, e.g. Exod. 16.10, 24.16, Isa. 6.3). It is more likely, though, that Paul recognizes that e.g. law-keeping and temple cult continue, for Jews, and are compatible with putting one's trust in God and Christ (so e.g. Stowers (1994), 130–1); there is also no reason to think that he thinks the 'law' in the broad sense of the scriptures is 'annulled' (cf. 3.31): see e.g. Williams (2002), 110.

[52] The importance of the pro-active and decisive power of God throughout Romans is emphasized by Flebbe (2008), *passim*, though he does not see God as replacing the covenant with Israel with the new relationship of trust.

of God consists in God's doing not necessarily what his people want or expect, but what God wills. This reaffirms and, if anything, sharpens the argument of 3.2–4, and Paul perhaps thinks he has sharpened it too much, because he emphasizes that Israel (unlike the gentiles) has actively sought the 'law of righteousness' (9.31) and is zealous for God (10.1),[53] even if she has acted wrongly by practising 'works' rather than trust (9.32, cf. 3.9–10, 5.20).[54] There is no suggestion, however, that if Israel had kept the law with *pistis*, the Christ event would not have occurred or the law would continue to be the way to righteousness. God has taken a new initiative and righteousness is now only possible through trust in Christ.

Paul's argument that no one is made right with God by keeping the law may have developed as an argument for why, in Paul's view, gentile Christ-confessors need not keep the law, but in Romans it is made as an argument about the law *tout court*.[55] At 10.4 Paul asserts that 'Christ is the *telos* of the law for righteousness for everyone who trusts.'[56] By identifying Christ with the word brought to Israel by Moses (10.8), and confessing and trusting in Christ with holding the word (about Christ, 10.17) 'in your mouth and in your heart' (10.8–10, cf. Deut. 30.14), Paul argues that confessing Jesus as Lord and putting one's trust in Christ does everything the law is intended to do. Confessing and trusting in Christ is, in practice, fulfilling the law, even though some Jews do not currently recognize this (cf. 10.2). As Robert Badenas puts it,

> the Christ event has revealed in history that the righteousness which the law promised was nothing other than the righteousness manifested to all by Christ. Israel, biased by its wrong understanding of the law in relation to righteousness, did not recognize in the Christ event the manifestation of 'the righteousness of God' to whom the law pointed. It did not see, therefore, that 'Christ is the goal, the aim, the intention, the real meaning and substance of the Law...'.[57]

---

[53] Like Paul himself, as a Pharisee (Gal. 1.13–14, Phil. 3.6).

[54] Wolter (2015a), 351 suggests that if Israel had kept the law with *pistis*, she would apparently have achieved righteousness, perhaps because this would have entailed recognizing Christ, in due time, as the *telos* of the law, but as it is, Israel has forgotten that righteousness comes from God, on God's terms, and requires *pistis* (Rom. 10.3–4, cf. 6–11, 9.30–2). The idea that works of the law (9.31, 32, cf. 3.20) act as a stumbling-block to righteousness (9.32–3) does not automatically cohere with the idea that Israel, as defined in the past, was entrusted with the word(s) of God, which have now been fulfilled in such a way that humanity now stands in a new trust relationship with God, but Paul wants to persuade his readers that it does.

[55] This view may stem in part from Paul's own experience that it was putting his trust in the risen Christ, not his law-keeping, that brought righteousness and new life (Massinelli (2015) suggests that Paul offers his own experience here as a model for other Jews). Paul may have seen gentiles being incorporated into the Antioch church without keeping the law, but his view is probably also pragmatic: insisting that gentile converts should keep the law would add complexity to becoming a Christ-confessor, shift some of its focus away from Christ himself, and bring new Christians into the sphere of influence of more conservative Jewish community leaders who had doubts about Paul's mission (cf. Gal. 2.2–10).

[56] On this translation of *telos* see the discussions of Cranfield (1979), Jewett (2007), *ad loc*.

[57] Badenas (1985), 117–18. On various, somewhat different ways in which Matthew's community may understand Jesus as fulfilling the law see Davies and Allison (1988), *ad* Mt. 5.17.

To the idea that God fulfils God's word as God chooses and human beings must accept this, Paul therefore adds that God's choice not only fulfils God's promise but also the law, and so God has been faithful and is trustworthy to Israel as Israel (could have) hoped and expected. The meaning of *telos* here has been much debated, but on any plausible interpretation it is hard to avoid the inference that nobody who is made right with God by confessing and trusting in Christ, gentile or Jewish, needs to observe the law as well.[58] Paul never says this in so many words, and that need not surprise us: it is one thing to insist that gentiles need not keep the law, and another to provoke a confrontation with Jewish Christians about their own observance.[59] Instead Paul urges all community members to be tolerant and compassionate towards each other's ritual preferences and 'weaknesses' (cf. Rom. 14.1, 1 Cor. 8.9), whatever they are (Rom. 14 *passim*, 1 Cor. 8),[60] and fix their attention on the one thing that matters for righteousness and salvation: serving Christ (Rom. 14.18) and enabling others to do the same (cf. 8.11–13).[61]

Romans 11 takes a further turn. Paul reiterates that all that has happened does not mean that God has rejected God's people (11.1, 2), but by grafting the gentiles onto Abraham's stock (cf. 11.17–18), God is acting 'to make them jealous' (11.11, cf. 10.19) so that eventually 'all Israel will be saved' (11.26, cf. 11.14). At the same time, Paul holds that some Israelites have repeatedly broken their side of their covenant with God (cf. 11.3, 7–8) and that only a remnant remains, by grace (11.5). If, with many commentators, we take the remnant that remains as Jews who have confessed Christ (having, as Paul has already claimed, previously been sinners (3.9–10)), we can infer that at least part of Israel failed her side of the covenant before the Christ event.[62] A covenant that has been broken is, by its nature, not operative as a covenant until it is renewed or replaced, so Israel needs to be reconciled with God, which is now possible only through Christ. The assurance that God has not rejected his people (11.1) is an assurance that God is still committed—faithful—to Israel, as he has been when she has broken covenants in the past. As Paul expresses it at the end of this section, Israel remains beloved by God 'because of the patriarchs' (11.28).

Eventually, after 'the full number of the gentiles' has come in (11.25), Paul is confident that God will take the (or some) Israelites' godlessness away from them and fulfil his gifts and his call to them (11.26, 28). Israel will then recognize and accept that God's faithfulness to her is fulfilled in Christ, that it is in Christ that God continues faithful, and that all humanity is now encompassed in the divine–human

---

[58] Cf. pp. 59–60, 91.
[59] Paul's concern, moreover, is not to work out systematically all the implications of his convictions, but to persuade people of them and meet objections as best he can as they arise.
[60] Not, of course, to the point of condoning cult to 'idols' (1 Cor. 10.7, 10.14, Gal. 5.19).
[61] This view is separately supported by Paul's insistence, in different contexts, that every community member, *qua* community member, has the same standing (cf. 1 Cor. 7.17–24, Gal. 3.28). There is no harm in keeping the law, as long as one does not think it leads to righteousness or salvation, any more than there is any harm in eating meat sacrificed to non-gods, but in itself it is not righteousing.
[62] Discussed by Fitzmyer (1993a), *ad loc.*

pistis relationship. This, Paul asserts, citing Isaiah 27.9, 'is my covenant with them when I take away their sins' (11.27). At first sight, this verse seems to refer to yet another new covenant with Israel in the future, but this would be so alien to Paul's fundamental conviction that everyone is now saved by trusting in Christ that Paul is more likely to be referring here to the 'covenant' in Christ which, he is convinced, Israel will eventually accept.[63]

On this account, God's *pistis* relationship with Israel in the present time, in Paul's understanding, has taken a radically unexpected turn. It can no longer be framed by the covenant as it was before the Christ event, nor, between God and Jews who do not confess Christ, can it be reciprocal in the way Paul might imagine that God would hope, but it persists. Whether within covenants, without them, or when they have been broken, human infidelity does not nullify the fidelity of God (cf. 3.3). At the culmination of the argument it becomes a little clearer how Paul imagines this situation. At 11.32, he returns to where he began in chapters 1–2 to say that 'God delivered everyone to disobedience, that he might have mercy upon everyone', but with a twist. Where, at the start of the letter, God's *pistis* reached out beyond Israel to the gentiles, though they lacked a covenant with God, now God's *pistis* reaches out beyond Christ-confessors to non-Christian Israel, though she does not recognize that the basis of the divine–human relationship has changed. At this time, for Paul (9.15), God's *pistis* is well expressed by God's announcement at Exodus 33.22 (in another narrative marked both by much *pistis* language and by recurrent tensions and Israelite failures of trust) that 'I will show mercy to whom I will, I will take pity on whom I will.'

The argument of chapters 9–11 is made more complex by the fact that chapter 9 invokes two pivotal moments in God's past relationship with Israel. The promise to Abraham and the covenant at Sinai are somewhat different, and the differences have been sketched both in earlier chapters of Romans, and in an earlier letter. The argument of Galatians 3 itself is somewhat different from that of Romans, but there are points of overlap. It is therefore worth looking at both in a slightly broader context, and saying a little more about Paul's understanding of the relationship between promise, covenant, and *pistis*.

Trust, Covenant, and Promise

Trust is widely recognized, across academic disciplines as in everyday life, as fundamental to individual and social relationships, but as chronically risky and often

---

[63] Using the language of covenant here in a way which would resonate with a Jewish audience: see e.g. Hegermann (1990), 301, Christiansen (1995), 225–32. Wolter observes ((2015a), 421, (2018)) that when and how Paul envisages the redemption of Israel remains highly uncertain; we can only be sure that he is convinced that Israel will be redeemed and that it will be by turning to Christ.

difficult.⁶⁴ To limit the risks of trust and make it easier, individuals and groups find ways to try to establish and ensure each other's trustworthiness, based on direct or indirect experience, evidence, attitudes ranging from belief to speculation, and a wide range of social instruments from oaths to laws, tokens backed by political or legal authorities, socially sanctioned customs, and forms of argument.⁶⁵

These instruments are sometimes described as objectivizations or reifications of deferred trust.⁶⁶ For example, when Roman soldiers take an oath of loyalty to the emperor, the oath, on one level, expresses a relationship of *fides*: the soldiers will be loyal and the emperor will be trustworthy. But the oath is not just the expression of a relationship (which may not be very robust: for instance, if the soldiers have no alternative source of income or the emperor has a poor military record). It is reified as a political and legal entity, with legal consequences if it is broken.⁶⁷ On another level, therefore, the oath itself defines the relationship between the emperor and his soldiers, and rather than having *fides* directly towards each other, which may be difficult, both parties trust the oath which guarantees *fides* between them. Similarly, a form of argument which guarantees that if your premises are true, you can trust your conclusion to be true, is reified and given its own identity with the term 'proof', and trust in the conclusion can be deferred to the trustworthiness of the proof. Instruments like these are ubiquitous and powerful in complex societies. By defining and reifying trust they enable the development and flourishing of all kinds of other relationships and practices, from friendship to marriage and justice to commerce. So integral to the practice of trust are social and legal instruments that, for instance, Greek *pistis* and Latin *fides* can mean, in addition to trust, trustworthiness, and faithfulness, (financial) credit, a pledge, argument, proof, testimony, a safeguard, a guarantee, and a legal trust.

Most scholars of the Hebrew Bible share with scholars of the ancient Near East and Mediterranean, and with modern social scientists and philosophers of law, the recognition that a covenant is a socio-legal instrument, which seeks to make trust easier by affirming that if one party is, say, trustworthy and faithful to the other, the other will be trustworthy and faithful in turn, and setting out the relevant scope of their trust.⁶⁸ In Genesis 17, for example, God establishes God's covenant with Abraham, affirming that as long as Abraham walks blamelessly in

---

⁶⁴ E.g. Erikson (1959), Masters (1986), Berg et al. (1995), Fukuyama (1995), Meyer (2002), O'Neill (2002), Wang (2002), Kohn (2008), Seldon (2009), Rose (2011), cf. Putnam (2000), Dasgupta (1999).
⁶⁵ On this in Greek and Roman mentality, see Morgan (2015a), 36–122.
⁶⁶ Nörr (1989), 43–4, Morgan (2015a), 6.
⁶⁷ If the emperor betrays his army, the consequences are not likely to be legal, but the role of the military in multiple *coups d'état* during the principate shows the consequences for emperors of losing the trust of their armies.
⁶⁸ McCarthy (1963), Behm and Quell (1964), 109–24, cf. 104–5, Weinfeld (1972), 59–157, Mendenhall and Herion (2001), 1179, Barton (2003), 24–5, Koch (2008), Hibbard (2015), Joosten (2019). On the variety of covenants see e.g. Freedman and Miano (2003), Buchanan (2003), Bautsch (2009), Bautsch and Knoppers (2015).

God's presence (17.1) and marks his and his descendants' commitment to God with circumcision (17.10), God will make Abraham 'the father of many nations' (17.5) and give them the land of Canaan as their possession (17.8). Abraham has, of course, already been said to have put his trust in God, at 15.6, but it emerges at 17.17–18 that his trust in God to give him and Sarah an heir (cf. 15.4) is still far from firm.[69] Genesis narrates what modern scholarship identifies as a classic pattern in the evolution of trust. For human beings (or even divinities) to have any relationships at all, they must take the risk of trusting, but once a provisional relationship of trust has been established, it can be fortified and developed by covenants and other instruments.[70]

It is worth emphasizing that to understand God's covenants with Israel as instruments of trust or reifications of deferred trust is not to undervalue them.[71] Such instruments, as noted, make possible all kinds of closer social relationships and enable all kinds of further activities. One of the striking aspects of many of the Jewish scriptures and other writings, in the context of the ancient Mediterranean and Near East, is the scale and sophistication of their explorations of what it means to live in a covenant with God, and the deeper relationships and new activities which covenants make possible.[72] No tradition takes more seriously the potential of covenants to transform and enrich human lives and divine–human relationships. The expectations of human beings within God's covenants with Israel are both practical and visionary: to keep the Sabbath (Exod. 20.8); to be just,

---

[69] Some might argue that Gen. 12.1 implies an existing covenant between God and Abram, of the basic 'I am your God and you are my people' type, which itself would plausibly rest on an act of trust (cf. Exod. 6.7, Jer. 30.22, though these and other instances in the Hebrew Bible occur at moments of renewal of an established relationship), but to see covenant in every relationship is to over-extend the concept. Albrektson (2003), 8 and *passim* attractively proposes that the MT of Gen. 15.6 should be translated 'He trusted Yahweh and considered it (i.e. Yahweh's promise) reliable [or "trustworthy"]', but Paul uses the LXX version. Paul may also derive some of his interest in trust and faithfulness from its relative prominence in Isa. 1–39, though Isaiah's trust is made possible by the covenant.

[70] The same pattern is visible in the story of the Exodus, where several incidences of trust, supported by various kinds of evidence (e.g. 4.5, 4.8–9, 14.31, 19.9), precede the giving of the Sinai covenant; see Morgan (2015a), 185–7.

[71] This concern leads some commentators (e.g. Blumenthal (1987)) to argue that Jewish covenants are expressions of e.g. faith, love, and grace rather than having any contractual dimension, but this requires us to assume that God's covenants with Israel are wholly unlike covenants elsewhere in the ancient world. Without very clear evidence it is difficult, historically, to argue for such radical discontinuity, and the range of scholarly views indicates that the evidence is far from clear (in addition, it is hard to see what the status of laws within such a non-covenant would be). Jewish covenantal thinking is surely better understood, with many modern commentators, as an exceptionally rich exploration of all that divine–human agreements make possible. Thielman (1989) argues that, for Paul, the covenant is not surpassed because Paul endorses its ethical commands—but Paul's key ethics, as often noted, are widely shared by Jews and gentiles and need not take place within covenants; Ware's (2011) view that one strain of covenantal thinking holds that grace and forgiveness are only found within the covenantal relationship has to assume covenantal thinking in Romans where it is not referenced.

[72] It is occasionally suggested (e.g. Fee (1994), 806–7) that Paul's description of the spirit as an *arrabōn* (2 Cor. 1.22, 5.5) implies a (new) contract with humanity; *arrabōn*, though, can mean 'gift' as well as 'pledge' or 'deposit', and is not connected by Paul with 'new covenant' language. Moule (1978), 34–6, while accepting the translation 'pledge', captures the sense in these passages that the spirit brings the faithful trustworthy confidence in the future.

merciful, and humble (Mic. 6.8); to enjoy and bless God for the land God has given Israel (Deut. 8.10–20); to write the law in human hearts and 'know the Lord' (Jer. 31.31). Living and thinking within covenants enables the people of Israel to ask challenging questions and engage in searching discussions about creation, suffering, and theodicy in the scriptures and elsewhere. It also allows them to express high hopes and profound confidence that God will take care of them and fulfil God's promises. In Israelite and Jewish tradition, covenantal thinking becomes such a fertile, powerful, and widespread way of conceptualizing the divine–human relationship that it comes as no surprise to find it applied to stories and relationships in which covenants are not mentioned (notably the relationship between God and Adam).[73]

That said, the concept of covenant is not equally important in all books of the scriptures, nor in all other writings.[74] Close in time to Paul, it receives notably little attention from, among others, Philo (like Paul, a Greek-speaking diaspora Jew) and Josephus (like Paul, a Pharisee and a writer to gentiles). Though the first covenants are made in the Book of Genesis, moreover, the first covenant identified as such is not made until Genesis 9.9, and, though we might be tempted to infer a covenantal relationship between God and Abram at Genesis 12.1, the first explicit covenant between them is made at 17.2.[75] There is therefore scope and authority for later writers to speak of the divine–human relationship without reference to covenants. In Greek and Roman cult, meanwhile, gods and humans have relationships, in which it is taken for granted that both sides benefit, and which are often stable and long-standing and fortified by various kinds of sacred laws, but which are not described as covenants.[76] Many of the gentiles who formed Paul's primary audience will presumably not have found covenantal language particularly resonant in their thinking about the divine–human relationship. There is also a strand of thinking in ancient Mediterranean and Near Eastern writings, as in modern sociology, philosophy, and psychology, which recognizes that there are direct relationships of trust which do not invoke supporting instruments, and in the ancient world these are sometimes seen as among the best trust relationships one can have.[77] In Paul's world, friendship is often taken as an

---

[73] See below, pp. 80–2. On the covenant with Adam as with all humanity see Polish (1985), 184–5.
[74] Childs (1992), 418–19 notes that covenant is a central concept in the 'Old Testament' as it has been transmitted, but that it may not have been central in every period; Grabbe (2003) argues that 'covenant' is far from a universally significant term in Second Temple Judaism and is strikingly little used by either Philo or Josephus. Feldmeier and Spieckermann (2011), 459 argue that the concept of covenant has been over-applied to biblical texts in recent years (though they too apply it where it does not appear, notably in Galatians 3.26–4.7, which they see as referring to a 'covenant of promise' which is the 'new covenant'. The concept of a 'covenant of promise' is unhelpful since the two are conceptually distinct and this passage concerns the fulfilment of the promise to Abraham as distinct from the Sinai covenant (3.17)).
[75] On creation and covenant see below, p. 89.
[76] On types of Greek sacred laws see Parker (2004), Harris (2015).
[77] On this view in Greek and Roman culture, see Morgan (2015a), 45–51, 55–60.

example of this kind of trust:[78] ideally, trust in one's close friends is not backed by laws, promises, or even by social convention, but is based on mutual liking and respect, shared interests, shared experience, and openness to a shared future.[79]

In contrast with the several covenants which God makes and renews, in the Hebrew Bible and the Septuagint God is not said to make promises as such (though *epangelein* in the meaning 'to promise' is used in the Septuagint of promises between human beings). Hellenistic Judaism and the rabbis, however, do speak of God as making promises (e.g. 3 Macc. 2.10, Ps. Sol. 12.8) and fulfilling them (e.g. Shebu., 35b, Or Pesikt. R., 42 (178a)).[80]

In Paul's letters, covenant (*diathēkē*) and *pistis* language appear explicitly in relative, though not very close proximity in just one passage, at Galatians 3.6 and 17, but they are also, more loosely or implicitly, connected in 2 Corinthians 3 and in Romans 3–4 and 9–11. At 2 Corinthians 3.7–18, Paul contrasts the 'ministry' which was carved on letters of stone with the 'ministry of the spirit' (3.7–8).[81] The first ministry was glorious, but the second will surpass it in glory (3.9–10). When people read the first, which Paul also calls the 'old covenant', it is as if they are veiled and their thoughts are dulled or hardened (3.14), but through Christ, 'whenever a person turns to the Lord', the veil is removed (3.14, 16).[82] 'This sentence', C. K. Barrett observes of verses 14–16, 'is full of obscurity and ambiguity', but it is reasonably clear that those who put their trust in the Lord are freed to be transformed 'from glory to glory' (3.17–18), while those who do not are dulled and cannot attain glory.[83] This, however, is not the whole story, because Paul's target here is not primarily (if at all) non-Christ-confessing Jews but his Jewish-Christian opponents in Corinth, who have put their trust in Christ but also keep the law. When these people read the 'old covenant', their hearts, Paul thinks, are still veiled; law-keeping puts a barrier between the faithful and the life of the spirit

---

[78] NB among the patriarchs Abraham, who put his trust in God before the covenant was made between them, is also known in the scriptures as God's friend (2 Chr. 20.7, Isa. 41.8, cf. Jas 2.23); Moses, who trusts in God many times before the Sinai covenant, is also said to be like a friend of God at Exod. 33.11.

[79] In the modern western world, lovers and life partners sometimes say that their trust in each other is so profound that they prefer not to marry or enter civil partnerships which seem to seek to back their trust with the force of law or covenant. In contrast, children who are friends sometimes get each other to promise that they will *always* be friends, or prick their fingers and swear blood-brotherhood: children seem to have an instinct that friendships made at a time when they are changing quickly, and relatively little in control of their own future, are precarious, and often try to fortify them with covenants.

[80] Schniewind and Friedrich (1964), 579–80. Gn, r., 76 (49a) attributes to R. Judan the view that there is no sure rest, even for the righteous, in God's promises in this world, suggesting, perhaps, that even the faithful cannot rely on God to do as they want or hope. In imperial and rabbinic writings God makes a number of eschatological promises (e.g. 4 Esr. 4.27, 5.40, 7.60, S. Bar. 21.25).

[81] Wolter (2015b) points out that the contrast between letter and spirit appears to be original to Paul and designates (p. 44) the difference between what is material and recognizable to human eyes, and the reality of God. On 3.6–18 as a response to the situation in Corinth see Thrall (1994), *ad loc.*

[82] *Epistrephein* is used elsewhere of conversion (1 Thess. 1.9, cf. Gal. 4.9).

[83] Barrett (1973), *ad* 3.14. Thrall (1994), *ad loc.* sets out the four most likely interpretations of v. 14b, but all point to the conclusion that only (non-law-keeping) Christ-confessors attain the greater glory.

(cf. 3.6).[84] We may note that when Paul refers elsewhere to the things written (e.g. Rom. 2.27, 2.29, Gal. 3.10) and the curse, sin, or death associated with them (e.g. Rom. 3.20, 5.20, Gal. 3.13, 3.19, 3.22), he is normally speaking of the law, but here he speaks explicitly of the covenant. It is perhaps his clearest indication of what we should surely expect, but is not always acknowledged, that Paul does not separate the law and the covenant (cf. Gal. 3.17), and understands both as surpassed in life-giving (3.6) and glory (3.10) by the Christ event.[85]

The argument of Galatians 3 reads a little more straightforwardly. Paul has been clear in Galatians 2.15-20 that what now makes human beings right with God is the *pistis* relationship between God, Christ, and human beings and the trust human beings put in Christ.[86] The paradigm for this relationship is Abraham, who put his trust in God and had it reckoned to him for righteousness (3.6).[87] Paul follows Genesis in not describing Genesis 15.6 as a moment of covenant-making,[88] but he associates it with the idea that God did something different, making a promise or promises to Abraham (Gal. 3.16, 17, 18, 22).[89] God's promise was that, through Abraham, all the nations of the earth would be blessed.[90] Paul later identifies this promise or these promises as made to Abraham and his seed (3.16).[91] The 'seed', Paul proposes, is Christ, and through Christ gentiles have, indeed, received the blessing of Abraham.[92] Much later, God made a subsidiary and temporary covenant with Moses to discipline the wayward Israelites until the

---

[84] Käsemann (1971a), 155 notes that if 'Moses' is read through Christ or the spirit it becomes readable in a new way, as 'a promise of the new, eschatological obedience'.

[85] So Furnish (1984), 233-4.

[86] As at 2 Cor. 3.7-18 he identifies this with life in the spirit (Gal. 3.2-5). On the meaning of *pistis Christou* at 2.16, and hence the mechanism of righteousing in this passage, see Morgan (2015a), 267-73.

[87] Schliesser (2007), 404-8 emphasizes that Abraham is not only a type of generic faith, but is the type of God's people (so also Monserrat (2016), 199-200; both note Paul's continuity here with tradition) and of the Christian believer. *Contra* Bultmann and Buber he sees trust as integral to this 'faith', together with belief and acceptance of a new way of life (pp. 408-9); I do not disagree that the latter two are important to Paul, but it is more helpful to distinguish, where possible, which aspects of *pistis* are to the fore in particular passages.

[88] At 3.15 and 17 Paul refers to a *diathēkē*, but most commentators, surely rightly, now take this not to refer to a covenant in the scriptural sense, but to a human will or disposition: so e.g. Porter (2003), 278-9, Dunn (2003b), 291, Welch and Rennaker (2019), 442.

[89] On God's trustworthiness in his promises to Abraham as a basis for human trust in God in Philo's writings, and in Judaism of this period generally, see Moxnes (1980), 158-63, 202. Niehoff (2003), 109-11 argues that for Philo, God's covenant with Abraham is a grace which follows Abraham's moral perfection through *pistis*.

[90] ὁ θεὸς προευηγγελίσατο τῷ Ἀβραὰμ ὅτι Ἐνευλογηθήσονται ἐν σοὶ πάντα τὰ ἔθνη, 3.8. At Gen. 15.2-5 God tells Abraham that his offspring will be as numerous as the stars, but the promise of blessing goes back to Gen. 12.3; at Rom. 4.13 the promise is said to be that Abraham and his descendants will inherit the world (cf. Gen. 12.7, 18.18).

[91] At 3.16 *epangeliai* appear in the plural, reflecting the fact that in Genesis there is more than one promise, and reference to Abraham's seed occurs in the promise that 'to your seed I will give this land' (Gen. 12.7). Paul explicitly describes only one promise, however; he glosses over the reference to land, mainly, presumably, because Christian inheritance of the land of Israel forms no part of his thinking.

[92] Cf. pp. 303-4.

fulfilment of the promise to Abraham (Gal. 3.17, 19).[93] The Israelites could expect God to be faithful to this covenant as long as they kept the law, but 'now that *pistis* has come, we are no longer under a disciplinarian' (3.25). The *pistis* that has now come is a new relationship which has been made possible through the promise to Abraham.

We may wonder whether the promise to Abraham has been fulfilled in the Christ event, or whether it will only be fulfilled eschatologically and is therefore still 'live'. Paul does not distinguish, and it is tempting to suggest that his reason for calling God's prophecy to Abraham a promise is to distinguish it from the covenant which he is arguing has been 'surpassed' (cf. 2 Cor. 3.10) by God's new initiative in Christ. This is certainly possible, but there is perhaps marginally better reason to think that Paul sees the promise as having been fulfilled in the Christ event. Blessings typically look forward, so it makes good sense to think of God as blessing all the nations through the Christ event by enabling them to be made righteous. The idea that all nations might be blessed, say, only at the *parousia*, surely understates what Paul thinks has already been given by God through Christ, and what is given when people put their trust in Christ and are righteoused. At 3.19, Paul says that the law was added 'until the seed came to whom the promise had been made'. The seed has done what he came to do, ransoming humanity 'from the curse of the law' (3.13), and the law is now no longer needed (cf. 3.25), both of which suggest that the promise has been fulfilled.[94] 3.22 is more ambiguous: 'scripture confined everything under sin so that the promise…might be given to those who trust'. In principle, this might mean that the promise is extended to those who trust, but this makes poor sense since the promise has always encompassed all nations; it is more likely that the content of the promise has been given to those who trust, and hence that the promise has been fulfilled. Paul seems to confirm this at 3.26–9: the faithful are in a new relationship with God and Christ, being 'children of God in Christ Jesus' (3.26), belonging to Christ, and being 'heirs according to the promise' (3.29). The significance of this is that a promise which has been fulfilled is no longer operative: the faithful have inherited what was promised, but they are 'under' neither the law nor the promise; their relationship with God and Christ, like Abraham's relationship with God (3.9), is now, as Paul says repeatedly, defined by *pistis* (2.16, 3.5, 3.9, 3.11, 3.14, 3.22, 3.24, 3.26). In this letter Paul does not suggest that there is a new covenant: perhaps

---

[93] Paul is also explicit that the covenant was given through a mediator, of whom now there is no need (3.19–20).

[94] So Schniewind and Friedrich (1964), 584, who agree that God's promises have been fulfilled in Christ, citing Rom. 15.8, 2 Cor. 1.20 in support. Käsemann (1971a), 90–1 takes the promise of Gal. 3.8 to be the 'anticipation or complement of the gospel' (p. 90), following Schniewind, but then, unexpectedly, claims that the gospel replaces the law but not the promise, but itself has the character of promise. Insofar as the gospel carries a promise, it is better to see this as a new promise implicit in the *pistis* relationship.

because his opponents in Galatia, unlike some of the Corinthians, are not making use of the term.[95]

Romans 4 invokes Abraham as an example to make a somewhat different argument.[96] 'Abraham put his trust in God and it was reckoned to him for righteousness' (4.3, cf. 4.9). This, Paul indicates, happened before the making of the covenant which was sealed by Abraham's circumcision (4.10-11, cf. Gen. 17.10-11). This is primarily a reference to Abraham's own trust, but a few verses later, it becomes clear that it also invokes the *pistis* which Abraham's seed have 'in the one who raised Jesus our Lord from the dead' (4.24).[97] The promise to Abraham (cf. 4.13), that is, is fulfilled when it becomes possible for people to trust in God and Christ.[98] For most of the interim, the people of Israel have had the Sinai covenant and law to keep, and God has undoubtedly also been faithful to that covenant, but the promise to Abraham is not fulfilled through it, and now that the promise has been fulfilled and human beings are invited into a new *pistis* relationship with God, keeping the law does not make one an 'heir' of Abraham (v. 14), nor does keeping it define or preserve one's relationship with God (vv. 14-15).[99] Paul elaborates further on the strength and effectiveness of Abraham's trust (4.17-22). It is through trust, above all, that Abraham is the father of the uncircumcised as well as the circumcised, and an example to both.

To underline the difference, in his view, between trust and covenantal law-keeping, Paul says that people (that is, in his world, mainly contract labourers[100]) work for a wage, which is not a gift (as Abraham's righteousness is a gift), but which is due to them (4.4). The righteousness that comes through the death of Christ and through trust in Christ, in contrast, is not earned, and is not due to the faithful on the basis of anything they have done (4.5). Without taking up at length the very conflicted history of interpretation of this passage, we can note that, as in chapters 9-10 (and despite the reference to gentiles at 3.29), Paul's argument about the works of the law here is not specifically about whether gentiles should keep the law, but is about the status of the law per se. Two objections to it are intertwined in chapters 2-4. People keep the letter—do the work—of it and think that thereby they are fulfilling the spirit of it (cf. 2.13, 2.25, 2.29) when they may be

---

[95] Gal. 4.24-6 speaks of two covenants but, as Dunn (2003a), 294 notes, this refers to two aspects of the covenant with Abraham, not to the old and new covenants.

[96] Abraham's exemplarity may be part of Paul's debt to Isaiah (e.g. 41.8, 51.2) as well as his reading of Genesis. Holtz (2018) sees in it a debt to Stoic ideas of the submission of the self to the divine (and is surely right (p. 221) that Abraham allows 'God to be God') but everything Paul says about Abraham can be derived from the scriptures.

[97] Cf. 4.23-4: 'it was not for him alone that it was written that "it was credited to him"; it was also for us...'.

[98] So Schliesser (2007), 401-3, Dunn (1988), Fitzmyer (1993a), Byrne (1996), *ad* 4.13.

[99] At 4.17 Paul quotes Gen. 17.5: 'I have made you father of many nations'; though this is said pro-spectively to Abraham, after the Christ event it also implies that the promise has been fulfilled.

[100] Since contract labourers form the lowest stratum of the workforce, below even slaves whose masters, in principle, take care of them, the comparison is designed to be as negative as possible.

doing no such thing (2.5, 2.21–5, 2.27), so the unintended consequence of law-keeping can be sin (4.15, 5.20, cf. 2.12). And, after the Christ event, it is *pistis* towards God and Christ that leads to justification (3.20, 3.21–6, 4.13).[101] Paul does not say explicitly here that the law, or the Sinai covenant, is no longer needed, nor that Jews should stop keeping it, but it is hard to avoid the conclusion that the Christ event, in the language of 2 Corinthians 3.10, surpasses both.[102] By likening law-keeping to contract labour, moreover, Paul turns it into a reification of deferred trust of a kind which is no longer needed where there is direct, open-ended personal trust.

Does Paul think that the new relationship between God, Christ, and humanity is itself a new or renewed covenant?[103] As we have noted, he uses the phrase only twice, and, though there are credible arguments on both sides of this debate, it is likely that he uses it largely in response to opponents, especially in Galatia and Corinth, who want gentile Christ-confessors to observe the Mosaic law,[104] rather than because it reflects his own thinking.[105] His own preferred language is that of

---

[101] Bearing in mind that trust is paradigmatically both an attitude and an action (so when e.g. Bultmann (1971), 175, Käsemann (1971a), 81–2 stress its close connection with practical obedience, they are right, but this does not diminish its cognitive aspect).

[102] In this I share some of the reservations of (friendly) critics of the New Perspective (e.g. Räisänen (1985), Seifrid (2000), Carson et al. (2004), Westerholm (2004), Gathercole (2006b), Watson (2007), Barclay (2015)), from a perspective closest to Barclay's. I agree with Hughes (2012), 34–55 that the Mosaic covenant is surpassed, though not with all aspects of his analysis of Gal. 2–3. Though Paul never says that Israel has been ransomed from the covenant, in places references to law must imply covenant (e.g. Gal. 3.19, 4.4, which refer to the law of Moses, in addition to 2 Cor. 3.5–16 where the covenant implies the law); moreover, Paul never explicitly distinguishes the law of Moses from the Mosaic covenant. Joosten (2019), 7–8 observes that Israel is unusual in linking covenant with law; this makes it easier for Israelites to associate the two and e.g. to assume, as Paul claims, that they are pursuing righteousness when keeping the law 'by works' (Rom. 9.31–2), but by the same token it would be hard for Paul to claim (as he never does) that the law and covenant are separable.

[103] Paul knows as well as anyone that God makes multiple covenants in the scriptures, with humanity as a whole, with individuals, and with Israel, and may share the view of most modern scholars that, after the Mosaic covenant, when scriptural or other texts refer to a new covenant, they are thinking of the renewal of the Mosaic covenant rather than the making of a completely new covenant. When Israel is unfaithful, God's faithfulness to her sometimes allows her to resume her existing relationship and covenant with God (Ps. 88.33–5 (32–4), Ezek. 16.59–63). The covenant can also be renewed without previous unfaithfulness: e.g. Deut. 29.1, Josh. 24.25, 2 Kgs 11.17, 23.2–3. Jer. 31.31–4, Hos. 2.18–25 refer to a 'new covenant', probably in the sense of the renewal of the existing covenant in a new form; the 'new covenant' of the Damascus Document is also probably the Mosaic covenant in an Essene interpretation (see e.g. Abegg (2003), 81–97, Murphy-O'Connor (2010), 56–9, Tallent (2012)). On God's reliable faithfulness as a basis for trust in the 'Hymn of the Maskil' in 1QS IX, 25B-XI, 15a see Gayer (2015). It is less clear whether, when early Christians talk of what Paul, quoting or paraphrasing, calls 'the new covenant in [Christ's] blood' (1 Cor. 11.24), they are thinking of the 'new covenant' as renewing or replacing the Mosaic covenant; there may have been room within *ekklēsiai* for both views: see e.g. Conzelmann (1975), Collins (1999), Fitzmyer (2008), *ad* 1 Cor. 11.24.

[104] The passages in which Paul talks about covenants are passages in which he is passing on a tradition (1 Cor. 11.25), speaking of the present situation and future of Israel (2 Cor. 3.6, 3.14, Rom. 9.4, 11.27), or disagreeing with law-keeping Christ-confessors (Gal. 4.24, arguably Gal. 3.15, 3.17). I follow e.g. Martyn (1993, 1997a), Dunn (2003b), Westerholm (2004), Murphy-O'Connor (2010), 51–9, *contra* e.g. Deidun (1981), Porter (2003), Gräbe (2006), Blanton (2012), W. Campbell (2012), Whittle (2015), Hafemann 2019); see also the discussion of Pitre (2019).

[105] Welch and Rennaker (2019), 447 are among those who suggest that we should look for covenantal thinking even where Paul does not use the language, but they do not offer examples, and this principle would apply equally to terms and concepts which Paul uses explicitly more often, so does not

relationship: above all the relationship of trust, but also love, righteousness, grace, obedience, and peace, all of which come from God and Christ and are offered back to them and (in most cases) to other community members.[106] All these relationships can be invoked within a covenantal context, but they do not require one.[107]

We can go further: I have argued elsewhere that Paul's intense interest in relationships is matched by a striking lack of interest in other ways of structuring communities or solving their problems.[108] He recognizes that community members have different gifts (e.g. Rom. 12.6–8, 1 Cor. 12.8–10), but says remarkably little about how communities should organize themselves or (other than by seeking his advice) handle the tensions that inevitably arise within them. Those who put their trust in God and Christ are a new creation (cf. 2 Cor. 5.17),[109] living for God like the risen Christ himself (cf. Rom. 6.11, Gal. 2.19), while Christ lives in them (cf. Gal. 2.20) and they live 'in Christ's hands'.[110] This life is envisaged as an aspect of eternal life already active in the present time even as the faithful wait for the *parousia*.[111] Jewish prophecies and visions of the messianic age or of heaven, in this period, have little to say about whether the covenant and the law are imagined as part of either heaven or the messianic age, but elsewhere in Paul's world it is common for depictions of a golden age (in the past or future), or of communities of the wise, to say explicitly that where everyone behaves virtuously, and in harmony with the divine, a society has no need for formal institutions and instruments of state such as covenants or laws.[112] Though we cannot be certain,

---

necessarily change what we understand as the balance of his thinking. Hays (1989) and Whittle (2015) argue for the influence of Deut. 32 on Rom. 9–11, in particular, and on this basis Whittle argues that Paul thinks of God's action through Christ as covenant renewal, but we should beware of assuming that the Paul who can think so radically about the Messiah cannot think equally radically about the covenant.

[106] Morgan (2020), 210–15. On the vision of God as leading to 'ethical replication' (in the covenant community of Isaiah) see Grey (2018).

[107] On divine–human relationships of trust etc. within covenants see Dietrich (2014).

[108] Morgan (2020), 215–35.

[109] Monserrat (2016), 202–5 attractively links Paul's treatment of Abraham with the theme of creation, on the basis that the God of Rom. 4.19–21 is the God who gives (new) life.

[110] Below, pp. 131–5.

[111] On life 'in Christ' see Morgan (2020), 172–4 and below, pp. 131–2. Jewett (2007) *ad* Rom. 11.26b–27 suggests that Paul looks forward to God's making a 'final and ultimate' covenant in the future, but does not explain why a covenant would be needed in the eschatological future or how it would relate to the 'new covenant' in Christ's blood. It is more likely that v. 27 refers to the 'covenant' in Christ: so Byrne (1996), *ad loc.*

[112] On the messianic age see especially Horbury (1998), 36–108, (2003), 35–64, 189–228; cf. Reynolds (2016) and, on messiahs, Collins (1988, 1993), Collins and Collins (2008). In Jewish literature, the nearest relatives of this vision are visions of the messianic age or of God's kingdom in heaven, and they also have Greek relatives in Stoic visions of what life is like in the cosmopolite community of sages (Schofield (1991), 43–8, 57–63, 67–74, 103). Prophecies and visions of the messianic age or of heaven tend not to spell out the status of the covenant and the law in them. In Stoic visions of the cosmic community of the wise, however, political institutions are explicitly not needed, because all members will enact, in themselves and towards each other and the divine, the virtues of the god with which the god has endowed humanity. On laws as not needed in golden ages see also Ov., *Met.* 1.89–92, Tac., *Ann.* 3.26, cf. Morgan (2015a), 488–500, Krauter (2020). Thielman (1989) argues that in Romans Paul gives a place to the law in the eschatological age on the basis of Gal. 5.14 and Rom. 8.4,

therefore, it seems very possible that, for Paul, where trust, love, and the rest structure the divine–human relationship and there is no need for other forms of organization, there is also no need for covenants or laws.

All this suggests that, for Paul, the new trust relationship between God, Christ, and the faithful takes the place of past promises, dispositions, and covenants, together with the 'works of the law' that go with the Sinai covenant:[113] either because they have been fulfilled in the Christ event, or because they have been broken by Israel and are therefore moot, or, more broadly, because they are no longer the means by which human beings come into and remain in their right relationship with God.[114] (As a partial alternative, it is conceivable that Paul rarely speaks in covenantal terms because he is willing to leave open to Jewish listeners the possibility of thinking in covenantal terms, without committing gentile listeners—to whom the concept of covenant was not native and must have sounded both strongly Jewish and closely involved with law-keeping—to doing so.[115])

In proposing this, it is worth highlighting that the new relationship of *pistis*, or the human side of it, is not only, as it is sometimes taken to be in later Christian thinking, an act of commitment to God and Christ. It has more specific content than that: as much as many covenants. Giving an account of that content, which, I hope, will show why *pistis* is a satisfactory expression of the divine-human relationship in its own right, is one of the aims of this study.[116]

---

but Paul only says, respectively, that those who love fulfil the law and those who walk according to the spirit fulfil the *dikaiōma* of the law, which is more likely to mean (cf. Rom. 10.4) that putting one's trust in Christ or following Christ's teaching on love (cf. 1 Cor. 13.2) does everything the law was designed to do.

[113] Barclay (2010a) sees Paul at Rom. 9–11 as drawing on Exod. 32–4, and shows how this is compatible with a radical view of the newness and creativity of God's mercy towards humanity: 'divine mercy for Paul is not, as we might expect from *our* use of the term, an act of pity that overlooks sins to restore the *status quo ante*; it is an act of creation that brings new reality to birth' (p. 101). Barclay does not discuss the idea of 'new covenant' in this context but his emphasis on newness and creation opens the possibility that God is doing more than renewing the covenant or framing a new one. On how Rom. 1–4 and 9–11 use the idea of covenant but separate it from the tradition to describe how God is acting anew and outside the law, see also Moxnes (1980), 32–55, 265; Eastman (2010a) emphasizes God's ongoing mercy towards Israel during the time when, for Paul, her destiny has been 'interrupted' by her obduracy (p. 367).

[114] Opinions about the status of a covenant which human beings have failed vary: e.g. Hibbard (2015), 203 observes (*in re* Isa. 24.5) that the establishment of even a perpetual covenant implies the possibility of its abrogation; Schüle (2015) argues that the eternal covenant in the Priestly Pentateuch and the major prophets is envisaged as standing whether human beings keep it or not (unlike the 'old covenant' which it replaces). But Paul does not speak of an eternal covenant and, we have argued, portrays the new divine–human relationship consistently as a relationship without covenantal language, so there is no reason to think that he did not conceive of the existing covenant with Israel as unbreakable (if so, and if Polaski (1998) is right that the 'eternal covenant' of Isa. 24.5–6 is the Deuteronomic covenant, this is one respect in which Paul does not follow Isaiah).

[115] None of the attitudes (such as love or humility) or states (such as holiness or righteousness) required by past covenants, of course, is incompatible with the new relationship of trust. On the contrary: Paul insists that the coming of the Messiah fulfils the law, and those who do good (2.10, cf. 2.7, 2.13–15, 2.28–9), Jewish or gentile, are fulfilling what the law asks of them.

[116] One might ask whether trust is in itself a covenant, and some forms of trust have some aspects in common with covenants: for instance, if I trust you to fetch me a carton of milk, you trust me to pay

This discussion inevitably raises the spectre of supersessionism. Was Paul a supersessionist? In the sense that he imagined that the Church superseded Israel or Christians Jews as God's chosen people, certainly not: the New Perspective has made abundantly clear how inaccurate and anachronistic any such reading is.[117] Nor does Paul think that everyone who puts their trust in Christ is automatically eventually saved; while for those who have not put their trust in Christ he sees that there is still time to be righteoused (cf. Rom. 11.25–6). Paul, with all preachers of the gospel, is radical in preaching that righteousness must now be sought by acknowledging what God has done through Jesus Christ and putting one's trust in Christ alongside God, but there is every reason to think that he (and all early preachers) understood this as a thoroughly Israelite proclamation. The Messiah is the Messiah of God's people Israel, even when the definition of God's people and the means by which they are called to seek righteousness change.[118]

We have argued that Paul is convinced that since 'the redemption in Christ Jesus', righteousness comes from the trust relationship between God, Christ, and humanity, that all God's past promises have been fulfilled, notably those to Abraham, and that the law, and the Sinaitic covenant of which it is part, no longer in itself keep Israel in its right relationship with God.[119] This indicates that, for Paul, the new trust relationship between God, Christ, and the faithful takes the place of past covenants, and this could be seen as a form of supersessionism. For Paul, however, this development is wholly within the spirit and history of God's relationship with Israel, which has been marked by renewed relationships, new and renewed covenants, new commandments, and unexpected new directions many times before.[120] That God should, in the words of the prophet Paul most often cites (Isa. 43.19), do a 'new thing' in Paul's day, is, for Paul,

---

you for it, and some agreement is in place which establishes that milk can be got for money and what happens if either party proves untrustworthy. But trust is not, like covenants, reciprocal per se, nor does it necessarily have specified terms, goals, or sanctions, so it is more directly relational and potentially less defined.

[117] Discussed by Longenecker (2007), who also argues persuasively against the 'two ways' interpretation of Paul, notably by Stowers (1994), Donaldson (2006): Paul is so clear that both Jews and gentiles have sinned, Jesus is the Messiah/Christ of Israel (including of Paul himself, e.g. Gal. 2.20) as well as the saviour of the gentiles, and both Jews and gentiles who become Christ-confessors trust in Christ, that a Paul promoting two ways to righteousness would be at odds with himself and surely with most, if not all other Christ-confessing communities. On Paul, Israel, and the gentiles see also the balanced assessments of Bachmann (2012), Bieringer and Pollefeyt (2012), Bird (2012); regrettably, Boccaccini (2020) reached me too late to be discussed here.

[118] So e.g. Boyarin (1994), 205, Longenecker (2007), 39–40 (though with an emphasis on salvation that not all would share), D'Costa (2017), cf. Langton (2005–6). *Contra* see e.g. Soulen (1996), Wyschogrod (1996) with the discussion of Plevan (2009).

[119] We could express this without trust language by saying that, for Paul, it is now humanity's relationship with God mediated by Christ rather than humanity's relationship with God mediated by the covenant and the law that righteouses. This formulation, by omission, highlights the centrality of *pistis* in the equation: what God and Christ have done constitutes (we have argued) an act of *pistis*, and for what they have done to be effective requires (all commentators recognize) a human response of *pistis*.

[120] Cf. Meeks (1993), 219 who concludes that God, for Paul, never abandons the faithful but can surprise them: 'A faithful hermeneutic of the Pauline kind...requires confidence in the God who,

wonderful and extraordinary—but for God, as Paul conceives of God, it is anything but extraordinary.[121]

While the faithful wait for the *parousia*, uncertain of the immediate future and sometimes under persecution, Paul affirms, invoking the *pistis* relationship without the language of promise or covenant, that if they remain faithful they can be confident that a faithful God will eventually save them.[122] At 1 Thessalonians 5.23-4, he prays that the Thessalonians may be 'preserved blameless for the coming of our Lord Jesus Christ. The one [God] who calls you is faithful, and he will also accomplish it.'[123] At 1 Corinthians 1.8-9, he assures the Corinthians that God will keep them firm to the end because God is faithful and called them to fellowship with his son, Jesus Christ.[124] At 1 Corinthians 10.13, God is faithful and, if the Corinthians suffer, God will not let them be tried beyond their strength. This passage is remarkable for using the Exodus story as an example of God's faithfulness (and a cautionary tale for anyone thinking of abandoning their own faithfulness), linking it with the faithfulness of Christ via a bold typology. The spiritual rock from which the Israelites drank in the desert was Christ (10.4), and that when some of the Israelites tested God (cf. Num. 21.5-9), they were really testing Christ. 'Let us not test Christ,' Paul says, 'as some of them did, and suffered death by serpents' (10.9).[125] Being faithful means trusting both God and Christ to the end.

If an appeal to the apostles' experience of the resurrection and their own reception of the spirit, together with the hope that Christ would return to vindicate their faithfulness, was not enough to assure all the faithful that God could be trusted to support them through the present time, then they could also draw inspiration from the example of Paul himself and their fellow Christ-confessors.[126] In his ministry, Paul says, he is 'afflicted in every way, but not constrained; perplexed, but not driven to despair; persecuted, but not abandoned; struck down, but not destroyed...', because he knows that God who raised the Lord Jesus will

---

determined to have mercy on all and to bring into being the things that are not, will astonish those who are loyal to the story of God's past action, but will not abandon them.' Cf. Meeks (1990).

[121] Paul does not cite this verse, but cf. e.g. 2 Cor. 5.17: 'the old things have passed away; behold, new things have come'.

[122] Cf. 1 Pet. 1.5, 5.8-9, likely influenced by Paul.

[123] Following references to the return of the risen Christ and the Thessalonians' reception of the spirit (5.19), this passage affirms the trustworthiness of God not in relation to past covenants but on the basis of Jesus' followers' experience of his death and resurrection, their conviction following his resurrection that he will return, and their experience of receiving the spirit (cf. 2 Cor. 12.7-10, where it is Christ who is implicitly reliable rather than God).

[124] Conviction of God's faithfulness is based on the 'testimony to Christ' which has been confirmed among the Corinthians by their reception of the spirit (cf. 1.6-7).

[125] This story takes place before the Israelites reach Sinai, so Paul leaves open whether it exemplifies divine-human trust within an earlier covenant, or the new (somewhat unstable) *pistis* between God, Moses, and the Israelites which has marked the story since Moses' call at the burning bush.

[126] On Paul as exemplar cf. 1 Cor. 4.16, Phil. 3.17, 1 Thess. 1.6; Hooker (1996), 92, Weaver (2013), Morgan (2020), 47 n. 22.

also raise him with Jesus (2 Cor. 4.8–9, 14). When he is given a 'thorn in the flesh', he is also given the assurance that 'power is made perfect in weakness' (2 Cor. 12.7–10). Towards the end of his life, Paul gives thanks to God, among other things, for the fact that even his imprisonment turns out to further the gospel (Phil. 1.3, 12–14). The faithful can, he says, not just endure, but even boast of their afflictions, because their experience is that affliction produces, in turn, endurance, character, and hope, and 'hope does not disappoint, because the love of God has been poured into our hearts through the holy spirit that has been given to us' (Rom. 5.3–5). Paul recognizes that, even if the covenant is no longer in force between God and humanity, sometimes the faithful need support to fortify their trust, and he offers them encouragement in the form of human exemplars.[127]

Finally, in this section, it is worth noting that the God who has acted anew and, from Israel's point of view, very unexpectedly through Christ, can be trusted, for Paul, not least because the Christ event is a revelation of God's righteousness. Paul's understanding of God's righteousness is much debated, in general and in particular at Romans 1.17 and 3.21, and this is not the place to seek to contribute to that debate,[128] though I remain broadly persuaded by Käsemann's view that God's righteousness is a characteristic of God's nature and activity which is given to human beings to enable their own right-standing with God.[129] But we can also observe that in the everyday Greek of Paul and his communities, *dikaiosynē* is not least a function of social (which is not limited to legal) regulation. *Dikaiosynē* and its relatives refer to divine justice, which decides when human beings are rightly rewarded or punished; the justness of laws, which define what behaviours and relationships are legitimate and due between members of a community; or what society and culture regard as normative or acceptable. In all three registers of meaning they express the aspiration that individuals and groups (divine and human) should behave appropriately towards each other within a community.[130] With this in mind, we can see the righteousness of God which is revealed in the present time as being, for Paul, not least an expression of God's will to bring the

---

[127] See below, pp. 76–7.
[128] In particular, the recent monumental contributions to the debate about divine righteousness and justification by Wright (2009) and Campbell (2012) and their interlocutors are regrettably beyond our scope here.
[129] Käsemann (1969), especially 169–80, and Way (1991), 177–236. Käsemann emphasizes that God's righteousness enters the earthly arena to establish the lordship of Christ which is the content of his righteousness; he also marks ((1969), 180) the connection between God's righteousness and God's faithfulness to creation, as creator (cf. Müller (1964), 265, Stuhlmacher (1965), 236). See also especially the discussions of Williams (1980) and Brauch in Sanders (2017) (though Williams over-identifies God's faithfulness, righteousness, and truthfulness (p. 268), and I doubt (p. 265) that the phrase refers to God's faithfulness in keeping his promise to Abraham, for reasons outlined above; nor do I share Wright's (e.g. 2009) emphasis on the covenantal context of the phrase; cf. also Lampe (1977), 34–5.
[130] On divine justice in the Greek world see especially Lloyd-Jones (1983); on justice and related concepts in Greek thinking see e.g. Gargarin (2002), Farenga (2006), Anagnostopoulos (2018) (though writing on justice in Greek thinking tends to focus on early Greece). On justice in modern philosophy see Miller (2017); on what is due see Scanlon (1998).

whole of humanity into its right relationship with God and one another, through Christ and through trust, such that all receive God's *dikaiosynē* on equal terms, offer to God what is acceptable, and behave towards one another as is due to each, whether Jewish or gentile, as fellow members of one people of God.[131]

Foundations of Divine–Human Trust

Like almost everyone in his world, Jewish or gentile, Paul takes the existence of the divine for granted.[132] When speaking of the trustworthiness of God, he feels no need to make the case for God's existence either to Jews, who share his assumption that the God of Israel is the one true God, or to gentiles, who have no difficulty accepting the existence of multiple divinities, whether or not they themselves worship them. Paul also takes for granted that God is supremely powerful, wise, and benevolent towards human beings,[133] though he does not debate whether God is omnipotent, omniscient, or omnibenevolent in the technical senses in which later Christian doctrine discusses them.[134] If, in the modern western world, one asks why anyone should trust in God, one response is likely to be because, if God exists, then God is necessarily all-powerful, all-knowing, and all-kind.[135] The difficult question, for many within and beyond the academy, is whether God exists.[136] In Paul's world, especially among gentiles, the difficult question is usually whether the gods who are assumed to exist are trustworthy.

Paul's trust in God, in the first place, is evidently inherited. He follows tradition in affirming that God is faithful and trustworthy to Israel. He also affirms, however, that God has fulfilled God's promises and shown his trustworthiness to all humanity through the Christ event. Paul's trust in the God who has acted

---

[131] Quell (1964), 174 observes that in general Greek *dikaiosynē* and related terms in the LXX match well the Hebrew terms they translate, and there is strong continuity in the use of these terms between the LXX and New Testament. Moore (1999) argues convincingly, in relation to some of the most influential contemporary theories of human justice, that justice presupposes care, which fits well with this model of divine justice and righteousness.

[132] On atheism, see Whitmarsh (2015).

[133] Rom. 3.3–4, 9.14, 11.1 are unusual in New Testament writings in allowing that humanity might challenge the faithfulness or justice of God, but Jewish scriptural and non-scriptural writing has a long tradition of debate about the nature, and even existence, of God's justice: e.g. Levinson (2008), especially chs 3, 4, 6, Estes (2010), Burt (2012), Shapira (2015), cf. Hayes (2015), ch. 1. On rabbinic discussions about justice and the law see e.g. Newman (1998), especially chs 1, 3; Novick (2010), chs 5–6. cf. Hayes (2002), Wyn Schofer (2005, 2010), and Fuller (2006).

[134] He does think that God's kingdom will take over heaven and earth (e.g. Rom. 9.17, 1 Cor. 15.24–8); cf. e.g. Dan. 4.35, Prov. 21.1 (God as omnipotent); Gen. 1–2, Ps. 95.5, 136.5–9, 148.1–6, Isa. 45.8–18, cf. Jn 1.1–3, Rom. 11.36 (God as universal creator); Ps. 147.5, Isa. 46.10, cf. Acts 2.23, Rom. 8.29 (God as uniquely knowing); Gen. 18.25 (God as ultimate judge); Ps. 86.15, 106.1, 135.3, 145.17, Nahum 1.7, cf. Mk 10.18, Jn 3.16, Rom. 8.37–9 (God as benevolent).

[135] Discussing recent scholarship on these claims and challenging them, however, see e.g. Wettstein (2012), Buckareff and Nagasawa (2016), Patterson (2016), Nagasawa (2017), Speaks (2018).

[136] See also pp. 68, 94–5, 101–3.

through Christ is presumably founded first on his acceptance of his own and others' experiences of seeing and/or hearing the risen or exalted Christ (cf. 1 Cor. 15.5–8, 2 Cor. 12.1, 4, 8, Gal. 1.16). Attitudes formed by (what are reported as) sensory experiences like these, are often called 'basic' beliefs, so Paul can be said to hold a basic belief that Christ was raised from the dead.[137] Paul also preaches that, in the Christ event, God has kept God's promises, that Christ died for (the sins of) others (cf. 1 Cor. 15.3, Gal. 2.20), that he was raised by God on the third day (1 Cor. 15.4), and that God has sent God's spirit to inspire and give new life to the faithful (e.g. 1 Cor. 1.7, 12.7).[138] These are interpretations of his and other people's experiences, based probably on a mixture of traditions about Jesus' own teaching, interpretations of Jesus' death in light of the resurrection experiences, and interpretations of scripture.[139] They are new convictions which Paul has consciously adopted, against the grain of his own previous views, and he undoubtedly thinks they are true, so they too are probably best understood as beliefs: what some philosophers call non-basic beliefs. Paul's affirmation that Christ will return to save those who trust in him and bring them to eternal life (e.g. Rom. 2.5, 1 Thess. 1.10), however, which is also based on a mixture of traditions about Jesus' own teaching, extrapolation from the resurrection experiences, and scriptural interpretation, both inherited and Paul's own, may be better described as an instance of propositional trust.[140] If so, Paul's trust in the God who has acted through Christ is based on a mixture of inherited assumptions, new basic and non-basic beliefs, and propositional trust.

This may seem a rather circuitous argument for what almost all modern Christians take for granted: that Paul, and all early Christians, held a number of beliefs which were both foundational to, and part of their relationship with God. (We are talking here about propositional beliefs, not the English concept of relational 'belief in', which is most nearly expressed in Greek with relational *pisteuein* and is better translated as 'trust'.) In Chapter 1, however, we saw that some philosophers of religion now argue strongly that faith need not involve beliefs, but can be based, for instance, on assumptions, hopes, or acceptance.[141] In this light, it is worth considering whether belief really is the basis, or a basis, for Paul's, or any New Testament writer's trust in God.

The argument above is not decisive because, although it seems implausible, given that Paul's call by Christ caused a dramatic shift in his world-view, that his trust in the God who has acted through Christ is based simply on acceptance or

---

[137] When he invokes the spiritual power with which he speaks, together with converts' experience of receiving the spirit when they respond to his preaching, he also appeals to something which he represents as self-evident or evident to the senses.
[138] On the spirit, for Paul, as combining inspiration and life-giving, see Morgan (2020), 118–19.
[139] See pp. 99–109. On Paul as interpreter of scripture see e.g. Hays (1989), Evans (1993), Porter and Stanley (2008), Stanley (2012), Watson (2016).
[140] Cf. pp. 117–18.   [141] p. 15.

an assumption, it could be based on propositional trust or hope. Nor is Paul's use of language definitive. When he tells the Corinthians, for instance, 'so we preach, and so you *pisteuein*' (1 Cor. 15.11), he could mean either 'so we preach and so you believe' or 'so you trust'. Does Paul (or do other New Testament writings) express belief using other, less ambiguous terms? We observed in Chapter 1 that Greek normally refers to believing using 'thinking' language: *nomizein*, *dokein*, *phronein*, and their cognates. *Nomizein* occurs only fifteen times in the New Testament, usually (including in Paul's two uses of it at 1 Cor. 7.26, 36) to refer to thinking or believing in the human sphere, but it can refer to thinking or believing something about the divine (e.g. Acts 8.20, 17.29). *Phronein* occurs only twenty-three times, nearly always with reference to the human sphere, usually in the sense 'have in mind' or 'have an attitude' rather than 'think' or 'believe', and does not offer a clear example of someone's believing something about the divine.[142] *Dokein* is more promising: of its sixty-three occurrences, a handful refer to thinking or believing something about the divine, some of which occur in Paul's letters. For example, at 1 Corinthians 4.9 Paul says 'I think [or 'believe'] that God has exhibited us apostles as the last of all...', and at 7.40 that 'I think [or 'believe'] I too have the spirit of God'.[143] We might add to these a few passages where Paul expresses the strength of a conviction with the language of persuadedness, witness, certainty, or propositional 'knowing' rather than thinking.[144] These comparisons are rather thinner than we might expect—and confirm the finding of *Roman Faith* that belief is not at the forefront of New Testament writers' thinking about the divine–human relationship—but they indicate that Paul, and other writers, can speak of thinking or believing things about the divine using common terms which are less ambiguous than *pisteuein*, so it is perfectly possible that they also sometimes use *pisteuein* to mean 'believe'. Chapter 8 will argue that trust in God and Christ can appropriately be based on propositional trust, and that, in the contemporary world, there may be value in articulating a commitment to God and Christ in terms of propositional trust rather than propositional belief. In light of the arguments above, however, particularly when Paul is referring to events in the past, of some of which he and others claim direct experience, it is overwhelmingly likely, if not absolutely provable, that Paul not only makes some claims on the basis of propositional trust, but that he holds some beliefs, and that his trust in God is based in part on beliefs.[145]

---

[142] Col. 3.2 refers to thinking about what is above, not what is on earth, but not in the sense of 'believing'.
[143] Cf. 1 Cor. 14.37.
[144] E.g. 2 Cor. 10.7, Phil. 1.6, 3.3–4, cf. 1 Cor. 2.4 (persuadedness), 1 Cor. 1.6 (witness and certainty), Rom. 6.6, 1 Cor. 2.11, 2 Cor. 4.6, 14 (knowing); see pp. 117–8. Cf. Jn 6.69, where *gignōskein* strengthens *pisteuein*; propositional knowing, as a stronger attitude than believing, encompasses belief.
[145] On how Christ's death and resurrection and the hope of eventual salvation are a basis for trust see further pp. 162–4.

The Trustworthiness of God in Other New Testament Writings

The authors of Hebrews and 1 John also affirm the trustworthiness of God, once each. At Hebrews 10.23, the one (God) who, through the prophets (10.16–17) promised humanity a new covenant (v. 16) and forgiveness of sins through the blood of Christ (vv. 18–19), is trustworthy (πιστὸς γὰρ ὁ ἐπαγγειλάμενος), and the faithful should therefore 'hold unwaveringly to our confession that gives us hope' (v. 23).[146] We might have expected the author of Hebrews to place more emphasis on the covenantal faithfulness of God to Israel than does Paul, but the focus here is again on God's trustworthiness, though foretold by the prophets, as revealed and confirmed through the death of Christ.[147] The one who has made possible the forgiveness of sins, moreover, is also worth trusting for the future, as the day (of judgment, cf. 10.30–1), draws near (10.25).

The writer of 1 John focuses even more closely on God's *pistis* as a new initiative enacted and revealed in the death of Christ. The blood of God's son Jesus cleanses human beings from all sin (1.7). The faithful must therefore acknowledge their sins in order to be forgiven: 'If we confess our sins, he [God] is trustworthy and just and will forgive our sins and cleanse us from every wrongdoing' (1.9).[148] The author doubtless takes for granted that God has always been trustworthy, but at this time God's trustworthiness is intimately linked with the Christ event and human beings' response to it.

Despite their similarities to Paul's letters, a slight difference of emphasis from Paul's is audible in both Hebrews and 1 John, which may be due to the fact that these writers are less likely actively to be preaching the gospel to new audiences. The author of 1 John quotes what may be an earlier hymn proclaiming that 'we have seen and heard' the Word of life, and 'we now proclaim it to you' (1 Jn 1.3, cf. 1–2), but both authors take for granted that Christ's death confirms the *pistis* of God without referring to other grounds for trust.

A small number of passages in other writings goes further, and suggests that trust in God may follow trust in Christ and beliefs about Christ. The author of Colossians tells the faithful that they are raised with Christ through trust in the

---

[146] Koester (2001), *ad* 10.23 underlines that God is faithful in granting through Christ's sacrifice the mercy promised in the covenant. Attridge (1989), *ad loc.* suggests that 'God is faithful' is a common early Christian affirmation, citing 1 Jn 1.9 and Rev. 1.5 together with the examples in Paul, but the argument above suggests that this does not do justice to the complexity of Paul's thinking.

[147] Unlike Paul, however, Hebrews undoubtedly thinks of the new divine–human relationship through Christ as a new or better covenant (e.g. 7.22, 8.6, 9.15, 12.24), on the model of Jeremiah's new covenant (Heb. 8.8–10), founded on *pistis* (4.2–3, 6.1, cf. 12.2, 13.7). This study will not do justice to new-covenantal thinking in Hebrews or elsewhere, on the basis that the significance of the divine–human relationship of trust is less explored than this and is of theological interest in its own right.

[148] ἐὰν ὁμολογῶμεν τὰς ἁμαρτίας ἡμῶν, πιστός ἐστιν καὶ δίκαιος ἵνα ἀφῇ ἡμῖν τὰς ἁμαρτίας καὶ καθαρίσῃ ἡμᾶς ἀπὸ πάσης ἀδικίας. Smalley (2007), *ad loc.* notes that God's faithfulness is typically linked with his covenant promises.

power of God who raised Christ from the dead (2.12).[149] Belief in the resurrection here appears to be the foundation of trust in God, as presumably in Christ himself. The author of 1 Peter is even more explicit: Christ

> was known before the foundation of the world, but revealed at the end of time for you, who *through him* are faithful/trusting towards God ($\pi\iota\sigma\tau o\grave{\upsilon}\varsigma\ \epsilon\grave{\iota}\varsigma\ \theta\epsilon\acute{o}\nu$) who raised him from the dead and gave him glory, *with the result that* your trust and hope are in God. (1.20–1)[150]

The jailer whose prison doors are shaken open to free Paul and Silas (Acts 16.25–34) asks them, 'what must I do to be saved?' (v. 20). They tell him, 'Put your trust in the Lord Jesus and you and your household will be saved' (v. 31). He does so, takes them home with him, and as he and all his family are baptized he rejoices at having come to trust in God (v. 34).[151] This is not an implausible scenario in the context of the gentile mission, where it is imaginable that preaching began with the proclamation about Jesus Christ. These passages, like that of 1 John, may also indicate that, over two or three generations, Christians felt a decreasing need to frame their trust in Christ with reference to God's relationship with Israel.

Trust and Risk

We have seen that in some of the passages discussed, the focus on the saving death and resurrection of Jesus Christ as reasons to put, maintain, or strengthen one's trust in God, together with the likelihood that many of the faithful were gentiles who had not previously worshipped the God of Israel, gives the trust at issue a strong flavour of novelty. Unlike many instances of new trust, however, whether between human beings or human and divine beings, this *pistis* is never presented as epistemically or existentially risky for human beings. It is recognized as carrying an element of this-worldly practical risk, since putting one's trust in God and Christ sometimes leads to exclusion from a synagogue or to persecution, but theologically it is presented as an opportunity whose outcome, if one takes it up wholeheartedly and does not waver, is assured.[152]

There may, however, be more risks, both epistemic and existential, implicit in this kind of *pistis* than are obvious at first sight. Jews who hear the gospel preached

---

[149] Col. 1.21 suggests that the church at Colossae was mainly gentile. 1 Pet. 1.1 suggests that the addressees of this letter were mainly Jewish, but 1 Peter also shows Pauline influence and may therefore show traces of gentile-focused discourse.

[150] Italics added.

[151] Though at 1 John 5.10 trust in the Son of God is based on testimony God has given about him, which suggests that in this dominantly Jewish community trust in God is primary.

[152] In contrast, putting trust in human beings may be both epistemically and practically risky for God: below, pp. 70–2.

are invited to take the risk of entering a new trust relationship with God, and of accepting that their long covenantal relationship with God has taken a radical new turn. Gentiles are invited to risk abandoning their other gods, nearly all of whom they think have some track record of trustworthiness, and worshipping exclusively the God of Israel. Everyone is invited to put their trust in the newly ascended being Jesus Christ in the yet unproven hope that he will come at the end time and save the faithful.

What is more, the life which the faithful are called to live, especially as Paul describes it, is conceptually, ethically, and relationally demanding. After they have died to sin (Rom. 6.2) and the 'deeds of the body' (Rom. 8.13), and are living as a 'new creation' (2 Cor. 5.17), embodying the spirit of God (cf. 1 Cor. 6.19) or Christ himself (2 Cor. 4.10, Gal. 2.20), the faithful are called to practise love, hope, and peace, without qualification, without exception, and without fail,[153] together with all the other fruit of the spirit (Gal. 5.22) and the many other positive attitudes and actions which Paul commends throughout his letters.[154] At the same time, they still live every day in the old world of sin and death, in which, as Paul's letters frequently attest, it is all too easy to fail in love, peace, and the rest.

The greatest risk of trust in God and Christ for the faithful may be the difficulty of living out its implications until the day of the Lord (cf. 1 Cor. 1.8, Phil. 1.6).[155] This is a very unusual form of risk. In most fields of study, the risk of trusting another person is taken to be that they will let you down, not that you will let them down.[156] In the history of Israel, moreover, Israel is remembered as having let God down at times, but not because God's covenant demanded a standard of attitude or action which human beings could all too easily fail to meet. The commendation of the Mosaic covenant which Deuteronomy puts in the mouth of God (30.11–14) emphatically asserts the opposite: 'this command which I enjoin on you today is not too mysterious and remote for you...No, it is something very near to you, already in your mouths and in your hearts; you have only to carry it out.' For Paul (and probably, more or less explicitly, for later writers), trust in God and Christ leads to the highest possible hopes, but also the risk that the faithful will fail to be as trustworthy as God asks them to be.

---

[153] Love: e.g. Rom. 12.9, 12.19, 13.8–10, 14.15, 16.5, 16.8–9, 16.12; 1 Cor. 4.14, 4.17, 4.21, 13 *passim*, 15.58, 16.24; 2 Cor. 2.4, 2.8, 6.6, 7.1, 8.7–8, 8.24, 12.15, 12.19; Gal. 5.13–14, 5.22; Phil. 1.16, 2.12, 4.1; 1 Thess. 2.8, 3.6, 4.9, 5.13; and Phlm. 1, 5, 7, 9, 16; cf. Rom. 9.13; references to love sometimes leave open whether Paul is referring to love of God or neighbour or both (e.g. 1 Cor. 14.1, 2 Cor. 2.8). Hope: e.g. 1 Cor. 2.9, cf. 8.3; 1 Thess. 1.3–4, cf. 3.6, 5.8; Phlm. 5; peace: e.g. Rom. 2.10, 3.17, 14.19; cf. Rom. 15.33; 1 Cor. 7.15, 16.11; 2 Cor. 13.11; Gal. 5.22.

[154] On the relationship between Paul's 'theological' and 'ethical' thinking, see especially Furnish (1968), Rosner (1994), Hays (1996), Keck (1996, 2015a), Martyn (1997b), ch. 15, Lewis (2005), Horrell (2016), ch. 1.

[155] Cf. pp. 79, 88, 110, 111–12, 115, 120.

[156] This points to the fact that God invests therapeutic trust in humanity (see below), and also marks what is not normally observed about therapeutic trust, that it also involves risk for the trustee. We can detect traces of the same concern in Greek religiosity.

Chapter 6 will argue that the gospels offer one response to this problem, recognizing that human trust is inevitably inchoate, imperfect, and prone to fail—and that, even so, God accepts it as adequate for salvation.[157] At 2 Corinthians 12.7-10 Paul offers his own answer. He describes being given some kind of 'thorn in the flesh' (v. 7), 'to keep me from being too elated' (v. 7). He begged to have the thorn taken away, but Christ told him, 'My grace is sufficient for you, for power is made perfect in weakness' (v. 9). Therefore, Paul says, 'I am content with weaknesses, insults, hardships, persecutions, and constraints... for when I am weak, then I am strong' (v. 10). Verse 10 lists circumstances which might present a risk to any faithful person, and this suggests that what Christ says to Paul is relevant to all the faithful in their sufferings. Christ's grace supports and empowers them in their weakness, and, by implication, mitigates the risk that they will not be faithful or trustworthy.

This interpretation fits with Paul's affirmation at Galatians 2.20 that 'I no longer live, but Christ lives in me', and with his recurring theme that he, and all the faithful, live 'in Christ's hands'.[158] If one is afraid of one's own frailty in the trust relationship, Paul's answer is to be more open to grace, more hospitable to Christ, and more obedient in service.[159] This theme also fits with Paul's sense, and that of all New Testament writers, of the love and care which God and Christ give to the faithful, and their attentiveness to human suffering. As Paul might argue, the God and Christ who love human beings and have made possible their salvation would not give them 'work of *pistis*' (cf. 1 Thess. 1.3) to do which was not possible for them to fulfil. There may be risks for the faithful in the demands of the divine-human relationship, but they must be, in the modern phrase, manageable risks. Implicit in the call to trust, therefore, is an assurance that God and Christ will not let the trusting person down: an assurance which, in this new relationship, is perhaps most likely to be based on hope, belief, propositional trust, or a combination of all three.

In this chapter so far we have not distinguished between trust as an attitude and as an action, but 1 Thessalonians 1.3 reminds us that even if attitude and action ideally go together, they do not always do so in practice. This suggests two more ways in which both the risk of putting one's trust in God and Christ and the risk of failing in one's trust may be mitigated. A human being may struggle to trust cognitively, but decide to act with trust and see what living in the trust relationship is like. Or he may decide to trust that, despite his own doubts, God has good reason to invite him to trust, and opt to trust those reasons.[160] Compare the situation when a person is learning to swim, and the teacher says, 'Trust me: you can take your feet off the bottom now, and you will float.' Even if the learner does

---

[157] pp. 258-63.   [158] See 131-2.
[159] Cf. pp. 132-3, 222-3.   [160] Cf. pp. 259-60, 347-8, 353-4.

not feel that she can trust herself to float, she may decide to take a risk and act as though she does. Alternatively, she may trust the teacher's assurance sufficiently to act with trust. Once she has acted, and found that she does float, the attitude of trust will presumably follow and reintegrate cognition and action.[161]

The idea that God might invite human beings to trust, even though God knows that their trust is likely to be fragile and imperfect, is an example of therapeutic trust. As discussed in Chapter 1, one person trusts another therapeutically when he expresses or enacts trust in another, even though he does not really think the other person is currently trustworthy, because he thinks (or believes, hopes, or trusts, perhaps) that being trusted will encourage the other person to become more trustworthy.[162] When, for example, as Paul describes it, God 'entrusted' Israel with God's oracles or words (Rom. 3.3), we may imagine that God was not necessarily certain that Israel was perfectly trustworthy at that moment, but hoped that she would grow in trustworthiness.[163] Paul does not speak explicitly of God as trusting or entrusting in the hope that humanity will become more trustworthy over time, but the idea fits well with the way he and other writers speak of the life of the faithful in the present time.[164]

The idea that God trusts therapeutically in human beings, however, raises a further question. If God is omniscient, and has foreknowledge of everything, how can God's trust be a risk? Presumably God knows whether or not human beings will, eventually, become trustworthy or not. One response would be to locate our discussion in an 'open theist' understanding of God, according to which God knows the many possibilities which the future holds, some of which will materialize and others not, as free human action interacts with God's love and hope for the world.[165] On this view, God could trust therapeutically, knowing that it is possible that human beings will become trustworthy, and working in love and hope for this to happen. A theology of trust, especially one strongly rooted in New Testament writings, fits well within a framework of open theism, but another possibility suggests itself in the context of this study. In Christian tradition, one strand of thinking about human knowledge of God has emphasized that such knowledge is not only, or mainly (or at all), knowledge about God, but is rather personal knowledge of God.[166] Personal knowing, moreover, is especially important when people seek to speak to God or serve God, or listen or be guided by God. Conversely, we can see God's knowledge of humanity, when God interacts

---

[161] On this as what God requires of humanity, specifically in relation to the Abraham narrative, see Magonet (1984).
[162] See p. 12.   [163] p. 44.
[164] E.g. pp. 109–12, 132–3.
[165] The term 'open theism' was introduced by Rice (1985) and developed e.g. by Pinnock et al. (1994); the concept continues to be widely debated. Rissler (2006) argues that in a model of open theism, God's relationship with creation is one of hope rather than risk, but his view of risk as simply 'playing the odds' (p. 73) is very thin, and it is better to see both hope and risk as involved.
[166] Going back to New Testament writings (and further).

with humanity, as not only, or mainly, knowledge about humanity, but personal knowledge of humanity.

God's personal knowledge of humanity is a recurring theme of the Jewish scriptures, especially in the Psalms, books of wisdom, and prophecy. Some of the most memorable passages of the Hebrew Bible affirm it: 'Before I formed you in womb I knew you...' (Jer. 1.5); 'O God, you have searched me out and known me...' (Ps. 139.1). It is an equally strong theme in New Testament writings. God is the God who knows the hearts of all (Acts 1.24, cf. 1 Cor. 4.5); who numbers the hairs on your head (Mt. 10.30=Lk. 12.7 and knows what you need before you ask (Mt. 6.31-2=Lk. 12.29-30); who knows his people (Gal. 4.9, 2 Tim. 2.19, cf. Jn 10.14-15); before whom nothing and no one is hidden, but is laid bare before God's accounting eyes (Heb. 4.13). There is therefore scope to argue (though we cannot make the case at length here) that in the few New Testament passages which refer to divine foreknowledge, God's knowledge of the future is founded on God's knowledge of humanity. For Paul, God has not rejected Israel (Rom. 11.2) because he has always known his people, for the present and the future, and it is because God has always known his people that Paul is confident that all Israel will eventually be saved (Rom. 11.26). It may be because of the kind of people the Jerusalemites and the Romans are that God knew that Jesus would be crucified (cf. Acts 2.23), but God also knows that they are capable of change, and still have time to repent and be baptized (Acts 2.38).

Like a parent who knows her children and deeply understands them, God knows God's creation, including God's human children. And, like a parent of young children or teenagers, we can imagine God as knowing there is a good in most, if not all his children, even if they are immature and unformed—a bit careless, not very considerate, a real tearaway, not always very kind; even mean, selfish, or cruel. If God trusts in them now, they will likely fail. They may need a good deal of therapeutic trust, together with both love and discipline, to become trustworthy. But most, perhaps all of them have it in them to turn out well, and so God trusts in them and accepts the interim risks.[167]

Is God Reliable?

In Chapter 1 we saw that trust often, though not always, goes hand in hand with reliance, and it is often argued or assumed by modern Christians and modern scholars, especially in connection with claims about divine omniscience and

---

[167] On the basis that among New Testament writers, perhaps only John sees some as pre-elected not to receive eternal life; but this model works equally well whether we envisage God as knowing all human beings as savable, or some as not.

justice, that God is absolutely reliable.[168] Should we therefore say that, despite the argument of the previous section, trust in God is not truly risky because God is absolutely reliable?

It is helpful to distinguish the two kinds of reliance we described earlier.[169] When we say that we are relying on something or someone, we often mean that we are relying on him or it to do something we want or need.[170] I may, for instance, rely on Joe to bring a bottle of wine when he comes to dinner, and on my corkscrew to open it. In line with this common usage, Christians sometimes say that God will not let them suffer, or will always protect them, with an implication that they assume that God's definition of suffering or protection reliably matches theirs.[171] But sometimes we rely on a person or thing to be and act as itself, independently of what we want or need. If I drop the bottle on my foot or poke myself in the eye with the corkscrew, I can rely on it to hurt. Should I suffer a psychotic break, I rely on a psychiatrist to commit me to hospital whether I want to go or not.

For Paul, as we have seen, by fulfilling his promises to Abraham, God has shown not only that he is trustworthy for the future, but also that he is reliable: God has done what he said he would do. God has, however, fulfilled God's promises in a radically unexpected way and 'apart from the law' which, for most Jews, frames Israel's relationship with God. Evidently human beings can rely on God to fulfil God's promises, but not necessarily to act as they want or expect. As Paul says in round terms at Romans 9.14–16, God enacts God's will, and human beings must respond as God requires.[172] This may have sounded as shocking to some law-keeping Jewish listeners in the first century as it does to some people of faith today. Having lived faithfully for centuries within the covenant, and assumed that God was faithful and reliable within that covenant, they heard Christ-confessors preach that God had made a new relationship or a (re)new(ed) covenant with humanity, redrawn the parameters of God's existing relationship with God's people, and redefined that people. Putting one's trust in God (even if, like Paul, one also understands God as gracious, merciful, loving, and just[173]) and living in

---

[168] E.g. Bultmann (1973), 160, Sequeri (2002), 64, Helm (2002a), Landau et al. (2018), cf. Artz-Grabner (2011) (in relation to Paul) Abraham (2018), 54–68. Arguing against divine immutability see e.g. Brown (2008). Claims of divine reliability, however, tend not to focus on the potential differences between what human beings believe or hope for and what God can be relied on to do.

[169] p. 24.

[170] Swinburne (2005), 144 says the same of faith more broadly: 'one who believes that God exists and believes the propositions of the Christian creeds about Him already believes that God will do for us what He knows that we want or need: this follows immediately from the goodness of God...'

[171] Büssing et al. (2015), Glassman (2018), cf. Dentale et al. (2018). On a similar view among Jews and Muslims see e.g. Bonab and Namini (2010), Bonab and Koohsar (2011), though Krause et al. (2000), Krause (2004) show that some of those who pray think God knows best how to answer prayers.

[172] The 'command of the eternal God' should bring about 'the obedience that is *pistis*' (16.26, cf. 1.5). With most commentators, I read ὑπακοὴν πίστεως as a subjective genitive; Jewett (2007) *ad* 1.5 argues that it refers to the obedience that follows from faith, but this is a distinction without much of a difference.

[173] E.g. Rom. 1.7, 5.15 (grace), 11.31, 13.9 (mercy), 5.8, 8.39 (love), 3.26, 9.14, cf. 11.1 (justice).

trust is therefore, as we have seen, profoundly risky in the sense that it may overturn both a person's sense of her existing covenant with God and her own agenda.

Separately (logically, if not theologically) from the question of God's reliability, we can note that, by putting their trust in the God who has acted so unexpectedly, through Christ, and in addition, if they are gentiles, giving up their trust in other gods, the faithful do, in practice, rely on God. Looking ahead to a number of passages which emphasize God's care for creation, we might add that affirming God's care for creation also affirms that God can be relied on. This is surely true, but later chapters will suggest that it is not the focus of Paul's discourse, nor that of New Testament writings in general. When we rely on someone, we tend to rely on them to do something specific or perform in a certain way. Trust in God and Christ involves much more than this, from entering a new life under new authority, to following and imitating Christ, to being entrusted with gifts and work for God's people and God's kingdom. Though the faithful do, therefore, rely on God in a sense, their relationship with God involves much more than reliance, and reliance is not what is most distinctive of it.

Most of this chapter so far has concerned the kind of trust that brings human beings into a relationship with God, rather than the kind that continues once they have become community members, though we saw some examples of the latter in 1 Corinthians and 1 Thessalonians. This raises the question whether those who have put their trust in God and been baptized are reliably saved. Paul is clear that they are not.[174] They must continue to trust and be faithful (e.g. 2 Cor. 6.4, Gal. 5.22, 1 Thess. 1.23) and strengthen and develop their trust and faithfulness (e.g. 1 Cor. 3.6, 9.4, 1 Thess. 3.2–3).[175] They can be excluded from the *ekklēsia* for certain kinds of behaviour (e.g. 1 Cor. 5.2). When Paul looks forward to salvation or eternal life in the future, he often links it with the language of divine gift, service to God, and hope: 'now that you have been freed from sin, and have become slaves of God, you reap the fruit for your sanctification, and the consummation is eternal life. For the wages of sin is death, but the gift of God is eternal life in Christ Jesus' (Rom. 6.22–3).[176] The faithful cannot rely on God to save them in any circumstances, but hope for salvation as long as they play their part of faithfulness, service, and hope. These examples underline what is true of every stage of the divine–human relationship: it is never one-sided. Human beings can rely on God to be God, and to enact God's will, but to be saved at Christ's coming they must respond with trust.[177]

---

[174] E.g. Stuhlmacher (1965), Roetzel (1972), Aune (2002), Donfried (2002a, 2002b), Boers (1994), 86–94, 120–32, all of whom see the eventual salvation of the faithful as dependent in part on their obedience between justification and final judgment; cf. Morgan (2020), 235–6, 238–9.

[175] Volf (1990).

[176] Cf. e.g. Rom. 8.24–5, 1 Cor. 15.19, Gal. 5.5, 1 Thess. 4.13–14 (hope), Rom. 14.7–8, 1 Cor. 15.58, Phil. 3.12–14 (belonging to God).

[177] Despite referring not infrequently to God's foreknowledge, choice, and calling of the faithful (e.g. Rom. 8.30, 9.24, 1 Cor. 1.1–2, 1.26, 7.17, 7.21, Gal. 1.6, 5.13, Phil. 3.14, 1 Thess. 4.7 (calling), Rom.

An Unusual Form of Three-Place Trust?

Speaking of salvation draws attention to the fact that trust in God, in the passages we have looked at so far, often (though not always, and not explicitly) looks like 'three-place' trust.[178] God is trustworthy in having enabled human beings to be saved from their sins and made right with God through the self-offering of Jesus Christ, and human beings put their trust in God in the hope eventually of being saved (though also, in more two-place and open-ended terms, in hope of both present and future existence with God and Christ). Salvation or right-standing with God is something which anyone might be imagined as wanting. We have seen, however, that the assumption of research on trust, across disciplines, that we normally trust others to do things we want, does not do justice to the thinking of New Testament writers.

The faithful trust God, through Christ, to extend God's power, righteousness, and peace to the whole of heaven and earth and, at the culmination of this process, to bring those who put their trust in God and Christ to salvation and eternal life.[179] They hope that they will be among the saved.[180] But they recognize that the primary agency and the agenda in the divine–human relationship are God's and Christ's, and human beings can only trust that God and Christ will do what they hope for insofar as they align themselves with that agenda and are obedient to God's will.[181]

Trust, Trustworthiness, and Exemplarity

We have seen that, in affirming the faithfulness, trustworthiness, and reliability of God, Paul and other writers draw on ideas about God's *pistis* in the scriptures. With the exception of several references to Genesis 15.6 and Habakkuk 2.4, it is rare for New Testament writers to quote or refer to scriptural passages containing *pistis* language. Several passages, however, refer to or gloss passages of scripture that do not contain *pistis* language, in such a way as to indicate that the writer

---

9.11, 9.19, 11.2–8, 1 Thess. 1.4 (choice and chosenness), cf. Rom. 9.16, 1 Cor. 15.38, Phil. 1.6. 1.28–9, 2.13), Paul does not develop a theory of predestination but takes for granted that human beings exercise free will (Morgan (2020), 183–7).

[178] Cf. pp. 11–12.

[179] E.g. Rom. 11.25–6, 1 Cor. 15.24–8, cf. Rom. 13.11, Phil. 3.20 (salvation); Rom. 6.23, Gal. 6.8 (eternal life); Phil. 3.20, 2 Cor. 5.2 (heaven). 1 Cor. 1.18, 2 Cor. 2.15 seem to allow the possibility that some are not saved, though 1 Cor. 5.5 suggests that someone might be handed over to Satan for the destruction of his body and salvation of his spirit.

[180] On whether Rom. 9–11 should be read as affirming the ultimate salvation of all see e.g. Fitzymer (1993a), *ad loc.*, arguing that Paul envisages the salvation of all people, whether Jews or gentiles; Levering (2011), 25–33 and Wagner (2011) see God's redemptive love for his creatures as absolute, while leaving room for them to choose to remain in their sins. Both Levering (2011) and Byrne (1996), *ad loc.* plausibly suggest that when Paul refers to 'all people' in this passage, he has in mind Jews and gentiles as groups rather than all individuals, but it does not follow that Paul excludes some Jews or gentiles.

[181] Even, in the gospels, when Christ is encountered as a baby: pp. 274–5.

understands *pistis* as implicit in them, and, moreover, as meaning what *pistis* between God and human beings means in and after the Christ event. Listeners are evidently meant to infer that the scriptures foreshadow the (re)new(ed) divine-human *pistis* relationship as Christ-confessors understand it.

At Romans 3.30, for example, Paul says that 'God is one and will righteous the circumcised on the basis of (*ek*) *pistis* and the uncircumcised through (*dia*) *pistis*'.[182] The phrase 'God is one' recalls Deuteronomy 6.4, but the key human attitude towards God, in response to God's promises to Israel (cf. Deut. 6.3), which the *Shema* characterizes as love, is reinterpreted by Paul as *pistis*, redefining God's relationship with humanity as based on the attitude and action which centrally characterize the new divine–human relationship after the Christ event. Human trust and faithfulness, for Paul, are responses to the trustworthiness as well as the righteousness of God, which was testified to by the law and the prophets (cf. 3.21) and has now been manifested through the death of Christ Jesus (cf. 3.21, 24–5).

Later in the letter (10.8), Paul quotes parts of Deuteronomy 30.11–14: the commandment or 'word' of God which promises life and prosperity to those who follow it (Deut. 30.15) is not up in the sky or down in the depths of the sea, but in the mouth and heart of the faithful. Paul glosses the 'word' as 'the word of *pistis* which we preach', which saves those who put their trust in Christ (10.9). The God who, for Deuteronomy 30, would fulfil his promise to the Israelites who kept the law now fulfils his promise and makes righteous those who confess Christ.[183]

Peter's speech at Pentecost (Acts 2.14–36) quotes Joel (3.1–5), prophesying that in the 'last days' (v. 17) God will send the spirit on 'all flesh', all kinds of people will prophesy, and 'everyone shall be saved who calls on the name of the Lord' (v. 21), and implying that God has fulfilled his prophecy on this day. Peter quotes Psalms 16.8–11 (vv. 25–8) and 110.1 (vv. 34–5) as prophecies of the resurrection and installation of Jesus as Lord and Messiah (v. 36) which have also been fulfilled.[184] Though no *pistis* language appears in this speech, its clear implication is that, in raising Christ from the dead, God has faithfully fulfilled the promises spoken through the prophets.[185]

Paul and other writers also use well-known stories from the scriptures as *exempla* of trust in God and God's trustworthiness to the faithful.[186] The point of all

---

[182] Assuming that we should not be looking for 'two-covenant theology' in Paul (so Sanders (1983), 192–5), this is probably simply stylistic *variatio*; Stowers' (1989) argument that Paul uses *dia* when referring only to gentiles and *ek* when referring to both Jews and gentiles does not distinguish the meaning of the prepositions clearly enough to be convincing.

[183] The gospels sometimes echo scriptural language in a similar way to affirm the trustworthiness of Jesus in his earthly life: pp. 212–14.

[184] God's faithfulness and trustworthiness, though without *pistis* language, are also a clear theme of Stephen's speech (7.2–53), Philip's teaching (8.32–5), and Paul's speech at Pisidian Antioch at 13.16–41 (with explicit references to the fulfilment of promises at vv. 23, 27, 32–3).

[185] Peter makes the same point in slightly different terms at Acts 3.18–24.

[186] Some of these are already models of trust in the scriptures: e.g. Neh. 9.8, 1 Macc. 2.52, Sir. 44.19–20 (Abraham), Sir. 45.4 (Moses), 46.15 (Samuel). Prov. 12.22, cf. 15.27–8, 15.27a affirm that faithfulness is always acceptable to God.

these stories, as New Testament writers use them, is that individuals and groups throughout history have held and enacted the same direct trust in God that they are commending, and have never been disappointed. The figure most often invoked is Abraham, in the story of God's first covenant with what will become Israel (Gen. 15.18). In Genesis chapter 12, God tells Abram to leave his fatherland and go to another land which God will show him, where 'I will make of you a great nation, and I will bless you' (12.2). Abram does as God directs until he arrives in Canaan, which God tells him will be his descendants' land (12.7). After further travels in Egypt and the Negeb Abram returns to Canaan, where God again promises all the land he can see to him and his descendants (13.3–4, 14–16). God tells Abram to walk the length and breadth of the land (13.17), which he does, and secures his place there (ch. 14). God yet again promises great rewards to Abram, but Abram pushes back: 'O Lord God, what good will your gifts be, if I keep on being childless...?' (15.2). God assures Abram that his descendants will be as numerous as the stars (15.5), and Abram 'put his trust in the Lord, and it was reckoned to him as righteousness (ἐπίστευσεν τῷ θεῷ, καὶ ἐλογίσθη αὐτῷ εἰς δικαιοσύνην)' (15.6). Abraham's story is one of continuously evolving *pistis*: each time he follows a divine direction it is an act of new or renewed trust.[187] At 15.2, however, Abraham asserts a degree of independence by challenging God, and it is after he has chosen to accept God's reassurance that he is described explicitly for the first time as trusting. 15.6 therefore marks a new departure in the divine–human relationship and the rest of Abraham's eventful story, and that of his descendants, confirms his trust in God and God's trustworthiness to him.[188]

In Galatians and Romans, as we have seen, Paul uses Genesis 15.6 to argue that it is *pistis* that brings human beings into their right relationship with God (Rom. 4.5–8, Gal. 3.5–6) and makes gentiles children of Abraham along with Jews (Rom. 4.9, Gal. 3.7). The second part of this argument relies not only on the call to trust God, but also on an affirmation of God's trust and trustworthiness towards both Jews and gentiles, which was enacted above all in the crucifixion (Rom. 3.24–5, cf. Gal. 2.19).[189] By repeatedly emphasizing the fulfilment in Christ of the promises made by God (Rom. 4.13, 14, 16, 20, Gal. 3.14, 16, 17, 18 (bis), 19, 21, 22, 29), Paul emphasizes God's trustworthiness towards everyone who acts like Abraham.[190]

---

[187] Stump (2010), 258–312, Morgan (2015a), 178–84.

[188] That this act of trust is not without risk is underlined by the fact that God makes a covenant with Abraham at 15.18: an act which both reifies the trust between them, and, like any agreement, acts as a reification of deferred trust. That uncertainties remain after 15.6 is indicated by 15.7, where God reminds Abraham that he has proved trustworthy in the past, and 15.17, where God performs a miracle for Abraham over a sacrifice to demonstrate his trustworthiness.

[189] God promised Abraham that 'through you shall *all* the nations be blessed' (Gal. 3.8), and this promise has been fulfilled through the death of Christ Jesus (Gal. 3.9, 14, cf. 16).

[190] Paul also thinks that *pistis* can evolve in the course of a community member's life and relationship with God and Christ (e.g. 2 Cor. 8.7, 10.15, 13.5, 1 Thess. 3.2–3, 5–6, 10), though he does not link this theme explicitly with his reading of Genesis. Gen. 15.6 is also invoked by James 2.23, arguing that Abraham is also justified by works, not by trust alone.

Abraham is also a model of trust for the author of Hebrews: for accepting God's call to leave home, settle in a new land, and have a child in his own and his wife's old age (11.8–12).[191] Abraham did all these things because 'he thought the one who had made the promise was trustworthy' (*pistos*) (11.11). The writer does not tell us whether Abraham thought God was trustworthy by nature, or on the basis of his own past experience, but the moments in Abraham's life which he chooses to demonstrate Abraham's trust are times when Abraham's life takes a new direction, so they illustrate moments of new or renewed trust.[192]

The narrative of Moses and the Exodus offers another paradigmatic example of God's trust and trustworthiness on which New Testament writers draw. The Septuagintal Exodus story is peppered with *pistis* language, emphasizing, at key turning-points in the story, God's trust in Moses to free his people and trustworthiness towards them; Moses' trust and faithfulness towards God; God's entrusting of leadership and of the law to Moses; Moses' entrusting of leadership to other Israelites; and the Israelites' (sometimes insecure) trust and faithfulness towards God and Moses himself (e.g. Exod. 4.1, 4.8–9, 4.31, 14.31, 19.9).[193] God, Moses affirms at the beginning of the Book of Deuteronomy, is *pistos*: he keeps his covenant with Abraham's descendants to the thousandth generation (7.9). God is a rock for Israel, a firm foundation for life: just, upright, without deceit, trustworthy (32.4). No listener to the Septuagint could hear a reference to Moses without recognizing the importance in his story both of new acts of trust as events unfold and of God's ongoing faithfulness and trustworthiness to his people. Like Abraham, Moses is most often referenced, especially in the gospels and Acts, to affirm that God's promises to Israel have been fulfilled in Christ, though without any indication whether the writer is also thinking of God as continuously faithful to his covenant.[194] For the author of Hebrews, however, Moses is a model

---

[191] Abraham presumably takes both epistemic and practical risks, e.g. when he leaves home or prepares to sacrifice his son.

[192] At Lk. 1.68–79, God has fulfilled his promise 'to be mindful of his holy covenant and of the oath he swore to Abraham our father' (1.72–3), suggesting that for Luke, as for Paul, God's promise to Abraham is fulfilled in Christ. The fulfilment of oaths is a key characteristic of trustworthiness throughout the ancient Mediterranean and Near East (Morgan (2015a), 59, 61, 78, 80–3, 86, 92–3, 102–30, 155–8), but Lk. 1.46–55 invokes something more like God's covenant faithfulness, affirming that God's mercy, so perhaps also his trustworthiness, 'is from age to age to those who fear him' (v. 50), and referencing Abraham with all his descendants (cf. Exod. 2.24, 32.13, Deut. 9.27, Ps. 105.8–11, 42 LXX, Mic. 7.20: so Fitzmyer (1981), Bovon (2002), Wolter (2016), *ad loc.*, though e.g. Green (1997), Edwards (2015), *ad loc.* see this too as a reference to the fulfilment of promises). Elsewhere (Mt. 1.2, 1.17, 8.11, 22.32=Mk 12.26; Lk. 13.16, 13.28, 16.19–31, 19.9, 20.37; Jn 8.31–59; cf. Mt. 3.9=Lk. 3.8) Abraham is invoked as the patriarch of patriarchs, who marks the length of God's relationship with Israel but without explicit characterization of the nature of God's faithfulness.

[193] Morgan (2015a), 184–7. Josephus presents the *pistis* of Moses towards God as enabling him to channel the power of God and mediate *pistis* to the Israelites and evoke it in them, making him, in turn, an object of their *pistis* (*Ant.* 2.276, 3.27).

[194] Mt. 17.3–4=Mk 9.4–5=Lk. 9.30–3, Mt. 19.16–20, Mk 12.26, Lk. 16.31, cf. Jn 5.46–7, Lk. 20.37, Lk. 24.27, 44, Jn 1.45, 5.45–6, Acts 3.22, 7.37, 13.39, 26.22–3, 28.23, Rom. 9.15, 10.5–13, 19, Rev. 15.3, cf. 2 Tim. 3.8–9. In a number of passages Moses (as a metonym for the law) is used as a contrast with

of faithfulness (though inferior to Christ): he was 'faithful in all his house' (3.2–5). Moses is contrasted with the other Israelites whose behaviour in the desert is *apistos* (3.12) and leads God, inexorably trustworthy, to fulfil his promise that '[t]hey shall not enter into my rest' (3.11).[195]

The same writer offers a 'great cloud' (12.1) of examples of *pistis*, who throughout history trusted in God and were vindicated, including Abel, Noah, Abraham, Isaac, Jacob, Joseph, Moses and his parents, the Israelites at the walls of Jericho, Rahab, Gideon, Barak, Samson, Jephthah, David, Samuel, and the prophets (11.4–40).[196] In a few cases it is unclear whether the act of trust by these *exempla* is a new departure or an expression of ongoing trust and faithfulness: as, for instance, when Abel makes his offering to God (11.4), or when Enoch is said to be taken up to God 'by' (i.e. because of) his *pistis* (11.5). Most of those referenced, though, seem to put new or renewed trust in God at a moment of crisis or a turning point in their lives: Noah when he built the ark (11.7); Abraham when he travelled to Canaan (11.8); Moses' parents when they hid him as a baby (11.23); Moses when he chose to identify with the Israelites rather than the Egyptians (11.24–5); the Israelites when they crossed the Red Sea (11.29); Rahab when she helped the Israelites to take Jericho (11.31). Many of those whose activities are not described individually, moreover, are remembered as having 'conquered kingdoms...closed the mouths of lions, put our raging fires, escaped the devouring sword...[become] strong in battle and turned back foreign invaders...received back their dead through resurrection' (11.33–5)—all actions that could be the fruit of ongoing trust and faithfulness, but equally, and perhaps more likely, could be consequences of (re)new(ed) trust in God.

This list of exemplars is offered in the context of the writer's urging his listeners to maintain their confidence in God (10.35), persist in trust (10.38, 39), and endure whatever sufferings may be imposed on them because they confess Christ (10.32–8), and, to his list of famous individuals from Israelite history, he appends many nameless faithful people who endured torture, imprisonment, mockery, and marginalization because of their *pistis* (11.35–8). Since the writer is addressing community members who are already in a relationship of trust and faithfulness with God, it is not surprising that some of his *exempla* are of ongoing trust/faithfulness. It is more striking how much emphasis he puts on the idea that, at a decisive moment in one's life, one might put new or renewed trust in God to be trustworthy at that moment. Evidently the importance of new or renewed trust to the mindset of the faithful does not diminish after baptism.

---

what Christians should put trust in; but the *pistis* of those who put their trust in Jesus is also occasionally contrasted, in the gospels, with the *apistia* of Israel: e.g. Mt. 8.10.

[195] Cf. Hos. 5.9; also 1 Cor. 10.1–13 where the Israelites are also unfaithful in the desert.

[196] Niedzwiedzki (2016) explores the evolution of traditions about Joseph in early Judaism with particular reference to his trust in God.

At the very end of this colourful series of examples, the writer offers a further reflection. He has already said that some of his early exemplars did not receive what they had been promised, but died in trust (11.13). Now he says that none of those who trusted in the past received what they had been promised: 'God had foreseen something better for us, so that without us they should not have been made perfect' (11.40). Just as, for Paul, God's promises are all fulfilled in Christ, for the author of Hebrews, God's trustworthiness, and the trust of people in the past, are fulfilled in the death and glorification of Christ (cf. 12.1–2).

Trust before Trust: God, Christ, and Creation

We noted above that the trust in God which we have outlined so far often looks three-place: the faithful trust God above all to forgive their sins and save them from the 'coming wrath' (1 Thess. 1.10). Behind this, however, we can glimpse indications of two-place trust. When Paul says to the Corinthians, '[a]s God is trustworthy, our word to you is not "yes" and "no"' (2 Cor. 1.18); when the writer of 2 Timothy says of Christ, as God's son, that he is always faithful 'because he cannot deny himself' (2 Tim. 2.13); when John's Jesus says, 'Do not let your hearts be troubled. Trust in God, trust also in me' (Jn 14.1), trust between God and human beings is not only a means to an end but constitutive of the divine–human relationship itself.[197] Two-place trust is of interest not least because it typically forms part of an open-ended relationship which is understood as good or worthwhile in its own right, and as this study progresses we will want to know more about what such a relationship between God, Christ, and humanity looks like, and what life is like in it. The place, in New Testament writings, where two-place trust in God is perhaps most powerfully attested, is in passages about God and/or Christ as creator.

Trust language appears for the first time in the scriptures with Abraham's trust in God at Genesis 15.6, but Genesis' picture of an identifiable relationship of trust between God and humanity begins with the beginning of the book.[198] Without delving into the complex history of the text and even more complex history of interpretation, and drawing on the discussion of trust in Chapter 1,

---

[197] Taking both instances of *pisteuete*, with most commentators, as imperative, though the first could be indicative.

[198] Divine–human trust in Genesis 2–3, in antiquity and today, is less discussed in explicit terms than one might expect (e.g. Philo, who is deeply interested in Abraham's and Moses' trust, does not attribute trust or mistrust to God or Adam and Eve in Gen. 2–3; nor does Josephus, who sees the narrative of the serpent and Adam and Eve as involving persuasion (*peithein*), belief (*peithesthai*), and disobedience rather than trust (*AJ* 1.40–8)). However, for Sequeri (1993), 42, 57, (1996), 132, 421), Mackey (2006, 2008), Lebens (2017), and Holtzen (2019), 153–9 the trust restored through Christ is that broken by Adam and Eve; the latter two also make the more general argument that God puts trust in human beings.

a brief sketch of Genesis' two creation stories points to the theme of trust that runs through them.[199]

God appears at the beginning of chapter 1 as the being who creates the world. As creator God acts (1.1, 2.4) and rests (2.2); speaks (1.3) and plans (1.3, 6). God recognizes and names goodness and beauty (1.4, 2.9), gives living creatures which he sees as good autonomy to multiply (1.22), and creates humanity in (some aspect of) God's likeness (1.26).[200] In these stories God is portrayed in personal terms, interacting with creation in such a way as to enable human beings to interact with God.[201] Human beings are connected from their creation with the being who made them, in a relationship which operates recognizably like human relationships. The fact that Adam and Eve exist from their creation in relation with God (and the rest of God's creation) means that they are never imagined (as Annette Baier criticizes some philosophers for imagining human beings) as autonomous subjects who begin their active life by deciding whether or not to forge social contracts. The first action of humanity is a reaction to being given responsibility for creation or for cultivating Eden by God (1.28-9, 2.15), and the next is the woman's reaction to the serpent (3.1-7).

From the beginning, God's relationship with humanity is one of care, evident in God's sense of what is good for creation and actions on its behalf.[202] At Genesis 2.18-24 God creates the woman because 'it is not good for the human to be alone' (2.18) and, in both stories, God provides humanity with the means of life (1.29, 2.15). In the second, God forbids the man (and by extension the woman), for their own good, to eat the fruit of one tree in the garden in which they live.[203]

---

[199] A long tradition, starting in the Second Temple period, sees Adam as in a covenantal relationship with God: e.g. Sir. 17.10, Jub. 2-3, cf. Hos. 6.7; see e.g. Mayes (1973), Levison (1988), Elgvin (1994), Noffke (2007), Berg (2013), Kelly (2014), but what follows suggests that the relationship may better be seen as one of trust. On the history of interpretation of Gen. 1 in general see Van Kooten (2005). Wenham (1987), *ad* Gen. 2.4-3.23 observes that the Yahwist has drawn on universal themes of human life to create an original story: 'Marriage, work, pain, sin, and death are the subject matter of this great narrative': on the basis that trust and failures of trust are also seen as fundamental to the divine-human relationship across the scriptures, we can add trust.

[200] On the history of interpretation of the image of God in Genesis see e.g. Jonsson (1988), Lorberbaum (2015); Barth (1986) 3.1.183-7 argues that humanity's divine image means that God can enter relationships with human beings, speak to them and make covenants with them, cf. Westermann (1966), *ad loc*. McDowell (2015), 185, 201-2 argues that the language of imagery does not only belong to Near Eastern statue manufacture, long thought by many commentators to be a source of Gen. 1.26, but is also language of sonship, and so Adam is being characterized here as God's son. All these suggestions strengthen the reading of God's relationship with humanity in Gen. 1-3 as one of care, and the last suggests an origin for Paul's Adam/Christ typology more satisfactory than that of the long-discredited Gnostic myth of the *Urmensch* (Käsemann (1933), 161-83; Brandenburger (1962); Conzelmann (1975), *ad* 1 Cor. 15.22; Bultmann (2007), vol. 1, 164-83).

[201] Though Burns (2009) argues that this does not commit us to assuming that the God of Genesis etc. *is* personal.

[202] The intimacy of this relationship, and the alienation that follows, is explored by Hauser (1982), though without discussion of trust. On Gen. 2-3 as concerning God's relationship with humanity, as distinct from his later relationship with Israel, see e.g. Westermann (1976), 277-8.

[203] Affirmed by Eve at 3.3. Translations from the MT are from the NAB unless otherwise noted; translations from the LXX are my own unless noted.

When they do eat it, he expels them from the garden and makes life much harder for them, but he does not abandon them, nor they him.[204] God resettles Adam and Eve east of Eden (2.24) and at the beginning of the next chapter we find their sons Cain and Abel making offerings to him (4.3-4). Outside Eden, God continues to care for humanity and give it work to do. He blesses human beings (1.28) and is generous towards them (1.29, 2.8, 15). He knows what is best for them and expects them to accept his authority (2.17-18, 3.11-24). When they do not, he reorders the relationship again on new terms (3.14-24). This pattern is repeated, with variations, throughout the Book of Genesis, in the stories of the flood, Sodom and Gomorrah, and Jacob, and beyond.

God's relationship with Adam and Eve fits the classic model of care developed by care ethicists and drawn on by theorists of trust such as Baier.[205] Like the parent God is often portrayed as being, God has an attitude of care towards the man and woman expressed in practice.[206] God's care, however, does not mean that the man and woman have no agency or responsibilities: at Genesis 1.28-30, God gives them dominion over the earth, and at 2.15 he gives the man Eden to cultivate and care for. As care ethicists regard as normal in caring relationships, God and human beings have different needs, roles, and rights: for instance, Adam and Eve need the means of life, while, in the second story, God needs to be able to exercise his authority to keep them safe in the garden (2.15-17). It is striking that one of the sharpest theological debates arising from Genesis 2-3 parallels one of the sharpest debates arising from the ethical theory of care: whether it is just that those who are cared for have their freedom or autonomy restricted in the interests of care.[207] (Should Adam and Eve, at their own risk, have been allowed to eat the fruit of the tree of the knowledge of good and evil? Should young children, at their own risk, be allowed to play with fire?[208]) Our focus, however, is on the trust between God, Adam, and Eve, rather than on God's injunction.

Ethicists of care argue that caring relationships are marked by trust, and so, at first, is the relationship between God and the man and woman. When God commands the man not to eat the fruit of the tree, he does not police his injunction; he seems to trust him to keep it, perhaps as part of his stewardship of the garden (2.16-17, cf. 15). When the sly serpent first approaches the woman (3.1), she affirms what she has been told about eating the fruit, quoting God's own words

---

[204] On God's ongoing relationship with erring humanity as corrective see Morgan (2015c).
[205] Above, pp. 11, 16.
[206] On the parenthood of God in Jewish writings see e.g. Strotmann (1991), Dille (2004), Tasker (2004).
[207] On justice and the ethics of care see Sevenhuijsen (1998), Engster (2007), Held (2015).
[208] Modern theologians, if not philosophers, are liable to think the first question much more problematic than the second because Adam and Eve seem to be imagined by Genesis, from their creation, as adults, and modern western culture takes a high view of the rights to freedom and autonomy of adults. Since, though, the gulf between the wisdom of God and that of humanity is surely conceived theologically as at least as great as that between a parent and child, it is probably better to think of the divine–human relationship as closer to a human relationship of care.

(3.3, cf. 2.17). The repetition of God's words has rhetorical force, but it also hints that the woman is trusting: she has accepted God's words as spoken and is willingly and unquestioningly doing what she has been told.

The serpent, significantly, does not try to persuade the woman that she ought to consider herself free or autonomous, that God is unjust in telling her what to do, or that it might be fun to break bounds. He attacks her trust, inducing her to doubt that God was telling the truth when he said eating the fruit would lead to death, and to doubt she was justified in trusting God.[209] He then invites her, if she is no longer sure she can trust God, to trust him instead, when he tells her that eating the fruit will give her, like Godself, knowledge of good and evil (3.5).

The eating of the fruit is normally portrayed as disobedience on the part of the man and woman, but the disobedience is based on the betrayal of trust.[210] It is quickly followed by another betrayal. When God asks the man whether he has eaten the fruit, he shifts responsibility onto the woman (3.12). The man and woman are also in a relationship of care: the woman is made because 'it is not good for the man to be alone', and she is twice described as his helper.[211] At the point when the man accepts the fruit, he evidently trusts the woman, but when, questioned by God, he shifts the blame for eating it onto her, he breaks their trust by implying that she was untrustworthy. The stage is set for trust, failures of trust, and renewals of trust between God and humanity to characterize the whole of human history.[212]

We saw in Chapter 1 that although relationships of care are an obvious form of three-place trust, they also have aspects of two-place trust. A parent and child, for instance, form a complex bond, involving trust, which persists when neither is in immediate need. They entrust themselves to one another not only for discrete goods, but as part of the relationship itself. This kind of trust, as Doris Brothers argues, is part of what makes people functional as people: without it, at the extreme, a person may fail to develop a sufficiently clear and coherent sense of

---

[209] Noted by Skinner (1930), *ad* Gen. 3.5, Holtzen (2019), 155–6. We can imagine that Eve's failure of trust therefore looks to her like a *reaction* to a failure by God; on sin and *apistia* as reactive see further pp. 144–5, 181–2.
[210] So Rom. 5.15–21; Wenham (1987), *ad loc.* describes this as the loss of the 'trust of innocence'; see also Kimelman (1996).
[211] *Boēthos* 2.18, 20 LXX.
[212] God's speech-act at 3.16–19 implies that the relationship between Adam and Eve will no longer be based on trust but on mutual need which is experienced with pain. Godfrey (2012), 30, 169 raises the question whether stories like the disobedience of Adam and Eve make sense. Can we trust someone we cannot help but depend on? Surely we can, assuming that we have any degree of free will (something the Jewish scriptures, like New Testament writings, take for granted), because even if we depend on someone, we can choose *not* to trust them. A small child, for instance, who depends on her parents to feed and clothe her, can in principle decide not to trust them to do so. Her choice will probably turn out badly fairly soon—she will get cold and hungry—but she can make the choice. Similarly, when people choose not to trust God in the scriptures, it eventually turns out badly for them or their descendants, but they can make the choice.

self to be able to engage in three-place trust at all.[213] Two-place trust is also implicit in the creation stories. When the man and woman initially obey and do not eat the fruit of the tree, one might argue that they are trusting God to have their best interests at heart, but in their just-created state it is hard to imagine on what basis they would make a judgment about God's motives, or make a decision to take a risk on them. The fact that the woman repeats God's words at 3.3 hints that they have not exercised any such judgment: they have simply done as they were told, accepting the injunction as part of their relationship.

The theme of trust remains implicit in the creation stories, but elsewhere in the scriptures, especially in the psalms and books of wisdom, the connection between trust and creation is explicit. Psalm 32 LXX, for example, has a strong creation theme. 'The word of the lord is upright,' proclaims the psalmist, 'and all his works are trustworthy [or perhaps 'performed in good faith'] (πάντα τὰ ἔργα αὐτοῦ ἐν πίστει)' (32.4). God loves mercy and justice and the earth is full of his mercy. By God's breath and word the heavens and all their hosts were established, and God gathers the waters of the sea and puts them in store (vv. 5–7). The Lord brought all the inhabitants of the world into being (vv. 8–9, cf. 15). He looks down on them (v. 13): 'the eyes of the Lord are on those who fear him, those who hope in his mercy to rescue their souls from death and to keep them alive in famine. Our soul waits for the Lord, because he is our helper and protector . . .' (vv. 18–20). The trustworthiness and care of God for his creation frame all, including human existence, and human beings' capacity to trust God is made possible by God's care and oversight.

Psalm 18 links the witness of the Lord, which is trustworthy (*pistos*, v. 8) and makes infants wise, with God's creation of the world and the world's celebration of God's glory. 'The heavens tell the glory of God, and the firmament proclaims the work of his hands . . .' (v. 1). Created beings are in a relationship of trust and care with God as creator, and grow in wisdom within that trust. Ben Sira begins by affirming both that wisdom is created before all things, and that she is created together with the faithful in the womb.[214] Human beings' trust in God exists from their conception, and their growth in wisdom is as dependent on that basic relationship of trust as on the gift of wisdom itself. In chapter 15 the author returns to the connection between trust and creation. God made humankind from the beginning and 'left [humanity] in the hand of his deliberation' (v. 14),[215] so that human beings can keep God's commandments if they want to, and it is their pleasure to trust (or perhaps 'to keep faith').[216] Their aboriginal relationship with God as God's creation, together with God's care for them, means that human beings can trust both God and each other and find trust a pleasure, and therefore

---

[213] Above, pp. 19–22.
[214] προτέρα πάντων ἔκτισται σοφία καὶ σύνεσις φρονήσεως ἐξ αἰῶνος (1.4); Ἀρχὴ σοφίας φοβεῖσθαι τὸν κύριον, καὶ μετὰ πιστῶν ἐν μήτρᾳ συνεκτίσθη αὐτοῖς (1.14).
[215] That is, gave him freedom of choice.
[216] ἐὰν θέλῃς, συντηρήσεις ἐντολὰς καὶ πίστιν ποιῆσαι εὐδοκίας (v. 15).

choose life and piety over sin and death (vv. 17, 20).[217] In passages like these, the trustworthiness of God as creator and carer evokes trust in human beings from their beginning, and this trust makes possible every other aspect of their relationship, from fear of the Lord, to wisdom and pleasure in the relationship itself.

The story of Adam and Eve is referenced rarely by New Testament writers, and then for purposes which are not explicitly linked with trust,[218] but the creation of the world is invoked regularly, often in a prominent position at or near the beginnings of books. In light of the scriptural connections between creation and trust, we should not be surprised to find New Testament writings invoking the trustworthiness of God as creator when they testify to the importance of putting one's trust in God. Occasionally they do, but more often they refer to creation to proclaim that Christ, as the one who pre-existed with God and participated in creation, is trustworthy as God is trustworthy, and exists in the same relationship of trust and care with the faithful as does Godself. They also refer to creation to claim that the faithful have been chosen and pre-elected by God, or to affirm that not only Jews, but gentiles can and should put their trust in God.[219] The complex of debates about the pre-existence of Christ is beyond our purview here, but it is worth considering briefly the passages in which Christ's pre-existence with God is linked with the themes of creation and trust.[220] This section therefore begins to explore the nature of trust between human beings and Christ.

The writers of John's gospel and 1 John may both be using existing hymns when they begin their texts by proclaiming that Christ was (with) God before creation, or was the firstborn of creation, through whom everything else was made:[221]

In the beginning was the Word, and the Word was with God, and the word was God. He was in the beginning with God. All things came to be through him, and apart from him nothing that did come to be came to be... (Jn 1.1–3)

What was from the beginning, what we have heard, what we have seen with our eyes, what we looked on and touched with our hands concerns the Word of

---

[217] In vv. 18–19 the writer affirms, like the psalmist, that God sees everything and he 'will know every human deed' (v. 19). As for Brothers, being seen and known here is part of what makes trust possible.

[218] 1 Cor. 15.22, 45; Rom 5.14; 5; Lk. 3.38.

[219] NB some of the passages discussed below are among those which virtually all commentators agree refer to Christ's pre-existence, while others may link trust in Christ with humanity's restoration to the right relationship of creation with God without assuming Christ's pre-existence. The theme of Christ's pre-existence also draws on wisdom literature, where trusting in God is also a theme (e.g. Prov. 3.3, 5, 16.20, 29.25, Wis. 1.2, 3.1, 10.7 cf. 10.5, 12.2, 16.24–5, Sir. 2.6, 8, 10, 13, 32.24; see Blowers (2012), 39–66) so linking Christ with God the creator via the idea that Christ is God's wisdom fortifies the idea that one should trust Christ as in the creator God; on this idea in post-testamental Christian writings see Blowers (2012), 245–312. Discussing the origins of the idea of Christ as creator see McDonough (2009).

[220] Cf. pp. 136–7.

[221] Though for our purposes the presence of these passages is more significant than their origin.

life—and the life was made visible, and we have seen and witness to it and proclaim to you the eternal life that was/is with the Father and was made visible to us... (1 Jn 1.1-2)

John's gospel uses *pisteuein* ninety-eight times, nearly always to refer to trusting or believing (relationally) in Jesus, and one of its key themes is that human beings can and must trust in Jesus as they do in Godself.[222] Throughout the gospel, Jesus reveals himself as God's son by his presence, words, and actions, and, in principle, only the foolish or wicked fail to recognize him. To those who do recognize him, 'he gave power to become children of God, to those who trust in his name (τοῖς πιστεύουσιν εἰς τὸ ὄνομα αὐτοῦ)' (1.12). By identifying Jesus with the pre-existent Word of God, John affirms that Jesus is trustworthy as the creator God is trustworthy.

Those who put their trust in Jesus in John's gospel do so, first and foremost, because they recognize him for who he is.[223] The relationship also brings goods: above all, eternal life (3.16, 4.14, 4.53, 5.21, 6.35, 6.68, 7.38, 10.28, 11.25, cf. 12.25, 14.6, 17.2-3) in the presence of God (14.6), but it would be misleading to characterize this trust as dominantly three-place.[224] Jesus' followers recognize him as the one with whom, with God, they are already in a relationship of trust from their creation: a relationship which is good in its own right. Some of the 'I am' sayings which punctuate the gospel hint that this relationship is also one of care. Jesus is the light of the world without which creation cannot come into being (8.12, cf. 1.9[225]), and the bread of life which feeds all those who come to him (6.35[226]). He is the shepherd who looks after the faithful even at risk of his own life; the protective door of the sheepfold (10.9, 11), and the vine on which its branches depend for life and sustenance (15.4-5). 1 John 1.1-4 treats some of the same themes in closely related language.[227] The Word of life has been made visible, so that human beings can see it and testify to it (1.2). Those who see and recognize it (cf. 1.1) are brought into fellowship or unity (*koinōnia*) with the Father and his son, Jesus Christ (1.3), and are cleansed once for all from all sin (1.7, 9).

Colossians 1.15-20 may draw on another existing hymn to the pre-existent Christ: 'He is the image of the invisible God, the firstborn of all creation, for in him were created all things in the heavens and on the earth, the visible and the

---

[222] Morgan (2015a), 397-403.   [223] E.g. pp. 204-5, 215.
[224] Not least because a theme of pre-election runs through the gospel, suggesting that those who recognize and trust in Jesus were chosen to do so (Morgan (2015a), 418-25).
[225] 8.12 also refers to lighting of lamps each night during the feast of tabernacles, which is the setting of this story.
[226] Beasley-Murray (1999) *ad loc.* points out the Law could be spoken of as 'bread'; Philo *Mek. Exod.* 13.17 speaks of manna's being assimilated into the bodies of the Israelites eating manna.
[227] Smalley (2007) *ad* 1.1 notes that if the letter's opening verses are intended to echo the prologue of John, then the 'Logos of life' may be meant to be personal, and to describe Jesus. Many commentators, however, think that the Logos is the word of life in the sense of the gospel; Smalley suggests the ambiguity is deliberate.

invisible, whether thrones or dominions or principalities or powers; all things were created through him and for him ...' (1.15-16). Here again, to have a relationship of trust and faithfulness with Christ (1.2, 1.4, 1.23, cf. 1.7) means to have a relationship which is tantamount to the relationship of human beings with the creator God.[228] It is, moreover, as the hymn says and the letter-writer echoes, to be reconciled and at peace with God and Christ (1.20, 21), to be part of the unity of all things (1.17), and to 'share in the inheritance of the holy ones in light' (1.12). This restored relationship is an end in itself, not an instrument of a further end: a few verses later, the author will characterize it as what he hopes and works for, for every person who has become 'perfect in Christ ($\tau \acute{\epsilon} \lambda \epsilon \iota o \nu$ $\acute{\epsilon} \nu$ $X \rho \iota \sigma \tau \hat{\omega}$)' (1.28, cf. 22).

The Letter to the Hebrews applies the creation passage of Psalm 101.26-8 LXX to Christ:

> At the beginning, Lord, you established the earth, and the heavens are the works of your hands. They will perish, but you remain; and they will all grow old like a garment; you will roll them up like a cloak, and like a garment they will be changed. But you are the same, and your years will have no end.   (1.10-12)[229]

The writer has already affirmed that Christ is God's son, 'the imprint of his being' (1.3), and that the universe was created through him (1.2).[230] Now God's 'sure word' (2.2) has been revealed through Christ (2.3-4), for the salvation (2.3) of those who put their trust in Christ (2.13). Christ the creator will outlast creation itself, but he never abandons those whom he has created, and through Christ it has become possible for God's children to be freed from slavery (2.15), restored to their right relationship with God, and brought to glory (2.10, 14). The right relationship of the faithful with God and Christ is the trust relationship of creation with the creator who cares for it and works for its good.

The opening of Ephesians blesses God,

> who in Christ has blessed us with every spiritual blessing in the heavens, as he chose us in him, before the foundation of the world, to be holy and unblemished before him in love; he destined us for adoption to himself through Jesus Christ, according to the favour of his will, for the praise of the glory of his grace that he granted us in the beloved...   (1.3-6)

---

[228] This holds whether we think *eikōn* here characterizes Christ e.g. as the manifestation or embodiment of God (Kittel (1964), 396), as creator and reconciler of the universe (Barth and Blanke (1994), 194-5), or as standing with God and acting on and with the world (so Lohse (1971), 48, who also argues that the use of *eikon* need not refer to Genesis, since the term is widely used in Jewish and non-Jewish literature).

[229] Hebrews text varies slightly from the LXX.

[230] Attridge (1989) *ad* 1.8 notes that the author takes Psalm 45 (44), 7-8 to be an address to the Son of God.

Ephesians makes more prominent the theme of pre-election which Paul touches on only occasionally.[231] Through Christ, God has chosen those who put their trust in Christ (cf. 1.1, 1.13) to be redeemed by his blood, forgiven their transgressions (1.7), and adopted into the family of God and Christ (1.5, cf. 1.14). The writer also calls this state an existence for the praise of [God's] glory (1.12). This existence, like eternal life with God and Christ in John's gospel, and the state of fellowship and unity in Colossians, is an end in itself. To put one's trust in Christ is to be restored to a relationship with God which God planned before the foundation of the world, but in which human beings have not lived—possibly not since the expulsion from the garden of Eden, or possibly never.[232]

Creation and eschatology are closely linked in all these passages. The end of what God has done through Christ is the restoration of humanity, by trust, to the relationship which it was created to enjoy with God. At Titus 1.2, the life and salvation through Christ (cf. 1.1, 1.4), which are given to those who are chosen, were promised by God 'who does not lie' before time began (1.2). The writer of 1 Peter also looks back to look forward. He urges the faithful to endure their sufferings because 'the end of all things is at hand' (4.7). Those who share the suffering of Christ, in accordance with God's will (4.13, 19), will hand over their souls to a 'trustworthy creator ($\pi\iota\sigma\tau\hat{\omega}$ $\kappa\tau\iota\sigma\tau\eta$)' (4.19) and 'receive the unfading crown of glory' (5.4).[233]

In two memorable passages, Paul (at Rom. 1.18-23) and Luke's Paul (at Acts 17.22-31[234]) invoke creation theologies to say that God makes Godself known to everyone, Jewish and gentile, and therefore that everyone can and should give glory and thanks to God (Rom. 1.21), and repent and put their trust in God and Christ before Christ returns to judge the world (Acts 17.30-1). In Romans, this is part of Paul's argument that everyone, Jewish or gentile, has sinned in some way and stands in need of grace. Paul's speech in Acts initially takes a softer line, telling the Athenians that the God for whom they have been groping (v. 27) is the creator God of Israel, who has overlooked their ignorance in the past (v. 30) but now requires repentance before the day of judgment (vv. 30-1). Both link the idea

---

[231] Newman (1996), cf. Muddiman (2001), 67-8, 76-7, who also notes (37-8) that their shared view of predestination is one of a series of non-coincidental similarities between Ephesians and the Johannine corpus (cf. Jn 15.19, Eph. 1.4-15).

[232] Barth (1974), 103-4 argues there is no reference to the Fall here. We have not discussed Phil. 2.6-11 in this section because, even if it concerns the pre-existent Christ (which continues to be debated), it does not refer explicitly to creation and is only indirectly linked with *pistis* language (which appears at 1.27, 2.17).

[233] Rev. 21.1-4 sees the end time as a new creation, though without trust language. Trust is not an explicit element of such visions of existence after the *parousia* as the New Testament offers, but we can infer that it continues to be part of the restored or fulfilled relationship between God and humanity: see Morgan (2015a), 473-5.

[234] Barrett (2002) *ad* Acts 17.24 notes that the idea of God as creator is common to Jews and Greeks (which is broadly true, though the landscape of Greek myth is complex), but also shows how many echoes of scripture are threaded through this speech, which is more Jewish than is sometimes assumed.

that gentiles are under God's judgment with the idea that they have failed to see and understand God for who and what God is (Acts 17.23–4, Rom. 1.20–1).[235] Luke's Paul underlines God's parental relationship with creation and care for it with two (alleged) citations from Greek authors: 'in him we live and move and have our being' and 'we too are his offspring'.[236] Paul tells the Romans that gentiles who reject their relationship with God (1.28) become incapable of other functional relationships: they become insolent, haughty, boastful, wicked, rebellious towards their (human) parents (1.30, cf. 31), and destructive of themselves and each other (1.26–7). For both writers, for human beings to be restored to their right relationships with God and one another means being restored to the right relationship of creation to its creator, and for both this means restoring a relationship of trust (cf. Acts 17.34, Rom. 3.26).

All these passages, apart from Acts 17, appear at, or close to the beginnings of books (we might add to them the vision of a new heaven and earth (21.1–5) which forms the climax of the Book of Revelation). From this position they frame their writers' arguments about what God has done for humanity though Christ, and how humanity is called to respond. They form one of several means by which these writers envision the restored relationship between God, Christ, and humanity, but, prominently located as they are, and often articulated in vivid, hymnic language, they are particularly powerful and memorable. Drawing on a scriptural vision of creation which puts a relationship of care, and the trust intrinsic to it, at the heart of the divine–human relationship, they proclaim that human beings can and should trust God and Christ because to be human is to be part of creation; to be part of creation is properly to be in a relationship of trust and care with God and Christ; and restoring that relationship also restores every other relationship between human beings and that of human beings with themselves.

In recent years, scholars of the Hebrew Bible have taken an increasing interest in the relationship between the biblical themes of creation and covenant.[237] Scholars of Paul, in particular, have drawn on their work to argue persuasively that an inherited creation theology underlies Paul's understanding of human redemption and also (especially in Romans 8) of the current suffering of the natural world.[238] Katherine Dell, for example, has argued that a theology of creation, expressed in the Noachic covenant, validates and underpins all God's later covenants with Israel, and, more broadly, the ordering of the human world, and that this

---

[235] e.g. Cranfield (1975), Fitzmyer (1993a), Jewett (2007), *ad loc.*
[236] The first is often thought to be Stoic but has no direct parallel; the second quotes Arat. 5.
[237] Notably e.g. Dumbrell (1984), Schmid (1984), Murray (1992), Rendtorff (1993), Miller (1995), Brueggemann (1996), Hayes (2002), Dell (2003), Fretheim (2005), Mason (2007), Hahne (2006), Bellinger (2015), cf. Barton (1979), Anderson (1994). Blowers (2012), 245–312 explores how patristic writers extend the idea that a theology of creation underpins God's relationship with humanity to the pre-existent Christ.
[238] E.g. Christofferson (1990), Murray (1992), Keesmaat (1999), Braaten (2006), Moo (2008).

vision powerfully influences the prophets, especially Isaiah and Jeremiah.[239] Steve Mason has argued that the 'eternal covenant' of Isaiah 24.5 looks back to the Noachic covenant, and that, in Isaiah's vision, its breaking brings catastrophic consequences not only to human beings but to the earth as a whole,[240] while W. H. Bellinger shows that some psalms use creation imagery to appeal to God's faithfulness to Israel in the context of God's wider faithfulness to creation.[241] Laurie J. Braaten proposes that both Genesis 9 and Isaiah 24 are in the background of Paul's thinking about the groaning of creation at Romans 8.22, and Douglas Moo develops this idea, arguing that, for Paul, borrowing from Isaiah 24-7, creation as a whole is enslaved to the consequences of human sin and divine judgment. Moo's conclusion points modern readers to the recognition that the connections Paul makes between human corruption and the suffering of the earth are even more compelling and challenging in the present day than in Paul's own.[242] In light of these insights, we can take our conclusions about the passages discussed in this section a little further. Those passages link the pre-existent Christ with God in an aboriginal relationship of trust with creation, care for creation, and trust in humanity to share in creation's care. They look forward hopefully to the restoration of that relationship through the Christ event and at the end time. For Paul, and possibly other writers too, the restoration of trust between God, Christ, and humanity is also humanity's best hope for the restoration of suffering creation, and creation's best hope for its own restoration.

Conclusion

The writings we have discussed have very little to say about trust in God or the trustworthiness or faithfulness of God separately from the proclamation about Jesus Christ. The call to Jews to a renewed trust relationship with God, and to gentiles to put their trust solely in the God of Israel, is based almost entirely on these writings' understanding of what God has done through Christ. This raises the question whether the strong modern Christian focus on trust in God as distinguishable from trust in Christ—notably in popular paraenetic literature—is as appropriate as is often assumed. At the same time (and potentially in some tension with the first point), Paul and other New Testament writers share with all ancient theists the assumption that a new divine figure must be understood with reference to at least one existing divinity. This raises the question whether the same is necessarily true for modern readers, in principle or in practice. Do we, or should we, seek to understand the trust and trustworthiness of God through

---

[239] Dell (2003), drawing on Nicholson (1986), especially 194. [240] Mason (2007).
[241] Bellinger (2015). [242] Braaten (2006), 147, Moo (2008).

Christ, or that of Christ through God? The dual witness of Paul and other New Testament writers to Jews and gentiles suggests that both routes may be accessible, and potentially appropriate to different individuals or groups.

Affirmations of God's trustworthiness and faithfulness, and encouragements to trust in God, appear in these writings mainly in two contexts: when they are speaking of the new relationship of trust which God offers to humanity through the death of Christ, and when they are speaking of God, or Christ, as creator. We have seen that Paul, especially, but also some other writers, offer a vision of the *pistis* of God which is active and innovative, reaching out through Christ to offer humanity a new relationship of trust, a new definition of God's people, and a new hope. God's action in the Christ event, though testified to by the law and the prophets, is radically unexpected, but new and unexpected actions are the prerogative and *modus operandi* of the God of Israel.

Through the 'redemption in Christ Jesus' (Rom. 3.24), all God's past promises are fulfilled, and the divine–human relationship reconfigured in a form which 'surpasses' (cf. 2 Cor. 3.10) the covenant and the law. Though this idea is controversial among contemporary commentators, there are several reasons why it may have made sense to Paul and others. Most early Christians do not envisage Christ as saviour or ruler of the state of Israel (as distinct from God's people Israel). Paul, and others, want Christ-confession to be as accessible to gentiles as to Jews, and to minimize differences between community members. They may not have seen the imminent *parousia* as needing covenants or laws at all, but, not unlike some contemporary visions of golden ages or communities of the wise, as existing under the direct rule of God and Christ without the institutions or problem-solving processes which ordinary societies need. (There are hints that Paul, in particular, sought to configure his communities as a foretaste of this eschatological vision, offering them little in the way of institutions or processes of problem-solving, but urging them regularly to live with love, peace, holiness, grace, freedom, and righteousness.[243]) Most significantly, New Testament writers attest to a widely shared view of Christ-confessors as in a life-changing, life-encompassing, open-ended personal relationship with Jesus Christ, and a commitment to living in a relationship with Christ which is characterized above all by the inter-personal attitude and action of trust.

That said, we noted that even if Paul thinks the covenant has been surpassed, other writers do not (or refer to the 'new covenant' in the death of Christ), and the trust relationship is central to all of them. As in the scriptures and elsewhere in Jewish tradition, being in a covenant and a divine–human relationship of *pistis* are by no means mutually exclusive, nor necessarily in competition. But the ubiquity of *pistis*, and its equivalents in other languages, in New Testament writings,

---

[243] Morgan (2020), 203–15.

some other very early writings, and patristic literature, suggests that, even where *pistis* coexists with covenantal language, trust, faithfulness, entrustedness, and, as the concept gradually evolves, faith, are more central to early Christian thinking.[244]

Within Christ-confessing communities, God and Christ continue trustworthy and the faithful, ideally, continue faithful and grow in faithfulness. *Pistis* is not only soteriological but ethical: central and essential to the ongoing divine–human relationship until the end time. This does not mean, however, that the faithful, any more than Israel in the past, can rely on God to act for them as they might want or hope. Trusting in God has always involved accepting that God enacts God's will, not necessarily that of human beings.

We argued that we can think of God as investing 'therapeutic trust' in humanity: the kind that one person puts in another knowing, or suspecting, that they may not be trustworthy at this point, but convinced (or hopeful) that the act of trust itself will encourage them to become more trustworthy through time. In this, God takes a risk on humanity which is potentially in tension with the tradition idea of God's omniscience, but which makes good sense if we envisage God as all-knowing in a personal, rather than a propositional sense. God deeply knows God's creation, so God can trust human beings, convinced that they have it in them, eventually, to justify God's trust.

Human beings, meanwhile, take their own risks: Jews by accepting that God is fulfilling God's promises to Israel in a highly unexpected way, and by renewing their trust in God in new terms by trusting in Jesus Christ; gentiles by not only trusting in God and Christ but relinquishing all their other gods.[245] In addition, human beings take the risk (one rarely recognized in modern accounts of trust) that they may let God down by not being faithful or trustworthy enough. Paul and others, however, offer encouragement to those who take the risk. God does not ask of humanity more than it is capable of; God and Christ strengthen those who trust wholeheartedly; and when people have trusted God in the past, their trust has always turned out well.[246]

---

[244] Among New Testament writings (where, strikingly, the covenant is not only referenced rarely in the Pauline corpus, but never in John, the Johannine letters, James, or the Petrine letters, only once each in Mark, Matthew, and Revelation, and four times in Luke–Acts), the only outlier is Hebrews, where it appears, at the most generous estimate, in nine passages, while *pistis* language appears, at the most economical estimate (counting, for instance, 10.38–11.39 as one), in ten. Nor is covenantal language common e.g. in early non-testamental writings in which *pistis* is relatively uncommon or does not appear: it does not feature, for instance, in the gospel of Thomas, Didache, Protoevangelium of James, Epistle to Diognetus, or 2 Clement; while in other early works in which *pistis* is common it is rare or does not appear.

[245] In addition, the idea that God has always been faithful to Israel may not have seemed, to many gentiles, a strong reason to put their trust solely in God at a time when Israel's God was not, from their perspective, obviously more powerful than e.g. the gods of Rome.

[246] Which is not to say it has been vindicated as they might themselves have understood vindication: Abel, for instance, died, and others were tortured and killed (Heb. 11.4, 35–7).

The divine–human relationship of trust rests, on the human side, on a number of assumptions, traditions, experiences, interpretations of experience and tradition, beliefs (basic and non-basic), and instances of propositional trust, together with a sense of the coherence of all these things. It is both 'three-place' and 'two-place': the faithful trust God for their eventual salvation, but also as part of the right-standing with God which trust itself makes possible. Two-place trust is a powerful bond, allowing both partners to look to a future which, for human beings, at least, is unpredictable, but towards which they can move with confidence.

The affirmation that the God who creates the world is trustworthy and caring, and that the relationship of trust with God and Christ restores humanity to the relationship it had with God before the expulsion from the garden, or leads to the fulfilment of its relationship in salvation, adoption, eternal life, and glory—or both—assures the faithful that God sees and knows humanity for who and what it was created to be and can be again. In the terms in which Doris Brothers talks of formative trust, God assures human beings that, even in their state of sin and alienation, they can and do show God who they are and can be, and God sees and recognizes them; at the same time, even in their state of sin and alienation, they are capable of seeing and recognizing God acting through and in Christ. This most basic ability to show and be shown, see and be seen, with which humanity is created, makes possible a life full of other relationships, actions, and possibilities rooted in the reality of the divine to human beings and human beings to the divine. The restoration of trust between God, Christ, and humanity, moreover, has implications beyond humanity itself. By locating Christ with God as creator, and linking *pistis* with the creative activity of both God and Christ, New Testament writings suggest that trust is characteristic of the right relationship between God, Christ, and creation as a whole. When trust fails in any part of it, creation is at risk. When it is fully restored, creation will be whole. The restoration of trust is therefore not only humanity's best hope for itself, but creation's best hope for restoration from its present state of suffering and ruin.[247]

The writings we have discussed look forward more than back. Though the God who acts through Christ is the God of Israel, and God has fulfilled God's promises to Israel, the trustworthiness of God is not rooted primarily in the conviction of God's covenant faithfulness. It is based above all on the very recent experience, together with interpretation of that experience, of God's action through Christ, and hope for what that action implies for humanity. The relationship offered by God through Christ reforms God's people and looks forward to the glorious culmination of humanity's 'race' (cf. 1 Cor. 9.4–5, Phil. 3.14). This trust is both

---

[247] This is not the place to explore whether or how far non-human creation has also broken trust with God, but it envisages creation at least in part as an innocent victim of human sin; on how the Christ event may offer a route out of innocent suffering for human, and possibly also other beings, see pp. 167–88.

three-place, working to an end, and two-place, good in its own right. Two-place trust relationships, in particular, have powerful possibilities. They enable both partners to contemplate a future together which human beings, at least, cannot predict; which may change them in ways which they cannot imagine; but towards which they can move with confidence because they know they are seen, known, and trusted in a way which is not context-dependent. We do not have to think for long about what life is like when we cannot trust the people around us to begin to sense how transformative an assurance this is. When we cannot trust, we have to be constantly alert and on guard, doubtful and sceptical. We limit ourselves, at best, to trusting people for specific purposes on particular occasions. We live with the constant fear of being cheated, disappointed, damaged, or destroyed. Our engagement with individuals and communities becomes narrow, shallow, fragile, and self-regarding.

One well recognized challenge to belief in God in the modern world is the classical doctrine of God's perfection, which includes God's reliability.[248] New Testament writings, however, do not offer the prospect that God reliably supports human beings as they might (think they) want. Rather, they offer the vision that the power that creates and sustains everything that is, can be interacted with, in trust, as a personal being who cares for and trusts human beings, and trusts them with work to do in collaboration with itself. In its trustworthiness, this power does not overlook nor abandon any created being. In its creativity, however, it can act afresh at any time, and change what is possible for created beings. The God so envisaged offers humanity not the reliability of a tool or an expert in their field, nor a relationship which they can negotiate through cult or law-keeping, nor one in which they are at the mercy of divine caprice, but a partnership with infinite possibilities, to which both parties contribute. The risk in this relationship, as we have seen it so far, is in the possibility that human beings will fail on their side of it, but Paul, in particular, is convinced that the more whole-heartedly they embrace the relationship the stronger it becomes.

We noted that, in the world of the first century, almost everyone took for granted that God or gods existed; the question, especially for gentiles, was whether the gods were trustworthy. Does the argument of this chapter have anything to say to the many people in the modern world for whom the primary question is whether God exists at all? For one thing, it suggests that, rather than beginning an exploration of faith with the question of God's existence, one might begin (as many first-century gentiles probably began) with the life, work, and death of Jesus Christ, together with the experience of his followers that his death was not the end of his life. Those who confess and follow Christ find in him more than an inspiring example of human goodness. His life and death are experienced as

---

[248] Above, p. 64.

making possible a transformation in others—new life and right-standing with the power which creates and sustains everything that is—which New Testament writers reach for metaphysical language to describe. Engaging with the experience of Jesus' followers therefore offers the possibility of thinking about God from the 'bottom up' rather than the 'top down'.

This chapter also recognized in the creation stories an intuition that human beings are connected, from their beginnings, with the God who creates and sustains all life, in a relationship which can be understood as good in human terms. Whether this intuition is a literal or imagistic response to the nature of ultimate reality, a by-product of consciousness, or an evolutionary adaptation of the human brain,[249] is irresolvable from a human perspective, but for those who are attracted by the possibility that there is a good way to be human as part of creation, the existence of a creative being which interacts with human beings in a relationship which they can understand as good in human terms is, at a minimum, an economical hypothesis.[250]

Last but not least, we can say a little more about the relationship between God, Israel, and humanity as a whole, of which we have argued that Paul, notably (and all New Testament writers, to a greater or lesser degree) take a new and controversial view. We argued that, for Paul, in the Christ event, all God's promises have been fulfilled, and God's earlier covenants have been surpassed. Paul, caught up in the power of his experience of Christ and his calling to preach, undoubtedly thinks that, in the Christ event, God has acted definitively for the righteousing of humanity. We, though, may note that, in taking for granted that right-standing with God now comes only through Christ and will only ever come through Christ, Paul's proclamation is inconsistent with his own view of God's relationship with humanity, and claims more than the gospel he has inherited gives him a basis to claim. If, despite the widely shared conviction in Israel that the covenant would stand forever, God, as Paul preaches, has exercised God's prerogative and done a new thing through Christ, then God can presumably exercise God's prerogative and do a new thing again.

Many Christians in the twenty-first century find themselves in the position of most first-century Jews: some groups (who might include, for instance, fellow children of Abraham Muslims, Mormons, or members of the Unification Church) proclaim that God has acted anew since the Christ event, and their own revelation surpasses that given to the first followers of Jesus. Christians who do not identify with any of these groups might respond by believing that their existing covenant and/or relationship with God holds, and newer proclamations are mistaken—though, as we have noted, it is far from clear that the logic of the kerygma itself offers a good basis for assuming it cannot be surpassed. They might accept that,

---

[249] On the last two see e.g. Tremlin (2006), Boyer (1994).
[250] Cf. e.g. Schaefer (2005), Swinburne (2008), Dalton and Simmons (2010).

whatever form of divine–human relationship is salvific, everyone will eventually come to it (though this is a view modern religious groups, like Paul in Romans 11, tend to hold for others rather than themselves). They might take the view that there is more than one way to salvation (I doubt that Paul, or other early Christians, believed that there were two or three ways to salvation, but I sympathize with contemporary scholars who seek in New Testament writings a basis on which Christians now may affirm that view). The following chapters of this study will suggest a further possibility: that trust in God is salvific, even though all human understandings of God and what God has done are always partial and imperfect, and human responses are equally imperfect. Indeed, trust is salvific precisely because knowledge, reason, and understanding, together with human trust and trustworthiness, are always imperfect: it is where apprehension and response are inadequate that God's trust in humanity, and humanity's in God, are most necessary, most appropriate, and hold out the greatest hope.

Whether or not divine grace, human behaviour, or the condition of creation has already led to a new divine response, however, Christ-confessors would be complacent to assume that they will never do so. God's trustworthiness, as Paul and others envisage it, is not a comfortable, or even entirely reassuring concept, but is always potentially as awful, challenging, and disruptive as it must have seemed to some who heard it preached in the first century. By the same token, the call to trust in God is as urgent, demanding, and potentially life-changing now as it was in the first generation after the crucifixion.

3

'So we preach and so you believed'

Pistis between God, the Risen and Exalted Christ, and the Faithful

In this chapter we turn from *pistis* between God and humanity, which draws on traditions familiar to both Jews and gentiles, to a new idea: that human beings can trust, and live in trust with Christ, very much as they live in trust with Godself.[1]

Why, of all the concepts used to describe divine–human relationships in Jewish and gentile religiosity, *pistis* so quickly became so important to Christians, remains one of the mysteries of Christianity's first ten or fifteen years. It is possible that the historical Jesus called people to put their trust in God: N. T. Wright has observed that every strand of synoptic tradition shows Jesus using *pistis* language, and that language and themes of which this is true have a good claim to authenticity.[2] It is certain that Jesus' followers began to call themselves *hoi pisteuontes* or *hoi pistoi*, 'the trusting' or 'the faithful', with reference to both God and Jesus Christ, from a very early date. Paul uses both phrases in 1 Thessalonians and 1 Corinthians as if they are already familiar, and these and related terms are used in every New Testament writing except 2 John, as well as in early non-canonical writings.[3] The fact that *hoi pistoi* and *hoi pisteuontes* are used interchangeably in our earliest evidence suggests that both may be translations of an Aramaic original. It also indicates strongly that the best translation for both is 'the trusting' or 'the faithful' rather than 'the believers', because although *hoi pisteuontes* could bear the meaning 'the believers', it is extremely unlikely that *hoi pistoi* would do so.[4]

Even if the historical Jesus called people to trust in God, the call by Jesus' followers to trust in Christ and be faithful to him, as one trusts and is faithful to God, almost certainly originated after the resurrection experiences.[5] If so, it was

---

[1] The chapter heading quotation is from 1 Cor. 15.11. [2] Wright (1996), 259–63.
[3] Morgan (2015a), 238–41.
[4] Morgan (2015a), 240, and below, pp. 106–7. In addition, as noted (pp. 5–6), to believe in the existence of a heavenly being and believe certain things about him, her, or it is not the same, for Jews or gentiles, as making a commitment to that being, and it is clear that the call to confess Christ involves the latter; since this commitment is described everywhere with *pistis* language it must refer to relational trust etc. as well as belief.
[5] The difficult question whether commitment includes worship (above, pp. 5–6 n.26) is not our main concern here, but it is worth noting that investigations of Jewish and gentile parallels for Jesus' titles (e.g. Horbury (1998); Fletcher-Louis (1997, 1999)) have tended to multiply rather than limit the

probably used first of the risen or exalted Christ, perhaps of Christ's coming in the future.[6] Trust between the risen or exalted Christ and the faithful is therefore a good place to begin our exploration of the trust between God, Christ, and humanity.

This and the next three chapters have aspects of a Christology: what we might call a *pistis* Christology. Although they will argue that *pistis* stands at the heart of the relationship between Christ and the faithful, as it is depicted by New Testament writers, however, they do not offer a Christology of any one writer, much less a 'New Testament Christology'. Nor do they try to tell a unified diachronic story of the trust between God, Christ, and human beings in Christ's pre-existence, earthly life, death, resurrection, and exalted life. Rather they seek to show a range of ways in which New Testament writings conceive of Christ in different instantiations of his existence, exploring the significance of trust in each.

That said, it comes as no surprise to find the call to trust in the risen or exalted Christ linked with the memory of Jesus of Nazareth's earthly life, ministry, death, or even with claims of Christ's pre-existence. In the thought-world of the first century, human beings, Jewish or gentile, are not taken up to heaven, nor do divine beings descend to earth and return, at random: there is always some connection between the earthly and heavenly life of an exalted figure. What follows will argue that, in the case of Jesus Christ, the connection is unusually close and rich (and becomes richer over time). Chapters 5 and 6 will propose that the gospels offer an image of Jesus and his *pistis* relationships which functions not only as an account of his earthly life and a proclamation of his identity and work, but as a guide for those who put their trust in the exalted Christ. At this point, we can observe simply that the language of trust is one of the means by which New Testament writings represent and reflect on the continuity of Christ's identity and relationships throughout his existence.

The relationship between the exalted Christ and human beings is nearly always referenced in these writings in the context of the relationship between Christ and those who are already community members.[7] Since community members are known as 'the trusting' or 'the faithful', every aspect of the relationship could be said to have an aspect of *pistis*, but what follows focuses on the most significant and widely attested ways in which *pistis* operates between the exalted Christ, God, and the faithful. Among these are the idea that Christ is faithful towards both

---

interpretative possibilities, suggesting that the definition of worship, or of a worshippable being, may not have been much clearer in the first century than it is now. Greek *latreia, therapeia, timē, proskynēsis* etc., moreover, are applicable to exceptional human beings, divine men, spirits, gods, and heroes, so gentile members of Paul's communities could have understood themselves as worshipping both God and Christ, but not necessarily as the same kinds of being, while gentile acclamations are also highly flexible, being offered to human beings, divinized human beings, or gods (e.g. Klauser (1950), Rouché (1984)).

[6] E.g. Bultmann (2007), 31–53, cf. Lührmann (1990), 248–9, Wannamaker (1990), 9–10.

[7] Though see below, p. 111 on Acts.

God and human beings; that he acts as mediator between them; that he is a model of trust and faithfulness for his followers; and that he oversees the daily life and work of the faithful in the present time.[8]

The Role of Resurrection Belief in Trust

We begin, however, not with trust, but with belief. In the last chapter we argued that (specifically for Paul, but almost certainly for all New Testament writers) trust in God is based on, or coheres with, various other attitudes, one of which is belief, basic or non-basic.[9] From the earliest Christian preaching, the call to trust in the exalted Christ and his future coming must have rested, in significant part, on the resurrection experiences of Jesus' first followers. When the resurrection is invoked in New Testament writings, it is, as we also saw in the last chapter, sometimes as something that can or must be believed (sometimes, though not always, using *pistis* language), and belief in it is sometimes invoked as a basis for trust, together with every other aspect of the relationship of the faithful with God, Christ, and one another. For many modern Christians, moreover, belief in the resurrection, in some form, is the indispensable basis of faith. It is therefore worth giving a little more consideration to the question, what is the relationship, in New Testament writings, between belief that Christ was raised from the dead and righteousing, life-giving, saving trust?

As a preliminary, it is worth noting that physical resurrections from the dead are reported occasionally in the world of the early principate outside as well as within Jewish and early Christian texts.[10] As in Jewish and Christian stories, they occasionally attest to the exceptional nature of the one resurrected, but more often to the fact that somebody loves the dead person and will not let them go, or to the exceptional power and authority of the wonder-worker who performs the resurrection.[11] The testimony that God raised Jesus from the dead, therefore, would not in itself have established all the claims Jesus' followers wanted to make about him.[12]

---

[8] On the gospels as offering further ways of thinking about how to relate to the exalted Christ, see p. 245.
[9] Cf. pp. 64–5.
[10] In the Hebrew Bible: 1 Kgs 17.17–24, 2 Kgs 4.32–7, 13.21; in addition, from the Roman period to the present day there is evidence of 'corpses' reviving in the grave (Barber (1988), Mikkelson (2006)). Allison (2021), 11–13 discusses the history of the argument that Jesus did not die at the crucifixion, but no canonical test canvasses that possibility.
[11] E.g. Hom., *Il.* 2.698–702, Pind., *Pyth.* 3.55–8, *Ol.*, 1.25–7, Eurip., *Alc.*, *Heracl.* 799–866, Plat., *Symp.* 179b, Theog. 702–12, Philostr., *VA* 7.4, 8.41, despite Acts 17.32; see Tappenden and Daniel-Hughes (2017), Johnston (2017).
[12] Though it does open the resurrection narratives to the interpretation, which would have made sense, for instance, to those who knew of the raising of Alcestis by Heracles, that Jesus' appearances to the disciples are a gift from God to those who loved him and were distraught at his death.

In mythical and historical narratives, it is also common for exceptional human beings to be taken up to heaven, sometimes after physical death and sometimes in lieu of it.[13] Roman emperors and some of their relatives, notably, in this period, were being offered cult as divinities after what was accepted as their physical death. The affirmation that Jesus had been taken up to heaven, therefore, did not need to be linked to a belief that he had been raised from the dead. In itself, moreover, exaltation would testify to Jesus Christ as an exceptional person, but not necessarily more than that. Greek and Roman mythical or historical heroes, kings, and emperors who were taken up to heaven were normally offered cult, but it is likely that not all dead heroes who were offered cult were understood as divine.[14] Within Jewish tradition, meanwhile, one could be taken up to heaven (like Enoch or Elijah) and even identified with another heavenly being (as Enoch becomes identified with the angel Metatron) without being worshipped.[15] Testimony to Jesus' resurrection and exaltation therefore affirms that Jesus was an exceptional person, but by no means establishes all his followers want to say about him: that he is unique, Son of God, to be confessed as Lord or even worshipped. Nor does it determine what kind of relationship it is appropriate for his followers to have with him for the future. When we consider what Jesus' followers write, and believe, about the resurrection, therefore, we need to bear in mind that neither resurrection nor ascension experiences are likely to have been reported in themselves to make a claim about Jesus' identity or the nature of his relationship with his followers, and we should be alert to alternative explanations of them in the texts.

Among New Testament writings, the most explicit affirmations that the resurrection occurred physically, was proven to have occurred, and can be believed on that basis, occur in Luke–Acts.[16] In the Acts of the Apostles, a series of speeches by Peter and Paul proclaims the believability of the resurrection:[17]

> This man, delivered up by the set plan and foreknowledge of God, you killed, using lawless men to crucify him. But God raised him up (ὃν ὁ θεὸς ἀνέστησεν), releasing him from the throes of death, because it was impossible for him to be held by it...God raised this Jesus; of this we are all witnesses... (2.23–4, 32)

---

[13] E.g. in myth Heracles, Achilles, and Asclepius ascend to heaven after death, Castor and Ganymede in lieu of death. Occasionally, as in the case of Enoch (Gen. 5.21–4), it is ambiguous whether an exalted figure died or was taken up alive (cf. Plu., *Rom.* 35 of Romulus).

[14] Though their divine status is debated in some cases: see Currie (2005), 89–200.

[15] Cf. pp. 5–6.

[16] His language of resurrection is properly that of resurrection (*anastasis, anhistēmi, egeiro*) rather than ascension or exaltation (cf. e.g. Gen. 25.8, 4 Rgns 2.11 LXX, Plu., *Rom.* 35).

[17] On these as drawing on memories of very early preaching see e.g. Stanton (1974), 67–85; cf. Fitzmyer (1997), 81–8. Friedrich (1982), 113 notes that belief leads to trust here and trust to confession.

> The God of our ancestors raised Jesus (ἤγειρεν Ἰησοῦν), whom you killed by hanging him on a tree...We are witnesses (μάρτυρες) of these things, as is the holy spirit that God has given to those who obey [or 'trust in'] him. (5.30, 32)
>
> You know the word that he sent to the Israelites as he proclaimed peace through Jesus Christ, who is Lord of all...We are witnesses (μάρτυρες) of all that [Jesus] did both in the country of the Jews and in Jerusalem. They put him to death hanging him on a tree. This man God raised on the third day (ὁ θεὸς ἤγειρεν τῇ τρίτῃ ἡμέρᾳ) and granted that he be visible, not to all the people, but to us, the witnesses chosen by God in advance, who ate and drank with him after he rose from the dead...To him all the prophets bear witness (μαρτυροῦσιν), that everyone who puts their trust in him (πάντα τὸν πιστεύοντα εἰς αὐτόν) will receive forgiveness of sins through his name (10.36, 38, 39–41, 43).
>
> The inhabitants of Jerusalem and their leaders failed to recognize [Jesus]...they asked Pilate to have him put to death...But God raised (ἤγειρεν) him from the dead, and for many days he appeared to those who had come up with him from Galilee to Jerusalem. These are his witnesses (μάρτυρες αὐτοῦ) before the people. (13.27, 28, 30–1)[18]

Luke makes much use of the language of witness: specifically, at 10.41, witnesses who ate and drank with the risen Christ. The witnesses are multiple, both first-person and third-party, and, given that the second speech above takes place at a trial (cf. 5.26–33), and in all four the speaker accuses the Jews of responsibility for Jesus' death, their claims have strong forensic overtones. Acts' description of how (some) people respond to this preaching is that they *pisteuein*.[19] The primary meaning of *pisteuein* in this context must be that people put their trust in (God and) the exalted Christ and become community members, but in a forensic or quasi-forensic context it is also strongly implied that listeners believe the witness reports.

Luke's connections with Hellenistic literary and intellectual culture are well recognized, and in his interest in belief he may be engaging with a debate in wider society. Many writers of the early principate, in various forms and genres, raise the question whether one can believe in the gods, or believe specific things about

---

[18] Translations NAB, modified at 5.30. At Acts 17.20–1 Paul says that 'God has overlooked the times of ignorance, but now he demands that all people everywhere repent, because he has established a day on which he will "judge the world with justice" through a man he has appointed, and he has provided confirmation [or "proof"] (*pistis*) for all by raising him from the dead' (17.30–1, transl. NAB): *pistis* here is often translated 'assurance'. Outside the NT this translation is used where *pistis* bears the meaning of a pledge of goodwill or good faith: the resurrection here could be a pledge of Good's good faith, following e.g. Paul's characterization of Christ as the 'first-fruits' of resurrection (1 Cor. 15.23), but following Lk. 24.25–7, 44–6 it seems more likely that the resurrection here is a proof of prophecy.
[19] E.g. 2.44, 13.39, 13.48, 17.34, cf. 5.39.

the gods, and if so, on what grounds.[20] A traditional view, according to Origen, is offered by the second-century philosopher and polytheist Celsus. People have worshipped the gods for centuries and found them trustworthy, and it beggars belief that so many people could be wrong about their experience.[21] Gods of the Greek and Roman worlds, moreover, appear to worshippers (especially in sanctuaries and often during incubation); they are experienced as helping and healing the faithful and punish wrongdoers (e.g. 3.24, 7.3, cf. 2.68, 4.6); and they offer advice, via oracles, which has proven reliable over centuries (8.45, cf. 3.35, 7.6).[22] All these, Celsus thinks, are sound reasons to believe in the reality and powers of the established gods.[23] At the other end of the spectrum, around the same time, Lucian constantly raises doubts (playfully, seriously, or something of both) about whether or how people can believe in the gods. In *The Lover of Lies*, for instance, the character Tychiades describes how he once attended a party at which the other guests told a series of increasingly tall stories about their supernatural journeys and encounters they or others had had with divine beings, all of which they claim to believe as fact.[24] Tychiades himself is prepared to believe that the gods exist, but he finds it impossible to believe much of what is attested about them. Between these extremes stands Plutarch who, as both a pious worshipper and a Platonist, seeks to distinguish rationally between what can and cannot be believed about the gods.[25] For example, he suggests, it is credible that gods want to associate with and advise the best and wisest human beings, who (following Plato) seek the beautiful and good, and therefore seek God,[26] but incredible that gods should want to make love to inferior human bodies, so it is plausible that the nymph Egeria advised the Roman king Numa, but implausible that she slept with him (*Num.* 4.3–4).

All these writers are interested in how worship of the gods is grounded in belief and belief in evidence. All accept, however, that evidence is diverse: it may be an object one can point to, or, for instance, the coherence of one experience with that of others, or with existing beliefs or authoritative texts. In the passages above from Acts, belief in the testimony of many witnesses to the physical resurrection is a reason to believe in the resurrection. Luke knows, however, that witnesses to the resurrection cannot prove who and what the Christ is in whom people are

---

[20] Morgan (2015a), 142–56, (forthcoming), cf. Whitmarsh (2015).

[21] Orig., *Cels.* e.g. 6.42, 8.68, cf. 1.67; Morgan (2021a), 152–3, 160–1. Celsus has a high view of the ability of human reason to decide whether a being is divine (e.g. 1.5, 3.17, 3.26–9, 7.42).

[22] Origen seems to struggle to respond effectively to these claims, which emerge as widely shared, rationally based, and sophisticated, suggesting that he is not misrepresenting Celsus here (Morgan (2021a), 160–1).

[23] Cf. Tert., *Ap.* 19, attesting that Greeks and Romans tend to believe what has been found credible by many nations, cities, and wise men over time.

[24] They often, though not always, use *pisteuein* of their belief: e.g. 7, 10, 13, 15, 17, 20, 28, 30, 32, 38.

[25] See especially *Sup.*, *De Isid.*, *Def. or.*, *Num.* 4.3–4.

[26] The relationship between the divine and e.g. good and beauty is debated among Platonists: see Boys-Stones (2018), 147–54.

called to trust, so belief in the resurrection in itself is not a sufficient basis for trust. To recognize who people are being invited to trust, and therefore why they can and should trust, one must recognize the coherence of what has happened to Jesus with prophecies about the Messiah; one must experience the gift of the spirit on trusting him; one must trust in preaching and hope that trust in Jesus Christ will lead to the forgiveness of sins.

Almost at the end of Luke's gospel, Jesus appears to the disciples (24.36–43), asks them why they are troubled and doubting (two conditions often linked with the failure of trust),[27] and shows them his hands and feet (24.40). While they still *apistein* (24.41), he proves his physical reality by eating a piece of baked fish (24.42–3). The experience and physicality of the resurrection are both important to Luke here, but Jesus' purpose in appearing to the disciples goes further. He emphasizes that he is the same person as he was before the crucifixion ('look…it is I, myself' (24.39)) and reminds them of his past teaching (24.44). He confirms that everything that has happened fulfils what was prophesied about him in the scriptures, that the Messiah would suffer and rise from the dead, and that repentance and forgiveness of sins would be preached in his name (24.44–7).[28] He allays their doubts that he is who he has always been and that he has always been the Messiah.[29] Similarly, earlier in the chapter, the two men whom the women encounter at the tomb remind them that, in Galilee, Jesus had told them that the Son of Man must be handed over to sinners and crucified before rising on the third day (24.7). On the road to Emmaus, the stranger explains that the death of the Messiah fulfilled what was written in the scriptures (24.25–8). Jesus' final appearance in the gospel, as noted, is to teach the disciples how his death and resurrection fulfil the scriptures (24.44–6). The experience of the resurrection, however powerful, is, once more, not a complete basis for trust. The disciples can believe not only that Jesus has been raised, but that he is the Messiah, and that trusting in him with repentance brings forgiveness, because they can recognize the risen Christ as the same as Jesus in his earthly life, and the scriptural prophecies about the Messiah as fulfilled in everything that has happened to him.

In 1 Corinthians 15, Paul reminds the Corinthians,

> I handed on to you as of primary importance what I also received: that Christ died for our sins according to the scriptures; and that he was buried; and that he was raised (ἐγήγερται) on the third day according to the scriptures; and that he

---

[27] Τί τεταραγμένοι ἐστέ, καὶ διὰ τί διαλογισμοὶ ἀναβαίνουσιν ἐν τῇ καρδίᾳ ὑμῶν, 24.38.

[28] Cf. Acts 2.30–2 (quoting Ps. 16.10), 10.43.

[29] At the beginning of Acts, recapping the disciples' resurrection experiences, Luke reports that the risen Christ 'presented himself alive to them by many *tekmēria* ("tokens" or "proofs")…' (1.3). Barrett (1994), *ad loc.* confirms that 'proofs' is used here in its regular, e.g. judicial sense; Conzelmann (1987), *ad loc.* compares the appearance of Luke's narrative with the appearance and miraculous acts of other *theioi andres*, and the founding of cults based on prophecies (cf. e.g. Lucian., *Peregr.* 22–42, especially 38–41).

appeared to Kephas, then to the Twelve. Then he appeared to more than five hundred brothers at once, most of whom are still living, though some have fallen asleep. Then he appeared to James, then to all the apostles. Last of all, as to one born abnormally, he appeared to me...so we preach, and so you believed/ trusted (ἐγήγερται). (1 Cor. 15.3-8, 11)

Some Corinthians were evidently asserting that (some) people do not rise from the dead. Exactly what they were claiming is not our main concern here, but we may note with many commentators that they need not have been claiming that Christ was not raised, but only that people in general are not raised, and they did not expect to be raised themselves.[30] Paul moves to quash their doubts, for at least two reasons. Doubts about resurrection might constitute the thin end of a wedge leading to doubts either about Christ's own resurrection or about his real humanity and the continuity of his identity in his earthly and exalted life (cf. 15.21). And doubts about resurrection might contradict Paul's eschatological conviction that where Christ leads, the faithful can follow, sharing his inheritance, glory, and eternal life in God's kingdom.[31]

Paul uses the Corinthians' alleged belief in Christ's resurrection as the rhetorical starting-point of his argument here, but belief in the resurrection is not the only foundation of his own trust in Christ or his preaching.[32] At 1 Corinthians 15.10 and at Galatians 1.15-16, Paul refers to God as revealing Christ to him and making him who and what he is as an apostle. Christ's appearance to him (and perhaps to other followers) is, for Paul a revelation by God of God's grace, which discloses Christ as God's son, the one who died for humanity's sins (1 Cor. 15.3) and will bring everyone who trusts in him to life (1 Cor. 15.22), and calls him to *pistis* and apostleship.[33] Paul's beliefs, as well as his trust, follow not just from what he undoubtedly thinks is the fact of the resurrection, but from the grace of God's revelation to him.[34]

---

[30] On what may have been the views of gentile or Jewish Corinthian community members see e.g. Barrett (2003), Keener (2005), 122-3, Holleman (2014), Taylor (2014), *ad* 15.1-58, with Bryan (2011), especially 45-64; on Paul's assumption that the physical resurrection occurred see Cook (2017). Paul's formulation at 15.13, 'If there is no resurrection of the dead, then neither has Christ been raised' indicates that the Corinthians' claim is not about Christ himself: if it had been, Paul would surely have tackled it directly.

[31] Cf. e.g. 15.43, 49, 50, 54; see especially Schrage (2001), 152-231. It may also be important to Paul to emphasize that even when the faithful die they do not fall out of the sphere of Christ's power and care: see below, p. 131.

[32] We do not know what Paul thought of the resurrection testimony before his call but he could, in principle, have believed it (for instance, as a work of necromancy) without inferring that Christ was exalted or to be confessed as Lord and Son of God. As a Christ-confessor, Paul undoubtedly believes in the resurrection, though he does not comment on its physicality, as part of the preaching he has inherited, but his own call depends on his experience of the exalted Christ rather than on the resurrection itself (cf. Acts 22.1-21, 26.2-20).

[33] As e.g. Boers (2006), 136-7 emphasizes, Christ's death and resurrection go together; without resurrection Paul would have thought Christ's death ineffective.

[34] On the relationship between revelation and trust see pp. 164-7, 237-41.

Paul also refers, in this passage (15.3-4), to the coherence of the death and resurrection of Jesus with scripture.[35] Many commentators take the first reference, linked with the proclamation that 'Christ died for our sins', as rooted in an early Christology drawn from Isaiah 53.4-12.[36] If this is right, Paul could have expected Jewish and godfearing listeners, and possibly even gentiles, to remember the beginning of that passage: 'Who would believe what we have heard (τίς ἐπίστευσεν τῇ ἀκοῇ ἡμῶν, Isa. 53.1 LXX)?'[37] The rhetorical question underlines the astonishing content of the prophecy while affirming its trustworthiness as an oracle of God.[38] This indicates not so much that the proclaimed fact of the resurrection in itself demands belief, as that the accepted trustworthiness of the scriptures coheres with many people's experience of the self-revelation of the risen or exalted Christ in such a way as to command both belief and trust.[39] Paul's affirmation, like that of Luke, suggests that one's own experience and that of others, and the coherence of that experience with tradition and one's existing commitment (if any) to God, together form an even more powerful basis for trust in the exalted Christ than truth claims about the resurrection in themselves.

John's gospel takes an equally nuanced approach to the relationship between belief in the resurrection and trust in Jesus. At 20.17, when Mary encounters Jesus in the garden (vv. 14-17), Jesus tells her, 'Do not touch me, for I have not yet ascended to my father.' John focuses not on the nature of Jesus' resurrection, which remains undefined, but on his imminent ascension, re-emphasizing the nature of Jesus' relationship with God which has been such a strong theme throughout the gospel, and recognition of which has been the basis on which people have trusted in him.[40]

At first sight, the two stories that follow seem rather different. Jesus appears to the disciples (20.19-23), showing them his hands and side, and they 'rejoiced when they saw the Lord' (v. 20). The implication seems to be that they take what they see as proof of physical resurrection, and so can John's listeners. Jesus then

---

[35] As did Luke: p. 103.
[36] Though *contra* see Hooker (1959), 117-20, Hahn (1963), 56-7. Breytenbach (2010), 83-94 shows that the use of *paradidonai* in Isa. 53.12g LXX draws on Greek and Hellenistic rather than Hebrew and Jewish thinking about dying on behalf of another; Paul, or some of his predecessors, could therefore have derived the idea both from LXX and everyday usage.
[37] Belief may be to the fore here, since the object is the content of a prophecy, but trust may also be implied.
[38] Cf. 1 Pet. 3.18. Fitzmyer (2008), *ad loc.* notes that it is unclear what passage Paul is pointing to here; modern commentators tend to suggest Isa. 53.5 on the basis of 1 Pet. 2.22-5. Pre-Pauline Judaism, however, did not apply the suffering servant song to the deaths of martyr or the righteous (Breytenbach (2010), 83-94).
[39] Elsewhere, Paul invokes his personal encounter with the exalted Christ to fortify his trustworthiness (e.g. 1 Cor. 9.1, 2 Cor. 12.2, 12.7). At 2 Cor. 12.7-10, Paul's thorn in the flesh evokes among *inter alia* Josh. 23.13 LXX, in a passage which warns the Israelites what will happen to them if they are not faithful to God (cf. Ezek. 28.44, Num. 35.55), so this reference underlines that Paul is being actively kept faithful and this is one reason why he is trustworthy.
[40] See further pp. 205-36.

appears to the sceptic Thomas (20.24-9), inviting him to test the evidence of his eyes by touching Jesus' hands and side (v. 27). This narrative, however, is more complex than the first and suggests that the first may also be more complex than it seems.[41] In the first place, we are struck by Thomas' focus on the nail and spear marks. Why does he need to see the wounds and not, for instance, simply Jesus' face? Other ancient discourses of ascension suggest a reason. The identity of human beings who ascend to heaven often changes significantly: Enoch, for instance, becomes identified with Metatron; Romulus with the god Quirinus. John's focus on Jesus' wounds underlines that the person of Jesus after Easter morning is identical with the person of Jesus in his earthly life and death.[42] The wounds and the reference to ascension at 20.17 perform analogous functions: not simply to assert the resurrection or its physicality, but to insist on the identity of Jesus in his earthly and heavenly life.[43] No doubt members of John's community believed that the resurrection occurred, but these stories tell them that trust in the ascended Christ is based on recognition of him as equally rabbi, Lord, and God; as equally the crucified and the ascended one; as the one who reveals to his followers not only his relationship, even identity, with God, as he has done throughout the gospel, but his identity with himself at every point in his existence.

The climax of Jesus' invitation to Thomas is often translated 'do not be unbelieving, but believe (καὶ μὴ γίνου ἄπιστος ἀλλὰ πιστός)' (v. 27). This, however, would involve an extremely rare meaning of *pistos* and probably an unparalleled meaning of *apistos*.[44] In itself, we should expect this phrase to mean, 'Become not untrusting [or "faithless"] but trusting [or "faithful"]'.[45] This fits well with what I have argued elsewhere is the strongly relational meaning of *pisteuein* throughout John's gospel, and with the following two verses.[46] On the basis of what he sees, Thomas is invited to reaffirm his commitment to Jesus, and he does, in triumphal terms: 'My Lord and my God!' But Jesus then says, 'Have you trusted because you have seen me? Blessed are those who have not seen and yet have trusted' (v. 29).[47]

---

[41] Especially if, as many argue, 20.20-9 has been developed out of the previous story (e.g. Lüdemann (1994), 163-5, Ashton (2007), 478, Allison (2021), 64).

[42] Cf. p. 122.

[43] Cf. Barton (1994), 112-14, Morgan (1994), 18, Hurtado (2003), 265-7 (who notes that, among early gospels, this is distinctively true of the canonical gospels), Orr (2018), 29-34. This, of course, is a point about the continuity between the earthly Jesus of faith and the exalted Christ of faith, not the 'Jesus of history' and the 'Christ of faith'.

[44] Thgn. 283, A., *Pr.* 917, *Pers.* 55 use *pistos* just possibly meaning 'believing', but more likely meaning 'relying on' (and are all early and poetic); LSJ wrongly cites 1 Cor. 6.6 as a semantic outlier, meaning 'unbelieving'.

[45] Aland (1993), half-recognizing this, translates *apistos* as 'faithless' but *pistos*, oddly, as believing.

[46] Morgan (2015a), 394-437.

[47] To complicate this passage further, the writer concludes (20.31), 'These [signs] are written that you may believe/trust that Jesus is the Messiah, the Son of God [both belief and the commitment of trust are likely involved here], and that through this belief/trust you may have life in his name', but this refers to the whole gospel and testimony not just to the resurrection experiences. Earlier, prophesying his death to a crowd, Jesus says, 'if you do not believe/trust that I am, you will die in your sins...when you lift up the Son of Man, then you will realize (*gnōsesthe*) that I am' (8.24, 28). The implication is that

What is vital, for John, is that people put their trust in Jesus, recognizing him as the same in his earthly and heavenly life, whether they have witnessed him risen or not.[48]

The end of Matthew's gospel also suggests that Jesus demonstrates his resurrection by appearing to the disciples, while arguably making even less of his physical presence than does John.[49] It has been suggested that 28.16–20 echoes the form of commissioning narratives in the Hebrew Bible.[50] This model offers an explanation of the otherwise startling phrase, in verse 17, 'and looking at him they bowed down to him, but they doubted'.[51] Do the disciples doubt the evidence of their eyes, or something else? Many commentators have assumed the former, but nothing is done in the narrative to address such a doubt; it immediately moves on to the commissioning. It makes better sense to see the disciples' doubt as Matthew's version of the moment of reaction or protest which sometimes occurs in commissioning narratives when the person commissioned doubts who is addressing them or their worthiness or readiness for the task. The disciples suffer a moment of doubt about their worthiness to bow to Jesus, whom they had deserted, or about whether bowing is appropriate, or about what Jesus' appearance means. Jesus moves, literally, to reassure them, coming closer to tell them, 'All power in heaven and on earth has been given to me. Go, therefore and disciple all nations…' (28.18–19), and promising, 'behold, I am with you always, until the end of the age' (v. 20). He addresses not the possibility that the disciples do not believe their own eyes, but their uncertainty about what his appearance means for them. In the process he emphasizes the continuity of his own identity before and after the crucifixion, teaching them as he taught them in life and sending them, as he sent them in life, on a new mission on his behalf, and assures them that in his exalted life he will still be with them.[52]

1 Peter echoes John's 'blessed are those who have not seen and yet have trusted' with an even more explicit focus on the importance of trust. He blesses God,

> who in his great mercy gave us a new birth to a living hope through the resurrection of Jesus Christ from the dead, to an inheritance that is imperishable,

---

not only knowing but trusting will come of the raising up which conflates the crucifixion and resurrection. Cf. 12.32, 3.14, 6.39, 6.40, 6.44, 6.54.

[48] And, for John, in his pre-existence (1.1–3).

[49] Michel (1995) points out that the commissioning of the disciples is linked with the exaltation and enthronement of Christ, not simply with his resurrection.

[50] Commissioning narratives typically take the form: introduction, confirmation, reaction, commission, protest (absent from Matthew), reassurance, and conclusion: see Hubbard (1974), Davies and Allison (1988–2004), *ad loc*. Woodington (2020), 88–9 reverts to the less satisfactory view that the disciples at Mt. 28.17 doubted Jesus' power, but is surely right in observing that, in general, 'doubt…never truly goes away in Christian life' (p. 175).

[51] καὶ ἰδόντες αὐτὸν προσεκύνησαν, οἱ δὲ ἐδίστασαν. On this translation see Grayston (1984), though my point here would also fit with the translation 'some doubted'.

[52] Michel (1995), 44–6.

undefiled, and unfading, kept in heaven for you who by the power of God are safeguarded through trust, to a salvation that is ready to be revealed in the final time. In this you rejoice, although now for a little while you may have to suffer through various trials, so that the genuineness of your trust, more precious than gold that is perishable even though tested by fire, may prove to be for praise, glory, and honour at the revelation of Jesus Christ. Although you have not seen him you love him; even though you do not see him now yet trust in him, you rejoice with an indescribable and glorious joy, as you attain the goal of your trust, the salvation of your souls (ὃν οὐκ ἰδόντες ἀγαπᾶτε, εἰς ὃν ἄρτι μὴ ὁρῶντες πιστεύοντες δὲ ἀγαλλιᾶσθε χαρᾷ ἀνεκλαλήτῳ καὶ δεδοξασμένῃ, κομιζόμενοι τὸ τέλος τῆς πίστεως ὑμῶν σωτηρίαν ψυχῶν).[53] (1 Pet. 1.3–9)

The resurrection experience is the catalyst for a new relationship between God, the exalted Christ, and Christ's followers. Most of these, the writer emphasizes, have not seen and do not see Christ for themselves; nevertheless, they love him, rejoice, and trust in him for the salvation of their souls at the end time.[54]

All these passages affirm Jesus' followers resurrection experiences, and their belief that the resurrection occurred, but none of them indicates that belief in the resurrection *in itself* is the definitive reason why people should put their trust in Jesus Christ. Trust is based as much on the experience of divine grace, which reveals Jesus as both the Messiah foretold by scripture and the one who is to come. It responds to the coherence of Jesus' death with prophecies that the Messiah would die for others. It affirms that the Jesus who taught and reassured his disciples and sent them out to speak and act in his name is the same person as the ascended Christ who continues to reassure them, and will be with them, in Matthew's words, to the end of the age.[55]

Some of the complexity of the passages we have discussed so far is no doubt due to the fact that all New Testament writings address, or encode addresses to multiple audiences. 1 Corinthians is written to a community, some or all of whose members' belief in their own future spiritual resurrection needs fortifying. When Matthew says that some people claimed, and still claim in his day that Jesus' disciples stole his body before proclaiming the resurrection (28.13–15), he implies that the resurrection stories have an apologetic function aimed at outsiders in

---

[53] Transl. NAB.
[54] Coherence with prophecy (1.10) and the preaching of the good news (1.12) are referenced immediately afterwards as bases for their trust. Elsewhere (Heb. 11.6, Jas 2.19), belief in God, rather than in the resurrection as such, is foundational for Christ-confession. On the emotions of the faithful see e.g. Elliott (2005).
[55] We have focused here on stories that include *pistis* language, but the same points could be drawn from those that do not; we can also note that at Mt. 28.5, 10 the disciples are told not to be afraid, and fear is often the opposite of trust.

addition to the meaning they bear for insiders.[56] Acts not only tells of how the resurrection experiences affected Jesus' existing followers, but reports that preaching about the resurrection brought people to trust in Christ. For community members who have already put their trust in Christ, resurrection stories are also their own stories: they not only describe something which they believe happened to Jesus Christ, but also act as a paradigm of the new life they have received in baptism and the new life they hope to receive at the end time.

It is also worth remembering what no early Christian writer can have forgotten: that only a limited number of people reported resurrection experiences, and, even in the early years, some of the faithful probably did not meet any of them. Proclamations of the resurrection always risked being regarded at best as hearsay, at worst as gossip and rumour, in a world in which hearsay was regarded as a fragile basis for trust and gossip and rumour were widely seen as wholly unreliable.[57] In such an environment, it is not surprising that all New Testament writers appeal to multiple foundations for trust, from the experience of Jesus' followers in his lifetime to community members' experience of receiving the spirit or meeting inspiring individuals who had been 'entrusted with the gospel' (1 Thess. 2.4).[58] It is arguably more striking, in this environment, that Christians continued so strongly to affirm the resurrection. Their affirmation attests both to the power of experiences of the risen or exalted Christ, and to the profound significance for the faithful of the continuity of the identity of the exalted Christ with that of Jesus in his earthly life and death.[59]

Trust in Christ and Christ's Future Coming

We noted above that one of the earliest Christological affirmations must be that which foresees Christ's future coming from heaven to deliver the faithful from the coming wrath (cf. 1 Thess. 1.10). In the last chapter we saw that God is sometimes described as faithful to human beings between the resurrection and the end time.[60] We might expect to find the exalted Christ, too, affirmed as faithful to the faithful in the present time, but New Testament writings prefer to imply that Christ is faithful by describing his activities on behalf of the faithful and their relationship in other terms.[61] One reason for this may be that these texts belong to the early stages of Christian thinking about who and what the exalted Christ is

---

[56] Even if non-Christians are not likely to have read Christian texts themselves, the texts may have been furnishing the faithful with possible responses to criticism; cf. Just., *Dial.* 108, Tert., *Spect.* 30.
[57] Morgan (2015a), 65–72.   [58] Morgan (2015a), 241–3.
[59] Barth (1932 –67), 64.2.144, 146.   [60] p. 62.
[61] Though 2 Thess. 3.3, 'the Lord is faithful' probably refers to Christ's faithfulness to the 'brothers' (cf. 3.1).

and what he does. They cannot yet simply affirm that 'Christ is faithful' and expect listeners to recognize the distinctive content of that affirmation.

New Testament writings do, however, affirm that the faithful can and should trust in the exalted Christ or be faithful to Christ while they wait for his coming. Since *pistis* language is part of Christian discourse before Paul's earliest surviving letter, this fits with the argument that Christ's future coming is one of the earliest Christological claims, and suggests that encouraging the faithful to remain trusting or faithful in a period of uncertain duration and outlook is one of the early uses of *pistis* language.[62] In addition to referring to the saving trust which people put in the exalted Christ because of Christ's death (Rom. 3.26, 1 Cor. 15.1–2, Gal. 2.16), Paul is keen for the Corinthians to 'stand firm in [your] trust/faithfulness (στήκετε ἐν τῇ πίστει)' (1 Cor. 16.13), possibly to both God and Christ, as they wait for the *parousia* (cf. 1.7, 15.23), and for the Thessalonians to 'remedy the deficiencies' of their trust/faithfulness (1 Thess. 3.10) and allow Christ to increase their love for one another (3.12).[63] Several writings refer to the possibility of growing in trust and faithfulness in this time (to Christ, and in some cases to God too: 2 Cor. 10.15, 2 Thess. 1.3, Jude 20–1, cf. Mt. 25.14–30=Lk. 19.11–27).[64] In such passages, Christ's coming is not explicitly a matter of trust or belief in itself, but is taken as accepted and hoped for.

In the synoptic gospels, Jesus prophesies wars, natural disasters, and persecution before 'the end', but promises the disciples that 'the one that endures to the end will be saved' (Mt. 24.13=Mk 13.13=Lk. 21.19). In the meantime, Jesus' followers must be careful whom they trust.[65] They must trust only the real Messiah, who, as the evangelists write, is the exalted Christ. Matthew and Luke also tell a series of parables which look forward to the arrival or return of a master-figure, representing Christ, to his household, and emphasize the importance of his slaves' being faithful while he is away (e.g. Mt. 24.45–51=Lk. 12.41–6 (the parable of the faithful and wise slave); Mt. 25.14–30=Lk. 19.11–27 (the parable of the talents, again featuring faithful slaves).[66]

These parables echo some of the epistles in suggesting that the faithful must not only remain faithful until the master returns, but work to steward and increase his resources.[67] Acts, in historiographical form, offers a similar vision of the work of the apostles after Pentecost. Like the faithful slaves of the parable of the talents, the apostles do not simply preserve their master's legacy but increase it, continually growing the community of the faithful. Like the faithful and prudent servant of Lk. 12.42, the apostles feed the master's servants as a group and

---

[62] Cf. p. 133.   [63] Either 'trust' or 'faithfulness' would make good sense here.
[64] At 2 Tim. 3.14–15, Tit. 1.9, cf. Jude 2–3 the faithful must remain faithful to the teaching they have received about Christ.
[65] Τότε ἐάν τις ὑμῖν εἴπῃ· Ἰδοὺ ὧδε ὁ χριστός, ἤ· Ὧδε, μὴ πιστεύσητε, Mt. 24.23–4=Mk 13.21–2, cf. Lk 17.23 (without *pisteuein*).
[66] Cf. Jn 14.1–4 (with *pisteuein*).   [67] Cf. pp. 290–7.

take care of them (cf. Acts 6.1-4). Acts' relatively rare explicit references to the end time, or time of 'universal restoration' (3.21), however, are usually linked with preaching which calls people to 'repent and return' (3.19, cf. 17.30-1, 24.25), in response to which some of those listening 'come to [believe and] trust' (e.g. 4.4, 17.34 cf. 5.14, 6.7).[68] In these responses, *pistis* is the new trust that justifies or saves (e.g. 13.26, 39) rather than ongoing faithfulness. Acts can also refer to the importance of the ongoing faithfulness of community members (e.g. 2.44, 4.32, 16.15) or their strengthening in trust (14.22-3, 16.5), but it speaks of the ongoing faithfulness of the faithful as a group infrequently and, in contrast with the epistles, offers almost no advice about what it involves. On one level, this is surprising: we might expect a history of the early church, especially one written when early expectations of an imminent *parousia* have begun to recede, to have more to say about faithful living in community. One explanation may lie in Acts' generic affiliations. Acts is an apologetic history of Christian expansion which owes much to Hellenistic historiography.[69] Like other histories of expansion—Polybius' history of the Roman empire, the imperial sections of Diodorus' universal history, Josephus' *Jewish Antiquities*, or Arrian's *Anabasis* of Alexander—it has more to say about how its subject extended its scope than how it governed the peoples who came under its authority.

New Testament writings also recognize that trust in the exalted Christ and faithfulness to Christ are demanding and therefore risky. References to the *pistis* of the faithful are often accompanied by exhortations to hold fast or endure, and by references to patience and hope (e.g. Mt. 24.45-51=Lk. 12.41-6, 1, 1 Tim. 3.9, Jas 1.2-3, 1 Pet. 1.5-7, Rev. 2.10, 2.19, 13.10, cf. Rev. 14.12). For Paul, the Thessalonians' main resources as they wait for God's son are 'your work of trust and labour of love and endurance in hope of our Lord Jesus Christ' (1.3, cf. 1.10, 3.6-8). At the beginning of 1 Corinthians, the God who is faithful 'will keep you firm to the end, [so that you may be] irreproachable on the day of our Lord Jesus Christ' (1.8, cf. 2 Thess. 1.4). In 1 Corinthians 15, Paul's vision of the end time begins by reminding the Corinthians that they are being saved by the gospel, 'if you hold fast to the word I preached to you, unless you trusted in vain' (15.1-2). At end of the letter Paul returns to the theme again: 'be on your guard, stand firm in trust, be brave, be strong' (16.13).

One of the most poetic and fertile expressions of the way trust can be expressed as the faithful wait for the coming of the Lord is that of James 5.7-11. Though these verses themselves contain no *pistis* language, the letter takes for granted that

---

[68] Belief, as discussed, is implicit in putting one's trust in God and Christ, but Acts never says explicitly that listeners believe propositionally in the apostles' teaching: either *pisteuein* is left without an object or converts are said to believe in God or Christ (Morgan (2015a), 384). At 17.11-12 the Jews of Beroea receive and examine the word before they *pisteuein*, perhaps marking the difference between their intellectual response and their commitment.

[69] Sterling (1992), especially 311-89.

pistis is part of what it means to be a Christian (not least at 2.14–26, where the writer insists that the attitude of trust or belief must be accompanied by good works), and these verses look back to the beginning of the letter, in which the author encourages community members, telling them that 'you know that the testing of your trust produces perseverance...' (1.3).[70] 5.7–11 is full of language of patience, firmness, and perseverance, qualities closely associated with faithfulness: 'Be patient (μακροθυμήσατε), therefore, brothers, until the coming of the Lord. See how the farmer waits for the precious fruit of the earth, being patient with it until it receives the early and the late rains. You too must be patient. Make your hearts firm, because the coming of the Lord is near' (5.7–8).[71] If you are patient and faithful, the writer suggests, what you sow in the present will grow and change like the fruit of the earth. It will become something quite different from what you invested in it, and beyond comparison greater; more than anything you could create for yourself. It will not simply realize your hopes, but will feed you and help you to grow in turn. The fruit of trust, for the faithful as for Elijah (5.17–18), the prophets (5.10), and Job (5.11), is life beyond anything they have power to generate: the life that comes with the coming of the Lord, which is like the abundance of creation itself (cf. 5.18). Even so, the writer recognizes that to trust in Christ to return in the future is risky.[72] Patience, firmness, and endurance do not palliate the risk, but they offer ways to live with it until the expected end.[73]

At Romans 5.1–5, Paul addresses the uncertainty of the future in a rhetorical *klimax*. He tells the Romans that the *pistis* of the faithful has brought them peace with God, through Christ, and grace (5.1–2), and with these the ability to 'boast in hope of the glory of God' (v. 2) and even to boast of their afflictions, because affliction produces endurance, endurance proven character, and character, hope, and 'hope does not disappoint, because the love of God has been poured into our hearts by the holy spirit' (vv. 3–5).[74] In this passage, hope has three distinguishable foundations: righteousing trust in Christ (cf. 3.26), the character that is built by afflictions, and the experience of God's love through the holy spirit. The faithful can trust their experience of the spirit, of how they were changed by trusting in Christ, and of their own character, and all three combine to enable them to hope on the grandest imaginable scale: for glory (5.2), salvation (5.9), and eternal life (5.21).[75]

---

[70] Γινώσκοντες ὅτι τὸ δοκίμιον ὑμῶν τῆς πίστεως κατεργάζεται ὑπομονήν.
[71] Transl. NAB, modified. [72] Cf. p. 133.
[73] On whether the call to practise these qualities still has equal force, see p. 282.
[74] The conventions of the *klimax* may discourage Paul from changing the verb between each clause; v. 4a is probably best understood as meaning 'endurance proves character (ἡ δὲ ὑπομονὴ δοκιμήν)', but the NAB translation 'endurance [produces] proven character' captures his meaning. Byrne (1996), *ad* 3–4 notes the connections between this sequence and wisdom tradition; Wolter (1978), 145 m. 488 compares *klimakes* elsewhere.
[75] Cf. 1 Cor. 15.1–2, 1 Thess. 1.8–10, where belief and trust in what has happened in the past is also a basis for trust in the future; Wolter (2015a), 177–81.

Hebrews 11.1 shares Paul's affirmation that trust is the basis of eschatological hope.[76] It is (only) in a relationship of trust in God (and, by implication, Christ) that the faithful can prove the reality of what God has promised them and what they hope for. Without trust, there is no possibility of inhabiting that reality. I have argued elsewhere that eschatological hope is the key to the interpretation of this verse: Ἔστιν δὲ πίστις ἐλπιζομένων ὑπόστασις, πραγμάτων ἔλεγχος οὐ βλεπομένων.

[Hans Dieter] Betz points to the two-part, arguably parallel form of the verse, suggesting that it imitates the parallelism common in Hebrew poetry and that its meaning derives from the Septuagint, in particular from Isaiah 28.16. On his interpretation, *pistis* is both a foundation (*hypostasis*) laid by God, and the attitude to God of the faithful human being.[77]...I share with Betz the view that 'foundation' is the most convincing translation of *hypostasis* here.[78] Any idea that *pistis* might be an intuition unsupported by evidence or experience which leads to the understanding of the divine, a right relationship with the divine, or the revelation of God's plan, fits badly with the way in which it is understood elsewhere in this letter or more widely. The idea of *pistis* as the foundation of what we hope for, however, fits well with what we have seen of the use of *pistis* in this letter and elsewhere. *Pistis* marks the beginning of human beings' relationship with God. This is a relationship which looks forward hopefully to the future (in this case, ultimately to the faithful being brought to 'glory' (1.10)). Moreover, the fact that people are in a relationship of *pistis* with God enables them to achieve what they hope for. *Pistis* is therefore foundational in two senses: it creates the divine-human relationship within which it becomes possible for human beings to hope for certain things, and the relationship within which those hopes become achievable...The first half of 11.1 can therefore be translated, '(The) *pistis* [of those who put their trust in God] is the foundation (in two senses) of the things that are hoped for.'[79] In accordance with the conventions of parallelistic Hebrew poetry, the second half of the verse may mean the same as the first, or may develop or modify it.[80] What, then, does it mean to say that '*pistis* is the *elenchos* of things not seen'?

---

[76] In the past half-century, Hebrews' *pistis* language has been seen as ethical, Christological, or eschatological, but perhaps best as all three (so Grässer (1965), Hamm (1990), 273–6, Rhee (2001), 64–79, 81–100). Käsemann (1984), 22–48 sees the faithfulness of community members as hopeful, obedient, and open to the future: 'faith becomes a confident wandering' (p. 44).
[77] Betz (1990), 434–8.
[78] Though 'reality' or 'substance' makes better sense at 1.3, at 3.14 the meaning is more debatable, and could be 'foundation'.
[79] This is close to Plu., *Mor.* 756a–b, where *pistis* is the 'basis and common foundation (ἕδρα τις αὕτη καὶ βάσις) for piety,' cf. Cic., *ND* 3.4.9.
[80] Even if this verse is not evoking Hebrew verse, common sense suggests that these constitute the range of likely relationships between the two halves.

Among the meanings of *elenchos* in Greek, most (such as 'argument', 'refutation', 'scrutiny', 'disproof') have no obvious relevance. The likeliest meanings (which are all closely related to one another) are 'evidence', 'proof' or 'test'.[81] The second offers a particularly tempting possibility, since 'proof' is also a common meaning of *pistis*.

'Things not seen' could be of two kinds: they could (like the things hoped for) be in the future, or they could be metaphysical, and so invisible to the physical eye but visible to the eye of faith. There are, however, strong reasons why the second option is unlikely to be the right one here. For one, putting one's trust in a metaphysical entity might be either justified or deluded, but it is wholly unclear how it would constitute evidence, a test, or a proof (in the sense of the means by which something is proven) of that entity's truth or reality (or any other quality). For another, though, as we have seen, doubt and scepticism regularly go hand in hand with *pistis/fides* in the ancient world, testing the divine to prove its reality, reliability etc. is rarely considered as a possibility and almost always frowned on when it is. There is, moreover, no sign that testing or proving anything about God is any part of the project of the author of this letter or of the models of *pistis* which he cites. Furthermore, the author is addressing people who already belong to the community of the faithful, who do not need persuading of the truth or reality of God, so it is hard to see why he would praise *pistis* for doing so.

There is no good reason to take 'things not seen' as referring to the metaphysical, but, paralleling the 'things hoped for', it could well refer to the future. It makes good sense to translate the second half of the verse, '(the divine–human relationship of) *pistis* is the means by which things which have not yet happened are tested/proven.' The particular things which have not yet happened are most likely to be those which we hope for, since these have just been mentioned: above all, what the author sums up in the previous verse (10.39) as 'possessing life'. Through being in a relationship of *pistis* with God, the author tells us, we come to prove the reality of what God has promised us and we hope for, but have not yet seen: eternal life.

The whole verse should therefore be translated, 'The divine–human relationship of *pistis* is the foundation [in two senses] of everything human beings hope for, the proof of everything [which God has promised] that they have not yet seen.' There follows a series of examples of people who put their trust in God in this way, and were not disappointed.[82]

---

[81] The common English translation 'conviction' (e.g. NRSV) bears a tenuous relation to any meaning of the Greek word and owes its currency to the later fideist view of *pistis*.
[82] Morgan (2015a), 338–40.

For the writer, the 'cloud of witnesses' to the validity of trust in God, and, implicitly, in Christ, inspires community members to 'persevere in running the race that lies before us' (12.1[83]).

In 1 Corinthians, Paul suggests that, while they wait for Christ, community members can foster *pistis*, among other qualities, in one another, to strengthen their relationship with God and Christ.[84] At 4.1–2 Paul describes himself as a servant of Christ and 'steward of the mysteries of God', and says 'it is of course required of stewards that they be found trustworthy (or 'faithful')' to their master, here both God and Christ (4.2). At 4.16–17, he urges the Corinthians to be 'imitators of me', and tells them that he is sending Timothy, 'who is my beloved and faithful son in the Lord' to remind them of his ways 'in Christ Jesus'.[85] Timothy's faithfulness to Paul seems to be one reason why he can help the Corinthians to imitate Paul (perhaps both by teaching and by acting as a model himself); by the same token, Paul's faithfulness to God and Christ enables others to imitate him.[86] In this passage (4.6–13) the qualities in himself which Paul indicates the Corinthians should be imitating are above all humility (4.6, 10–13), and what the world sees as foolishness (vv. 10, 12), but they also include endurance under persecution (v. 12), which elsewhere Paul also links with *pistis*.[87]

Paul's followers and those influenced by him also see ongoing trust or faithfulness as vital to the lives of the faithful as they wait for Christ, and occasionally represent the faithful as models of trust for one another. The author of 2 Thessalonians thanks God for those who endure and remain faithful under persecution, who will be vindicated 'at the revelation of the Lord Jesus from heaven' (1.4–7, cf. 11–12). At 2 Timothy 3.10–14, [Paul] exhorts Timothy to remain faithful to what he has learned from Paul himself in the way of teaching and of Paul's example of faithfulness, patience, and endurance, among much else. Presumably Timothy, like Paul, if he 'keeps faith' (cf. 4.7), can hope to inherit the 'crown of righteousness' on the day of judgment (4.8). The author of 1 Peter exhorts his communities to be sober and vigilant, 'steadfast in trust (or 'faithfulness') ($\sigma\tau\epsilon\rho\epsilon o\grave{\iota}$ $\tau\hat{\eta}\ \pi\acute{\iota}\sigma\tau\epsilon\iota$)' (5.9), because the devil is prowling round to corrupt them, and after they have suffered 'a little' they will be called to eternal glory through Christ Jesus (5.8–11).

The reference to glory reminds us, last but not least, that the uncertainty of the future and the fragility of trust and hope, are counterpoised, especially in the epistles and Revelation, with multiple dramatic visions of what the faithful can hope to receive when the end time comes and they are judged to have remained faithful. For the author of Revelation, the faithful can hope for nothing less than a

---

[83] Without an explicit mention of judgment day.
[84] Particularly by deflating their pride (cf. 4.6, 18).
[85] This section also suggests that Paul is imitating Christ (Morgan (2020), 47). At 11.1 he returns to this theme: 'Be imitators of me, as I am of Christ.'
[86] Cf. pp. 243, 286–7. [87] E.g. 1 Thess 1.2–10, Tit. 2.1–13.

new heaven and earth and a new Jerusalem in which God will live with humanity (21.1-4). The words in which this vision is delivered, the 'one who sat on the throne' tells the writer, are 'trustworthy and true (πιστοὶ καὶ ἀληθινοί)' and the faithful can trust them (21.5). As for the *apistoi*, those who fail in trust or faithfulness: with the cowards, the depraved, murderers, magic-workers, idol-worshippers, and all kinds of deceivers, they will be consigned to 'the pool of fire and sulphur' (21.8). Paul envisions the faithful as heirs of God, and siblings and co-heirs with Christ (Rom. 8.17 and 8.23, Gal. 3.26 and 4.1-7, cf. 2 Cor. 8.9).[88] At Romans 8.32, the God who gave human beings his own son will, eventually, 'give us everything else, with him'. The Lord is the firstborn of many brothers who will all be glorified (Rom. 8.29-30, cf. 1 Cor. 15.20). On his return, the faithful will share his victory (1 Cor. 15.57) and be taken up to be with him after the *parousia* (1 Cor. 15.52-7; 1 Thess. 4.16-17 and 5.10; cf. 2 Cor. 5.8, Phil. 1.23) into the presence of God (2 Cor. 4.14) for eternal life (e.g. Rom. 2.7, 6.23; Gal. 6.8). Christ will transform their earthly bodies to conform with his glorified body (Phil. 3.21, cf. 1 Cor. 15.52-4).[89] 1 Peter, similarly, celebrates the hope of those who are 'safeguarded through trust (φρουρουμένους διὰ πίστεως)' (1.5, cf. 1.7, 8) of coming 'to an inheritance that is imperishable, undefiled, and unfading, kept in heaven for you' until the end time (1.4-5). For the authors of Ephesians, Colossians, and 2 Thessalonians, those who trust inherit the riches of glory (Eph. 1.18-19, cf. Col. 1.26-8, 3.4) and the 'surpassing greatness of his power' which belong to the kingdom of Christ and God (cf. Eph. 5.5). In Hebrews, the faithful are receiving 'the unshakable kingdom' (12.28); for the writer of 2 Timothy, 'we will reign with [Christ]' (2.12). For Matthew and Luke, the faithful are invited to sit and feast with the patriarchs and prophets in the kingdom of heaven (Mt. 8.11, cf. Mt. 22.1-14, 26.29, Lk. 14.15-24).[90]

It is easy to read passages like these as expressions of uncomplicated confidence, and, on one level, their writers no doubt want them to be read that way.

---

[88] Whatever earlier uses of the phrase 'Son of God' Paul knew, he uses the phrase to emphasize Christ's closeness to God, especially in his death and future coming (Dunn (1989), 37-8); by calling the faithful also God's children and Christ's siblings, he underlines how high their expectations can be for their present and ultimate relationship with God and Christ. This language does not erase the difference in status between Christ and the faithful: in a Greek, Roman, or Jewish family, there may be many beloved siblings, and several co-heirs, but there will still be one head of the family and the eldest sibling takes precedence.

[89] The faithful will gaze unveiled on the glory of the Lord and 'be transformed into the same image, from glory to glory' (2 Cor. 3.18, cf. 4.4, 6) (see especially Holleman (1995), 161-99, arguing that the emphasis on eschatological resurrection as participation in Jesus' resurrection is Paul's own). Paul refers often to the glory that awaits the faithful through and with Christ: God has predestined and prepared them for glory (Rom. 9.23, 1 Cor. 2.7) and calls them into his kingdom and glory (1 Thess. 2.12), their current light sufferings are a preparation for a glory beyond all comparison greater and weightier (Rom. 8.21, 2 Cor. 4.17); whatever the nature of this glory, Paul treats it as aspirational and motivational. On glory as the presence of God in Romans, see recently Grindheim (2017), cf. Newman (1992); on glory as 'participation' by the faithful in Christ's messianic rule, see Jacob (2018).

[90] O'Neal (2013) explores how, for the author of Hebrews as for Paul, Christ brings all the faithful with him to glory.

But, visions as they are of a future which, from the human perspective, cannot be certain, they also ask listeners some searching questions. What, ultimately, do you put your trust in? What are the risks you run, and are they worth running? What risk is being taken on you, and how are you responding to it?

Trusting in Christ to come or return at the end time not only challenges the faithful to remain faithful, support each other, grow in faithfulness, and steward their master's resources in the interim, but also contributes to their understanding of who the Christ is in whom they are putting their trust. He is not simply someone who did something, however important, in life and was then exalted by God. He bridges the gap between the resurrection and the end time by continuing trustworthy. Just as God did not abandon his holy one, Christ does not abandon the faithful, in life, death, or exalted life.[91] It is very uncertain what, if anything, Jesus said about his death or its significance beyond, perhaps, that a prophet must die in Jerusalem (Lk. 13.33), but if he was remembered as saying anything more about the future, the affirmation that he will come at the end time forms another connection between his earthly and exalted life, acting as an assurance that what he said before his death was trustworthy, and hence that he was and is trustworthy equally in each aspect of his existence.[92]

So far we have been focusing on the trust relationship between the risen and exalted Christ and the faithful, but when Paul looks forward, he also occasionally speaks of 'trusting that' something will happen:

> If, then, we have died with Christ, we *pisteuein* that we shall also live with him... (Rom. 6.8)

> Since, then, we have the same spirit of *pistis*, according to what is written, 'I *pisteuein*, therefore I spoke', we too *pisteuein* and therefore speak, knowing that the one who raised the Lord Jesus will raise us also with Jesus and place us with you in his presence. (2 Cor. 4.13–14)

> For if we *pisteuein* that Jesus died and rose, so too we *pisteuein* that God will, through Jesus, bring with him those who have fallen asleep. (1 Thess. 4.14)

No doubt there is an element of belief in these affirmations, based on Paul's beliefs about Christ's death and resurrection, but he is doing more here than extrapolating beliefs about the future from the past. At 2 Corinthians 4.14, he underlines the strength with which he wants the Corinthians to *pisteuein* in the future by saying, not that 'we believe that the one who raised the Lord Jesus will raise us

---

[91] Morgan (2020), 44.
[92] Theissen and Merz (1998), 275–8 and Wedderburn (2013), 47–66 give balanced summaries of opinions with plausible arguments that Jesus did reflect on his likely fate and its significance; for recent maximalist views see e.g. Pitre (2005). Emphasizing the salvific activity of Christ in every aspect of his existence see e.g. O'Collins (1973), ch. 10, Moule (1998), 15–16.

also...', but, 'we *know*...'. He cannot, of course, know the future, and he is not literally claiming to: he is expressing the strength of his conviction, hope, and commitment to the preaching that the faithful will eventually be raised and saved. This suggests that the best translation of *pisteuein hoti* when Paul uses it (explicitly or implicitly but clearly) of future life or resurrection in Romans 6.8 and 1 Thessalonians 4.14, and when it is implied at 2 Corinthians 4.14, is 'trust that': propositional trust.[93]

Not only, for Paul, do the faithful put their trust in God and Christ, who make it possible for human beings to come to right-standing with God and ultimately to be saved, but, in light of that trust, together with their belief in the resurrection of Jesus, and probably their experience of what happened to themselves when they embraced Christian preaching, they are also able to trust that the God who raised Jesus from the dead will raise them. For the faithful, that is, propositional trust in the future is possible based on beliefs about the past and present, combined with personal trust in God and Christ.

We have observed that the kind of trust that is part of close relationships, for instance between lovers or among family members, facilitates the development of a shared and expanded world-view. The possibility of propositional trust in the future is another consequence of relational trust in the present. Because the faithful live in a relationship of trust now, they can look forward to a future that continues to be shaped by that relationship, with a confidence which those who lack trust find difficult or impossible.

This section has focused on the future coming of Christ, but even here the theme of staying faithful until Christ's return is often intertwined with advice and exhortation about how to live in the interim: with love, enacting the gifts of the spirit, and so on. Even if looking forward to Christ's return constitutes one of the earliest Christologies, the earliest books of the New Testament are already deeply interested in the restoration of trust between God, Christ, and humanity and what it means to live in a relationship of trust with God and Christ in the present time.

Trust in Cosmic Conflict

Some of the passages we have just discussed refer not only to the coming of Christ but to the cosmic conflict which most writers, in some form, envisage as ongoing in the meantime.[94] The vision of God as engaged in a cosmic conflict with the

---

[93] See further Chapter 8, *passim*.
[94] So e.g. Käsemann (1962, 1964a), cf. (1945), 10, (1952), 146, (1957), 24, with Way (1991), 124–38; Beker (1982), Martyn (1985, 1997a, 1997b, 2000), Middleton (2006), Adams (2007), Thom (2012), Grabiner (2015).

powers of evil highlights the riskiness and uncertainty of the present time, and, by the same token, the importance of being able to trust someone, and in knowing whom to trust. In 1 Corinthians 15.24–8, Paul's vision of Christ's triumph over every sovereignty, authority and power (v. 24) comes after the passage in which he has emphasized that the Corinthians have not trusted in Christ in vain (15.2–4). Christ was raised not least for this final battle, and his subjection of everything (v. 27) before his own final subjection to God (v. 28). It follows, for Paul, that the Corinthians can trust Christ to battle on their behalf of the faithful.[95]

At 1 Thessalonians 5.8 those who have chosen to put their trust in God and Christ have a supporting role to play in this conflict: 'since we are of the day, let us be sober, putting on the breastplate of trust and love (ἐνδυσάμενοι θώρακα πίστεως καὶ ἀγάπης) and the helmet that is hope for salvation…'. The Thessalonians must be vigilant, in case 'the tempter' puts their trust to the test (cf. 3.5).[96] Romans' 'armour of light' image (13.11–14) also looks forward to the conflict that will precede end time, without explicitly referring to *pistis*, but Ephesians follows 1 Thessalonians in making trust part of the 'armour of God' (6.11) in which the Ephesians play their part in the cosmic conflict:

> Therefore, put on the whole armour of God, so that you may be able to resist on the evil day, and, having done everything, hold your ground. So stand fast with your loins girded in truth, armed with righteousness as a breastplate, and your feet shod in preparation for the gospel of peace. Whatever happens, hold on to the shield of trust [or 'faithfulness'] (τὸν θυρεὸν τῆς πίστεως,), on which you will be able to quench all the flaming arrows of the evil one. And take the helmet of salvation and the sword of the spirit, which is the word of God. (6.13–17)

Both the breastplate and the shield of trust, together with all the armour of God, are defensive armour, not offensive weapons, so the Ephesians, like the Thessalonians, may be involved in the conflict, but apparently only defensively.[97] For the writer of 2 Thessalonians, the role of those who have put their trust in God and Christ in fending off 'the one whose coming springs from the power of Satan' (2.9) and, in general, the lies of those who do not love truth (2.10–11), is

---

[95] This is also an example of trusting that, for the future, as at pp. 118, 121. Bates (2017), 77–100, (2020) emphasizes the 'allegiance' aspect of *pistis*, which is especially strong (if not the whole of *pistis*, as he recognizes e.g. at (2018), 64–6 where Christ is envisaged as triumphant over every other power).

[96] The faithful also have to resist being 'yoked' with *apistoi* (6.14–16), on the grounds 'what accord has Christ with Beliar?' (6.15), but the boundaries of the community are Paul's immediate focus there (and e.g. at 1 Cor. 7.5) rather than cosmic conflict.

[97] Strawbridge (2015), 57–96. The *machaira* of the spirit is the short sword used for engaging and defending oneself at close quarters, not the long sword or spear used in an initial attack.

even less combative: it is to believe and/or put their trust in the truth (2.12) and 'stand firm and hold fast to the traditions that you were taught' (2.15).[98]

It is not surprising to find a connection between trust in God or Christ and cosmic conflict in Revelation, but we may be surprised not to find it a more prominent theme than it is.[99] At the beginning of the book (1.5), Jesus Christ is the witness faithful to God who rules the kings of the earth, and who will reappear at the culmination of the cosmic wars as the one 'called Faithful and True' (πιστὸς καλούμενος καὶ ἀληθινός) (19.11).[100] This figure wages war and judges (19.11), and also entrusts others with judgment (20.4). 'The armies of heaven' follow him (19.14), but these are probably supernatural forces rather than the human faithful.[101] Members of the churches to which the author writes at the beginning of the book are sometimes commended for trust or faithfulness in the present time (2.10, 2.13, 2.19, cf. 2.2, 3.8). In the writer's vision of the Lamb surrounded by the 144,000 elect (14.1–5), the elect 'follow the Lamb wherever he goes' (14.4), and this may hint that in their faithfulness they follow and imitate the faithfulness of Christ to God.[102] But following the Lamb is a reference to their relationship with the one who has ransomed them (14.4) in general, not to the cosmic conflict specifically. The role of the faithful in cosmic war is to endure it, remaining faithful until the triumph of Christ. In this, Revelation is broadly in line with most other New Testament (and later) writings that reference cosmic conflict.[103] It is not for human beings to take part actively, but to remain faithful and endure until they are saved.[104]

Another writer from the Johannine communities links *pistis* with cosmic conflict in slightly different terms. 1 John 5.4–5 tells listeners,

> everything begotten by God conquers the world. And the victory that conquers the world is our *pistis*. Who is the conqueror of the world if not the one who

---

[98] Cf. 1 Pet. 5.9, where Christians are urged to remain 'steadfast in *pistis*' in order to resist the devil: given the strongly relational language of vv. 6–8 and 10 it makes good sense to read this as 'trust'. At Col. 1.10, the role of the faithful (cf. 1.2) is to please the Lord with, among other qualities, endurance and patience (1.11), because God has 'delivered us from the power of darkness and transferred us to the kingdom of his beloved son' (1.13); the emphasis here is less on cosmic conflict than on triumph already achieved, as also at Eph. 1.18–22; at Titus 2.13–14, the faithful await the appearance of God and Christ and the delivery of the faithful from 'all lawlessness', but without closely associated *pistis* language.

[99] Unlike John's gospel or even 1 and 3 John, Revelation does not use *pisteuein* and uses other *pistis* language only a dozen times.

[100] Cf. pp. 219–23.

[101] Koester (2014), *ad loc.* notes that these could be armies of saints or angels; Charles (1975), *ad loc.* suggests that the heavenly armies are composed of angels and glorified martyrs.

[102] Cf. pp. 135–6.   [103] Morgan (2020), 167.

[104] Unlike the idea of coming judgment, cosmic conflict is little referenced to encourage people to remain faithful: so e.g. Rom. 8.38, 13.12, 16.20, 1 Cor. 5.5, 7.5, 10.20, 2 Cor. 2.11, 10.4, 12.7, Eph. 2.2, 1 Thess. 2.18, Heb. 2.8, 2.14, Jas 4.7, 2 Pet. 2, *passim*, refer to Satan to cosmic conflict or the triumph of Christ without referencing *pistis*.

believes/trusts that Jesus is the Son of God (ὁ πιστεύων ὅτι Ἰησοῦς ἐστιν ὁ υἱὸς τοῦ θεοῦ)?

Pisteuein hoti is usually taken to refer to 'belief that', and belief is doubtless involved here, but since the affirmation that Jesus is the Son of God cannot be objectively proven, and is a matter of life-changing commitment, we can also hear propositional trust in it. This letter moves several times between the relational and the propositional: when the writer speaks of the life and activities of community members, he writes of love, fellowship, family, and relational trust (e.g. 3.23, 4.1, 5.10), but when he is drawing boundaries and speaking of the conflict between those who do and do not belong to the community, he uses propositional language (cf. 5.1). He implies that, for his community, it is important to know not only whom, but what to believe and trust, and that what one believes and trusts, no less than whom, is a weapon in the fight against 'the world'.[105]

The idea of cosmic conflict with evil and the ultimate triumph of God and Christ is, in some form, part of the thinking of all New Testament writers. Not unlike children of trustworthy parents, the faithful trust that the God and Christ in whom they trust are acting for them, not only directly, in their relationship, but elsewhere, on a bigger stage. In the last chapter we saw that the trust between parents and children is very like that between God as creator (and Christ as, in some writings, the one through whom God creates) and human beings as God's creation. The same theme reappears in visions of the end time. The trust of the faithful not only affirms the restoration of humanity's relationship of trust with God, but looks forward to a time when they will be changed or recreated (e.g. 1 Cor. 15.52-7, Heb. 12.22-4, Rev. 21.1-8, cf. Col. 3.4). On judgment day, the author of 1 Peter says (4.19), 'those who do good will hand their souls over to a faithful creator'.[106]

At the same time, it is striking how few New Testament writings make much of the theme of cosmic conflict. Almost all are more interested in what the relationship of the faithful with God and Christ means for human beings in this world. Without saying so explicitly, they convey that the faithful need not worry too much about what is beyond their horizon, let alone their power to affect, but can focus on the human plane, the nature of the divine-human relationship of trust, and how trust changes human being and human life.

---

[105] The importance of what, as well as whom one believes and trusts is an early instance of an idea which will become much more important in later centuries, when orthodoxy is routinely used as a determinant of true faith and community membership.
[106] Looking back to 1.21, 2.23. Elliott (2000), *ad* 4.19b notes that the idea of God as faithful creator is closely related to the subordination of all creatures to God. God has given both life and new life (cf. 1.3), and 'as the power...to preserve those who entrust themselves to his care' (cf. 5.7).

The Exalted Christ as Mediator

We have observed that the connections New Testament writers make between the earthly and exalted life of Christ, and arguably also his pre-existence, form a theme which runs throughout this and the next three chapters. It is worth reiterating a point we have already made more than once, that the presence of these connections is significant in itself. Granted that human beings, in the ancient world, are not taken up to heaven at random, but always for some reason, it cannot be assumed, in Jewish, Near Eastern, Greek, or Roman mythology, that writing about them will give significant space to both their earthly and heavenly existence, or make many links between the two. All we learn in Genesis, for example, about Enoch son of Jared is that he became the father of Methuselah at the age of 65; he had other children and lived for 365 years; then he 'walked with God, and he was no longer here, for God took him' (Gen. 5.21–4).[107] This brief passage gives no hint of the rich and varied mythology which would develop around Enoch's heavenly life in the Hellenistic period, in 1 Enoch and the Book of Giants, and later in rabbinic literature.[108] In contrast, Genesis includes several well developed stories about Abraham, but it is not until around the period of the New Testament writings or slightly later that stories of his heavenly life and activities begin to proliferate.[109] Similarly, many stories collected around the name of Romulus, mythical founder of Rome, but very few around the god Quirinus with whom he was identified after his death or ascension.[110] The activities of Alexander the Great and the Hellenistic kings in their lifetimes were diverse and well documented, but their cults tended to simplicity: they were guardians and saviours of cities and pious individuals, and few stories circulated of divine epiphanies or other activities.[111]

In contrast to these and many other heavenly figures, Jesus Christ is remembered, from an early date, as active in his earthly life, as actively accepting his betrayal and death, and also as active in his exalted life, in some similar and some distinct ways. He also quickly attracts a significant number of titles (what gentile Christians probably thought of as cult epithets[112]), some, and perhaps all of which—Messiah, Lord, Son of Man, Son of David, Son of God—can, in early use, already be seen as referring to both his earthly and his heavenly existence and activities. Scholars of early Christianity tend, for understandable reasons, to focus on the diversity of Jesus' titles and traditions about his earthly and heavenly life,

---

[107] Transl. NAB from MT.   [108] VanderKam (1995), Alexander (1998).
[109] Levenson (2012), Adams and Domony-Lyttle (2019).
[110] Casquillo Fumanal (2008), Rose and Scheid (2014).
[111] A rare example is D.S. 18.60.4–5 (Alexander appears to Eumenes); see e.g. Boehm (2015), Kholod (2016), Petridou (2016), Jim (2017), Caneva (2020).
[112] It is normal for Greek and Roman divinities to attract multiple epithets, and the many epithets of the exalted Christ would not have been seen as unusual by many early Christ-confessors.

their varied sources and the potential tensions between them, but the simple fact of their existence and abundance is just as significant. Within a few years of the crucifixion, it was important to Christians to be able to honour Christ, and to attribute various activities to him, in every instantiation of his existence, and to make connections between those activities. With the possible exceptions of the brief letter to Philemon and 3 John, every New Testament text refers to at least two aspects of Christ's existence. I doubt one could parallel this complexity in this period in the case of any other Jewish or gentile figure with both an earthly and a heavenly life.[113]

Chapter 4 will consider the ways in which New Testament writers link the language of trust with that of Christ's mediation between God and humanity in his death. A few passages, however, suggest that Christ continues his work of mediation in his exalted life. Where the focus in passages which speak of Christ's death as mediation is on the new relationship with God which becomes possible for those who put their trust in (God and) Christ, the focus in passages which speak of the exalted Christ as mediator is on his relationship with those who have already put their trust in him. This testifies not least to the concern of early writers with the risks and uncertainties of the present time. Trust and faithfulness are fragile and assailable: always liable, despite the best efforts of the faithful, to wax and wane. Those who have been forgiven may fail and need to be forgiven again; to recover and reaffirm their trust.

For the writer of 1 John, the blood of Jesus not only has cleansed but continues to cleanse those who 'have fellowship' with God (1.6–8). He addresses community members: 'My children, I am writing the things to you so that you may not sin. But if anyone does sin, we have an advocate (*paraklētos*) with the Father, Jesus Christ the righteous. He is the expiation for our sins, and not for our sins only but for those of the whole world' (2.1–2). The reference to Jesus' blood indicates that human beings are cleansed primarily through the crucifixion, but 2.1 acknowledges that they may sin again as community members. If they do, they have an advocate in Christ, in the present and future. The writer also affirms that 'if we acknowledge our sins, [God] is faithful and just (πιστός ἐστιν καὶ δίκαιος) and will forgive our sins…' (1.9). We infer that one aspect of God's faithfulness lies in his enabling humanity's cleansing not only in the past but in the present and future, and, further, that Christ's willingness to continue to act as humanity's advocate attests to his faithfulness both to God and to his followers. Community members are not described here as trusting or being faithful to God and Christ, but it is strongly implied that the Father and Son who are faithful to them are beings they can (continue to) trust. The writer completes this passage by emphasizing another connection between Christ's earthly and heavenly life: community members are

---

[113] On pre-existence see below, pp. 136–7.

urged to 'know' Christ (2.4) in the present by living 'just as he lived' in his earthly life and keeping his word and his commandments (2.4-6). The Jesus who taught and gave his blood to cleanse others is the same Jesus with whom community members are in fellowship in his exalted life (1.3).[114]

A handful of passages in other books hints more obliquely at the same theme. The author of Hebrews affirms that the Son of God has purified human beings from their sins (1.2), acting like a high priest in his faithfulness to God and, implicitly, to his people (e.g. 2.17, 3.1-2). The brothers must respond with trust and faithfulness, and 'watch out...that none of you may have an evil heart of unfaithfulness, so as to forsake the living God' (3.12). The writer seems to acknowledge the possibility that the brothers, like Israelites in the past, may fail in their faithfulness: 'let us be on our guard while the promise of entering into his rest remains, that none of you seem to have failed...' (4.1, cf. 4.11). In this time of risk, however, the brothers can 'hold fast to our confession' about Christ (4.14), because 'we do not have a high priest who is unable to sympathize with our weaknesses, but one who has similarly been tested in every way' (4.15). They can therefore 'confidently approach the throne of grace to receive mercy and to find grace for timely help' (4.16). The exalted Christ remembers the trials of his earthly life, and his relationship of faithfulness with his people is such that he has compassion on them when they find themselves in need of ongoing grace.

At Romans 8.34, Paul tells the Romans that Christ, who died for the faithful and was raised, continues to intercede for them at the right hand of God. In 2 Corinthians, he hints that Christ's work of mediation also continues indirectly. Describing how his ministry conforms to the shape of Christ's saving activity, Paul says,

> We are...always carrying about in the body the dying of Jesus, so that the life of Jesus may also be manifested in our body. For we who live are constantly being given up to death for the sake of Jesus, so that the life of Jesus may be manifested in our mortal flesh. So death is at work in us, but life in you. Since, then, we have the same spirit of trust (πνεῦμα τῆς πίστεως), according to what is written, 'I trusted, therefore I spoke (Ἐπίστευσα, διὸ ἐλάλησα)',[115] we too trust and therefore speak (καὶ ἡμεῖς πιστεύομεν, διὸ καὶ λαλοῦμεν), knowing that the one who raised the Lord Jesus will raise us also with Jesus and place us with you in his presence.   (2 Cor. 4.10-14)[116]

---

[114] Cf. pp. 162-3.   [115] Ps. 115.1 LXX.

[116] Transl. NAB, modified. *Pistis* language is translated 'trust' here because of the suggestion that an act of *pistis* leads to inspired speech, but Paul could also be referring to his ongoing faithfulness. Cf. Col. 1.24-5, where Paul is 'filling up on my part what is lacking of the sufferings of Christ in my flesh for the sake of his body, which is the church...'.

Paul identifies with Christ via the singer of Psalm 115 LXX, who asks, 'how shall I make a return to the Lord for all the good he has done for me?' and answers, 'I will take up the cup of salvation...O Lord, I am your servant...to you I will offer sacrifice of thanksgiving...' (vv. 4, 7, 8), affirming that 'precious in the eyes of the Lord is the death of his holy ones' (v. 6). Paul thus identifies with Christ in his earthly life and death, and sees himself as continuing the work of mediation which was performed in Christ's death (cf. 5.19-20) by his ministry. Not only Christ's death, however, but also 'the life of Jesus' is manifested in Paul's body (4.10, 11). The genitive could be objective, referring to the life given by Jesus, but since in verse 10 it parallels 'the dying of Jesus', it is most straightforwardly read as subjective, referring to the exalted life Christ lives.[117] This parallel suggests that if Paul's ministry continues Jesus' work of mediation in his death, he also sees himself as continuing the mediating work of the exalted Christ through his ministry. Romans 8.34 suggests that that work includes intercession, and, indeed, Paul often describes himself as praying for the faithful.[118]

Christ is able to mediate between God and humanity not least because he is faithful both to God and to human beings and so worthy of trust by both.[119] Trust/faithfulness and trustworthiness are such well recognized qualities of mediators that we can assume that wherever in New Testament writings Christ is envisaged as mediator, or more broadly as acting for both God and human beings, he is also envisaged as faithful to both and worthy of trust by both.

2 Timothy 2.13 may follow Paul in affirming the double faithfulness or trustworthiness of the risen Christ. 'This saying is trustworthy,' he says: 'If we have died with him, we will also live with him; if we persevere, we will reign with him; if we deny him, he will also deny us; if we are unfaithful, he remains faithful; he cannot deny himself (εἰ ἀπιστοῦμεν, ἐκεῖνος πιστὸς μένει· ἀρνήσασθαι ἑαυτὸν οὐ δύναται)' (2.11-13). Since 12b-13 is in the present tense, it evidently refers to the exalted Christ. In the verses immediately preceding, [Paul] reminds Timothy of his gospel about Christ's death and resurrection, reminding Timothy of Christ's faithfulness and obedience to God. Verse 13 can be read as meaning that even if human beings do not die and live with Christ, it is the nature of Christ to remain faithful to God: human unfaithfulness does not nullify what God and Christ have done. Since, however, in his exalted life with God, it is also part of Christ's identity, as it is of God's, to be faithful and trustworthy to human beings, the phrase is productively ambiguous and probably deliberately bivalent.[120]

---

[117] Elsewhere it is God who gives life through Jesus: e.g. 2 Cor. 5.18, cf. Rom. 6.23.
[118] E.g. Rom. 1.8-10, 10.1, 2 Cor. 13.7-9, Phil. 1.3-4, 1.9, 1 Thess. 1.2, 3.10. Elsewhere, Paul is explicit that he understands himself as being 'entrusted' with the gospel and his mission by God, and as being 'trustworthy' in that mission, and speaks the power which he wields from God because of his relationship with God and the exalted Christ.
[119] Cf. pp. 153-62.
[120] The faithfulness of the exalted Christ, primarily to the faithful, is rightly identified by Downs and Lappenga (2019) as under-explored (though in seeking examples of the *pistis* of the

Revelation refers at 14.12 to *pistis Iēsou*, in what may also be a reference to Christ's trustworthiness or faithfulness both to God and to community members. In chapter 14, the writer has a vision of three angels (14.6–12). One flies over the earth, calling human beings to 'Fear God and give him glory, for his time has come to sit in judgement' (14.7). The second announces the fall of 'Babylon the great' (representing Rome) (14.8). The third proclaims that anyone who worships 'the beast or its image' will invite the wrath of God (14.11). 'Here,' says the author, 'is what sustains the holy ones keeping (*hoi tērountes*) God's commandments and τὴν πίστιν Ἰησοῦ (14.12). As in Paul's letters, this phrase is often translated 'faith in Jesus', but Sigve Tonstad has argued convincingly that what is referred to here, and throughout the book, is the faithfulness of Jesus in his unveiling of evil and his disclosure of God's character.[121] The elect follow the Lamb, Jesus Christ, (14.4), and their faithfulness follows his faithfulness. If Tonstad is right, *hē pistis Iēsou* is primarily to God, but it may also point to Christ's faithfulness towards human beings. This possibility is made stronger by the fact that at 1.5 and 3.14 Christ, as a witness, can be understood as faithful both to the human beings to whom he testifies, and to God about whom he testifies.[122] It is also the faithfulness of Christ to both God and human beings that makes his words 'trustworthy and true' (πιστοὶ καὶ ἀληθινοί) at 21.5, where he tells the author to write who Christ is, what he gives to his sons, and how he punishes the *apistoi* (21.6–8), and again at 22.6. Jesus sends his angel to call people to worship God (22.9). He also reassures the faithful, 'I am coming soon.' (22.20)[123]

In the last chapter, we argued that the relationship of *pistis* between God and humanity, through Christ, is understood, especially by Paul, as fulfilling God's promise to Abraham and, in some sense, both fulfilling the covenant at Sinai (because Christ is the *telos* of the law (Rom. 10.4)) and surpassing it (because it was added because of transgressions until Christ came (Gal. 3.19, cf. 2 Cor. 3.10)). This trust relationship needs no covenant of its own (and, we argued, Paul's occasional use of the phrase 'new covenant' probably does not reflect his own thinking). How does the image of Christ as mediator sit with this argument? In one sense, mediators act as instruments of trust very much as do laws, customs, covenants, and so on, making trust between two parties possible where it is difficult

---

post-resurrection Christ they underplay the well recognized role of *pistis* in Christ's death). They see Christ's faithfulness here (pp. 4–10) and elsewhere (like that of Godself) as to the faithful, but on its own this meaning sits oddly with 12b.

[121] Tonstad (2006): see especially pp. 159–93, comparing the structure and content of 14.12 with thematically related passages; cf. Boxall (2006), *ad loc.*, Harrington (1993), 152–3, and 1 Jn 1.9. DeSilva (2009) shows how Jesus' trustworthiness encourages faithfulness in his followers.

[122] In this book, though, the twofold faithfulness of Jesus is invoked not to explain how Jesus saves those who put their trust in him, but to confirm the strength of the divine–human relationship which enables human beings to endure faithfully.

[123] Christ's twofold trustworthiness gives the author's book such truth that God will punish anyone who adds to or detracts from it (22.18–19).

or fragile. The difference is that human beings are agents as well as instruments, and to act as mediators they must be trusted and trustworthy in themselves to both parties. A three-way trust relationship is therefore still a trust relationship rather than an instrumental relationship.

The richness of the language of reconciliation as it is used in both Greek and Jewish discourse, especially in public and political life, has recently been demonstrated by Cilliers Breytenbach.[124] His analysis points to a significant aspect of the trustworthiness of Christ to God and the faithful and the trust both have in him: notably, but not solely in the Pauline corpus. In the world of the early principate, those who use their *pistis* or *fides* to reconcile others are makers and leaders of communities; they end wars, resolve disputes, form and reform societies at every level from the local to the imperial. By speaking of Christ's *pistis*, New Testament writers identify Christ, in strongly social terms, as one who creates and strengthens communities. We can go further: the exalted Christ who has the *pistis* of God and humanity, works actively for the salvation of the faithful, acts as ongoing mediator between God and the faithful, and reigns until he has put all his enemies under his feet (1 Cor. 15.25), is a leader, military commander, bringer of peace, restorer, reformer, and overseer of communities. Under God and for God he reigns and rules, and those over which he reigns form the society of God's kingdom.

Further Activities of the Exalted Christ

Among New Testament writers, Paul and his followers are particularly interested in how Christ acts in relation to the faithful in the present time. At the right hand of God, Christ, with God, is a continual source of grace and peace for the faithful (Phil. 1.1, 1 Thess. 1.1, cf. Rom. 1.7; 1 Cor. 1.3; 2 Cor. 1.2, 13.13; Gal. 1.3; Phil. 1.1; Phlm. 3). At 1 Thessalonians 3.12, Paul prays, 'May the Lord make you increase and overflow with love for one another and for all.' Paul thinks of Christ as laying the foundation of communities of the faithful as well as being their foundation (1 Cor. 3.11). Christ welcomes new members into a church: at Romans 15.7, Paul

---

[124] Breytenbach (2010), especially 171–86, with 207–38 on *charis* and *eleos*. On mediators in Judaism in this period see Lightstone (2006), Balogh (2018); on Jewish mediatory figures as precursors of Christ, see also Grindheim (2011), 134–67. Davis (1994) identifies three types of mediation (from the past, e.g. via covenants made with Adam, Moses etc., in the present, and in the future) in Jewish writings, and argues that New Testament writings (following some, but not mainstream Jewish writings, especially about angels, and especially in the DSS) attribute all three to Christ. Against this line of argument see especially Bauckham (2008), arguing that Jesus is included by early Christians within the identity of God, rather than being represented in any way as a mediator, but this does less than justice to the language of mediation in New Testament writings and, more broadly, the complexity of their presentations of Jesus in relation to God.

encourages the Romans to 'welcome one another as Christ welcomed you' (cf. Rom. 14.1, 3).

For Paul, Christ is undoubtedly near in time, in the sense that he is expected soon. He may also be spatially close. At Philippians 4.5, Paul assures the Philippians that 'the Lord is near'. *Engus* can mean 'near' in place or time, but Paul's concern in this passage is with how the Philippians should be living: standing firm in the Lord's hands (4.1), rejoicing (4.4), and being kind (4.5), without anxiety but with prayer and thanksgiving (4.6), so that the peace of God, in Christ's hands, will guard their hearts and minds. (4.7).[125] Paul may therefore be thinking of Christ here as near in space, overseeing and taking care of the Philippians.[126] Christ's nearness in space is implied in a number of other passages: he can hear those who call on him (1 Cor. 1.2); and Paul portrays himself as acting ἐν προσώπῳ Χριστοῦ, 'in the presence of Christ' or 'before the face of Christ' (2 Cor. 2.10), and ἐνώπιον κυρίου, 'in the sight of the Lord' (2 Cor. 8.21).[127] At Galatians 5.4, in contrast, the state of having fallen from grace is described as being 'separated from Christ' (κατηργήθητε ἀπὸ Χριστοῦ οἵτινες ἐν νόμῳ δικαιοῦσθε, τῆς χάριτος ἐξεπέσατε) (cf. Rom. 8.39, 9.3).[128] Matthew's Jesus, in the context of giving the disciples guidelines about how to solve disputes in their assemblies, tells them that 'if two of you agree on earth about anything for which they are to pray, it shall be granted to them by my heavenly father. For where two or three are gathered together in my name, there am I in the midst of them' (18.19-20). This passage looks forward to the relationship of the faithful with the exalted Christ, whose presence, as is often noted, is imagined like the *shekinah*, the presence of God with those who keep the law (cf. Mt. 1.23).[129] Jesus' final saying in the gospel reaffirms the same theme: 'behold, I am with you until the end of

---

[125] This is a change of focus and mood from Paul's eschatological vision of 3.20-1; cf. 2 Thess. 3.3, where [Paul] asks the brothers to pray for him so that his mission may continue and he may be delivered from the wicked who lack *pistis*: 'But the Lord is faithful; he will strengthen you and guard you from the evil one.' Since the writer of the letter is following Paul, for whom, outside scriptural quotations, 'the Lord' is consistently Christ, we can assume that the reference here is to Christ and Christ's relationship with the faithful.

[126] Most commentators take *engus* as temporal, linking it with the age to come, but see Gnilka (1971), *ad loc.* and Fowl (2005), *ad loc.* (citing Ps. 118.18 LXX: 'the Lord is near to all who call on him'); Bockmuehl (1997), *ad loc.* sees it as both spatial and temporal.

[127] Cf. 1 Cor. 9.2, 15.8, though these may refer to resurrection appearances which do not continue indefinitely, while 2 Cor. 12.3 (if it refers to a different experience) may refer to an atypical experience of being 'caught up to the third heaven' (2 Cor. 12.3), rather than something any of the faithful might experience.

[128] Related to this may be Paul's view, in different passages, that the word of God (1 Thess. 2.13), spirit of God (e.g. 1 Cor. 6.19-20, cf. 14.15, 25), or Christ himself (2 Cor. 13.2-5, Phil. 1.20, cf. Gal. 1.24) is in the faithful. In these examples, Paul's focus is on the work that God, Christ, or the spirit do through the faithful (Morgan (2020), 110-19); 1 Thess. 2.13 explicitly says that the word of God is at work in 'you who trust'.

[129] Pirqê 'Abôt 3.3.

the age' (28.19–20).¹³⁰ In some passages, Christ also directs his apostles, especially Paul himself, as they serve him.¹³¹

None of the passages above says in so many words that these activities are an expression of the *pistis* of Christ, or the result of the *pistis* of the faithful towards Christ, but *pistis* language appears in proximity to most of them and it can plausibly be heard as involved in each case. At 1 Thessalonians 3.12, Paul has just said that he is praying to be able to see the Thessalonians in person and 'remedy the shortfalls in your trust' (3.10), so when he prays that the Lord will increase their love, we can assume that this is one way in which their relationship of trust may be developed. At 1 Corinthians 3.11, Paul has just observed that the Lord gave all the apostles, through whom the Corinthians came to trust, their ministries (3.5), so when Christ lays and acts as the community's foundation (3.11) he is also, through the apostles, the ongoing foundation of their trust.¹³² All the ways in which Paul encourages the faithful to behave in Philippians 4.1–9 are part of standing firm in the Lord (4.1), and standing firm, like enduring, is elsewhere related to faithfulness.

We noted earlier that there are few references to ongoing trust and faithfulness between Christ and the faithful in Acts, and the same is true of other activities of the exalted Christ, especially if the 'Lord' who tells Peter that all meat is clean (10.13) and confirms the teaching about his grace by Paul and Barnabas at Iconium (14.3) is God rather than Christ.¹³³ It is well recognized that Acts is more explicitly concerned with the activity of the spirit than that of Christ. That said, Christ is present, especially in the early chapters, in his name and power, by which the apostles baptize (2.38, 8.16, 10.48, 19.5), heal and exorcize (3.6, 3.16, 4.7, 4.10, 4.30, 19.11–20), and preach (4.17–18, 5.28, 5.40, 9.27–8), and on which the faithful

---

[130] The idea that human beings live and act in the sight or presence of the divine is shared by Jews and gentiles. In the scriptures, worshippers sometimes pray to be seen and heard with compassion (Strawn and Bowen (2003), Thomas (2009), Tracey (2015)); when God reveals his countenance to human beings, it is an assurance that God sees them and is near to give grace or peace (e.g. Num. 6.25–6); when God hides his countenance, people have sinned and are separated from God (e.g. Deut. 32.20, Mic. 3.4). In Greek and Latin myth, the gods are often imagined as overseeing the activities of human beings, and sometimes as intervening in them: see especially Myers (2019) on the Homeric gods. The 'holy ones' who call Jesus Christ Lord call on his name, in the confidence that they will be heard (1 Cor. 1.2), and the nearness of Christ also means that Christ is an active arbiter of right behaviour (2 Cor. 2.10, 8.21).

[131] Cf. p. 284.

[132] Tilling (2012), 137–54 sees the exalted Christ as active on behalf of the faithful in similar terms.

[133] E.g. Barrett (1994) *ad loc.* avoids specifying. It seems odd, if Christ is speaking at 10.13, that he does not identify himself or is not identified by Peter, and since the reference is to the dietary laws of the Law of Moses, it would make sense if Godself was interpreting them for Peter. When, however, at 18.9, 'the Lord' tells Paul, in a dream, not to be afraid of staying in Corinth, Paul has just converted Crispus the synagogue official, who 'came to believe in the Lord with his whole household' (ἐπίστευσεν τῷ κυρίῳ σὺν ὅλῳ τῷ οἴκῳ αὐτοῦ, 18.8); 'the Lord' here must be Christ since Crispus already trusts in God, so is presumably also Christ in the next verse. At 14.3 it is possible that the reference to the Lord is to Christ because the author knows Paul or his letters, but if the author knew Paul he also knew that, for Paul, grace comes from God, through Christ, except in greetings. At 27.23 Paul is directed by an angel of God.

call (22.16).[134] At 3.16, for instance, Peter says that 'his name has made strong' the man whom he has healed outside the temple, underlining that not only has Peter acted with power in Christ's name, but that the power of Christ himself is active in every such act.[135] At 10.43 Peter proclaims that, as the prophets bear witness, everyone who puts their trust in Jesus will receive forgiveness of sins through his name,[136] suggesting that forgiveness comes not only from God because of what God has done through Christ by his death, but also from Christ in his exalted life.[137] Not all these passages explicitly mention trust or faithfulness, but they all refer to situations—preaching, healing, forgiveness of sins—so widely linked with the putting of trust in Christ elsewhere in Acts, in Luke's gospel, and in Paul's letters, that we can infer that (mostly new or renewed) trust from human beings to Christ is involved in each case.

The most striking exception is at Acts 9.3-6 (cf. 22.6-10, 26.13-18), when Christ speaks to Paul to reproach him for persecuting him and give him a new mission: a mission which at 26.16-18 is specified as witnessing to what Paul has seen and will be shown of Christ, and preaching to the gentiles so that they turn to God and obtain forgiveness and an inheritance among those (the Jews) 'who have been made holy by the trust that is in me [i.e. Christ]' (26.18). Luke makes much of this unique story, no doubt, because Paul is a key figure in his narrative and the only one of the early apostles who had not met Christ in life. Thematically (though not linguistically) the story echoes both the way Jesus in his earthly life presents himself to his disciples and summons them to follow him (cf. Lk. 5.10), and Jesus' commission to the eleven before his ascension (cf. Acts 1.8), as well as acknowledging Saul's distinctive situation as a persecutor of Christians, and giving him his unique ministry. Christ can therefore be seen as calling Paul, as he called the disciples, to put his trust in God and in Christ himself, and as entrusting him with the gospel.[138] We can also assume that, in carrying out this mission, Paul must remain faithful, but Acts, in line with its greater interest in the expansion of the Christian mission than on the nature of life in the divine-human relationship of trust, does not say so in those terms.

---

[134] See e.g. Moule (1977), Stählin (1973), Menzies (1993), Turner (1996), Levison (2009), pt 3, Zwiep (2010), Tuckett (2014). Luke several times says that Paul, or Paul and Barnabas, are set apart for their work, sent out on their mission, or directed by the holy spirit (13.2, 13.4, 16.6, 20.22, 20.23) or God (16.10), where Paul might have said of himself that he was directed by Christ (cf. 1 Cor. 1.17, 2.4, Phil. 3.12, 1 Thess. 3.11, cf. 1 Cor. 16.7).

[135] As God is active wherever God's name is invoked, cf. 8.12, 9.15-16, 15.26, 19.17, 21.13, 26.9.

[136] ἄφεσιν ἁμαρτιῶν λαβεῖν διὰ τοῦ ὀνόματος αὐτοῦ πάντα τὸν πιστεύοντα εἰς αὐτόν...

[137] Ziesler (1979), 37 notes that the name is seen to be particularly powerful where faith is present, but thinks this does not mean that Jesus himself is present in any direct or personal way, at least if the background of such stories is in Hellenistic magic.

[138] Below, pp. 283-7. Pickett (2005) argues attractively that the resurrection is represented in Mark's gospel as a form of empowerment of Jesus' followers; on the relationship between being empowered and entrusted see pp. 305-10.

The grace, nearness, and oversight of the faithful by Christ are all additional reasons to trust Christ, and form part of the focus of these writings on the importance of the trust relationship in the present time. They also suggest that the relationship between Christ and the faithful is one of care. Like a good parent, or like Godself, Christ is envisaged as guarding and guiding community members, welcoming them in, building them up, and enabling them in their own ministries.

Living 'in Christ's Hands'

In a number of passages in Paul's letters and those of his followers, *pistis* language is used, including of the relationship between the exalted Christ and the faithful, in proximity to the language of being 'in Christ', which itself is closely related to Paul's language of belonging to Christ and God.[139] *En Christō* language, together with its relatives *en Christō Iēsou*, *en kyriō*, *en hō*, and *en autō*, is widespread in the Pauline corpus, much discussed, and has, over the past century, generated little consensus as to its meaning. I have argued that the phrase is used essentially in two ways: instrumentally, to speak of what God has done 'through Christ', by Christ's death, and 'encheiristically', to speak of the life the faithful now live 'in Christ's hands'—that is, in Christ's power, under his authority, under his protection, and in his care.[140] It is worth briefly outlining some of the main points of that argument here, because in the Pauline corpus life 'in Christ's hands' has good claim to describing much of the content of the trust relationship between the exalted Christ and the faithful.

One of the many locative meanings of *en* with the dative in Greek is the meaning which modern dictionaries, in many languages, render 'in the hands of'.[141] When something or someone is 'in the hands of' another person, divine or human, he, she, or it is that person's responsibility (*en soi* is the standard way to say in Greek that something is 'up to you'). Being *en* a person in this sense always involves an imbalance of power, but it never means that the less powerful person has no agency.[142] When one person is 'in the hands of' another, he may feel at risk, or that he is taking a risk, but the other may also be his best hope, or an agent of opportunity or positive change. Being in somebody's hands is therefore closely involved, like trust, with risk, fear, doubt, and hope. Last but not least, when one

---

[139] Below, p.132, pp. 174–5.
[140] Morgan (2020). What follows draws especially on Chapters 2-4.
[141] Including standard Greek dictionaries and grammars in German, French, Italian, Spanish, and English. The possibility that 'in the hands of' may translate very occasional instances of *en Christō* is (unknown to Morgan (2020)) suggested, though not discussed, by Talbert (2007), 36–7.
[142] *Entheos* also exists, meaning 'full of the god', 'inspired', or 'possessed', and is used of prophets, bacchanals, and others who are overtaken by a god. Greek usage distinguishes between being *entheos*, which implies that a god is working through a person, and sometimes that they have lost control of themselves (normally temporarily), and being *en theō*, in the hands of a god, which is not used to describe being possessed or driven out of one's mind.

person is said to be 'in the hands of' another, the situation is often a crisis of some kind; a matter of life or death.[143]

Paul especially, and those influenced by him, both in and beyond the New Testament, use *en Christō* and related phrases in both the instrumental and the encheiristic senses.[144] Because of what God has done through Christ, it has become possible for those who put their trust in God and Christ to be brought to right-standing with God and to live a new life in Christ's hands. By living in Christ's hands in the present time, the faithful are able to remain in right-standing with God until Christ's return. It is insofar as they remain in Christ's hands until his return that the faithful can hope eventually to be saved.[145]

For Paul, the present is a time of crisis, of decisive significance and unprecedented hope for humanity. *En Christō* language emphasizes that Christ is overseeing everything that happens in this time. The faithful have been chosen and called to belong to God and Christ, and their relationship with God and Christ is exclusive and permanent. They are in Christ's hands not (as they might be in the hands of a gentile god) for as long as Christ can be persuaded to favour them, but until they are, Paul hopes and trusts, saved on Christ's return. Even the dead are safe under Christ's protection: there is no power in whose realm the faithful are beyond Christ's reach.[146]

En Christō language forms one of the ways in which Paul and his followers explore and articulate the role of Christ as the new figure in their inherited understanding of the relationship between God and humanity and the cosmic drama of God's engagement with the world. God remains the creator, the source of everything human beings need, and their ultimate authority, but lordship and oversight of the faithful in the present time are given, through Christ's death and resurrection, to Christ, and are in his hands.[147] It is vital to this vision that the exalted Lord in whose hands the faithful live is also the human being who allowed himself to be crucified for others. His power and authority over others are grounded in his own faithfulness and obedience to God.[148]

The key roles of the faithful in this relationship are to remain faithful and to serve. They live for God and Christ, freed from sin, the flesh, their old life, or the law, in order to serve God and Christ. The value of their lives in Christ's hands, on the one hand, is the infinite value of human beings whom God has chosen to

---

[143] Morgan (2020), 17–20.

[144] Outside the pastoral, Petrine, and apostolic letters, which are all clearly influenced by Paul, John's gospel also uses *en* in what may be an encheiristic sense (Morgan (2020), 256–7). Løgstrup (1997), 28 uses the image of being in someone else's hand to describe what he argues is the inescapable dependence of human beings on one another out of which arises trust and our responsibility to be trustworthy.

[145] Morgan (2020), 90.   [146] Morgan (2020), 43–4.

[147] Morgan (2020), 245.

[148] This also means that, though unique in his role in God's plan of salvation, Christ is an example for the faithful: see also pp. 219–23.

sanctify through Christ.[149] On the other hand, their value is defined wholly by what God and Christ ask of them. The ability to serve is also sometimes seen as something with which the faithful have been entrusted: under Christ's authority, they are trusted to live and serve in ways which would be impossible without the intervention of God and Christ.[150]

Even for those who put their trust in God and Christ and live in Christ's hands, salvation is not guaranteed. It is possible for the faithful to lapse or to be led astray by Satan. The present is therefore a time of jeopardy, in which the faithful are accountable for their actions and relationships. Paul's and others' encheiristic use of *en* draws attention to their sense of the importance not only of what God has done through Christ and what the faithful hope for, but also of the present and what happens now; and not only on the cosmic, but on the human plane. If God's grace is to receive the fullest possible response, and those who respond are to be saved on Christ's return, then it is vital that the faithful remember that they are living under Christ's protection and act accordingly. This message of jeopardy is interwoven with a vision of the new life which the faithful live in Christ's hands. Just as the exalted Christ lives for God, so, despite the persistence of the world of sin and the flesh, the faithful already live for God and Christ as a new creation. Life in Christ's hands is therefore not a temporal or temporary condition, but an aspect of eternal life already active in the present age. This life is imagined as all-encompassing: a whole life lived in a multi-dimensional society. To be a Christian is to belong not only to a new cult, a new family, or a new school, but to a new existence. As such it is a very practical state of life, closely linked not only with Paul's and his followers' soteriology, Christology, and eschatology, but with their ecclesiology and ethics.[151]

It is apparent even from this brief summary that to be 'in Christ', especially in the encheiristic sense, is closely related conceptually to living in a relationship of trust with Christ.[152] When the faithful put their trust in Christ they put

---

[149] Morgan (2020), 54. [150] Morgan (2020), 245–6.
[151] Morgan (2020), 169–74, 246.
[152] Morgan (2015a), 304, suggested that *en pistei* and *en Christō*, in this and other passages, are close in meaning for Paul, both referring to being in the relationship or bond created by the *pistis* between God, Christ, and the faithful. Though both refer to the same relationship, however, *pistis* and *en Christō* language, at Gal. 2.16–20 and elsewhere, are better seen as expressing two complementary perspectives: God acts through Christ, which emphasizes God's ultimate responsibility for salvation, and God acts through the double *pistis* between himself, Christ, and humanity, which emphasizes Christ's active role in the process (Morgan (2020), 108). After the faithful have put their trust in God and Christ, Paul's *pistis* language expresses the continuity of their initial trust with ongoing life of trust and faithfulness, while the idea that they are *en Christō* reminds them that they are live under the authority and in the care of Christ. This treatment of the two ideas suggests that Paul inherited both and adapted them to express his own understanding of the new divine–human relationship made possible by God's grace (Von Dobbeler (1987) develops a similar view, though using the language of participation, arguing that, for Paul, *pistis* leads to participation in God and Christ and in God's community; Neugebauer (1961), 171–4 sees *pistis* as an aspect of life *en Christō*, understood as the existence that has been made possible by God's saving action through Christ, and though he positions his understanding of *en*

themselves under Christ's authority for the present and the future, under his protection, and in his care, even if they die before the *parousia*. Like living in a relationship of trust, being 'in Christ' is far from a passive existence. It involves active service of God and Christ, and living in the world and in the community of the faithful as God and Christ require. We can go further, and conclude that the encheiristic use of *en Christō* is one of the most important ways in which Paul and those influenced by him describe what it means to live in the trust-relationship with Christ in the present time.[153]

In an earlier section, we saw the exalted Christ mediating and interceding for human beings with God, in an extension of his saving action in his death for them. In this section and that on Christ's other activities, we have seen the exalted Christ, behind the apostle, laying the foundations of communities, welcoming new members, overseeing communities, giving Paul his mission, and exercising authority and protection over those who are 'in his hands'. It is tempting to see these activities too as reflecting activities and relationships with his followers which are attributed to Christ in his earthly life, at least by the time of the composition of Mark's gospel. In broad terms, there is something in this: both the earthly and the exalted Christ, for instance, exemplify love and care for those who follow him. The parallels, however, are only partial: for example, Christ in his earthly life does not oversee communities, and the exalted Christ, in New Testament writings, does not teach.[154]

The activities of the exalted Christ also mirror those of apostles, as described in the epistles and in Acts, and leaders of early churches. One concern of these writers in these passages may therefore be to validate and authorize the activities of apostles and community leaders by linking them with those of the exalted

Christō under an 'umbrella' of instrumentality, this too amounts to a view of the relationship between *pistis* and *en Christō* language similar to von Dobbeler's and mine).

[153] Since both *pistis* and *en Christō* language are common, especially in Pauline texts, it is not surprising that they appear in some of the same passages: e.g. at Rom. 3.22, 24 Paul uses both in proximity (*en Christō* instrumentally) as complementary ways of referring to God's righteous and righteousing act through Christ. Occasionally Paul uses *pistis* and *en Christō* in proximity in different spheres of their operation: e.g. at Gal. 2.16, a person who trusts in Christ is made right with God through the *pistis* of Christ towards God and human beings (below, pp. 157–8), but at 2.17 being 'in Christ' refers encheiristically to an aspect of the life of the faithful who have already trusted and been righteoused *pro tempore* (Morgan (2020), 64–7). Matera (1992), ad 2.17 notes that some commentators have proposed a locative interpretation of *en Christō* here on the grounds that the faithful are not only justified through Christ but are transferred into a new sphere of life 'in Christ'; their sense of the complexity of *en Christō* in this verse is surely right, though a different interpretation is proposed by Morgan (2020), 64–7, but Matera cannot be right in taking *en* as locative in this verse on the basis that in v. 20 Paul says that Christ lives in him, since the two are not equivalent (Morgan (2020), 110–19). In many passages, *pistis* and *en Christō* language appear separately, but both describing God's saving action through Christ or life in the salvific relationship with God and Christ. I cannot detect any pattern in these appearances which suggests that Paul sees them as in tension or competition. They are two lexica, both centrally important to him—not least, perhaps, because both were inherited—both of which he adapts creatively.

[154] Though the exalted Christ does teach in later texts, notably several of the Nag Hammadi writings.

Christ. Above all, however, Christ's continuing attention to his followers in his risen and exalted life, his presence with them, authority over them, and care for them, tell the faithful something about the Christ they trust, and what kind of trust they can have in him. The one who made the restoration of their relationship with God possible through his death does not leave them to maintain the restored relationship by themselves, but stays close to them, acting for them, and helping them to survive the risks of the present time. Pressing this theme a little further, we can see the Christ who, as he is remembered in his earthly life and envisaged in his exalted life, adapts his activities to the needs of different times, as an adaptable saviour: one who expresses his love and care for humanity in different ways at different times and in different circumstances.

We mentioned above that, in New Testament writings, the exalted Christ does not teach, as Christ is remembered as teaching in his earthly life. Nor does he teach in the sense in which gentile deities regularly teach, through oracles, dreams, and visions.[155] Between the resurrection and ascension, Christ is occasionally seen teaching. Matthew's Christ instructs the disciples to 'go, and make disciples of all nations' (28.19), while Luke's twice explains to the disciples how his death and resurrection have fulfilled the scriptures (24.26–7, 44–5).[156] Even in these passages, there is much the risen Christ does not say: he does not, for instance, instruct the faithful in how to worship or behave, or tell them how to respond to persecution or whether to undertake a new mission; nor does he, as gentile divinities occasionally do, appear to tell them that they have misunderstood their relationship with him.[157] One reason for this is probably that all early writers accept the continuing authority of the scriptures.[158] Another may be that Jesus is remembered as a teacher in his earthly life and his teachings are remembered as authoritative. It is notable that Paul's (admittedly few) references to Jesus in his earthly life, before his death, are references to his teachings,[159] while all the gospel writers and the double tradition record significant quantities of teaching material.

Imitation of the Exalted Christ

Those who trust in the exalted Christ are offered, especially in the epistles, an unsystematic but substantial picture of what this relationship involves. One aspect

---

[155] See especially Artem. with Thonemann (2020), and e.g. de Villiers (2000), Burkert (2005), Johnston and Struck (2005), Brodersen (2006), Platt (2011), Morgan (2013), Renberg (2016), Petridou (2016), de Jong (2016), Driediger-Murphy (2018), 51–126, Driediger-Murphy and Gayle (2019).
[156] Paul believes that Christ, at least on some occasions, directs his travels (e.g. 1 Cor. 16.7, 1 Thess. 3.11), but this is distinct from teaching.
[157] Morgan (2013), 16–19.
[158] Though not all continue to accept the law.
[159] Gathercole (2018); Riesner (2003), argues that Paul knew the ransom logion Mk 10.45, but its connections with the undisputed letters are fragile.

of it, on which we touched in the previous section, is the imitation of Christ. The next three chapters will have more to say about the imitation of Christ in his death and earthly life, but a few passages in Paul's letters suggest that the faithful can also imitate Christ in his exalted life.[160]

At Romans 6.10–11, having said, in various ways, throughout chapter 5, that God acted through Christ in his death to reconcile human beings to himself, Paul affirms that Christ died to sin once for all and now lives for God, 'so you too must think of yourselves as dead to sin but living for God in Christ'. This passage can be read as combining instrumental and encheiristic meanings of being 'in Christ': the faithful have died to sin because of what God did through Christ, and now they live under Christ's authority.[161] By saying, however, not only that the faithful are dead to sin because of what God has done through Christ, but that they must *think* of themselves as dead to sin and living for God, Paul tells them not only to recognize what has been done for them, but to follow the example of the exalted Christ by 'living for God'. At 2 Corinthians 13.4 Paul tells the Corinthians that Christ was crucified out of weakness (and implicitly out of obedience to God), but lives (and acts for the faithful) by the power of God. Paul too, in imitation of both the crucified and the exalted Christ, is weak under Christ's authority (*en autō*), but lives with him by God's power for the sake of the Corinthians. Elsewhere, the faithful should imitate the exalted Christ in loving one another (e.g. 1 Thess. 3.12) and by welcoming one another into the community of the faithful (Rom. 15.7).[162]

The accent in these passages is on Christ's faithfulness and obedience to God and the power that follows from it. By imitating the *pistis* of both the crucified and the exalted Christ, the faithful are empowered to imitate, on the human plane, his activities in both his earthly and his exalted life, not least by enabling others to place and maintain their trust in him. The Lord in whose hands the faithful live, as both crucified and exalted saviour, is the new paradigm for human life both in the present time and in eternal life, and by imitating him the faithful become more like him in his relationship with his Father and with the world.

Trust and the Pre-existent Christ

In the last chapter, we saw that several New Testament writings invoke the creation of the world in passages which are seen by some commentators as affirming

---

[160] The idea that the Lord is an example for the faithful is strengthened further in a number of other passages in which Paul tells the faithful to obey God, to endure whatever suffering their faithfulness brings in this life, and perhaps even to live as a sacrifice (Rom. 12.1; 1 Cor. 11.1; 1 Thess. 1.6; cf. 1 Cor. 4.9–13). Against sacrifice as Paul's main model of Jesus' death, however, see e.g. Breytenbach (2010), ch. 5.

[161] Morgan (2020), 81–4.

[162] Perhaps also by their trust, love, and hope, if 1 Thess. 1.6a is to be heard as referring back to 1.3 as well as forward to 6b–7. On Christ as a model of faithfulness in Hebrews see Marohl (2008), 125–48.

that Christ pre-existed with God and participated in creation.[163] It is debatable which New Testament writings affirm the pre-existence of Christ; the arguments are finely balanced and beyond the scope of this study.[164] We can, however, observe that in passages which affirm Christ's pre-existence, or arguably allude to it, it is likely that trust, trustworthiness, and faithfulness form part of the relationship between the pre-existent Christ and humanity as they do between humanity and God. *Pistis* language does not appear in any of these passages; it appears shortly before or after some of them (e.g. Jn 1.12, Phil. 1.29), but not specifically with reference to the trustworthiness or faithfulness of Christ to humanity in creation, or trust in or faithfulness by human beings to Christ as the one through whom they are created. Nevertheless, since God is affirmed as *pistos* towards humanity both in the scriptures and in New Testament writings, and a good case can be made that God is *pistos* not least as creator, where Christ is associated with creation we can infer that the pre-existent Christ is imagined as trustworthy and faithful towards humanity, and human beings as appropriately trusting and faithful towards him. We can go a little further, and infer that the idea that *pistis* is part of the appropriate relationship between the pre-existent Christ and humanity reinforces the hope of some writers that the restored relationship between God, Christ, and humanity restores, or will ultimately restore humanity to the relationship of trust in which they were created.

Conclusion

We noted at the beginning of this chapter that this and the following chapters on Christ do not offer a Christology of any one writer, much less a New Testament Christology. Nor do they claim that New Testament writings, between them, tell a unified story of the trust between God, Jesus Christ, and human beings in Christ's pre-existence, earthly life, death, and risen or exalted life. We have seen that some themes (notably the resurrection) are treated somewhat differently by different writers, and that some (Christ's pre-existence, the importance of imitating the exalted Christ) are treated only by a minority. We have also seen, however, several themes (Christ's future coming, cosmic conflict, the exalted Christ as mediator, the importance of the faithful remaining faithful) widely referenced and connected with the trust relationship. Inexhaustive and unsystematic as New Testament writings are, occasional and multi-focal, we can conclude that the

---

[163] Especially Jn 1.1–3, Eph. 1.3–6, Phil. 2.7–11, Col. 1.15–20, Heb. 1.10–12, 1 Jn 1.1–2.
[164] It is likely, on balance, that D-Paul and even Paul speak of pre-existence, along with John and Hebrews, though for Paul little, if anything seems to rest on the idea. Surveying the range of views see e.g. Hamerton-Kelly (1973), Hurst and Wright (1987), Habermann (1990), Kuschel (1992), Schneider (1992), 333–56, Brown (1994), 103–52, Davis, Kendall, and O'Collins (2002), Talbert (2011), Fewster (2015); Byrne (1997), Bauckham (2008), 26–30 in favour of pre-existence in Paul; Dunn (1989), ch. 4, Murphy-O'Connor (2009), 58–75 against pre-existence in Paul; Kunath (2016) on pre-existence in John.

relationship of trust, trustworthiness, and faithfulness between the exalted Christ, God, and the faithful is a significant theme of their thinking and that of their communities. Equally significantly, it is important to virtually all (very likely, in fact, all) New Testament writers, and presumably a wide range of early communities, to speak of trust between God, Christ, and the faithful in every part of Christ's existence.

In the last chapter, we saw that the trustworthiness of God and trust between human beings and God are typically referenced when writers (especially epistle writers and, above all, Paul and his followers) are talking about what God has done through Christ, and the new relationship which the Christ event makes possible between God, Christ, and the faithful. We also saw that both God and Christ are sometimes envisaged as caring for humanity in an aboriginal relationship of trust which human beings have lost but which the faithful hope to regain. This chapter, which has discussed a wider range of authors, but in which Paul and the Pauline corpus have also featured largely, has argued that the trust relationship between the faithful and the risen or exalted Christ is dominated by the twin themes of looking forward to Christ's coming, and concern with what life in the relationship of trust with Christ looks like in the interim.[165] In some passages, Christ is seen as acting with God; in others, as mediating between God and humanity or acting in his own right. The measure of the trust relationship between the exalted Christ and the faithful is the extent to which it reinterprets the past of the faithful and shapes their present and future. They trust in the exalted Christ for his role in what God has accomplished through him, for what he does now, in his exalted life, and for what they trust and hope he will do.

Multiple New Testament writings attest that the faithful can and do trust in Christ to come to save them at the end time. Meanwhile, Christ acts on behalf of the faithful in a cosmic conflict; he continues to mediate and advocate for the faithful with God; and he oversees the communities of the faithful in their earthly lives. The faithful live in what is imagined as a full-scale society under Christ's authority and in his care, and even when they die they do not move out of his protection. Just as Israel has long been a society with its own social structures, customs, laws, and relationships, so the community of the faithful is not an aggregate of individuals righteoused by trust and hoping for eventual salvation, but the renewed and reconfigured people of God in every aspect of its life and activity.

Images of the exalted Christ are well recognized as owing much to multiple near-contemporary Jewish visions of the Messiah. The ideas that Christ judges and saves, is engaged in cosmic conflict, and oversees communities, and that the faithful live 'in Christ's hands', under Christ's authority and in his care, suggest that early Christians' visions of the exalted Christ in whom the faithful trust draw

---

[165] Trust for the future is strongly three-place, but trust in the present has both three-place and, as a foretaste of eternal life already active in this age, two-place aspects.

especially on scriptural and other Jewish traditions about the kingly messiah.[166] In addition, writing in the world of the early principate and often for gentile audiences, Paul and other writers can draw on the tradition of honouring emperors, kings, and other military leaders as 'saviours'.[167] At the same time, they can tap into a strong strand of criticism, especially in the eastern Roman empire, of worldly rulers as untrusting and untrustworthy.[168] It is often suggested that Paul contrasts the righteousness of God with the unjust power of the Roman emperor.[169] He may well be contrasting the trust and trustworthiness of both God and Jesus Christ with that of worldly powers.[170]

In the following centuries, the image of the exalted Christ as ruler will, of course, remain centrally important to Christians. In the next three chapters, however, we will see how, in New Testament writings, this image is already complicated and nuanced by reflection on the trust and trustworthiness of Jesus Christ in his earthly life and death.

The role of the faithful in the trust relationship is above all to serve Christ, remain faithful, and strengthen their faithfulness until they are saved, in the process imitating Christ, becoming more like Christ in his relationship with both God and humanity, building earthly communities, and stewarding God's and Christ's resources. Chapter 7 will explore further the activities of the faithful in the present time, especially the idea which has begun to emerge here, that those who trust in God and Christ are also entrusted by God and Christ with work for God's kingdom. In this chapter we have also seen that writings which affirm the pre-existence of Christ suggest that Christ is trustworthy as the one through whom all things are created, and that the relationship of trust to which the faithful are restored is, or will be, a restoration of the aboriginal trust between God and creation.[171]

The exalted Christ is always (and, in the thought-world of the first century, by no means inevitably), identical with Jesus of Nazareth, who died for human sins. The proclamation of the Letter to the Hebrews could stand as an epigraph to New Testament writings as a group: 'Jesus Christ is the same yesterday, today, and

---

[166] This fits well with the argument of Horbury (1998) that the kingly messianic model predominates in the Hebrew Bible, is stronger in the Second Temple period than is sometimes allowed, and is a likely model for the exalted Christ and early Christ-cult (see especially pp. 31–5, 37–42, 56–63, 66–71, 109–14, 140–50); see also Witherington (1998), Collins and Collins (2008) especially 48–74, 101–22, Novenson (2012), 34–63. On Christ as kingly messiah in Hebrews see Bertolet (2017).

[167] Jim (2021).

[168] E.g. D.S. 10.34.2, 20.63.3, Plu., *Mor.* 152a–b, 522f, *Dion* 9.3, D.Chrys. 2.75, 37.12.1, 46.19.3, Philostr., *Ap.* 1.38.1, cf. Cic., *Off.* 1.26, Tac., *Ann.* 15.68, MA, *Ad M. Caes.*, 2.10.1 (Morgan (2015a), 87–8).

[169] Though for a slightly different view see Morgan (2020), 181–92.

[170] Harrison (2013) notes that Paul is as concerned with the difference between living under the authority of Christ and that of worldly powers as with the difference between living under God and the emperor.

[171] Cf. Johnson (2009) arguing that the resurrection should be understood as not only for humanity but for the whole of creation.

forever' (13.8). Not least, Jesus Christ is faithful and trustworthy as God is faithful and trustworthy, from the beginning of existence to the end time. In this continuity of identity, however, Christ is also adaptable: his activities evolve in his earthly life, death, and exalted life, as his relationship with those who put their trust in him evolves.

Pierangelo Sequeri has emphasized that trust in God and Christ is not generalized trust or belief in the divine, but is personal and specific: trust in the particular persons that God and Christ are.[172] This chapter has begun to illustrate the specificity of the trust between Christ and the faithful to the person of Christ himself as he is encountered and recognized. It is worth noting, however, that in this chapter we have not seen a great deal of light and shade in the relationship: less, for instance, than we will encounter in Chapters 5 and 6. When New Testament writings speak to the faithful of their trust and faithfulness to the exalted Christ, they exhort them to stay faithful and not to renege on their trust; there is a strong sense of the jeopardy of the present time, in which no one can yet be certain that they are faithful enough to be saved; but, outside the resurrection appearances, there is little explicit recognition that fear, doubt, or scepticism are much involved in *pistis*. The likely reason is not far to seek: the strong eschatological focus of most of the epistles and Revelation means that their focus is on what the faithful must do to be saved, while the apologetic historiography of Acts encourages listeners to focus on the church's successes.

The picture of the relationship between Christ and the faithful also tells us something about what the faithful entrust to Christ when they *pisteuein*. The exalted Christ is the Christ who will come to save; who seeks to ensure that the faithful remain in right-standing with God; who plans to bring the faithful with him to the inheritance of God's kingdom. The faithful entrust to him their safety and security, individually and as a group; their place of both service and honour in God's kingdom. By the same token, trusting in Christ expands the perspective of the faithful: inviting them, in their new life, to share something of God's view of humanity as something worth hoping for, fighting for, working with, and endowing with God's gifts.

In the last chapter we considered whether God is reliable, as God is often thought to be by modern Christians, philosophers, and theologians. We concluded that God can be relied on to enact God's agenda, but not necessarily to do as the faithful want or expect. The same is true of Christ. New Testament writings assume that Christ will always be faithful and trustworthy to the faithful, as well as to God, but they do not assume, for instance, that if the faithful fail to remain faithful, Christ will ensure that they are saved. The trust relationship is full of promise, potential, and empowerment, but it is not a guarantee that Christ will do

---

[172] E.g. (1996), 97, 378–88, (2002), 64, cf. (2007), 143.

as human beings want or expect. That said, the last chapter also argued for an understanding of divine omniscience, and in particular divine foreknowledge, in New Testament writings, as relational rather than propositional. God, we argued, can take the risk of trusting humanity because God knows God's creation. Just as a parent can recognize that her child, though a bit of a scatterbrain or a real tearaway, is basically a good kid, and be confident that he will come good eventually, God invests therapeutic trust in humanity knowing that it will probably fail repeatedly, but confident that, in the end, it will prove trustworthy. From a human point of view, therefore, the trust relationship may not be a guarantee—and it may be that for humanity to learn to be trustworthy, it is necessary that it is not a guarantee—while, from God's perspective, there may be great confidence that it will eventually come good.

We noted at the beginning of the last chapter that most New Testament writings have more to say explicitly about the *pistis* relationship between Christ and humanity than that between God and humanity. It would be an oversimplification to say that, for early Christians, trust and faithfulness towards God are expressed by trust and faithfulness towards Christ, but discourse about the divine–human trust relationship focuses strongly on Christ. No doubt this is partly because that relationship is new, and early writers are working out how they understand it, for themselves and their communities. It may also be because increasing numbers of Christ-confessors do not keep the law of Moses, but see themselves as directly under the authority and care of Christ.[173] Beyond that, the richness of early Christian depictions of the exalted Christ affirms that—and illustrates how—the faithful are in a trust relationship with Christ which is as complex, as far-reaching, and as significant as their relationship with Godself.

---

[173] This must have been especially novel to gentiles: e.g. tutelary gods of cities are not normally imagined as working constantly and on their own initiative on behalf of their people, though their support is often sought. Emperors may be portrayed as active on behalf of their subjects on the earthly plane (Saller (1982), Millar (1992), *passim*), but even where living or dead emperors receive cult, they are not normally envisaged as continuing to work for their subjects among the gods (though lesser divinities in myth sometimes supplicate to more powerful gods on behalf of human beings (paradigmatically Hom., *Il.* 1.496–516)).

4

'The righteousness of God has been revealed...through the *pistis* of Jesus Christ, for all who trust'

Trust and Atonement

Early Christians inherit from both Jewish and gentile tradition a wealth of ways of thinking about the significance of a death.[1] A death may be good or bad, heroic or tragic, accidental or the outcome of bad moral luck.[2] It may come as divine reward or punishment or express the complexity of a person's relationship with the divine.[3] Some people offer their death for the safety of their community; some are martyred for a cause; some are punished for transgressing a community's boundaries. Occasionally people are sacrificed—especially, in what by the first century was the distant or mythical but not forgotten past, children or the unblemished—to seal an agreement between peoples or between human beings and gods.[4]

We noted in the last chapter that New Testament writers pay attention to every part of Jesus Christ's existence to a degree that is very unusual. It is especially notable, given the prominence of the exalted Christ in early thinking, how extensively they reflect on Christ's death.[5] In Mediterranean and Near Eastern myth and history, human beings who were also divine, or were believed to have been taken up to heaven, sometimes died painful or degrading deaths (Osiris was dismembered by his brother; Heracles was accidentally killed by a poisoned shirt; Julius Caesar was publicly stabbed[6]). Their deaths are sometimes described and sometimes veiled in myth (Plutarch suspects that Romulus was murdered, but reports the official story that he was taken up to heaven in a storm[7]), but they do

---

[1] The chapter heading quotation is from Rom. 3.21–2.
[2] Bad moral luck puts a person in a position in which they cannot make a morally good choice (Nagel (1979), Williams (1981)). Deaths can also be functional and morally unmarked in antiquity, as when unwanted infants are put out to die by exposure (Patterson (1985)).
[3] E.g. Num. 20.1–12, Deut. 1.37–8.
[4] Stager and Wolff (1984), Castleden (1990), 121–2, Brown (1991), Smith (2002), 172–8, Rundin (2004), cf. Levenson (1993).
[5] In light of the resurrection experiences, it seems unlikely that the main reason for this is, for example, a need, in modern terms, to process the trauma of the crucifixion.
[6] Plu., *Mor.* 355d–358b, Soph., *Trach.* 734–806, 983–1277, Suet., *Caes.* 82.
[7] Plu., *Rom.* 27.4–8.

not normally take centre stage in the overall narrative of the earthly and heavenly life of the divine figure. Being taken up to heaven trumps death, sometimes to the point where a person is not said to have died at all, but simply to have been taken up to be with God (e.g. Gen. 5.24, 2 Kgs 2.11). In contrast, both the death of Jesus Christ and the manner of it have always been central to Christianity. The role of *pistis* in Christ's death is correspondingly significant for this study.

Early writings explore multiple models of the death of Christ, even within a single text, including sacrifice, ransom, recapitulation, expiation, offering, and example.[8] It is evident both that Christ-confessors were convinced from an early date that Christ's death was decisively significant, and that they found many ways of thinking about it fruitful.[9] Among these, one of the most distinctive was that God and humanity had been brought back into their right relationship by the *pistis* enacted in the death of Christ and human beings' response to it. The writer who makes most use of *pistis* language in connection with the death of Christ is Paul, so this chapter begins once more with Paul.[10] Paul links *pistis* language with Christ's death in a number of contexts, including when he is arguing that people are brought into right-standing with God by *pistis*, not by works of the law; when he is contrasting the foolishness of the cross with the world's wisdom; when he is speaking of the new creation 'in Christ'; and when he speaks of the faithful as sharing in Christ's death or, in their new life, in his sufferings. Beginning from these passages, this chapter will seek to develop a trust-based model of the significance of Christ's death. Like all theological models of human 'at-one-ment' with God, this will not be purely a reading of the texts, but an extrapolation from them which seeks both to capture something of the spirit of what Paul says and to speak to modern readers.[11]

Sin, Suffering, and *Apistia*

By calling Jesus 'Christ', early Christians invoke two distinct but sometimes interwoven Jewish models of messianic activity: that which saves a people from

---

[8] For Paul the crucifixion can be e.g. a 'supplicatory gift' (*hilastērion*, Rom. 3.25), an act of redemption (*apolytrōsis*, Rom. 3.24, 1 Cor. 1.30), ransoming (*exagorazein*, Gal. 3.13, 4.5), release (*exairein*, Gal. 1.4), or a curse (*katara*, Gal. 3.13). He evidently inherited a number of models, no one of which dominated his understanding of Christ's death; in all the relevant passages, however, *pistis* is a recurring theme.

[9] Studies of early Christian understandings of Christ's death and the models of atonement that have developed from them abound, and both their strengths and weaknesses are well explored: see e.g. Aulén (1931), McIntyre (1992), van der Watt (2005), with Stump (2018), 3–112.

[10] It is occasionally suggested (e.g. Martin (1981), 36–7, 153–4) that Paul's language of mediation and *pistis* is intended to be particularly accessible to gentiles, but cult-based ideas such as sacrifice and supplicatory gift would have been as understandable to gentiles as Jews.

[11] 'Atonement' is hyphenated periodically throughout this chapter to draw attention to its original meaning in English.

suffering or oppression, and that which enables their release from sin and guilt.[12] Interpretations of Christ's death, ancient and modern, tend to focus on Christ as enabling or securing the restoration of humanity's relationship with God through the forgiveness or annulment of sin and guilt. There are, though, indications in New Testament writings that Christ is also thought of as saving those who trust him from suffering—not only the suffering caused by one's own sin, but also suffering caused by others. In the gospels, a significant part of Jesus' messianic activity is healing the sick. A healing is once explicitly identified with the forgiveness of sins (Mt. 9.2=Mk 2.5=Lk. 5.20[13]), but it is striking how rarely the connection is made explicitly, and equally striking how often the emphasis in healing stories seems to be on the ending of the suffering of one who seeks healing, whether for him- or herself or for another, for its own sake.[14] The gospels also hint at a memory that, in his lifetime, some people saw Jesus as a potential political leader and deliverer from their suffering under Roman rule: a suffering which they could be understood as having brought on themselves, but which need not have been understood in that way.[15] The fact that Jesus did not become a political leader, and probably never saw himself as one, does not mean that the idea of his delivering his people from suffering was abandoned. Images of ransom, redemption, and salvation, meanwhile, widespread in New Testament writings, fit the idea that human beings need to be saved from innocent suffering as well as that they need to be saved from sin or guilt, while the language of mediation implies that God and humanity need to be reconciled but does not specify why.

It should not surprise us to find that Jesus Christ enables humanity's release from sin, guilt, and guilty or innocent suffering alike. The relationship between God and humanity is widely portrayed by early Christians as ideally one of love, peace, trust, generosity and thanksgiving, mercy and the acceptance of mercy, righteousness, freedom, hope, and joy. Experience, however, tells us that all these can be hard to feel or enact when we are suffering, whether we have caused our own suffering or it has been caused by others. Those whose love or trust has been betrayed often struggle to love or trust again. Those who have been treated unjustly or unkindly may cease to look for justice or mercy. Those who live in an atmosphere of conflict become hardened to it and pessimistic about the possibility of peace. Even when those who suffer long to be released from suffering, it can

---

[12] 'Suffering' throughout this chapter refers to the suffering caused by human sin (one's own or another's), not 'natural' suffering. On messianic models see e.g. Schürer et al. (1973–87) 2.488–554, Neusner et al. (1987), Horbury (1998, 2016), Novenson (2012), Baxter (2017), Johnson (2017); on messiah-type figures elsewhere in the ancient Near East e.g. Thompson (2001); on the spectrum of Greek and Roman thinking about saviours in this period Jim (2021).

[13] At Jn 9.2–3 Jesus' opponents make the connection but Jesus denies it.

[14] On the nature of the suffering that is relieved in these stories, however, see further pp. 250–4.

[15] E.g. Mt. 20.21=Mk 10.37, Mt. 27.11=Mk 15.2=Lk. 23.3, cf. Jn 18.33, Mt. 27.37=Mk 15.26=Lk. 23.38, cf. Jn 19.19–21, Mk 11.10=Lk. 19.38, Jn 19.14; see e.g. Theissen and Merz (1998), 537–41, Baxter (2017).

be extraordinarily difficult or impossible to release oneself without help. We should expect that a God who sought a relationship of love, peace, trust, and the rest, would act to enable humanity's release from either guilty or innocent suffering, if either might form an obstacle to the relationship.

Sin and suffering, both guilty and innocent, moreover, are often entwined, not only in messianic discourse and elsewhere in Jewish and gentile tradition, but in everyday experience and in discourses about trust. Most of us have had the experience of saying or doing something damaging to another person or betraying their trust, and feeling bad afterwards: if we have a tender conscience, we suffer for our wrongdoing. At the same time, when we say or do something damaging, it is often in reaction to something which we perceive has been said or done to us: we lash out because we feel hurt or betrayed. Something of the same pattern is familiar to psychologists investigating trust. Even very young children, when they do not feel they can trust those around them, can become both untrusting and untrustworthy. The perception that others are failing in trust or trustworthiness leads to withdrawal from relationships or antisocial behaviour, and withdrawal or antisocial behaviour in turn undermine trust.[16]

We can see similar dynamics at work in the paradigmatic scriptural stories of Genesis chapters 3 and 4. In Chapter 2, we noted that when the serpent induces the woman to eat the fruit he offers her the suspicion that God has told her not to do so not because it will kill her, but because it will make her godlike.[17] If she is influenced by the serpent's suggestion, she perhaps feels betrayed in her trust in God or hurt by God's economy with the truth, and reacts by taking the fruit. When Cain kills Abel, his offering to God has been rejected, while Abel's has been accepted (Gen. 4.4–5). Cain is angry and upset: he can see no reason for this rejection (4.5). God's response is to imply that Cain, unlike Abel, is being tested; apparently he cannot be trusted not to be sinful (4.7).[18] When Cain takes his brother out into the fields and kills him, we might infer that, hurt and resentful at not being trusted when he has not done anything wrong, he thinks that if God is not going to trust him, he may as well deserve it. In both stories what, from one perspective, is an aboriginal sin against God and a betrayal of trust can be seen, from another, as a reaction to a perceived hurt or betrayal of trust.

---

[16] Psychological models assume that children are born with the capacity and impulse to trust, which, for instance, a theory of original sin would not, but this chapter follows most New Testament writings in assuming that everyone has the capacity to trust, though people sometimes trust mistakenly.

[17] pp. 82–3.

[18] Wenham (1987), 104 notes that of the many explanations that have been proposed for God's rejection of Cain's offering, several attribute no blame to Cain; he notes further that 4.7 is perhaps the most obscure verse in the book, and as it stands is probably corrupt. Ancient commentators recognize that the text offers no reason for the murder of Abel and offer various explanations; I have not come across the explanation offer here in ancient texts, but speculating beyond the text is an ancient tradition (see e.g. Grypeou and Spurling (2013), 99–145).

When we think of Jesus Christ as giving his life for humanity, we should take seriously the possibility that his death is envisaged as making possible human beings' release from both sin and suffering, guilty and innocent. Specifically, in the context of this study, when we think of the relationship with God and Christ to which the faithful are called as one of trust, and when we think of that relationship as made possible through the *pistis* of Christ and *pistis* towards Christ in his death, we should expect to find that Christ's death makes possible human beings' release from the suffering which damages trust, as well as from sin.[19] We can, I think, go further, and say that a model of atonement which shows how the death of Christ makes possible human beings' release from innocent suffering—or, better, as we will see, the power of suffering[20]—as well as sin, is stronger and more satisfying than a model which shows only how Christ's death enables humanity's release from sin.

Paul has more to say about sin, and the suffering which sin imposes on human beings, in Romans than in any other letter. Romans is also the letter in which he speaks of *apistia* and *apistein* in connection with both sin and suffering, and one (together with Galatians and Philippians) in which he speaks of right-standing between God and humanity as restored through *pistis*.[21] Romans accordingly is our starting-point.

At Romans 1.16-17 Paul proclaims, invoking the authority of scripture, that 'the righteous one will live by *pistis*' (cf. Hab. 2.4).[22] The possibility for life-giving *pistis* comes through the gospel, which is the power of God 'for salvation for everyone who *pisteuein*' (1.16).[23] The gospel reveals the righteousness of God 'from *pistis* to *pistis*', which, we have argued, refers in part to the trust and trustworthiness of God which is answered by human trust and faithfulness.[24]

---

[19] The problem of innocent suffering is usually treated separately from atonement as part of the problem of theodicy, and the two are not regularly connected except in discussion of the innocent suffering of Jesus. Among recent theories of atonement, those that come closest to seeing atonement as releasing human beings from innocent suffering as well as from guilty suffering and sin are those of liberation theologians, but e.g. Gutierrez (1973), 263 argues that '[l]iberation from sin is at the root of political liberation. The former reveals what is really involved in the latter.' Stump (2010) considers innocent suffering and is explicitly linked with Stump (2018), but the latter focuses on atonement as the resolution of sin and guilt. Jegen (1989), in a brief study, explores reconciliation as release from both sin and suffering, though without discussing trust.

[20] Cf. pp. 168-9, 170-1, 182-3.

[21] *Apistos* appears in 1 and 2 Corinthians, usually referring to non-community members, but at 2 Cor. 4.4 it refers to those who actively refuse to put their trust in God and Christ. Paul occasionally refers to sin as disobedience (e.g. Rom. 5.19 using *parakoē* of Adam's sin, 10.21 with *antilegein*), and once or twice speaks of the 'obedience of faith' (ὑπακοὴν πίστεως, Rom. 1.5, 16.26), but he also uses other terms of Adam's sin, e.g. *parabasis* Rom. 5.14, *paraptōma* 5.15, *hamartanein* 5.16, suggesting that disobedience does not dominate his concept of sin.

[22] On Hab. 2.4 see pp. 42-3.

[23] *Pisteuein* should probably be read here as both believing in the content of the gospel and trust in God as a response to it.

[24] pp. 42-3.

Paul then says that the wrath of God is also being revealed against the impiety (*asebeia*) and unrighteousness (*adikia*) of those who 'suppress the truth by their wickedness' (1.18). These are gentiles, who have no excuse for not giving God glory or gratitude (1.21) because God has always made 'what of God is knowable'— including perhaps the *pistis* to which Paul has just referred—known to the gentiles through the created world (1.19–20).[25] They, however, were made fools in their reasoning (1.21); by claiming to be wise they became fools (1.22), and exchanged worship of God for worship of created beings (idols) in various forms (1.23). The gentiles' failure to worship God, including perhaps their rejection of God's *pistis*, has led to every form of vice, from murder to gossip by way of unnatural relations (1.24–31).[26] (These sins are enacted mainly on the human level, but verse 30 includes 'God-haters' (*theostygēs*) followed by two other terms, 'hybristic' and 'arrogant' (*hybristēs, hyperēphanos*) which are also strongly associated, in the New Testament and in gentile discourse, with the kind of arrogance and self-will towards the divine which invites devastating retribution and often death.[27]) And indeed, Paul continues, gentiles know that those who practise such things deserve death by divine decree. Even so, they not only go on practising them but approve of them in others (1.32), fomenting yet more sin.

Most of the vices Paul lists here, however, are not only sins, but also forms of suffering. Communities marked by greed, malice, murder, treachery, insolence, untrustworthiness, ruthlessness, strife within families, impiety, and the rest, are dangerous, frightening, painful places to be. The gentiles who need forgiveness just as urgently need release from their suffering.[28]

If, however, Jews think they are in a position to pass judgment on gentiles (2.1), they are not. They are condemned by their own standard (2.2). They are stubborn (2.5) and disobedient to the truth (2.8). They claim to know God's will and to be

---

[25] On knowledge of God a relational rather than objective see pp. 71–2.

[26] At 1.24 Διὸ παρέδωκεν αὐτοὺς ὁ θεὸς...εἰς ἀκαθαρσίαν is usually translated something like 'Because of this God handed them over...to impurity' (cf. 1.26), suggesting that all the sins that follow are punishments, but *paradidomai* may be better read more neutrally, as meaning 'surrendered': i.e. God let them go rather than consigned them to sin. Among commentators who tend in this direction, Dodd (1932), *ad loc.* argues that we should not take *paradidomai* as a judicial act by God; Dunn (1988), *ad loc.* that God 'hands over' responsibility for the gentiles.

[27] Cf. Paul's use of *asebēs* at Rom 1.18, 4.5, 5.6, 11.26. In classical Greek *theostygēs* means 'hated by the gods' but commentators agree that it must be active here (as e.g. the Vulgate takes it). Both *hybristēs* and *hyperēphanos* are used in similar ways elsewhere in the New Testament: e.g. the invitees to the wedding feast of the king's son (Christ) who treat the king's messengers with *hybris* are destroyed (Mt. 22.6–7); Luke's Jesus predicts that the Son of Man will be treated with *hybris* by the gentiles at the crucifixion (18.32); Paul speaks of himself as having been treated with *hybris* at Philippi (1 Thess. 2.2); Mark's Jesus lists *hyperēphania* with blasphemy among the evils that come from within people and defile (7.22); in Mary's song, God scatters the *hyperēphanoi* (Lk. 1.51); 2 Tim. 3.2 also links *hyperēphania* with blasphemy as qualities of God's enemies in the last days; and at Jas 4.6 and 1 Pet. 5.5 (echoing Prov. 3.34) God is the enemy of the *hyperēphanoi*.

[28] In light of our interpretations of Genesis 3 and 4, we might wonder whether the gentiles turned from God because they felt rejected by the God of Israel, but Paul does not speculate.

able to discern what is important (2.18, cf. 2.20), but in practice they break the law in all directions (2.21-5) or fail to observe it in the proper spirit (2.29).[29]

At 3.3 Paul describes the failing of Jews, before as well as after the Christ event,[30] as *apistia*, lack of trust or faithfulness (either translation would make good sense where Paul is talking about Israel's covenantal relationship with God).[31] He returns to this theme in chapters 9-11, where he says that some of the branches of Israel have been 'broken off by lack of trust [or 'faithfulness'] (τῇ ἀπιστίᾳ ἐξεκλάσθησαν, 11.20)'.[32] Israel 'pursued the law of righteousness' (9.31) but sought to establish their own righteousness rather than recognizing that righteousness has always comes from God by *pistis* (9.32) and now comes through Christ and trust in Christ (10.4, 8-11, cf. 14, 17).[33] When Paul speaks of some branches of Israel as having been 'broken off', he implies that *apistia* brings not only alienation from God but also suffering. For a branch to be wrenched off its tree means the dessication and death of that branch. For Israel, to be alienated from God is the definition of pain and grief.[34]

The idea that valuing one's own judgment over trust in God and/or Christ, for whatever reason, is both a disastrous error and a source of suffering recurs in other letters. At 1 Corinthians 1.18-23, one of the themes in Paul's praise of the 'foolishness' (*mōria*) of the cross is that God will demolish the wisdom of those who think they are wise (1.19, cf. 18) and show it for the foolishness it is (1.20).[35] It is not human wisdom but trust in God and Christ that saves (1.21).[36] 'Jews ask for signs and Greeks seek wisdom, but we proclaim Christ crucified, a stumbling-block for Jews and a foolishness to gentiles' (1.22-3). Here, as in Romans 11, Paul's imagery is evocative. When some people stumble over the stumbling-block of the cross, we hear in their stumble not only the sin, but also the pain of failing to trust.

---

[29] *Bdelussomai* (v. 22), which normally refers to idolatry (cf. Isa. 2.8, 20, Dan. 11.31, Wis. 14.11, Rev. 21.8), here probably refers to some less dramatic form of lawbreaking, since there is no suggestion of idol-worship elsewhere.

[30] p. 44.   [31] Cf. pp. 43-4.

[32] Or, even more brutally, 'by lack of trust', implying that Israel has mutilated herself by her lack of trust.

[33] Paul speaks in these passages of *apistia* in collective terms, but, since he thinks that individuals have a choice whether or not to trust (and not all do), implies that individuals have responsibility too.

[34] As in the case of the gentiles, we may wonder why Jews, who, as Paul acknowledges at Romans 10.2 'have zeal for God', sin, or fail in trust. Does Paul's attack on Jews who trust their own judgment about the law hint at some loss of confidence that the God who 'long ago...spoke to our ancestors through the prophets' (Heb. 1.1), still speaks to his people to guide them amid the political upheavals and increasing oppression of recent decades?

[35] Tilling (2012), 76 notes that Paul opens 1 Cor. 'in a way that expresses true faith in the one God as the relational commitment of believers to this God over against idolatry'; idols may include one's own wisdom as well as foreign gods. Even in the aftermath of the resurrection, both Jews and gentiles are still relying on themselves to know God (cf. 1.21) and discern God's will and the way to 'righteousness, sanctification, and redemption' (1.30), instead of answering God's call in trust (1.21, 24).

[36] Since the focus of the passage is on both God and Christ as the power and wisdom of God (1.24) trust in both may be implied here.

Though Jews and gentiles have arrived at their present condition by different routes, and though God's people are still and always God's people (cf. Rom. 11.1), for Paul, especially in Romans, Jews and gentiles have much in common.[37] Instead of recognizing the *pistis* of God and answering it with their own, both groups have preferred to rely on their own wisdom (Rom. 1.22) or knowledge (2.20) and judge for themselves whom they should worship or how they should worship.[38] Both have failed in trust and fallen under the domination of sin (cf. Rom. 3.9). Both are suffering in their sin.

Paul hints that his own wrongheadedness in the days when he persecuted the 'assembly of God' was also a failure of trust. At Galatians 1.14 he links it with his zeal for his ancestral traditions, pre-echoing Romans 10.2 and perhaps making the same point, that in those days he relied improperly on human wisdom.[39] The same theme in mirror image recurs at Philippians 3.9, where Paul no longer has (or, we may hear him saying, even aspires to have) 'any righteousness of my own based on the law', but only that which comes from God and through the *pistis* relationship between God, Christ, and the faithful. Living in *pistis* here is the opposite of trusting one's own judgment and seeking to determine for oneself where righteousness lies, which Paul implies was his approach in the past. Earlier in Philippians, Paul urges the faithful to 'have among you the same attitude that is also yours in Christ Jesus' (2.5),[40] who, though he was in the form of God, did not

---

[37] *Contra* notably Stowers (1994), and more broadly the 'New Perspective' view that Romans deals more with the incorporation of gentiles into God's people than the sinfulness of gentiles and Jews alike, and following e.g. Barclay (2015), 15.5. This is not the place to take up discussion of the New Perspective (see e.g. the discussions of Seifrid (2000), Bieringer and Pollefeyt (2012), Bird (2012), Yinger (2011), and pp. 57–8 n.102), but, for instance, it makes doubtful sense, as Stowers (1994), 100–3 does to read Rom. 2.1–2 as an attack on gentiles' passing judgment on each other, given that Paul's attack in 1.18–32 has been on gentile claims of wisdom in relation to God, not in competition with each other, but it makes good sense to read him here as turning to Jews as a group, since he can assume that Jews in general think gentile wisdom is wrongheaded about the divine. It is also beyond reasonable doubt that Paul thinks everyone, Jewish and gentile, must confess Christ to come or return to right-standing, and salvation, and by implication both groups are therefore in need of justification and salvation, and 3.19–20 fit unambiguously with this picture. This fits more broadly with Paul's use of the title *Christos*: messiahs characteristically save or reconcile human beings with God; Paul everywhere indicates that confessing Christ frees one from sin and hostile metaphysical powers; if Israel is not sinful, it is hard to see why Jesus should be identified as 'Messiah', rather than, for instance, simply as a missionary to gentiles.

[38] That is, they have practised inappropriate self-trust, relying on their ability to assess who is God and how to worship God, rather than trusting God to communicate what God requires. It is worth noting that many gentiles would probably have recognized this account of their religiosity, and, absent its negative value judgment, endorsed it: e.g. in the second century the polytheist Celsus presents as mainstream the view that ordinary worshippers are equipped to decide who is and is not a god, and who deserves worship (e.g. Or., *Cels.* 1.2, 1.5, 3.17, 3.26–9). Parker (2011), 2–13, 34–9.

[39] At Galatians 5.19 most of the 'works of the flesh', which people perform when they are not inspired by the spirit of God, are immoral; the exception is idolatry (and arguably sorcery), which again, implicitly, is the choice to worship the wrong gods.

[40] NAB, which does more justice to Paul's wording than most translations. Τοῦτο φρονεῖτε ἐν ὑμῖν ὃ καὶ ἐν Χριστῷ Ἰησοῦ is usually translated in English something like, 'Let the same mind be in you that was in Christ Jesus' (NRSV), which makes sense in context but treats Paul's wording slightly impressionistically. On the grammatical difficulties of the verse and the history of interpretation, see

regard equality with God something to be grasped. Rather, he emptied himself, taking the form of a slave...he humbled himself, becoming obedient to death, even death on a cross...'[41] Without taking on the dense history of debate over this passage, we can hear clearly that Christ's attitude to God was one of service, humility, and obedience; he was the opposite of arrogant, self-serving, or self-willed. Among Paul's followers, the writer of 1 Timothy 1.13 picks up Paul's language of *hybris* and connects it with both blasphemy and *apistia*, making Paul say of himself, 'I was once a blasphemer and a persecutor and a man of *hybris*, but I have been treated with mercy, because in my *apistia* I did not know better.'[42] Having *pistis* means behaving towards God as God requires. *Apistia* means trusting one's own judgment rather than God's about how to achieve righteousness, and, as a result, behaving with arrogance, blasphemy, and hostility towards God.

Paul does not tell us much about his state of mind before his call, except that he was zealous and implicitly arrogant in trusting his own judgment, but at Romans 7.14–24 he sketches vividly the mental pain and stress of life under 'slavery to sin' (7.14). Such a person is at war with himself (v. 23); he does not do what he wants, but what he hates (vv. 15, 19), and does not understand his own actions (v. 15). 'Miserable one that I am!' he cries out, and gives thanks to God for his deliverance from this suffering (vv. 24–5).

The *apistia* of both Jews and gentiles is broadly of two kinds: they fail to trust in God and Christ, who are trustworthy, and they opt instead to trust in untrustworthy powers, including both false gods and themselves.[43] It has broadly two

---

especially Martin (1998), Brown (1998), Morgan (1998), Reumann (2008), *ad loc.*, with the discussion of Bockmuehl (1997), *ad loc.* Bockmuehl proposes the translation 'have the attitude among yourselves, which is also in Christ Jesus', which fits with an ethical interpretation of the passage and Paul's use of the hymn in that context, but also refers to the present reality of the risen Christ as well as Christ Jesus' nature and action in the past.

[41] The fiercest debate in relation to the 'Christ hymn' of 2.6–11 in the past half-century has been over whether its meaning is ethical (as was commonly assumed before Käsemann (1950)) or Christological and soteriological (as Käsemann argued and many since have accepted): e.g. Thurston and Ryan (2005), Holloway (2017), favouring ethical readings; cf. Fowl (1990), chs 3–4. Christological readings since Käsemann's include Martin (1967), Wanamaker (1987), Dunn (1998), ch. 4, and Bauckham (1998). Bertschmann (2018) suggests persuasively that Christ's *kenōsis* at 2.7 is a model for Paul's own in ch. 3.

[42] τὸ πρότερον ὄντα βλάσφημον καὶ διώκτην καὶ ὑβριστήν· ἀλλὰ ἠλεήθην, ὅτι ἀγνοῶν ἐποίησα ἐν ἀπιστίᾳ. *Hybristēs* and *hyperēphanos* are also found together at Arist., *Rhet.* 1390b, D.S. 5.55.6, Rom. 1.30.

[43] *Apistia* is not linked, here or elsewhere in the New Testament (or, normally, elsewhere in Greek or Roman culture), with the kind of scepticism about the divine, widespread in the modern western world, which holds that human beings should take responsibility for their views and actions and not seek to defer responsibility to a higher power. This is not only because most inhabitants of the early Roman empire took the existence of gods for granted; they also, as individuals and groups, had little experience of the kind of material, social, or legal security which encourages modern westerners to value material and intellectual self-determination above trust in a deity. In addition, in a world without intergovernmental organizations, a universal declaration of human rights, or international law, it was effectively impossible for small groups or states to be autonomous or politically neutral: small states had some power to pick their allies, and even, occasionally, play larger states against each other, but ultimately they had, for their own safety, to be aligned with larger powers. This mindset is reflected

consequences: they are sinful and they suffer.[44] Paul's emphasis in these passages is on the suffering that comes from sin, but he also hints that the sinful cause suffering for the innocent. When he criticizes some people at 2.17–24 for constituting themselves 'a guide for the blind and a light for those in darkness' (v. 19), and teachers of the foolish and simple (v. 20), he suggests that the sinful lead the innocent astray. We should add what Paul does not say here, but implies of himself at Galatians 1.14, that taking a wrong view of the law may not be a matter of sin, but may be an honest mistake, in which case it may lead to suffering which is not the result of wilful sin.[45]

Within this outline, we can discern more varied and subtle failures of *pistis*. When, for instance, at 1 Corinthians 1.22, 'the Jews demand signs', they speak as though they want to trust in God, but because they ask God to send what they recognize as a sign, rather than simply trusting God to reveal to them what God chooses, as God chooses (1.21), they fail to recognize Christ and the proclamation of Christ crucified (cf. 1.23) as trustworthy. When the Galatians allow themselves to be persuaded to keep the law—perhaps more out of suggestibility or naivety than anything else, but against Paul's gospel (e.g. 1.6–9)—Paul implies that, despite their experience that their trust in his preaching led to their receiving the spirit (3.2), they have lost trust in experience to confirm which apostles are trustworthy, casting themselves instead on whoever preached to them most recently.[46] The gentiles' choice to worship many gods rather than one (Rom. 1.21–3) implies a lack of trust, not only in God, but in themselves to discern which god is trustworthy; as a result, they put themselves at the mercy of all kinds of false gods who are not trustworthy or 'true'.[47]

Paul's sketch of Jewish and gentile *apistia*, whether wilful, misguided, or naive, and the enslavement to sin and suffering which follow from it, will resonate with many modern readers' experience. The *apistia* of Jews and gentiles, as Paul describes it, is the misplaced trust of the gambler who trusts her system to make her fortune; the mistrust of the patient who refuses a life-saving therapy from his doctor. It reminds us of the person who puts his trust in a loan shark or a cult leader, and struggles to extricate himself from the relationship. It is the mistake that Jane makes, when she lets Hayley pressurize her into breaking off her friendship with Sarah, though experience suggests that Sarah is the more trustworthy of the two. It is the failure of most people today when we fail to trust

---

in the thinking of New Testament writers about *pistis* and *apistia*: not to be in a relationship of trust with God and Christ does not mean being intellectually or existentially independent, but putting one's trust in some other being, variously characterized as Satan, evil, demons, sin, or death. On sin and other powers as personified in Paul see e.g. Forbes (2001), Gaventa (2004), Williams (2009), cf. Brown (2015).

[44] This is not to assume that the failure of trust is the only cause of sin or suffering, only that it is one that interests us here.
[45] Emphasized more strongly on Paul's behalf by 2 Tim. 1.12–13.   [46] Cf. pp. 359–60.
[47] E.g. Rom. 1.25, 3.4, 1 Thess. 1.9.

environmentalists who point to the evidence of global warming sufficiently to reduce our individual carbon footprint. The consequences of failures of trust, of all kinds, are far-reaching. They put us in toxic relationships. They make it more difficult for us to see and respond to those who are trustworthy.[48] They make us behave in ways which hurt ourselves and others. They undermine our trust in ourselves and our sense of self-worth.

Potentially most damaging of all, where we put our trust affects our sense of how the world works. When we trust people, we tend to trust their values and (at least some aspects of) their world-view. We entrust ourselves and (at least some aspects of) our world-view to them. The linguistic link in English between what matters and physical matter well captures that what matters to us is material to us; it is real to us. The people we trust (and also the ideas and things, but our focus, like Paul's, can be on persons) matter to us; they are material in our world; they shape its reality. In toxic trust relationships, the assurance, for instance, of an abusive husband that his wife will never find anyone else to love her may seem more real—more trustworthy—to her than the possibility of making a new life for herself. To someone who distrusts the government, the media, or big business, a world of conspiracy theories shared in internet chat rooms may seem more real than what most people regard as reality.

All our trust relationships help to frame our sense of reality and what matters to us. The toxic relationships and worlds we enter by trusting the wrong people, or trusting ourselves misguidedly, or by not feeling able to trust ourselves or others, may be extremely difficult to leave, even if part of us wants to. We often talk about people who do leave them as having 'got out', as if a set of relationships and a world-view were a physical box or a prison, or as 'survivors', as if of a disaster in which others have been injured or died. For Paul, the world of *apistia* is a world which shapes us and our lives for nothing but death and destruction (cf. 2 Cor. 6.14–15).[49] We have to get right out of it: to die to it and live in a different reality.[50] God makes this possible for all humanity through Christ, and a key element of what makes it possible is *pistis*. One of the most distinctive contexts in which Paul uses *pistis* language is when he is talking about Christ as restoring

---

[48] No New Testament writer apart from the final redactor of John suggests that sinful human beings are incapable of responding to God's action through Christ with *pistis* (cf. the nuanced discussions of Barclay and Gathercole (2008) with the Introduction by Barclay (pp. 1–8), *contra* e.g. Wells (2015), 209–23).

[49] Not only for Paul: John's gospel consistently links *apistia* with sin and the inability to receive eternal life (e.g. Siker (2020), 87–104); cf. 1 Tim. 5.8, Tit. 1.15, Heb. 3.8, 3.12, 1 Pet. 2.7, Rev. 21.8.

[50] In passages which are not about atonement Paul can offer a more practical, pragmatic, and perhaps charitable or optimistic approach to those without trust: e.g. 1 Cor. 7.12–15, where *apistoi* who are family members of the faithful may be 'made holy' by their association with community members and should remain part of their Christian families. At 14.22–4, Paul urges the Corinthians not to speak in tongues, because speaking what appears to be gibberish is liable to put off any *apistos* who come to a meeting of the church; instead they should concentrate on prophecy, which is more liable to convince non-community members that 'God is really in your midst' (14.25).

life-giving, saving trust between God and humanity, so to these passages we turn next.[51]

Pistis and Reconciliation

At Romans 5.10 Paul says that 'we were reconciled to God (κατηλλάγημεν τῷ θεῷ) through the death of his son' and that this reconciliation, which is also identified with being made right with God (5.1, 5.9), having peace with God (5.1), standing in grace (5.2), and living in hope of salvation and glory (5.2, 5.9), comes about through *pistis* (5.1).[52] Paul has just referred (5.1) to the trust human beings put in 'the one who raised Jesus our Lord from the dead' (4.24) so *pistis* here is most readily heard as human trust in God, but at 3.21-6 he has used *pistis*, together with *dikaiosynē* and *charis*, in a more complex configuration to proclaim what God has done through Christ.[53]

Paul has been claiming that Jews and gentiles alike are impious and under sin and suffering (e.g. 1.18, 3.9-10, cf. 2.1), and at 3.3 has said that some Jews have

---

[51] It is worth mentioning in this context Paul's much debated exhortation to the Galatians not to turn back to slavery to τὰ στοιχεῖα τοῦ κόσμου (Gal. 4.3, cf. 9). Discussion of this phrase has sometimes been made more difficult by the assumption that these entities, whatever they are, must primarily be things to which the Galatians used to be enslaved as gentiles, and only 'at least to a certain extent... equivalent to being ὑπὸ νόμον (4.5)' (Roth (2014), 2, cf. e.g. de Boer (2007), 213, Woyke (2008), Martin (2018)). But Paul says that an under-age heir, under the supervision of *epitropoi* etc., is like a slave, and, in his first mention of the phrase, he says, 'in the same way we too [or 'even we', i.e. Jews], when we were infants, were under τὰ στοιχεῖα τοῦ κόσμου', but then God sent his son to ransom those under the law so 'so we might receive adoption', that is, be treated like heirs, no longer slaves (cf. 3.23-6). Being under the law clearly *is* being under τὰ στοιχεῖα τοῦ κόσμου. The Galatians have come to know God (through Paul's preaching, according to which they do not need to follow the law), but now they are turning back to the *stoicheia*, for instance by keeping (presumably) whatever cultic calendar they kept before. Paul's point must be that the law, like the worship of other gods, is part of the 'sphere of human activity which is temporary and passing away' (Bandstra (1964), 55), and cannot in itself bring salvation (cf. e.g. Roth (2014), with a thorough discussion of past interpretations), which puts the argument of 4.1-11 well in line with that of chs 2-3. If, as some commentators argue (e.g. Davies, Meyer, and Aune (1981), Wessels (1992), Trebilco (1991), 137, 243 n. 49, Mitchell (1993), 5), some of Paul's converts were godfearers or Jews, Paul could also be referring to them as turning back to the *stoicheia*—in which case both the scale of Paul's criticism of the law and his references to himself as a (formerly) paradigmatic law-keeper have even more point.

[52] Cf. 2 Cor. 5.18: although there is no *pistis* language in these verses, we noted in the last chapter that, for Paul, being 'in Christ' in the encheiristic sense amounts to a description of what it means to be in a *pistis* relationship with God and Christ: Christ's act of reconciliation makes it possible for human beings to trust (cf. 4.13) and makes possible the new relationship of trust in which the they live (cf. 1.24). On Paul's reconciliation language and reconciliation as a model of atonement, see notably Taylor (1946), Stuhlmacher (1979, 1983, 1986), 1-15, Martin (1981), Thrall (1982), Hultgren (1987), 43-4, Gunton (1995), 118-25, Moule (1998), 1-18, Hales (2012); *contra* see Käsemann (1971) with the critique of Martin (1981), 71-9; on atonement as the overcoming of alienation (closely related to *apistia*) and restoration of relationship in Paul see Moule (1982), 250-60; on the relationship between various early models of atonement, including mediation revelation, and exemplarity, all discussed here, see Slusser (1983).

[53] This passage, with its close relatives at Gal. 2.15-21 and Phil. 3.7-11, is discussed at greater length in Morgan (2015a), 267-74, 288-94, 302-4.

been *apistos*.⁵⁴ Despite God's unique relationship with Israel, there is, at this moment, no distinction between Jews and gentiles in their standing before God (3.22–3).⁵⁵ God, however, remains *pistos*, specifically towards Israel (3.3) and implicitly towards everyone.⁵⁶ God's righteousness is revealed in the gospel 'from *pistis* to *pistis*', which, we have noted, suggests that *pistis* belongs first to God and eventually to human beings too.⁵⁷ Paul also affirms that when the people of Israel are in their right relationship with God they have *pistis*; he says that he has been sent to bring about the 'obedience of *pistis*' among the gentiles too (1.5⁵⁸); and at Romans 1.12, as in many other passages, he describes Christ-confessors as having *pistis*. At 3.21–6 he turns to Christ's role in the process by which human beings return to right-standing with God, employing several phrases which he likely inherited and which lie outside the scope of this discussion, but also using *pistis* language three times.

God's gracious righteousness has been revealed 'apart from the law' (3.21, cf. 24), διὰ πίστεως Ἰησοῦ Χριστοῦ (3.22) for all who trust (which again may refer to trust in God, Christ, or both⁵⁹), through the death of Christ (however that is understood). Debate about the meaning of the phrase διὰ πίστεως Ἰησοῦ Χριστοῦ, here and at Galatians 2.16 and Philippians 3.9, has focused on whether it refers to the faithfulness of Christ to God, or the trust or 'faith' which human beings put in Christ. *Roman Faith* argued that Paul's meaning encompasses both of these, exploiting the fact that *pistis* is an 'action nominal', a noun which describes both ends of a relationship in complementary terms,⁶⁰ together with the fact that Paul understands Christ, in general, as being in relationship both with God and with human beings, and his position 'between' God and humanity, in relationship with both, as a crucial aspect of the new relationship between God and humanity.

Paul has affirmed the *pistis* of God (3.3) and now affirms that the renewed possibility of right-standing with God is a manifestation of God's righteousness (3.21). Whatever has happened through *pistis Christou* is God's initiative; at the same time, it is clear that human beings must actively trust in order to be made right with God (3.22, 26). What of the role of Christ?

In this and other letters, Paul assumes that Christ's obedience to God and death are undertaken freely.⁶¹ If God does not determine that Christ will die, however,

---

⁵⁴ Above, pp. 43–4.   ⁵⁵ Cf. pp. 45–6.   ⁵⁶ pp. 42–5.   ⁵⁷ pp. 42–3.
⁵⁸ Taking this with most commentators as a subjective genitive. Cranfield (1975), *ad loc.* offers a list and discussion of possible alternatives, and Dunn (1988), *ad loc.* discusses the history of interpretation.
⁵⁹ This reference is normally taken as to trust in Christ, but given that gentiles must come to trust in God too, we should probably hear both as involved.
⁶⁰ Morgan (2015a), 31, 53, 263 n. 7, 273. *Charis* is another action nominal whose two-endedness is exploited by Paul.
⁶¹ Cf. Rom. 5.6–7, Gal. 2.20, Phil. 2.6–7. On Christ's willingness to suffer and die elsewhere see e.g. Mk 10.43–5=Mt. 20.26–8, Mt. 26.39=Mk 14.36=Lk. 22.42, Jn 12.26–7 with Brown (1966), *ad loc.* For the author of Hebrews, Christ's faithfulness to God is that of a son of the house (3.6), whose loyalty to his father is presumed by their relationship but must also be enacted; in 1 Peter, the faithful are urged

he might, for instance, assume, wager, hope, trust, or know that he will be willing to die.[62] Assuming that, to adapt Einstein's phrase, God does not play dice with humanity, it seems frivolous to suggest that atonement might rest on an assumption or a wager. It might, though, rest on a relationship of trust, itself based on personal knowledge, between God and Christ (which might, as we have seen elsewhere, also have aspects of hope). As many commentators have argued in recent years, it makes good sense of Christ's willingness to die for humanity to see it as an expression of his active faithfulness towards God and trust in God's new initiative towards humanity.[63] If, moreover, we assume that *pistis Christou* at 3.22 refers to the trust of those who put their trust in Christ rather than the action of Christ himself, then Christ plays no active role in Paul's account of justification in this passage. It makes for a richer and more satisfying reading, and one which fits better with Paul's view elsewhere (and that of other writers) that Christ does play an active role in divine–human at-one-ment, to take *pistis Christou* here as referring to both Christ's trustworthiness by God and his trust/faithfulness towards God. This yields a grammatically and semantically unproblematic reading of 3.22 that the righteousness of God has been manifested through God's trust in Jesus Christ to be faithful to God,[64] together with Jesus Christ's trust/faithfulness towards God, to enable the possibility of human righteousing through his self-giving death.[65]

This, however, does not capture everything that is needed for human beings to be made right with God by putting their trust in Christ. If God acts for humanity through Christ, with whom he is in a relationship of mutual trust and faithfulness, that might be a reason for people to trust in God, but it is not necessarily a reason for people to put their trust in Christ, separately and in addition to trusting God. Even less is it sufficient reason to affirm what Paul unambiguously affirms, that it is trust in *Christ* that justifies. It seems clear, here and elsewhere, that Paul and others envisage the faithful as having a strong and life-changing

---

to let themselves be built up into a spiritual house in imitation of the 'living stone' Jesus Christ (2.4–5). Even sacrificial victims in mainstream cult were taken to assent to their sacrifice (Burkert (1966); few have followed Naiden (2007) in disagreeing).

[62] In the relational sense of knowing.

[63] See especially Hooker (1990), ch. 14, Hays (2002), ch. 4; on the history of the debate see e.g. Easter (2010), Kugler (2016). Stowers (1989) argues, against what he acknowledges as the consensus, that there is a difference (at Rom. 3.30 and by implication elsewhere) between gentiles' being righteoused *dia pisteōs Christou Iēsou* and Jews and gentiles together *ek pisteōs* (citing Rom. 11.36 and 1 Cor 11.12 in comparison), but Paul speaks of himself as righteoused *dia pisteōs* at Phil. 3.9, and in other passages *dia* and *ek* are interchanged almost certainly for stylistic *variatio*, so the majority view is surely right.

[64] Cf. Rom. 5.6–7; God also entrusts Paul and the Jews with his plans for humanity, e.g. Rom. 3.2, 1 Thess. 2.4.

[65] As a willing collaborator he does more than simply obey, but when Paul speaks of the crucifixion he tends to emphasize the humanity of Christ (e.g. 1 Cor. 15.3–4, 21), his self-emptying and subordination (Phil 2.7–8), and distinguishes Christ's 'gracious gift' from God's own grace (Rom. 5.15), rather than suggesting that as God's son or God's wisdom Christ knew what his death would achieve.

pistis relationship with Christ in his own right. This too makes good sense, if we envisage that, in parallel with God's trust in Christ to 'die for the ungodly' (Rom. 5.6), Christ must trust human beings to respond to his death by putting their trust in him.[66] He cannot compel them to do so, and it is hard to see how human repentance, the desire to die to sin, or the desire to be part of God's kingdom would be of any value to God, Christ, or the faithful themselves if it were forced. Christ therefore seeks a relationship of trust with human beings, in which he trusts them to respond to God's action through him, and they trust him as faithful in his actions both towards God and towards them. As for the trust that human beings put in Christ, Paul is explicit at Romans 3.26 and elsewhere (e.g. Gal. 2.16, cf. 3.13–14) that human beings trust in God, Christ, or both, to be made right with God.[67]

This double nexus of trust, between God and Christ and Christ and humanity, is what makes it possible for human beings to return to right-standing with God through Christ. As one without sin (2 Cor. 5.21) in a world in which all have sinned (Rom. 3.23), Christ is uniquely trusting towards God and worthy of divine trust.[68] By the same token he is uniquely trustworthy towards human beings and worthy of their trust.[69] The trust between God and Christ makes it possible for Christ to be faithful to God even to death and offers a vehicle for God's grace. The trust between Christ and human beings makes it possible for human beings to trust that Christ has acted for them and for Christ to trust them to respond to his actions and God's actions through him. Through this double bond of trust and trustworthiness—which is slightly laborious to describe, but simple and intuitive to understand—not only right-standing but trust itself is restored between humanity and God. To this nexus we should add one further element, which remains implicit but which we have argued must underlie it all: God's therapeutic trust in humanity to be able to respond, immediately or eventually, to the revelation of God's righteousness and trustworthiness through Christ.[70]

---

[66] Furnish (1993), 109–10, 113–17, points out that when Paul refers to Christ as giving himself up or being given up, the verb *paradidonai* can bear the meaning 'entrust' as well as 'hand over', and may have that resonance e.g. at Rom. 8.32.

[67] Hays (2002), 170 argues that Romans is strongly theocentric and Paul never says explicitly that people put their trust in Christ. Since Paul affirms unambiguously elsewhere that people trust in Christ, though, it seems perverse to refuse to recognize the possibility that trust in Christ is implicit in Romans; there is no reason to think that trust in Christ diminishes Paul's sense of the importance of God.

[68] Taking 5.21 with Thrall (1982), 229–30 as meaning that Christ was made like sinful humanity, though sinless himself.

[69] This, of course, does not explain how atonement comes about, only the configuration of relationships that allows it to do so. Seifrid's (2009) argument that *pistis Christou* is the faith that comes from Christ is, on its own, rather abstract, forfeiting something of Paul's intense sense of relationship with Christ, but we could hear it as a further resonance of Christ's *pistis*.

[70] NB this argument assumes that Christ's mediation makes divine forgiveness possible, not that the mediator is the one who forgives: on this as the norm in early Judaism see Johansson (2011).

The passages of Galatians 2 and Philippians 3 which are most closely related to Paul's thinking in Romans 3.21-6 are not exactly parallel to it, partly because in both Paul's argument about how God acts through Christ and human beings respond is entwined with a defence of his own apostleship. Both Galatians 2.15-20 and Philippians 3.7-11, however, sketch the same understanding of how trust operates between God, Christ, and human beings in Christ's death.

At Philippians 3.9-11, Paul affirms that any right-standing he has with God comes

> through *pistis Christou*, the rightness from God depending on *pistis* to know him and the power of his resurrection and the sharing of his sufferings by being conformed to his death, if somehow I may attain the resurrection from the dead.

Though the role of *pistis* is alluded to rather than spelled out in this passage, Paul is clear that right-standing with God comes from God through Christ and on a basis of *pistis*. It makes good sense to read *pistis Christou*, as at Romans 3.22, both as the trust and faithfulness between Christ and God which makes renewed right-standing with God available to humanity, and as the trust Christ puts in human beings to put their trust in him, together with the trust Paul has put in Christ.[71]

At Galatians 2.15-20, Paul refers several times to *pistis* in an argument which also has much to say about the law.

> We, who are Jews by nature and not sinners from among the gentiles, [yet] who know that a person is not justified by works of the law if he is not justified through the *pistis* of Jesus Christ (διὰ πίστεως Ἰησοῦ Χριστοῦ), even we have put our trust in Christ Jesus, so that we are justified by the *pistis* of Christ (ἵνα δικαιωθῶμεν ἐκ πίστεως Χριστοῦ) and not by works of the law, because by works of the law no one will be justified. But if, seeking to be made right in Christ we ourselves have been found to be sinners, is Christ a minister of sin? Of course not! But if I am building up again those things that I tore down, then I show myself to be a transgressor. For through the law I died to the law, so that I might live for God. I have been crucified with Christ; yet I live, no longer I, but Christ lives in me; insofar as I now live in the flesh, I live in [the] *pistis* of the Son of God (ἐν πίστει ζῶ τῆι τοῦ υἱοῦ τοῦ θεοῦ) who loved me and gave himself up for me. I do not nullify the grace of God; for if right-standing comes through the law, then Christ died for nothing.[72]

---

[71] Paul does not say here that he has responded to God's actions through Christ with *pistis*, but it may be implied by 'depending on trust' in v. 9, and he has already described the Philippians as actively trusting in Christ (1.29, cf. 1.25): so e.g. Vincent (1897), Holloway (2017), *ad loc*. A few verses later, Paul describes himself as having been taken possession of by Christ (3.12); this may relate to the idea elsewhere that Christ is 'in' him, on which see Morgan (2020), 112-19.
[72] NAB, modified.

Leaving aside many of the complexities of this passage, which are not our current focus, it is clear that Christ loves Paul, has given himself up for him, and has died to make possible Paul's right-standing with God (2.20–1). To this we can add that Christ 'gave himself for our sins that he might rescue us from the present evil age in accord with the will of God...' (1.4). These formulations, like those of Romans 3.21–6, show Christ facing two ways. He does God's will, so he can be described as being trusting and faithful towards God, and we can infer that God has trusted Christ to make possible human at-one-ment with God.[73] At the same time, he loves and acts on behalf of human beings. Elsewhere in the scriptures and the New Testament, as we have seen, God's care for human beings and action on their behalf is sometimes linked with his being *pistos*, in the sense of 'trustworthy', towards them, and, similarly, Christ is worthy of trust by human beings by virtue of his self-giving care for them. Christ can therefore be seen as *pistos* towards both God and human beings. Finally, human beings trust Christ to enable them to come into right-standing with God. As in Romans and Philippians, Christ stands at the centre of a nexus of divine–human *pistis*, at once faithful, trusted, and trustworthy by both God and humanity.

The idea that *pistis* in these passages is doubly reciprocal not only cuts the Gordian knot of debate about whether the genitive in the phrase *pistis Christou* is subjective or objective, but well expresses Paul's understanding of what is made possible for humanity by God's acting through Christ in his death, and how human beings can respond. As an interpretation, moreover, it should come as no surprise: taken alongside Paul's language of reconciliation and seen in the context of the first century, it is an obvious way to read the *pistis* of Christ.[74] One of the most important qualities of conciliators, mediators, ambassadors, and anyone in public or private life who seeks to reconcile or enable a new relationship or agreement to be made between individuals or groups, is that they are willing to trust both parties and are seen as trustworthy and are trusted by both.[75] It is only by being trusting, trustworthy, and trusted that one can bring together people who have not trusted one another in the past or whose

---

[73] On the relationship between *pistis Christou* and Jesus' faithfulness and obedience in the gospels see Bolt (2009), Salier (2009).

[74] Explored by Dognin (2005), cf. Bash (1997), Morgan (2015a), 99–104, 114–6, Lee (2019). It is less likely (cf. Cox (2007), 24–5) that Paul draws on middle-Platonist theories about intermediaries in the divine–human relationship because there is little evidence in general that Paul drew on Platonism, while models of human mediation are ubiquitous; Segal's (1977) exploration of intermediary powers offers closer parallels: particularly the Son of Man in the Parables of Enoch (pp. 202–3).

[75] Modern mediation theory also fits this reading notably well, emphasizing the importance of the personal qualities of mediators (e.g. Bowling and Hoffman (2003), and that in the process of resolving conflicts, mediation can change participants' sense of identity and sense of belonging and the 'truth' they inhabit (Beer et al. (2012), Asmussen (2018), Nadler, Malloy, and Fisher (2008), Nadler and Shnabel (2018)), and the practice of mediation combines care, the creation of new structures and life goals, and the creation of new (secular) belief or faith (Katz (2006), esp. 374–6).

trust has failed.[76] We can go further, and note that although Paul does not use explicit 'reconciliation' language very often, *pistis* language, when used as Paul uses it in these passages, is itself language of reconciliation, and adds to the strength of the 'reconciliation' theme in the letters.

Several of Paul's followers pick up his image of Christ as reconciler and add to it the closely related language of mediation which Paul himself does not use. They also use *pistis* language in proximity to it even more often than does Paul himself, suggesting that they understand Paul's *pistis* language and his language of reconciliation as closely related. For the author of Ephesians, listeners have 'become near' to God 'through the blood of Christ', through which both Jews and gentiles are reconciled with God (2.13, 16). The death of Christ achieves this salvation *dia pisteōs*, 'through faith' (2.8). This *pistis* could be, in the context of this passage, Christ's faithfulness to God or the doubly reciprocal *pistis* between God, Christ, and humanity, though I have argued that in the context of the letter as a whole it may be more likely to be the first.[77] Nevertheless, the Ephesians are also called to put their trust in God and Christ: there is 'one Lord, one trust, one baptism; one God and Father' (4.5) and every community member should aim for unity of trust in, together with knowledge of the Son of God (4.11–13).[78] At Colossians 1.19–20 the writer (or the hymn he may be quoting) says that 'in [Christ] all the fullness was pleased to dwell, and through him to reconcile all things for him, making peace by the blood of his cross…'.[79]

The author of 1 Timothy understands Christ as mediating between God and humanity to reconcile them: 'for there is one God, and one mediator between God and humanity, the man Christ Jesus, who gave himself as a ransom for all…' (2.5–6). Paul was appointed to preach this message of salvation as 'teacher of the gentiles in *pistis* and truth' (2.4, 7). This may refer primarily to Paul's entrustedness with the gospel and faithfulness as Christ's slave, and only implicitly to the trust and recognition of truth for which he hopes for the faithful, but both trust and truth originate with God, so Paul's and the community's trust is also a response to God and Christ and what Christ offers as mediator.

---

[76] The kind of trust at stake in righteousing is more, for instance, than loyalty, which is an attitude and practice which persists over time within a positive relationship. Although we can imagine that the trust between God and Christ, which presumably never fails, involves loyalty, what is centrally involved in God's gracious outreach to humanity through Christ, Christ's allowing himself to be the means of God's outreach, and the restoration of the divine–human relationship, is at every stage a new act of trust. Paul may have inherited the idea that the *pistis* between God, Christ, and humanity made possible the reconciliation of the world to God, but it also fits well with his use of a wide range of political and military language and, in general, language of public life elsewhere (Morgan (2020), 169–92).

[77] Morgan (2015a), 308–10. At 6.23 *pistis* comes from both God and Christ.

[78] On trust in Christ at 1.13 and 1.15 see Morgan (2015a), 311.

[79] The writer goes on to say (vv. 21–3) that Christ has reconciled human beings in order to present them, 'without blemish', before God. Wilson (2005), *ad* 1.23 notes that both *hagios* and *amōmos* may be linked with sacrifice (though *hagios* has a much wider application too), but *anenklētos* has legal associations so the thought here is both cultic and legal: 'provided that you persevere in trust…'.

2 Timothy may go further in understanding *pistis* as doubly reciprocal. The writer affirms that even if community members fail in trust (*apistein*), Christ remains *pistos*.[80] Since this affirmation is the last of a sequence of four, all of which concern Christ's relationship with human beings, the simplest reading of *pistos* here is as referring to Christ's faithfulness to humanity.[81] This and the previous couplet, however, run: '[I]f we deny him, he will deny us; if we are unfaithful, he remains faithful (εἰ ἀπιστοῦμεν, ἐκεῖνος πιστὸς μένει), for he cannot deny himself.' This suggests that Christ also remains faithful to God, because for Christ to 'deny himself' would mean denying his role in the salvation which, as the writer has just said, God has brought about through him (cf. 1.8, 10). Although the writer's language does not directly echo Paul's, therefore, he may be drawing on Paul's understanding of Christ as reconciling God and humanity through his *pistis* towards God in his salvific death and resurrection.

A later passage may offer further support for this reading. At 2 Timothy 3.10–16 [Paul] is praising Timothy for continuing, under persecution, to follow his 'teaching, way of life, purpose, *pistis*, patience, love, endurance...' (3.10), and warning him that he can expect to be persecuted further. 'But you, remain in what you have learned and been entrusted with (*epistōthēs*), knowing from whom you learned it, and knowing that from infancy you have known [the] sacred scriptures, which can give you wisdom for salvation διὰ πίστεως τῆς ἐν Χριστῷ Ἰησοῦ' (3.14-15). The writer understands community members as saved and called to a holy life (1.9) not by their own works, but by God's plan and 'the grace given to us through Christ Jesus before time began' (1.9). Grace is not something Christ's followers achieve for themselves: it is given to them. This suggests that the salvation that comes διὰ πίστεως τῆς ἐν Χριστῷ Ἰησοῦ at 3.15 is also not achieved by them, but by Christ, perhaps in faithfulness both to God and to humanity. On the other hand, [Paul's] own *pistis* is also invoked in this letter (3.10), and so is Timothy's (1.5, 3.14), which hints that *pistis* ἐν Χριστῷ Ἰησοῦ may be something that Timothy enacts too, and therefore that *pistis* here is both the double faithfulness of Christ and the trust of those who are in Christ's hands.[82]

For the author of Hebrews, the *pistis* of Christ operates within the rather different framework of the new covenant, but he too sees Jesus Christ both as *pistos* in his death and as mediating between God and humanity. Christ is first described as *pistos* to God at 2.17: 'he had to become like his brothers in every way, that he might be a merciful and *pistos* high priest before God to expiate the sins of the people.' The high priest whom the author has in mind is Melchizedek, the high priest of Genesis 14.18–20 and Psalm 109.4 (LXX) who, by the late first century CE, could be treated as a divine being who descends to the human sphere or is

---

[80] In what may be another pre-existing unit of tradition.
[81] So e.g. Downs and Lappenga: above, p. 125 n.120.   [82] Cf. pp. 132–3, 134–5.

taken up from it.[83] We cannot be sure that the author has these strands of tradition in mind, but even if he does not, he has already affirmed the divine sonship of Jesus, so the *pistis* of Jesus is introduced in the context both of his divine origins and of the special importance of his *pistis* during his lifetime. The high priest, as representative of the people of Israel, intercedes for them, and also behaves as God would wish all his people to behave: loyal and obedient to God, even in suffering, merciful and helpful towards his fellow human beings (2.17–18). To carry out his duty he must therefore be faithful or loyal to God and trusted by God, and faithful or loyal to his people and trusted by them, and the author, by comparison, affirms the same of Jesus both as pre-existing son of God and in his earthly (life and) death.[84]

Immediately after this passage, Jesus is described as 'the apostle and high priest of our confession', who was *pistos* to the one who appointed him, just as Moses was 'in all his house' (3.1–2). By the late first century, Moses could be portrayed as angelic or divine, especially in connection with his role as mediator between God and the people of Israel.[85] The author then says that Moses was '*pistos* in all his house' (quoting Num. 12.7), but that Christ was 'like a son placed over his house' (3.5–6).[86] The *pistis* of Christ, here, it seems, exceeds that of other mediators appointed by God, but is analogous to it: Christ is both faithful to God and trusted by God, and faithful to and trusted by his people.

In the early chapters of Hebrews, the *pistis* of Jesus, though enacted especially in his earthly life, is understood as an aspect of his identity as God's son and the unique position from which he mediates between God and humanity. So far, the author has much in common with Paul, who also locates Jesus Christ between God and humanity and, in some passages, makes *pistis* integral to Christ's expiation of sins. In one respect, however, the role of *pistis* in the formation of the new covenant, as the author of Hebrews understands God's new relationship with humanity, is significantly different from its role in Romans, Galatians, and Philippians. God, in Hebrews, is faithful (*pistos*) to human beings. Jesus may also be understood as faithful to human beings, though the author does not say so explicitly. Jesus is explicitly faithful to God and his faithfulness (together with that

---

[83] Cf. 5.6, 6.20, 7.1–17. Melchizedek is divine or angelic at 11Q13. For Philo (*Som.* 1.214–15, *Spec. Leg.* 1.116, 189) the divine Logos is High Priest of the temple of God that is the cosmos, while the human High Priest is the image of his representative; both represent and intercede for God's people (Leonhardt (2001), 128–9, 230–3, Horton (1976), 64–82, 152–64); cf. 2 Enoch 71.12–72.11, where Melchizedek is miraculously born of a virgin and soon after is removed to the Garden of Eden by the angel Gabriel.
[84] Cf. Gen. 14.17–20, Ps. 109.4 LXX.
[85] Cf. Ezek. Trag., *Exod.* Fr. 6–7 (Eus. Hist., *Praep. Ev.* 9.29.4–6), Philo, *Vit. Mos.* 1.158, *Test. Mos.* 1.14, 4Q374, 377 (though here the writer may have Moses' humanity mainly in mind).
[86] Mitchell (2007), 81 argues that Jesus is not only faithful to God here but worthy of God's trust. The omission may be only for reasons of stylistic balance: at 3.2 the author calls Jesus *pistos* but omits the word from his quotation about Moses; this time he leaves *pistos* in his quotation about Moses but omits it from his description of Christ.

of many biblical figures) is a model for others, who are exhorted repeatedly to be faithful to God.[87] But in Hebrews, people are never exhorted to put their trust in Christ. The author does not take the final step that Paul and other writers take of placing *pistis* towards Christ alongside traditional *pistis* towards God.

These passages all suggest that the double nexus of trust between God and Christ and Christ and humanity makes possible a new or renewed relationship of right-standing between God and humanity. But this model also raises further questions. Why, in the view of these writers, especially Paul, do the participants in this nexus trust one another? For the new relationship of trust between God, Christ, and humanity to be established, did Christ have to die, and if so, why? And, given that we have argued that a model of atonement should ideally show how Christ's death makes possible humanity's release from both sin and suffering, how does this model do so? These questions are all aspects of the key question about the atonement, to which multiple answers have been, and continue to be offered: how does it work? We can add one more: is trust ultimately a means to right-standing, or is it also an end in itself: an intrinsic part of the right relationship between God, Christ, and humanity?

Why do Participants in the Nexus of Trust Trust One Another?

From a post-resurrection perspective Paul has certainly one, possibly two, or even three ways of thinking about the trust between God and Jesus Christ. It is a maximally powerful form of the trust that pertains between God and any faithful human being, such as Abraham or Moses. If, as James Dunn and others have argued, Paul has heard of Jesus as having been anointed by the spirit at the beginning of his earthly ministry, then the trust between God and Christ is part of their common purpose for humanity's reconciliation with God.[88] If Paul thinks of Christ as pre-existent, then the trust between God and Christ is also an expression of their relationship from before creation.[89]

The trust between Christ and the faithful takes a little more teasing out. We can assume that Paul and his followers knew something of Jesus' earthly life and ministry, and is it possible, though unprovable, that his followers thought of themselves as trusting Jesus in his lifetime.[90] As we saw in the last chapter, affirming the continuity of Jesus' identity in his earthly life and resurrection is essential to Paul,

---

[87] E.g. 6.1, 10.38, 13.7, cf. 4.2, 6.12, 10.22, 10.39, 11 *passim*.

[88] So e.g. Dunn (1975), 318–26, (1998) 1.126–53, cf. Dodd (1952), 123, though *contra* see Fee (1994), 831–4, Turner (1998). Coulson (2016), 81–2 argues that Paul's calling Jesus 'Christ' implies that he accepts that Jesus was anointed by the spirit as Messiah and Son of God in his lifetime, despite what may be the partially inherited formulation of Rom. 1.4 (on which, Coulson (2016), 83 rightly notes, e.g. Dunn (1998), 130–42 is unconvincing).

[89] Cf. pp. 136–7.   [90] See especially Gathercole (2018).

as to all New Testament writers. But (unlike the gospels, for instance) Paul makes nothing of the idea that people were healed or saved by trust during Jesus' earthly ministry. The trust that concerns him begins with Jesus' suffering and death on the cross.[91] We suggested that, at the crucifixion, Christ trusts in humanity to be able to respond to what God is doing through him, but human beings' response begins when they experience the resurrection or hear the gospel preached. For Paul as a preacher and for his followers, therefore, those who put their trust in Christ crucified trust the one whom they have also experienced or heard of as raised. Trust in the crucified Christ is, in practice, trust simultaneously in the crucified and risen or exalted Christ.

This means that in a *pistis*-based model of atonement (unlike, for example, in a sacrificial or penal-substitutionary model), nothing is accomplished on the cross per se. In Christ's crucifixion, both God and Christ take the greatest imaginable risk, maintaining their trust in one another and in humanity even when it leads to betrayal, humiliation, and death. The resurrection is a sign that this trust is stronger than death, but it, too, does not accomplish anything in itself. Nothing changes until human beings respond to trust with trust. Paul's (and other writers') connection of *pistis* language with the idea of reconciliation underlines this point. An ambassador, for instance, cannot simply be authorized by one people to make peace with another and consider that by that token peace has been achieved. Any movement to reconciliation exists only in potential until both parties opt into it.

This observation points to some of the differences between a *pistis* model of atonement and, for instance, the doctrine of justification by faith, which it may seem superficially to resemble. For one thing, most models of justification by faith assume that something is achieved in the crucifixion itself. For another, notably in Luther's classic formulation, models of justification distinguish between the revelation of 'the invisible things of God' (as the 19th Heidelberg Thesis puts it), which Luther does not describe with *fides* language, and the response of faith which, by grace, makes possible salvation, rather than uniting them in a single relational nexus of trust. Thirdly, Luther's *fides* is as much belief as trust, while in the 'trust' model, though belief is always likely to underlie trust, it is the commitment of trust that is decisive in making possible at-one-ment.[92] Fourthly, the trust model lacks the fideistic aspect of Luther's theology, in which God's self-revelation on the cross is concealed and can only be discerned with the 'eye of faith'.[93] Fifthly, Luther's *fides* is cast as an attitude, but we have already seen, and later chapters will argue further, that legitimate trust can be either an attitude or an action or (ideally) both.

The last point recalls an observation we made in Chapter 2: that even if, in most situations, the attitude and action of trust ideally go together, they do not

---

[91] Though on gospels see below pp. 200–2, 251–4.
[92] Vainio (2008), 1–61, McGrath (2011), 201–32.   [93] McGrath (2011), 212.

always do so, and an act of trust without the attitude can constitute genuine trust and vice versa.[94] In Chapter 6 we will see several examples of people who trust in Jesus failing, at a particular moment, in the attitude or action of trust. In the context of this chapter, the distinguishability of the action and attitude of trust means that human beings may put their trust in God and Christ and enter a relationship of trust with them with a trust which is still imperfect. Ideally, their trust will strengthen and widen in scope through time. But one can imagine, for example, a person who does not yet fully, in her mind or heart, trust in Jesus Christ as her only saviour opting to act with trust in him (for instance, by being baptized), and this trust as being adequate to bring her into right-standing with God.[95]

We observed in the last chapter that the call to trust in the risen or exalted Christ is likely to be one of the earliest uses of *pistis* language among Christ's followers. In that context, it is likely that early Christ-confessors trust in the crucified Christ in light of their trust in the risen or exalted Christ. The crucified one is the one whose trust and trustworthiness have been revealed as vindicated in the resurrection. We will return to the question why, in that case, it is appropriate for the faithful to put their trust in Christ crucified.[96] First, though, it is worth noting that the way Paul describes how 'the righteousness of God' is revealed (Rom. 1.17, 3.21) fits well with his narrative of trust.

Trust and Revelation in Christ's Death and Resurrection

Paul affirms that God's self and God's righteousness have been revealed repeatedly to Israel and, through Israel, to the nations, throughout history and the scriptures.[97] At Romans 3.21, the righteousness of God has now been revealed through 'the redemption through Christ Jesus' (3.24) for all those who trust.[98] The crucifixion and resurrection are a revelation of God's grace and love for humanity (cf. Rom. 5.6).[99] At Galatians 3.23, Paul says, also of the Christ event, that 'before *pistis* came, we were held in custody under the law, confined for the

---

[94] pp. 70–1, cf. 4–5.   [95] Cf. p. 263.   [96] pp. 276–9.
[97] E.g. Exod. 34.6, Num. 14.18, 1 Kgs 3.5, Pss 98.2, 103.8, 17, 145.8, Jer. 32.18–19, Dan. 9.4, Joel 2.13, Jonah 4.2, Nahum 1.3. Partially rehabilitating the long unfashionable view that early Christians make use of Hellenistic models of epiphany in their developing Christologies, see Zeller (2001).

[98] pp. 45–6. At 16.25–6 the doxology (probably non-Pauline, but Pauline in tone) reaffirms that 'the mystery kept secret for long ages' has been manifested through the prophets, proclaimed, and made known to all nations.

[99] Returning to Israel's *apistia* and the inclusion of the gentiles among God's people in ch. 9, Paul (quoting Exod. 9.16) affirms that God has raised up Israel, 'so that I may show my power through you, and so that my name may be proclaimed in all the earth' (9.17). God has also endured the failings of Israel 'so that the riches of God's glory might be made known' (9.23) to those, Jews and gentiles, whom God has called (9.24). The theme of people thinking they know better also recurs here, when Paul imagines a Jew objecting to God's finding fault with Israel, if Israel's history is all part of God's plan (9.19, cf. 14); Paul's response is, 'Who are you, a human being, to talk back to God?'

pistis that was to be revealed'.[100] Only God's self-revelation can reveal God's mercy and the power of *pistis*, which are far beyond human understanding: 'For who has known the mind of the Lord, or who has been his counsellor?' (Rom. 11.34).[101]

It is not only the death and resurrection of Christ themselves that reveal: so does the preaching of the gospel and even the presence of the preacher. At Romans 1.16–18 the gospel is the power of God for salvation for everyone who trusts, first Jews, then Greeks, 'for in it is revealed the righteousness of God...'. At Galatians 1.15–16, Paul tells how 'God...was pleased to reveal his son to me, so that I might proclaim him to the gentiles...'.[102] At 2 Corinthians 2.14, God 'manifests through us the odour of the knowledge of him in every place', and a little later (4.10, cf. v. 11), Paul tells the Corinthians that he is 'always carrying about in the body the dying of Jesus, so that the life of Jesus may also be revealed in our body'.[103] At Galatians 4.9, Paul upbraids the Galatians, who have come to know God through the son whom God sent (4.4) and through Paul, who appeared to them like an angel of God or like Christ Jesus himself (4.14), for turning away from God again. At Philippians 3.15, in contrast, he reassures the Philippians that if they do happen to have the wrong attitude towards the 'pursuit towards the goal, the prize of God's upward calling in Christ Jesus' which Paul exemplifies and commends to others (3.14–15), God will reveal it to them (3.15).[104]

The revelation of God and Christ also continues after the resurrection through the holy spirit. 1 Corinthians 2.4 Paul reminds the Corinthians that 'my message and my proclamation were...with a demonstration of spirit and power (cf. 1 Thess. 1.5). A few verses later, Paul affirms that God revealed to the faithful, through the spirit, what he prepared for those who love him (2.10). The spirit uncovers (cf. 2.7) what human eyes and ears cannot (cf. 2.9), and by the spirit the faithful can understand what has been given to them by God (2.12). Later in the letter, it is the spirit that enables people to recognize Jesus as Lord (12.3). The Corinthians are evidently spiritual enthusiasts, who hardly need Paul's encouragement to 'strive eagerly for the spiritual gifts' (14.1), and we can infer that the revelations (*apokalypseis*) which Paul speaks of as coming to them (14.26, 30, cf. v. 6) are gifts of the spirit (cf. 12.4). At 14.25, Paul imagines how a non-community

---

[100] Longenecker (1990) argues that this is both the faithfulness of Christ and humanity's *pistis* response; Martyn (1997a) that it refers to God's eschatological act, and therefore the faith that is (everywhere in?) God's deed in Christ.

[101] Cf. Job 15.8, Wis. 9.13, Isa. 40.13, Jer. 23.18.

[102] Cf. 1 Cor. 15.5–8, Gal. 1.12, Phil. 3.8, with reference to Paul's resulting *pistis* at Phil. 3.9, cf. Gal. 1.23.

[103] At 2 Cor. 4.6 God's revelation of Christ continues through Paul's preaching; cf. Gen. 1.3; at 2 Cor. 3.18 human beings are able to gaze with unveiled face on the revealed glory of Christ after they have put their trust in Christ (van Unnik (1963)). His preaching, Paul affirms (with what to modern readers may seem a degree of optimism) makes the gospel clear (2 Cor. 11.6), while at Phil 1.12–13 even Paul's imprisonment has become well known for the advancement of the gospel.

[104] Doubtless the signs and wonders Paul performs also reveal God's power: e.g. Rom. 15.19, 2 Cor. 12.12, cf. 1 Thess. 1.5.

member (*apistos*, v. 24) might join a Corinthian assembly and be so convinced by what he saw that the secrets of his own heart would be revealed and 'he will fall down and worship God, declaring, "God is really among you"' (v. 25).

The process of revelation will not be complete until the end time.[105] The 'day of wrath', Paul says (Rom. 2.5), will also be the day of revelation, and the sufferings of the present time are nothing to the glory that will be revealed in the eschatological future (Rom. 8.18). At 1 Corinthians 1.7, Paul reminds the Corinthians that they are waiting for the 'revelation of our Lord Jesus Christ' at 'the end' (1.8), and at 4.5 he reminds them that when the Lord comes, 'he will bring to light what is hidden in darkness and will manifest the motives of our hearts...'.[106]

Paul hopes that every stage of the revelation of God and/or Christ will lead to a response of trust, and, since trust needs to be maintained, and even strengthened through the present time, it is appropriate that revelation also continues until the 'day of the Lord'. The divine–human trust relationship will not be a 'done deal', beyond failure, development, or extension to new participants, until the *parousia*. In some form or other, moreover, revelation is indispensable to trust.[107] A person, whether human or divine, who seeks to establish trust with another must not only be trustworthy, but must show herself and be recognized as trustworthy. Commentators who, in recent years, have rightly emphasized the importance of apocalyptic in Paul's thinking, have tended to link it with the idea that, for Paul, God and Christ are 'invading' this world to liberate humanity from the powers of Satan, sin, and death.[108] Our discussion so far suggests another possibility (not necessarily incompatible with the first). Godself, God's righteousness, and the person of Christ are, and continue to be revealed to the world to make possible the new relationship of trust which enables human beings' right-standing with God and will eventually make possible their salvation.

As noted, it is a recurring theme of the scriptures that God reveals Godself to restore or renew God's relationship with Israel, and Paul's language of revelation continues in that tradition, emphasizing what he recognizes as the continuity of God's actions in the past, present, and future, together with his conviction that God's new act in Christ is more powerful and transformative than any in the past. We saw in Chapter 3 that we should probably take the response of Paul and others to the revelation of the resurrection as belief, leading to trust.[109] Modern readers may assume that revelation should also lead to belief or knowledge rather than

---

[105] Cf. pp. 240, 245–6.   [106] At 1 Cor. 3.13 everyone's work will be revealed on the day, too.
[107] Though qualifying this in relation to the gospels, see pp. 237–41.
[108] Especially Käsemann (1962, 1964) with Way (1991), 124–8, J. Collins (1979). A. Collins (1979), Beker (1980, 1982), Martyn (1985, 1997a, 1997b, 2000), Wright (1996), chs 6–9; Matlock (1996), Gaventa (2013), the gospel as 'God's liberating invasion of the cosmos' is Martyn's phrase ((2000), 246). Morgan (2020), 165–8 argues that even though Paul doubtless does envisage a cosmic conflict as taking place, his concern is more with human life in the present time.
[109] pp. 100–8.

trust.¹¹⁰ For Paul, however (and other New Testament writers, notably John), knowledge is less knowledge about God or Christ than personal, relational knowledge of God and Christ, of a kind which enables trust.¹¹¹ I have argued elsewhere, and we have already seen in this study, that the *pistis* which is initiated by the Christ event is not primarily propositional belief, but the trust that involves putting oneself in another's hands, based on a complex combination of experience, belief, assumptions, tradition, interpretation, propositional trust, and hope. As in human relationships (and as, for instance, in Abraham's or Moses' trust relationships with God), there is nothing anomalous in this trust being fostered by what one person reveals to another of him- or herself and what the other perceives and believes: quite the opposite. Just as, for instance, my partner and I may decide to entrust ourselves and our future to each other in marriage, based on our experience of each other in the relationship so far, so human beings are invited to entrust themselves and their future to God and Christ, based not least on their experience of what God has revealed through Christ in and since the Christ event.¹¹² The ultimate aim of what we reveal to each other, however, is not knowledge or belief but an ongoing and developing relationship.

Did Christ Need to Die, and if so, Why?

Our second question on page 162 was whether, to restore human beings to trust and right-standing with God and establish a new relationship of trust between God, Christ, and humanity, Christ needed to die, and, if so, why. The model we have sketched so far does not answer this, not least because mediators and conciliators in Paul's world did not normally need to die to accomplish their work, and because there is no reason to think that a death is required for divine self-revelation. On one level, of course, Christ-confessors simply inherit the fact that Jesus did die, and seek to account for his death by seeing it as part of a divine plan. As we have seen, however, the deaths of great men who are taken up to heaven can be treated, in the ancient Mediterranean and Near Eastern worlds, in very varied ways. Even if they are remembered, and even if they are traumatic,

---

[110] Wahlberg (2020), 1 notes that 'revelation has usually been understood as an epistemic notion'.
[111] Cf. pp. 71–2; this, as noted (p. 140), is also central to Sequeri's (1996) understanding of divine–human trust.
[112] It is significant that what Paul describes as revealed is normally God's or Christ's self or a quality of God; he does talk of knowledge of God being revealed at 2 Cor. 2.14, but this is not the knowledge that implies that human beings can understand God (cf. Rom. 11.34, 1 Cor. 2.16) but knowledge in the sense of personal, relational 'knowing' or acquaintance. (That said, an underlying anxiety is detectable in Paul's writing, not so much about the current gap between God's self-revelation and humanity's response, which he sees as growing, but about his own effectiveness as an apostle to convey that revelation; some of his sharpest criticisms (e.g. 1 Cor. 1.10–17, Gal. 1.6–9) are directed at those who have, at some point, trusted as a result of his preaching but since fallen away.)

they are not necessarily seen as central to the significance of the person's earthly or heavenly life. Interpretations of Jesus' death as necessary are expressions of early Christ-confessors' sense that it not only occurred but was decisively significant, and it is in that light that it demands interpretation.

We have noted that, for Paul as for other New Testament writers, it is important to affirm that Christ, in his earthly life and death, is wholly continuous with who and what he is in his exalted life, and perhaps already is in his pre-existence. One possibility must therefore be that Christ dies because he cannot be other than he is.[113] The one who is and has been unconditionally and always trusting and trustworthy towards both God and humanity, and seeks to restore trust between God and humanity on that basis, cannot show, for instance, that he does not trust God to work through him by trying to evade arrest, but must allow himself to be taken, trusting that God will bring the possibility of a new *pistis* relationship even out of his death, and trusting human beings to be able to respond despite his death. God, for God's part, must allow Christ to show himself trustworthy by allowing himself to be betrayed, trusting him to be trusting and faithful even to death, and humanity to be able to come to trust even after the trauma of his death. Christ's death demonstrates the reality of the trust relationship in which he and God live, which physical death does not overcome, and this revelation is itself an invitation to trust.[114] In this vision, Christ needs to die not, like a sacrifice or a penal substitute, in place of others or to seal a new covenant between God and humanity, but because he is the person he is, and it is as that person that he is able to reconcile humanity with God.

To Christians who are used to the idea that Christ's death changes the state or status of humanity, however, this will seem a relatively weak explanation of why Christ had to die. Without depending on ideas of sacrifice, ransom, or substitution, but drawing on the *pistis* relationship between God, Christ, and humanity, can we understand Christ's death as doing something in itself? I think we can. If Christ's death only affirms the continuity of who and what he is, for Paul, it changes radically what it is possible for human beings to be. It enables them to die—because it is, above all, human beings who have to die—not, in this context, physically, but to the power of sin and suffering.[115] To explore further why Christ

---

[113] That a trusting or trustworthy person, to be or remain trusting or trustworthy, cannot evade dire or tragic circumstances, is a common idea: e.g. Abraham had to be willing to sacrifice Isaac because he had put his trust in the 'unwavering steadfastness' (*anendoiaston bebaiotēta*) of God (Philo., *Atrept.* 4); Regulus had to keep his word as a prisoner-ambassador from Carthage to Rome and, having advised the Romans not to come to terms with the Carthaginians, return to Carthage to die (Liv. 18, Sempr. *apud* Gell. 7.4.1, Hor., *Carm.* 3.5).

[114] Among recent theologies of the cross with which this argument has points of contact, Haight (2005), 86–101 argues that, through his death, Jesus can be understood both as involved in the process of salvation and as revealer of it, and that the cross itself does not save, but God saves in spite of it; he sees the same pattern of thinking in Paul.

[115] Phil. 1.21–3 indicates that having come to right-standing with God, Paul sees his physical death as insignificant; all the more, perhaps, if at the coming of Christ the faithful, dead or living, will alike be taken up (cf. 1 Thess. 4.16–17).

needed to die, we therefore turn to some of Paul's most distinctive soteriological language, that of dying and living with Christ.

Paul, as we saw in the last chapter, has the highest hopes for humanity's relationship with God.[116] He looks forward to the day when the faithful will be with Christ under the kingdom of God (cf. 1 Cor. 15.50, Gal. 5.21), co-heirs with Christ (cf. Gal. 4.1–7), victorious (1 Cor. 15.57) and glorified (cf. Rom. 8.29–30) in the presence of God (cf. 2 Cor. 4.14) for eternal life (cf. Rom. 2.7, 6.23).[117] This vision will finally be fulfilled after the *parousia*, but after the resurrection the faithful are already a 'new creation' (2 Cor. 5.17) who must think of themselves as already 'dead to sin and living for God in Christ Jesus' (Rom. 6.11).[118] Those who put their trust in God and in Christ aspire to live and relate to God, Christ, and one another, here and now, with the qualities and relationships that characterize God's kingdom, including grace, truth, mercy, peace, freedom, holiness, and love.

To enter the relationship of trust which both makes right-standing with God and new creation possible and is part of them, however, human beings must leave behind their present way of life: their sins and failures of trust, misguided self-trust and trust in others, and the painful life which is created by those relationships. They must, as is often said of those who suffer abuse or addiction, 'get out', abandoning a way of life that leads only to death and destruction in order to be survivors in a different world. They must dare to let trust give them access to a new reality, new relationships, a new way of life, and a new hope. For Paul, the world of sin and *apistia* has no future but death and destruction. In 2 Corinthians, the faithless are dying (2.15, 4.3) and in Philippians, the very hostility of the faithless to the faithful is 'proof to them of destruction' (1.28).[119] Life comes from trust in God and Christ: human beings must be connected by *pistis* with the power that creates and sustains creation in order to flourish.

To cease to trust in one circle of relationships, set of circumstances, way of life, and world-view, and let a new trust make possible new relationships and a new life, is a kind of death: metaphorical but, in many people's experience, transformatively powerful. In a number of passages Paul describes the effects of trust as dying with Christ, being buried with him, and living a new life with him, using a cluster of unusual *syn-* compounds, including 'suffer with' (*sympaschō*, Rom. 8.17), 'be crucified with' (*systaurōmai*, Rom. 6.6, Gal. 2.19), 'be buried with' (*synthaptomai*, Rom. 6.4), 'live with' (*syzaō*, Rom. 6.8), and 'be conformed to'

---

[116] E.g. pp. 113, 115–16.
[117] On Paul's *syn-* language see the useful survey of McGrath (1952) and discussions of Sieber (1971) and Campbell (2012), 217–36.
[118] Fitzmyer (2008) suggests that even at e.g. 1 Cor. 15.35–54 Paul leaves open the possibility that the faithful share Christ's risen life already.
[119] Cf. 1 Cor. 1.19 if this refers to physical beings.

(*symmorphizomai*) (Phil. 3.10), together with 'grown together with' (*symphytos*, Rom. 6.5) and 'in the same shape as' (*symmorphos*, Rom. 8.29, Phil. 3.21).[120]

Human beings' trust response to Christ's crucifixion and resurrection makes possible their release from the domination of the flesh, sin, suffering, and death, into a new life and world in the power and under the authority of Christ.[121] At Galatians 2.19-20, Paul's affirmation 'I have been crucified with Christ' is part both of an affirmation of what Christ's death means to him, and an assertion of his authority as an apostle to insist that *pistis* leads to justification (cf. 2.16).[122] By trusting, Paul was crucified to this world; now he lives for God (2.19); Christ lives and works in and through him (2.20); and he cannot 'nullify the grace of God' (2.21) by denying that it is *pistis*, not works of the law, that make possible righteousness (cf. 2.16).[123] At Romans 6.5, Paul speaks of being 'grown together with Christ' through the crucifixion and resurrection. We can translate the verse, literally, 'If then we have grown together with [Christ] by the likeness of his death, so we will be [grown together with him by the likeness] of the resurrection.'[124] Those who trust do not physically die and rise in baptism, but they go through a death to (the power of) sin (cf. 6.2), and the suffering sin brings with it, and a rising into new life (cf. 6.4) which is analogous to the death and resurrection of Christ. In this death and new life they grow 'with' him like plants on the same rootstock.[125] Later in the letter (11.17-24), Paul uses another plant image to speak of the gentiles as being 'grafted', through trust, like a wild olive shoot onto the 'rich root' of the olive tree of Israel, which thrives (implicitly, at 11.20) because of its historic relationship of trust with God.[126] At the same time, some branches of Israel have been broken off 'because of *apistia*' (11.20). If they do not return to trust in both

---

[120] Paul's followers use *pro rata* even more and more varied *syn-* language than he does, including *synkakopatheō* (2 Tim. 1.8, 2.3), *synapothnēskō* (2. Tim. 2.11), *syzōopoieō* (Eph 2.5, Col 2.13), *synthaptō* (Col 2.12).

[121] Morgan (2020), 145-55 substantially following Tannehill (1967), 30, 39-40, argues that these passages are not references to 'participation' in the person of Christ, but represent the death of Christ as an 'inclusive event' which frees human beings from the dominion of the old aeon and releases them into the power of Christ in the new. Tannehill's study is also illuminating in tracing the connections between God's actions through Christ, human beings' response, their life under Christ's lordship, and their ethical behaviour.

[122] Morgan (2020), 64-8, 114-15.

[123] Martyn (1997a) shows that Paul is summarizing his refutation of the Teachers' charge against him here, arguing that they, not he, nullify God's grace, which is located not in the law but in God's rectifying power and hence in Christ's faithful death. Later in this letter, Paul will refer to those who already belong to Christ as also crucifying their own flesh, with its passions and desires (5.24).

[124] Εἰ γὰρ σύμφυτοι γεγόναμεν τῷ ὁμοιώματι τοῦ θανάτου αὐτοῦ, ἀλλὰ καὶ τῆς ἀναστάσεως ἐσόμεθα, Morgan (2020), 153. Wolter (2014), *ad loc.* notes that in using *symphytos* Paul may have an agricultural image in mind, as at Rom. 11.17-24.

[125] In the wider context of the chapter, much of which concerns the life of the faithful as God's 'weapons of righteousness' (6.13), 'slaves of righteousness' (6.18,) or 'slaves of God' (6.22), being *symphytos* may also imply that the faithful are following Christ's example in his earthly life, death, and exalted life. This fits with the language of *homoiōma* which Paul also uses at 6.5, and which Morgan (2020), 148-55 argues is also ethical.

[126] Because the branches that were broken off were severed because of their *apistia*.

God and Christ (cf. 11.23), then they will wither and die.[127] These images express the literally vital importance, for Paul, of being with God and Christ. Being in the relationship of trust means life itself and growth; the absence of it means corruption and death.[128]

Why, though, to enable human beings to die 'with' him to *apistia*, sin, and death, should Christ have had to die physically? And how can we conceive of his death as making a difference? We suggested above that, once his betrayal is planned, Christ accepts what follows because he cannot be other than who and what he is. One possibility is therefore that the continuity of Christ's identity and relationship with God before and after his death reveals the inviolability of the divine–human relationship of trust, which no human sin or destruction can disrupt, and that only this revelation can be imagined as powerful enough to enable human beings to take the risk of putting their trust in God and Christ and dying to the world of *apistia*. This is imaginable as far as it goes, but it still does not do justice to the idea that human beings die 'with' Christ. On one level, Paul's *syn*-language expresses vividly, metaphorically, how real—how material—human beings' death to *apistia* and new life of *pistis* are for them.[129] We can, however, hear more in it even than that.

From one perspective, Paul's *syn*- language tells those who trust that they 'died-with' Christ, live 'in Christ's hands', and will 'live-with' Christ at the resurrection (Rom. 6.8, 11, cf. 5). That is, their old self has died, lives, and will live in a way which Christ has made possible, and which is, in some way, like Christ's own physical death and resurrection. From another perspective, Paul's *syn*- language tells those who trust that they died and will live 'with-Christ'. As they go through a death to the world of *apistia* and enter the new life of right-standing with God which God has made possible—and which, in some sense, would form part of any reconciliation with God at any time—they do so *with* Christ, who died and was raised.[130] In either reading, both elements are important, but the emphasis is slightly different. Commentators usually emphasize the first perspective, but the second offers something distinctive in the context of a *pistis* model of atonement.[131]

---

[127] This is not as mixed a metaphor as it may sound, since cracked and even broken branches can be bound onto a tree and healed.

[128] At Gal. 6.8, in another agricultural analogy, those who sow 'for the flesh' reap corruption—which, pursuing the image further, they will then have to consume, and which will not fortify their life, and might poison them—while those who plant 'for the spirit' reap life; at 1 Cor. 3.6–7, Paul planted the faithful in their new relationship of trust, Apollos watered, and God caused and continues to cause the faithful to grow. Colossians, following Paul's lead, describes the faithful as 'rooted' in Christ and established in the trust which they were taught (2.7).

[129] Using a metaphor which appears elsewhere in the context of initiation into ancient cults, though there is no strong reason to think that Paul consciously borrowed it from elsewhere: cf. e.g. Apul., *Met.* 11.41–6, and the discussion of Dunn (1988), 308–12.

[130] On similar lines, Moule (1956), 40 cites with approval Dodd (1932), 88, who suggests *ad* Rom. 6.3 that human beings have died and risen again in solidarity with Christ.

[131] Elsewhere in Greek, for instance, when one person *syngignōskein*, 'agrees with' another, the emphasis is on the agreement, because, within the term itself, no 'withness' between those involved

Imagine that, as a small child, I am invited to visit my grandparents in their beautiful home in the country. I want to see them more than anything, but to get there I need to leave my own home and everyday life, and take a long train journey. I cannot do this alone; someone will have to take me. My mother may not, herself, feel a great need to visit her parents at this time. Their home is her childhood home; part of her is always with them in spirit, and she is in touch with them regularly. But if she arranged for me to travel alone, I would be afraid and might get lost or even kidnapped. If we go together, I will be joyfully confident, trusting her to get us both there safely. Because she loves and cares for me, she makes the journey so that I can go with her.

I trust my mother because we have an existing relationship; because she is an adult; and because, as an adult, she has done the journey before. I feel safe because she is with me and I am with her. Though I am with her, however, in a significant sense we are not on the same journey. My mother is an adult, and she has taken this journey before as an adult for whom it held no terrors. For me, the journey is ground-breaking. I am exploring new worlds, and the trip alters my view of the world and my sense of what is possible for me. By the time we arrive, I will have taken a step towards growing up, and I will never be quite the same again.

The Christ with whom those who trust have a relationship is both the crucified and exalted Christ. As we saw in the last chapter, Paul envisages the exalted Christ as near the faithful: he guides them and they are in his hands. Because the exalted Christ is with them, those who trust, like the child on the journey, can undergo their death to the world of sin and *apistia* with confidence, knowing that Christ, who has taken the journey before and is with them now, has shown that where there is trust with God, there is, ultimately, no death, but only renewed life. Their journey is not the same as Christ's, because Christ never needed to die to sin, and his identity and relationship with God were not changed by his physical death.[132] But from the perspective of the one who trusts, as of the child, the presence of one who knows and has shown that leaving one's old life leads to new and more glorious life enables trust to persevere and allows the trusting one to be taken to the journey's end.

On one level, both the mother's past journeys and Christ's death operate as a sign of what the child, or those trapped in sin and suffering, can hope to attain.[133] On another, the journey that has been made before has created and mapped a route for others. On yet another, the mother's journey and Christ's death are an example, but the fact that the child, or the one who trusts, travels 'with' Christ or the mother, makes both journeys more than exemplary. If my mother had told me

---

exists except in the agreement. But if one person *syngēraskein*, 'grows old with' another, he is (by nature) growing old anyway, and the word emphasizes that he is also doing it with another.

[132] Though if Paul thinks of Christ as having been anointed at the beginning of his ministry, we may imagine Christ as having died to sin and death at that point.

[133] Cf. pp. 179-80.

that she had taken this journey before, perhaps I would have been sufficiently encouraged by her example to travel alone, but when she comes with me, my experience is completely different. When the faithful experience themselves as 'with' the dying and rising Christ, they are not just making a journey that has been made before. They are affirming the presence with them of one who knows what it is to have arrived, who guides them and reassures them at every point.[134] By being with the Christ who is with them, they can be sure that, unless they wilfully lose themselves on the way, they will reach the destination to which they have been invited.

In this scenario, Christ did not have to die to negotiate humanity's release from sin and death. His death remains a scandal and an act of human evil. But it is also an act, and perhaps a necessary act, of grace, on his part and on God's, which makes possible what might otherwise have been impossible—too big a step, too risky, utterly unimaginable—for human beings. In this act of grace, Christ dies not as humanity's representative, but as humanity's leader, brother, and carer. Just as we may imagine my grandparents trusting my mother to deliver me safely to their home, my mother trusting them to welcome me when I arrive, my mother trusting me to stay close to her as we travel, and my trusting her to guide me on the journey, so the double nexus of trust between God and Christ and Christ and humanity enables human beings to be delivered safely to God. For humanity, the call to trust is trustworthy and possible to respond to with joyful confidence because Christ knows the journey they will have to take and is with them as they take it.[135]

We said that this model of grace, mediation, and companionship would not refer to other traditional models of Christ's death, as sacrifice, ransom, and so on. But we can now see that some of this language could, in fact, be applied to our model, within a slightly different frame of reference from that in which it is usually used. By allowing himself to be arrested, by trusting God to use even his death to bring humanity to trust and new life, and by showing humanity the way through death to life, Christ can be seen as allowing himself to be sacrificed on humanity's behalf, and as enabling humanity's redemption or release from the power of sin and suffering.

We have seen that psychologists emphasize the importance of trust relationships for giving us the sense that we are real in the world around us and that the world is real to us. Trust relationships help to create our social reality: the reality in which we can see ourselves, live, and act as real, and make relationships with

---

[134] Here Christ's mediation in his death converges with the mediating activity of the exalted Christ: cf. pp. 122–7.

[135] Cranfield (1975), 296, discussing Rom. 6.1–14, rightly recognizes that the Christian dies and is raised in several senses, between which Paul moves throughout this passage: at the beginning of the relationship, as 'a matter of present obligation', and in the eschatological future. For a wide-ranging exploration of the exemplarity of Jesus' death in the New Testament see Hurtado (2004).

others who are real to us. Paul grasps this thoroughly and profoundly. To choose trust in God and Christ is to choose to be real in the reality of God and Christ, and live, work, and make relationships with other human beings in that reality.[136] It is, for Paul, to be alive in that world which is both already partly realized in the present time and which will be fully realized at the *parousia*: a world which the faithful reach by travelling with Christ through death. Paul therefore presents his listeners with a question. Who you trust will determine the reality you live in, your life, and your future. Whom do you trust?[137]

Jesus' Suffering and Death as Exemplary

The previous section touched on the role of exemplarity in Christ's death.[138] A number of scholars have observed recently that the imitation of Christ plays a larger role in Paul's letters than is often recognized, and deserves more attention.[139] We have seen that the faithful can imitate aspects of Christ's exalted life,[140] but above all, for Paul and his followers, it is Christ's earthly suffering that is exemplary. When they imitate Christ in his suffering, the faithful can be seen as expressing their trust and trustworthiness towards God and Christ, as becoming more Christ-like, and even as continuing Christ's saving work in this world, while the imitability of Christ can be seen as its own contribution to divine–human at-one-ment. For all these reasons, imitation deserves a little more exploration.

At 1 Thessalonians 1.6, Paul tells the Thessalonians, 'You have become imitators (*mimētai*) of us and of the Lord, receiving the word in much affliction with joy from the holy spirit, so that you became a model (*typos*) for all the faithful in Macedonia and Achaia.' The Thessalonians' affliction seems to be that they have been attacked in some way for putting their trust in God. At 2.14 Paul adds that they have become imitators of the churches of Judaea 'because you suffer the

---

[136] So Martyn (1997b), 121.

[137] Most of us are further familiar with the experience that relationships of trust, for instance, within families or between lovers, lead to the sharing of experience and perspective. One of my close friends, as she was getting to know the man she would marry, observed, 'There's definitely a sense of an expanded world-view': 'we' as a couple or a family, involved as we are in our shared histories, ongoing exchange of experience and ideas, developing our in-jokes and catch phrases, learn, more or less deeply, to identify with one another and to recognize our perspective on the world as communal. Paul's language of dying and being raised with or like Christ is, not least, a way of capturing this perspective-changing nature of trust.

[138] Duyndam (2004) offers a helpful philosophical analysis of exemplarity, particularly in relation to sainthood, but which is also relevant to Christ's exemplarity.

[139] See especially Meeks (1986), 136–43, Hooker (1996), 92, Hays (1997a), 215–24, Weaver (2013), 1–45. Keck (1996), 10 emphasizes that the language of imitating Christ should not be conflated with practising virtue, which has implications of self-regulation and self-control inappropriate to early Christian (or Jewish) writers whose focus is on trust, obedience, and service to God and Christ. On the role of imitation in the gospels see notably Beck (1981, 1989), Lampe (1981), Ruthven (2000), Burridge (2007), chs 3–6.

[140] pp. 135–6.

same things from your compatriots as they did from the Jews'.[141] These passages are sometimes taken to mean that the Thessalonians can console themselves in their suffering by remembering that Christ, Paul, and other churches have suffered too,[142] but Paul's language of imitation suggests more than, 'These things happen to us all.' It indicates that suffering, if not actively to be sought, makes the faithful more like Christ, while expressing their trust and perhaps also strengthening it (cf. 1 Thess. 3.10, cf, 13).

At 1 Corinthians 4.16–17, Paul urges the Corinthian *pistoi* to become imitators of him who has become their father 'in Christ'.[143] Paul has been arguing since 1.10 that the Corinthians should not divide into factions loyal to different apostles but preserve unity, because all apostles are ministers of God and Christ and the Corinthians belong, ultimately, solely to Christ and through him to God (cf. 3.23). At the beginning of chapter 4 he affirms his own trustworthiness as a 'slave of Christ and steward of the mysteries of God' (cf. 4.1–2) who, he says, will be judged by God (4.3–5),[144] and at 4.6 says that he has applied 'these things'—probably the preceding point—to himself and Apollos for the Corinthians' benefit, so that the Corinthians may learn from them not to 'go beyond what is written' and be 'puffed up in favour of one person against another'.[145] We saw above that in chapter 1 Paul is scathing about those *apistoi* who rely on their own wisdom to know God (1.21) and the way to 'righteousness, sanctification, and redemption' (1.30), rather than putting their trust in God and Christ and the 'foolishness' of the message of the cross (cf. 1.18). Here he turns the same critique on the Corinthian *pistoi*. They are 'puffed up' with pride (4.6) in that they think they are in a position to assess the relative merits of ministers from whom they received everything they 'possess' about the gospel (4.7). Paul draws a contrast between what, in the Corinthians' own eyes, is their wisdom, strength, and honour (4.9–10), and the humiliations endured by himself and, very likely, his co-workers. They have become a spectacle to the world, fools on Christ's account, weak and disreputable. They have been ridiculed, persecuted, slandered, and treated like scum. He is telling the

---

[141] This clause, which creates an awkward turn in the argument, may well be a post-Pauline gloss.

[142] So e.g. Michaelis (1964), IV, 666–7; *contra* de Boer (1962), Proposition 4; 210. The Thessalonians and others, of course, have not suffered in the same way as Christ: in practical terms, there is no indication that they are being persecuted to the point of death, and their suffering is not salvific for others. Bultmann (1969), 239, 245–6 argues that Christ's divine nature and the uniqueness of his atoning sacrifice make imitation impossible, so Paul's (and others') language of imitation in itself suggests that the model of sacrifice is not central to Paul's thought (cf. Michaelis (1964), 671, Betz (1967), 187, Outka (1972), 149, Marxsen (1993), 53–5).

[143] 'In Christ' here is probably encheiristic: Paul is the Corinthians' father insofar as he, as an apostle, lives and works under Christ's authority and 'in his hands' (cf. Tuckett (2001), 45).

[144] The reference to the mysteries may be linked with the concept of imitation: Betz (1967), 138 argues that the language of mimesis itself comes from the mysteries.

[145] The Corinthians are regularly 'puffed up' (cf. 4.18, 19, 5.2, 8.1, 13.4, 2 Cor. 12.20; elsewhere only Col. 2.18); Barrett (1968), *ad* 1 Cor. 4.6 connects it with the Corinthians' arrogant determination to choose their own leaders. Conzelmann (1975), *ad loc.* notes that this verse and section warn against human beings' passing judgment in general, since judgment is reserved to God at the *eschaton*.

Corinthians this, Paul says (14–15), not to shame but to admonish them: he is their father in Christ and they should imitate him. He is sending Timothy to remind the Corinthians of his 'ways in Christ Jesus' (4.17), just as he teaches them elsewhere. 'Ways' suggest more than teachings (especially if we want to avoid tautology at 4.17): probably the whole package of Paul's teaching and example as a servant and fool for Christ.[146]

This passage is occasionally read as demanding that the Corinthians should accept Paul's apostolic authority despite everything he has suffered, but this does not do justice to the connection between chapter 4, in which Paul calls the apostles fools on Christ's account (4.10), and chapters 2–3, where Paul repeatedly describes the message of the cross as foolish in the world's terms and the wisdom of God as the opposite of the wisdom of the world.[147] By being trustworthy servants and stewards of the message of the cross, Paul and his co-workers embody the foolishness of the cross and the mysteriousness of God's wisdom in their lives and actions, as they speak of it in their teaching.[148] Like Christ to God, Paul is trustworthy to Christ and Godself, and Timothy to Paul (4.17), and through their imitative *pistis* the power of God (cf. 1.18) spreads wider and wider to bring more people to trust. To understand this, the Corinthians must stop trying to be wise or to judge Paul (cf. 4.5), but trust and imitate him as he trusts and imitates Christ.[149]

At 1 Cor. 10.31–11.2, Paul says

> whether you eat or drink, or whatever you do, do everything for the glory of God. Be irreproachable, whether to Jews or Greeks or the assembly of God, just as I try to please everyone in every way, not seeking my own benefit but that of the many, that so they may be saved. (11.1) Be imitators of me, as I am of Christ (μιμηταί μου γίνεσθε καθὼς κἀγὼ Χριστοῦ). I praise you because you remember me in everything and keep the traditions, just as I handed them on to you.

At some point, a scribe dividing the letter into chapters took 11.1 as closely linked with 11.2. Imitating a person, though, is not the same as following their teachings, and 11.1 reads more naturally as the culmination of the previous few verses, in which Paul has been telling the Corinthians to do as he does. 11.2 then makes sense as a coda to the whole passage, in which Paul praises the Corinthians both

---

[146] Conzelmann (1975), *ad loc* is surely right to see Paul's sufferings as imitating Christ's, but limits 4.17 unnecessarily to Paul's teaching; cf. Blendinger, Müller, and Bauder (1975) I. 491.

[147] So Fitzmyer (2008), 210. Collins (1999), 192–3 notes that 4.8–13 echoes the list of tribulations or peristatic catalogues of Hellenistic, including Hellenistic Jewish literature, which demonstrate the virtue of the subject by his ability to overcome adversity. The reference to Paul's toil may refer to his apostolic work as much as to his work with his hands (so Barrett (1968), *ad* 4.12.)

[148] Helpfully discussed by Thistleton (2000), 365–8.

[149] Cf. 1. Cor 15.4 with its possible allusion to Ps. 16.8–11 (15.8–11 LXX) (God will not allow his holy one to see corruption (v. 10)), and 2 Cor. 4.13 with its reference to Ps. 116.10–15 (115.1–6) (the psalmist puts his trust in the Lord because the death of his holy ones is precious in the Lord's eyes).

for remembering him and for following his teachings. On this reading, 11.1 means, 'Imitate me, as I imitate Christ, in seeking the benefit of the many, so that they may be saved.'[150] Both Paul's preaching and his actions and sufferings as one who is *pistos* continue the salvific work of Christ in the world.[151]

Imitation is also implicit in a number of passages where the language of *mimēsis* does not appear. As we have seen, Paul introduces the 'Christ-hymn' in Philippians (2.5–11) by exhorting the Philippians, 'Have among yourselves the same attitude that is also yours in Christ Jesus', the 'mind' that led Christ to empty himself, take the form of a slave, humble himself, become obedient to death on a cross.[152] As Morna Hooker has argued, it seems likely here that the Philippians are being invited not only to exercise humility and obedience but also, in some sense, to identify with and model their life of faith on the self-emptying of Christ.[153]

Imitating Christ, then, expresses one's trust in Christ, makes one more like Christ, and continues Christ's saving work in the world. These are not the only passages in which Paul commends to followers of Christ activities that are also associated with Jesus during his lifetime. At 1 Corinthians 12.8–10, for example, community members are described, among other things, as healing, doing mighty deeds, prophesying, and discerning spirits. But here and elsewhere, such activities are described by Paul as gifts of the spirit rather than as ways in which the Corinthians follow Christ.[154] When Paul speaks of people following or imitating Christ (directly or indirectly), it is consistently in connection with Christ's suffering and death.[155]

Returning to the image of the child taking the train journey, we can see how the idea of imitation might also play a part in helping the child travel and arrive safely. The small child who carefully imitates everything her mother does is a familiar sight on public transport. She has her own small suitcase, and perhaps a backpack. She follows closely in her mother's footsteps as they climb up into the train. She stows her suitcase next to her mother's and sits down by her side. It is not just her mother's presence with her and the fact that her mother has taken the

---

[150] On imitating God or Christ see also Eph. 5.1–2, 1 Pet. 2.21, 23–4; on imitating Paul see also 2 Thess. 3.7–9.

[151] Michaelis (1964), 667–8 raises the question why Paul does not simply tell the Corinthians to imitate Christ, but that would circumvent his own authority which he is here emphasizing. Paul is probably not explicitly looking forward to his physical death here, nor does he conflate his apostolic activity with Christ's salvific activity, but there is reason to think that, as elsewhere, he sees following Christ as a death to the world; he has just described the celebration of the Lord's supper as a sharing in the body and blood, i.e. the sacrificial death of Christ (10.16–17, cf. 18).

[152] Transl. NAB.

[153] Hooker (1979), 74–6, cf. Lohmeyer (1928), 91, Hays (2002), 73–117. At Rom. 15.1–3, the faithful should tolerate the failings of the weak and not please ourselves, as Christ did not.

[154] Rom. 12.6–8, 1 Cor. 12.28–31, 14.1–2, 1 Thess. 5.19–20, cf. Eph. 4.11.

[155] Hebrews also speaks of imitating Christ in suffering and death: e.g. 12.1–3, with Richardson (2012).

journey before that reassures her, but also the fact that she can model her actions on her mother's every step of the way.

If the child has a younger sister, then in due course she may, in turn, become her sister's model and reassurance when they travel together. In much the same way, when Paul speaks of himself as *pistos* and encourages others to imitate him as he imitates Christ, he understands himself as continuing, in his life and work, what was done through Christ's suffering and death, and thereby as playing a part in God's ongoing action and revelation which enables others to come to trust and remain in trust until the *parousia*.

It is worth noting that Paul's and others' discourse of imitation of the suffering of Christ does not fit easily within the typology of imitation developed by scholars of exemplarity in the Greek and Roman worlds and adopted by some New Testament scholars.[156] When, in Greek and Roman moralizing literature, great men and women are held up as examples to be imitated, their exemplarity normally consists in either a virtue or an action. Horatius Cocles defends Rome from the invading Etruscans in the sixth century BCE by holding the Sublician bridge with two comrades until it can be destroyed behind them.[157] Achilles and Ajax, in different ways, exemplify courage, Odysseus and Nestor wisdom.[158] Suffering, however, is neither a virtue nor an action. A follower of Christ may undergo suffering, and even welcome it as a way of coming closer to Christ, but Paul never suggests that it is an intrinsically good thing, that Christians should actively seek it out, or that it should take any particular form. To do justice to Paul's understanding of *imitatio Christi*, we need a third category of imitation, which we might describe as 'embracing the consequences of a commitment one has made', in the trust, hope, and conviction that, however apparently negative, they will ultimately be justified.

For Paul and his followers, willingness to suffer, like Christ, for the gospel, is an expression of trust in what has been revealed and preached to them.[159] It is, further, an expression of trust in the process by which God and Christ are righteousing and ultimately saving all nations.[160] Equally importantly, it is an expression of trust in their own part in this process: their entrustedness with the gospel and with new life in the present time, by which they become part of God's and Christ's

---

[156] See e.g. O'Brien Wicker (1978), Pelling (1988, 1995), Duff (1999), van Hoof (2010), 42–54, 74–7, with notably Plu., *Quomodo adulescens, passim,* and *Mor.* 439e. Edwards (2006) is unusual (and, I think, right) in resisting the assumption that exemplarity in New Testament writings follows the pattern of Greek and Roman exemplarity.

[157] Polyb. 6.55, Liv. 2.10.

[158] Plu., *Mor.* 243c–d. For highly nuanced recent discussions of the workings of Greek and Roman exemplarity see Langlands (2018), Roller (2018).

[159] Bultmann (1964), 208–9 calls this an attitude and *praxis* in which trust and faithfulness are closely entwined with obedience and hope.

[160] In the trust that 'all things work for good for those who love God', Rom. 8.28.

ongoing self-revelation in the world and the spread of *pistis*.¹⁶¹ Not least, it is an expression of their willingness to serve: to offer their lives and actions, as Christ did in his earthly life and death, in service to God and to the exalted Christ himself.¹⁶² We might also pick up a hint in 1 Thessalonians 1.6, and see suffering as the dark counterpart of life in the spirit. The more vibrant and distinctive life is within the Christian community, the more liable it is to attract suspicion and hostility from outside, but if the former is to be sought, then the latter must be borne.¹⁶³

In the landscape of early imperial exemplarity, imitation of Christ, involving both trust in what God has done and is doing through Christ, and acceptance of the consequences of that trust as exemplified by Christ, has a further implication. It commits those who practise it not only to holding an attitude (like courage, say, or wisdom) or practising one type of action, but to following a path of action. Following a path informed by a (religious, intellectual, moral, or other) commitment is the beginning of what Christians, and others in their world, call a *hodos*, a 'way'; and following a way, with acknowledged leaders and authorities, in company with others who are following it, creates a not only a moral or intellectual, but a social identity for the follower.¹⁶⁴ Paul's call to *pistis*, as he himself never forgets, therefore invites people into not only a new relationship with God and Christ, but a new community and way of life, even in the present age.

Finally, the suffering and death of Christ, and preaching about it, change human beings' understanding of how it is possible for human beings to live transformatively for God. By this token, we can see the imitability of Christ as contributing to divine–human at-one-ment in its own right. We might compare what happens when the first athlete runs a four-minute mile or a sub-ten-second hundred metres. Almost immediately, a number of others find that they can also run a time which until that moment was widely seen as impossible, because the first athlete has changed their understanding of the possible.¹⁶⁵ Christ's trust, trust-

---

¹⁶¹ At 1 Thessalonians 1.6–8 willingness to suffer seems to strengthen other *pisteuontes* and even to speak to non-community members. For the idea that commitment to one's allegiance or values might convert one's enemies cf. Dan. 3.1–30, Liv. 5.27.14, cf. Plu. *Mor.* 90f–91a.

¹⁶² Cf. Rom. 1.1, 1 Cor. 7.22, Gal. 1.10, Phil. 1.1.

¹⁶³ Paul may also see imitating Christ by being willing to accept suffering as marking the difference between God's values and those of this age and revealing the faithful as belonging to God's kingdom (cf. Betz (1967), 186–9). Embracing the consequences of a commitment one has made has something in common with martyrdom, of which Christ's suffering is treated as a model elsewhere, but is a broader category.

¹⁶⁴ Noted by Michaelis (1968), 668. McKaughan (2016) discusses the combination of trust in a person and commitment to following that person or a way of life (though he characterizes this as 'faith', a term which this study avoids because Christian faith is a complex concept, practice, and concatenation of relationships within which we are discussing the strand of trust; cf. Rice et al. (2017), 1–6).

¹⁶⁵ This phenomenon is recognized in the slogan 'You can't be what you can't see', attributed to the American civil rights activist Marian Wright Edelman and widely referenced in arguments for equal rights and opportunities, and explored in relation to the idea of Christ as mediator in the African American systematic theology of Evans (2012), especially 89–113.

worthiness, and faithfulness to God, even to death, show his followers a way which makes possible their at-one-ment with God and enables them to act as a model for others. For all the writers of the New Testament, the crucifixion, and, more broadly, the Christ event, are unique, but they also enable a relationship with God and a form of life which until that moment might have seemed impossible. The imitation of Christ cannot be understood as a model of atonement in itself, because 'atonement by imitation' would not do justice to the active and proactive relationship of Christ with humanity: his love, trust, trustworthiness, and self-giving.[166] But the imitability of Christ contributes both to the salvation of the faithful at the *parousia*, and to the spreading of the gospel to bring more people to trust.[167]

Trust, Suffering, and Sin

So far, this chapter has argued that Christ, in his death and resurrection, acts as a mediator between God and humanity: his trust, faithfulness, and trustworthiness to both parties make it possible for human beings to return to a relationship of trust and right-standing with God. God and Christ trust one another either because they have coexisted since before creation, or because Christ received the spirit of God at his baptism. God and Christ trust human beings to respond to God's action in Christ. For human beings, however (certainly for Paul, who is little concerned with Jesus' earthly ministry), not only the crucifixion but the resurrection is needed to reveal the transformative possibilities of trust in God and Christ. On a model of atonement centred on the restoration of trust, Christ did not need to die, for instance, as a sacrifice or a substitute for sinful humanity, but his trusting and trustworthy nature meant that he could not have been himself and tried to evade death. In addition, his death is a gracious, and perhaps necessary gift, which makes it possible for humanity, by dying 'with Christ', to take the risk and the step of trust by which they die to sin and the suffering which sin imposes on this world. As a model of trust and trustworthiness, moreover, Christ changes what is thinkable and doable for the rest of humanity.

All this does not amount to a simple, unifocal model of atonement, but that is not necessarily a problem, given that its elements are mutually compatible, and since neither New Testament writers nor later Christians have found any one, simple model universally acceptable or adequate to their thinking. So far, however,

---

[166] Some feminist theologies, unhappy with the violence inherent in many theories of atonement (e.g. Finger (1988), Hopkins (1994), Van Dyk (1996), Carlson Brown and Bohn (1989), Solberg (1997), Keshgegian (2000), Weaver (2001), Streufert (2006), Vandenberg (2007), Gudmundsdottir (2010), Geneva Cannon et al. (2011)), identify exemplarity as one alternative model; as above, I do not think that exemplarity can act as a complete model of atonement, but it can contribute.

[167] See also pp. 286–7, 319, 320–1.

our argument has not answered the third question we posed on page 162: how the restoration of divine–human trust makes possible the release of humanity from both sin and suffering.

The second section of this chapter argued that sin, suffering (both guilty and innocent), and the failure of trust are closely entwined in the scriptures, in Jewish tradition, in everyday experience, and in Paul's thinking. Sin is often presented as a response to a perceived failure of trust, which can also be experienced as suffering. The absence of trust is a cause of both suffering and sin; and sin can be experienced as slavery to a power which, whether internal or external, is beyond the sufferer's control. Some people suffer and struggle to trust because of other people's sins, without sinning themselves. To illustrate how the double relationship of *pistis* between God, Christ, and humanity addresses sin, both kinds of suffering, and *apistia*, it may be helpful to consider another fictional scenario. Readers should be warned that this scenario refers to the trauma of adult-child abuse.

Daphne is 15 years old, and is the victim of a violent stepfather. Her abuser Delius was abused himself as a boy and, as an adult, unable to handle his suffering or his anger, has turned to abusing others.[168] Daphne cannot physically stop him. She does not know of any way to take away his suffering or his anger, or to address the brutality with which he is replicating his own experience. Trapped in her suffering, she is slipping into ever deeper fear and misery. Having long ago lost trust in her abuser, she is losing trust in anyone else to help her, and withdrawing from friends and relatives, who, in turn, are hurt and annoyed by the change in her behaviour. At the same time, Delius, pathologically, is becoming the one person she can rely on, at least, to need her; in the absence of help from any other quarter, it becomes harder to imagine breaking out of the relationship.

The organization Help for Adult Victims of Child Abuse (HAVOCA) describes the damage abuse does to victims' ability to make and sustain relationships of trust:

> If I had a pound for every time somebody emailed HAVOCA and said they had trust issues, I'd be a rich man. It is the one characteristic that raises its ugly head on a regular basis—trusting oneself and trusting others...Lack of trusting yourself can manifest itself in a lack of trusting others and ultimately a lack of trust in your relationships...Learning to trust yourself and others is a big step—it takes time and practise...[169]

---

[168] Tenkorang et al. (2018) examines help-seeking behaviour in victims of domestic abuse and finds it strongly correlated with existing trust in formal and informal support networks, which, however, themselves tend to be weak in the group studied. Buck et al. (2012) finds that male batterers tend to suffer from insecure attachment, including lack of trust, cf. Scully (1988).

[169] <https://www.havoca.org/survivors/trust>. The second page goes on to emphasize that changing one's mindset is an essential first step, but only the first step.

Even those who believe in a God of justice and love, or live in a culture shaped by the idea of such a God, find it extraordinarily difficult, or impossible, not to retaliate when we are hurt, not to lose faith in the people around us when we are suffering, or to trust when trust has been betrayed in the past. It is all too easy to see how the sin and suffering of Daphne's situation might continue, generating more abuse and more suffering for more people through time.[170] Most classical theories of atonement, moreover, struggle to meet the problems of human sin, guilt, or suffering since the Christ event.[171] Models of atonement are always in danger of seeming too theoretical, too broad-brush, and too distant from a situation like Daphne's and her stepfather's to have any real bearing on it. At the same time, if a model is worth discussing at all, we must consider how it might speak to such a situation.

The vision of the death and resurrection of Christ which this chapter has sketched is, like all models of atonement, a vision of a God who does what humanity cannot do alone, bringing life and renewal out of the most extreme human sin and suffering. Like a good gardener, who takes the weeds she has removed from among the cultivated plants, the dead flower-heads, and rotten fruit, and adds them all to her compost heap, where gradually they turn back into nutritious soil which is returned to feed the garden the next year and grow into fresh flowers and fruit, God accepts the worst of human action and experience and 'composts' it, turning it back into earth in which new life grows and flourishes. Both sin and suffering can be likened to what the gardener composts, because both militate against new and renewed life and relationships. Our sins damage ourselves, our relationships, and other beings. Our suffering also damages ourselves—our sense that we have any human value, for instance, or that we are loveable, or have anything to hope for—and our relationships, and therefore, indirectly and often unintentionally, other beings too. Plants do not choose whether to be composted by the gardener but, for Paul and almost all early Christian writers, human beings can entrust themselves, their sin, and their suffering, through Christ, to the transformational power of God. How God 'composts' human suffering and evil remains a mystery and, given the limitations of human understanding, perhaps it must; but it is not the mechanics of the process human beings most need to understand, but the outcome.

In this gardening image, the sins or suffering human beings entrust to God and Christ are not strictly the actions they commit or damage that is done to them, in themselves. They cannot assume (as Paul does not assume) that trusting in God and Christ mean that they will never think or behave badly again, or that they will

---

[170] This scenario cannot begin to do justice to theological discussions of abuse and theories of atonement in light of the fact of abuse, on which see e.g. Carlson Brown (1992), Houts (1992), Schertz (1994), Deaver (2017).
[171] Stump (2018), 3–39.

never suffer again, much less that, if they trust, the damage they do to themselves and others or that is done to them no longer matters. What they entrust to God is the power their sins and our suffering have over them, to entrap them in their situations and toxic relationships. What the trust and trustworthiness of God and Christ offer them is the power to be renewed and to make new and life-giving relationships even out of what is most toxic in their lives.[172]

Neither Daphne nor Delius can see a way out of their suffering, his violence, or their alienation and loss of trust, that would lead to a new and better life.[173] But Daphne might see in God and Christ persons who do not, in any circumstances, collaborate with evil, and who act always and only for life and human flourishing. This vision of God as righteous and life-giving is a vision of a God who assures Daphne that suffering at the hands of an abuser is not normal or right. Beyond the violence in which she feels trapped, however, there is life, and the possibility of renewed life in trusting and trustworthy relationships.

Christ has suffered as Daphne suffers, though not in the same way, and he is with her in her suffering, and will always be with her. But Christ's trust relationship with God brought him and, with him, his people, out of suffering, into new life. Where he has been, Daphne can go. The first assurance this vision offers to Daphne is that her suffering is an intolerable evil. The second is that a wholly different life is imaginable and possible. The third is that, in company and in trust with Christ, there is a way out of this evil. The fourth is that, if Daphne can trust in God and Christ, she can also be entrusted with the power to act with God for the practical renewal of her life.[174] At first, God's power might be experienced in the courage and determination to seek help which can extricate Daphne from her impossible situation. Later, it might be the power to remake her life with new relationships, or to support others who are in the evil place where she has been.

Trusting in God does not remove Daphne from the violent relationship in which she is suffering, nor negate the damage that is being done to her. But it may free her from the power which suffering has over her to make her believe that her life could not be different, or that she does not deserve any better. It has the potential to change her vision of the world, and with it her capacity to act, to seek help, and to accept it. It opens up the possibility that her suffering can be 'composted' into new self-confidence, new power to make new, life-giving relationships, and even, eventually, the power to inspire and support others who are suffering as she has suffered.

---

[172] On being released from the power of sin, see Rom. 6.7, cf. 5.21, 6.6, 6.9, 3.9 (Gaventa (2004), 234).

[173] The trust model suggests one reason why, for Christ-confessors, it quickly became important to connect Christ's death and trust in God's action through Christ with the person of Jesus in his earthly life, because the more people know about the Jesus in whom they were invited to trust, the more content trust could accrue.

[174] And that of others: cf. pp. 283–97.

We have argued that sin can be a response to suffering, and it may be that the assurance that suffering is not normal or right could reach Delius too, and find a response. But Delius has already put his trust in himself and in violence to satisfy his needs and solve his problems, so it may be that this assurance is not enough to change his sense of what is possible for him. For Delius, the invitation to trust may be less an assurance than a challenge to recognize that his abuse of his stepdaughter, and, in general, his self-trust are not solving anything. Rather, they are reinforcing his alienation from those closest to him, making others suffer, involving him in further toxic relationships, and putting him at risk of being arrested and imprisoned. For Delius, the invitation to trust is an invitation to trust less in his own ability to solve his problems or meet his needs, and be open to the possibility of more abundant life in a different reality.[175]

God's action in Christ here acts as a sign that this is not a world in which evil is acceptable, nor in which the evil that is done stays done forever. It is not a world in which, when people fail, their failures work themselves out inexorably in suffering and lost opportunities, and those who are damaged, stay damaged and pass their damage on. Rather, this is a world in which evil is always being interrupted by new life and new possibilities for action and relationships, and in which entering a new relationship of trust with God and Christ can change those who enter it for good.

Familiar as we are with models of atonement which understand Christ's death, for instance, as an atoning sacrifice or penal substitution, we may be tempted to think of trust as a weaker or less direct means of atonement than these. In fact, a wealth of recent research in social science and psychology, most notably on the role of trust in the rehabilitation of offenders and ex-offenders, testifies to the opposite. Trust relationships change people and change the course of their lives in direct and decisive ways.

In many western countries, governmental and not-for-profit organizations work side by side, offering support and mentoring to ex-offenders—many of whom are victims of crime and abuse as well as perpetrators—to help them to make new lives after their release from prison and not to reoffend. One story from an initiative in Cleveland, Ohio, may stand for many. In the 1980s and 1990s, six Christian denominations in Cleveland jointly administered a Community Re-Entry (CR) Program, which sought to enable ex-convicts to re-enter and remain part of mainstream society. Part of the programme was Care Team, a group of ex-convicts who were trained to assist vulnerable elderly residents in a local housing authority. Although the CR Program had invested trust in team members, and team members had affirmed their intention to be trustworthy, the vulnerable residents initially found it hard to trust them—for instance,

---

[175] On openness to a new perspective as a precursor to trust in the gospels see pp. 255–8.

with money for buying groceries and other necessities. Gradually, however, reassured by what they saw as the trustworthiness of the programme's administrators, the residents took the risk. Team members proved highly trustworthy, and trust relationships began to develop. On one landmark day, a team member came into the CR office with $300 in cash which a resident had entrusted to him to deposit in her bank. There were tears in his eyes. 'No one has trusted me like this since I was 13 years old,' he said.[176]

The denominations which administered this programme were committed to the possibility that ex-offenders could, by trusting, and being trusted therapeutically by an organization whose own trustworthiness was rooted in its trust in God and Christ, become trusting and trustworthy in turn, and be rehabilitated.[177] They acted as we have suggested Christ acts in his death, to enable, by their trust and trustworthiness towards both parties, trust to develop between the ex-convicts and community residents. Between about 1980 and 2000, when the programme was described in an article by Richard E. Sering, more than 1,000 offenders took part in the programme every year and at least 93 per cent annually stayed out of prison. Trust, together with practical help and the opportunity to practise a new way of life, changed thousands of lives. Not the least striking aspect of this, and many similar stories of rehabilitation, is that ex-offenders were invited not only to trust the Re-Entry Program and let themselves be helped, but to become trustworthy and help others. We will explore the significance of being entrusted and trustworthy in Chapter 7, but here we can note that becoming trustworthy towards others is not only a consequence of learning to trust, but part of entering a trust relationship, and integral to the change that trust can bring about. Returning to the situation of Delius, it may be that hope for change for him lies not only in the challenge to trust in God and Christ and enter a new life, but also in the affirmation that God and Christ are ready to trust him, despite his record, with a new and different life, and new and life-giving relationships.

Life-changing trust can take place between two parties, or, as in the Cleveland CR Program, it can be mediated through a third party. In a recent report into government-administered Youth Offending Teams (YOTs, part of HMI Probation services) in the UK, one young offender attests to the role of his parents in mediating trust between the Youth Offending Team and himself:

If your YOT worker gets on well with your parents...then you, you form a bond, it's like that trust circle in'it? It opens up a bit more because you think well yeah, my parents trust them maybe I can trust them that little bit more. And if, if they

---

[176] Serling (2000), 1263, cf. Armstrong (2014), Obatusin and Ritter-Williams (2019) on the role of trust in the employment of ex-offenders.
[177] On the role of human mediators in imitation of Christ see also pp. 190–1.

get on well and they're chatting and that then it's like it's a good thing because then it makes you feel better about yourself.[178]

This young offender not only recognizes the role of his parents in mediating between himself and the YOT, but also puts his finger on a key aspect of therapeutic trust. At a time when many young people feel worst about themselves and their prospects, mired in the grip of past errors and present difficulties, 'it makes you feel better about yourself'.

Another group of recent studies has shown the effectiveness of inviting ex-offenders to share their experience of crime, punishment, and rehabilitation with other offenders or groups who, because they have grown up in difficult circumstances, are deemed at higher than average risk of offending.[179] Meeting people with whom they can identify, who have offended, whose lives and values have subsequently changed, and who encourage and support them in taking a different path, can change the course of offenders' or potential offenders' lives. As Sean Creaney observes, change is brought about less by tools or programmes than by 'the existence of a trusting, empathetic and consistent relationship which provides sources of hope'.[180] This model reminds us of what Paul and other New Testament writers never forget, that the death of Christ makes possible the release of sinners from sin not only through encounter with Christ himself, but also through the testimony of those who have encountered him and been changed. It may be, for instance, that one hope for change for both Daphne and Delius lies in the testimony of others that there is a different and better life beyond violence and abuse, as much as in the sign that God brings life out of Christ's suffering and death. Not only does trust between God, Christ, and humanity enable the at-one-ment of humanity with God in itself, but the trust and trustworthiness of those who trust cascades through the world to enable change for others.

On this model, God is ready to act for humanity at any time, but not without human willingness to be part of the process. If human beings turn away from God in distrust, or prefer to trust themselves or other powers, real or imagined, to govern their lives and solve their problems, God does not intervene by force. In the Christ event, however, God reveals God's righteousness and invites (re)new(ed) human trust. The Christ who trusts God and is trustworthy towards God allows God to bring new life out of his suffering and the evil of his death and, with his suffering and death, that of his people.[181] Christ's trustworthiness and trust not only in God but also in his fellow human beings invites them to trust him, and the new life God brings out of his death shows them their opportunity to

---

[178] Larkins and Wainwright (2014), 15.
[179] E.g. Barry (2000), Boyce et al. (2009), Weaver (2015), Buck (2017a, 2017b), Creaney (2020).
[180] Creaney (2020), 24 (italics original), 22.
[181] Envisaging Christ here as leader but not necessarily as representative.

enter new life in trust with God.[182] The trust into which human beings are invited is not only trust in God and Christ, but also trust (which is closely related to hope) in a new future and trust in others who embrace that future.

The previous paragraph, however, raises a further question about Daphne's situation. I have not suggested that Daphne's suffering is in any way a result of her own sin (nor did I intend to imply that she inherited original sin): she is an innocent victim. Is it not cruel that Daphne's unmerited suffering damages her ability to trust, and potentially puts an obstacle in the way of her salvation through no fault of her own? Can we countenance the vision of a God who allows obstacles to salvation to be put in the way of the innocent because they have suffered?

It is cruelly unjust that Daphne's suffering damages her ability to trust. Part of what makes sin sin and evil evil is the often life-changing damage it does to the innocent, and we should surely envisage that one reason why God seeks reconciliation with the sinful is for the sake of the innocent who are damaged by their sins. The model we have outlined does not even help Daphne by arguing, for instance, that God gives her grace or the gift of the spirit which enables her to trust. (Even such a gift would not necessarily fully compensate for her lack of trust.[183] In models of atonement in which grace or the spirit does enable trust, or, more broadly, faith which encompasses trust, unless they are also predestinarian, a person under grace must still actively trust or have faith in order to be saved, so the grace that enables trust or faith does not itself free one from sin or the damage done by sin.) I think, however, that the model we have outlined can answer this challenge in a way that is not glib. It is a brutal fact of our experience that sin damages the ability of the guilty and the innocent alike to trust, and one which no model of atonement should gloss over. But Paul, and probably all New Testament writers, affirm that those who are suffering through no fault of their own *can* respond to other persons with trust.[184] Trust, for many people, may not be easy, but it remains possible. This conviction fits well with the examples we have seen in the psychological and sociological literature, which attest that trust can be built or rebuilt even among offenders and ex-offenders, victims of crime, the vulnerable, and those who have suffered abuse. The (re)building of trust may be a slow process, but a model in which salvation is not a 'done deal' until the end time

---

[182] This model focuses on Christ's death rather than specifically on the cross. Though the humiliating circumstances of Jesus' death are clearly and understandably a 'scandal' for his followers, I am doubtful that we should read them as focusing on the cross itself as strongly as many interpreters do (especially those writing after the abolition of crucifixion in the Roman empire). Crucifixion was a horrific and disgraceful death but a common one, which must, to some degree, have affected perceptions of the horror of it; it was not regarded as the cruellest form of execution in the first century; and the relatively short duration of Jesus' crucifixion, according to the gospel accounts, may have made it less brutal than some.

[183] Cf. pp. 299–300.

[184] Even the final redactor of John, for whom some people are not elected to be able to trust, shows those who are suffering (on behalf of others, in these instances) as trusting (4.50, 11.25–7).

allows for that (all the more as the time before the end continues to lengthen). It also allows for the possibility that trust will periodically falter and fail, and affirms that this need not be a deal-breaker in the divine–human relationship.

In this process, both the incarnation and the imitation of Christ by the faithful are also key elements. New Testament writings affirm that encounters with Christ in both his earthly and his exalted life bring people to trust. So do encounters with those whose trust in God and Christ, and entrustedness by God and Christ with work in the present time, communicate the *pistis* of Christ to humanity until the end time.[185] Daphne's suffering may have damaged her capacity to trust, but she may still be able to trust that the capacity has not been destroyed, and that it can respond to the trust which God, Christ, and the faithful, as followers of Christ, offer in the world.[186]

We have observed that not only human experiences of evil, sin, and suffering since the resurrection, but also the language of trust which this study is tracing through New Testament writings, suggest that what God made possible through Christ in Christ's death need not—even should not—be thought of as having been done once for all. However carefully a gardener cultivates her flower beds, fresh weeds will spring up every year until the last day. Many people have not put their trust in God and Christ, and the trust of those who have is liable to waver and fail periodically. Even right-standing with God is only provisional until the final judgment. The crucifixion and resurrection, when they act as a sign, make best sense of subsequent human experience as a sign not only of what God has done, but of what God, through Christ, continues to make possible for humanity.

The Absence of Trust in the Passion Narratives

Although Paul, as we have seen, speaks of trust in God and Christ regularly in connection with the suffering and death of Jesus Christ, *pistis* language is rare in the gospels' passion narratives.[187] The partial exception is the farewell discourses in John's gospel, where *pisteuein* occurs a handful of times (13.19; 14.1, 10-12, 19; 16.9, 27, 30; 17.8, 20-1), but even here it is noticeably less common than in other passages.[188] Elsewhere it is extremely sparse. At the last supper, Luke's Jesus tells Peter, 'I have prayed about you, that your trust [or 'faithfulness'] may not fail' (22.32). In Matthew's gospel, the chief priests and scribes mock Jesus on the cross, saying, 'He trusted in God (πέποιθεν ἐπὶ τὸν θεόν); let him deliver him now if he wants him' (27.43), and implying that if Jesus' trust in God is visibly vindicated,

---

[185] See especially Chapter 7.
[186] This is an example of propositional trust.
[187] Though see p. 222 and pp. 261-3 on the cry of dereliction.
[188] Cf. pp. 279-80.

they themselves will trust in him (27.42). In Chapter 6 we will suggest that Jesus' agony in the garden, in which he prays for 'this cup' to pass by him, but then says, 'your will be done', uses language of obedience which elsewhere is associated with trust (Mt. 26.39=Mk 14.36=Lk. 22.42).[189]

We can assume that one reason for the paucity of *pistis* language in these chapters is that, elsewhere in the gospels, it is most prominent in teaching and healing scenes. Another is that it is normally put in the mouth of Jesus. During the passion narratives Jesus speaks little and not to call people to trust in God, and this is not a narrative in which most of the actors are seeking Jesus' help or are receptive to a call to trust.[190] But we may also note that where *pistis* language does appear in the passion narratives, it echoes some of its uses in connection with Christ's death and resurrection in the epistles. The taunt of the priests and scribes in Matthew's gospel looks to modern readers, in light of Romans 3 and Galatians 2 (and conceivably also to Matthew or his source), unintentionally ironic, because, for Paul, Christ's trust in God is indeed active in the crucifixion—not to save him from the cross, but to bring the resurrection and the possibility of life-transforming *pistis* out of Jesus' death. We suggested above that, in a *pistis* model of atonement, *pistis* is a process which begins in Jesus Christ's lifetime, continues through the crucifixion and resurrection, and is only brought to full fruition at the *parousia*.[191] In this light, we can hear Jesus' prayer for Peter in Luke's gospel as referring in part to what Jesus hopes may be Peter's trust and faithfulness through the crucifixion, but also, perhaps more importantly (since 22.32b suggests that Luke wants us to think that Jesus foresaw that Peter's *pistis* would fail after Jesus' arrest), to the *pistis* which will enable Peter to preach the gospel after the resurrection. Some of the references to *pisteuein* by John's Jesus in the farewell discourses echo that of earlier passages in the gospel. Jesus exhorts the disciples to trust in him (14.1) and to recognize (using *pisteuein*) the closeness of his relationship with the father (14.10-12, cf. 16.27, 16.30, 17.8[192]). Jesus is, as he has always been, aware of all

---

[189] Brownsberger (2013) emphasizes Jesus' human consciousness' of himself as mediator in his death.
[190] Nor does Jesus use *pistis* language when foretelling his suffering and death earlier in the gospel narratives (in Matthew, Jesus' second passion prediction occurs just after the saying about the power of *pistis* the size of a mustard seed (17.20), but 17.22 marks a break in the narrative so there is no connection between the two). This adds to our impression that the absence of *pistis* language from the passion narratives themselves is likely to be deliberate; it is doubtless possible that both synoptic and Johannine narratives are drawing on existing passion narratives which, for whatever reason, did not use *pistis* language, but there is no direct evidence for this, nor can we assume that the evangelists would not have added *pistis* language for their own purposes had they seen fit.
[191] References to process here and elsewhere are not intended to invoke process theology, since in the understanding of the *pistis* relationship we are developing, the trust, faithfulness, and trustworthiness of human beings, in their relationship with God, may evolve, but God's does not. (We have, of course, talked of God as trusting therapeutically, but I take this not to be one kind of trust which develops into another kind, as the person trusted becomes more trustworthy, but as trust *tout court* which is offered for a particular reason when the person trusted is likely not to be trustworthy.)
[192] 14.12 also refer to trusting or believing in Jesus' works, echoing 10.38.

those who sin by not trusting in him (16.9). But he also foretells the future for the disciples, as he did in chapter 2 (v. 19), so that later, when the events happen that he has prophesied (cf. 2.22), their trust in him may be reinforced or renewed (13.19, cf. 14.29, 2.22).

Pistis in Healings, Exorcisms, and Resurrections: Christ as Mediator and Imitating Christ

If *pistis* language plays very little part in the passion narratives, elsewhere in the gospels people approach Jesus for healing, putting their trust in him, and in the synoptic gospels Jesus sometimes describes their trust as having healed them, using a verb (*sōzein*) that also means 'saved'.[193] In other passages the disciples call on Jesus to save them when they are caught by storms at sea, and Jesus, even as he responds to their appeal, castigates them for not trusting, or not enough. For the evangelists, such stories not only act as testimony that Jesus in his earthly life was the Messiah, but prefigure the saving trust that people will put in him after his death and resurrection.

We can see Jesus' healing and other saving miracles as involving the same double nexus of salvific trust as Paul finds in Christ's death. Jesus is occasionally explicit that to perform great deeds requires trust in God (e.g. Mt. 21.21-2=Mk 11.22-4), and we infer that God entrusts Jesus with power.[194] Those who appeal to Jesus for help put their trust in him (if sometimes far from perfectly), and he implicitly trusts them to be trusting in him (however imperfectly).

Even more strikingly, in several healing stories we can see human beings as playing the role in this double nexus that Jesus plays in his death. When, for example, the friends of the paralytic bring him to be healed (Mt. 9.1-8=Mk 2.1-12=Lk. 5.17-26), Jesus, 'seeing their trust' (Mt. 9.2=Mk 2.5=Lk. 5.20), both healed and forgave him. The friends put their trust in Jesus (and therefore, of course, also in God), and we can infer that they also trust the paralytic to be open to healing.[195] Jesus apparently trusts the friends to be right in their trust in the paralytic, and the paralytic to respond to his power. When the paralytic obeys

---

[193] Cf. Jn 11.12, if, with most commentators, we take *sōzein* as referring to the healing of Lazarus as well as looking forward to his ultimate resurrection.

[194] Christologically some might prefer to say that Jesus shares God's power, but in passages in which Jesus tells the disciples that they must, like him, trust in God to exercise power, or that the exercise of power requires prayer (e.g. Mt. 17.20, Mk 9.29), his human distinctness from God and dependence on God are marked more strongly than his closeness or identity with God.

[195] Especially since Mk 6.6 specifies that Jesus cannot, and Mt. 13.58 that Jesus does not heal where there is no *pistis*; cf. Jas 5.13-15: if a person is sick the prayers of his presbyters will heal him, and if he has committed any sins, they will be forgiven. The sick person implicitly entrusts himself to both Christ and the presbyters, who, entrusted with their office by God and Christ, trust the sick man to be open to healing and Christ to heal him.

Jesus' command to rise, take up his bed, and go home (Mt. 9.6–7=Mk 2.11–12=Lk. 5.24–50), it is clear that he too trusts Jesus.[196] Among other stories which explicitly invoke *pistis* and show it in operation in the same configuration are the healing of the centurion's servant (Mt. 8.5–13=Lk. 7.1–10), the exorcism of the boy possessed by a spirit (Mt. 17.14–21=Mk 9.14–29=Lk. 9.37–43), the healing of the royal official's son (Jn 4.46–54), and the raising of Lazarus (Jn 11.1–44), while one or two further stories, notably that of the Canaanite or Syro-Phoenician woman (Mt. 15.21–8, Mk 7.24–30), imply the same configuration without mentioning *pistis* explicitly.

In none of these stories, of course, do those who intercede for others die, as Christ does, but they do act in extreme ways, and sometimes give up the behaviour expected of self-respecting people. In the process, they are humiliated and occasionally reviled.[197] Within the gospels, their behaviour pre-echoes the humiliation which Christ will undergo, and which Paul describes those who imitate Christ as undergoing at the hands of society. Obliquely and subtly, therefore, gospel stories of the way in which people are inspired by the presence of Jesus among them, in his earthly life, both to put their trust in him and to act in trust as mediators between him and other people, prefigure both Christ's own death and the way his followers will be encouraged to imitate him. By doing so, they add to listeners' sense that Christ's saving activity begins in his earthly life, and underline the continuity between his earthly and risen life and the new life of his followers. They hint that part of what it means to be *pistos* and to imitate Christ is to undertake a mediating role between God and Christ and other human beings, to help to bring the good news and the possibility of salvation to others.[198]

Conclusion

This chapter began with the role of *pistis* in Paul's writing about the death of Christ, taking it as a starting-point from which to outline a *pistis* model of atonement. Both Jews and gentiles can be seen as both sinful and suffering, and as both enacting and suffering from various forms of *apistia*: not trusting in God, trusting in the wrong gods; trusting themselves and their judgment to choose their gods or decide how to worship them, rather than attending to what is revealed to them; trusting their own judgment as to what constitutes a sign; or not trusting themselves to recognize that what the gospel has taught them is 'the power of God for

---

[196] We do not need to assume, from this parallel, that Mark knew Paul's preaching or writings; the model may have been widespread among early communities.
[197] Cf. 1 Cor. 4.9–13.
[198] On those who are healed as mediators of healing and salvation see Estévez López (2009).

salvation'.[199] The failure of Jews and gentiles alike to trust where trust is due may be well meaning (as Paul implies when he talks of his own zeal or that of other Jews) or wilful (as when he talks of the gentiles' failure to see what is revealed in creation). It may even be a response to the perception that one's own trust has been let down. In the case of Daphne, we described how lack of trust may result from abuse, through no fault of the person who is abused. We drew on psychological theories of trust to underline how powerful mistrust or wrongly placed trust can be, putting us in toxic relationships which may be extremely difficult to get out of, and disastrously shaping our sense of reality and our own value.

The failure to trust may be culpable, or it may not, but it is always a problem that needs to be overcome, because it alienates those who do not trust from God and leads to self-destruction, damage to others, and, for Paul, to death. Like a conciliator in the human sphere, however, Christ, by being both trusting and trustworthy towards both God and humanity, makes possible (re)new(ed) divine–human trust and right-standing with God.

We saw how Paul's narrative of reconciliation through *pistis* is closely bound up with the revelation of God's righteousness through the Christ event, because trust and trustworthiness, to be effective, must both exist and be seen to exist. Trust, for Paul, begins when people respond to divine self-revelation. In this context, we argued that Christ allows himself to be taken and crucified because he cannot be other than he is: wholly trusting of God to make possible what God plans, in any circumstances. Christ dies trusting God to bring life even from his death, and trusting human beings to be able to come to trust even out of his death, even as God trusts him to be trusting even to death, and trusts humanity to be able to come to trust even after his death.[200]

Paul's language of dying and living 'with' Christ, in addition to its metaphorical meaning, offers a further insight into why Christ died to enable a new divine–human relationship. Christ's death graciously maps a new route to trust and right-standing with God, showing human beings the way. The exalted Christ accompanies those who put their trust in him on their journey, guiding them and caring for them as they die to sin and are raised to new life, and giving them hope and confidence. Like a mother who travels with her child so that the child can be with her mother—each, in one sense, on the same, and in another sense, on a quite different journey—Christ enables the faithful to trust that with him they will not fail to reach their destination. We noted that, seen in this way, Christ's death can be seen not only as an act of mediation, but also, in some of Paul's and other writers' other terms, as a sacrifice, and an act of redemption and release.

The relationship of 'withness' has aspects of exemplarity, though it is more than an example. Elsewhere, however, for Paul, Christ is also an example to be

---

[199] On appropriate self-trust see pp. 359–60.
[200] On the cry of derelection see pp. 261–3.

imitated. Exemplarity is not a sufficient reason for Christ to die, but it has a capacity to change the way people think and act which can make saving trust possible. In addition, by accepting the consequences of his commitment to God, even to suffering and death, Christ shows his followers a new way to live in this world, while dead to the world's sin and *apistia*, and living, like the exalted Christ himself, for God. Not only, moreover, can Christ himself act as this kind of example; so can those, like Paul, who have put their trust in Christ and been entrusted with authority over others. When human beings put their trust in God and Christ, they also become able to trust that they will eventually be saved: to look forward to the future with propositional trust and hope.

Just as sin and suffering are closely entwined in scripture, tradition, human experience, and New Testament writings, and both are closely entwined with *apistia*, trust has the capacity to bring people both out of suffering and out of sin. This is an advantage of this model over most traditional models of atonement, which focus on Christ's role in releasing people from sin and guilt. The *pistis* of Christ can rescue both Daphne from her struggle to trust as a result of the evil that she has suffered, and Delius from the sins he has committed, in part out of his own suffering. We argued that while trust does not erase suffering, nor nullify sins or make them of no account, nor prevent people from making errors in the future, it makes possible release from the power of sin and suffering, and enables people to seek and accept further help and to change. Through some recent studies of the role of trust and trustworthiness in rehabilitating ex-offenders—many of whom are victims as well as perpetrators of crime—we saw how powerful the role of trust can be in enabling the return of modern *apistoi* into mainstream society, or their entry into it for the first time. Being trusted therapeutically, and being invited to trust individuals and bodies which have a record of trustworthiness, is well documented as having the capacity to change lives, radically and permanently. Those whose lives have been changed, moreover, can become sources of trust and trustworthiness for others, extending the working of trust further through society.

In Chapter 3, we noted that the call to trust in Christ was likely first applied to the risen Christ, on the basis of the resurrection experiences and the interpretations of those who experienced or heard about those experiences. Because the gospels play such a large part in public worship, and because in the modern era there has been intense interest in the historical Jesus, modern Christians tend to think of the crucifixion as the climax of Jesus Christ's earthly life and ministry. Paul and other early Christ-confessors, especially those who did not know Jesus in his earthly life, probably thought intensively about the crucifixion first in the context of their commitment to the exalted Christ and their anticipation of Christ's future coming. They could trust in Christ crucified, and trust that the crucifixion was part of God's action through Christ, because of, and in light of, the resurrection experiences and their future hope. In that context it is not surprising that Christ crucified, for Paul, is always also Christ raised and exalted, and to die to sin and death is always also to be raised to new life. Neither the crucifixion nor the atonement that is made possible by it are self-contained salvation events; both are part of a sequence of events and restoration of relationships which continues until the end time.[201]

We have seen throughout this study so far that trust makes possible new life and new relationships in God's kingdom and in the society of the faithful. For Paul, the death and resurrection of Christ are central to the inauguration of a new age and the salvation of humanity. Trust between God and Christ, Christ and humanity, and God and humanity is both the catalyst and the expression of the new age and of Paul's eschatological hope. In Paul's vision, and in the model outlined in this chapter, human beings are both the beneficiaries of this new age and new hope, and active participants in it through their trust and, ideally, trustworthiness.

Chapter 3 also noted that in many of his aspects and activities, the risen and exalted Christ evokes the messianic king of some contemporary Jewish hopes. The Christ who mediates between God and humanity, and who dies on the cross, plays a lowlier role than the exalted Christ: in his suffering and death he is fully and destructibly human. In the next two chapters Jesus will, in some ways, be more emphatically human still. At every stage in surviving early writings about salvation, the humanity and human accessibility of Christ are more vividly drawn and form a more important part of what it means to trust in him.

This chapter has touched on the role of therapeutic trust and human trustworthiness in at-one-ment and human beings' right-standing with God. Chapter 7 will explore this theme at greater length, but we can note here that being trusted, recognizing oneself as entrusted, and responding to that trust are a significant part of the process of human at-one-ment with God and eventual salvation. Trust means not only entrusting oneself and trusting for something, but accepting trust, and with it activities, responsibilities, and partnership in the life and hope of God's kingdom.

In Chapter 1, we observed the intimate connection between trust and care: that care depends on trust, and our earliest relationships of trust, if we are fortunate, develop in contexts of care. In Chapter 2, we saw that one of the contexts in which New Testament writers, including Paul, affirm that God and Christ are trustworthy, is when they envisage God as creator, and Christ with God as involved in creation, and that the relationship between God and creation is also one of care. At the end of this chapter, we can propose that the right-standing which is made

---

[201] This is true even of the passage which focuses most strongly on the cross, 1 Cor. 1.18–2.10. Paul focuses on the 'foolishness' of the cross (1.18) here to make the point that human wisdom, left to itself (before or after the Christ event), cannot understand God's purposes, but what Paul describes himself as preaching, through the spirit (cf. 2.4, 10), is God's hidden wisdom (cf. 2.7, 9–10) which is revealed after the resurrection of the 'Lord of glory' (2.8).

possible for human beings through God's actions in Christ and through trust, which Paul can also describe as new life and new creation, should also be thought of as a relationship of care for creation.[202] In this relationship, as we have begun to see, human beings are both cared for, as part of creation,[203] and carers, as imitators of Christ. This raises a further question for Paul's readers. What does trusting in Christ's death and resurrection, and trusting in God and Christ to bring humanity through death to new life and new creation, imply about the relationship of care to which human beings are called with the rest of creation?

---

[202] Whether this is understood as a restoration of the divine–human relationship as it was when Adam and Eve were created, or the formation of a new and even more glorious eschatological relationship: both possibilities can be drawn from different passages, and both may be in the minds of Paul and others.
[203] Cf. Schneider (1992), 357–71, especially 368–70.

5
'Because you have seen me, you have trusted'
The Trustworthiness of Jesus Christ in his Earthly Life

In previous chapters we saw how New Testament writers, especially Paul and his followers, encourage Christ-confessors to put their trust in a God who is trustworthy and caring towards all God's creation, and who, through Jesus Christ, has done a 'new thing', inviting humanity into a new relationship of trust with God.[1] We have seen how this invitation is made, and human beings' response to it made possible, through the death and resurrection of Christ, who, in his exalted life, continues to be near and to work for the faithful as they seek to remain faithful and serve God in the hope of eventual salvation. Throughout these narratives, these writers strongly affirm the identity of Jesus Christ and of his relationship with God and other human beings in his earthly and heavenly life.

The gospels bring together in complex narratives, probably for the first time, the memory and interpretation of Jesus' crucifixion and resurrection with that of his earthly ministry.[2] In broad terms, the gospels share with the epistles their central themes that God has acted anew through Christ; Christ is the same in his earthly and exalted life (and, for John, embodies the pre-existent Logos[3]); and Christ (his identity variously described) is a trusting and trustworthy mediator of what God is making possible for humanity (also variously described).[4] The gospels also attest to Jesus' earthly ministry as a locus of saving or life-giving activity and relationships in its own right. For these writers, it seems, every context in

---

[1] The chapter heading quotation is from Jn 20.29.
[2] This and the next chapter will tend to refer to 'Jesus' rather than to 'Christ', to emphasize his humanity in his earthly life, but not to imply that any of the evangelists holds a 'low' Christology. We may note with de Jonge (1993), 13 that 'Christ' does not appear in 'Q' and is rare in Mark, suggesting that it may not be an equally significant title to all Jesus' followers.
[3] Assuming with almost all commentators that John is not an adoptionist (e.g. Haenchen (1984), 109–13, Watson (1987), Habermann (1990), Kuschel (1992), Talbert (1993), cf. Smit (2015)), and that Christ's pre-existence is not a concern of the synoptic gospels, though for an alternative view see Gathercole (2006a), with Downing (2007). The identity of the Logos is beyond our purview, but Fossum (1995) argues against mainstream 'wisdom' interpretations, reading the Logos, as in some Hellenistic Jewish texts, as the Angel of the Lord; this fits well with John's theme of revelation (cf. de Jonge (1988), 191–2).
[4] Trusting in God and Christ, in the gospels, may lead to healing, forgiveness, new or greater life, admission to the kingdom of God or heaven, the giving of power to become children of God, the giving of eternal life, righteousness, glory, and more.

which people put their trust in Jesus Christ is salvific or life-giving. As, in the Jewish scriptures, any encounter with God is life-changing, one way or another, so any encounter with Jesus changes the future of those who encounter him.[5]

This chapter and the next explore how the gospels present the relationship of trust between God, Jesus, and humanity in Jesus' earthly life and ministry. We will also touch on Jesus' call to his followers to be trustworthy to God or to himself, which will be explored further in Chapter 7. Although, as already noted, it is possible that the historical Jesus called his followers to trust in God, these chapters do not try to resolve that question, nor in general to further the 'quest for the historical Jesus'.

Large parts of these chapters will discuss the four canonical gospels side by side in what, to many, will be a counterintuitive arrangement. In some respects, John's treatment of *pisteuein* is one of the most distinctive features of his gospel and very different from that of the synoptic gospels. For one thing, the synoptic gospels often leave open whether *pistis* is *pistis* in God, Jesus, or both, while, for John, *pisteuein* is almost always trust in Jesus. In John's gospel, moreover, the earthly Jesus in whom people are invited to trust is closely identified with the risen and glorified Jesus, and trusting in Jesus is sometimes explicitly coupled with trusting in Godself. This treatment of *pisteuein* reflects John's dominantly realized eschatology, in contrast to the dominantly future eschatology of the synoptic gospels.[6]

Roman Faith, however, argued that the differences between the gospels' treatment of *pistis/pisteuein* are not as stark as may first appear, and should not distract us from their similarities.[7] In addition to the passages in which the synoptic gospels refer explicitly to trust in Jesus, there are reasons to think that they sometimes intend objectless *pistis* to be heard as referring to Jesus, or to both Jesus and God together.[8] For example, when those seeking healing are commended for

---

[5] Though sometimes, it seems, more incrementally than decisively. This chapter will not discuss whether Jesus or his followers saw him as an eschatological prophet or messianic figure in his lifetime, though the first is likely and the second conceivable (see especially the discussions of de Jonge (1998), Tuckett (2001), 202–26, Dunn and McKnight (2005), 269–344, Evans (2006), Schnelle (2009a), esp. 146–65, cf. Giambrone (2019)).

[6] Though see the argument of Hylen (2009), 69–73, 156–8 that John's eschatology is more future-oriented than we often assume, which she links with the imperfection of the disciples' *pisteuein* and with an interpretation of 'belief' as 'a process or spectrum rather than an all-or-nothing affair' (cf. p. 257 n.41).

[7] In particular, *pisteuein* in John's gospel is more relational (trust-centred) than doxastic (belief-centred) (Morgan (2015a), 394–432), and involves not only (or even primarily) acceptance of the Word (see especially Bultmann (2007), 2.70–4), but also persists through time.

[8] We can assume that trust in God is always implied. Trust in Jesus: Mt. 18.6=Mk 9.42 (though εἰς ἐμέ is weakly attested there), 27.42; cf. Mk 13.21 (where the warning may be not to trust in the news about false messiahs, or in the claimants themselves, or both), Lk. 22.67 (where Jesus' response to the Sanhedrin may mean that if he told them who he was, they would not believe his testimony or would not trust him, or both). In these cases the object of trust is Jesus or testimony about Jesus rather than God, but where the object is not specified it is usually possible to supply both God and Jesus, and this ambiguity may be one of the evangelists' ways of marking Jesus' closeness to God without defining its nature; see Grindheim (2016, with a discussion of earlier views, pp. 79–80), who also argues that

their *pistis*, they are likely to be trusting both in God as the ultimate source of healing and in Jesus as its immediate source. Through their resurrection stories, the synoptic gospels identify the risen Jesus with Jesus in his earthly life as strongly as does John, so we should assume that they too understand Jesus as trustworthy in his earthly, as in his risen life. Although they look forward, and portray Jesus, as eschatological prophet, as looking forward to the coming of God's kingdom and salvation in the future, the synoptic gospels also point periodically to the idea that the kingdom, or salvation, is already here (e.g. Mt. 9.37=Lk. 10.2, Mt. 11.4=Lk. 7.22, Mt. 12.28=Lk. 11.20, Mt. 13.31–2=Mk 4.31=Lk. 13.19–21, Lk. 2.30, 17.21), while John occasionally implies that final salvation lies in the future (5.24, 12.32, 14.3). In all four gospels, moreover, it is the commitment of trust and ongoing faithfulness to Jesus, rather than the belief that he is the Son of God or the Messiah, that is life-giving and salvific (though beliefs are often, perhaps always involved). In exploring how people come (or do not come) to trust in Jesus, and what happens when they do, what follows will argue that in some key respects all four gospels paint a similar picture, and that even where John is significantly different from the synoptics, they share more ground than is often recognized.

In Chapter 2, we saw that New Testament writers' affirmation of the trustworthiness of God is rooted partly in the existing assumption and scriptural attestation that the God of Israel exists and is trustworthy, together with the revelation and interpretation of what God has done through the death and resurrection of Christ. For the gospel writers, as Christ-confessors, affirmation of the trustworthiness of Jesus Christ in his lifetime rests, in significant part, on experience, interpretation, and proclamation of the death and resurrection of Jesus, and interpretation of Jesus' earthly life on that basis, and their depiction of Jesus' trustworthiness in his earthly life and ministry is partly from that perspective. But they are also concerned to show how, and sometimes reflect on why, many people, during Jesus' ministry, did not put their trust in him.[9] Their picture of Jesus' activities is therefore in part an exploration of what makes, or does not make, God's Messiah trustworthy when his appearance, so urgently hoped for, comes in an unexpected form.

The gospels' representation of Jesus mainly as an adult who, in his various activities, engages *de novo* with other adults, means that we should expect trust in Jesus in his earthly life to be marked, within the gospel stories, as a new departure and a choice. In addition, when some of those whom Jesus meets recognize him as 'the one who is to come', Son of David, Messiah, or Holy One of God (e.g. Mt.

---

people are invited to trust in Jesus in the synoptic gospels, as in John, and that the historical Jesus may have invited trust in himself.

[9] The synoptic gospels offer less explicit reflection than John on why people do not trust Jesus in his earthly life, but hints of it appear at Mk 4.11–12, cf. Mt. 13.11=Lk. 8.10; Mt. 12.39, 16.4=Mk 8.12=Lk. 11.29, Mt. 11.21–4=Lk. 10.12–15.

11.3, 15.22, 20.30, Mk 8.29, Lk. 2.30, 9.20, Jn 1.41, 6.69), they recognize Jesus as speaking and acting in some way with divine authority and power. Trust in him is therefore not only a choice to make and pursue a new relationship of trust with Jesus himself, but (for Jews) a choice to reaffirm trust in God in a new context or (for gentiles) to put their trust in the God of Israel for the first time (e.g. Mt. 8.5–13=Lk. 7.1–10, Mt. 15.21–8, Mk 7.24–30, Jn 4.46–54). On this basis, we might expect the trust people put in Jesus to be more like, for instance, the trust Abraham puts in God in Genesis 15, than the aboriginal trust between God, man, and woman. We might also expect this kind of trust to be based extensively on what people see and hear of Jesus—on his eschatological prophecies, teachings, miracles, or signs—and, like Abraham's trust, to be incremental.[10] As it turns out, however, the picture is somewhat different. Jesus' preaching, teaching, signs, and miracles also point to the aboriginal relationship of care between God and humanity, whose restoration is made possible through Christ. Jesus' words and actions, however, though they are represented by all the gospel writers as real and significant indicators of his identity, often do not engender trust by themselves, and can even be treated as if they should not do so.

This and the next chapter are closely related. This chapter focuses on who, according to the gospels, the Jesus Christ is, in whom, with God, people *pisteuein*, and how he calls (or does not call) people to believe, trust, or be faithful. Chapter 6 explores how and why people come to *pisteuein*, and how *pistis* may be partial and insecure, cut with fear, doubt, and scepticism, but nevertheless lead to salvation, forgiveness, or new life. It will emerge that one of the gospels' contributions to Christian understandings of human *pistis* is their rich depiction of its imperfection and instability. As a coda, Chapter 6 also considers some of the ways in which the gospels themselves, as narratives, seek to foster trust in their listeners.

Contexts and Consequences of Trust

Though not ubiquitous, *pistis* language is widely distributed throughout the gospels: especially in healings and other miracles or signs, parables of the end time and other teaching material, and in Jesus' disputes with various authorities and crowds. It is characteristic of Jesus' relationship with his disciples (in principle, though it is more mentioned in the breach than the observance), and its absence is characteristic of those who oppose Jesus throughout the gospels, even at the crucifixion (Mt. 27.42=Mk 15.32). *Pistis* expresses a need and answers it. It creates and maintains a new relationship, brings trusters into God's kingdom, empowers, and, ideally, defuses fear and doubt. *Pistis* language treads a distinctive path

---

[10] Stump (2010), 260–76, Morgan (2015a), 178–85.

through the gospel narratives: ubiquitous in John and closely associated with Jesus' self-identification as Son of God; in the synoptic gospels, present in multiple sources, layers of tradition, and narrative forms, but not closely linked with any of Jesus' messianic titles.[11] As we have noted before, the sense of the significance of *pistis* is clearly widely shared among early Christ-confessors, and Christians are distinctive in putting *pistis* and *pisteuein* at the centre of their understanding of the relationship between God, Christ, and humanity.

The consequence of trusting in Jesus Christ, or in God through him, is indicated in the synoptic gospels whenever Jesus tells a suppliant that their *pistis* has healed them, using a verb (*sōzein*) that is also regularly used to mean 'saved'.[12] It is explicit in the healing of the paralytic when, having seen the *pistis* of the man's friends and healed him, Jesus glosses his action by telling the Pharisees that 'the son of man has authority on earth to forgive sins' (Mt. 9.2-6=Mk 2.5-11=Lk. 5.20-4).[13] In John's gospel, the first person shown to 'receive' Jesus and 'trust in his name' (cf. 1.12) is John the Baptist.[14] Directing his followers' attention to Jesus, John says, 'Behold, the Lamb of God, who takes away [or 'is taking away'] the sin of the world' (1.29).[15] Those who put their trust 'in his name' become children of God (Jn 1.12), are given life or eternal life (e.g. Mk 5.22-3, 35-42=Lk. 8.40-2, 49-55, Jn 3.16, 6.35, 10.26-8, 11.25-6, cf. 4.36, 5.21), enter the kingdom or house of God or heaven (e.g. Mt. 8.11=Lk. 13.29, cf. Jn 14.1-3), or are vindicated at the coming judgment (e.g. Mt. 12.39-42, 24.45-51=Lk. 12.41-6, Mt. 25.14-30, cf. Jn 9.39).[16]

---

[11] Below, pp. 229-31. These chapters focus on the role of *pistis* in the gospels in their current form rather than the history of their composition.

[12] *Sōzein* refers to divine salvation at Mt. 2.21, 10.22, 16.25=Mk 8.35=Lk. 9.24, 19.25=Mk 10.26=Lk. 18.26, Mt. 24.13=Mk 13.13, Mt. 24.22, Lk. 8.12, 13.23, 19.10, 23.35, Jn 3.17, 5.34, 10.9, 11.12, 12.47. Lk. 7.50 makes the connection when Jesus says to the sinful woman who anoints his feet, 'Your sins are forgiven... Your faith has saved you'; cf. Mt. 9.22=Mk 5.34=Lk. 8.48, Mk 10.52=Lk. 18.42, Lk. 17.19, cf. Mt. 14.30.

[13] Cf Mk 1.15, where Jesus calls people to repent and believe or trust in the good news; trusting in his words requires trust in him, and presumably leads to forgiveness. On sickness as a result of sin cf. e.g. Exod. 20.5, Lev. 26.14-33, Deut. 28.15-68, 2 Chr. 21.15, 18-19, Ps. 103.3, 4Q510, 1QapGen. 20.16-29, 1QS 3.20-4. Though human healers or exorcists can seemingly forgive sins in the thinking of at least some groups Davies and Allison (1988-2004), 2.90, Broer (1992)), Jn 9 captures something of the view of all the evangelists when he represents Jesus' healing of the man born blind as sign of his coming from God (v. 33) to judge the world (v. 39) and enable those who trust to 'see' and be released from their sins (cf. vv. 39-41).

[14] Since *pisteuein* is a life-changing commitment here it is well expressed as trust.

[15] Whatever John's point of reference for the phrase 'lamb of God' (discussed e.g. by Brown (1966), 58-63), the present tense refers to what the lamb does, whenever he does it, so this verse does not indicate whether those who trust receive life now or in the eschatological future, but 5.24 suggests both.

[16] Taking 'his name' to refer to that of Jesus rather than the Word, with e.g. Brown (1966), *ad loc.*, following Büchsel, Bauer, and others, since Jesus is the one to whom John testifies, who is also called the light that is in the world in v. 10 and the Word become flesh that lived among us in v. 14, and since it is once he is in the world that he is or is not received by humanity (implied by Moloney (1998), *ad loc.*). Mt. 12.1-32 offers a good example, in brief compass, of the many ways in which gospel writers

Just as gospel writers can speak of salvation, eternal life, or the kingdom of God both as if those who follow Jesus will attain it in the future, and as if it is already with them, so they speak of *pistis* both as something that will be rewarded in the future, and as something that receives an immediate response.[17] The slaves of Matthew 24.45-51 (=Lk. 12.41-6) and 25.14-31 (=Lk. 18.11-27) must be faithful now to be rewarded in the future, when their master returns. The paralytic for whom healing is sought, however, is forgiven immediately (Mt. 9.2=Mk 2.5=Lk. 5.20), while those who are not *oligopistos* and do not worry about their life (Mt. 6.30-1=Lk. 12.28-9) can expect, it seems, to be looked after by God in the present.[18] At John 5.24, Jesus combines both perspectives: 'whoever hears my words and trusts in the one who sent me has eternal life and does not come to condemnation, but has passed from death to life'.[19]

As these examples begin to show, *pistis* language expresses many of the gospels' key theological themes.[20] It is soteriological: *pistis* follows repentance, releases from sin, heals, and leads to new life or new birth.[21] It is Christological: when people trust in Jesus, they are responding to something distinctive about him, even if their belief or understanding about what that is, is imperfect.[22] It is often eschatological: people are called to trust because the kingdom of God is at hand, or the time when the faithful will be vindicated or entrusted with true riches, or will be with God.[23] In a handful of passages, it is charismatic: Jesus promises the disciples that trust in God will bring them a power like Jesus' own.[24] Occasionally, those who trust are cared for by God;[25] and once (in a Markan phrase which echoes the trust that responds to preaching in the Acts and epistles), *pisteuein* is explicitly kerygmatic.[26] More than almost any other single theme or lexicon, *pistis* language weaves together the overall narratives of the gospels, from what God has done through Christ to Christ's identity and work; from how human beings are

---

can represent Jesus as saviour, including as Davidic king, priest, Son of Man, Isaianic servant, and one who is empowered by the spirit of God.

[17] And occasionally as something that anticipates Jesus' hour: cf. Jn 2.1-11.

[18] On Matthew's treatment of *oligopistos* in its narrative context see Olivares (2015).

[19] Cf. Jn 6.25, 27-40, 10.27 (the shepherd protects the sheep in life as well as by laying down his life), 12.44.

[20] The main exception is that it is not used ethically of relationships between community members; the same is true in the epistles if we take *pistis* at 1 Cor. 12.9 to refer to the gift of trustworthiness in leadership, at Gal. 5.22 to refer to faithfulness to God (below, pp. 287-8).

[21] E.g. (among many examples) Mk 1.15 (following repentance), Mt. 9.2, Jn 8.24 (release from sins), Mt. 8.10, 9.21 (healing), Mk 5.34, cf. 16.16, Lk. 18.42 (salvation), Jn 3.12, 6.47-8, cf. 4.50 (new life).

[22] Indicated e.g. by use of a title or the conviction that he can heal: e.g. Mt. 9.27, 15.28, Jn 1.49-50, 11.26-7.

[23] E.g. Mk 1.15 (the kingdom of God is near), Lk. 18.1-8 (vindication), Lk. 16.10-12 (true riches), Jn 14.1-3 (Jesus goes to his father to prepare a place for his followers).

[24] E.g. Mt. 17.20, 21.20-2=Mk 1.20-6. *Pistis* is only once described in the gospels as the direct precursor to receiving the spirit (Jn 7.37-9, though cf. Mk 16.7), as it is occasionally elsewhere (Gal. 3.2, Eph. 1.13, cf. Acts 19.2), though the connection is also implied where *pistis* precedes baptism.

[25] Mt. 6.30=Lk. 12.28, Mt. 8.26, cf. Mk 4.40=Lk. 8.25.

[26] Mk 1.15; both belief and trust can be heard in *pisteuein* since people are called to respond to Jesus' words and commit to their message.

invited to respond to God and Christ to the consequences of their response for themselves and for the world.²⁷

It is worth noting, since Jesus' messiahship is so closely connected with salvation in all four gospels, as elsewhere, that trust language is not as strongly connected with salvation elsewhere in the ancient world as we might, on this basis, expect. When Mediterranean and Near Eastern peoples seek salvation, of any kind, from an earthly or heavenly agent, we often see them hoping, praying, and sometimes negotiating for it. When they have been saved, whether by divine or human agency, from some natural or supernatural threat, we find them displaying gratitude, thanksgiving, and, where appropriate, worship.²⁸ In the scriptures, the God who saves Israel can be described (almost always with reference to the covenant) as *pistos* (e.g. Deut. 7.9, 32.4, Ps. 32.4, 110.3–6, Isa. 49.7). The people of Israel occasionally trust in God or an agent of God to save them, particularly in the Exodus narrative (Exod. 4.5, 14.31, Ps. 105.12), and occasionally in the books of wisdom (e.g. Wis. 3.8–9, Sir. 11.21). But it is not a *topos* of salvation that it involves trust.²⁹ We have observed, however, that *pistis* is strongly associated in the ancient world with processes of mediation and reconciliation, and that Paul seems likely to be drawing on this association when he speaks of the role of *pistis* in atonement. In the last chapter, we also observed that Jesus acts as a mediator, with *pistis*, in the synoptic gospels, in his healings and exorcisms, which are also key signs of his messiahship. It seems possible that one reason why both Paul and the synoptic gospels—and other writers—make much use of *pistis* language is because their understanding of the kind of Messiah Jesus is, draws significantly on the theme of reconciliation and mediation. (What this implies about relationships between surviving early writings is an interesting question beyond our scope to pursue.)

The (Un)trustworthiness of Signs, Miracles, Prophecy, and Teaching

The gospel writers, like Paul, take for granted that the new relationship which is made possible for humanity through Jesus Christ is God's initiative. We might assume, on this basis, that divine self-revelation would form a major theme of this chapter, but we will defer discussion of the relationship between revelation and trust until the end. We begin with a topic much discussed in recent literature, but

---

[27] No other theme or lexicon is equally common across all the gospels, though e.g. *dikaiosynē* language is marginally more common than *pistis* in Matthew and the term *Christos* is used with similar frequency in Luke and Acts combined.

[28] Deichgräber (1967), Danker (1982), Zeller (1990), Chow (1992), Forbis (1996), Harrison (2003), Jim (2021).

[29] More broadly, God is often said to preserve those who trust in him, but my concern here is with discrete moments and acts of salvation.

not usually from the perspective of trust and trustworthiness: the striking fragility or ambiguity of signs, miracles, prophecy, and teaching as a basis for trust between Jesus in his earthly life and those around him.

In Chapter 3 we saw that, for the epistolographers and the author of Acts, people can put and maintain trust towards God and the exalted Christ based not least on their experience and interpretation of miracles and signs: above all, the experience of the resurrection or preaching about it, and the power of the spirit which some people experienced when they came to trust. Peter's speech at Pentecost (Acts 2.14-36) tells listeners, both within and outside the text, that Jews, at least, should also have been able to recognize and respond to Jesus' relationship with God through the signs and wonders he performed in his lifetime.[30] 'You who are Israelites,' says Peter, 'hear these words':

> Jesus the Nazorean—a man revealed to you as from God with mighty deeds, wonders, and signs (ἄνδρα ἀποδεδειγμένον ἀπὸ τοῦ θεοῦ εἰς ὑμᾶς δυνάμεσι καὶ τέρασι καὶ σημείοις), which God worked through him in your midst, as you yourselves know—this man, given up by the plan and foreknowledge of God, you killed, crucifying him through the agency of lawless men. But God raised him up, releasing him from the pains of death, because it was impossible for him to be held by it. (Acts 2.22-4)[31]

In the gospels, miracles or 'signs' and other works performed by Jesus in his earthly life are never misleading. They testify authentically to Jesus' identity and to the coming or presence of the kingdom of God, and trust which arises from them is never misguided in itself.[32] Seeing a miracle or sign not infrequently leads people to begin to trust in Jesus, or to trust more strongly, especially in John's gospel, where we find individuals (20.27-9) or groups (2.11, 2.23, 7.31, 12.10b-11), coming to *pisteuein* in Jesus because of signs.[33]

---

[30] Lüdemann (1989), 47-9, cf. Stanton (1974), 67-85.

[31] Conzelmann (1987), 20 notes that the derivation of *Nazōraios* is uncertain (cf. Schaeder (1967), 874-9).

[32] Dulles (1992), 131-54 discusses the widespread distinction in twentieth-century theology between signs and symbols, arguing that 'a symbol is a special type of sign to be distinguished from a mere indicator...A symbol is a sign pregnant with a plenitude of meaning which is evoked rather than explicitly stated...In symbolic communication, the clues draw attention to themselves. We attend to them, and if we surrender to their power they carry us away...' (p. 132). From John's perspective, Jesus' signs are well described as symbols, but within the narrative they only work as symbols for those who are capable of trusting; for everyone else, they act as signs whose point of reference people do not understand (see Schnackenburg (1968-72), 1.521-5, Warren (2018), Lee (2018), 265-6, cf. Lee (1994)). On miracles as pointing to Jesus' divine identity or divine Sonship in Mark see e.g. Twelftree (1999), Brower (2009), Grindheim (2012), 35-80.

[33] In the synoptic gospels, healings or exorcisms lead people to flock to Jesus, bringing more people to be healed or simply following him, in what we can envisage as an expression of trust, though the term is not used: e.g. Mt. 4.23-5, Mk 3.8-10, Mt. 14.34-6=Mk 6.53-6, cf. Mt. 8.16=Mk 1.32=Lk. 4.40, Mt. 9.35-6, Lk. 6.16. According to Acts, the numbers of *hoi pisteuontes* several times grow because of 'signs and wonders' performed by apostles or by God (e.g. 5.12-14, 9.42, 16.25-31).

Sometimes, however, in John's gospel, the trust that arises from seeing a sign explicitly goes with a lack of understanding of what the sign points to (e.g. 3.2, 9.30), or is fragile or short-lived (e.g. 2.23-5).[34] In addition, all the gospels indicate that people should not rely on signs. 'Unless you see signs and wonders,' John's Jesus says critically to the Galileans, 'You do not trust' (4.48). In the double tradition he says, even more trenchantly, 'An evil and adulterous generation seeks a sign' (Mt. 12.39, 16.4=Lk. 11.29, cf. Mk 8.12, Lk. 11.16, 23.8).[35] Those who seek signs which they can recognize as such, as proofs of Jesus' identity, implicitly, and occasionally explicitly lack trust.[36]

John 10.22-39 explores the relationship between trust and signs in a passage which also illustrates the writer's view of the relationship between trust and belief. At the Feast of the Dedication in Jerusalem (10.22), some of the Jerusalem crowd want a plain statement from Jesus that he is the Messiah.[37] Jesus says, 'I told you and you do not *pisteuein*' (10.25).[38] The works he does in his father's name testify to him (v. 25).[39] The crowd do not *pisteuein* because they are not his sheep: they do not belong to him, he does not know them, and they do not follow him (10.26-7).[40] At first sight, it makes sense to translate *pisteuein* here as 'believe', since belief is something one typically has in words or testimony to a proposition (here, that Jesus is the Messiah). If *pisteuein* does means 'believe', however, Jesus immediately indicates that belief should not be based on words or works, but can only arise within a relationship with himself. He does not give this relationship a name, but his sheep follow him, are safe in his hand, and will never perish with him (vv. 27-8). Following, being saved, and being given life are all associated with trusting Jesus elsewhere in the gospel, so it is no great stretch to hear this as a relationship of trust, or at least a relationship in which trust is possible.[41] If so,

---

[34] Agreeing with e.g. Becker (1969), Bultmann (1971), 696, Haenchen (1984), 1.237, 2.212, Carson (1991), 184 that John's gospel views signs as problematic, though not because for John *pisteuein* must be based on the word (below, p. 208, pp. 209-10). Hofbeck (1966), Brown (1966), 195-6, are right that signs sometimes cause *pisteuein*, but not, it seems, reliably, or usually long-lived trust (though Nathanael's trust does persist, cf. 1.50).

[35] Though, unusually, at Mt. 24.3=Lk. 21.7 the disciples ask what sign there will be of Jesus' coming and the end of the age, and he describes what will apparently be reliable signs.

[36] Or, as we saw in the last chapter, trust misguidedly in themselves rather than in God.

[37] Cf. Jn 10.24. At G.Th. 91, the disciples say to Jesus, 'Tell us who you are, so that we might believe in you,' and he replies, 'You inquire into the appearance of the sky and the earth, but the one who is in front of you, you do not know, nor do you know this season and inquire into it' (transl. Gathercole (2014), 533). As Gathercole (2014), *ad loc.* notes, Jesus criticizes not only the disciples' ignorance of Jesus, but also 'their *method* for discovering what is of supreme importance' (italics original), which recalls less the disciples' exchanges with Jesus in the canonical gospels than those of non-followers. The canonical gospels avoid attributing this kind of scepticism to the disciples.

[38] Cf. Lk 22.67 in a similar context: the Sanhedrin cannot or will not trust anything Jesus says.

[39] Believing in the works may refer back to 9.31-3, where the man born blind says that only a man 'from God' could open the eyes of the blind.

[40] On God as shepherd cf. Ps. 23.1-4, Isa. 40.11, 49.9-10 (following a reference to God's faithfulness at v. 7).

[41] Trusting is associated with being a follower at e.g. 1.50, cf. 1.37, 14.1-3; being saved at e.g. 3.17-18, 12.44-7, cf. 10.9; receiving life at e.g. 3.15-16, 11.26. If we keep 'trust' for the active

then Jesus is saying, in verses 25–8, not simply that the crowd should believe who he is on the basis of his words and works, but that, even though these things testify to him as the Messiah and giver of eternal life, the crowd cannot believe or receive eternal life because they do not have the kind of relationship with him that makes trust possible.[42] On this basis, we can hear a secondary meaning in *pisteuein* in verse 26: the crowd (as they themselves know) do not believe because, more fundamentally (as Jesus and the gospel's listeners know), they do not trust, or have the kind of relationship with God and Jesus that makes trust possible.[43]

The next few verses may seem at first sight to contradict this claim. Jesus says that the Father has given his sheep to him, and 'I and the Father are one' (10.29–30). The crowd prepare to stone him for blasphemy (10.33).[44] He says, 'If I am not doing my father's works, do not *pisteuein* in me, but if I am doing them, even if you do not *pisteuein* in me, *pisteuein* in the works, so that you may know and recognize that the Father is in me and I am in the Father' (vv. 37–8). If they seem initially to affirm that belief or trust in (the divine origin of) Jesus' works can lead to trust in him, however, these verses turn out to do the opposite. Jesus challenges the crowd to recognize that he is performing his father's works. If they cannot see this, the unmistakable implication is that they are failing to recognize God's activity among them. But failing to recognize God's activity in the world is tantamount to failing to recognize God in God's relationship with the world: it is an admission that one is not in one's right relationship with God, or not in relationship with God at all. When Jesus invites the crowd to recognize that his works are God's works, therefore, and points out that, if they are, then they must come out of his relationship with God, he affirms that if the crowd do not recognize this, then they are not only not among Jesus' sheep; they are not among God's people. Recognizing Jesus' works for what they are, believing and trusting in them, does not lead people to become part of Jesus' flock; it shows that they are.

A brief coda shows some people actively putting their trust in Jesus. Jesus crosses back over the Jordan to where John baptized, where many people came to him and said that what John said about him was true (10.41), '[a]nd many trusted in him there' (10.42).[45] We do not hear how these people came to think that John's

---

relationship which those who respond to Jesus make with him, then this is best seen as a relationship in which trust is possible.

[42] So e.g. De Jonge (1977), 135–6, Schnackenburg (1968–72), 1.519, Boismard (1982). It is tempting to identify this relationship with the pre-election to which John refers elsewhere: Morgan (2015a) 418–25.

[43] On the foundational nature of relational trusting see e.g. Koester (2008), Morgan (2015a), 425–32. McWhirter (2006), followed by MacGregor (2020), 110–17 argues that John's πιστεύειν εἰς alludes in particular to a 'personal commitment analogous to a marriage' (MacGregor (2020), 110).

[44] Jesus invokes Psalm 82.6: all those to whom the word of God came are called gods, so it cannot be blasphemy for the one whom the Father has consecrated and sent into the world to call himself the son of God (10.36).

[45] 'Trust' makes the best sense of *pisteuein* here because it refers to an act of commitment following acceptance or belief in the truth of John's testimony.

testimony was true, but the position of this vignette in the narrative suggests that they are contrasted with the Jerusalemites of 10.22–39.[46] They can recognize the rightness of John's words and trust in Jesus because they are among his sheep.[47]

Trusting on the basis of miraculous works or signs is never unequivocally or unproblematically positive in the gospels. At best, they have limited power to create trust. They are often requested by those who lack trust. They may be understandable only by those who already trust in Jesus or are pre-elected to trust.[48] One likely reason is that, despite the tradition that he performed many such works, the gospels remember how many people did not come to trust in Jesus his lifetime and are concerned to explain it. Another reason is surely that, for all the gospel writers, to encounter Jesus in his earthly life is to encounter, through Jesus, the saving power of God. The gospel writers all affirm that scepticism, demanding a sign, trusting one's own judgment about what constitutes a sign, or even relying on signs are not appropriate responses to such an encounter.[49] In this, they have much in common with Paul, for whom, as we saw in Chapter 4, seeking signs, or trusting one's own judgment about what constitutes a sign or about the meaning of signs, is itself a sign of sin or *apistia*.[50]

---

[46] Cf. Jn 8.12–20, where Jesus also seeks to shift his interlocutors away from the idea that trust in Jesus can be based on others' assessment of his self-revelation, towards the recognition that trust is relational: see Morgan (2015a), 429–31. Each of the 'I am' sayings is followed by an explanation of how the image describes the relationship between God and Jesus, or Jesus and those who follow him, or both (Ball (1996), 204–54, Veres (2008)).

[47] This takes a somewhat different view of John's language of witness and testimony from e.g. Harvey (1976), Lincoln (2000). Jesus speaks truly about himself, and testifies e.g. to what he has seen (cf. 3.11), but such testimony cannot prove his identity or persuade the sceptical of it because a human being cannot prove that he is the Son of God, and a human being cannot assess another person's testimony that he is the Son of God. Any flavour of the lawcourt about Jesus' exchanges and discourses, therefore, serves only to highlight that one cannot put the divine or divine truth on trial, and that the capacity to trust is a gift of God, not something arrived at by human reason.

[48] At Jn 5.38, Jesus uses the unusual phrase 'you do not have [God's] word remaining in you (τὸν λόγον αὐτοῦ οὐκ ἔχετε ἐν ὑμῖν μένοντα)'. The closest New Testament parallel is perhaps Lk. 8.12 (the devil takes the word away from the hearts of those who are like a hard path, so that they 'may not trust and be saved'); cf. also Jn 2.23–5. Both are reminiscent of the famous illustration by Zeno of Citium of the relationship between perception, assent, comprehension, and knowledge, according to which perception is like an open palm, assent like the hand with the fingers half closed, comprehension (*katalēpsis*) like a closed fist, and knowledge like a fist with the other hand closed over it (Cic. *Acad.* 2.145[147]). Perception and assent are insecure states in which what one assents to may always run out of one's hand; it is not enough to receive and accept a sense impression to know the truth of it, but one must bring to it something one already has: ideally a knowledge which, for Stoics as for Platonists, ultimately derives from the divine which is the only source of reality, truth, and knowledge. If John's or Luke's image owes anything to popularized philosophy, it may be indicating that Jesus' critics may encounter, and may even receive an impression of the Word of God, but they are not equipped by their relationship with God to know the truth and securely retain it. On (cognitive) knowing as following sight and hearing in John's gospel see Bennema (2002), 124–35, though on the greater importance of relational knowing for John and others see pp. 214–19.

[49] As Jesus tells Satan in the double tradition (Mt. 4.7=Lk. 4.12, cf. Deut. 6.16), the appropriate response to a new initiative from God is not to put God to the test, but (by implication) to trust and obey. Morris (2016), 292 notes that Jesus' reference to Deuteronomy demonstrates his faithfulness to Torah; and, we might add, to God.

[50] pp. 147–51.

The association between *pistis* and Jesus' prophetic ministry is similarly complex. Jesus makes a number of prophecies about the coming of God's kingdom and the end time, and he occasionally identifies himself (Mk 6.4, Lk. 13.33, Jn 4.44), and more often other people identify him, as a prophet (e.g. Mt. 21.11, Mk 6.15, 8.28, Lk. 7.16, 9.8, 24.19, Jn 4.19, 6.14, 7.40). The scriptures, however, offer abundant examples of prophets who were not listened to and were persecuted for their words by their own communities, so it is not entirely surprising that, for all four evangelists, prophecy and trust have, at best, an uncertain relationship.

Mark creates an expectation that prophecy about the kingdom will be the central theme of his gospel when his Jesus begins his ministry by proclaiming, 'This is the time of fulfilment. The kingdom of God is at hand. Repent, and trust in the good news' (1.15).[51] Later in the chapter Jesus says to his new disciples, 'Let us go on to the nearby villages that I may preach there too. For this I have come' (1.38=Lk. 4.43). Matthew, however, omits the phrase 'trust in the good news' from Jesus' opening proclamation (4.17), while Luke omits the proclamation altogether, substituting the scene in the synagogue at Nazareth when Jesus applies the prophecies of Isaiah to himself (4.16-30).[52] When Jesus sends out the Twelve (Mt. 10.1-16=Mk 3.13-19a=Lk. 6.12-16) he tells them to preach the kingdom of God and to heal, and talks about how people may respond.[53] Jesus' prophecies of the end time (Mt. 16.2-3=Lk. 12.54-6, Mt. 24.1-36=Mk 13.1-27=Lk. 21.1-28, cf. Mt. 7.22-3=Lk. 13.25-8) include, in Matthew's version (24.23-6), a warning that his followers should not trust the false Christs and false prophets who will arise before the end, which implies that he, and some other prophets and their words, are trustworthy.[54] But although, for these three evangelists, Jesus' prophetic words are an important part of his ministry and undoubtedly trustworthy, they do not show Jesus calling people to trust in prophecy, or in himself on the basis of his prophecies. Unlike trust in God or Jesus personally, or trust in Jesus' power or willingness to heal, the importance of trusting in prophecies (whether scriptural, those of Jesus, or, occasionally, those of John the Baptist) is not explicitly a major theme of any of the synoptic gospels.[55]

---

[51] Belief or acceptance of the news is implied here, but trust is vital, since Jesus is calling people not only to think that the good news is true, but to respond to it by repenting and, presumably, seeking forgiveness.
[52] Isa. 61.1-2, 58.6.
[53] *Pistis* language does not appear in this passage, but since the disciples are following in Jesus' footsteps and seek the same response to their preaching and healing as people have given to Jesus', it is implied.
[54] Luke shows more interest in belief/trust in prophecy in the birth and resurrection narratives (1.20, 1.45, 24.25-7). In Acts, after the resurrection, people several times come to trust as a result of miracles (e.g. Acts 5.12-15, 13.12, 11.21, 15.7, 17.10-12).
[55] At Mt. 21.23-7=Mk 11.27-33=Lk. 20.1-8, the religious authorities challenge Jesus' authority, and he replies by asking by what authority they think John the Baptist baptized. They argue among themselves, saying, 'If we say "From heaven," he will say, "Why then did you not trust him?" But if we say, "Of human origin," we are afraid of the crowd, for all regard John as a prophet.' John's authority from

In John's gospel, with its strong focus on the identity of Jesus and whether or not those whom he meets in his lifetime 'know' and 'receive' him, it is even less surprising that we find few references to believing or trusting in prophecy.[56] On his first visit to Jerusalem, Jesus prophesies that the 'temple of his body' will be destroyed and raised up again in three days (2.19, 21), but only after the resurrection, the evangelist says, did the disciples remember what he had said and come 'to trust [or 'believe'] (*episteusan*) in the scripture and the word Jesus had spoken' (2.22).[57] In chapter 3, before prophesying that the Son of Man must be lifted up as Moses lifted up the serpent in the desert (v. 14), Jesus highlights the difficulty of trusting on the basis of prophecy, asking Nicodemus, 'If I tell you about earthly things and you do not *pisteuein*, how will you *pisteuein* if I tell you about heavenly things?' (3.12).[58] (Nicodemus' problem is undoubtedly partly one of belief—he expresses confusion at the idea of being born again (v. 4)—but Jesus emphasizes that what is at stake is not simply what Nicodemus thinks is true, but whether he is able to make a commitment that will bring him to eternal life (3.15, 16), and therefore not just belief, but trust.) On his last evening, Jesus foretells that the Advocate will come to the disciples (14.15–17, 16.12–15); the world will persecute them (15.18–25); and they will see him again after he has left them (16.16–24). He consciously speaks, however, in figures or parables (*paroimiai*, 16.25), and does not ask them to believe or trust in what he says at this point. Throughout the gospel, the focus of John's extensive use of *pisteuein* is firmly on trusting Jesus himself.[59]

Jesus' teachings form such a significant part of all the gospels that we might expect to find them regularly portrayed as an expression of his trustworthiness and a reason to trust him. In the synoptic gospels, Jesus' teaching is sometimes mentioned, without *pistis* language, as one of several reasons why crowds flock to him.[60] Occasionally listeners are said to be astonished at Jesus' teaching—for example, at the end of the Sermon on the Mount (Mt. 7.28, cf. Mk 1.21, Lk. 4.32)—though they are not said to *pisteuein* as a result. One might argue that the fact Jesus seems to speak to anyone who comes to hear him implies that it is

---

heaven suggests that his words and works should be trusted, but the passage speaks explicitly of his being trusted himself.

[56] *Pisteuein* in Jesus' name, at 1.12 and elsewhere (cf. 2.23, 3.18, 1 Jn 3.23, 5.13) which is equivalent to *pisteuein* in him (MacGregor (2020), 124–5), must involve making a trust commitment, since it changes the status of those involved.

[57] Both belief and trust may be implied here. After the resurrection, the disciples presumably believed, in the sense that they recognized that the scripture pointed to Jesus and what Jesus had said was true, but the more significant point must be that this belief fortified their relationship with Jesus, i.e. strengthened their trust in him. This reading highlights the juxtaposition between 2.22 and 2.11. The sign at Cana encouraged the disciples to trust in Jesus, unlike the saying about the temple, which did not affect them until after the resurrection.

[58] Cf. 12.20–36, but without *pisteuein*. This recalls Wis. 9.16–17 (without *pistis* language).

[59] Morgan (2015a), 425–35.

[60] E.g. Mt. 4.23–5=Lk. 4.40–4 (cf. Mk 1.39, but this does not mention people following him); Mt. 9.36, cf. Mk 6.34, Lk. 10.2.

possible for anyone to put their trust in him or to follow him as a result of hearing him.[61] But understanding or recognizing the importance of Jesus' teaching is only explicitly attributed to those who are already followers, so have already put their trust in Jesus, and even they are never said to grow in *pistis* as a result of hearing Jesus' teachings.

This pattern is visible, for example, in the interpretation of the parable of the Sower (Mt. 13.10–17=Mk 4.10–12=Lk. 8.9–10). Before offering an explanation of the parable, Jesus tells the disciples that he talks to the crowd in figures of speech either (in Mark and Luke) so that they will not understand him (or in Matthew) because they do not understand him. Only the disciples, who are already in a relationship of trust with Jesus, can learn from the story.[62]

Even John's gospel, in which discourse plays such a large part in Jesus' ministry, connects trust with teaching less often and less directly than we might expect.[63] For the disciples who already trust in Jesus (cf. 1.50, 2.11) Jesus has, as Peter says, the 'words of eternal life' (6.68). Even on the last night of his life, though, Jesus expects the disciples to *pisteuein* some of what he tells them only when it has happened.[64] Those outside the circle of the disciples, meanwhile, who come to trust in Jesus, or who are hinted at, through the gospel, as being on a journey towards trust, are not, even when they engage in long conversations, brought to trust through Jesus' teaching. The Samaritan woman at the well does not understand Jesus' words about the water of life (4.13–15), though she is attracted by them, but she is amazed by his knowledge of her past (4.29). It is apparently what Jesus knew about her that brings her to ask whether he might be the Messiah (4.29) and her fellow-townspeople to trust in him (4.39). Nicodemus (3.1–21) persistently fails to understand what Jesus says, so whatever keeps him interested in Jesus through the rest of the gospel (7.50, 19.39), it is not obviously trust based on Jesus' teaching. We have seen that, after the 'Good Shepherd' discourse, Jesus tells some of his interlocutors that they do not believe or trust in his words or his works (10.24–5), 'because you are not among my sheep' (10.26). To recognize Jesus' testimony on his own behalf, one must recognize that it comes from God (3.34, 5.31, 7.16, 8.12, cf. 8.14); for those who do not already recognize Jesus' relationship

---

[61] Matthew's 'Whoever has ears, let him hear' (11.15, cf. Mt. 13.9=Mk 4.9=Lk. 8.8, Mt. 13.43, Mk 4.23, Lk. 14.35) is ambiguous: it could suggest that anyone can hear and understand what Jesus says, or that only those who already e.g. trust will understand.

[62] Mark's and Luke's version appears to suggest that some people are not given the chance to hear and repent, implying that they are not destined for salvation, but this would be so atypical within either gospel that it is more likely that both mean that people must trust in Jesus before they receive teachings about the kingdom, and that Matthew has emended Mark to make that clearer (so e.g. Taylor (1957), *ad* Mk 4.12, with a discussion of the history of interpretation). John's Jesus, however, uses Isa. 6.9–10 explicitly to affirm that some people are not chosen to trust (12.37–40).

[63] This tends to be overlooked by those who view the words of Jesus, as the Word, as the soundest basis for believing or trusting in the gospel: e.g. Schottroff (1970), Bultmann (1971), Koester (1989).

[64] 13.19, 14.29; here, as at 2.22, *pisteuein* after the event must refer to trusting as well, perhaps, as believing.

with God, his testimony cannot be credible. Such people cannot even learn what they need to learn through the teachings of scripture (cf. 5.39) because, though the scriptures testify to Jesus, only those who trust in him can see it. The crowds who hear Jesus speak in the course of the gospel are divided about what he says, some saying that he is the Prophet, the Messiah, or even more (e.g. 7.40, cf. 7.40, 8.30, 10.21), while others hold that he is nobody special, or even that he is possessed (e.g. 6.42, 7.26-7, 7.41-2, 8.48, 9.24, 10.19). Not only does the evangelist not show trust in Jesus as being founded on his teaching, but he sometimes seems to indicate that it is not, or cannot be.

On one level, we need not be surprised that it is only those who have already put their trust in Jesus who are represented as understanding his teachings or having parables interpreted to them.[65] On another, we may be surprised that stories which say that Jesus preached and taught wherever he went, which were told in communities which presumably knew that Jesus' disciples went on to preach themselves to very diverse audiences, do not say that Jesus called people to trust him on the basis of his teaching, or that people came to trust him on the basis of his teaching. This is all the more notable when some early Christian communities spoke of *ho pistos logos* (though they applied the concept to teaching about Jesus rather than to Jesus' own teachings).[66]

One explanation may be the ambivalent attitude to words and rhetoric which is widely attested in this period (and both earlier and later).[67] Language is recognized as extremely powerful but also alarmingly slippery. What is said need not be rooted in the integrity of the speaker or the truth of what is being said, and when it is misleading, it is dangerous. Trust in persons, on the basis of personal encounter and the whole complex of what they do and say and how they relate to others, is not perfectly reliable either, but it offers a broader, more complex, and so potentially firmer basis for trust.

Another explanation may lie in what philosophers identify as the nature of trust in words in principle. If, for example, I say, 'I trust in these words', I am saying that I trust that these words are true. In most cases, this will involve believing (or perhaps accepting or assuming) that these words are true.[68] There are two

---

[65] Jesus also speaks of the Jewish law as authoritative (and implicitly trustworthy) when he tells people to keep the commandments, or what the greatest commandment is (e.g. Mt. 19.16-19; Mt. 22.34=Mk 12.28-34=Lk. 10.25-8). In these passages, he is speaking to Jews who are already community members, not telling non-Jews to hear and understand the Jewish scriptures, so the Law is implicitly *pistos* for those who are already in relationship with God.

[66] 1 Tim. 1.12, 3.1, 4.9, 2 Tim. 2.11, Tit. 3.8.

[67] In a tradition which goes back to Plato's *Gorgias* and Phaedrus: e.g. Kennedy (1994), *passim*, Fortenbaugh (2002), Ryan (2003), Connolly (2007), Day (2007), Nichols (2014), Amato, Citti, and Huelsenbeck (2015), 1-5, Morgan (2015a), 65-74, Petrucci (2017) (cf. e.g. Mt. 23.3, where Jesus criticizes the Pharisees for not practising what they preach).

[68] Acceptance might involve, for instance, using a proposition as a premise in practical reasoning within a limited context, without committing to belief or trust (Bratman (1992), 7).

possible bases for this. Either I am in a position to assess the truth of the words for myself—for instance, on the basis of existing knowledge—or I may trust the person who speaks them. Trust in the person who speaks the words will need more than one component. I will need to trust her to know what she is talking about, and I will also need to trust in her integrity, at least in this particular context, so that I can trust that she is not lying to me. (I cannot base my trust on her integrity alone, because she might be honest but mistaken.) I must, however, have a reason to trust in her integrity, such as that I have prior experience of her, or that someone else testifies to her integrity—but in the latter case, I have to have a reason for trusting what the other person says.[69] Trust in the truth of a person's words, therefore, either invites an infinite regress of trust, or must be rooted in my own ability to test those words, or in my trust in the person based on my own experience of her.[70] If I cannot test what the person is saying against my own knowledge or reason—if, for example, she is talking about God—and if I do not already know her—if, for instance, she is a new prophet—then I cannot reasonably trust her based on her words alone.

The same is true, *mutatis mutandis*, of signs and miracles. Signs and miracles, in the thought-world of the first century, may be either genuine or faked. Everyone in the gospel stories takes for granted that Jesus' signs and miracles are genuine, but they sometimes raise the question where they come from: God, or the devil (Mt. 9.34, 12.24=Mk 3.22=Lk. 11.5, cf. Jn 10.20).[71] Jesus himself offers an argument for the genuineness of his signs: 'How can Satan cast out Satan?' (Mk 3.23, cf. Mt. 12.26, Lk. 11.18). None of the gospels gives his opponents an answer to this, but they might fairly have responded that Satan is a highly devious being, so he might do anything to gain credence. It follows that if people cannot assess what Jesus is doing against their own knowledge or reason—which, in the case of miracles or signs, by definition they cannot—and they do not already trust Jesus, then they cannot reasonably trust Jesus based on his wonder-working.[72] I am not

---

[69] We might see the Transfiguration as offering such a reassurance, when Peter, James, and John hear the voice of God (whom, presumably, they already trust), saying, 'This is my beloved son: listen to him' (Mk 9.7=Mt. 17.5=Lk. 9.35). John's Jesus says at 5.31–2: 'If I testify on my own behalf, my testimony cannot be verified. But there is another who testifies on my behalf...'. (God only once audibly testifies on Jesus' behalf, at 12.28, though cf. 1.32.)

[70] Discussed in detail by Godfrey (2012), 176–212 as relating to trust both in human beings and in God.

[71] As it happens, this is unusual in this world where the authenticity of miracles is often disputed (Remus (1983), 54, Cotter (1999), 175–200).

[72] This fits with the view, widespread particularly in Protestant theology, that those who trust God can be expected to believe in God's words (though this need not be based on an account of God as omnipotent, omniscient, and omnibenevolent). This argument, though, sometimes takes a simplistic view of 'God's words' (e.g. Millar (2002), cf. Helm (2002), 245–6; concern with the view that any words attributed to God in the scriptures must be divine goes back in the modern era to Locke and Kant, and see e.g. Lamont (2009), 115). But New Testament writers would agree with the general proposition that those who trust God and Christ believe what they say (and, more broadly, reveal, though on the distinction between the two, and on divine speech-acts more broadly see Wolterstorff (1995), 19–36,

suggesting that the gospel writers arrived self-consciously at this view through this kind of argument, but they may have grasped intuitively that words and miracles, and human judgments about them, are fragile things to which to entrust oneself, one's life or salvation.

At the beginning of this section we noted that, to all four evangelists, miracles or signs performed by Jesus, and teachings and eschatological prophecies delivered by him, are never misleading. For their audiences, they testify authentically to Jesus' identity and to the coming or presence of the kingdom of God, and, within their narratives, trust which arises from them is never misguided in itself. But, in all four gospels, signs, miracles, prophecies, and teachings generate, at best, limited and fragile trust; human beings cannot rely on themselves to judge what, if anything, they prove; often, only those who already trust Jesus (or have the capacity to do so) can even begin to recognize or understand them; and, most importantly, *pistis* language is connected much less with words or miraculous acts than with the person of Jesus. Common sense, of course, suggests that if you trust a person, you will, in practice, trust (at least some of) their words and actions, and nothing in the gospels contradicts such an assumption, but their focus is on trust in Jesus himself.

Finding *Pistis* in the Scriptures

In Chapter 2, we saw that the epistles sometimes evoke and gloss scriptural passages which do not explicitly use trust language, in such a way as to make clear that the writer sees them as testifying to the trustworthiness of God. The gospels occasionally use scripture in a similar way, to testify to the trustworthiness of Jesus, for their listeners, by associating him with the God of Israel whom they take for granted as trustworthy. In Matthew's story of the storm at sea (8.23-7), for example, the disciples think they are going to die and beg Jesus to save them. Jesus says, 'Why are you terrified, you of little trust (*oligopistoi*)? (8.26). He gets up, rebukes the winds and the sea, and there is calm. Matthew's language echoes that of Psalm 107.23-30, in which God raises storms, terrifying sailors and making them cry to God in their distress, before stilling the winds and sea so that sailors rejoice. There is no trust language in the psalm, but Jesus' words to the disciples show that Matthew sees fear of a storm as a failure of trust in God, and

---

75-94, and *passim*). Bekken (2008) links the controversies in John's gospel 5.31-40, 8.12-20 about Jesus' self-testimony with Philo's argument (*Leg.* 3.205-8) that only God can testify to Godself. No doubt this is right in the sense that John's Jesus invites those around him to recognize him by his self-testimony as they would recognize Godself (cf. e.g. 14.9), but where Philo is making an argument in principle, the gospel is keenly aware of the practical difficulty of recognizing a human being as revealing himself as God's son.

Jesus as trustworthy because of his relationship with God, which gives him power over the elements.[73]

In the meeting between Jesus and Nicodemus in John's gospel (3.1–21), Jesus says, 'If I tell you about earthly things and you do not trust, how will you trust if I tell you about heavenly things?' (3.12). His question evokes the Book of Wisdom 9.16–17: 'scarcely do we guess the things on earth, and what is within our grasp we find with difficulty; but when things are in heaven, who can search them out? Or whoever knew your counsel, except you had given Wisdom and sent your holy spirit from on high?'[74] Again, no trust language appears in the scriptural passage, which is about the understanding that comes from God's gift of wisdom, but John shifts the emphasis to underline the importance of trusting in Jesus, and to imply that Jesus is as trustworthy as the wisdom that comes from the spirit of God. A little later in the gospel, Jesus says to his sceptical interlocutors, 'If you had trusted Moses, you would trust me because it was about me that he was writing (5.46). His words recall Deuteronomy 18.15, where Moses says that God will raise up a prophet like him from among the Israelites, and the Israelites will listen to him. Deuteronomy uses the language of listening rather than trusting, but John's Jesus again adapts the scripture to emphasize the importance of trust in himself, and also to imply that he should be trusted because Moses, who was trusted by God and trustworthy to both God and Israel, wrote about him.[75]

It is sometimes observed that Matthew envisages Jesus as the human embodiment of the law.[76] In the gospels, Jesus does not tell his listeners explicitly to put their trust in the law, but trust in God's commandments is a recurring theme of the Jewish scriptures.[77] When Matthew's Jesus tells his followers to trust in him, therefore, or leaves open the possibility that an exhortation to trust refers to trust in him, listeners to the gospel may also hear in the exhortation that Jesus is trustworthy as the embodiment of God's law.

In none of these passages which draw on the scriptures are people said to come to trust Jesus, or to grow in trust (allowing that the disciples have an ongoing relationship of trust with him). Within the gospel narratives, invoking the scriptures or the law cannot in itself convince people of Jesus' trustworthiness, any

---

[73] Held (1963), 275–95 draws out the several connections between *pistis* and miracle stories in the synoptic gospels, noting that *pistis* is active as well as cognitive trust, emphasizing that faith is always 'praying faith' (284–8), especially for Matthew, and that it also brings participation in the miraculous power of Jesus.

[74] Transl. NAB.

[75] Here, the coherence of Jesus' call to trust him with scripture and John's interpretation of scripture offers a basis for both belief and trust. See also Exod. 4.1–5, 14.31, 19.9 (at Num., very unusually, 14.11 God complains to Moses that the people do not trust him, despite his signs, but what is described as a failure of trust here is a rejection of God (14.11), not a failure to recognize God's signs or see them as trustworthy).

[76] Especially by Matthew, e.g. 5.17 (Davies and Allison (1988-2004), *ad loc.*), but cf. Jn 1.14, 17.8, and Rom. 10.4; Allison (2008).

[77] E.g. Ps. 88.29, 110.7, 118.66, Wis. 16.26, Si. 35.24, 36.3, Isa. 55.1–3 LXX.

more than can Jesus' own words or signs. For the gospel writers and their communities, however, who have already put their trust in Christ, scripture does testify to Jesus' trustworthiness. Allusion to scripture is also one of the ways in which *pistis* language attests to the personal closeness of Jesus to God. In the scriptures, God's prophecies and promises have proved trustworthy through time (as those of Jesus are sometimes said to do: e.g. Mt. 26.75=Mk 14.72=Lk. 22.61, Lk. 24.6-8, 24.44, Jn 2.22, 12.16, 16.24). God may demonstrate God's power and implicitly God's trustworthiness by a great act at a given moment. But human beings are not entitled to expect that God will prove God's trustworthiness, at any moment, by either speech or action, and the gospel writers affirm the same about Jesus. It is for human beings, as beneficiaries of God's new initiative in Christ, to recognize, acknowledge, and trust in God and in Jesus Christ.

Trustworthy Encounters

Signs, miracles, prophecy, and teaching are all, in scripture and tradition, paradigmatic means by which the intentions, instructions, and judgments of a trustworthy God are communicated to human beings. All, in the gospels, are problematic as ways of demonstrating the trustworthiness of Jesus or bringing those who do not already trust to trust in Jesus, and even those who already trust in Jesus do not always understand them. In part, as we have noted, this may reflect and interpret a memory that most people, in Jesus' lifetime, did not recognize him as the Messiah, but it goes further than that. It tells listeners that, in the presence of Jesus, people should not be seeking words or signs to testify to his identity, any more than, in the presence of God, they would seek words or signs to testify to God.[78] Without ever fully and formally articulating their understanding of Jesus' nature in relation to God, all the gospels imply that the relationship between God and Jesus is such that the implications of encountering Jesus are inseparable from the implications of encountering Godself (cf. Mt. 1.23, 18.20, Jn 14.9).[79] Nowhere is this more clearly illustrated than in the paradigmatic stories in which people come to trust in Jesus: the calls of the disciples.[80]

---

[78] Though we need not look for close models for encounters with Jesus e.g. in scriptural stories of encounters with God, because those who encounter Jesus, at least in the synoptic gospels, do not need to recognize his identity e.g. as Son of God to follow him (below, pp. 231-4). Dalferth (2006), 228-31 discusses trust as a response to the sense of the presence of God. See also Pope (2018) on an argument by C. S. Peirce, that direct perception of God leads to trust, which, in turn, leads to belief.

[79] Emphasized especially by Mt. 1.23, 18.20, 28.20 (Gerhardsson (1994)), cf. Jn 1.14. Bauckham (2015), 28 observes: 'in incarnation God is not present merely *with* or *in* one or more of his creatures, but *as* the particular human Jesus of Nazareth...To put the matter the other way around, incarnation means that Jesus *is* the human presence of the eternal Son...'. Matera (2006), 250-1, cf. (1999), 215 argues in relation to John's gospel (but the same point could be made of the synoptics) that God entrusts Christ with the work of revelation and life-giving.

[80] Cf. pp. 269-77.

It is a puzzling feature of the gospels how little is said about the calls of most of the disciples, some of whom have significant roles to play later in the narrative, and all of whom, apart from Judas, were presumably leading figures in primitive churches. The only story, moreover, which makes explicit use of *pistis* language is the call of Nathanael in John. Nevertheless, it is tempting to see these stories as exemplifying trust, and later occasions when the disciples are referred to as trusting, or Jesus criticizes them for *apistia* or *oligopistia*, attest that trust is foundational to their relationship with Jesus.[81] How then does this *pistis* come about?

In the stories of the call of Simon Peter and Andrew (Mt. 4.18–20=Mk 1.16–18, cf. Lk. 5.1–11), James and John (Mt. 4.21–2=Mk 1.19–20), and Levi or Matthew (Mt. 9.9=Mk 2.14=Lk. 5.27–8) in the synoptic gospels, Jesus is passing by the Sea of Galilee or Matthew's customs post. Among all those who we can assume are in the vicinity, he sees these individuals; he invites them to follow him, and they do.[82] John 1.35–51 offers a more elaborate set of linked stories. John the Baptist (who is both unique and exemplary in the gospel in being able to say on his own behalf (1.34), 'I have seen and testified that he is the Son of God'), points Jesus out to two of his own disciples (who, we can infer, already trust John as a prophet): 'See, the Lamb of God' (1.36). Hearing him, they follow Jesus, though they hardly seem sure why: when Jesus asks them what they are looking for, all they can say is, 'Where are you staying?' (1.38). Jesus, however, tells them, 'Come and see', and they stay with him. One of these is Andrew, who finds his brother Simon and brings him to Jesus, saying, 'We have found the Messiah' (1.41). When Simon arrives in Jesus' presence, Jesus looks at him, and tells him who he is and that he will be called Kephas (1.42). The next day, Jesus travels to Galilee and 'found Philip' (1.43). He tells Philip to follow him, and he does. Philip finds Nathanael and brings him to Jesus despite his expressed scepticism (1.45–6). When Jesus sees him, he says, 'Here is a true Israelite. There is no duplicity in him' (1.47). Nathanael asks, 'How do you know me?' and Jesus tells him that he has seen him under a fig tree (1.48). Nathanael, instantly impressed, says, 'Rabbi! You are the Son of God; you are the King of Israel' (1.49). Jesus asks, 'Do you believe [or, since Nathanael's affirmation amounts to a commitment to Jesus, 'trust', or both] because I saw you under the fig tree? You will see greater things than this…' (1.50). Nathanael, however, does (probably both believe and) trust because he is seen; and so, it seems, does Simon Peter in John's account, and all the disciples in the synoptic gospels.

---

[81] These stories may also attest to Jesus' trust in the disciples. Spencer (2005) explores the political as well as theological overtones of Jesus' 'imperious call'.

[82] James and John are with their father (Mt. 4.21=Mk 1.20) and, in Mark, also hired hands (Mk 1.20), while Matthew is at his post at the custom house, presumably dealing with people all day. It is often noted (e.g. Taylor (1952), 167–8) that the call of the disciples is reminiscent of, and may be based on, that of Elisha (1 Kgs 19.19–21), where Elijah identifies Elisha as his follower by throwing his cloak over him; cf. also Jn 20.14–15, where Jesus approaches and speaks to Mary, asking her whom she is looking for.

The common themes of these stories are presence, seeing, hearing, calling, and following: terms of proximity, personal connection, and change. Jesus comes to where a person is (or, occasionally, someone comes to him), and sees and calls them, and when they see and hear him seeing and calling them, they follow.[83] We will return below to whether or in what sense these stories are best characterized as examples of revelation. At this point, we may note that they fit remarkably well with the four bases of everyday trust described by Doris Brothers: the experience that we are seen by the people around us for who (we understand) we are; that we are able to communicate who we are to those people; that others are able to communicate who they are to us; and that we can understand (at least something of) what they are communicating about themselves. The call stories invite us to imagine that, in the moment of the call, Jesus and the future disciples are in each others' presence, and that, in Brothers' rich fourfold sense, they see, hear, and respond to each other, and each sees and hears that the other responds to him. This process, as Brothers recognizes, is not without risk on all sides. Everyone involved, moreover, must not only trust in another person but trust propositionally that their trust will be justified. As we have already seen, and will see further in Chapter 8, both risky trust and propositional trust also involve an element of intersubjectivity: everyone involved must acknowledge and respect the subjectivity of the other and allow themselves to be changed by it.[84] At the moment when the future disciples respond to Jesus' call, therefore, they not only see and are seen, communicate and are communicated with, but they take a risk and open themselves to the subjectivity of the other. For Brothers, all four foundations of trust must be present for people to make and sustain good relationships. These stories lay the foundations on which the disciples will make and sustain a relationship with God and Jesus Christ that will change their lives.[85]

Luke develops further the theme of trusting on the basis of proximity, personal connection, and change in his story of the call of Simon (Lk. 5.1–11). Jesus, teaching by the lake of Gennesaret, sees two boats which have put in after a night's fishing. He gets into one and asks the owner, Simon, to put out again so that he can better address the crowds (v. 3). When he has finished preaching, Jesus tells Simon to put down his nets again (v. 4). Simon is sceptical (v. 5). When they catch almost more fish than the boat can hold, he is astonished and frightened, and begs Jesus, 'Get away from me, Lord, for I am a sinful man' (v. 8). We might have expected to hear, at this point, that Jesus' miracle impressed Simon, even led him

---

[83] John's use of *lambanein* at 1.12 is probably also a term of personal and physical proximity. On the importance of being seen and heard in Genesis see Tracey (2015).

[84] pp. 29, 30, 338, 340.

[85] An interesting 'near miss' in this context is the story of the rich young man at Mk 10.17: though Mark does not indicate specifically that he seeks to become a disciple, Jesus looks at him, loves him, and tells him to follow him, but the young man apparently cannot do so. At Mt. 7.23 Jesus says of those who are false followers that, on the day of judgment, he will say, 'I never knew you'.

to *pisteuein*, but the story takes a different turn. The miracle does give Simon a flash of insight into Jesus' identity—he is, after all, a future disciple—but the insight is as much wrong as right, because Simon fundamentally misunderstands the relationship in which Jesus stands to him. Luke underlines Simon's failure to understand by making his words echo the words of the unclean spirit which Jesus cast out of a man a few verses earlier (4.31–6): 'What do you have to do with us, Jesus of Nazareth? Have you come to destroy us? I know who you are, the Holy One of God' (4.34).[86] As a human being, Simon is less hostile to Jesus than is the unclean spirit, but he also understands less of what he is seeing, and he is awe-stricken and afraid (5.9, 10).[87] Where the spirit is silenced by Jesus, however, Simon is reassured: 'Do not be afraid [a regular opposite of trust]; from now on you will be catching men' (v. 10). This, rather than the miracle, is the turning point in Simon's story. Together with James and John, he allows himself to accept Jesus' reassurance, takes a risk on trust, and throws in his lot with Jesus. 'When they brought their boats to the shore, they left everything and followed him' (v. 11).[88]

Throughout the rest of the gospels, until Judas' betrayal, Jesus takes for granted that he and the disciples are in a relationship of trust. Though he several times chastises them for not having enough trust (e.g. Mt. 8.26, 14.31, 16.8, 17.20=Lk. 17.6) or for failing in trust (e.g. Mk 4.40=Lk. 8.25), his treatment of them on these occasions is quite different from his treatment of others who do not trust at all. The disciples' failings are failings within a trust relationship, not failures of trust *tout court*.[89]

Being approached or approaching Jesus, seeing him and being seen by him, are not the same thing, but either, in different stories, can lead to the other, and the work of Brothers shows how intimately seeing and being seen cooperate in the creation of trust and the ability to trust.[90] The trust which is created in this way has both two-place and three-place aspects. The gospels all emphasize that putt-

---

[86] Unclean spirits and demons recognize Jesus for who he is, but cannot respond with trust because their allegiance is elsewhere (e.g. Mt. 8.29=Mk 5.7=Lk. 8.28, Mk 1.24=Lk. 4.34).

[87] Plummer (1989), 145 underplays the significance of Simon's verbal echo of 4.34 when he argues that Simon does not think Christ's holiness is dangerous to a sinner, only that he is sharply aware of the contrast between the two, so the presence of Christ is a reproach, not a peril.

[88] In general, in the world of the first century, sight is the most trustworthy of the senses (Morgan (2015a), 39–42). The gospels use the language of sight for everyday seeing, for seeing without understanding, as an image for understanding, and as a proxy for other kinds of closeness (e.g. John's Jesus speaks of seeing the Father to emphasize his closeness to God and his authority to reveal him (1.18, 3.11, 3.32, 6.46, 8.38, cf. 5.19, 8.57)). Seeing can lead to belief or trust: e.g. in the case of the man born blind, and we are not surprised to find sight widely connected with the idea of revelation (e.g. Mt. 24.30=Mk 13.26=Lk. 21.27, Mt. 26.24=Mk 14.62=Lk. 22.69, Lk. 3.6, 9.36, Jn 1.18, 1.29, 1.51, 11.40), but the relationship between sight and trust can be problematic itself if sight is treated as evidence and not as a medium of experience (e.g. Nathanael and Thomas both come to *pisteuein* through seeing, but in both cases Jesus' response is ambivalent (1.50, 20.29)).

[89] Morgan (2015a), 356–8.

[90] Those who see before they are seen are usually looking for help.

ing one's trust in Jesus Christ leads to forgiveness of sins, eternal life, participation in God's kingdom, and more: that is, it has an aspect of the three-place. At the same time, trust in Christ, as in God, is also two-place: an expression in its own right of being in one's right relationship with God and Christ.

In Brothers' model, trust, and the ability to trust, should develop from birth. When the disciples and others see and are seen by Jesus and put their trust in Jesus, John's gospel tellingly describes them as reborn: not by natural generation nor by human choice nor a man's decision, but 'of God' or 'from above' (1.13, 3.3). They have new life or a new kind of life, eternal life (e.g. 4.14, 6.27-9, 6.68-9, 11.25). Their life is restored or renewed: they are healed, exorcized, or raised from the dead.[91] Elsewhere, the disciples are promised that those who lose their life for Jesus' sake find it or save it (Mt. 16.25=Mk 8.35=Lk. 17.33). The gospels share this vision of trust and new life going hand in hand, notably, with Paul, who speaks of the death to sin and new life in which the faithful live for God.[92] Whether the gospels derive their vision of the new life which those who trust God and Jesus Christ inhabit from earlier teachings about the relationship of the faithful with the risen Christ, or whether they arrive at their vision independently from traditions about Jesus in his lifetime or post-resurrection reflection, their narrative links the new and transforming relationship which Jesus' followers have with him in his earthly life with that which the faithful have with him in his risen life.[93] Seeing and being seen enables trust, and trust, for those who follow Jesus, makes possible rebirth, a new life, new kinds of relationships, and a new identity.[94]

Why the disciples, at their call, follow Jesus remains, within the texts, mysterious. What the gospel writers choose to say and not to say, however, is intriguing, and points us away from the idea that the disciples make their own assessment of Jesus' identity based on evidence or testimony,[95] towards the idea that they

---

[91] Cf. Williams (2018), emphasizing the relationality of both *pisteuein* and eternal life for John, and the connection between them. Valentin (2016), discussing the connections between the treatment of eternal life in the Wisdom of Solomon and John's gospel, notes that in Wisdom, immortality is associated with being 'in the hand of God' (e.g. Wis. 3.1, (2016), 164–72), as well as that, for John, eternal life is above all a relationship with God (pp. 243–71).

[92] Above, pp. 169–71.

[93] On the importance of the experience of the presence of the risen Christ, as of Christ in life, for recognizing his identity and responding to him with relational faith, and the role of the gospels in making possible this experience, see especially Frei (2013). Frei also notes (p. 32) the difficulty of defining presence, even when our experience of it is ungainsayably powerful.

[94] We observed above that the epistles treat resurrection experiences and the reception of the spirit as bases for new or ongoing trust; in light of this discussion we can note that they are both signs of God's action and/or direct experiences of God or Christ, so they also function as divine encounters.

[95] Except at Jn 1.36–7, 1.41 where John the Baptist is sent by God to bear witness to Jesus (1.6–7), and his followers trust his words because they know him. Thompson (2008), 174 argues that Jesus is revealed by other 'trustworthy witnesses' too (e.g. 4.42, 6.68, 20.28), but the Samaritans, and even the disciples, are not trustworthy as John is trustworthy by virtue of being a prophet. Schnackenburg (1968–72), 1.251–2 observes, more helpfully, John's interest in the problematic nature of witness: *martyrein* occurs thirty-three times in the gospel, and is linked with *pisteuein* from the prologue (1.7) onwards.

respond to his presence, sight of them, and invitation to relationship.[96] By the same token, it suggests that the disciples' relationship with Jesus centres less on propositional belief than personal trust. In this connection, we may briefly mention the unclean spirits who see and know and are seen and known by Jesus, but are not forgiven or given new life by the encounter because they are as fixed in their identity and allegiance as human beings are changeable in theirs. The themes of presence, seeing and being seen, and relational knowing, in the narrative of salvation, are also part of the narrative of the insuperable gulf and unavoidable conflict between good and evil, in which human beings may end up on either side. Accordingly, when Jesus approaches, or is approached by others, the trust which can follow is not only transformative for individuals, but strikes a blow in the conflict between God and evil which will only be concluded at the end time.[97]

The *Pistis* of Jesus as a Model for Others

So far we have argued that, for all four evangelists, healing, saving, or life-giving trust in Jesus is not paradigmatically, and in some passages cannot be based on belief in, or any other cognitive response to signs, miracles, prophecies, teachings, or anything else which might, at first sight, be supposed to prove or testify to Jesus' identity or work. Trust is portrayed as personal and relational: arising from Jesus' presence with those who encounter him and his invitation to trust in him, together (as we will see further in the next chapter) with the willingness and ability of those who encounter him to respond to him. In a number of passages, however, the invitation to trust both in God and in Jesus himself does appear to be based on a form of testimony. This, however, is not a type of testimony which those around Jesus can assess for its truth, but one which, like Jesus himself, can only be responded to with trust and self-commitment. This is the idea that Jesus' own trust in God is an example for others.[98]

A number of passages point to Jesus' trust relationship with God in his earthly life as exemplary.[99] *Pistis* language appears explicitly in most of these passages,

---

[96] See further pp. 229–36 on what the gospel writers think people should have been able to recognize about Jesus in his earthly life. Mk 1.15 and Mt. 4.17 give only a hint that the disciples, before their call, could have heard of Jesus as a preacher of repentance, while Jn 1 refers to no activities by Jesus before the first disciples come to him; Luke's Jesus, though, preaches and performs several cures before the call of Simon.

[97] In this context the 'loyalty' aspect of trust is to the fore.

[98] Cf. pp. 135–6, on the role which imitation of the exalted Christ by the faithful plays in the epistles, and pp. 175–6, 178–80, on how, in the epistles, those who trust imitate Christ's suffering and death. The gospels do not always connect Jesus' exemplarity with *pistis* language: e.g. not at Mt. 10.24, cf. Lk. 6.40, Jn 13.16, 15.18–21; Mt. 16.24=Mk 8.34=Lk. 9.23, cf. Jn 12.25; Mk 10.39=Mt. 20.23; Mk 10.42–5=Mt. 20.25–8=Lk. 22.25–7. On Jesus as an ethical example, thought without particular attention to trust, see e.g. Burridge (2007).

[99] So e.g. Ebeling (1963), 223–46 (taking up a question raised by Bultmann (1958), 159), Fuchs (1964), 48–64, Tuggy (2016). O'Collins and Kendall (1992) argue for Jesus' having (a commitment,

but occasionally it is implied by the use of terms which are associated with it elsewhere.[100] The story of the healing of the centurion's slave, for example (Mt. 8.5-13=Lk. 7.1-10), describes a moment of insight by the centurion which marks both Jesus' exemplarity and his own. Jesus is willing to visit the centurion's home to heal the slave, despite the fact that the centurion is a gentile and a member of the oppressing power, but the centurion declines:

> Lord, I am not worthy to have you come under my roof; but just say the word, and my slave will be healed. For I am also a man under authority, with soldiers under me; and I say to one, "Go," and he goes, and to another, "Come," and he comes, and to my slave, "Do this," and he does it. (Mt. 8.8-9=Lk. 7.6-8)

Jesus wonders at the *pistis* of the man (Mt. 8.10=Lk. 7.9). The centurion recognizes Jesus' power, like his own, as that of a man under authority.[101] The paradigmatic virtue of Roman soldiers to their superiors, and above all to the emperor—visible and audible to every subject of the empire on coins and inscriptions and in imperial communications—is *pistis* or *fides*, involving trust, trustworthiness, and faithfulness, with a strong accent on loyalty.[102] The centurion's recognition that Jesus does what he does as a man under authority points not only to his own willingness to trust Jesus, but to his recognition of Jesus' trust and loyalty towards God as a basis for that trust.[103]

---

rather than a confession of) faith in God, with a discussion of those, especially within Roman Catholic tradition, who have assumed or argued the opposite. Collins (2014) shows that when Jesus speaks of himself as one who serves, he refers to serving God rather than other people, and links service with trust when he says that 'his…service is to carry out the mission entrusted to him by his Father' (p. 78). In later tradition, the exemplarity of saints functions similarly: see e.g. Cuneo (2017), Tuggy (2017). NB since almost everyone in the ancient world takes the existence and qualities of gods for granted, where *pistis* language appears in connection with God we should assume it refers to trust rather than belief unless there is a strong reason to assume otherwise.

[100] E.g. (though this story is exemplary for readers but not for Jesus' followers within the gospel, since he is alone when it takes place) during Jesus' vigil in the wilderness, the devil tempts him to throw himself off the parapet of the temple to be caught by angels. Jesus refuses: 'it is written, "You shall not put the Lord your God to the test"' (Mt. 4.6-7=Lk. 4.9-12). Testing is frequently associated elsewhere with scepticism and the desire for proof, both of which are represented as antithetical to trust (e.g. Mt. 12.39=16.4=Mk 8.12=Lk. 12.29, Mt. 13.54-8=Mk 6.1-6, Mt. 21.28-32, Mt. 22.23-33=Mk 12.18-27=Lk. 20.27-40, Mt. 27.43), so Jesus' refusal, in the double tradition, to test God is exemplary both of his own relationship with God and for other people. Ironically, in this passage, the devil appears to be encouraging Jesus here to show his trust in God, but Jesus is not misled: to test God is to fail in trust, not to practise it.

[101] Ammonius' catena on Acts 3.16 (CGPNT 3.64) observes that 'someone is healed through the faith that is directed to Christ. For it is necessary that the faith of both concur, that is, the faith of the one healed and the faith of the one praying over the sick person. This we see in the case of the paralytic and the women with the flow of blood' (transl. Martin with Smith (2006), 43); i.e. Jesus could not do what he does in these stories without *pistis* of his own, which is exemplary for others who pray over the sick.

[102] Morgan (2015a), 77-85.

[103] 'Trust' is the best translation here since the man not only believes that Jesus can help him but puts his trust in him to do so, and he is not in an existing relationship of e.g. loyalty.

In this story Jesus' own *pistis* remains implicit, while the centurion's is explicit. '[I]n no one in Israel have I found such trust,' Jesus says, hinting that the Israelites should imitate the centurion if they want to be invited to the banquet in the kingdom of heaven (Mt. 8.11).[104] More often, however, trust that is explicitly exemplary is Jesus' own. After the transfiguration, Jesus descends from the mountain with Peter, James, and John to find that the other disciples have been trying to expel a demon from a young boy (Mt. 17.14-18=Mk 9.14-27=Lk. 9.37-42). They do not seem to lack belief that demons can be expelled, but, rather, trust in God of the kind that gives power.[105] Jesus criticizes them: 'O untrusting [or 'faithless'] and perverse generation, how long am I to be with you?... Bring him here to me' (Mt. 17.17=Mk 9.19=Lk. 9.41). He heals the boy. When the disciples ask why they could not heal him, Matthew's Jesus tells them it is because of their *oligopistia*: if they had *pistis* even the size of a mustard seed, they would be able to move mountains (Mt. 17.20, cf. Lk. 17.6).[106] Mark's Jesus explains that this kind of demon can only be driven out by prayer (9.29). Jesus' trust (and, perhaps, ongoing faithfulness) towards God is both a reason for the disciples and the father of the boy to trust him (cf. Mk 9.24), and an example to the disciples, who, Jesus says, will be able to do deeds of power as great as his own if their trust becomes more like his.

The vision of *pistis* as giving those who trust the power to move mountains recurs at Matthew 21.18-22 (=Mk 11.20-4). On the road between Jerusalem and Bethany, Jesus curses a barren fig tree, and the next morning the disciples notice that it has withered. When they ask how this happened, Jesus tells them, 'if you have *pistis* and do not doubt, not only will you do what has been done to the fig tree, but even if you say to this mountain, "be lifted up and thrown into the sea," it will be done. Everything you ask for in prayer, trusting, you will receive' (Mt. 21.21-2).[107] Jesus indicates that the disciples must be more like him in their trust towards God, and promises that it will bring to them a power like his. In this passage Matthew also marks the connection between *pistis* and prayer which Mark makes after the healing of the boy with the demon: the way Jesus prays is another example of his trust which can be imitated by his followers.

The idea that imitating Jesus' trust in God will bring the disciples power highlights another dimension of the divine–human *pistis* relationship. For God to entrust the disciples with power, God must presumably think them trustworthy, or at least be willing to act therapeutically as if they are trustworthy. The call to imitate Jesus is therefore not only a call to put one's trust in God and in Jesus

---

[104] Verse 12 goes on to say that (if they go on as they are, presumably), the 'children of the kingdom' will be driven out into the outer darkness.
[105] Together, perhaps, with trustworthiness in handling that power.
[106] Since this follows from Jesus' healing of the boy, it must refer to trust in God.
[107] Again primarily trust in God, though from the perspective of listeners to the gospel, we might hear an implication of the possibility of praying to the risen Christ.

himself, but a call to become worthy of trust, or to be open to the possibility that by being trusted one may learn to be more trustworthy, and so to become more like Jesus in his relationship both with God and with other people. This theme also reaches out beyond the text and Jesus' earthly life to the post-resurrection life of his followers and early churches. It suggests that if his followers not only put their trust in Jesus but become more like him in trust and trustworthiness, they will be entrusted with a power, authority, transformative presence, and exemplarity like Jesus' own. Trust in God and in Jesus is therefore not only salvific, but ecclesiological and missiological.[108]

Outside John's 'farewell discourses', as we have noted, there is very little *pistis* language in any of the passion narratives, but Matthew makes those who mock Jesus on the cross say, 'He trusts in God ($\pi \acute{\epsilon}\pi o\iota \theta \epsilon v$ $\grave{\epsilon}\pi \grave{\iota}$ $\tau \grave{o}v$ $\theta \epsilon \acute{o}v$); let God deliver him now, if he wants him...' (27.43). At the culmination of his story, Matthew indicates that Jesus was known for trusting God.[109] In the context of Jesus' warnings that those who would follow him must take up their own cross (e.g. Mt. 16.24), this not only attests to Jesus' own relationship with God (cf. Mt. 26.39=Mk 14.36=Lk. 22.4, cf. Jn 12.27) but calls others to recognize that they can imitate his trust in God as they take up something of the role that he played in this world.

John uses a range of other terms and images for the relationship between Jesus and the Father, preferring to keep *pisteuein* mainly for the relationship between Jesus and his followers as an extension of the traditional relationship between God and humanity (cf. 14.1). Jesus is in God and God in him (14.10–11, 17.21); he glorifies his father (13.31–2, 17.4) and honours him (8.49); the Father and he are one (10.30); no one has seen the Father except the one who is from God (6.46). Several passages, however, draw attention to Jesus' obedience to God: 'My food is to do the will of the one who sent me and to fulfil his work' (4.34).[110] 'I cannot do anything on my own; I judge as I hear, and my judgment is just, because I do not seek my own will but the will of the one who sent me' (5.30). 'My teaching is not my own but from the one who sent me.' (7.16)[111] Since obedience is often an aspect of *pisteuein*, these passages can also be heard as indicating that Jesus is faithful towards God. They do not go further and say explicitly that Jesus' trust or obedience are models to be imitated, but in the farewell discourses John's Jesus does explicitly characterize the disciples as following in his footsteps and imitating his example, though mostly without using *pisteuein*.[112] 'I have given you

---

[108] See pp. 312–19.   [109] On the cry of derelliction see pp. 261–3.

[110] Cf. 12.44, 17.8, 16.30. At 5.19–20, the phrase '[the Father] shows [the Son] everything that he himself does' has been identified (Dodd (1962)) as a formula widely used in apprenticeship agreements, and may also reference Jesus' obedience.

[111] Cf. 5.17, 5.19, 5.31–67, 6.37–8, 6.56, 8.28, 8.50, 12.27, 12.49, 16.28, 17.21, 17.25.

[112] Cf. Rev. 1.5 and 3.14, where Christ is called *pistos* as a witness to God, 19.11, where the exalted Christ is called $\pi\iota\sigma\tau \grave{o}s$ $\kappa\alpha\grave{\iota}$ $\grave{\alpha}\lambda\eta\theta\iota\nu\acute{o}s$, 'faithful and true', and 14.12. Allen (2009), chs 2–3 argues that as

a model to follow, so that as I have done for you, you should also do' (13.15). 'As I have loved you, so you also should love one another' (13.34, cf. 15.12–13). '[W]hoever puts his trust in me will do the works that I do, and will do greater ones than these...' (14.12). The rule of love may be intended as a rule for life as well as for suffering and death, as it is in the Johannine letters, though in this passage it is linked with giving up one's life for one's friends.[113] But the language of modelling and following in this section in general focuses on the disciples' future suffering and persecution, founded on their trusting in Jesus and in God (cf. 14.1), as an imitation of the suffering and persecution of Jesus founded on his trust relationship with God.

Stories and sayings like these link Jesus' trust and trustworthiness towards God with his obedience, the way he prays, his refusal to put God to the test, and his power.[114] All these qualities encourage his followers, both within and beyond the gospel stories, to trust both in God and in him, and sometimes they are explicitly exemplary, to be imitated by his followers, praised when they are, and criticized when they are not. In Chapter 3, we saw Paul encourage the faithful to imitate the risen Christ in living for God and for one another. In Chapter 4, we saw him encourage them to imitate Christ in his death by accepting the consequences of their commitment to God and to Christ.[115] For the gospels, too, to imitate Jesus is to imitate his commitment and obedience to God. When, moreover, Jesus indicates to the disciples, who will become the apostles, how imitating him will enable them to act with power, we are reminded of Paul's conviction that, in his apostolic imitation of Christ, he wields power. Though the language and context of the call to imitation in these corpora are different, therefore, they bear a family resemblance. In both, moreover, the call to imitation is one way in which the faithful develop from trusting in Christ to acting for Christ. The faithful are called to imitate the trust and trustworthiness of Jesus both in order to play their part in the spreading of the good news and the struggle against evil, and in order to live as humanity should live in its right relationship with God. In both, imitation of Christ, in various ways, plays a role in a world in which the kingdom has not yet come on earth as in heaven, and in the kingdom which is near, or has already come upon the world. *Pistis* belongs to human relationships with God both in heaven and on earth, in both the present and the eschatological future.

---

faithfulness is appropriate to Jesus as a human being, it is also appropriate to see Christ exercising it on earth, though Barrett (1978), 82 is sceptical. In these passages, *pisteuein* is a response both to Jesus' unity with God and his subordination as God's agent; it is difficult, if not impossible, to separate the two and perhaps to try to do so misses the point.

[113] So Brown (1970), *ad loc.*
[114] Cf. pp. 306–8.   [115] pp. 178–9.

Jesus with God as Creator and Carer

Earlier in this chapter, we saw that trusting in Jesus in his earthly life can be seen as bringing new life to those who trust. This raises the question whether, for their listeners, the gospels invoke the creation narrative in the Book of Genesis in connection with their language of trust. In Chapter 2 we saw that, although trust language does not appear in Genesis until the story of God's covenant with Abraham, Genesis 1–3 can be read as a narrative of aboriginal trust and care between God and humanity, and the undermining and betrayal of that trust. We also saw that creation imagery is used in several New Testament writings to speak of the closeness of Christ, especially the pre-existent Christ, to God. In recent years, students of the canonical gospels have taken an increasing interest in creation theology and in the use the gospels make of the scriptural story of creation, though they have not linked the themes of creation and care extensively with that of trust.[116] Paul Minear, for example, in *Christians and the New Creation*, finds echoes of Genesis in, among other passages, the proclamation of the angels to the shepherds in Luke 2.8–14, the battle between Jesus and Satan in Luke's gospel, Jesus' writing on the earth in John 8.2–11, and Paul's vision of resurrection and the end time in 1 Corinthians 15. Minear argues that Genesis, especially the early chapters, is important to New Testament writers because it reflects their interest in the relationship between God and the whole of humanity; it shares their sense of 'the abysmal depth and age-long power of evil'; and the Genesis narratives speak to God's original and eternal concern for what God has made.[117] More broadly, the visions of early Christians for the future and the end time are shaped by their stories of the past and the beginning of all things.[118]

The gospel which has most often been seen as connecting creation imagery with the person of Jesus is John's. In *Creation Imagery in the Gospel of John*, for instance, Carlos Sosa Siliezar argues that creation imagery can be seen not only in John's prologue but in Jesus' claims to be performing his father's works, his walking on the sea, his healing of the man born blind, his prayer in chapter 17 where he prays to God to glorify him 'with the glory that I had with you before the world began' (17.5), and when he gives the holy spirit to the disciples.[119] Sosa

---

[116] Though Miller (2012) demonstrates the connections between John's 'I am' saying and other language about the earth, *pisteuein*, and eternal life, arguing that salvation is not purely individual but restores the right relationship between God, humanity, and the earth, and Rabie-Boshoff and Buitendag (2020) emphasize that the relationship between God, Christ, and creation, rather than the nature of God or Christ, must stand at the centre of a modern theology of creation. Siliezar (2015), 1–24 gives a helpful summary of work to date on John; on the New Testament and environmental theology more broadly see notably Lucas (1999), Bauckham (1999, 2015), Gregersen (2001, 2015), Johnson (2009), Bredin and Bauckham (2010), Horrell (2010).

[117] Minear (1994), xiv.

[118] Minear (1994), xiv–xv. Mackey (2006) also finds the theme of creation embedded throughout the New Testament.

[119] Siliezar (2015).

Siliezar limits his study to passages which he argues use creation imagery in ways which show the clearest linguistic or formal links with Genesis.[120] His caution is understandable, but the identification of intertextuality is a notoriously inexact science, and there is also room for studies which are interested in identifying shared patterns of thinking as well as quotation, allusion, and shared vocabulary.[121]

The gospels' creation theology and their use of Genesis in general are beyond our scope here, but we can point to one or two passages in which the trust between God, Jesus in his earthly life, and Jesus' followers can be seen as reflecting, and perhaps invoking, the original, paradigmatic relationship of trust and care between God and man and woman. In the Sermon on the Mount, Jesus tells his followers not to worry about their lives: what they will eat, drink, or wear (6.25-34). Like the birds and the flowers which neither toil nor spin, they should let God care for them. 'If God so clothes the grass of the field, which grows today and is thrown into the oven tomorrow, will he not do much more for you, O you of little trust (*oligopistoi*)?' (6.30). The business of human beings is to seek the kingdom of God and God's righteousness (6.33).[122] Commentators have heard an echo here of the creation narratives, and specifically an inversion of God's proclamation to Adam when he ejects him from the Garden of Eden (Gen. 3.17-19).[123] Because of what we identified as their failure of trust, Adam and Eve are no longer in right-standing with God. From now on, Adam will have to work the land in order to eat: 'Cursed be the ground because of you! In labour shall you eat its yield all the days of your life...' (3.17).[124] When he has made this pronouncement, God clothes Adam and Eve in leather garments as a sign that their new knowledge of good and evil has brought disgrace on them. In contrast, Jesus says, those who put their trust in God need no longer worry about what they will eat or wear, but can concentrate, once more, wholly on their relationship with God. Since much of what Jesus says in this discourse sharpens or elaborates on the law, his listeners must not only trust the tradition in which he teaches, but also trust him personally. Matthew indicates as much at the end of the sermon, when he says, 'the crowds were astonished at his teaching, for he taught them as one having

---

[120] Siliezar (2015), 11-14. He is critical of studies which find many more, looser, allusions to the creation narratives: for instance, in mentions of the garden in John 18 and 19, in Jesus' sleeping at John 19.30, or in almost any reference to light, life, or the adjective 'good'; to Jesus as the Son of Man, or to women (2015), 1-10.

[121] E.g. Moore (2013), who sees the creation theme as more widely distributed through the gospel, though cf. the reservations of Menken (2015).

[122] Matthew links *pistis* with *dikaiosynē* in several passages (e.g. 8.11-12, 21.32, 23.28, 24.51, cf. 23.23); he does not say, as Paul does (and Genesis does) that one leads to the other, but they go together in his concept of right relationship with God.

[123] Reworking the theme of e.g. Ps. 145.15-16, 147.9, as noted by Davies and Allison (1988-2004), *ad loc*. It is a sign of how far environmental theology has developed that Betz (1995) *ad loc*. sees no echo of Genesis here, and observes that the natural order is of little interest in the New Testament.

[124] Though there is no overlap of vocabulary.

authority, and not as their scribes' (7.29). Jesus' authority, confirmed before the Sermon at his baptism, comes from Godself (Mt. 3.16–17, cf. Mk 1.10–11, Lk. 3.21–2, Jn 1.32–3). Although Matthew does not say so of the listeners in the story, therefore, the listeners to the gospel recognize that the trust they put in Jesus the teacher is trust in him as God's son. In this sermon, the one in whom the faithful trust is, not least, the son of God the creator and carer through whom they are restored to the relationship with God which was lost by Adam and Eve.

In John chapter 11, Jesus arrives at the home of Mary, Martha, and Lazarus to find that Lazarus has died. When Martha goes to meet him, expressing confidence in him, with a hint of reproach ('Lord, if you had been here, my brother would not have died. But even now I know that whatever you ask of God, God will give you', 11.21–2), Jesus assures her that her brother will rise. Martha says that she knows he will rise on the last day, but Jesus tells her, 'I am the resurrection and the life; whoever trusts in me, even if he dies, will live, and everyone who lives and trusts in me will never die' (11.25–6). A few verses later, Jesus approaches Lazarus' tomb and tells the bystanders to take away the stone. Martha's matter-of-fact response never fails to shock: 'Lord, by now there will be a stench; he has been dead for four days' (11.39). Jesus says only, 'Did I not tell you that if you *pisteuein* you will see the glory of God?' (v. 40). They remove the stone, and Lazarus, 'the dead man', comes out (v. 44). Lazarus is a man of the world after Adam and Eve. In his tomb, John emphasizes, his body is decaying, just as God foresees for Adam at Genesis 3.19: 'you [will] return to the ground, from which you were taken; for you are dirt, and to dirt you shall return'. But Jesus not only brings life: he is life, and life takes life from him (cf. 1.3). Like God creating Adam, he makes the clay of the ground to which Lazarus has returned breathe and walk (cf. Gen. 2.7). What is more, he affirms that the life he brings to those who trust in him is eternal (cf. v. 26). Whether or not Adam and Eve would eventually have died, even in Eden, those who trust in Jesus will never die.

Genesis is not the only text John references in this passage, but one other possible intertext has, to my knowledge, not been discussed.[125] The raising of Lazarus is unique to John's gospel, where it holds a pivotal place in the narrative, as the last major incident before Jesus enters Jerusalem for the last time (though three short scenes intervene). Its position in the narrative closely matches that of the transfiguration in Mark's gospel, and, like the transfiguration, the raising of Lazarus takes place on a high mountain, the Mount of Olives.[126] After a long period in

---

[125] Many commentators have noted that John may be using synoptic stories of raisings from the dead and material about Martha, Mary, and Lazarus. In later sequences of images of gospel stories, the transfiguration and the raising of Lazarus often appear together.

[126] In Mark the transfiguration is the last major event before Jesus turns towards Jerusalem, though two short scenes intervene. John may have seen the Mount of Olives, which, by Jesus' day, had long been used as a cemetery, some of whose occupants had probably looked forward to resurrection and/or the messianic age; where Ezek. 11.23 envisages the glory of the Lord as standing on leaving the temple; and where Zech. 14.4 prophesies that the Lord will stand before his final victory at the end of

which John was not regarded as having known Mark, there is now increasing interest in the possibility that he did, and if this is right, it may be no accident that John places the raising of Lazarus where Mark places the transfiguration. The transfiguration reveals Jesus in glory to Peter, James, and John (Mk 9.2-3), the presence of Elijah and Moses (though exactly what they stand for is debated) pointing to his identity as the Davidic Messiah who helps to bring in God's kingdom (9.4). The voice of God is heard, saying, 'This is my beloved Son. Listen to him' (9.7). In John 11, Jesus says twice that Lazarus' illness and death are 'for the glory of God, that the son of God may be glorified through it' (11.4, cf. 40), and when he is about to raise Lazarus, Jesus speaks to God to confirm that God has sent him (v. 42).[127] Both the transfiguration and the raising of Lazarus, moreover, are well established as looking forward to Jesus' own death and resurrection.[128] They prefigure the new life which Jesus will enter, and into which he will eventually bring all those who trust in him. Both the transfiguration and the raising of Lazarus therefore reveal Jesus not just as son of God (Mk 9.7, Jn 11.27), but as the son of God the creator, who gives life to all. Martha makes the connection audibly when she echoes John's prologue: 'the true light, which enlightens everyone [who is also the Word through whom everything is created (1.3-4)], was coming into the world (ἐρχόμενον εἰς τὸν κόσμον)' (1.9). When Jesus asks whether she believes (or, perhaps, trusts[129]) that 'everyone who lives and trusts in me will never die' (11.26) she says, 'Yes, Lord. I have come to believe that you are the Messiah, the son of God, who is coming into the world (ὁ εἰς τὸν κόσμον ἐρχόμενος)' (11.27).

All four gospels also incorporate stories of Jesus' control over inanimate creation: stilling a storm (Mt. 8.23-7=Mk 4.35-41=Lk. 8.22-5), walking on water (Mt. 14.22-33=Mk 6.45-52, cf. Jn 6.16-21), and cursing a fig tree (Mt. 21.18-22=Mk 11.12-14, 20-6).[130] The links between the Jesus of these pericopes and the God of the scriptures who not only brings the world into being but sets bounds on the sea and stills it, controls the weather, and rides on the winds, are well recognized.[131] In the synoptic gospels, in particular, some of these stories also show Jesus caring for his followers by saving them from danger, and, in the

---

days, as a symbolically richer location for the revelation of Jesus' identity and glory than Mark's mountain in Galilee.

[127] Chs 11 and 12 are well recognized as closely connected, and at 12.28 God speaks to affirm that God glorifies God's name through Jesus.

[128] After the transfiguration Jesus tells the disciples not to mention it to anyone until after his resurrection from the dead (Mk 9.9). When Jesus gathers the disciples to go to the dead Lazarus, Thomas says to the others, 'Let us also go to die with him' (11.16), in an apparent *non sequitur* which, nevertheless, signals that the disciples are following Jesus in the direction of Jerusalem to his death and eventually, their own.

[129] Since Martha not only believes in her declaration but has made a commitment to Jesus, and we have also argued that *pisteuein* in the future may be best seen as propositional trust.

[130] Cf. Mt. 17.27.

[131] E.g. Gen. 7.4, Exod. 9.33, Deut. 11.17, 2 Sam. 22.11, Job 37.6, 38.8, 11, Ps. 33.7, 65.7, 89.9, 104.3, 104.9, 107.29, 148.8, Prov. 8.29, 30.4, Jer. 5.22, 10.13.

process, emphasizing the importance of trusting both God and himself. During the storm at sea, as we have already seen, the disciples, terrified, wake Jesus from sleep and beg him to save them.[132] In Matthew's gospel he responds, 'Why are you afraid, *oligopistoi*?' (8.26), before calming the winds and sea. In Mark and Luke he first stills the storm and then asks the disciples, 'Have you no trust (οὔπω ἔχετε πίστιν)?' or 'Where is your trust (Ποῦ ἡ πίστις ὑμῶν)?' (Mk 4.40, Lk. 8.25). Jesus himself leaves open whether he is urging the disciples to trust in God, as the controller of nature, or in himself, but the gospel writers make clear, and also show the disciples recognizing, that it is trust in Jesus himself as the controller of nature that is at issue. 'What sort of person is this,' they wonder, 'that even the winds and sea obey him?' (Mt. 8.27, cf. Mk 4.41, Lk. 8.25). In the story of the walking on the water, when the disciples first see Jesus, they are terrified (Mt. 14.26=Mk 6.50, cf. Jn 6.19) and Jesus has to tell them not to be afraid (Mt. 14.27=Mk 6.50, cf. Jn 6.20). Matthew's gospel continues with a story which becomes explicitly about Peter's trust and doubt. John's version ends with the disciples reassured and gladly taking Jesus into the boat (6.21), Mark's with the disciples astonished but baffled (6.51), and Matthew's with the disciples doing *proskynēsis* to Jesus as the son of God (14.33). The message, unstated in so many words but clearly heard, is that the disciples trust in Jesus and revere him as one who, with God the creator, rules the natural world and keeps them safe within it.

The story of the fig tree is another 'nature miracle' in which Jesus calls his followers explicitly to trust.[133] Walking into Jerusalem one morning in the last week of his life, Jesus looks for fruit on a fig tree by the road, finds none, and curses it. The fig tree withers. When the disciples see this (either immediately or later, in different versions), they are amazed. Mark's Jesus tells them to trust in God (11.22): if they have trust, God will command the natural world for them (11.23), and whatever they pray for, they will receive (11.24). Matthew's Jesus further tells the disciples that 'if you have trust and do not doubt', they will be able to cause mountains to be uprooted (21.21); whatever they ask in prayer, they will receive, if they have trust (21.22). Implicitly or explicitly, the disciples are being exhorted to trust in God, and we have seen that one point of this passage is to illustrate Jesus' own exemplary trust in God, but we can go further.[134] The disciples are exhorted to pray for God to command nature on their behalf, but Jesus commands the fig tree himself, so the story ties him closely to the God who commands creation, and tells listeners to the gospel that they can put their trust not only in God to answer their prayers and command nature for them, but in Jesus too.

---

[132] Jesus' sleep testifies to his own trust in God: cf. e.g. Ps. 4.8, Prov. 3.24.
[133] As Böttrich (1997) shows, in this case, strongly eschatological trust.
[134] Explored in relation to Matthew by Jones (2017).

We saw in Chapter 2 that an implicit theme of trust and the betrayal of trust runs through Genesis 2-3. That trust is bi-directional: God entrusts Eden to the man and woman, and they are implicitly invited not only to trust in God for everything but to be trustworthy in looking after God's creation. When they trust the serpent and eat the apple they fail on both counts. By the same token, when Jesus is identified by the gospels with God the creator, the disciples are not only invited implicitly to trust him but to be trustworthy when they are entrusted with his power or his ministry.[135] As we have begun to see, they frequently fail, but the invitation stands, to themselves during and after Jesus' earthly life, and to Jesus' later followers.

Who is the Jesus in Whom Trust is Placed?

The previous sections tell us something not only about how Jesus is trustworthy and why it is appropriate for people to respond to him with trust, but also about how they understand his identity. He invites trust not least as one who is uniquely closely connected with God the creator and life-giver. This invites us to consider what more the gospels affirm about the identity of the earthly Jesus who invites people to trust, and in whom they are called to trust. One of the first places commentators turn in seeking to understand how the gospels represent Jesus' identity is his messianic titles. The synoptic gospels are significantly different from John in their treatment of some of these, so we will take them separately.

Though both *pistis* language and messianic titles, between them, are widespread in the synoptic gospels, the connections between them are weak. In Mark's gospel, two titles are linked with *pistis* language once each. Soon after the healing of the paralytic, Jesus refers to himself as 'Son of Man' (2.10), and, when Bartimaeus asks him for healing, he calls him 'Son of David' (10.47). 'Son of David' is a title for an earthly Messiah, while Jesus most often (though not always) seems to use 'Son of Man' to refer to his suffering humanity.[136] Elsewhere, when

---

[135] A parallel reciprocity is explored by Daube (1972) in the mutual accountability of Jesus and the disciples to one another as master and followers, though without reference to *pistis*.

[136] He also uses it eschatologically, but arguing that 'Son of Man' refers to Jesus' humanity in a majority of instances see Hooker (1967), cf. Kingsbury (1981), 38–40 (though Hurtado (2011), 163–8 argues that the title refers to Jesus rather than characterizing him, so we should be less concerned than most commentators are with its precise meaning in particular passages). Bartimaeus calls Jesus both Son of David and rabbi (10.47-8) in a story which occurs just before Jesus' triumphal entry into Jerusalem, from which point he is associated with David more strongly (11.10, 12.35, 12.37, cf. 2.25), so Bartimaeus' identification may look forward to that development, or it may have been affected by a form of conceptual attraction. Occasions of *pistis* are also associated with people wondering who Jesus is (4.41, 6.1-6, cf. 11.28), while at 15.32 the chief priests and scribes say, 'Let the Messiah, the King of Israel, come down now from the cross that we may see and believe,' but evidently think he is neither the Messiah nor the King of Israel, nor expect to come to believe. On recent discussions of 'Son of David' in Mark see Botner (2019), 1–38; he argues that the title is important to Mark, but does not see it as closely linked with *pistis* language.

people put their trust in Jesus or are urged to do so, they usually call him, if anything, *didaskalos,* teacher (4.38, 9.17), or 'rabbi' (10.51, 11.21). We can be confident that the evangelist himself thinks that Jesus' followers, in his own day, can and should put their trust in Jesus as Messiah, Son of God, and eschatological Son of Man. But the lack of close connections between *pistis* language and Jesus' Christological titles suggests that, for Mark, those who put their trust in Jesus in his earthly life do not need to see him in whatever terms these titles suggest. Those who trust see Jesus as a human being, a figure of authority among the people of Israel, someone who wields exceptional power, and someone who can help or save them; their trust is focalized through his presence and actions among them rather than through traditional images of saviour figures.

Matthew follows Mark in making a pair of blind men who seek healing, and also the Canaanite woman, call Jesus 'Son of David'.[137] Unlike Mark, Matthew also several times links *pistis* language with the title *kyrios,* which is most often translated 'lord' or 'master' (e.g. 8.6, 8.8, 9.28, 15.22, 25[138]). However, the man who brings his possessed son to be exorcized, who in Mark addresses Jesus as 'teacher' (9.17), in Matthew addresses him as *kyrios* (17.15), during the storm at sea, Mark's disciples wake Jesus by calling him 'teacher', Matthew's by calling him *kyrios* (8.25), and when Matthew's Peter tests his *pistis* by getting out of his boat to walk to Jesus across the sea, he twice calls him *kyrios* (14.28, 30). Among other things, *kyrios* can be used to translate *rav* or *rabbi,* so it is perhaps most likely that Matthew is using it to mean 'teacher' or 'master' rather than the more hierarchical 'lord'.[139] The elasticity of the term, however, allows listeners to hear other possibilities. It suggests that for Matthew, as for Mark, those who trust Jesus trust him primarily on the basis of his presence and actions among them, as a human being, an authority figure in Israel, and a person of power who can help or save them— but it hints that, in some undefined sense, some people may also be beginning to see Jesus as more than a rabbi, or be beginning to suspect that he may be more than they understand.[140]

---

[137] 9.27 (though there are two men, the story is closely related to Mark's Bartimaeus story), 15.22. John's references to the Davidic line are more submerged; the clearest, at 7.42, is not connected with *pisteuein.* Here, and in his linking of *pistis* with the title *kyrios* and with *dikaiosynē,* we see Matthew actively connecting themes that are particularly important to him with *pistis.* Baxter (2006) argues that the link between healing and the title 'Son of David' in Matthew refers to the Davidic shepherd of Ezek. 34, and so to the theme of God's Messiah as carer.

[138] Mt. 8.8=Lk. 8.6, the only one of these uses of *kyrios* that derives from Q.

[139] Rowland (1985), 247–8. On New Testament connections with Jewish traditions about Lordship see Longenecker (1970), 120–47.

[140] Matera (1999), 38 argues that more people recognize more about Jesus' identity in Matthew than in Mark, e.g. confessing him as Son of God and performing *proskynēsis.* Equally significantly, Matthew links *pistis* several times, more or less explicitly, with *dikaiosynē* (e.g. 21.32, 23.23, cf. 23.38), which is paradigmatically the quality of those who seek the kingdom of God or heaven (5.6, 5.10, 5.20, 6.33, cf, antithetically, 22.13 with 25.26–30).

Luke too links *pistis* language with the title *kyrios*, but less often than Matthew (e.g. 7.6, 22.33). The disciples, frightened by the storm at sea, call on Jesus as *epistata*, 'master', where Mark uses 'teacher' and Matthew, 'lord'.[141] The ten lepers whom Jesus heals also call on Jesus as *epistata* (17.13). When the man whose son is possessed appeals to Jesus, Luke follows Mark in making him call Jesus 'Teacher'.[142] Simon Peter uses *kyrios* more than once to address Jesus (5,5. 8.45, 9.33), and the disciple John once (9.49).[143] The semantic range of *epistatēs* in Greek in general is similar to that of *kyrios*, so these usages are hard to separate; Luke is likely using *epistatēs* as an equivalent of 'rabbi' or *kyrios*, but, like *kyrios*, its elasticity also allows listeners to wonder whether those who encounter Jesus are uncertain of his identity, or suspect there may be more to it than they realize.[144]

We will see in the next chapter that those who come to Jesus in trust have, at best, a partial understanding of who and what he is. The weakness of the connections between *pistis* language and the messianic titles in the synoptic gospels suggests that the origins of Christian *pistis* discourse do not lie in these messianic traditions, but also—for our purposes, more significantly—that none of the evangelists chooses to link the trust people put in Jesus with any of these titles, with all their complex (and, to us, only partially audible) overtones. Not only do most of those around Jesus not trust in him as Son of God, Son of David, and so on, but the gospel writers do not indicate to their listeners that trusting in Jesus in his earthly life should entail trusting in him in those terms.[145]

We can go a little further. The synoptic gospels and Acts, from their post-resurrection perspective, all point to what we might call a minimum understanding of Jesus in his earthly life, which, they imply, those who encountered him could and should have grasped, and in which they could and should have put their trust.[146] Some people within these stories, of course, recognize more than this, but this is apparently what everyone should have been able to grasp.[147] This understanding is both limited and flexible. It offers food for thought not only in

---

[141] Lk. 8.24=Mk 4.38=Mt. 8.25.   [142] Lk. 9.38=Mk 9.17=Mt. 17.15.

[143] It is tempting to make something of the fact that every time the disciples use it, they are expressing doubt or saying something inappropriate, demonstrating the inchoate nature of their *pistis*, but since that is true of other utterances by the disciples too, and 17.13 does not fit the pattern, this is probably pressing the text too hard.

[144] E.g. S., *OC* 889, though it is used less commonly of gods than is *kyrios*. Oepke (1964), 623 notes that Luke sometimes uses it to translate the Hebrew/Aramaic 'Rabbi', which he avoids.

[145] The passages of Isaiah invoked by Jesus' healings and resurrections, which, especially in the synoptic gospels, are closely linked with *pistis* language, refer to prophecies of the time when God will bring the world to rights, but not to Messiah figures (e.g. Isa. 26.19, 29.18–19, 35.5–6).

[146] At least, the Jews who encountered him should have grasped it: cf. p. 233. On Jesus as enabling God to be seen, in Mark's gospel, in a way which most more readily associate with John's, see e.g. Chronis (1982), Tuckett (2001), 114–16.

[147] The cognitive nature of this understanding is never specified, but it is based on things people saw, heard, and experienced as done for them, which elsewhere are foundations of belief.

relation to Jesus' earthly life, but also to listeners to the gospels reflecting on their relationship with the risen Christ.

We have already mentioned Peter's speech at Pentecost, in which he tells the Jerusalem crowd that they should have been able to recognize the 'mighty deeds, wonders, and signs' that Jesus performed in his earthly life as worked through him by God (Acts 2.22). In the next chapter, Peter, speaking in the portico of the temple, proclaims that God has 'glorified his servant Jesus' whom the Israelites handed over and denied in Pilate's presence (3.13). As God's servant, Jesus was holy and righteous (ἅγιον καὶ δίκαιον) (3.14). Among the various words for 'holy' in Greek, *hagios* usually means dedicated or devoted to the divine, and is used in the same way by early Christians.[148] *Dikaios* has a very wide range of meaning, but in connection with service and dedication probably refers to Jesus' righteousness as one who was wholly dedicated to God.[149] This Jesus was 'the founder of life (τὸν δὲ ἀρχηγὸν τῆς ζωῆς)' (3.15). Some commentators treat this as a reference to Jesus as the first to rise from the dead, or to the risen Christ as the head of the new community, the emerging church, but the order of the sentence suggests that the phrase refers to Jesus before his death: 'The "founder of life" you killed, but God raised him from the dead, of which we are witnesses' (3.15).[150] The reference, in line with a theme we have seen running through the gospels, is to Jesus as the leader who makes possible new life through *pistis* (referenced immediately afterwards, at 3.16) in his earthly life, as through his death and in his exalted life.[151] In this speech, therefore, Peter affirms that in his earthly life it should have been possible for those who encountered Jesus to recognize him, at a minimum, as a human being who was God's servant, dedicated and devoted to God, and the bringer of life. Peter's later speeches and those of other apostles (4.9-12, 5.29-32, 7.2-53) return to the same themes: Jesus was recognizable in his earthly life as the Nazorean (4.10), righteous (7.52), and *archēgos* (5.31).

In the synoptic gospels, Jesus himself criticizes people for not recognizing him in passages which also hint at what the evangelists think people could have understood about him in his earthly life. In Mark's gospel, for example, during altercations with crowds or religious authorities, Jesus describes himself as a prophet (6.4), sent to call sinners (2.17, cf. Lk. 5.32). He is amazed (6.5-6) by the *apistia* which makes the people of Nazareth unable to recognize his prophetic

---

[148] As opposed to made holy by association with the divine or intrinsically holy as divine.
[149] Cf. 22.14. Johnson (1992), *ad loc.* links this phrase with the *dikaios* of Hab. 2.4 who lives by trust and the *dikaios* servant of Isa. 53.11.
[150] Fitzmyer (1997), *ad* 3.15 notes that *archēgetēs* is normally used of pathfinders, founders, and eponymous heroes, and thinks it refers to Jesus here as the first to rise from the dead; Johnson (1992), *ad loc.* observes that the word appears again in combination with 'saviour' at 5.31 and suggests that its likeliest meaning is 'the one who gives life'. 5.31 as a whole suggests that Jesus is the exalted head or leader of the new community of his followers, through whom come salvation and remission of sins.
[151] References to the (eternal) life to which Jesus gives access are less characteristic of Luke than John, but see 10.25, 18.18, 18.30, cf. 12.22-3.

words and works. He points out, as noted above, that it is perverse of his critics to claim that he exercises power, in casting out demons, by the power of Satan rather than of God (3.23). In several passages he contrasts his and his followers' actions with the hypocrisy of the religious authorities who keep the letter but not the spirit of the law. He criticizes the scribes and Pharisees for honouring God with their lips but not their hearts, when they ask why his disciples do not wash before meals (7.1–7). When his followers are criticized for not fasting, he refers to himself as the bridegroom (2.18–19), a traditional image for Godself or God's representative.[152] He demands, 'Why does this generation seek a sign?' (8.12). It should be clear that he is a prophet, a healer and exorcist by divine authority; a person who knows what constitutes authentic piety; a person through whom God acts.

At first sight, these passages seem to contradict what we argued above, that, although signs, miracles, prophecies and teachings are never misleading, they do not in themselves prove Jesus' identity to the sceptical, and those who seek to prove Jesus' identity via his words or miraculous actions lack trust. It is significant, however, that in none of these passages are Jesus' words or deeds said to prove his identity: rather, those who witness them should have recognized what they signified. They should have recognized their significance because, in each case, they are Jews; they already trust in God and accept the authority of the scriptures, with their prophecies of salvation and stories of the great works of those chosen by God to lead Israel. (The complex basis on which gospel writers imply that those around him should have recognized Jesus recalls the complex basis on which, in Chapter 2, both gospels and epistles described people recognizing the trustworthiness of God, and, in Chapter 3, the way they described people recognizing the resurrection, and trusting in the risen and exalted Christ.[153]) The Jews, to put it another way, should have been able to recognize Jesus, form certain beliefs about him, and put their trust in him, because they already recognized and trusted in God and their own tradition, and everything Jesus was, did, and said was recognizable within that relationship and tradition. By the same token, the failing which Jesus criticizes in the passages discussed above is that, despite being Jews, his interlocutors seek proof of his identity independently of their existing relationship with God and the scriptures.[154]

What the synoptic evangelists think that Jews should have been able to recognize and believe is notably limited: that Jesus was a teacher and leader; that he was holy, righteous, and obedient to God; that he acted by God's power, understood

---

[152] Collins (2007), *ad* 2.19; cf. Jer. 2.2, 3.14, 31.32, Hos. 2.6–7, 14–16, 19–20, Ezek. 16.13–15, 32, Isa. 54.4–5, Isa. 62.4–7.

[153] This highlights that even at the resurrection, it is not the miracle alone that leads to belief and trust; tradition and interpretation, and therefore reason, also play a role. Human reason, though, appropriately interprets scripture and tradition and their coherence with experience, rather than seeking to prove truths about Godself.

[154] In addition to their function in the narrative, these passages also emphasize, for the gospels' listeners, the coherence of the proclamation about Jesus with scripture and tradition.

what constitutes a right relationship with God, and called people to repentance and new life. In no passage, moreover, does Jesus criticize his interlocutors for not recognizing him in all these aspects at once. Most strikingly, none of these passages suggests that those who encountered Jesus in his earthly life should have understood him as more than human. During his earthly life, it seems, everything human beings need for forgiveness, salvation, or eternal life, can be gained through trust in Jesus in his human person.[155]

All these, of course, are post-resurrection perspectives. They are instructive not least because they by no means encompass everything which the synoptic gospel writers want to say on their own or their communities' behalf about the nature of Jesus Christ, his relationship with God, or his relationship with humanity. They recognize a significant difference between what the evangelists think people should be able to see in Jesus and put their trust in, after the resurrection, and what they claim people should have been able to see and trust in, in his earthly life.[156]

All three synoptic evangelists undoubtedly think that, after the resurrection, people should put their trust in Jesus as the one who had to die for others (e.g. Mt. 20.28=Mk 10.45, Mt. 26.28=Mk 14.24=Lk. 22.19-20) and be raised by God (e.g. Mt. 16.21=Mk 8.31=Lk. 9.22, Mt. 17.23=Mk 9.31=Lk. 9.44, Mt. 20.18-19=Mk 10.33-4=Lk. 18.32-3, Lk. 24.46), to whom power has been given (e.g. Mt. 28.18, Acts 2.33-6), in whose glorified name repentance and forgiveness of sins are to be preached (e.g. Lk. 24.47, Acts 2.38), and who will return as eschatological judge (e.g. Mt. 25.31-2, Mt. 26.64=Mk 14.62, Acts 10.42, 17.30-1). Nor is there much doubt that most other early Christians understood and preached Jesus Christ as all these things. But by creating a narrative of the Jesus whom people encounter before his death, these writers create a vision of Jesus in his earthly life which later listeners and readers can also encounter. They tell stories whose significance reaches beyond their immediate context in Jesus' earthly life to shape the relationship of Christ-confessors with the exalted Christ. They hint that those whose trust, even after the resurrection, is limited or imperfect, may still be saved or attain eternal life.[157]

---

[155] The gospels therefore suggest that those around Jesus in his earthly life could trust themselves to recognize enough about him to trust him, but this the trust that arises from intersubjectivity rather than trust in their autonomous ability to establish objective truths about Jesus.

[156] Cf. e.g. Frey (2011), arguing that the historical Jesus' likely self-understanding, together with that of his followers even before his death, sketches him as an eschatological prophet and wonder-worker through whom God was understood as acting and signalling the coming of God's kingdom, and that this picture is consonant with some contemporary views of the Messiah. On this view, most of whose elements are widely shared (cf. Theissen and Merz (1998), 235-6, 275-8, 309-13, Stanton (2002), 241-4, Keener (2009), 256-67), the synoptic evangelists draw on pre-resurrection traditions of how Jesus and his followers represented him in earthly life which they could claim would have been comprehensible within the world-view of (especially, but not necessarily only Jewish) contemporaries.

[157] On this idea in relation to John see Williams (2018), 140-50.

John's gospel takes a significantly different approach to the question what people who encountered Jesus in his earthly life could have been expected to recognize about him. He seems to want to preclude the possibility that people might understand the Jesus in whom they trust differently before and after the resurrection, identifying the earthly Jesus much more closely with the Jesus of his own post-resurrection perspective.[158]

John's approach is well illustrated by his use of Christological titles, some of which are more closely connected with *pistis* language than are titles in the synoptic gospels.[159] At 1.12, the proclamation that those who received Jesus and trusted in his name were enabled to become children of God is surrounded by references to Jesus as the Word which is both godlike and God, and as the light of the world (1.1–14, cf. 8.12).[160] John's Jesus several times refers to himself as the Son of Man, but where in the synoptic gospels the phrase tends to highlight his suffering humanity, in John it is more closely connected with his divine descent, putting trusting in the Son of Man very close to trusting in Godself.[161] The story of the man born blind shows that it is not enough for someone who encounters Jesus to trust him, for instance, as a healer. After the man has been expelled from his synagogue, as we have seen, Jesus seeks him out and asks whether he puts his trust in the Son of Man (9.35). The man asks who the Son of Man is, and Jesus says he is himself. The man affirms his trust in Jesus, doing *proskynēsis* to him (9.36–8), and Jesus says that he came into the world 'for judgment, so that those who do not see might see, and those who do see might become blind,' (v. 39). The Son of Man in whom the blind man ultimately trusts is both the pre-existent Word made flesh of the prologue, and the one who executes final judgment on God's behalf.

The title 'Son of God' occurs only a handful times in John's gospel in that form (1.34, 1.49, 3.18, 5.25, 10.36, 11.27, 19.7, 20.31), but most of these occur in close connection with *pisteuein*. At 1.49–50, Nathanael calls Jesus Rabbi, Son of God, and King of Israel, and Jesus asks him, 'Do you [believe and] trust because I saw you under the fig tree?'[162] Martha too, when Jesus challenges her to confirm that

---

[158] If John knew and, at times, was reacting to Mark's gospel, his approach may be a self-conscious 'correction' to some of the implications of Mark's picture of trust. NB, though, John's Jesus often uses *pisteuein* without an object or a dependent clause, leaving ambiguous, as in the synoptic gospels, what people are to trust/believe in.

[159] Schnelle (2018), 311, 317–20.

[160] The title 'Lamb of God', which appears only at 1.29 and 36, is not closely connected with *pisteuein*.

[161] Freed (1967), Martyn (1979), 134 (though at 3.14 the reference is equally to Jesus' suffering humanity). Even in John, not many references to the Son of Man are closely linked with *pisteuein* (e.g. 1.51, 5.27, 6.26, 6.53, 8.28), though alongside 9.35–7, see 12.34–6.

[162] Nathanael both recognizes something about Jesus and makes a commitment to him, so we can hear both belief and trust as involved; cf. 4.26, where Jesus reveals himself as the Messiah, and 12.37–41, where 'the Jews' fail to believe and trust in Jesus as the one foretold by Isaiah. On aspects of the background to the phrase see e.g. Cooke (1961), Bühner (1977), Hengel (1977), Byrne (1979), J. Collins (1993), Chaniotis (2003), Levin (2006), Peppard (2011).

she believes that resurrection and life come through trusting in him (11.25-7), calls Jesus 'Son of God' and 'Messiah'. At 3.18, Jesus says that whoever trusts in the name of the only Son of God will not be condemned, and whoever does not, will be.[163] At 10.36-7, he refers to himself Son of God, and immediately afterwards says, 'If I do not do my father's works, do not trust me...'. In his concluding words, the evangelist says that 'these things are written so that you may believe [or "trust"] that Jesus is the Messiah, the Son of God...' (20.31).[164] In addition, Jesus refers repeatedly to God as father and to himself as (God's) son, and many of these passages also link his sonship with the importance of trusting in him. 'Trust in God; trust also in me,' he tells the disciples on the last night of his life. 'In my father's house there are many dwelling-places...' (14.1-2). 'Whoever has seen me has seen the Father...Do you not believe/trust that I am in the Father and the Father is in me?' (14.9-10). 'The word became flesh and made his dwelling among us,' affirms the Prologue (1.4), 'and we [who trust in his name, cf. v. 12] saw his glory, the glory as of the Father's only Son...'. Nearly all these passages concern judgment and/or eternal life. To bring those who trust to life is *par excellence* the work of the Son of Man or Son of God, and, for John, it is by recognizing and trusting in him as God's son and agent in his earthly life, as in his pre-existence and ascended life, that human beings gain eternal life.[165] Where, however, for the synoptic evangelists, those who encounter Jesus could and should have been able to understand something of his identity based on their location in their own tradition, for John, the capacity to recognize and respond to Jesus is given by pre-election.[166]

---

[163] At 5.25, those who hear the voice of the Son of God will live, but in the previous verse Jesus has said that whoever hears his word and trusts in the one who sent him has eternal life.

[164] At 20.31 belief is probably to the fore, but perhaps with an implication of trust commitment.

[165] As noted, Jesus is occasionally addressed as *kyrios* in contexts where more than human lordship is indicated. Most strikingly, on meeting him after the resurrection, Thomas calls him 'My Lord and my God' (20.28) and Jesus responds that those *pisteusantes* (in him as Lord and God) without having seen him are (even more) blessed. John does not, though, seem to use the language of lordship as the synoptic writers sometimes do, to mark the complexity of Jesus' identity by showing how trust/belief in Jesus as a man of power and authority involves followers in a deeper and further-reaching relationship with God than they anticipated. *Pisteuein* is closely linked with three of Jesus' 'I am' sayings (6.35, 8.24, 11.25-6); in these passages, as in the 'Son of Man' sayings, Jesus' identity is closely linked with his divinely judicial activity and trusting with eternal life, while John's imagery seems to locate Jesus both as God's instrument (the bread that gives life) and as indistinguishable from God (as bringer of resurrection and life itself).

[166] Bultmann (2007), 3.70-4, cf. (1925), 57-8, while emphasizing the importance of revelation for John, notes that believing, knowing, seeing, hearing, and trusting or believing are virtually indistinguishable for John: that is, that what Jesus 'reveals' is not saving truth so much as the possibility of a life-giving relationship with himself, as with God. This kind of interpersonal knowledge (particularly between humanity and God as creator) is also explored e.g. by van Beeck (1979), Sequeri (1996), Eastman (2018); Eastman draws on recent research on relational knowing in philosophy and psychology, specifically in relation to Paul, but her argument is also relevant to the gospels. Even the 'Johannine thunderbolt' at Mt. 11.27 is couched in relational language ('No one knows the Son except the Father...'), though Luke (10.22), modifies this to, 'No one knows who the Son is except the Father...'; the latter is one of the most striking claims of propositional knowledge in the gospels, but does not outweigh the assumption in the gospel as a whole that what people are called to is a

Trust and Revelation

As we have explored how people are called to put their trust in Jesus in his earthly life, and for what, and the portrait of the Jesus in whom they are called to trust, we might have expected the theme of revelation to play a larger role. The previous section began to indicate why it has not, but we can say a little more about the relationship between *pistis* and revelation in the gospels in its own right.

In the world of the early principate, across Jewish, Near Eastern, and Mediterranean traditions, divinities are thought of as revealing themselves quite often: in visual or aural manifestations to the waking or sleeping; in signs, portents, and oracles, oral or written; through human agents; through texts composed to preserve divine communications (like books of prophecies) or used for bibliomancy (like the books of Homer and Virgil and books of the scriptures[167]). Human exegesis plays a role, especially, in the understanding of signs and texts, whose interpretation is often contested.[168] When divinities intend to reveal themselves, however, in person or through personal emissaries, their appearances are normally unmistakable,[169] and appropriate responses include reverence, fear, gratitude, and worship.[170] In the thought-world of the first century, divinities or their emissaries also visit earth in disguise: to help mortals, test them, seduce them, rape them, or take them to their own realm.[171] Those who encounter divine beings in deliberate disguise do not normally recognize them, and their response varies from abuse to hospitality and from contempt to compliance.[172] But the idea that God, or a god, might intend to reveal him- or herself, or his or her emissary, to mortals and fail to be recognized, is very odd, and arguably unparalleled in this

---

relationship with God and Christ. On Matthew 11.27 as expressing Jesus' entrusting of himself to God, and the disciples' relationship with Jesus as replicating this self-entrusting, see Grundmann (1965); on Matthew's gospel as a whole as written to enable personal knowing of Jesus see Franke (2012).

[167] Van der Horst (1999, 2000), Rutgers et al. (1999).

[168] Driediger-Murphy and Eidinow (2019).

[169] An arguable exception is manifestations of emperors, whose appearances were not normally in doubt but who were an unusual group among divinities, whose divinity could be disputed (cf. pp. 100, 281).

[170] For this reason e.g. Bauckham (2015), 28 is problematic: 'in incarnation God is not present merely with or in one or more of his creatures, but *as* the particular human Jesus of Nazareth'. One would expect, if this were the case, that he could not fail to be recognized unless he was deliberately disguising himself, and the gospels do not represent Jesus as straightforwardly revealing or disguising himself, nor, where he does reveal himself, as being straightforwardly recognizable.

[171] E.g. Smith (1988), Morgan (2013), 14–20, Strauss Clay (2019).

[172] Outside the gospels, the fact that a human character does not recognize a divine one in a story can be marked without this being understood as a paradox of revelation (e.g. Gen. 18.1–16, Tob. 6.4–5, Heb. 3.2, Hom., *Od.* 6.1–40, *h.Cer.* 91–291 (where something of Demeter's divine glory is seen without being recognized by some of those among whom she moves in disguise, 188–215), Ov., *Met.* 8.611–724), and this is probably one model for the evangelists. The misidentification of Silas and Paul as Zeus and Hermes in Acts 14.8–13 suggests that the crowd thinks not that it has penetrated a divine disguise (cf. 14.15), but that it is witnessing an epiphany.

period, and we should be wary of attributing it to early Christ-confessors if other interpretations of Jesus' earthly life are available.

In the gospels, the birth narratives of Matthew and Luke are well in line with stories of revelations elsewhere: God's plans and the identity of Jesus as God's son are revealed to certain people, and they see, hear, and recognize what is revealed to them.[173] During Jesus' earthly ministry, however, God rarely intervenes directly, in any of the gospels, to reveal Godself or Jesus (Mk 1.11=Lk. 3.22, cf. Mt. 3.17; Mt. 17.5=Mk 9.7=Lk. 9.35, John 1.33 and 12.28-9).[174] Of these instances, only Mark 1.11, if it is meant to indicate that Jesus' identity and work were conferred on him at his baptism, and John 1.33, where John the Baptist implies that God spoke to him and passes on what he has heard to two of his followers, affect the course of events (and only the Baptist's testimony directly affects anyone other than Jesus himself).[175] In the synoptic gospels, outside the passion narratives,[176] Jesus does not explicitly reveal his identity,[177] and, although those who encounter him sometimes seem to sense that they are encountering someone more than ordinarily human, normally, whatever the gospel writers understand as Jesus' identity and relationship with God, those around him do not recognize it in the same terms.[178] Much of Jesus' earthly ministry has more in common with stories of divinities or their messengers visiting earth in disguise than with divine revelations: those who encounter Jesus, without recognizing him, or much about him, are variously tested, helped, and cared for, and some are promised that they will eventually be with him in heaven or in God's house.[179]

This narrative pattern is usually taken to mean that, for the evangelists, most people's non-recognition, or very limited recognition of Jesus in his earthly life is a problem that needs explaining. It may, however, be read equally, or more satisfactorily as meaning that, for the evangelists, it is part of God's plan that

---

[173] Zechariah expresses doubt about the content of the revelation he receives rather than the revelation itself (Lk. 1.18–20).

[174] At Mt. 16.17 Jesus tells Simon Peter that God has revealed to him that Jesus is the Christ, and at Mt. 27.19 Pilate's wife has been warned in a dream to have nothing to do with 'that righteous one' (a messianic title, so we assume that the dream comes from God or an angel).

[175] *Ad* Jn 1.33 Haenchen (1984) notes the difficulty of squaring an account of Jesus' baptism similar to that of the synoptics with the Prologue, and suggests that this consists of inherited tradition, which might explain why it is an outlier. Lk. 3.22, unlike Mk 1.11, cannot be meant to confirm Jesus' identity to him, since Luke's Jesus has always known it, cf. 2.49.

[176] Mark's Jesus responds to Caiaphas' question, 'Are you the Christ, the son of the blessed one?' with the apparent affirmation 'I am', which is, however, altered by both Mt. 26.64 and Lk. 22.67–8.

[177] On Simon Peter's moment of insight in response to a question from Jesus at Mt. 16.15–16=Mk 8.29=Lk. 9.20.

[178] E.g. Mt 7.28–9=Mk 1.22, cf. Lk. 4.31–2, Jn 7.46, Mk 1.27=Lk. 4.36, Mt. 12.23, cf. 9.33=Lk. 11.14.

[179] Taking *pistis* as a significant strand in Mark's Christology also reduces the tension between Jesus' identity as Messiah and non-recognition of him during his ministry because (1) it puts the trust relationship rather than revelation of identity at the centre of the narrative of salvation, (2) it gives due weight to the responsibility of those who encounter Jesus to trust in what of him *is* visible to them, and (3) trust does not need to recognize Jesus in his full identity to be salvific in his earthly life.

forgiveness, salvation, or eternal life are given to those who put their trust in Jesus even though, during his earthly ministry, they do not fully recognize who or what he is.

Modern models of revelation fall into several types,[180] but they share, in broad terms, the view, as Avery Dulles expresses it, that '[r]evelation is God's free action whereby [God] communicates saving truth to created minds, especially through Jesus Christ...'.[181] The 'saving truth', which is communicated is by its nature something that human beings could not know by other means, and what it enables is most often described as knowledge, right belief, or faith which involves belief.[182] Chapter 3 spoke of the resurrection as God's revelation of Christ and Christ's self-revelation, which invites a positive cognitive response (almost certainly belief) together with a commitment of trust.[183] The way the gospels describe Jesus and his interactions with others in his earthly life is somewhat different, and puts revelation and trust in a different relationship.

We have just noted that the gospels are marked, if anything, by the absence of the kind of divine revelation that would be widely recognizable to first-century Jews or gentiles. One reason for this may be that, at least in the vision of the synoptic evangelists, as earlier sections of this chapter sought to show, to put one's trust Jesus in his earthly life does not need any such revelation. The synoptic gospels and Acts suggest that those who encountered Jesus should have been able to recognize certain things about him: above all, that Jesus was a human being devoted and dedicated to God, who could only have spoken and acted as he did by the power of God. Jews, especially, should have recognized and trusted Jesus because he was recognizably a man of God within their own tradition.

To put it another way: Jesus should have been trustworthy, the synoptic gospels imply, precisely because no new or special revelation was needed to communicate that a person who said and did what he did could and should be trusted, and no understanding of him greater than this was required as a starting-point for

---

[180] Among discussions of modern approaches to revelation see especially Pelikan (1971), 29–61, Dulles (1992), Ward (1994), Sauter and Barton (2000), Abraham (2006), Schillebeeckx (2014). Bultmann and Lührmann (1974) note that both Hebrew Bible and New Testament revelation is less the communication of knowledge than the self-disclosure of God (cf. Baillie (1956), 28). Gunton (1995), in part following Lindbeck (2009), also seeks to steer away from the idea that revelation reveals propositional knowledge, towards the idea that it reveals (e.g. God's) self, and so, by implication, human relational knowing and relationship with God. New Testament language of knowing God or Christ is much more often relational than propositional.

[181] Dulles (1992), 117.

[182] Few scholars discuss the relationship between revelation and trust, as opposed to 'faith'. Baillie (1956) argues (broadly following Luther) that revelation generates *notitia*, *assensus*, and *fiducia*, the last of which, however, he characterizes as reliance rather than, as we might expect, trust (though he does not distinguish the two, so he may, unlike most contemporary philosophers, think they are equivalents).

[183] So e.g. Jansen (1980), 44–6; what Wilckens (1978), 111 calls 'the actuality of the event of Jesus' resurrection as the decisive inauguration of the eschatological self-revelation of God'.

forgiveness or salvation.[184] During Jesus' earthly ministry, all that was needed for other Jews to trust him was general and historical divine revelation coupled with long experience of its validity for God's people.[185] Gentiles, meanwhile, could, as some did, trust Jesus on the basis that individuals, from any people, who heal and give life, who visibly trust in the divine and teach trust in the divine, are likely to be trustworthy.[186]

As we also noted, moreover, whatever Jesus thought about himself and his mission at any point (which remains highly uncertain), the synoptic gospels do not show him as calling people to trust in God or in himself based on his explicit self-revelation as Messiah. He invites trust because his words and actions resonate with actions and attitudes which those around him already accept as good, godly, and life-giving. He invites people to trust in him in a present and personal relationship, and to be open to where that relationship might take them and how its meaning and significance might grow. From the post-resurrection perspective of the gospels, Jesus thereby invites people to trust not only in God and in himself, but in what may happen in the future: a future in which Jesus will make possible the salvation, not only of individuals but of humanity as a whole, through his death and resurrection and in his risen life, the empowerment of the faithful to spread the gospel around the world, and the creation of a community greater than his first followers could have dreamed of.

John's gospel takes a different approach, in which the Jesus in whom people trust in his earthly life is much more closely aligned with John's vision of the glorified Christ. Accordingly, like the exalted Christ elsewhere, his Jesus reveals himself: especially as Son of God and as co-operative with God.[187] But, strikingly, such revelations are not shown in themselves as bringing people to firm and lasting trust, and in some passages it seems that only those who already have the capacity to trust can recognize enough of Jesus to trust in him. Jesus' self-revelation is therefore less the basis of trust *de novo* than an education in the trust relationship for those who are pre-elected to trust, through which Jesus helps his followers to understand what it means to trust in him and how trust in him relates

---

[184] We may ask why, then, as we argued in the previous chapter, the risen Christ was understood as revealed to his followers. One answer is probably simply that the resurrection was experienced as a revelation. We might also suggest that revelation is needed when Christ is not with humanity in his earthly person. Another possibility is that God's therapeutic trust in humanity is (as therapeutic trust tends to be) only partly successful during Christ's earthly life and at his death, and the resurrection offers another opportunity and basis for trust. This possibility would fit well with the longer story of God's relationship with Israel, in which Israel repeatedly fails God but God graciously re-establishes the relationship through a new revelation of Godself, as well as underlining that trust between God, Christ, and humanity is an ongoing relationship in which human failures, at least before the end time, are not deal-breakers.

[185] This implies that divine self-revelation is part of the traditional thinking and expectations of the evangelists, and probably their listeners, which is what we should expect.

[186] As true in a polytheist as an Israelite world-view (Morgan (2015a), 102–3, 106–7, 140–2, 157–8).

[187] Most explicitly at 8.58, 10.30, both of which elicit violence from the crowd (8.59, 10.31), while the second provokes the accusation of blasphemy (10.33).

to trust in God. In John's gospel, moreover, as the farewell discourses make clear, even the disciples, whose trust in Jesus is presumably meant to be understood as stronger than that of most other people, trust while holding beliefs about Jesus which are, at best, partial, uncertain, and fragile.[188] The basis of their trust lacks the clarity or assurance which are normally associated with divine revelation of a kind that leads to belief or knowledge of saving truth.[189]

On one level, for all four evangelists, revelation is undoubtedly involved in the incarnation, but, outside the birth stories, it is not their driving theme. It is more important that the Jesus in whom people trust in his earthly life is a human being who shares their human, social, and cultural situation, and in whom they can trust on the basis of their existing experience and understanding of the world, however imperfect that experience as a basis for recognizing and acknowledging Jesus as Son of God. Through their language of trust, the gospels express the paradox which has intrigued and stimulated Christian thinking for centuries: that new life and the restoration of humanity's relationship with God come through a human being, in the context of a particular time and place. They suggest that, by meeting God, through Jesus, in their time and place, even through what Paul called the 'dark glass' of their limited understanding, people can make the kind of trust relationship that brings them to eternal life, and begin the chain of trust and entrustedness, discipleship and apostleship, which, with the aid of the risen Christ and the spirit, continues into every time and place.

Conclusion

In this chapter, we have seen how *pistis* language is distributed throughout the gospels, especially in connection with healings and other miracles or signs, teaching material, and Jesus' disputes with various authorities and crowds. It appears in every layer of tradition and most types of story, though it is rare in the passion narratives. It expresses almost all the gospels' main theological themes: it is soteriological, Christological, eschatological, charismatic, kerygmatic, and linked with motifs of creation and care.

For all four evangelists, everything Jesus says and does attests to his trustworthiness. The idea, however, that what he says and does—notably in the form of miracles, signs, prophecy, or teaching—constitutes evidence for his trustworthiness which the people around him can rely on themselves to assess, is consistently

---

[188] The trust of one or two other characters, notably Martha and Mary, seems to be as firm as that of the disciples (e.g. 11.25–7).

[189] NB this is a point about the basis of the disciples' trust rather than its nature. Compare e.g. the Exodus story, in which the Israelites periodically lose heart or doubt Moses (i.e. their trust is fragile in nature, e.g. Exod. 16.3, 17.2, 32.1), but in which divine revelations are not doubted and sometimes explicitly engender trust (e.g. 14.31, cf. 4.5).

problematized. Those who demand proofs of Jesus' identity or trust in him because of something he has done cannot see what is before their eyes, or begin to trust only to fall away again. 'An evil and adulterous generation seeks a sign', as Matthew puts it. In the presence of Jesus, as in the presence of Godself, one does not demand proof of identity or rely on one's own judgment of what one is experiencing. One responds: above all, for the gospel writers, with trust.

Trust often arises in contexts which are vividly drawn, and which fit well with some psychological models of how trust develops, especially in the very young, but which remain, in many ways, mysterious: stories of Jesus' coming to people—especially the disciples—seeing and hearing them, being seen and heard by them, calling and being followed by them. Trust begins above all with proximity, presence, and interaction: *pistis* is personal. Of the four canonical gospels, John's is the only one which, in some passages, offers an explanation, in the idea of pre-election, as to why proximity may lead to trust for some people and not others. In all the gospels, however, as we will see in the next chapter, trust also arises where Jesus' presence meets another person's need, curiosity, or openness to challenge, which leads them to trust whether or not they understand much about him. The centurion, for example, puts his trust in Jesus, as a man under God's authority, to heal his son. The disciples trust Jesus, as in some little-understood way connected with the power that rules the natural world, to save them from shipwreck. In these stories those who interact with Jesus often recognize and respond to something of his own relationship of trust with God and trustworthiness towards God, and this also seems to be a factor in their trust.

Stories in which people put their trust in Jesus, or fail to do so, tell listeners to the gospels something about the Jesus in whom people trust. He is implicitly connected with God as creator, life-giver, and source of power. In the synoptic gospels, however, the theme of trust is not closely linked with Jesus' messianic titles, suggesting that, for the gospel writers, it is not the recognition of Jesus as Son of God, Son of David, or Son of Man that leads, or should lead to trust in his earthly life. The synoptic gospels and Acts all hint, moreover, at what we might call a minimum understanding of Jesus, which Jews, and even gentiles, who encountered him in his earthly life could have grasped and in which they could have trusted. Jesus was holy, righteous, and obedient to God; a teacher, prophet, and leader. He performed great deeds by God's power; understood what constitutes a right relationship with God; and justly called people to repentance and new life. This is a very limited cluster of ideas compared with what the gospel writers themselves hold about Jesus and, no doubt, expect their communities to hold, but it says much about their vision of the nature of trust between Jesus and those around him in his earthly life. Trust that heals, enables forgiveness, or gives life, need not, in Jesus' earthly life, recognize any more than that Jesus is a godly human being of a kind with which those around him are familiar, especially from the scriptures and Jewish tradition. John's perspective here, however, is different. He strongly suggests that those who trust in Jesus in his earthly life recognize him as the Son of God, seeing whom is tantamount to seeing Godself (14.9–10)—but that only those who have been chosen to do so can see and trust Jesus in this way.

The idea that those who encounter Jesus in earthly life need not, to begin to trust, recognize more than that he is a godly human being, raises two further questions for modern readers. Do they, to come to healing or life-giving trust, need to trust in Jesus as more than a godly human being? And could people come to a new or restored relationship of trust with God through trust in someone other than Christ?

The first question has generated a range of answers throughout Christian history, but on basis of this and previous chapters, I suggest that, in principle, the answer is 'no'. It is, however, widely agreed that in practice all the gospel writers do understand Jesus of Nazareth as more than a godly human being. Following their conviction offers Christ-confessors a much richer vision of divine grace, in the image of a God who is Godself present in the world with his son, offering and calling humanity to trust not through a revelation of power and glory, but human person to person out of human beings' everyday experience.

The second question has, throughout Christian history, received a resounding 'no'. This 'no' involves more complexity than at first appears when we bear in mind that an apostle like Paul can tell a community to imitate him as he imitates Christ (1 Cor. 11.1), suggesting that apostles (and other Christians) can act as Christ's representatives in enabling trust. But with that proviso, the centrality of trust in the divine–human relationship, as we have outlined it so far, strongly indicates that one can only come into *this* divine–human relationship through Christ. Trust is not only personal: it is person-specific. I might compare my trust relationships with my mother, my best friend, and my partner. They may have features in common, but they are all also unique. I trust each person in a particular way and for some distinctive things; I entrust them and they entrust me with some distinctive things; our trust, in each case, involves a distinct kind of care and stewardship. One cannot be in a trust relationship with God, as Christians conceive of it, without being in a trust relationship with Jesus Christ. That said, as we observed in Chapter 2, it is not self-evident that Christians can rule out that the God who has done a new thing through Christ might choose to do a new thing again, and establish a new relationship of trust with humanity, perhaps through another mediator. With the confidence that trust in God and Christ encourages goes the recognition that human beings, however faithful, do not control the choices of God.

Jesus' relationship of trust with God is also a relationship of power, and Jesus promises the disciples that, if they trust, God will entrust them too with power, and, by implication, with a reason for using it; a mission and ministry that follows

Jesus' own.[190] In the double tradition, Jesus' sermon on the mount or the plain tells his followers that they can trust in God for every aspect of their life, while the parables of the end time encourage them to remain faithful until the end time.

Chapter 4 argued that Christ's double trust and trustworthiness to God and to human beings enable him to act as mediator and make possible the return of human beings to right-standing with God. We have seen the same pattern implicit in many gospel stories, especially in healings and resurrection miracles. Jesus saves by mediating. He trusts in God and is entrusted by God with his ministry. He is trustworthy to God and to the people who come to him for help in healing them or raising those they care for. Those who come to him for help manifest trust and are often praised for it, and their trust completes the circuit of *pistis* which makes possible the transmission of God's power into human life. By the same token, where there is no *pistis*, the circuit is not closed and Jesus does not, or cannot do, many or any acts of power (Mt. 13.58, Mk 6.6).[191] The Jesus who mediates in his death and, for the epistolographers, in his exalted life, already, for the evangelists, mediates in his earthly life, and those who trust in him in his lifetime, however imperfectly, already experience healing, forgiveness, or new life.

All the gospels, sometimes in different ways, show those around Jesus in his earthly life as invited to trust in him as they trust in God. All, simultaneously, recognize that most people, in his lifetime, recognize very little of Jesus' identity. All agree that such recognition or understanding are not what matter most; what matters is relational trust, which is willing to encounter and be encountered, to follow, to imitate, and to be entrusted.

Some readers will think that this reading makes too little of the corporate and eschatological foci of Jesus' preaching, which are central especially to the synoptic evangelists. I do not intend to underplay the role of God's kingdom or eschatology in their accounts of Jesus' ministry, nor to argue against the likelihood that the coming of the kingdom of God was central to the preaching of the historical Jesus. But this chapter has sought to show that the *pistis* relationship between God, Christ, and humanity develops in the earthly present and continues to be part of that present, as long as it lasts. *Pistis* both looks forward to the coming of God's kingdom, and is part of what it means to be under God's rule and in God's care in the present time (cf. Mt. 12.36, Jn 12.48, Acts 17.31). No doubt the evangelists and their communities continued to look forward to the last day, if with

---

[190] See pp. 221, 228, 296, 297.
[191] Schillebeeckx (2014), 172 argues that this verse does not mean that miracles presuppose faith (he attributes the scepticism of the Nazarenes to their conviction that Jesus' power was demonic, but the passage does not suggest this, but indicates rather that they see Jesus as an ordinary man—the carpenter's son (Mt. 13.55=Lk. 4.22) or a carpenter himself (Mk 6.3)). Rather than seeing faith as unilaterally preceding miracles, however, I suggest that *pistis* is a response of trust to the trustworthiness of Jesus within which healing is possible; this is also in line with the gospels' narratives of forgiveness/ salvation, which indicate that it does not take place without a human response to God's and Christ's initiative.

decreasing urgency, but it is also clear that they were actively concerned with how to live and maintain their relationship with God and Jesus in the interim, and in stories of Jesus' earthly life they find both a basis for trust and a pattern for a life of trust with God and the exalted Christ.[192]

Whether it is drawn mainly from the synoptic gospels, from John, or from themes they share, a focus on *pistis* adds something to Christologies focused, for instance, on the *parousia*, the model of the *theios anēr*, the cross, or divine wisdom.[193] A *pistis* Christology is less concerned than most with defining the identity of Christ, or with what of Christ needs to be revealed for belief or the recognition of truth, and more concerned with exploring the conditions for saving trust: what kind of relationship it takes to be forgiven or to enter eternal life. In this relationship, it evidently matters who the person is in whom one trusts, but the gospels suggest that what it matters to perceive or believe about Jesus is rather less than we might expect. They also reaffirm a theme which we have seen throughout these chapters so far: that saving or life-giving trust is double-ended and comes from both above and below; from God entrusting humanity with the life and ministry of Jesus and from humanity responding with trust.

In line with these observations, we have suggested that the theme of revelation is less important in the gospels (especially in the synoptic gospels, but even in John) than is usually assumed. In the thought-world of the first century, Jewish or gentile, it would be very odd indeed to posit that God revealed Godself or God's son, that most human beings failed to recognize the revelation (unless they were pre-elected to do so), and that this was a problem which needed to be explained. It is preferable to see the synoptic gospels, in particular, as convinced that it was God's plan that forgiveness and new life should come through trust in Jesus in his earthly life as well as through his death and resurrection; that to trust in Jesus in life, those around him needed only recognize him as a man of God who acted by God's power; and so that no new or special revelation was needed as he went about his earthly life and work. Though, moreover, by the time the evangelists were writing, Jesus' earthly life had ended a generation earlier or more, they hint that the relationship of trust between Jesus and his disciples forges the beginning of a chain of trust, trustworthiness, and entrustedness, which ensures that human beings may continue to encounter the good news in their own time and place, and respond to it out of their own culture and tradition.

All this suggests that trust is a present relationship with the potential to develop and grow in significance into the eschatological future. Salvation, wherever its culmination (in God's kingdom, at the end time, in the material or metaphysical sphere) begins here and now, in and through the material world. It is trust forged

---

[192] On Paul's concern with the present time see Morgan (2020), 161–242.
[193] Schillebeeckx (2014), 370–400: or, we might add, Christologies focused on Jesus' birth, preaching, or resurrection.

here that changes the future for humanity and, perhaps, for creation as a whole. At a point in the future, from the perspective of most of the narrative of the synoptic gospels, a new revelation will occur: God will raise Jesus from the dead. That revelation will disclose, and invite people to respond to, more about Jesus than Jesus, in the gospels, asks people to respond to in his earthly life. That revelation, however, will have a double purpose, because it will show the risen and exalted Christ as continuous in identity and work with Jesus in his earthly life, so it will also vindicate trust in Jesus in his earthly life and ministry. In the next chapter we will see how those who come to Jesus only ever see and respond to part of who he is. The validation of even partial trust as salvific hints that, even after the resurrection, trusting in Jesus partially and imperfectly may still be an acceptable starting-point for those who hope to be saved.

6
'Your trust has saved you'
Coming to Trust

In the last chapter we argued that the synoptic gospels and Acts sketch a minimum understanding of Jesus which, they suggest, Jews and even gentiles should have been able to recognize and respond to during Jesus' earthly ministry.[1] Compared with what the evangelists themselves, from their post-resurrection perspective, want to say about Jesus, this understanding is limited. Even this limited understanding, however—even when it is imperfectly held—makes possible forgiveness and new life. In this chapter, we explore further the attitudes and actions with which, in all four gospels, people respond to Jesus in his earthly ministry.

Coming to Trust: Healing Stories

When Jesus preaches, heals, or performs other miracles or signs; when he is depicted as sharing God's creative activity or as a model to be imitated, the gospels are always, implicitly if not explicitly, concerned with what it is about Jesus that invites trust and how he invites it. But the gospels also sketch the motivations that bring others to trust in Jesus during his earthly life. Two things, above all, bring people to Jesus: an acute sense of need, and an openness to challenge and change.

A cluster of healing stories, most, but not all in the synoptic gospels, refer to the *pistis* of those who seek healing on their own behalf or that of others: the friends of the paralytic (Mt. 9.1–8=Mk 2.1–12=Lk. 5.17–26), the archon or synagogue leader whom Mark and Luke call Jairus (Mt. 9.18–26=Mk 5.21–43=Lk. 8.40–56), the woman with a haemorrhage (Mt. 9.20–22=Mk 5.25–34=Lk. 8.43–8), Bartimaeus or the two blind men (Mt. 9.27–31, 20.29–34, Mk 10.46–52=Lk. 18.35–43), the Roman centurion's slave (Mt. 8.5–13=Lk. 7.1–10), the Syrophoenician or Canaanite woman (Mt. 15.21–8=Mk 7.24–30), the cleansing of ten lepers (Lk. 17.11–19), and the royal official of Capernaum (Jn 4.46–54).[2] To

---

[1] The chapter heading quotation is from Mk 5.34.
[2] It is notable how often characters are driven by someone else's need, suggesting that care for others is itself a form of *pistis* and indicates readiness to be restored to one's right relationship with

these we may add the woman with the ointment (Lk. 7.36-50), who is told that her *pistis* has saved her (v. 50), and the persistent widow of the parable (Lk. 18.1-8), who seeks resolution of an injustice and is also commended implicitly for her *pistis*.[3]

We can infer that those who seek healing hold certain attitudes towards Jesus (most likely, perhaps, beliefs, though they could also, for instance, be hopes or assumptions[4]): at a minimum that he is able and may be willing to heal. When Jesus sees their *pistis*, however (cf. e.g. Mt. 9.2=Mk 2.5=Lk. 5.20), he commends more than a belief. When he sees the *pistis* of the paralytic's friends, he sees an action which may be motivated by need, desire, belief, and/or hope. The friends not only believe that Jesus can heal their friend, but entrust him to Jesus and trust Jesus to respond. When Matthew's Jesus says of the centurion that 'in no one in Israel have I found such *pistis*' (8.10), he is referring not only to the fact that the centurion believes that Jesus can heal his slave or that he believes that Jesus, like himself, is a man under authority, but to the fact that the centurion has acted on his belief: he has entrusted himself and his slave to Jesus' goodwill, and is trusting him to respond (cf. 8.5).

It is tempting to invoke an account of these stories which, for many modern readers, would be both familiar and powerful. These characters are driven to seek Jesus by a catastrophe, a dramatic reversal, subjugation, or undoing which has overtaken their lives, which they and normal forms of help cannot address. Mark reports that the woman with the haemorrhage had tried to help herself over twelve years, spending all her money on doctors, but that her illness had only grown worse (5.25-6). Jairus, the centurion, and the Roman official are figures of power and high status, but their status only emphasizes their powerlessness to save those they love.[5] Blindness and illnesses like leprosy could drive people to a life of fearful vulnerability on the edges of society.[6] Jesus' healings restore people

---

God: Mt. 4.24, Mt. 14.35=Mk 6.55, Mk 1.32=Lk. 4.40, Mk 8.22. Jesus' response to those who come to him in need sometimes marks his relationship of care with them: he calls the paralytic 'child' (Mt. 9.2=Mk 2.5) and the woman with the haemorrhage 'daughter' (Mt. 9.22=Mk 5.34=Lk. 8.48), and reassures the ruler of the synagogue, telling him not to be afraid (Mk 5.35=Lk. 8.50).

[3] Other healing stories act as messianic signs without reference to *pistis*: in these stories Jesus typically approaches the person he heals rather than the other way round (e.g. Mt. 12.9-13=Mk 3.1-5=Lk. 6.6-10, Lk. 13.10-17, Jn 5.1-9). *Pisteuein* becomes an important theme of the man born blind (and the *ou pisteuein* of 'the Jews' is mentioned at Jn 9.18), but the man does not come to *pisteuein* until some time after the healing, in conversation with Jesus (9.35, 36, 38).

[4] E.g. when Mark's woman with a haemorrhage says to herself, 'If I touch even his garments, I *will* be saved ('Ἐὰν ἅψωμαι κἂν τῶν ἱματίων αὐτοῦ σωθήσομαι)' (5.28, cf. Mt. 9.21), rather than 'I may be saved', we are invited to hear not only trust and hope but belief.

[5] Among (mostly) recent studies of healing miracles and exorcisms see notably van der Loos (1965), Theissen (1983), Twelftree (1993, 1999) Eve (2002), Sorensen (2002), Miller (2004), Porterfield (2005), Bazzana (2009), Witmer (2012), Verheyden and Kloppenborg (2018), Bersee (2021), with a discussion of recent scholarship.

[6] Though not always, and recent work emphasizes the diversity of experiences of disability in antiquity: e.g. Rose (2003), Garland (1995), Laes et al. (2013), Laes (2014), Draycott (2015), cf. Avalos et al. (2007); cf. Brawley (2011).

both to individual wholeness and to their community, freeing them from physical disease and contagion, ritual pollution, or forced indigence.

The shared structures, and often the wording of these stories, convey that, in the need that drives trust, everyone is the same. These characters are as socially diverse as the villages of Galilee and its environs: Jewish, Samaritan, Syrophoenician or Canaanite, Roman; a royal official, a synagogue leader, a widow, a 'sinful woman', beggars. They not only represent all social groups but transgress normal boundaries: the centurion seeks Jesus' help on behalf of his slave; the ten lepers of Luke 17.11–19 seem to be a mixture of Jews and Samaritans. Jesus responds similarly to all of them. In their need and in his eyes, everyone driven to trust is equal.[7]

These stories also recognize that the need which compels trust is not proud or pretty. It is ruthless and sometimes offensive or bizarre. Matthew's Canaanite woman first emerges from indoors, where respectable married women normally stay, to shout to Jesus for mercy (15.22–5), and then pursues him and does *proskynēsis* in front of him, blocking his path.[8] The disciples are embarrassed: 'Send her away, she is shouting after us!' (15.23). She is beyond embarrassment. Matthew's first group of blind men are equally disinhibited: they too follow Jesus down the street, shouting for mercy (Mt. 9.27).[9] Luke's persistent widow, who either has no male relatives, declines to rely on them to get her justice, or is in dispute with them—any of which would diminish her social standing in its own right—goes to law on her own behalf and pesters the judge until he (claims he) fears for his safety and gives her justice (Lk. 18.3–5).[10] In several stories disciples or bystanders highlight the transgressiveness of the protagonists by trying to stop it (e.g. Mt. 15.23, Mt. 20.31=Mk 10.48=Lk 18.39). They never succeed.

Some of those driven by need to trust are not only determined, but devious or argumentative. The woman with a haemorrhage, perhaps because she is afraid that Jesus will not help her, or that other people will not let her approach him, plans just to touch his garment from behind (Mk 5.27=Lk. 8.44). The Canaanite or Syrophoenician woman argues back when Jesus appears reluctant to help a gentile: 'even the dogs eat from the scraps that fall from their masters' table' (Mt. 15.27=Mk 7.28). Though his disciples sometimes do, Jesus never comments

---

[7] The Syrophoenician/Canaanite woman is an outlier in that Jesus needs some persuading to help her: probably, within the story, because she is a gentile (though Matthew's centurion does not meet the same resistance).

[8] On *proskynēsis* see Cotesta (2015), Lozano (2019) (though he is over-optimistic in arguing that the term always points to Jesus' divinity).

[9] Others shout from where they are sitting (Mt. 20.30, Mk 10.46–8=Lk. 18.37–9); Luke's ten lepers shout for help from a distance (17.12–13); the one thankful leper falls on his face when he thanks Jesus (17.16). The friends of the paralytic strip the roof off a house (Mk 2.4, Lk. 5.19), and Luke's woman with the ointment kneels at Jesus' feet, wiping them extravagantly with her hair in a formal dinner (7.38).

[10] For women to go to court is regarded as disreputable at Rome but is not uncommon in practice around the empire: see e.g. Cantarella (2016), Halbwachs (2016), cf. Czajkowski (2017), 14–22.

on the abnormality of their behaviour; he simply commends the trust which it expresses.

This reading can go further, and suggest that the gospel writers show how extreme need may be the only thing that drives some people to make the new relationship of trust which is capable of bringing them to salvation or new life. Those who seek healing see Jesus as healer; in their need, they are compelled to show themselves to him; they trust themselves to see him rightly and they trust him to see them. Their trust fits Brothers' model of trust closely.[11] That said, throwing oneself on the mercy of Jesus does not drive out all contradictory attitudes or emotions. Even after she knows she has been healed, the woman with a haemorrhage is afraid (Mk 5.33, cf. Lk. 8.47). Her fear may be appropriate fear of great power, or it may be fear such as the disciples sometimes show, which continues to coexist with trust even when one has become a follower of Jesus Christ. Either way, Jesus does not condemn her for it: it is enough that she has acted with trust.[12]

Readings along these lines have a long history going back to antiquity, and resonate with the experience of many people that it is when all human help fails that they turn to God and to Christ. They invoke the Isaianic tradition that the Messiah will heal the sick, and a widespread assumption, in the ancient and modern worlds, that illness and disability are, at the least, misfortunes from which it is 'natural' to want to be released. They speak of the compassion of Jesus Christ which responds to human need regardless of ethnicity, gender, wealth, or status. They also fit with an idea which we criticized in Chapter 2, that God can be relied on to respond to human beings' agenda and requests.

At a minimum, we surely want to retain the ideas that people frequently turn to Jesus in need, and that Jesus has compassion on those who are suffering. In some recent scholarship, however, this type of reading has also been powerfully criticized. Anti-ableist commentators have argued that it objectifies those with disabilities or chronic illnesses, equating the way they live with sin, incapacity, inadequacy, abnormality, diminishment, and failure. It invites pity for the sick or

---

[11] People who seek something, usually healing, from Jesus are classic examples of three-place trust: they trust that he can and will help them. We can also identify an element of two-place trust in these stories: e.g. when Jesus commends the centurion (Mt. 8.10) he indicates that the man has done more than trusted him to perform a single healing; he has entered a relationship with Jesus which will bring him to heaven. After Bartimaeus has been healed he follows Jesus (Mk 10.52), apparently for Jesus' own sake. After a period in which declining church attendance and self-identification by subjects as people of faith was correlated by many social psychologists with the increased provision of medical and social services in the developed world (Gill and Lundsgaarde (2004), Paul (2009), Franck and Iannaccone (2014)), some recent studies suggest the correlation between three-place trust or hope in God for healing, wholeness etc. and lack of social services is not as strong as we might expect: e.g. van Tongeren et al. (2020), Hook et al. (2021).

[12] Jesus often sends people away after healing, especially in Mark, which is usually connected with Mark's theme of secrecy, though cf. pp. 237–9.

disabled in these stories, but not much respect.[13] This, it has been pointed out, at the least involves a failure to listen to and understand those who live with disabilities or long-term illnesses, many of whom reject decisively the assumption that non-normative bodies, minds, and ways of life need to be pitied or 'cured', and at worst discriminates against the non-normative, marginalizes, and degrades it.

A less ableist approach to some of the gospels' healing stories invites us to interpret their main characters in different ways. The woman with a haemorrhage is a powerful and resourceful figure, who has not only lived and coped with her physical non-normativity for many years, but is a woman of substance who has been able to choose to put resources into changing her situation. The paralytic who had such good friends was surely both fortunate and socially gifted. The Canaanite woman's daughter, who inspired such self-giving love in her mother, can be seen as both a blessing and as blessed.

To my knowledge, anti-ableist readings of these stories have rarely considered the role of *pistis* in them, but seeing their protagonists differently also invites us to reconsider their *pistis*.[14] Ironically, this approach may seem to take away from characters who seek healing the one thing which, in traditional readings, they have going for them: strong and transformative trust. An alternative reading, however, brings these stories closer to the representation of *pistis/pisteuein* elsewhere in the gospels.

In several stories, Jesus seems to give someone what they ask for, but not in the terms they expect. The paralytic is told not simply that he can walk, but that his sins are forgiven. Jesus' response to the woman with the haemorrhage hovers semantically between healing and salvation. Jairus and Martha respectively seek or hoped for healing for those they love (Mk 5.23, Jn 11.21), but witness a resurrection. The woman who anoints Jesus' feet does not ask for anything, so within the story it comes as a surprise when she is told both that her sins are forgiven and that her *pistis* has saved her (Lk. 7.48, 50). The persistent widow seeks justice for herself, but the logion which is added to the end of the parable seems to commend her for a much greater trust/faithfulness in justice as ultimately the quality and gift of God.[15]

Jesus' responses suggest that, although those who come to him can be commended for having *pistis* at all, their *pistis* is not everything it might be: not big enough in scale or angled quite right. Jesus' words to the paralytic hint that, although he is willing to enable him to walk, it is not really release from paralysis

---

[13] E.g. Eiesland (1994), Yong (2009), Belser and Morrison (2011), Reynolds (2012), Lawrence (2014), Belser (2015), Hull (2015), Melcher et al. (2017). Tillotson et al. (2017) explores how people living with disabilities describe the interaction of their disabilities with their faith, defined (p. 320) as their experience of and commitment to God and Jesus Christ, and how traditional readings of healing stories can be disempowering.

[14] Yong (2009), 179 n. 30 notes an exception: John Hull suggests that Lk. 18.35–43 is told as much to illustrate the *pistis* and 'conversion' off the blind man as his desire for healing; cf. Hull (2002), 44–5.

[15] 'When the Son of Man comes, will he find trust [or 'faithfulness'] on earth?', Lk. 18.8.

he needs, but release from his sins. The haemorrhaging woman's trust in Jesus heals her, but, more importantly, it saves her—and a modern reader may wonder whether Jesus implies that it was really her relationship with God, more than her body, that needed healing all along. Jairus and Martha may trust in Jesus for healing, but they have not fully understood that they can and should be trusting in him for life itself: resurrection and eternal life.[16] In Chapter 2, we argued that, for Paul, God can be trusted to fulfil God's agenda, not that of human beings. We see the same theme emerging in these stories, in which people come to Jesus with real, but imperfect trust, wanting one thing, and receive something different and much greater.[17]

What the protagonists of healing stories do right is that, by trusting Jesus, they entrust themselves to him. This brings them close, in both the nature and the limitations of their trust, to the disciples, who also put their trust in Jesus and entrust themselves to him, but do not fully understand what that relationship involves, and sometimes ask for the wrong thing, or are given something they did not expect. The parallel is underlined in some of the stories of what those who have been healed, or exorcized, do next.[18]

In many cases, after the moment of healing, we hear no more about the healed person, or nothing that indicates ongoing trust. When Simon's mother-in-law, for example, is healed, she waits on Jesus and the disciples (Mt. 8.15=Mk 1.31=Lk. 4.39). This could be taken as an expression of her own faithfulness, but is not described as such. In some stories, however, healing or exorcism leads to an ongoing relationship with Jesus. According to Luke (8.2–3), Mary Magdalene, Joanna, Susanna, 'and many other' women who followed Jesus and subsidized his ministry, had been 'healed of evil spirits and infirmities'. The Gerasene or Gadarene demoniac, having been exorcized, begs to accompany Jesus, and when Jesus refuses, he begins to proclaim around the Decapolis how much Jesus has done for him, generating wonder at his testimony (Mk 5.18-20=Lk. 8.38-9).[19] After Jesus heals Bartimaeus, on the outskirts of Jericho, Bartimaeus 'followed him on the way' (Mk 10.52=Lk. 18.43, cf. Mt. 20.34[20]). If Jesus' saying that many will come from all points of the compass to feast with the patriarchs, while the 'sons of the kingdom' (Mt. 8.12) will be excluded (Mt. 8.11–12, cf. Lk. 13.28–9), is inserted by Matthew into the story of the centurion's servant to imply that some

---

[16] For a nuanced analysis of the shortcomings of Martha's *pisteuein*, and comparison with Mary's, in this chapter see Moloney (1994), cf. Moloney (2003), 525–7.

[17] Cf. stories in which Jesus expels demons from people who, speaking for the demon, resist (e.g. Mk 5.7=Lk. 8.28, Mk 1.23=Lk. 4.34).

[18] It is debatable whether exorcisms should be counted as a class of healings or separately, but stories of what the exorcized do next draw a parallel with healings in this respect.

[19] Collins (2007), *ad loc.* suggests that Jesus may refuse to let the man follow him because he is not an Israelite.

[20] Luke adds that he glorified God; in Matthew's version two unnamed blind men are healed and follow Jesus.

gentiles will enter the kingdom of heaven and some Jews will not, it suggests that the centurion's trust (Mt. 8.10=Lk. 7.9) may persist after the healing, and bring him into the kingdom.[21] Given that the *pistis* even of Jesus' closest followers is far from consistent or secure, we should not expect to hear that all those who put their trust in Jesus to be healed continue to trust, but the gospel writers suggest that at least some do. Their trust is the beginning of a relationship, and a literal and figurative journey, which points beyond the narratives themselves.

It is also worth noting the obvious points that the gospel stories do not suggest that Jesus healed everyone in Israel or beyond, and healing and physical resurrection are not permanent in themselves. Those who are healed may acquire a disability or fall ill again; in the synoptic gospels some, in the natural course of events, may die before the unknown hour and day of the coming of the Son of Man.[22] Jesus' activities as physical healer and exorcist, moreover, though for all the gospel writers they are a sign of his identity as Son of God and Messiah, are not the *raison d'être* of his ministry.[23] Jesus comes to call people not to physical normativity, but to their right relationship with God. It may be (though they never tell us so) that the evangelists imagine every body in the kingdom or house of God as illness- and disability-normative, much as others at the time imagine everyone under God's rule as enjoying a life of luxury and leisure in gardens that bear fruit unfarmed or cities built of precious stones.[24] Visions of heaven, however, always reflect the social aspirations of their time and place. (In contemporary society, we might want to resist not only the idea that in heaven everyone must be physically normative, but, for instance, that eternal life will involve constant heavy eating or perpetual daylight.) The real concern of those who trust in God and in Jesus before the end time lies elsewhere. This theme is further underlined after the resurrection, when Jesus shows his followers that the body that has been raised has not been 'healed' of its wounds. It is not physical normativity, let alone physical perfection, that is at issue in Jesus' life and ministry, but humanity's relationship with God.[25]

On this reading, the teaching which Jesus implicitly offers to those who are healed, is equally a teaching for wider society. The paralytic's trusting friends, Jairus, the centurion, the Roman official, and the Canaanite woman stand for the social networks around individuals who are identified as in need, and their trust may also betray a set of social assumptions which seek to 'normalize' those within society whose bodies, minds, or behaviour are not 'normal'. When Jesus gives the

---

[21] The fact that the Samaritan leper returns, healed, to praise God and give thanks to Jesus (Lk. 17.15–19), may also suggest that the trust that made him well (v. 19) is still operative.

[22] Unless the end time comes before their death: cf. Mt. 24.34=Mk 13.30=Lk. 21.32.

[23] Carroll (1995).

[24] E.g. Goodman (2010), Macaskill (2010), Schaper (2010), Morrison (2017).

[25] The striking contrast between this view and the Mediterranean cultural norm, which takes for granted that height, beauty, and strength are always desirable and gods and heroes are taller, more beautiful, and stronger than others, is well recognized.

person who is healed not quite what they asked for, he also challenges society's assumptions, reminding all those present that what they should be seeking is not the normalization or uniformization of the rich variety of the human form and lived experience, but a saving, life-giving relationship of trust with God and with Jesus himself.

We have observed more than once that these chapters offer a series of sketches of the trust relationship between God, Christ, and humanity, in different New Testament writings, which we cannot take for granted form a single picture. Nevertheless, at this point, we may wonder whether or how this reading of the gospels' healing and exorcism stories relates to the argument we developed out of Paul's letters in Chapter 4, that the trust relationship offers human beings release from the power of suffering as well as sin. That chapter, however, considered the suffering that arises from human sin, not 'natural' suffering, and the reading we have just offered fits better with it than perhaps we might expect.[26] Jesus' healings and exorcisms have a dual purpose: they show him acting with God's power and authority, and they illustrate the purpose of his mission. That mission is not to bring everyone to physical or mental normativity, but to bring humanity into its right relationship with God. Jesus' physical interventions, explicitly or implicitly, act as a visual symbol of people's release from the suffering of not being in that relationship. What brings people to Jesus, however, and makes them open to the healing of their relationship with God, may be very varied: in particular, it may involve an acute sense that healing is needed, but an imperfect understanding of what it is that needs healing.[27] In that context, these stories tell their listeners that to approach Jesus, or respond when one is approached by him, with a trust that is not big enough in scale, or not angled quite right, is good enough. It is a starting-point for trust which has the potential, eventually, to bring one to salvation and eternal life. This theme—the adequacy of imperfect trust—is one we will see repeated throughout the gospels and throughout this chapter.

Elsewhere in the synoptic gospels, Jesus' teaching sometimes resonates with the theme of the healing stories that it is often a sense of need that brings people to trust, in terms which also highlight that trusting in God and in Jesus is preferable to securing conventional physical and material goods in this life, not a route to doing so. The Sermon on the Mount begins with blessings, among others, on those who mourn, those who hunger and thirst for righteousness, and those who are persecuted for righteousness' sake (5.4, 6, 10 cf. 11). All these recognize that

---

[26] We noted that the problem of natural suffering is beyond the scope of this study, but the argument here and in Chapter 4 would be consistent with the view that where there is trust between human beings and God, the regular operation of the physical world, which includes death and decay, need not be experienced as unnatural or evil, and therefore as causing suffering.

[27] This is not to suggest that physical or mental suffering is a sign of the need for forgiveness (a suggestion which John's Jesus explicitly repudiates at 9.3), but that a person may experience suffering without fully understanding where its root cause lies, and may rightly seek help without fully understanding what she needs help for.

their situation, or their world, is not as it should be, and turn to God for help. Help from God is on God's, not human terms: Jesus teaches his followers not only to pray for their daily needs (earthly or spiritual) (Mt. 6.11=Lk. 11.3) and for deliverance from evil (Mt. 6.15), but also for the coming of God's kingdom and the enactment of his will (Mt. 6.10=Lk. 11.2). Nor does trusting in God necessarily bring security in this world: Jesus tells his followers not to store up treasure on earth (Mt. 6.19–21, cf. Lk. 12.33, cf. Lk. 12.16). But trusting in God, and in Jesus himself, means that the risks and dangers of this world are less fearful. Jesus tells his followers, 'Do not worry about your life (μὴ μεριμνᾶτε τῇ ψυχῇ ὑμῶν)' (Mt. 6.25=Lk. 12.22). Alongside not worrying about what you will eat, drink, or wear, we might add, do not worry about how you will get about, or work, or how your neighbours look at you. Not worrying is close to not fearing; fear is often antithetical to trust, and a few verses later Jesus says explicitly that if one is anxious, one is *oligopistos*, of little trust (Mt. 6.30=Lk. 12.28).

We noted in the last chapter the resonances between this passage and the creation story, with its underlying theme of trust between God, man, and woman, and it also echoes the link between trust and vulnerability in the healing stories.[28] Divesting oneself of the things that make one feel comfortable and secure in this life increases one's sense of fragility and need, which encourages one to put one's trust in God and in Jesus. At the same time, trusting in God and Jesus makes it easier to divest oneself of the securities of this life. Where there is *pistis* in God and Jesus, human frailty and vulnerability are no longer disabilities to be 'healed', but signs of orientation to righteousness, life in relationship with God, and ultimate hope.

Coming to Trust: Challenge and Openness

Stories of trust and healing are especially characteristic of the synoptic gospels, where they form an important aspect of those gospels' account of *pistis*. In every gospel, however, alongside stories of those who approach Jesus out of need, runs a series of stories about people who are less aware, or unaware of their need, but who respond to an invitation or challenge to trust.[29]

Writings from all over the early Roman empire offer us a picture of a lively, varied, sometimes competitive religious marketplace populated, alongside

---

[28] pp. 225–6.
[29] There is now a rich bibliography exploring the characters who surround Jesus in the gospels, especially in John, increasingly emphasizing their complexity and even how they develop in the course of their interactions: see notably Tannehill (1977), Bassler (1989), Gowler (1991), Staley (1991), Burnett (1993), Darr (1992), Lee (1994), R. Collins (1995), Beck (1997), Fehribach (1998), Malbon (2000, 2009), Brown (2002), Bennema (2009, 2014), Hylen (2009), Hunt et al. (2013), Skinner (2013), Dinkler (2017), Shin (2019).

established cults and forms of worship, by new cults, new forms of existing cults, new patterns of worship, new ideas about the divine, and all kinds of wandering prophets, healers, and other miracle-workers.[30] New cults, communities, and religious practitioners seem to meet a widely shared openness, even an appetite for new religious leadership, new objects of worship, new worshipping communities, and new forms of religious life. There are signs of this appetite in the villages of Galilee as elsewhere, both in the gospel writings and outside them.[31] Some of the people who listen to Jesus' preaching seem to know what they think they are looking for.[32] More often, the gospels describe crowds congregating around Jesus because they have heard of his healings or to hear him teach, without indicating that they are looking for anything in particular.[33] Jesus' teaching, however, often takes place in informal contexts, in private houses or out of doors, sometimes some significant distance from any village (e.g. Mt. 14.13=Mk 6.32-3, Jn 6.1-5). The people who gather around Jesus in such places do not just happen to be there; they have gone out of their way to hear him, and so, the gospels imply, have at least expressed curiosity and willingness to listen.[34]

In all four gospels, the disciples are paradigmatic of people who are open to being called by Jesus, and continue to try to trust even when they periodically fail. In addition, John's gospel offers a series of stories of individuals and groups who respond to Jesus' teaching and ask for more.[35] Nicodemus visits Jesus (3.1–21) at night, which hints that he has mixed feelings about his visit (half fearful or sceptical, perhaps), and also reflects his not-yet-illuminated condition.[36] His initial affirmation (3.2), 'no one can do these signs which you are doing unless God is with him' reminds us of Jesus' dispute with a different group of Jews in chapter 10, in which he indicated that only those who were 'among my sheep' (10.26), and had at least the capacity for trust, would be able, on the basis of that relationship,

---

[30] Beard et al. (1998), Ando (2008), Rüpke (2014), Wendt (2016), Maier (2018).

[31] Strange (1979, 2019), Meyers (1999), Zangenberg et al. (2007).

[32] Notably, at Jn 6.15, a king.

[33] At Mt. 9.36=Mk 6.34, the crowd is like a shepherdless flock. Crowds are several times, in all four gospels, said to congregate around Jesus because they have witnessed or heard about his healings (Mt. 4.23–5.1, cf. 14.14–15, Mk 1.45–2.2, Jn 6.2, cf. 2.23, 4.45. 6.26–7), and some people are sufficiently interested in the teaching to congregate to hear Jesus speak or seek him out (e.g. Mk 1.35–8=Lk. 4.42–3, cf. Jn 3.1–2); elsewhere the evangelists preface a passage of teaching simply by saying that a crowd gathers.

[34] Jesus occasionally tells crowds explicitly what they are looking for: a form of sustenance which is more than human (Mt. 6.11=Lk. 11.3); family and community beyond the communities of this world (Mt. 12.48–50=Mk 3.33–5=Lk. 8.21, Mt. 19.29=Mk 10.29–30=Lk. 18.29); the greatest imaginable treasure (Mt. 6.19–21= Lk. 12.33, Mt. 13.44–6), and, in the double tradition, says, 'Ask! You will receive!' (Mt. 7.9–10=Lk. 11.11–12, cf. Jn 14.14). Jesus therefore challenges his listeners both to trust in God for what they need, and to consider or reconsider what they do need: cf. Jn 4.10–14, 6.27, 7.37–8.

[35] See especially Culpepper (1983), Hylen (2009); cf. Mt. 19.16–22=Mk 10.17–22=Lk. 18.18–23; cf. Lk. 19.2–10.

[36] On Nicodemus see notably de Jonge (1971), Bassler (1989), Hylen (2009), 23–40, Ford (2013). Night is symbolic of hostility and evil at 13.30, but Nicodemus does not betray Jesus as Judas does.

to believe in (the divine origin of) his words or signs. Nicodemus, his opening words suggest, is among that group.[37] The conversation that follows is notorious for the obliqueness of Jesus' pronouncements and Nicodemus' failures of understanding, but it makes some telling observations about believing and trusting. First, Jesus implies that it is reasonable for Nicodemus to believe first when Jesus tells him about earthly things, and subsequently when Jesus tells him about heavenly things.[38] This suggests that those who have the capacity to trust may also be able to believe, and progress in believing.[39] Verses 15–16 move from believing in Jesus' words to the life-giving commitment of trusting in Jesus himself. Next Jesus says that though those who do not trust in him have already been condemned (3.18), those who do trust are not condemned but 'do what is true' and come to the light (3.21). Nicodemus, we infer, is in an intermediate position: he has the capacity to trust but he has not yet done so, or not to any great extent, so his future is in the balance.[40] Despite Jesus' apparent dissatisfaction with Nicodemus, John tells us that Nicodemus continues to take an interest in Jesus to the end of Jesus' life (7.50, 19.39). He shows a willingness to persevere which suggests, at least, the beginnings of life-giving trust.

The Samaritan woman at the well (Jn 4.4–42) makes more progress. From a sceptical beginning (4.9, 11) she first comes to acknowledge Jesus as a prophet (v. 19), and then returns to her village saying, 'Come and see a man who told me everything I have done. Could he possibly be the Messiah?' (v. 29). She is not said to put her trust in Jesus herself, but it is implied when John says that she brings many of her fellow-townspeople to *pisteuein* (v. 39). Even the crowd which Jesus chastises for following him because he fed them with ordinary bread (6.26) is willing to learn. 'What can we do to accomplish the works of God?' they ask (6.28). Jesus tells them to 'trust in the one whom he sent' (6.29). 'What sign can you do,' they ask, 'that we may see and trust in you?' (6.30). The request for a sign reveals the limits of both their understanding and their trust, but they seem to be open to trusting Jesus: 'Lord, give us this bread always' (6.34). They too, perhaps, are among Jesus' sheep.[41] The trust that arises from openness to Jesus' teaching

---

[37] Alternatively, but less likely, the writer may not have pre-election in mind in this passage, and Nicodemus may have become interested in Jesus (not necessarily to the point of trust) because of his signs.
[38] 3.12. *Pisteuein* here is probably belief since its object is what Jesus tells Nicodemus.
[39] Cf. pp. 38, 71, 92, 110, 117.
[40] If Nicodemus' visit means that he has the capacity to trust, Jesus is surely unfair in classing him with other Pharisees (3.11), who elsewhere he condemns as having no capacity to trust, but this may be a 'wake-up' call to Nicodemus to take the next step in trust.
[41] Hylen (2009), 119–21 argues that the twin openness and grumbling of the crowd in this story is not unlike that of the disciples, and shows they are not straightforwardly unbelievers, even if their believing is imperfect. Throughout this study Hylen shows both the imperfectness with which a series of characters in John's gospel *pisteuein* (including the disciples and Jesus himself), and how their openness to more or better believing (as she translates it) highlight the gospels' eschatological hope for all who encounter Jesus. Cf. Matera (1999), 8–9, emphasizing that the understanding of those around Jesus is always partial and changing.

may be slow to develop (even, or paradigmatically in the disciples), but the gospel leaves open the possibility that it does develop, perhaps even beyond the pages of the text.[42]

The Adequacy of Imperfect Trust

Most New Testament writings, including the synoptic gospels and some passages of John's gospel, indicate that anyone can put their trust in God and in Christ (and, by the same token, that anyone can be worthy of trust by God and Christ).[43] However damaged human beings' relationships with God and with one another, they can be restored through *pistis*. None of the gospel writers, however, indicates that anyone, during Jesus' earthly life, puts their trust in him in every aspect of his life and work. Many encounter the prophet, teacher, or healer, but we do not hear that all those who come to be healed, for instance, have heard Jesus teaching, while many of those who hear his teaching do not appear to seek physical healing. There is no sign that this is problematic: it seems that one may be forgiven or brought to life by trusting in Jesus in any of his activities. One may also encounter Jesus first in one role and later in others, like the man born blind in John chapter 9, who understands Jesus first as his healer, then as a prophet and a man from God, and eventually as Son of Man and Lord (9.15, 17, 25, 33, 35). We can assume that those who come to put their trust in Christ after the resurrection, and who hear stories of his life, teaching, actions, death, resurrection, and ascension, are expected to develop a multi-faceted relationship with him. No New Testament writing, however, insists that, to come to one's right relationship with God, one must form a relationship with Jesus Christ in every aspect of his identity and work.[44]

We can go further, and propose that to be able to put one's trust in every aspect of Jesus' identity and work (in his earthly or exalted life) is no more within human capacity than it is within human capacity to comprehend the full identity and

---

[42] Godfrey (2012), 49–51 develops a category of trust called 'openness-trusting', which is close to what other philosophers call one-place trust, though with a greater emphasis on the truster's readiness to be changed by his encounters; he describes this as 'an orientation or disposition towards the whole world, a readiness to receive what the world has to give...a readiness to be affected: to be changed, to be confirmed, and, indeed, to be harmed...' (p. 49). This, however, is rather different from the kind of openness discussed here, because it precedes relationships, while openness to Jesus' teaching begins within an encounter with him.

[43] Though, as noted, John's final redactor indicates that some of those to whom the gospel is preached are not chosen to receive it, and so cannot trust.

[44] At Jn 14.9–10 Jesus tells Philip that whoever has seen him has seen the Father—but this affirms that in Jesus human beings *can* see all that God chooses to reveal of Godself to them, not that they must do so.

work of God.[45] In the synoptic gospels, the only beings, apart from God, who know exactly who Jesus is from the beginning of his ministry are the devil with whom he disputes (Mt. 4.1–11=Lk. 4.1–13) and the unclean spirits whom he expels (Mk 1.24=Lk. 4.34, Mt. 8.29=Mk 5.7=Lk. 8.28).[46] In the double tradition, Jesus proclaims that 'no one knows the Son except the Father' (Mt. 11.27=Lk. 10.22); in John's gospel, even as Jesus makes his father known (1.18), he himself, in some ways, remains mysterious. But the gospels (and other New Testament writings) do not indicate that this is a barrier to trust: on the contrary. One may—perhaps inevitably must—see and trust partially and imperfectly, and still be saved or come to eternal life.

The adequacy of imperfect human trust is repeatedly illustrated, especially in the synoptic gospels, by the *apistia* and *oligopistia* of the disciples. Their relationship with Jesus is a tapestry of light and shade: trust, confidence, fear, doubt, and scepticism. We have seen that during the storm at sea, Jesus identifies fear as hampering the disciples' *pistis* (Mk 4.40).[47] At Mark 9.19, he seems to recognize that they have sincerely tried to expel the mute spirit, but do not have *pistis*, or were not practising it properly (cf. 9.29). At Mark 11.22, his teaching on *pistis* is a response to Peter's surprise that the fig tree had withered since the previous day, suggesting that Peter had been doubtful or sceptical that Jesus' curse would work (or work so quickly).[48] At 16.14, in the long ending of Mark's gospel, Jesus rebukes the disciples for their *apistia* and 'hardness of heart' (*sklērokardia*) because they did not believe those who reported seeing him risen from the dead. The writer evidently thought that attributing doubt or scepticism to the disciples at this moment would fit with Mark's portrayal of them.

In retelling Mark's story of Jesus' walking on the sea, Matthew adds an extra scene which highlights the complexity of Peter's trust. Jesus has come towards the disciples, who are at sea during a storm, walking on the water (14.24–5). The disciples, thinking he is a ghost, cry out in fear (v. 26). When Jesus tells them to be brave and not to be afraid because he is not a ghost, they are apparently reassured up to a point (v. 27). But Peter then says, '*if* it is you, Lord, command me to come to you on the water' (v. 28). The fact that he addresses Jesus as 'Lord' suggests that he trusts Jesus' self-identification, but his 'if' indicates his trust is not perfect. Jesus says, 'Come'. Peter gets out of the boat and begins to walk on the water, but becomes afraid. He starts to sink; in his fear, calling out, 'Lord, save me' (v. 30).

---

[45] Gaventa and Hays (2008), 22 observe that 'the identity of Jesus is something that must be learned through long-term discipline', citing the disciples as a paradigmatic example of people who 'follow him around for years without fully grasping who he is'.

[46] On unclean spirits see e.g. Sorensen (2002), Witmer (2012); on deliverance from Satan throughout the New Testament see Bell (2007).

[47] Cf. 5.36.

[48] Lk. 17.5 links Jesus' saying that if the disciples had faith the size of a mustard seed they would be able to uproot a sycamore tree (cf. Mt. 17.20) to the disciples' plea, 'Lord, increase our trust', so the disciples themselves are aware here of the inadequacy of their trust.

Jesus reaches out and catches him, saying, '*Oligopiste*, why did you doubt?' (14.31). Matthew leaves open whether Peter fails here to trust in Jesus or in himself—or both, since, to perform miracles, one must not only trust in God and Christ but in one's own capacity to be empowered by them.[49] The story is a rollercoaster of trust and self-trust undermined by fear, partially restored, seeking to test the strength of its relationship, reassured, demonstrated, undermined again by fear, renewed in desperation, and reassured again with the censure, 'you of little trust'.[50]

Luke incorporates a scene in the last supper which indicates how the disciples' trust may continue to wax and wane even after the resurrection (22.31-4). Jesus says to Peter, 'I have prayed about you, that your *pistis* may not fail; and once you have turned back yourself, strengthen your brothers' (v. 32).[51] The failure of *pistis* to which Jesus refers is probably not Peter's denial of Jesus, which, as Jesus tells him immediately afterwards (v. 34), is already certain. It is more likely to refer to events around that betrayal and its aftermath. As such, it probably has aspects of belief, faithfulness, and trustworthiness, perhaps towards both God and Jesus himself. Jesus prays that, even though he denies him, Peter will not fail permanently in his commitment to Jesus, but that he will rally and be able to rally the other disciples.[52] Both these stories also illustrate the cognitive-active complexity of the gospels' understanding of trust. When Matthew's Peter gets out of the boat, he acts with trust without holding a secure attitude of trust. Luke's Jesus prays that, once Peter's own (attitude and relationship of) trust has been strengthened, he will act trustworthily in strengthening the other disciples.

Even after the resurrection, imperfect trust, and even radical failures of trust, may not be deal-breakers. Matthew, of the synoptic gospel writers the most emphatic that those who reject Jesus are destined for the 'outer darkness' (e.g. 22.13) or 'fiery furnace' (e.g. 12.42), hints that, until the Son of Man returns, even those who have trusted and then resiled may be restored to the community of the faithful. When Jesus describes how community members should solve their tensions and problems (18.15-20), he concludes that when all avenues of reconciliation have failed, the problematic community member should be excommunicated: treated 'as you would a gentile or a tax collector' (18.17).[53]

---

[49] On when self-trust is appropriate see pp. 181, 322, 359-60.
[50] Matthew does, however, cut Mk 6.52 from his version of the story, softening Mark's criticism of the disciples (so e.g. Luz (1995)).
[51] Marshall (1978), 821 notes that 'in the interests of' may be a better translation of *peri* here (cf. 6.25), and discusses Bultmann's observation that since *epistrephein* is usually associated with conversion, it sits oddly in a passage which is essentially about Peter's faithfulness; perhaps two different sayings underlie this one.
[52] At Jn 16.32 Jesus, similarly, foretells that though the disciples trust now, the hour is coming when they will be scattered—but with the implication that this will not be a permanent failure in trusting.
[53] On parallels to 18.17 in synagogue regulations and parallels to the passage as a whole in 1QS 5.24-6.1, CD 9.28, as well as early Christian parallels, see e.g. Luz (2001-7), 1.453-4.

Gentiles and tax collectors are paradigmatic outsiders, but they are also among those with whom Matthew's Jesus associates (8.5–7, 9.11–13, 15.21–8), those to whom he preaches (9.10), those whose *pistis* he praises (8.10, 15.28), and those who become his disciples (9.9). If gentiles and tax collectors can put their trust in Jesus and become followers in Matthew's gospel, then 18.17 suggests that the door remains open even for those who have been expelled to return to the community, as long as they trust in God and Christ. Until the Son of Man returns, binding and loosing on earth remain provisional.[54]

Among human beings, in the gospels, Jesus himself exhibits the most consistent trust and faithfulness towards God. Even Jesus, however, may be portrayed, especially by Matthew and Mark, as wavering in the attitude of trust, though he always acts in accordance with God's will. In Gethsemane, Jesus prays to God to take away his imminent suffering: 'but not as I will, but as you will' (Mt. 26.39=Mk 14.36=Lk. 22.42).[55] Though *pistis* language does not appear in this scene, elsewhere obedience to God's will is characteristic of trust and faithfulness. In the context of the gospel so far, Jesus' prayer in Gethsemane comes as a shock, and some commentators see it as reflecting a historical memory of the trauma of that night.[56] Whether it does or not, it is significant that the synoptic gospels all include it. Jesus' affirmation of obedience suggests that he has not lost trust in God, but it may suggest that he has lost trust in himself to will what God wills. He responds to himself by reaffirming his obedience to God. 'Not as I will' indicates that, just as it is God's will, not his own, he is serving, it is by God's will, not his own, that he will remain faithful. If so, this prayer adds to what we have already seen of Jesus as a paradigm of trust and faithfulness. We have seen Jesus refuse to test God in the desert; the centurion recognizing him as under God's authority; and his affirmation of the importance of prayer, not least in making possible deeds of power. In Gethsemane, we see Jesus' trust in God not as giving him power or fortifying his self-trust, but, *in extremis*, as replacing his self-trust and his power. In the hours that follow, trust in God will mean complete self-surrender.

For some commentators, complete self-surrender to God describes every aspect of Jesus' relationship with God, and equally describes how all those who follow Jesus should live at all times in relation to both God and Christ. The passages we have discussed suggest that this view does not do full justice to the complexity of *pistis* in the gospels or in other New Testament writings. If, however, Jesus' prayer in Gethsemane indicates a failure of self-trust together with an expression of self-surrender to God in that moment, does his cry on the cross

---

[54] This is compatible with Mt. 16.19, 18.18 if we assume that the disciples have the authority to readmit the penitent into the community.
[55] Jn 12.27 also knows of this tradition and shows Jesus not asking for relief.
[56] Noted by Davies and Allison (1988–2004), *ad loc.*

(Mt. 27.46=Mk 15.34) point in the same direction?[57] Without delving deeply into the complex history of interpretation of this verse, it is worth considering its connection with *pistis*.

Psalm 22.1 (21.1 LXX), which Jesus' cry quotes, ends with a triumphal affirmation of God's justice. Much closer to the beginning, however, the psalmist's first words (vv. 1–3) are immediately followed by the affirmation that God is in his temple, and that 'our fathers hoped in you; they hoped, and you delivered them…in you they hoped and were not disappointed' (vv. 5–6). The psalmist expresses his pain that God has not yet responded to his prayer, but no fear that God is absent or will not save him. By analogy, we can see Jesus as speaking out of the depths of the agony of crucifixion, but without losing trust that he will be delivered. Alternatively, we can see him, as in Gethsemane, as momentarily losing trust in himself to remain trusting or faithful in mind and heart, even at this moment when he is beyond escaping the physical consequences of his faithfulness. Yet another possibility is that on the cross he loses trust in God.

In Mark's gospel, all three readings seem possible.[58] Matthew, however, points us to one or both of the first two. Three verses earlier, he gives the priests, scribes, and elders their own near-quotation of Psalm 22: 'He trusts in God; let God deliver him now, if he wants him (πέποιθεν ἐπὶ τὸν θεόν, ῥυσάσθω νῦν εἰ θέλει αὐτόν)' (27.43).[59] In this paraphrase of Psalm 22.9 (21.9 LXX), the most striking change is that where both the Masoretic text and the Septuagint say '[h]e hoped in God', Matthew changes the verb to 'trust'. Having just heard this, it is hard not to hear Jesus' cry of dereliction, drawn from the same psalm, as also a cry of trust, or the failure of trust.[60] It would be consonant with Matthew's portrayal of Jesus' *pistis* towards God in the rest of the gospel to hear it as an expression of pain that has not lost trust in God's nearness and righteousness. It would also fit Matthew's account of the scene in Gethsemane to hear this as Jesus, in agony, losing trust in himself to be faithful to the end. But Matthew cannot, I think, intend listeners to hear this as a loss of trust in God. Almost immediately after this cry, Jesus dies (v. 50). Matthew says, emphatically, καὶ ἰδού, 'and behold', the veil of the temple is torn in two, the earth shakes, rocks are split, tombs open, and many of the dead

---

[57] Davies and Allison (1988–2004), *ad loc.* suggest that this is not loss of faith but a cry of pain. Stump (2018), 143–75 suggests that Jesus' connection with God means that, on the cross, he 'mind-reads' the whole of human evil and, '[f]looded with such a horror, Christ might well lose entirely his ability to find the mind of God the Father' and so his trust (p. 165).

[58] All three views have had supporters, though usually without explicit consideration of the possible role of trust here. Rivkin (1984), 108 suggests that Jesus may have stopped believing in his mission, which could involve ceasing to believe in himself or in God as having given him a mission.

[59] Mt. 27.43, cf. Ps. 22.9: 'He hoped in the Lord; let him deliver him, let him rescue him, if he loves him.'

[60] Jesus does not waver in trust in John as arguably in the synoptic gospels; the closest he comes is at 12.27: 'I am troubled now. But what should I say? "Father, save me from this hour"? But it was for this purpose that I came to this hour.'

are raised (vv. 51–3). This portent is God's response to the jeering challenge of verse 43: Jesus' trust in God is answered and vindicated. He has remained faithful and God confirms God's faithfulness to him. What this story, whether in Mark's or (more clearly) in Matthew's version, together with the story of Jesus' prayer in Gethsemane, does suggest, however, is that if even the *pistis* of Jesus, in this moment, is in some way imperfect, that does not make it insufficient in God's sight.

Trust, as scholars in multiple disciplines have shown in recent years, makes us vulnerable, and vulnerability makes us fearful. Trust is always a risk, on another person and/or ourselves. Even if Mark and Matthew suggest that even Jesus, in his earthly life, does not always maintain an attitude of perfect trust, in God or himself, they never represent him as other than perfectly trustworthy towards God or other people. His trustworthiness places him, in the view of the gospel writers, very close to God. But the gospels also recognize the challenge posed to those who encounter Jesus, whether in his earthly or exalted life, and, in stories of those who put their trust in Jesus, Jesus' disciples, and even Jesus himself, they offer encouragement to the faithful. For God and Christ, even trust that is muddied with fear, scepticism, or doubt can lead to salvation. If one fails in the attitude of trust, it may be enough to act with trust, and vice versa.

In Chapter 2, we observed that if God is always trustworthy, then what God asks of human beings must, in some way, be possible to fulfil. This section has pointed to several ways in which this might be true. If human beings see and trust only part of who Jesus is, their sins may still be forgiven. If their trust is limited and imperfect, they may still come to eternal life. If trust wavers or fails, but they remain trusting or faithful in action, they may still enter the kingdom. If they fail to act with trust or faithfulness, they may still, eventually, be saved.

The Failure to Trust

The negative forms of *pistis* language—*apistia, apistos, apistein, ou pisteuein*—are much less common throughout the gospels than *pistis, pisteuein,* and so on, but they feature in every gospel (most often in John), in some of the same contexts as the positive forms: especially in relation to forgiveness, eternal life, power, or the end time. In Chapter 4 we saw that for Paul, especially in Romans, *apistia* can be seen as tantamount to sin, and arguably is the paradigmatic sin, for both Jews and gentiles, both before and after the Christ event.[61] It is sometimes suggested that something similar is true for John, but, though all four gospels connect *apistia* or

---

[61] pp. 148–52.

ou pisteuein with sin in some way, they are closer to each other in the pattern of their usage than any of them is to Paul.[62]

For John, as we have seen, some cannot believe or trust in Jesus because they are not 'among [his] sheep' (10.26, cf. 3.18, 4.48, 8.45-6, 12.39, 16.9).[63] The synoptic gospels seem to assume that everyone is capable of trust. In all four gospels, most references to the failure of *pistis* involve people who can trust, so are culpable for not trusting, or not trusting enough.

The clearest identification of the failure to trust and/or be trustworthy with wilful sin occurs in Matthew's attack on the scribes and Pharisees (23.1-36). 'You pay tithes of mint and dill and cumin', he tells them, 'and have neglected the weightier thing of the law: justice and mercy and *pistis*' (Mt. 23.23, cf. Lk. 11.42).[64] Matthew attributes to the scribes and Pharisees a series of failings which prevent them from recognizing their need to come to a (re)new(ed) relationship with God. They are arrogant, more interested in their own status than in serving God and the Messiah (23.6-12). They do not practise what they preach (23.3, 13-15, 23-30).[65] Their interpretation of the law places insupportable burdens on the shoulders of those who listen to them (23.3-4). They betray those who rely on them as guides, blocking the entrance to the kingdom to them (23.13), making their converts as wicked as themselves (23.15-16, cf. 10.1-36, Lk. 10.12-15), and leading them into hell (Mt. 18.6-9, cf. 15.1-20=Mk 7.1-23, Lk. 11.37-44).[66] They have persecuted and continue to persecute the prophets, wise men, and scribes sent by God (23.30-6, cf. 11.18-19, cf. 21.23-7, 23.37).[67]

These behaviours point to three key ways in which people may fail in trust, which we also encountered in the epistles. They may fail to put their trust in God and those who speak in God's name; they may put too much trust in their own judgment of how to serve God; and they may fail to be trustworthy towards God,

---

[62] John connects *ou pisteuein* twice explicitly with sin; in both cases the sin is failure to trust in Jesus (8.45-6, 16.19). Elsewhere we can infer that *ou pisteuein* is linked to condemnation (e.g. 4.48, 5.38, 5.47, 6.64, 10.25-6, 12.39; at 3.18 those who *ou pisteuein* have already been condemned); but in some passages it is disciples or those apparently open to trust who *ou pisteuein* (3.12, 14.10, cf. 20.25), so their failure is part of a positive process.

[63] Above, pp. 204-5.

[64] This must be an issue of trust rather than belief, since the Pharisees' belief in God is not in question.

[65] Luz (2001), 209 notes that 'the Athanasian understanding of the blasphemy of the spirit [Mt. 12.31-2=Mk 3.28-30=Lk. 12.10] as a deliberate denial of the divinity of Christ by non-Christians and heretics comes closer to the text than does the interpretation of Origen or Augustine as a specific sin of Christians for which a "second repentance" is impossible.' We can go further and suggest that the blasphemy is not only refusal to make a certain belief-claim about Jesus but refusal to trust him; if so, this verse connects trust and the spirit. Elsewhere, some of Jesus' sharpest challenges are reserved for those who express the desire to follow him but do not commit fully: e.g. Mt. 9.21-2=Lk. 9.59-60, Mt. 19.24=Mk 10.25.

[66] Lk. 6.43-4 links this image with the bearing of rotten fruit.

[67] To justify their refusal to listen they make perverse claims about Jesus and try to mislead others with them (e.g. Mt. 12.24-30=Mk 3.22-7=Lk. 11.15, 17-23).

or towards those who trust in their relationship with God.[68] Commentators assume that these passages testify to a conflicted relationship between Matthew's communities and some other Jews, as well as to the relationship between Jesus and the religious authorities. They also stand as a warning to Matthew's own community: to fail in trust towards God and in Jesus is indefensible, and equally indefensible is to fail in trustworthiness.[69] We can add to these two other passages, one of which is explicitly, and one implicitly, addressed to the disciples rather than to the religious authorities. Matthew 18.6 warns against untrustworthiness, both towards God and towards those who trust in Jesus: 'whoever causes one of these little ones who trust in me to sin, it would be better for him to have a great millstone tied round his neck and to be drowned in the depth of the sea'.[70] Luke 18.9–14 tells a parable unique to him but rather Matthaean in spirit, 'to some who trusted in themselves that they were righteous ($\tau o\grave{u}s$ $\pi\epsilon\pi o\iota\theta\acute{o}\tau as$ $\dot{\epsilon}\varphi'$ $\dot{\epsilon}a\upsilon\tau o\hat{\iota}s$ $\ddot{o}\tau\iota$ $\epsilon\dot{\iota}\sigma\grave{\iota}\nu$ $\delta\acute{\iota}\kappa a\iota o\iota$) and despised others' (18.9). A Pharisee, who trusts his own judgment of how to serve God, is found to be less righteous than a sinner who beats his breast and prays for mercy.[71]

In the passages of John's gospel in which *ou pisteuein* is most clearly linked with sin (3.18, 16.9), the sin is always the failure of personal trust in Jesus. At 3.17–18, Jesus says that God sent his son into the world so that the world might be saved through him. 'The one who trusts in him will not be condemned...' (v. 18). At 16.8–9, 'when [the Advocate] comes he will examine the world in regard to sin and righteousness and condemnation: sin, because they do not trust in me....'[72]

We have seen that even the trust of the disciples, who we assume are (outside the birth narratives) the most trusting and trustworthy of those who encounter Jesus in his earthly life, is unreliable and prone to fail at moments of crisis. In those who have put their trust in Jesus and (as far as we can judge from the narrative) continue to want to trust and be faithful, however, occasional failures of trust do not lead to the failure of the relationship as a whole.[73] When, for example,

---

[68] Similar themes appear e.g. at Mt. 4.1–7, Lk. 4.1–4, 9–12 (Jesus resists the temptations to serve himself or exercise inappropriate power over others, but remains obedient to God); Mt. 9.13 (the Pharisees serve God inappropriately).

[69] Acts continues the challenge, particularly to Jews, to repent and *pisteuein*, but post-resurrection repentance is focused on past failures to recognize Jesus' identity and mission (e.g. 2.22–40, 3.11–26, 7.51–3, 9.4). Outside Jerusalem, the call to trust is sometimes offered as an opportunity rather than a call to repentance: e.g. 8.37–8, 13.16–39, but 17.30 suggests (perhaps based on knowledge of Paul's letter to the Romans) that gentiles too need to repent as they recognize the 'unknown God' as the God of Israel.

[70] Mt. 18.6=Mk 9.42, though there $\epsilon\dot{\iota}s$ $\dot{\epsilon}\mu\acute{\epsilon}$ is probably a late addition.

[71] Mt. 18.6 is part of a discourse addressed to the disciples and there is no sign that others are present. Lk. 18.9–14 is one of a series of stories and sayings which are addressed to the disciples from 17.22, and there is no indication of a change of addressee at 18.9.

[72] In both passages, both grammar and context suggest that *pisteuein* refers primarily to trusting, since the *pisteuein* that saves is not only cognitive but an act of commitment.

[73] Except, we assume, in the case of Judas.

the disciples fail to cure a boy with a demon (Mt. 17.14–18=Mk 9.16–27=Lk. 9.38–42), Jesus says, 'O faithless and perverse generation, how long am I to be with you?' (Mt. 17.17=Lk. 9.41, cf. Mk 9.19). Then, however, he heals the boy, and the disciples stay with him, so his rhetorical question sounds more exasperated than condemnatory. In the same story, in Mark's version, the boy's father, who both expresses trust and asks for help with his *apistia*, receives help in the same way as do others who come for healing and are commended for their *pistis* (9.24).[74] Jesus does not comment on the man's unique form of words, but Mark may have intended his audience to hear it and note that *pistis* which asks for help, however imperfect, receives it.[75] In Luke's account of the resurrection, the disciples do not believe the women who first report having seen him (24.11), and when they see him themselves, are *apistos* with joy (24.41), but (unlike in John's gospel) they are not chided for it.[76] In John's gospel, Jesus occasionally criticizes those who (in the case of the disciples) have trusted in him or (in the case of Nicodemus at 3.12) have perhaps shown the capacity for trust, but who, at some point, falter in trust or belief. 'Do you not believe [or 'trust'] that I am in the Father and the Father is in me?' Jesus demands of Philip when Philip asks to be shown the Father (14.8, 10).[77] After the resurrection, Thomas' insistence that 'unless I see the mark of the nails in his hands...I will not believe [that Jesus has risen, or that the person the other disciples have seen was indeed Jesus]' (20.25) is met by Jesus' exhortation, 'Become not untrusting, but trusting' (20.27), together with the affirmation, both chiding and encouraging, 'Blessed are those who have not seen and yet have believed/trusted' (20.29).[78] In these pericopes, however, there is no sign that Jesus rejects those who want to trust but fail.[79]

That said, all the gospels envisage that some people fail in trust in such a way that their relationship with Jesus cannot continue. *Pistis* language does not appear in the narratives of Judas' betrayal, but since he has been a disciple, we can assume that he has been in a relationship of trust with Jesus. Foreseeing his betrayal, Jesus

---

[74] Joseph Spooner, in private correspondence, offers the translation of Mk 9.24, 'Lord, I find you trustworthy; help me with my struggle to trust you [perhaps specifically on this occasion]'.

[75] This could be heard as an example of the action of trust without the attitude of trust, of the kind explored by McKaughan (2017, 2018a, 2018b). If so, it is hard to see it as more than a starting-point for human trust in God and Christ. New Testament writings abound with affirmations about the nature of the relationships between God, Christ, and the faithful, God's and Christ's actions in the world, and what is made possible by God through Christ's death, the resurrection, Christ's return, and coming judgment, to which the faithful are invited to take an attitude, probably of both belief and trust.

[76] Cf., in the long ending, Mk 16.11, 14, 16.

[77] Elements of both belief and trust may be involved here, since *pisteuein* is part of the disciples' commitment to Jesus as well as their knowledge of him (cf. v. 9).

[78] On this translation of 20.27, see above, pp. 106–7. At 20.29 both belief and trust are implied, since Thomas has just come both to believe that Jesus has indeed risen, and affirmed him as Lord and God (v. 28).

[79] *Apistia* therefore refers either to absolute non-trust or inadequate trust within a relationship with Jesus; this complexity is what Matthew seeks to clarify by referring sometimes to the disciples' *oligopistia*.

says, in the synoptic gospels, 'woe to that man by whom the Son of Man is betrayed. It would be better for that man if he had never been born.'[80] At John 6.64, Jesus foresees not only Judas, but other disciples deserting him. 'There are some of you,' he says, 'who do not trust' (6.64). He 'knew from the beginning the ones who would not trust and the one who would betray him' (v. 65). Since these people have begun to follow him, and so presumably to *pisteuein*, Jesus seems here to acknowledge the possibility that his followers can lapse fatally from trust.[81]

Some of the most vivid expressions of this idea are those prophecies and parables of the end time in which Jesus foretells that, at the return of the master, his slaves, who have been entrusted in his absence with some action on his behalf (typically looking after his household or estate), will be assessed for their *pistis*, and some of them may be found wanting. At the end of the parable of the talents, for example, the slaves who have multiplied their talents are commended as *pistos* (Mt. 25.21=Lk. 19.17, Mt. 25.23), while the slave who has not is castigated as wicked and worthless (Mt. 25.26, 30, Lk. 19.22) and, in Matthew's gospel, flung into the eschatological outer darkness where there is weeping and gnashing of teeth (25.30). As Luke's Jesus warns, the 'master will come on an unexpected day and at an unknown hour' (12.46). He will punish severely the servant who he finds has not been faithful and prudent (12.42), and will 'assign him a place with the *apistoi*' (12.46). All the gospels recognize, and show Jesus recognizing, that trust is not easy, and even those who most want to trust and be faithful make mistakes. Wavering in trust, in the present time, is not a deal-breaker in itself—but all the gospels also convey to their listeners that *pistis can* fail catastrophically and find no way back. Moreover, there will come a time when the *pistis* of Jesus' followers is judged once for all, and, on that day, they must show the divine judge that they have been more *pistos* than otherwise.

Last but not least, Matthew and Mark both make, in slightly different terms, an observation about *apistia* which further highlights its relationality. Faced with the people in the synagogue at Nazareth, who respond to his preaching by taking offence at Jesus (Mk 6.3), Jesus, in Mark's words, 'was not able to exercise any power there, except that he laid his hands upon a few sick people and healed them. And he was amazed at their lack of trust' (6.5–6). God's and Jesus' will to exercise power requires a response of trust; human beings must do their part to forge and maintain the relationship within which they are saved.[82] Matthew changes 'was not able' to 'did not' (13.58), presumably to suggest that divine

---

[80] Mt. 26.24=Mk 14.21, cf. Lk. 22.22. John's gospel marks Judas' change of heart equally decisively by saying that 'Satan entered him' (13.27).

[81] John continues, 'As a result of this, many of his disciples returned to their former way of life and no longer accompanied him,' but he cannot intend Jesus' saying to be read as a self-fulfilling prophecy. We noted above John's unusual turn of phrase at 5.38 (p. 206 n.48), which may imply that those who do not trust in Jesus may forfeit (what they believe is) their existing relationship with God.

[82] Assuming that here, as elsewhere in the gospel, those who are cured have trusted.

power chooses to accept the human response rather than that it is constrained by it, but in his form of the story *pistis* is equally relational, and the responsibility of human beings within the relationship equally marked.[83]

The gospels, unlike Paul in Romans, show relatively little interest in the nature of the earlier sins or *apistia* which led John the Baptist and Jesus to call God's people to seek forgiveness and *dikaiosynē*. Though Matthew's Jesus accuses the Pharisees of failing in *pistis* towards God separately from their response to Jesus, in all four gospels *apistia*, like *pistis*, is almost always a reaction to Jesus. All four gospels, moreover, share the assumption that trust in Jesus rescues people from the power of evil, sin, and the suffering imposed by sin, but are less interested in exploring whether sin and evil are metaphysical or moral, individual or collective, inherited or brought on oneself, than in sketching what is involved in trust, and what those who trust can hope for.[84] Accordingly, it is never explicit whether *apistia* is tantamount to sin (however understood) or *pistis* to repentance; whether *pistis* is a new initiative which must follow repentance or is simultaneous with it (either of which might be implied e.g. by Mk 1.15), or whether it precedes repentance (as implied e.g. by Jn 9.1–7, 35–8); or whether gentiles are sinful, as Jews, by failing in their covenant relationship with God, can be sinful, and therefore whether gentile *pistis* stands in the same relationship to sin and repentance as Jewish *pistis*. We can assume that this choice of focus on the evangelists' part reflects their shared view that what matters most, in light of the Christ event, is not the precise nature of humanity's state before it, nor the detail of the order of events as people come to trust, but the universal and vital significance of that trust, how it changes the lives of those who trust, and how it frames their relationship with Jesus Christ in the present time.

The Gospel Narratives and the Creation of Trust

The genre of the gospels and their working as narratives have become sizeable fields of research in recent years, and the many debates they have generated are largely beyond our scope. It is, though, worth making some brief comments about

---

[83] Though even Mark qualifies the statement of 6.5a at 6.5b, while Luke omits this section of the story, presumably reluctant to suggest that human beings can hinder the Son of God in any way. The qualifications in Matthew's and Mark's versions hint at a tension in their thinking about the relationship between *pistis* and healing/salvation: salvific *pistis* is relational, but one would not expect an act of divine power to be constrained by human beings. What is remarkable, however, is that the relationality of *pistis* is so dominant in these narratives. Moss (2010) points out that the story of the woman with the haemorrhage shows her as 'the active agent in her own healing', who 'pulls power' from the porous, unregulated body of Jesus (p. 519).

[84] On sin see e.g. Marshall (2002), Nel (2017), Siker (2020), 38–107, Stack (2020).

how the texts present Jesus, and create an imaginative space in which to encounter him, in such a way as to foster trust in those who hear or read them.[85]

Compared with most ancient narratives with a strong focus on an individual, however we classify them, the canonical gospels are abnormally short of those descriptions of the subject which tell the reader so much about how to evaluate him (usually him).[86] Was Jesus tall and beautiful or sallow and hunchbacked? Did he have a gift for friendship or a horror of snakes?[87] In particular, someone used to reading about ancient orators and teachers might wonder, how did Jesus look and sound? Was his voice naturally strong or weak?[88] Was he lavish with gestures or notably economical? Later writers do take an interest in Jesus' appearance, claiming variously that he was small, plain, or ugly (to the ignorant, at least), or, alternatively, tall and handsome.[89] With the minimal exception of Luke 2.40, 'the child grew and became strong', however, the gospels do not draw listeners' attention to Jesus' appearance at all.[90] Their focus is firmly on the fact of his presence and the content of his interactions with those around him.

---

[85] On the genre of the gospels see recently e.g. Burridge (2000, 2018, 2020), Vines (2002), Carter (2004), Diehl (2011), Pennington (2012), Smith (2015), Walton (2015), Evans and Licona (2017), Pitts (2020), Calhoun et al. (2020), Dinkler (2020), Kelber (2020), cf. Adams (2013) on Acts as 'collected biography'. Most accounts of the gospels currently see them as some form of biography, but the most innovative move beyond arguments about genre *per se* to consider 'what it means to say that [e.g.] Mark's gospel is an ancient biography' (Bond (2020), 5); see also Lincoln (2005), 14–17, Keener and Wright (2016). Arguments about genre, however, may be more distracting than productive. One of the most prominent features of early imperial writing in general is generic fluidity, so we should not necessarily expect the gospels to conform to any existing genre. On the other hand, even narratives identified as historical can be difficult to distinguish from biography when one individual dominates a period of history: cf. e.g. Alexander's domination of D.S. 17, Arr., *Anab*. I am sympathetic to those who argue that the gospels cannot be seen as life-writing without, at the least, heavy qualification (e.g. Edwards (2006), Frein (2008), Ashton (2014), 31–7, Shively (2020)), and to the argument that they are a type of historical narrative (see especially Collins (1990), though Vorster (1983) argues for the limitations of history as a genre for the gospels). Their resonances with Greek tragedy have also been well explored, e.g. by Burch (1931), Exum (1992), Berube (2003), McCuistion et al. (2014), Oakeshott (2015), Larsen (2018), especially pp. 67–120, while on New Testament writings and comedy see Via (1975), Zakowitch (1984), and on the connections between tragedy, biography, and epic see Mossman (1988). In the ancient world in general, the idea of a biography of a heavenly figure, even in his or her earthly life, sounds odd; there is too much about such a figure that a biographical framework cannot encompass, whereas mythico-historical narratives, both Jewish and gentile, in which divine figures are central are common. (Jesus Christ, from this perspective, is a different type of subject from e.g. Moses, even if the synoptic gospels do not think in terms of his pre-existence.) In addition, thinking of gospels as biographical risks distracting attention from their focus on what *God* does through Christ, and also from the unusually large role played by Jesus' followers (below, pp. 271–3).

[86] See the discussion of Bond (2020), 162–6.

[87] On the relationship between depictions of appearance and character in ancient biography and other genres see Rohrbacher (2010).

[88] Mt. 26.73, uniquely, marks Peter as having a Galilean accent, but nothing is said about how Jesus sounded outside his home region.

[89] Taylor (2018), 139–54.

[90] Discussed in relation to the synoptic gospels by Fleddermann (1979), Vearncombe (2014), cf. Brock (1982), Cleland et al. (2007). Clothes are sometimes mentioned with symbolic significance, though mostly not Jesus' own: e.g. Mt. 9.20=Mk 5.27=Lk. 8.44, Mt. 17.2=Mk 9.3=Lk. 9.29, Mt. 23.5=Lk. 20.46, Mt. 28.3=Mk 16.5=Lk. 24.4, cf. Mt. 3.4=Mk 1.6.

Once Jesus' ministry has begun, the only activity of which we hear that is not directly (though it is indirectly) connected with his ministry is that periodically he retires to a quiet place to pray. The gospels report no anecdotes of his relationship with the disciples or others that do not culminate in sayings, teachings, or significant actions. Between episodes of teaching, healing, or controversy, we hear nothing of Jesus' daily life.[91] Only a handful of pericopes (the pre-birth stories, John the Baptist's preaching and death, Peter's denial, Pilate's interaction with the crowd) do not centre on Jesus himself, and no story is reported about Jesus which is not directly about his relationship with God and his mission. Even compared with collections of exempla or abbreviated thematic biographies such as Diogenes Laertius' *Lives of the Philosophers*, the gospels are parsimonious of detail concerning Jesus' life beyond his ministry (to the point that the idea of Jesus' having a life beyond his ministry may strike readers as odd). Even in the passion narratives, which offer, relatively, a wealth of detail, the details virtually always directly serve the significance of the story.[92]

The gospels are powerfully focused on Jesus, and present Jesus as wholly focused on God and on his work. No stories are told of Jesus before the passion narratives in which he does not speak for God or of God, or act with divine power. The gospels offer notoriously little in the way of scene-setting and geographical or chronological connections between stories (though Luke, the closest to a Hellenistic biographer or historiographer, offers a little more than the others). When Jesus arrives in a new place or begins a new activity, his movements are usually summarized, at most, in a clause or a short sentence before he begins to teach or someone approaches him for healing.[93] The stories' economy of framing directs all the listener's attention to Jesus' words and actions.

All four canonical gospels include lengthy sequences of teachings by Jesus in the second person, which draw eclectically on forms of Near Eastern and Mediterranean discourse from hymns and prayers to prophecy, scriptural wisdom, Greek collections of fables and proverbs, public speeches, and collections of philosophical teachings. Explicitly directed at the disciples or larger crowds, they can equally be heard as addressing anyone who is reading or hearing the text in any context.

---

[91] Outside Lk. 2.46, the gospels give no details of who, if anyone, taught Jesus: if he was a follower of John the Baptist they suppress or do not know it. Given that one of Jesus' brothers apparently became a leading figure in the Jerusalem church (Gal. 1.19), and others may also have followed him (cf. Mt. 12.46–50=Mk 3.31–5=Lk. 8.19–21), it is striking (and hints at partisanship) that they do not say more about his siblings. Doole (2017) argues that Jesus had a home in Capernaum where his early ministry was based, but if so, the gospel writers make little of it.

[92] One or two which do not obviously do so stand out and are much puzzled over: the young man in Gethsemane who loses his linen cloth and runs away naked (Mk 14.51–2) (on which see Lohmeyer (1937), 324, Vearncombe (2013), (2014), 168–94); the unexpected and ineffectual appearance of Pilate's wife (Mt. 27.19), on which see Van Der Bergh (2012).

[93] Jn 7.1–9, in which Jesus and his brothers debate over several verses whether to leave Galilee for Judaea, is unique in this respect.

Jesus' engagement with those around him is also represented as focused wholly on their relationship with God. In the synoptic gospels, his interactions are almost all short and decisive, and the details of the story contribute directly to its message. In some stories Jesus' concern for others is expressed as extraordinary knowledge: of the Samaritan woman's sexual history (Jn 4.17–18), or the long illness of the man by the pool called Bethesda (Jn 5.6). They emphasize Jesus' attentiveness to those around him: an awareness of need, sometimes before it is articulated, which reflects God's own attentiveness to humanity and awareness of human need.[94] The Syro-Phoenician or Canaanite woman has to argue her case (Mt. 15.26–8=Mk 7.27–9) and the Roman official to press Jesus for help (Jn 4.47–9), but in no story does Jesus fail to respond to someone who appeals to him or fail to answer a need which he has noticed. Nor, until his trial, does he ever fail to answer a question, though his answers are often oblique or unexpected.

When characters within the story, therefore, are called to put their trust in God or in Jesus, or when those listening to the story hear Jesus' words as addressed to them, they are called to trust in one whose life and work are focused entirely on God, whose awareness and response to human need reflects God's own, and whose concern for those around them is concentrated on their relationship with God. The consistent tightness of this focus, in all the canonical gospels, is highly unusual in early imperial writing.

Alongside Jesus' orientation to God and his work runs another theme which is equally unusual in ancient narratives of great men, Jewish or gentile: his close relationship with, and even dependence on those around him.[95] Elsewhere, accounts of leading political and military figures rarely tell us much about their close friends and allies.[96] In stories of famous teachers, their pupils rarely play a large role and are often not named (the exception being Plato's dialogues, where many of Socrates' interlocutors are named and a few play a role in more than one dialogue).[97] In the synoptic gospels, twelve of Jesus' closest male followers are named (Mt. 10.2–4=Mk 3.16–19=Lk. 6.14–16) together with several of his closest female followers (e.g. Mk 15.40=Mt. 27.56, Mk 16.1=Mt. 28.1, Lk. 8.1–3, 10.39–42, 24.10, Jn. 11.17–44, 12.1–8), and appear, named, in at least one story. In all four gospels, several, together with a scatter of other followers, male and female, appear in multiple stories. Some have not only names but distinct personalities.

---

[94] Cf. e.g. Mk 5.30=Lk. 8.45, Mt. 12.10=Mk 3.1=Lk. 6.6, Lk. 7.12–13, 13.11–12.

[95] On the wealth of these relationships see e.g. Theissen and Merz (1998), 213–25.

[96] An exception is some of the narratives about Alexander the Great, who was surrounded by a group of Macedonian nobles who acted as his generals and advisers, in most cases throughout his campaigns. These had either been close to his father or had been his near-contemporaries as he grew up.

[97] In Philostratus' *Life* of Apollonius of Tyana, we hear several times of Damis, a follower who took notes on which readers are meant to think the biography draws, but very little about what was apparently, over the years, a sizeable number of followers who travelled with him. Many of these are only listed by name as an appendix at the end of the work.

In addition to acting as foils for Jesus' exemplary faithfulness, his miracles, or his teaching, by listening, answering questions, being afraid in storms, or failing in prayer, disciples and other followers have their own views on Jesus' mission (e.g. Mt. 15.23, 16.22, Jn 7.3-4) speak to Jesus on behalf of the crowds he is teaching (e.g. Mt. 14.15, Jn 6.9), mediate between Jesus and others (not always to Jesus' approval (e.g. Mt. 19.13, Jn 12.20-2)), ask questions on their own account (e.g. Mt. 19.25, 20.21, Jn 13.25), argue (e.g. Mt. 26.33, Jn 2.3-5, 13.6, 13.37, 14.5 cf. Jn 3.4-9, 6.7), seek reassurance (e.g. Mt. 26.22), seek to heal even when Jesus is nearby (e.g. Mt. 17.16), fall out among themselves (e.g. Mt. 20.24, 26.8-9, 26.69-75), fight against Jesus' arrest (e.g. Mt. 26.51, Jn 18.10), and struggle to accept the resurrection (e.g. Mk 16.8, Lk. 24.27, Jn 20.25). The twelve (and, at Luke 10.1-12, 17-20, the seventy or seventy-two) are portrayed as helping Jesus to extend his ministry in his lifetime (Mt. 10.1, 5=Mk 6.7=Lk. 9.1, cf. Mk 3.13-19=Lk. 6.13). Luke mentions a group of Galilean women who not only follow Jesus but provide for him out of their own resources (8.1-3). After Jesus' death, some of the women and one or two men peripheral to the main narrative give him a decent burial (Mt. 27.57-61=Mk 15.43-16.1=Lk. 23.50-24.1, Jn 19.38-42).[98]

We might expect that Jesus, acting for God with the power of God, would need close relationships with other people, if anything, less than most historical or biographical subjects. The gospels propose the opposite. The representation of the disciples in the gospels is much discussed, not least because, despite the fact that at least some of them became major figures in early churches, they are so often portrayed as failing in trust, failing in prayer, asking the wrong questions, or doing the wrong thing. Is this simply the handing on of a cluster of complex, warts-and-all traditions? Did the writers have axes to grind against some of the twelve?[99] This and the previous chapter have offered a more optimistic interpretation of the disciples' shortcomings: that they represent the limitations and failings in trust which are inevitable in ordinary human beings, but which do not prevent either the disciples or later followers from trusting and, ultimately, being faithful, being forgiven their sins, and gaining eternal life.[100] We can go further and suggest that, although no gospel writer says so explicitly, the strong presence of the disciples in the gospels communicates that the trust God and Jesus put in

---

[98] Arguably we should add Jesus' enemies to this list: since all the gospels understand the death of Jesus as necessary, he also depends, in a sense, on his enemies to bring it about.

[99] Particularly Mark, in most commentators' view (e.g. Tannehill (1977), Best (1981), Donahue (1983), Matera (1987), 38-55, Kingsbury (1989), Hanson (1998)), though Bond (2020), 198-9 balances this by pointing out that Mark expects his audience to know of the disciples' post-Easter life and work (cf. Best (1976-7), 400).

[100] This suggests that the disciples can be seen, if not quite as role models, as offering encouragement to the faithful, as examples of flawed but savable humanity. Williams (1994), 151-71 explores how we are invited to identify even with minor characters in Mark's gospel as models.

them is almost as significant as the trust they put in God and Jesus.[101] His followers constitute a key element of Jesus' life of ministry, and their inevitable failings do not disqualify them. It is a powerful message to the evangelists' audiences.

The importance of the people around Jesus to his life and ministry is also illustrated in the birth narratives. Birth narratives and allusions to significant births, of course, appear both in the scriptures and in gentile history and life-writing.[102] Samuel's birth, in particular, is a partial type for that of Jesus for Luke: unlike that of Jesus it is an answer to prayer (1 Sam. 1.20), but when Hannah dedicates her child to the Lord she sings a song which foreshadows Mary's Magnificat (2.1–10), and when Samuel is called by God he is still a young child (*paidarion* at 1 Sam. 3.1 LXX). Matthew's and Luke's birth narratives, however, are on an unusually large scale: Matthew offers five pericopes of Jesus' birth and early childhood, Luke eight (counting the brief reference to Jesus' circumcision and naming), which incorporate, between them, two substantial songs and an extended cast of characters from family members to kings, paupers, and foreigners.

Luke's birth narrative, especially because of his story of Jesus in the temple as a boy, is often compared with stories of the birth and boyhood of great men in Greek biographies (though his use of 1 Samuel would be enough to account for the presence of a story of Jesus' boyhood).[103] The differences, though, are as striking as the similarities. It is common for a biographer to introduce his subject by listing something of his genealogy, but unusual for readers to hear much, if anything, about the circumstances of his birth. It is sometimes recorded, in retrospect, that signs and portents marked the birth, but these are not normally responded to, or even registered at the time. (It is far more common for signs and portents to be noticed and responded to before the subject's death, which does not happen in Jesus' earthly lifetime, though he foretells that it will happen before the coming of the Son of Man.[104]) It is unusual, though not unknown, for biographers to include stories about the subject's parents or other adults who surround him as a baby. The divergencies between Matthew's and Luke's birth narratives and broadly comparable stories in either Jewish or gentile life-writing underline that generic parallels do not explain why Matthew or Luke write as they do. Greek and Jewish life-writing takes varied forms, and we need not expect

---

[101] Explored further in the next chapter.
[102] Scriptural stories are not common but see e.g. Exod. 2.1–10, Judg. 13.3–5, 1 Sam. 1.19–12.1, cf. Isa. 7.14, 9.5.
[103] Luke's story of Jesus' boyhood (2.41–52) foreshadows something of Jesus the man (the teachers in the temple are amazed by his understanding (2.47), and Jesus refers to the temple as his father's house (2.49)), but in other ways, this story, like the earlier story of Jesus' presentation in the temple, is more striking for its differences from later stories than its similarities, since Jesus is presented here as in harmony with the temple teachers, sitting among them, listening to them and asking and answering questions which they admire (2.46–7).
[104] Only at the sixth hour, during the crucifixion, does the sky go dark (Mt. 27.45=Mk 15.33=Lk. 23.44), and the veil of the temple is torn after Jesus' death (Mt. 27.51=Mk 15.38), and according to Matthew, the earth shakes and tombs are opened (27.51–2).

early Christian writings to follow any particular model, but the distinctiveness of Matthew's and Luke's narratives suggests that we should look for explanations of their stories in their own understanding of Jesus. An explanation, moreover, needs to encompass more than their concern to link Jesus to the history and promises of God's relationship with Israel.

No doubt the main point of both birth narratives is to represent Jesus as Son of God from the moment of his conception, and not only (as Mk 1.10–11 suggests) from his baptism. But even this does not explain the scale and complexity of these narratives, which, with their multiple named characters and stories of Jesus' birth and early childhood as well as conception, are more elaborated than many of the scenes of the adult Jesus' ministry. It is tempting to look a little further into their significance. Both narratives both describe the significance of Jesus' babyhood and boyhood as the fulfilment of prophecy in its own right (Mt. 1.22–3, 2.15, 2.18, cf. Lk. 1.31–3, 1.54–5, 2.25–32), and emphasize the importance of the people who surround him. This raises two further possibilities for interpretation: that Jesus begins to act as saviour as a baby, and that the people around him have a significant role to play in his life, and perhaps also as types of those who surround and follow him later.[105]

The idea that a saviour might be a saviour even as a baby would be highly unusual in historical context, though it has passing scriptural warrant at Isaiah 7.16 and 8.4 (both much invoked by later Christian writers). Usually, however, human messiahs, whether kingly, priestly, or military, are envisaged as men: if a people is looking for a saviour, it is normally looking at least for a capable adult. Isaiah 9.6 seems to affirm this: when the prophet says, 'To us a child is born; to us a son is given', he foretells that the government *will* be on his shoulders and he will be called wonderful counsellor; he is not the saviour yet.[106] There are signs, though, that, in the evangelists' imaginations, some of those around Jesus respond to him as if he is already acting as saviour as soon as he is born, if not before.[107] If the gospels draw on Isaiah 7.16 and 8.4, together with 9.2–3, which suggests that those who walk in darkness already see the light and rejoice at the news of the birth of the future saviour, they elaborate significantly on them. Matthew's magi think that Jesus not only will be, but is born king of the Jews (2.2), and pay honour to him with the kind of rich gifts that one offers not to a prospective, but to a reigning monarch (2.11).[108] The shepherds hear that a saviour has been born,

---

[105] The *Protoevangelium of James* and *Infancy Gospel of Thomas* both take up both these themes: e.g. *Prot. Jas* 4.1, 19.2–20.3, *Inf. Gos. Thom.* 9–10, 15.2–19.4.

[106] Assuming, with most commentators, that this passage does refer to a baby (e.g. Brown (1993), 310–11), though it may celebrate the accession of an adult ruler rather than a birth (Blenkinsopp (2000), 248–9).

[107] Explored by Aletti (2017).

[108] If Origen's interpretation (*CC* 1.60) of their gifts, widely accepted by later tradition, is right, they also acknowledge his divinity and worship him. The gifts recall Isa. 60.6, and also 1 Kgs 10.1–5, where

who is—in the present tense—Messiah and Lord, and that God's favour has (already) rested upon some who presumably include themselves.

The announcements of Jesus' birth in Matthew's and Luke's gospels change the status of Joseph and Mary.[109] From being one, presumably, of thousands of members of the house of David, Joseph accepts that he is the member through whom the Son of David is identified as such (Mt. 1.20-1). Mary not only proclaims the greatness of the Lord, following in Hannah's footsteps, but identifies herself as the one through whom God has fulfilled his promise to Abraham and his descendants (Lk. 1.48, 54-5). Jesus' birth changes others too. Luke's shepherds, having seen what God has made known to them (2.15), become preachers, passing on what they have been told about the child (2.10-18). Simeon not only recognizes Jesus as Israel's salvation (Lk. 2.30[110]), but receives the gift of prophecy, telling Mary that 'this child is destined for the fall and rise of many in Israel...' (2.34). Anna, who, though a prophet (2.36), seems to have spent her time since her husband's death in worship rather than prophecy (2.37), discovers or rediscovers her gift, and 'spoke about [the child] to all who were awaiting the redemption of Jerusalem' (2.38). Embroidering on this story in the style of ancient midrash or biography, what might we imagine that Anna said? 'I have just seen a newborn baby who will be very exciting in about thirty years' time [cf. Lk. 3.23], so if you are looking for redemption, you have just three decades longer to wait'? Surely we should rather imagine her saying, 'I have seen the Messiah, today!' Before and around Jesus' birth, God is not only with humanity, as Matthew affirms (1.23), but, through Jesus, is already acting to save, to transform, and to give those who acknowledge the Messiah new gifts and new work to do for God's people.

Matthew's Joseph and wise men, Luke's Mary, Zechariah and Elizabeth, shepherds, Simeon and Anna, are paradigmatic of those who encounter Jesus in his later earthly life, as well as after the resurrection: precursors of the disciples and other followers. Because the saviour they encounter is a baby, however, they also highlight how much God and Jesus will rely on human beings to respond to Jesus. The saviour who is a human being, above all the saviour who is a baby, appeals to those around him not only to trust but to be trustworthy; to allow themselves to be entrusted with him.

It will not have escaped notice that no *pistis* language has been cited in this connection. Matthew's birth narrative does not make use of *pistis* language, but it does use language closely associated with *pistis* language later in the gospel. When the first angel appears to Joseph, for example, it tells him not to be afraid to take Mary into his home (1.20), and Joseph 'did as the angel of the Lord had

---

Solomon, Son of David, receives gifts from Arabia: the only place, according to Hdt. 3.107, that produces both frankincense and myrrh.

[109] We might also suggest that Jesus' birth creates a family, the first community he creates of those who love and serve God; cf. Mt. 2.13-15, Lk. 2.41-50.

[110] Using the aorist: 'my eyes saw your salvation' (εἶδον οἱ ὀφθαλμοί μου τὸ σωτήριόν σου).

commanded him' (1.24). He obeys the order of the second angel to 'Rise, take the child and his mother, flee to Egypt...' (2.13–14) and that of the third to return to Israel (2.20–1). Elsewhere in the gospel, trust is often linked with obedience and not being afraid. What Matthew leaves implicit, Luke makes explicit. When the angel appears to Zechariah, he is afraid and he too is told not to be (1.12–13). The angel foretells the birth of John the Baptist, but Zechariah is sceptical: 'How shall I know this...?' As a punishment, the angel strikes him dumb because, despite recognizing him as a divine messenger, 'you did not believe my words' (1.20). In contrast, when Gabriel appears to Mary, tells her not to be afraid (1.30), and foretells the birth of Jesus, she responds, 'See, I am the handmaid of the Lord' (1.38). Again, obedience and not being afraid are both linked, later in the gospel, with trust. When Mary visits Elizabeth, Elizabeth confirms the connection, saying, 'Blessed are you, who believed [or "trusted"] that ($\dot{\eta}$ πιστεύσασα ὅτι) what was spoken to you by the Lord would be fulfilled' (1.45). Later, both Mary and Zechariah, in their songs, affirm the trustworthiness of God in fulfilling his promises to Israel. The shepherds are initially afraid but seem to respond to being told not to be (Lk. 2.9–10). As we have seen, *pistis* language, in all the gospels, is almost always put in the mouth of Jesus, so it is perhaps not surprising that it does not feature more prominently in the birth narratives. Nevertheless, *pistis* or concepts connected with it appear often enough to suggest that trust in God and Christ and the importance of trustworthiness to God and Christ are themes in these stories, as in the rest of the gospel.

It is also worth noting the role of narrative itself in the creation of trust in Jesus and the ongoing relationship. In modern theory, trust tends to have a strong narrative aspect: I trust you because of my experience of you in the past, or because others whom I have reason to trust testify to your trustworthiness, and my trust typically looks forward, to our future relationship and/or to something I trust you will do or be for me. Some aspects of trust in Jesus in the gospel stories have this narrative quality, notably the trust of those who come to Jesus for healing, but others do not. Most strikingly, before the passion narrative, though all the gospels make some effort to link discrete pericopes with indications of the chronology or topography of the story, the pericopes are essentially distinct, and most could appear in almost any order. As narratives of the creation of trust, therefore, large parts of the gospels are weak. Most of those who encounter Jesus in his adult life encounter him *de novo*, and anyone, whether in Jesus' earthly life or in the pages of the gospels, can encounter Jesus and be changed by the encounter at any point in his life or their own. Moreover, the shared argument of the gospels that one should not seek signs or proofs of Jesus' identity and work, argues against the significance of narrative, particularly in the creation of trust.[111] To trust in Jesus

---

[111] It is plausibly argued that gospels were early bound as codices in order to facilitate not simply linear reading, but to be consulted and dipped into like a recipe book or prayer book (Letteney and

in his earthly life, they imply, one should not need to do more than encounter him, whether in life or in the gospel stories.

Conclusion

In a series of influential studies, the psychologist and psychoanalyst Ana-Maria Rizzuto has distinguished two ways in which people conceptualize or (in psychoanalytic terms) represent God: using the 'God concept', an 'intellectual, mental-dictionary definition of the word "God"', or the 'God image', a 'psychological working internal model of the sort of person that the individual imagines God to be'.[112] The God image, she argues, is especially important to people of faith, across multiple traditions, because it is so much easier to understand oneself as in a life-governing, life-changing relationship with a being whom one can conceive of imagistically, than as governed and changed by a concept or definition (such as, for instance, that God is 'that than which nothing greater can be conceived'[113]). The 'God image' is also important because, for those who see themselves as being, hope to be, or trust they are in a relationship with God, that relationship describes not only something of God but something of themselves: for instance, that they are acceptable to God, loveable, worth saving, or worthy of trust.[114]

What Rizzuto argues is true of God must also have been true, for early Christians, of Jesus Christ. It is often suggested, for instance, that relatively little in the way of a picture of the exalted Christ emerges from the letters of Paul (though Chapter 3 argued that more emerges than is sometimes acknowledged). Assuming that Paul never encountered Jesus in his earthly life, moreover, and while recognizing that he evidently knew something of Jesus' teachings, we may wonder how much Paul was in a position to tell his communities about Jesus' earthly ministry before his crucifixion, and even whether he felt the need to tell them much. Other apostles who had known Jesus during his earthly ministry presumably did talk about him, but, before the gospels were written, testimony (oral or written) about Jesus' earthly life, at least before his last night and crucifixion, probably circulated as individual stories and sayings or groups of stories or sayings rather than extended narratives. Perhaps the most decisive contribution of the gospel writers (canonical and non-canonical) to the evolution of Christianity was to offer the faithful a 'Jesus image': not only a collection of words and deeds but a portrait of a person with whom they could conceive of

---

Larsen (2019), Coogan (2021)). If so, then trust is even less likely to be created through linear reading of their narratives.
    [112] Rizzuto (1970, 1979, 1982); these definitions of Rizzuto's terms are offered by Lawrence (1997), 214.
    [113] Anselm, *Proslogion* 1077–8.
    [114] See Lawrence (1997), with a discussion of earlier literature.

themselves as being in a relationship, and whom they could conceive of as being in a relationship with them.

By drawing, for the second or third generation of the faithful, images of Jesus in his earthly life and death, it is worth noting that the evangelists were not only seeking to establish, as modern readers sometimes assume, that the man Jesus of Nazareth was really the Lord Jesus Christ, heavenly Son of God. They were writing primarily for Christians who already confessed or even worshipped the exalted Christ as Lord and their theme is equally that the heavenly Christ was really the man from Nazareth: a human being with whom other human beings had relationships on the human plane, not least relationships of *pistis*.

Within that theme, the evangelists are concerned to show especially what it is about Jesus that is trustworthy, how people come to trust in him, and what difference trust makes. In the previous chapter we argued that, despite their own high Christologies and rich and complex understanding of Jesus, all the gospels indicate that it is, above all, personal encounter with Jesus that makes trust possible. For the synoptic evangelists in particular, moreover, to put their trust in Jesus, nobody, whether Jewish or gentile, needs to recognize more than that Jesus is, by the standards of their own tradition, a man of God, dedicated to God and empowered by God.[115]

This in itself would mean that trust in Jesus in his earthly life could only ever be inchoate and partial. In addition, the limitations of those who put their trust in Jesus make their trust not only partial but also vulnerable to fear, doubt, and scepticism. Just as nobody fully understands Jesus' identity or work before his resurrection, so nobody has perfect trust in him. For the evangelists, this does not matter: any degree of trust, on any basis, is an adequate starting-point for the relationship. All that God and Jesus need of those who first encounter Jesus in his earthly life is that they have a reason to approach him and/or openness to the encounter. Every encounter with Jesus in trust is life-changing, and trust forms the basis for a relationship which looks forward far beyond the gospel narratives to the eschatological future.

In Chapter 3, we observed that New Testament writings take for granted that the *pistis* of the risen and exalted Christ towards God and humanity is perfect, and affirm that the *pistis* of the faithful towards God and Christ should also be as steady as possible, and, if anything, only grow and develop. The gospel writers offer a somewhat different picture: of the fragility and imperfection of human trust, and, at the same time, of the adequacy of imperfect trust—and even perhaps, on his last night, of the assailability of Jesus' trust in God. In part, this

---

[115] Though the synoptic gospels and John diverge where John insists that those who trust Jesus recognize him as God's son, in a unique relationship with God; in addition, though John seems to indicate that Jews, and perhaps even gentiles, should have been able to recognize this on the basis of their existing religious commitments, the final redactor, at least, suggests that only those pre-elected to trust can do so.

difference is doubtless due to the fact that the evangelists are writing mainly about the relationships between God, Jesus, and humanity during Jesus' earthly life and ministry. We have suggested, though, that the gospels' image of Jesus in his earthly life also offers the faithful a vision of the exalted Christ, who, as Hebrews puts it, is 'the same, yesterday and today and forever' (13.8). In this light, the image of human *pistis* sketched by the gospels offers a strikingly compassionate and encouraging picture of the possibilities for trust for community members in the evangelists' own day and beyond. If Paul, in particular, offers an ideal of *pistis* for the faithful to aspire to, the gospels offer the reassurance that, in the present time, human trust is always likely to be less than ideal. Until the end time, however, there is time, within the divine–human relationship of trust, for trust to develop and strengthen.

Chapter 3 also noted that where, for Paul, the *pistis* of the faithful to Christ is strongly marked by obedience, service, and acceptance of the consequences of one's commitment, in the gospels, those who put their trust in Jesus, especially for healing, sometimes seem to have scope to make demands, and even negotiate with him. This might seem to put the gospels at odds not only with Paul's vision of *pistis*, but also with the argument we made in Chapter 2, that, although God can be relied on to be Godself and to enact God's agenda, God cannot be relied on to do what human beings want or hope. Our discussion of the healing stories, however, suggests that there is less tension between these images of the trust relationship than may appear. People do come to Jesus with their needs, but, we have argued, what Jesus gives is not simply what people (or their friends or relations) think they need, but what they most fundamentally need. People may come, or be brought, to Jesus to be made physically normative—and, as a sign of the Messiah's activity, they may, within the story, be made normative, though with no promise that they will not become disabled or ill in the future, and die. But, vitally, they also receive what they did not ask for, and presumably did not know they needed, but fundamentally need: forgiveness, salvation, and new life.

We saw above that, in comparison with earlier chapters, there is very little *pistis* language in the passion narratives of any of the gospels, though Jesus' own *pistis* towards God is referenced by Mark and Matthew during the crucifixion, and may be implicit in Gethsemane. Nor is there a close connection earlier in the synoptic gospels between *pistis* language and, for instance, the language of ransom (though there is an explicit connection between *pisteuein* and eternal life, both present and future, in John). Where Paul, for instance, in some letters, sees *pistis* at work in the death of Christ and at the heart of the act of atonement, all four gospels, in different ways, focus rather on the life-changing *pistis* between Jesus and those who encounter him during his earthly life and ministry. If Jesus did indeed, as part of his proclamation of the kingdom, call people to trust in God in his lifetime; if his own trust in God was seen early as exemplary and people were remembered as responding to him with trust, the gospels may, in this, preserve some of the earliest strands of tradition in relation to Christian trust. Whether they do or not, they offer listeners an image of Jesus as trusting and trustworthy in earthly life to respond to, and in the process, an image of the exalted Christ, so strongly marked as wholly continuous in his identity with Jesus of Nazareth, to whom to continue to relate.

Extrapolating further from these points, we may see the gospels as developing a model of *pistis* which may be particularly helpful for those whose trust, in themselves and others, has been damaged. Those who encounter Jesus in these stories do not face a demand for trust *ex nihilo*, nor are they asked to believe more about Jesus, or trust in him for more than they are already asking of him (Mt. 9.28).[116] Jesus responds to what they think they need from him, even though this may not, in Jesus' or the gospel writer's view, be what they most fundamentally need. Trust is given an opportunity to grow, and is sometimes shown as growing, from the concrete, immediate, provisional, and partial, into something wider in scope and bigger in implications for the life of the truster and their relationship with Jesus and with God. In this process, failures of trust are represented as practically inevitable, and never as deal-breakers as long as the truster is willing to continue with the relationship. Those who trust are invited, in words which the gospels do not cite but the gospel writers must have known, to taste and see that the Lord is good (Ps. 34.8); to bring their need and desire to Jesus, to experience his response, and to respond in turn as they can.

Since the Reformation, one of the corollaries, in Reformed churches, of the centrality of the idea of justification by faith has been a strong focus on the relationship of the individual with God and Christ. In recent decades, this focus has been challenged by scholars who emphasize the centrality to New Testament writers of apocalyptic, of God's action through Christ as the creation of a (re)new(ed) Israel, and/or of ideas of Christians' corporate identity 'in Christ'. The focus of this chapter and the last has been largely on individual relationships with Jesus in his earthly life, not least because the gospels' paradigmatic stories of how the *pistis* of God and Christ encounters and engenders the *pistis* of human beings are told as encounters between individuals. *Pistis*, whether in response to Jesus or, for instance, to the preaching of apostles, is most often described as an individual attitude and act, but it is worth noting again that this is fully compatible with the corporate aspects of belonging to God's people and kingdom. Just as every citizen or subject of the Roman empire, for instance, knew that they lived under Roman power, as one of many peoples subject to the emperor, and normally that they had become part of the empire as part of a people, not as an individual, yet a great many individuals are attested as expressing a personal relationship with the emperor via acts of cult, private letters, petitions, or complaints, so those who put

---

[116] John's Martha (11.27) responds to Jesus' 'Do you believe this?' (v. 26) with an affirmation of what she already believes, though this belief can be seen as incomplete (p. 226).

their trust in God and Christ enter both a personal relationship with God and Christ and God's household and kingdom, under Christ's authority, as part of the body that belongs to Christ (cf. 1 Cor. 12.27).[117]

Chapter 2 proposed that God acts towards human beings with therapeutic trust, of the kind which one person puts in another when they suspect that the other is not entirely trustworthy, but they hope to foster trustworthiness in the future.[118] Though none of the gospels expresses it in this way, we can see the earthly life and ministry of Jesus, as a whole, as an act of divine therapeutic trust. From the gospel writers' perspective, it would not have taken divine wisdom to foresee that the sending of such an untraditional Messiah to preach repentance, the coming of God's kingdom, and eternal life, and to die for others on a cross, was not, in first-century Israel, the most likely way to compel recognition of Jesus or trust in him. That they understand this as God's action through Jesus points to the importance of the trust relationship to which those who encounter Jesus are called. It is not enough for God (as Zeus, Cybele, or the emperor might do) to compel worship or obedience by an unmistakable self-revelation. In Jesus, God seeks to entrust humanity with the kind of trust relationship in which both parties take a risk, but in which both can hope to develop and contribute to an ongoing and open-ended relationship. God's therapeutic trust implies that God holds human beings capable not only of trust, but also, as we will see in the next chapter, of trustworthiness and of being entrusted with God's trust and all that it implies. Human beings can therefore trust not only God and Christ, but also themselves to be able to respond to the trust of God and Christ. Therapeutic trust has the capacity to foster not only trustworthiness and trust themselves, but also related confidence, aspiration, and hope.

---

[117] On individuals petitioning etc. the emperor see Millar (1992), Hauken (1998), Tuori (2016); on individuals and imperial cult see McGraw (2019), cf. Jim (2017) on private cult offered to Hellenistic rulers. The idea that entering a personal relationship with God and Christ is in tension with e.g. becoming part of the new Israel may reflect in part the modern distinction between the public and private spheres, a distinction which is much weaker in the ancient world (e.g. Veyne (1987), with Nelson (1990), Ando and Rüpke (2015), Russell (2015), 25–42, Tuori and Nissin (2015), Hylen (2020)).

[118] pp. 71–2.

7

'Guard this rich trust'

The Entrustedness of the Faithful

Previous chapters have argued that we can see God as trusting or entrusting Christ with the means by which God's grace is communicated to the world and enacted for the world;[1] Christ as entrusting God with his life and death; and both as entrusting human beings with the opportunity to respond.[2] Human beings are called to put their trust in God and Christ when God is preached as reaching out to them in grace through the death and resurrection of Christ (what we have called soteriological and Christological trust). They are called to trust in the hope that their trust will be vindicated in the future (eschatological trust), even while they recognize that trusting in a new saviour-figure is risky, because compared with existing gods, heroes, and other heavenly powers, he has no record of trustworthiness, or because (especially in modern western cultures) the idea of trusting in a metaphysical saviour is risky in general.[3] We have also begun to see how human beings who put their trust in Jesus Christ are invited to imitate Christ and share his work: for instance by enduring suffering, mediating between God and other human beings, or acting as an example.[4] Imitation, we noted in Chapter 5, is one way in which the faithful develop from trusting in God and Christ to acting for God and Christ.

This chapter develops further the last of these themes by turning to the entrustedness of those who have responded to God's and Christ's act of trust and entered a relationship of trust with them. Compared with *pistis* language in general,

---

[1] The chapter heading quotation is from 2 Tim. 1.14. καλή is difficult to translate in the phrase τ is καλ ḍ παραθήκην: 'good', 'fine', or 'fair' sound too generic; 'noble' and 'precious' have strong secular overtones; 'auspicious' has implications of ritual which are not intended here. 'This rich trust' (NAB) captures both the richness of the teaching which is being referred to and its preciousness to the faithful.

[2] The only explicit reference to Jesus as entrusting himself to human beings occurs at Jn 2.24, where Jesus will not entrust himself to the crowd that has begun to *pisteuein* in his name because he knows them (and presumably that they are untrustworthy). Elsewhere in Greek, the verb most commonly used to mean to (en)trust is *encheirizein*, literally to 'put [something] in [someone's] hands', which does not occur in New Testament writings, so the choice of New Testament writers to use *pisteuein* for entrusting, linking it linguistically with *pistis*, is significant. *Paratithenai* can also mean 'entrust', and so occasionally can *paradidonai* (see e.g. pp. 8, 147 n.26, cf. 155–6 n.66 (*paradidonai*), pp. 45, 295–6, 297–98 (*paratithenai*)), both of which do occur in the New Testament.

[3] pp. 31–2.   [4] E.g. pp. 135–9, 174–5, 190–1.

The New Testament and the Theology of Trust: 'This Rich Trust'. Teresa Morgan, Oxford University Press.
© Teresa Morgan 2022. DOI: 10.1093/oso/9780192859587.003.0007

explicit references to the faithful as entrusted with something are rare in the New Testament, appearing only a handful of times in the Pauline corpus, though where they appear they play a significant part in the writer's understanding, in particular, of ministry and authority.[5] Trustworthiness or faithfulness, expressed especially by the adjective *pistos*, is more common, notably in the Pauline corpus and the synoptic gospels, and in some passages trustworthiness or faithfulness is clearly linked to entrustedness. The Pauline corpus and the synoptic gospels are accordingly the focus of this chapter.[6]

In Chapter 2, we saw that when God trusts human beings, God acts therapeutically, taking a risk on humanity's ability and willingness to respond, and, even if it fails in the short term, to become more trustworthy over time. We also noted that responding to therapeutic trust is also a risk for human beings, because one may fail, but that neither Paul nor any other writer entertains the possibility that God trusts in people beyond their ability to respond eventually. In Chapter 4, we saw that not only being trusted, but being entrusted with certain activities may be part of a process which helps people to become both more trusting and more trustworthy. Being entrusted can therefore be not only a consequence of a trust relationship, but part of the relationship which helps to strengthen it. In this chapter, too, we will see that entrusting and entrustedness are risky, and those who are entrusted do not always prove trustworthy immediately, but that the vision of the Pauline corpus and the gospels is strikingly optimistic. Both those who entrust, and those who are entrusted, can have confidence that ultimately they will be vindicated.

Entrustedness and Trustworthiness in the Pauline Corpus

All but one of the explicit references to someone's being entrusted in the Pauline corpus refer to Paul himself.[7] When Paul describes himself as entrusted, using *pisteuein* in the passive, he is always entrusted with something specific. At

---

[5] Patristic writers pick up the idea of entrustedness and use it relatively often: e.g. 1 Clem. 42–4, Clem., *Paid.* 1.11, *Strom.* 2.6, Or., *Cels.* 4.28. Some recent studies of authority in the Roman Catholic Church have made unusually extensive use of the concept of entrustedness, arguing that lay people should be, and within canon law, could be, entrusted with more roles in mission or ministry than they currently have: e.g. Beaudoin (2001), Wabgou (2005); cf. St-Pierre (2001), 97 (which also (p. 141) points to the possibility of propositional trust, and (p. 155) to the importance of being able to trust oneself, on which see below).

[6] Acts, in line with its interest in the spirit, has more language of the action of the spirit than of entrustedness, but e.g. when Paul takes his final farewell of the Milesians (20.17–38), he tells the community leaders, 'Keep watch over yourselves and over the whole flock of which the holy spirit has appointed you overseers, to shepherd the church of God that he acquired with his own blood' (v. 28). In addition to attesting to the importance of community leaders' caring for their 'flock', this suggests that Paul sees himself as entrusting the community to its local leaders.

[7] At Rom. 3.2 the Jews are entrusted with the oracles of God: p. 43.

1 Thessalonians 2.4 he says of himself, 'as we were judged worthy by God to be entrusted with the gospel (πιστευθῆναι τὸ εὐαγγέλιον), so we speak, not to please men but [to please] God, who judges our hearts'.[8] All the key aspects of entrustedness for Paul are here: it is God, ultimately, who entrusts;[9] it is, above all, the gospel with which Paul is entrusted; and he preaches as one who, first and last, is accountable to God. Galatians 2.7–9 adds a little more to this picture:

> when [those of repute] saw that I had been entrusted with the gospel (πεπίστευμαι τὸ εὐαγγέλιον) to the uncircumcision, just as Peter had with that of the circumcision (for the one who worked in Peter for the apostleship of the circumcision worked also in me for the gentiles) and they recognized the grace given to me, James and Cephas and John, who were regarded as pillars [of the community], gave their right hands in fellowship with me and with Barnabas...

Having been entrusted with the gospel, Paul fulfils his trust with God's help.[10] The gospel is described here as a grace or gift, pre-echoing Romans 1.5, where Paul says that through Christ 'we have received the grace of apostleship, to bring about the obedience of *pistis* among all the gentiles'.[11]

At 1 Corinthians 9.17 Paul describes himself as 'entrusted with a stewardship (οἰκονομίαν πεπίστευμαι)' which he also calls 'a necessity imposed on me' (9.16).[12] What God and Christ have entrusted to him is not something Paul feels he can refuse to accept.[13] This idea fits well with the language of stewardship, service, and belonging to God and Christ which abounds throughout Paul's letters. Earlier in this letter (4.1–2), Paul has already described himself as a servant of Christ and steward of the 'mysteries of God' (4.1), and asserted, 'it is required of stewards

---

[8] The fact that Paul has been judged worthy to be entrusted with the gospel should probably not be heard as implying that he thinks he cannot fail: i.e. this is an instance of God's therapeutic trust.

[9] Though in some passages God entrusts with or through Christ. Paul says the same of other qualities and gifts: e.g. Rom. 1.7, 1 Cor 1.3, 2 Cor. 1.2, Gal. 1.3, Phil. 1.2, 1 Thess. 1.1 (grace and peace); Rom. 5.2, 5.15, cf. 1 Cor. 8.9 (grace); Rom. 5.1 (peace); Rom. 3.22–4, and 2 Cor. 5.21, cf. Rom. 5.1; Gal. 2.17, 2.21; Phil. 1.11 (right-standing or righteousness); Rom. 5.2 (hope).

[10] Christ also works 'in' or 'through' Paul at e.g. 2 Cor. 13.2–5, cf. 4.12, Gal. 2.20. On Paul as the 'reconciled reconciler', working for the salvation of those to whom he preaches see especially Hofius (1980), cf. Schröter (1993). On Paul as mediator more broadly, especially in the Corinthian letters, see Martin (1981), 65–6; cf. Sandnes (1991), 154–71 (Romans), Schütz (1975), 204–48, Ashton (2000), 214–37 (on Paul as shaman), Collins (2014).

[11] Taking χάριν καὶ ἀποστολήν with many, though not all commentators, as implying that Paul received grace and his apostleship at the same time (see the discussion of Jewett (2007), 109–10). Here and at Gal. 1.15–16, Paul's point is that he was called to be an apostle, so there seems no reason for him to mark that he received grace and apostleship at different times, but good reason for him to mark his apostleship as a grace.

[12] 9.17 is notoriously difficult to interpret but the relevant point here is that Paul is emphasizing both that he is under obedience to God and Christ (cf. vv. 14, 16) and that he finds satisfaction in doing what is expected of him.

[13] Though some of the language linked to this claim is specific to the rhetoric of this chapter: there is no hint elsewhere that he accepts the trust unwillingly (v. 17). 9.14 probably refers to Christ, in line with Paul's usage of 'the Lord' elsewhere, but the reference to temple services at v. 13 and the echo of 4.1 at 9.17 invite listeners to hear Paul as referring to entrustedness by God too.

that they be found trustworthy (*pistos*)' (4.2). *Pistos*, as we have seen, most often means 'trustworthy' or 'faithful' in Greek in general, and all Christians, including Paul, must always be faithful (as the name *hoi pistoi* affirms they are, or seek to be). Paul, however, is talking about himself here as more than a faithful Christian: he is an apostle who acts for the benefit of the 'brothers' (4.6). As an apostle he is fulfilling a particular role, in which he needs to be not only faithful but effective: worthy of trust. A steward (typically a slave) is trustworthy when he fulfils duties, in Paul's language elsewhere, given to him, imposed on him, or entrusted to him, so it is no stretch to hear Paul's trustworthiness here as a correlate of his entrustedness. At 7.25 Paul offers some advice to virgins and widows, which, he admits, does not come from the Lord, but which he offers 'as one who by the Lord's mercy is *pistos*'. Here again, Paul is *pistos* not simply as a community member but as an apostle, and this is the basis on which he gives his opinion, so we can hear him as affirming not only that he is faithful but that he has been entrusted as trustworthy. Being trustworthy, in these passages, has a significant corollary: it implies that the rest of the faithful can trust not only God and Christ, but Paul himself, insofar as he is fulfilling the stewardship with which God and Christ have entrusted him. Entrustedness therefore begins to define not only the relationship between God, Christ, and the faithful, but also relationships of responsibility and authority within the earthly community.

We may wonder, in connection with these passages, at what point in his existence Paul understands himself as having been judged worthy to be entrusted with the gospel. The only clue is offered by Galatians 1.15–16: God set Paul apart 'from my mother's womb' and called him through God's grace.[14] If we take it that Paul thinks of himself as having been marked, if not specifically called, as a future prophet before or at his birth (cf. Isa. 49.1, Jer. 1.50), and that he would, in principle, have been free to reject his calling (as prophets very occasionally do), then God's setting him apart may be an instance of therapeutic trust.[15] We can add that if Paul intends the comparison with the scriptural prophets to be taken seriously (and there is no reason to think otherwise), he understands the ministry with which he has been entrusted not only as one of preaching, but as prophetic: more particularly, in his context, as eschatological. Paul has been entrusted not only with calling people (especially gentiles) to put their trust in God and Christ, but doing so with urgency, in light of the imminent *parousia*.[16]

---

[14] Paul's language of calling probably does not imply pre-election, but emphasizes that the gentiles are wanted by God and Christ: Morgan (2020), 183–8.

[15] 1 Tim. 1.12 and 2 Tim. 1.12 both affirm that Christ considers Paul trustworthy and appoints him to his ministry, and imply that this happens at or after his call to trust in Christ, hinting that they step back from Paul's implicit self-identification as a prophet called before birth.

[16] A small number of passages use *paratithenai*, to 'give in charge', in a way which is closely reminiscent of entrusting. Paul's entrustedness with his calling is linked by 2 Timothy to Paul's own trust in 'our saviour Christ Jesus' (1.10): Paul is suffering, 'but I am not ashamed, for I know him whom I have trusted, and am confident that he is able to guard what has been given into my charge (οἶδα γὰρ ᾧ πεπίστευκα, καὶ πέπεισμαι ὅτι δυνατός ἐστιν τὴν παραθήκην μου φυλάξαι)' until the day (1.12). At

Paul uses *pistis* language, or images of his relationship with God, in a handful of other passages in ways which point to the idea that he not only trusts but is entrusted. When, for example, he describes himself and Apollos, at 1 Corinthians 3.9, as God's co-workers, he implies that God trusts him to share in God's work, creating the field or the building that is the community of the faithful (3.9). At 2 Corinthians 4.13-14 Paul says of himself, 'Since, then, we have the same spirit of *pistis*, according to what is written, "I trusted, therefore I spoke",[17] we too trust and therefore speak, knowing that the one who raised the Lord Jesus will raise us also with Jesus...'. The 'spirit of trust' here could, in principle, be 'the gift of the spirit that follows trust'. Not everyone who trusts in God and Christ, however, can speak as Paul does, and the idea that he speaks simply because he trusted does less than justice to the theme of this section of the letter as a whole, in which Paul is justifying his ministry and emphasizing that everything he does is for the benefit of the Corinthians (cf. 4.15). The idea that Paul's speech arises simply from his trust is therefore insufficiently specific, and the word 'same' points in a different direction. Paul's 'spirit of *pistis*' cannot be the same as that of the Corinthians, since not all the Corinthians are called to preach, and that he and the Corinthians are the same is not the point he is making in this passage. Paul must be suggesting that he has the same 'spirit of *pistis*' as the singer of the psalm, which leads him to speak.[18] It makes good sense to hear this as tantamount to entrustedness with the spiritual gift of speaking: in Paul's terms, with preaching. Later in the same letter, Paul hopes that, as the *pistis* of the Corinthians increases, 'our influence among you may be greatly augmented' (10.15). The *pistis* of the Corinthians here must be primarily their trust in God and Christ, but Paul implies that their greater trust in God and Christ will lead to the increase of his influence; the connection must be that the more the Corinthians grow in trust, the more they will recognize Paul as trustworthy as one who has been entrusted with his apostleship by God.

Though preaching the gospel is the heart of his calling, there are signs that Paul sees himself and his co-workers as entrusted with more than preaching.[19] In a few passages, as we have seen, he encourages the faithful to imitate his actions as he imitates Christ (cf. 1 Cor. 11.1), not least by enduring the suffering that faithfulness can bring.[20] He refers to himself as founding and building communities (e.g. 1 Cor. 3.5-9), and he continues to oversee his communities when he is not with them, writing letters and sending his co-workers to act as his proxies, to 'remind

---

1 Peter 4.19, 'those who suffer in accordance with God's will hand their souls over to a faithful creator as they do good (οἱ πάσχοντες κατὰ τὸ θέλημα τοῦ θεοῦ πιστῷ κτίστῃ παρατιθέσθωσαν τὰς ψυχὰς αὐτῶν ἐν ἀγαθοποιΐᾳ)'; these passages assume that being effectively entrusted depends on the trust of the one entrusted in the one who entrusts.

[17] Ps. 115.1 LXX.

[18] So e.g. Thrall (1994), *ad loc*. The psalmist is thanking God for helping him in need, but Paul repurposes the phrase to mean that his preaching is based on his trust.

[19] Though perhaps less than some parables point to: pp. 291-4.

[20] E.g. pp. 115, 175-7, 243.

you of my ways in Christ Jesus' (1 Cor. 4.17) and to report to him on their activities (e.g. 1 Thess. 3.1–8). This suggests that he understands himself, like a trustworthy steward, as entrusted not only with specific tasks, but with a degree of discretion in how he shapes and supports the communities of the faithful. In this, however, Paul is never unaware—and never unaware of the value of affirming to his communities—that he never has a completely free hand. As he says to the Corinthians (2 Cor. 10.15), he hopes that his influence among them may be greatly enlarged 'in accordance with our schedule', or literally, 'according to our rule [that is, God's rule for Paul]'.[21] Entrustedness always acts within guidelines determined by God and Christ.

Paul and his followers several times describe Paul's co-workers as *pistos*, not only to God and to Christ but to Paul himself. At 1 Corinthians 4.17, Timothy is 'my beloved and *pistos* son in the Lord'. Timothy is not only faithful to Paul; he must also be worthy of trust, because Paul is sending him to remind the Corinthians of Paul's own 'ways in Christ Jesus' (4.17), and this suggests that, as God entrusts Paul with his ministry, so Paul entrusts Timothy with his. Similarly the writer of Ephesians, in Paul's voice, tells the Ephesians that, 'So you may know how things are with me and what I am doing, Tychicus, my beloved brother and *pistos* minister in the Lord, will tell you everything. I am sending him to you for this very purpose...' (6.21–2).[22] Tychicus is trustworthy as a minister both to Christ and to Paul, who entrusts him with news for the community. I have called the trust that is transmitted from God, through Christ, to apostles, and from apostles to community leaders and community members who offer it back to God and Christ, a 'cascade' of trust.[23] We can equally call it a cascade of entrusting and trustworthiness, which not only connects God, Christ, and the faithful in, as Ephesians puts it, 'one [relationship of] trust' (4.5), but articulates their relationships in terms of the authority to entrust and the responsibility of being entrusted.[24]

Within churches, community members have different gifts with which they exercise aspects of leadership, and at 1 Corinthians 12.9 one of these is said to be

---

[21] '[I]n accordance with our schedule' transl. Thrall (2000), *ad loc*.

[22] Also Col. 1.7, 4.7–9; cf. Phil. 2.25–30, though without *pistis* language. At 1 Peter 5.12, the writer, in Peter's voice (possibly influenced by Paul's letters) says that 'I write you this briefly through Silvanus, whom I consider a *pistos* brother...'.

[23] Morgan (2015a), 217–18.

[24] *Pistis* language is therefore invoked to describe the emerging organization and authority structure of churches, because some people are entrusted with leadership and others are not, but this theme does not dominate the use of *pistis* language in these texts, where there is more emphasis on the *pistis* that all Christians have in common and what everyone can contribute to the community. In all but the latest New Testament writings, moreover, everyone trusts in God in the same way: for Paul, for instance, men and women, or those with different gifts, may play different roles in a church, but there is no difference in the way they are described as practising trust. In some later writings this begins to change, such that men and women, free people and slaves, are exhorted to enact their *pistis* towards God and Christ in different ways: e.g. slaves by obeying their masters, and women by obeying their husbands (Morgan (2015a), 316–17, 320–1).

pistis. At Galatians 5.22, *pistis* is fruit of the spirit, and, in that passage, the fruit of the spirit seems to encompass qualities and practices (such as love, joy, peace, and generosity) which all the faithful can and should have and enact. In that context, *pistis* is not likely to be righteousing trust in God and Christ, which Paul can assume community members already have, but it could be persistent faithfulness or the trustworthiness which would enable the faithful to undertake any role they might be given. At 1 Corinthians 12, the gifts of the spirit (such as wisdom, healing, and prophecy) are qualities and practices which are not common to all community members, but are given to some for the benefit of all (12.7). In this context, *pistis* again cannot be righteousing trust in God and Christ, which Paul can assume all community members have. It cannot be persistent faithfulness, which should also be the property of all the faithful. It could be the trustworthiness which would enable a community member to undertake a particular role. Alternatively it could, with the other terms in the list, refer to a specific gift, and, given that Paul speaks of himself, as an apostle and preacher, as entrusted with the gospel, a likely candidate is the 'trust' of apostleship or preaching.[25] This interpretation also makes good sense given that we might expect apostleship to appear in this list alongside prophecy, mighty deeds, and the rest, but, unless *pistis* refers to it, it does not. If this is right, then *pistis* here bears the same meaning as at 2 Corinthians 4.13: it is the spiritual gift with which apostles are entrusted, which inspires them to preach.[26]

At Romans 12.3, Paul makes the unusual statement, 'I tell everyone among you not to think of himself more highly than one ought to think, but to think soberly, each according to the measure of *pistis* ($\mu\acute{\epsilon}\tau\rho o\nu$ $\pi\acute{\iota}\sigma\tau\epsilon\omega s$) that God has apportioned.' The phrase $\mu\acute{\epsilon}\tau\rho o\nu$ $\pi\acute{\iota}\sigma\tau\epsilon\omega s$ has occasioned a great deal of debate, and I have suggested that it refers to 'different quantities of *pistis* [in the sense of trust or faithfulness] which God has apportioned...to different people as a gift or grace (12.6) and which allow them to exercise different ministries (12.6–8)'.[27] Though many commentators have accepted the idea that Paul thinks it is appropriate for the faithful to have different quantities of trust and faithful, I am less comfortable with the idea now than I was in *Roman Faith*. Such an idea appears nowhere else in Paul's letters, and C. E. B. Cranfield is surely right when he objects that it would open the door to Christians of greater *pistis* looking down on those of less.[28] But Paul could be referring here to the different degrees to which community members are entrusted: some with heavier responsibilities, such as apostleship, and

---

[25] If so, we have noted that Paul describes his apostleship in prophetic terms, but here (12.10) prophecy is a distinct gift, which presumably can be received by those who are not apostles (cf. ch. 14, *passim*). Brown (1997), 581 suggests that *pistis* at 1.29 is 'a faith especially effective in sustaining others', but there is no explicit parallel for this elsewhere; Fitzmyer (2008), *ad loc.* suggests that it is the power to move mountains, but the other gifts of the spirit in this list are more everyday qualities, suggesting that *pistis* should be, too.

[26] Cf. pp. 27–8. [27] Morgan (2015a), 298.
[28] Cranfield (1962), 345–6.

others with lighter. This reading (which would yield the translation '...think soberly, each according to the measure of entrustedness that God has apportioned') fits with Paul's language of entrustedness elsewhere, without suggesting that this means that, for instance, those entrusted with apostleship can look down on the *pistis* of others.[29] This reading would also fit well with the image of the body that follows: those who are entrusted with particular responsibilities each form just one part of a body which lives as a whole under Christ's authority.[30]

Not only individuals, but groups can be entrusted with something. At Romans 3.2, Paul affirms that Israel was entrusted with the *logia* of God.[31] This raises the question whether, for Paul, Christians are entrusted with anything as a group. One of their names, *hoi pistoi*, in itself suggests that they can be: as we have noted, *pistos* can mean either faithful or trustworthy, and those who are asked to be trustworthy have often been entrusted with something.[32] A handful of other references point in the same direction.

At 2 Corinthians 13.5, Paul exhorts the Corinthians, 'Test yourselves to see whether you are in *pistis* (ἐν τῇ πίστει); examine yourselves. Do you not realize that Jesus Christ is in [or 'among'] you?—unless, of course, you are unsatisfactory.' Ἐν τῇ πίστει is a slightly unusual phrase in Paul; it could refer to being in a state of trust, or to being in the relationship or the bond of trust with God and Christ.[33] When Paul refers to Christ as 'in' the faithful, it is always to a purpose—Christ is working in and through them—so it sounds as though Paul is warning the Corinthians here to examine whether they are sufficiently firmly in (the bond of) trust to enable Christ to work through them.[34] If so, then another way of expressing this would be to say that the Corinthians have been entrusted with Christ and Christ's work and must ensure that they are worthy of the trust. Paul does not specify whether the Corinthians have been entrusted with Christ as individuals or as a group, but elsewhere he both speaks of Christ as in him individually and uses ἐν ὑμῖν to mean 'in' or 'among you' as a group (e.g. 1 Cor. 3.16, 6.19, cf. 2 Cor. 13.3, Phil. 2.13), so both could be intended here.

---

[29] Benjamin Schliesser notes in conversation that a number of patristic authors interpret this verse in terms of human entrustedness. Käsemann (1980), 333–4 notes the 'anti-enthusiastic thrust' of this passage, which recognizes that ecstasy and miracles are possible signs of the spirit, but are ambivalent since they can also be produced by demons; they are only validated when they are used in the faithful service of Christ and the community.

[30] On the meaning of 'in Christ' here see Morgan (2020), 86–7. At 3 Jn 5, the beloved are said to be faithful in all they do for the brothers, and especially for strangers. They are urged to help strangers 'in a way worthy of God', suggesting that they have been entrusted by God with acting on God's behalf.

[31] p. 43.

[32] On Jesus' messianic mission, in the synoptic gospels, as deliberately involving his followers as participants in his mission and so as entrusting them *qua* those who trust, see e.g. Henderson (2009). On the responsibilities which follow the trust between master and disciples in the gospels (though without a discussion of trust language) see Daube (1972).

[33] The 'relationship' or 'bond of trust' is also a likely meaning of *pistis* at Gal. 1.23, 1 Tim. 1.2, 4.1, 5.8.

[34] Cf. 2 Cor. 4.10, 13.2–5, Gal. 2.20.

Though apostles are particularly entrusted with the preaching, and hence with the content of the gospel, Paul never says that those who are not apostles cannot preach, teach, or spread the gospel by example. In other writings, the example of those who spread the news of their healing, or of Stephen who speaks to the Jerusalem crowd, suggests that Christians other than the twelve or the apostles can also be entrusted with spreading the good news. At 2 Corinthians 3.2, Paul describes the Corinthians as his letter, 'known and read by everyone', suggesting that their lives promulgate his teaching, and perhaps also his example. In 1 Thessalonians, Paul talks about the churches of Judaea acting as an example for the Thessalonians (2.14), and of the Thessalonians acting as an example for all the faithful in Macedonia and Achaea (1.7).[35] Paul's immediate point is that churches, by their reception of the word and the holy spirit (1.6) and their endurance of suffering (2.14), fortify each other, but he follows this point in chapter 1 by saying, 'For from you the word of the Lord has sounded forth not only in Macedonia and Achaea, but in every place your trust in God has gone forth, so that we have no need to say anything' (1.8). What Paul characteristically needs to articulate is the preaching that brings people to trust in God and Christ for the first time, and 'not only in Macedonia and Achaea, but in every place' hints that the word has 'sounded forth' from Thessalonians beyond even the surrounding churches, so this verse may suggest that the Thessalonians, by their trust, are also effectively preaching to non-Christians. If so, then they can be seen as entrusted with the gospel in their own right, as a group.

The idea that Christians can be entrusted as a group also emerges in the Pastoral letters, which several times use the phrase, 'the saying is trustworthy (πιστὸς ὁ λόγος)' (1 Tim. 1.15, 3.1, 4.9, 2 Tim. 2.11, Tit. 3.8).[36] The sayings in question are a mixed bag of affirmations (including that Jesus Christ is saviour (1 Tim. 1.15), that the faithful die and live with him (2 Tim. 2.11), and that God's grace righteouses 'us' (Tit. 3.8)), together with advice about how the faithful should live (1 Tim. 4.9) and instructions about church order (1 Tim. 3.1). Some *logoi* may be quotations from written or oral sources of teaching that are lost to us (e.g. 1 Tim. 1.15). Some echo phrases from the scriptures or from Paul, or similar phrases in the synoptic gospels (1 Tim. 1.15, 2 Tim. 2.11, 3.14, Tit. 3.8), while one looks like an adaptation of a gentile aphorism (1 Tim. 4.8).[37] 2 Timothy 3.14 implies in addition that the scriptures are trustworthy, especially if interpreted in

---

[35] At Rom. 1.12, Paul looks forward to himself and the Romans' being encouraged by each other's *pistis* when they meet.

[36] The writer of Jude 3 encourages his audience to contend for 'the *pistis* that was once for all handed down to the holy ones (τῇ ἅπαξ παραδοθείσῃ τοῖς ἁγίοις πίστει)'. We do not learn whether 'the *pistis*' is the relationship of trust between God, Christ, and the faithful itself, or the written or oral tradition about it, but either way, it is something which has been entrusted to the faithful and which they must work to preserve (cf. v. 4).

[37] 4.8 invokes the *topos* of the relative value of physical *vs* intellectual activity (here recast as *eusebeia*): cf. Arist., *Pol.* 1339a-b, Isoc., *Antidosis* 181-2, Dio Chrys., *Or.* 7.11, Juv. 10.356, D. L. 137; see

such a way as to give the faithful 'wisdom for salvation through trust in Jesus Christ' (3.15). Whatever their origin, however, the affirmation that these teachings are trustworthy suggests that, just as the *logia* of God are entrusted to Israel, so these *logoi* are entrusted to the faithful as a group.[38]

In Paul's letters and those of his followers, God, sometimes explicitly with or through Christ, entrusts human beings with a wide range of activities. People—both individuals and the faithful as a group—are always entrusted with something specific (such as a gift, a ministry, or a teaching) for a specific purpose and for the common good of the faithful and potentially faithful. Being entrusted is a gift and an obligation, and is strongly eschatological in focus. Those who are entrusted with a particular ministry are ideally trustworthy (though we may note what Paul glosses over, that they might, like many of Jesus' followers whom we discussed in the last chapter, sometimes fail in their trust), and are always accountable primarily to God. In New Testament writings, *pistis* is rarely, arguably never, a human-to-human attitude and practice; unlike love, for example, which human beings are widely encouraged to practise towards one another, it is an aspect above all of the divine–human relationship. When human beings are invited to find another human being trustworthy, it is insofar as that person has been entrusted by God and is trustworthy towards God.[39]

Entrustedness in the Synoptic Gospels and Acts

If, in Paul's letters, God's actions through Christ can be seen as an act of trust and entrusting, some of Jesus' parables in the synoptic gospels also point to the trust that is placed in humanity to respond to the coming near of God's kingdom and Jesus' preaching about it. Mark's parable about the growing of the seed sown by a farmer says,

> the kingdom of God is as if a man should scatter seed upon the earth, and should sleep and rise night and day, and the seed should sprout and grow, he does not know how. The earth bears fruit of itself, first the blade, then the ear, then the full grain in the ear. But when the grain is ripe, he immediately applies the sickle, because the harvest has come. (Mk 4.26–9)

---

the discussion of Young (2005), and, more broadly, Onians (1954), Ostenfeld (2018) on contemporary understandings of the relationship between mind and body.

[38] In Paul's undisputed letters, *pistis* is always between persons (though e.g. to trust a person may, in practice, involve trusting their words). Trust explicitly in words, discourses, or traditions is a later development, though Rom. 6.17 (using *paradidonai*) anticipates it.

[39] Cf. pp. 316–18.

This parable, unusually, emphasizes the limits of the farmer's control: he can sow the seed, but he is implicitly entrusting it to the earth which 'bears fruit of itself'.[40] The image of people as the earth into which something is sown is familiar to Mark's listeners from the preceding parable of the sower (4.1-9, 14-20), and perhaps also from other contexts: it is, for instance, a common image for the processes of elementary education or moral formation. As one early imperial educationalist, says, 'nature without learning is blind, learning without nature is imperfect, and practice without both is pointless. As in farming, first the land must be fertile, then the sower knowledgeable, then the seed sound, so [the] nature [of the child] is like the land, the teacher is like the farmer, and his precepts and instructions are like the seed...'.[41] The teacher must entrust his teaching to the child and hope that the ground is fertile.

The idea that Jesus' followers, especially the twelve and, in Luke, the seventy-two, are entrusted by him with their own mission and ministry begins implicitly, in the synoptic gospels, in Jesus' lifetime. When Jesus appoints twelve disciples and sends them out to preach, heal, and cast out demons as he has been doing, we can hear him as entrusting them with a share in his ministry (Mt. 10.1=Mk 3.13-15=Lk. 6.13, 9.1, cf. Lk. 10.1-9). When, moreover, Jesus tells the disciples that 'whoever receives you receives me, and whoever receives me receives the one who sent me' (Mt. 10.40-2, cf. Mk 9.41, Lk. 10.16), he identifies the disciples as his representatives and intermediaries, and implies that—like other kinds of representatives and intermediaries from legal mediators to inter-state ambassadors—they are entrusted with the authority and responsibility of speaking and acting for him.[42] But it is in Jesus' parables of the end time, which point to how the faithful should behave between the resurrection and the coming of the Son of Man, that we find explicit language of trustworthiness with the implication of entrustedness. Since Jesus identifies himself elsewhere in the gospels as Son of Man, the trustworthiness of the faithful in these stories is apparently to him rather than directly to God.

In Matthew 24.45-51 and Luke 12.41-8, Jesus' followers should be like 'the trustworthy and prudent slave (ὁ πιστὸς δοῦλος καὶ φρόνιμος)' whom his master has set over the household to feed and take care of his fellow slaves (cf. Mt. 24.49=Lk. 12.45). *Pistos* is usually translated 'faithful', and no doubt the good slave is faithful in general, but here he has been given a specific role and task, so 'trustworthy' is a better translation. The description of the slave as trustworthy

---

[40] The limits of the farmer's control are marked more clearly here than they are, for instance, in the parables of the sower and the wheat and the tares. In the explanation of the parable of the sower, the seed is the word (4.14), so listeners to Mark probably understand the seed the same way here, though at Mt. 13.30 the grown seed is those who have responded to the word.
[41] Ps.-Plu., *De lib. educ.* 2b, cf. Cic., *Leg.* 1.46, Sen., *Ep.* 34.1-2, Quint., *Inst.* 2.19.1-3, 10.3.2.
[42] Cf. the convention in both Near Eastern and Mediterranean culture that 'the one sent by a man is as a man himself' (Rengstorf (1964), 415). At Lk. 9.54 Jesus makes clear that the disciples, like any representatives, must not abuse the power that has been entrusted to them.

suggests that he is not simply given, but entrusted with his role.[43] On one level, the duty with which the slave has been entrusted is complex, being, first and foremost, to the master, but also to the household itself and other household members. On another level, it is simple, since the same actions will serve all three. If the servant is trustworthy in executing his trust, he will be praised; if he does not, he will be punished on the master's return.

The parable of the talents (Mt. 25.14-30=Lk. 19.11-27) explores entrustedness and trustworthiness in the present time a little further. A man embarking on a journey leaves three slaves in charge, respectively, of five talents, two, and one. When he returns, one has turned his five talents into ten and one his two into four, and each is commended as a 'good and trustworthy slave' (vv. 20, 22).[44] Since they were *pistos* in small matters, both will be given greater responsibilities (vv. 21, 23). The slave with one talent, however, was afraid of his master, whom he knows as a hard man (v. 24). He thought the least risky prospect was to bury his talent, and now he returns it undiminished. The man is furious, calling the slave 'wicked and lazy' (v. 25). He takes away his talent and orders that he be thrown out (v. 30). The master does not call this slave *apistos*, perhaps because, on one level, he clearly has been both faithful and trustworthy—he has not embezzled or thrown away his talent—though he has not acted according to his master's standards. This story, like the last, suggests that the faithful must both remain faithful, in general, and must be trustworthy in fulfilling specific responsibilities with which they are entrusted. It further implies that the faithful must be faithful not only in attitude but in action, according to the trust placed in them, and that they must not only care for what is entrusted to them, but grow it too.

Like other parables of the coming of the Son of Man, which affirm that it will bring universal final judgment, this story takes a hard line: those who do not measure up to what their master has asked of them will be cast out (cf. Mt. 24.50-1, 25.10). The story also hints at what we have seen before, that the greatest risk in trusting God or Christ may be the truster's own lack of understanding, or weakness, which means that they fail in trust or trustworthiness despite their best intentions. Though the fate of the slave fits the point of the parable in its immediate context, however, it is also significant that many modern readers of this story feel he has been hard done by. Perhaps, we think, he did not know what to do for the best. Perhaps he did know but was afraid to do it, or did not trust himself to succeed. Being entrusted with something is demanding, and many fail in one way

---

[43] At 12.48 Jesus concludes that 'much will be required of the person to whom much has been given'. The related saying at 16.11, 'If you are not trustworthy with dishonest wealth, who will entrust (*pisteuein*) you with true wealth?' suggests that being given and being entrusted are closely related here, as sometimes in Paul.

[44] As in the previous parable, 'trustworthy' is a better translation of *pistos* than 'faithful', because the issue is not simply whether the slaves are, in general, faithful, but whether they have been trustworthy in executing a particular task they have been given.

or another. As we have seen, in fact, the gospels often recognize and accept this idea. Ideally those who put their trust in God and Christ will not waver or fail—but probably they will, and, outside this parable, if their desire to trust and/or to be trustworthy persists, the relationship need not be broken.[45]

Luke 16.10–12 returns to the theme that those who prove trustworthy in a little will be trusted with more, in a saying appended to his parable of the unjust steward. This end-time parable contains no *pistis* language, but Luke follows it with,

> He who is trustworthy (*pistos*) in a very little is trustworthy also in much; and he who is dishonest [or 'unjust'] in a very little is dishonest in much. If then you have not been trustworthy in the unrighteous mammon, who will entrust (*pisteusei*) to you the true wealth? And if you have not been trustworthy with that which belongs to another, who will give you that which is yours?

This is one of several sayings appended to this parable, which are usually seen as only loosely connected with the parable or with each other.[46] Leaving aside its role in context, however, in itself this saying is reasonably clear and adds a little more to the theme of the parable of the talents. In the first place, it is explicit that the faithful are entrusted, until the end time, with the things of this world, and specifically with care for them. The faithful are to hold a double attitude towards these things. On the one hand, they are 'unrighteous mammon', not the 'true wealth' which God will ultimately give them. On the other hand, in the present time the faithful have been given 'unrighteous mammon' to look after, so it is precious, even if only for now. But the faithful must look after the things of this world in a strictly faithful and eschatological spirit, always serving God (cf. 16.13) and looking forward to the time when they will be called by God to account. At that time, they will be given what is God's, to be theirs (16.12): as Paul or John might have said, they will no longer be slaves, but friends or heirs.[47]

It is notable that, among parables of the end time, *pistis* language occurs distinctively in, or appended to those which are set within households.[48] The parable of the tenants in the vineyard, for instance (Mt. 21.33–46=Mk 12.1–12=Lk. 20.9–19), in which the tenants have a lease on the vineyard, involves no *pistis* language.[49] It is perfectly possible to conceive of one person as entrusting another

---

[45] Cf. pp. 258–61.
[46] This verse may be a Jewish proverb (so Bovon (2001–12), *ad loc.*; Wettstein et al. (1996–), 2.764–5 gives parallels.
[47] Cf. Jn 15.15, Gal. 4.7.
[48] Not all parables set in households include *pistis* language (e.g. Mt. 25.1–13, cf. Mk 13.33–7, Lk. 12.32–8 do not). The relationship of master and slave is not contractual because the master owns the slave.
[49] In the gospel of Thomas' version of this parable (21.1–4) the similitude has been interpreted as concerning an owner and his servants, not his tenants, and as beginning, 'They [the disciples] are like servants who have been entrusted with a field...' (Plisch (1999), 524). Gathercole (2014), 303–4,

with a contract such as a lease (for instance, in an act of therapeutic trust), but *pistis* is associated, in these stories, with non-contractual domestic relationships.

To this developing picture of entrustedness another Lukan parable (10.29–37) can be seen as adding (though without explicit *pistis* language) a little more. When the good Samaritan has given first aid to the robbery victim, he takes him to an inn and cares for him for the rest of the day. The next day, he gives the innkeeper two silver coins with the instruction, 'Take care of him. If you spend more than what I have given you, I will repay you on my way back' (10.35). The Samaritan entrusts both the injured man and his own funds to the innkeeper, trusting him to prove trustworthy. He also invites the innkeeper to trust him when he says that he will return on his way back, and pay any extra money the innkeeper has spent.

The Good Samaritan is not an end-time parable, but is told as a response to the lawyer who asks Jesus who the neighbour is whom the law tells him he must love (10.25–9). Commentators since the early church have read it as a parable of grace and salvation, a reading which fits well with our reading of the role of trust in salvation.[50] The Samaritan, like God or Christ, comes to the man who is injured and suffering and, through the agency of the innkeeper, saves him. The Samaritan trusts the injured man to respond to his help and trusts the innkeeper to help him help the man. We do not hear the end of the story, but since Jesus tells the parable to illustrate good neighbourliness, and the Samaritan's turning the man over to an innkeeper who let him die would surely mean that his neighbourliness failed, we assume that the innkeeper does trust the Samaritan and cooperates with him, and the man is saved. Since, however, the story is told explicitly to answer the question 'Who is my neighbour?', we can also hear it as speaking to the faithful in the present time. The Samaritan has been entrusted with the means to help the robbery victim, and he does. In the process, he entrusts the man to the innkeeper, enrolling his trust and his help. Here, as in Paul's letters, we can see the development of a cascade of entrusting, which spills over from those who trust in God and are entrusted with God's work in the world, to those with whom they come into contact and whom they trust and entrust in turn.

Elsewhere in Greek, as we have noted, *encheirizein* and *paratithenai* are as common or more common than *pisteuein* in the meaning 'entrust'. *Encheirizein* does not occur in New Testament writings, but *paratithenai* and its cognates occur several times, and in some of these passages can be read as involving entrusting.[51] At 1 Timothy 1.18, [Paul] tells Timothy, 'I entrust this charge [of

---

however, argues that a better translation is, 'They are like children who are sojourning in a field which does not belong to them.'

[50] See also modern readings by Mansfield (1849), Carroll (2003), and Clark (2014), who draws on care ethics to read the God who offers grace in this parable as a God of care.

[51] Elsewhere *paratithenai* means 'to set before' (e.g. Mt. 13.24, 31) or 'provide' (e.g. Mk 6.41, 8.6, Acts 16.34).

ministry] to you (Ταύτην τὴν παραγγελίαν παρατίθεμαί σοι), my child, in accordance with the prophetic words once spoken about you.'[52] 2 Tim. 1.14 urges Timothy to, 'Guard this rich trust (τὴν καλὴν παραθήκην φύλαξον) [the words which Timothy has heard from Paul] with the help of the holy spirit which lives within us'. At 2 Timothy 2.2 [Paul] says, 'what you heard from me through many witnesses, entrust to faithful people (παράθου πιστοῖς ἀνθρώποις) who will be able to teach others too'. The author of 1 Peter describes how 'those who suffer in accordance with God's will entrust their souls to a faithful creator (πιστῷ κτίστῃ παρατιθέσθωσαν τὰς ψυχάς) as they do good', 4.19). At Acts 14.23, newly appointed presbyters in various churches are entrusted to the Lord in whom they have put their trust (παρέθεντο αὐτοὺς τῷ κυρίῳ εἰς ὃν πεπιστεύκεισαν), and at 20.32 Paul, making his final farewell to the Ephesian elders at Miletus, entrusts them to God (παρατίθεμαι ὑμᾶς τῷ θεῷ). All these passages fit well with uses of *pistis* language in the sense of entrusting which we have already discussed. 1 and 2 Timothy refer to the cascade of entrustedness which descends from God and Christ through the apostles to their communities. In the two passages of Acts, those who are entrusted with the responsibility of overseeing communities entrust them to God. 1 Peter attests that to put one's trust in God is also to entrust oneself to God, not only as an act of identification with Christ and in hope of future salvation (cf. 4.13–14, 17–18), but because to entrust oneself to God is to be in one's right relationship with the creator as his creation.

To this point, the entrustedness of the faithful has emerged as a more significant theme than commentators have recognized, especially in the synoptic gospels and the Pauline corpus, even if it is sometimes expressed indirectly or imagistically. Those who are entrusted are entrusted by God, with or through Christ, with a specific 'trust', a message, activity, or mission. Israel is entrusted with the scriptures; Christians with the scriptures as interpreted to refer to Christ, and with their own, evolving traditions. Paul is entrusted with the gospel and his ministry, which includes the overseeing of communities and giving of advice: what, in general terms, we might call care of the faithful. All the apostles are entrusted with taking up Jesus' ministry (preaching, healing, and exorcizing); with leadership; with care for God's 'household' and its members, with growing what belongs to God in this world, in preparation for the end time; and with mediating, like Jesus himself, between God and humanity. All the faithful are entrusted with being faithful, and with being models for one another. Those who are entrusted are, by that token, trustworthy and can entrust others, and so a network of trust and entrustedness grows and spreads.

---

[52] Fiore (2007), *ad* 1.18 notes the 'loose ecclesiastical structure akin to that of Acts' here: Timothy is given the task of service to the gospel (cf. 2 Tim. 4.5) and he 'entrusts duties to others' (5.22, cf. Acts 6.6, 14.23).

God's trust is sometimes explicitly a grace or gift which seeks a voluntary response. The entrusted, both as individuals and as a group, are also entrusted with a variety of gifts, as Paul puts it, which, first and foremost, serve God and God's action in the world, but which also serve the body of those who put their trust in God and Christ in their common life. To be entrusted by God for something is always to be looking ahead in hope to the end time, but those who are entrusted and the gifts with which they are entrusted also play an important role in the present. The faithful are entrusted with things of this world not least to care for them now.

The images in which these ideas are expressed root them in everyday experience and add weight to them. The faithful are like the earth, which must take the seed entrusted to it and help to produce a harvest. They are stewards, who serve God but also hold responsible positions in God's household, looking after the material environment of the household and their fellow slaves. They are children or co-workers with their master, underlining that they are loved as well as entrusted, and always entrusted to a purpose. They trust others, as sons, siblings, fellow-slaves, or co-workers, to share their work. If they prove trustworthy, the faithful may be entrusted with more and greater work, helping to grow the kingdom in which they eventually hope to share. To be entrusted is to be entrusted with something precious: the practice of nurturing, care-taking, growing, fruit-bearing, relationship-, family-, and community-forming, inheritance-building, which brings more and more people to righteousness, salvation, or eternal life.

Throughout New Testament writings, to put one's trust in God and Christ and be trusted by them also means to serve and obey. At the same time, those who are entrusted are often shown, or show themselves, as exercising their own judgment, debating new courses of action, and taking new decisions. In Acts, in particular, the apostles are shown creating a way of life and discipline for community members (2.42–7, 4.32–5, 5.1–11), appointing some people to serve others (6.1–7), defining the boundaries of the community (8.18–25), and debating whether gentiles must keep the law (15.6–29). Paul and his followers make their case for their views on matters of debate from gentile law-keeping to the reality of resurrection from the dead, support for the Jerusalem community, and various forms of behaviour in community gatherings or everyday life. In being entrusted with a wide variety of roles in service to God and Christ, the faithful are also entrusted with responsibility for the way they enact their roles and shape their communities.[53]

Entrustedness and the Scriptures

We have seen in earlier chapters that the call to trust in God and Christ and the concept of God's trustworthiness towards humanity have roots in Jewish

---

[53] Below, pp. 322–3.

scripture and tradition, as well as being innovative in some respects. What of the idea of being entrusted? Whether using *pisteuein, encheirizein, paratithenai* or another term, the idea that human beings are entrusted with something by God is not widespread in the scriptures, but it is used in some memorable contexts.

At Numbers 12.7 LXX, God proclaims that Moses is '*pistos* in my whole house'. *Pistos* is usually translated 'faithful', but the point of God's declaration is that because Moses is *pistos*, God will speak directly to him, 'mouth to mouth' and without riddles. This may be in part a reward for Moses' faithfulness, but it implies more than that: that Moses is deemed trustworthy because he can be trusted with a unique form of divine communication. Samuel is several times described as *pistos*, including at 1 Reigns 2.35 LXX, when God sends a messenger to Eli to foretell that 'I will raise up for myself a trustworthy priest, who shall do everything that is in my heart and soul'; at 3.20, when Samuel is said to be trustworthy to God, and God continues to appear to him; and at Sirach 46.15 LXX, when Samuel is said to have been made accurate as a prophet because of his *pistis*, as a result of which the trustworthiness of his vision (to other people) was known through his words. In these passages, as in the case of Moses, the specific responsibility which God gives Samuel as a prophet suggests that he is not simply being rewarded for faithfulness, but being entrusted with a role, first in an act of divine therapeutic trust, and later because of his proven trustworthiness.[54] Other prophets are similarly said to be trustworthy, both towards God and God's people and in their vision: Isaiah at Isaiah 48.22 LXX, and the *pistos* prophet of the future to which 1 Maccabees 14.41 LXX looks forward.

The entrustedness of Israelite prophets pre-echoes that of Christian prophets and preachers, but also that of Christ himself (of whom Moses too is a type, and specifically, at Heb. 3.2, the *pistis* of Moses at Num. 12.7). New Testament writings may be drawing directly on scriptural examples when they speak of the trustworthiness or entrustedness of the faithful, but it more likely that the *pistis* of the faithful is conceived as inspired by that of Christ, and Moses, Samuel, and the great prophets in their trustworthiness and entrustedness as types of Christ.

Trust, Power, and the Gift(s) of the Spirit

We have seen that being entrusted is sometimes described as a grace or gift, and that it is linked with obedience and service. Both trust and entrustedness are also linked, especially in the synoptic gospels, Acts, and the Pauline corpus, with power. At Romans 4.20, Abraham is said to be empowered by trust. Trust in God (Mk 11.22) moves mountains (Mt. 17.20, 21.21=Mk 11.23, cf. Lk. 17.6, cf. 1

---

[54] Though e.g. at 2 Rns 23.1 LXX, where David is looking back over a lifetime of being entrusted and trustworthy towards God, 'faithful' is a better translation, emphasizing his *pistis* through time.

Cor. 13.2). Paul reminds the Thessalonians that the gospel with which he has been entrusted (1 Thess. 2.4) came to them 'in power and in the holy spirit' (1.5). Modern commentators focus more on the connection between power and the spirit, but the connection between power and trust raises two related questions. What is the relationship between trust and the gift, or gifts, of the spirit? And what is the relationship between being entrusted and being empowered?

It is sometimes argued, particularly on the basis of 1 Corinthians 12.9, 2 Corinthians 4.13, and Galatians 5.22, that *pistis*, in the sense of the trust in God and Christ that righteouses or saves, is a gift of the spirit.[55] A number of considerations, however, make this less likely than the reverse. If Paul thought that the gift of the spirit was needed to enable people to trust in God or Christ, it would imply a belief in pre-election of which there is no indication in these passages.[56] A number of passages, in Paul and other authors, indicate that putting one's trust in God and Christ is envisaged as preceding reception of the spirit. At Galatians 3.2, Paul asks the Galatians rhetorically, 'Did you receive the spirit from works of the law, or from trust in what you heard?'[57] Trust, like the law, comes before the gift of the spirit. At 3.14 Paul reiterates the point: Christ ransomed humanity from the 'curse of the law' (cf. 3.13) in order that 'we might receive the promise of the spirit through trust'. The writer of Ephesians 1.13 lists what seems to be an order of events: 'In him you also, who have heard the word of truth…and have trusted in him, were sealed with the promised holy spirit…', and at Acts 15.7-8 Peter describes events in the same order: 'God made his choice among you that through my mouth the gentiles would hear the word of the gospel and trust. And God…bore witness by granting them the holy spirit just as he did us.'[58] In the gospels, the disciples trust in God and in Jesus long before they are promised or receive the spirit (cf. Jn 14.16–17, Acts 1.5). At Acts 19.1–6 Paul encounters a group at Ephesus who have put their trust in the one who is to come, but have not yet received the spirit, while the Samaritans of Acts 8.14–17 have been baptized in

---

[55] E.g. Fee (1994), 853, Lindemann (2000), *ad loc.*, Wagner (2014); see also Colson (2017). Thrall (1994), *ad* 2 Cor. 4.13 notes this as a possibility, but without much conviction, and thinks that at 1 Cor. 12.9 the *pistis* in question must be a particular gift of the spirit which follows *pisteuein* in God and Christ in general. At 2. Cor. 3.17, in a much discussed verse, Christ himself is the spirit, and one can envisage both Paul and his followers and the evangelists as recognizing the life and ministry of Christ as an act of grace and gift of God to the world, but it would not follow that they understood the whole world as having received the spirit: at most one could infer that everyone has been given the opportunity to receive the spirit, by responding to Christ.

[56] See e.g. Byrne (1996), *ad* Rom. 11.29, Levering (2011), 25–33 and ch. 1, *passim*, Wagner (2011), and the nuanced discussions of divine *vs* human agency in Paul in Barclay and Gathercole (2008). Trust is often mentioned before baptism; reception of the spirit often goes with baptism, but not always (e.g. Acts 8.14–17), so this is not a clear indicator.

[57] This is trust rather than simply belief because commitment is implied.

[58] So e.g. Fitzmyer (1997), *ad loc.*; cf. 10.44, where listening to the word, and presumably responding to it, is followed by reception of the spirit and baptism.

the name of the Lord Jesus, suggesting that they have put their trust in him, but have not yet received the spirit.[59]

We have already argued against interpreting 2 Corinthians 4.13 as saying that trust comes from the spirit, or interpreting 1 Corinthians 12.9 and Galatians 5.22 as referring to trust in God and Christ as a gift or fruit of the spirit.[60] Galatians 5.22 lists qualities which all community members should share *qua* community members: that is, as people who have already put their trust in God and Christ. 1 Corinthians 12.9 refers to gifts which are given to some community members for the good of the community as a whole.

The diachronic relationship between putting one's trust in God and Christ and receiving the spirit is significant not least because it implies that being given the spirit depends on trust not only chronologically but logically: only those who are and remain (even if, perhaps, imperfectly) trusting and faithful receive the spirit. Equally significant for us, however, is a further question. Granted that trusting and receiving the spirit are both central to these writings, are they significantly linked, or do they sit side by side without being closely connected?

The terminologies of trust in God and Christ and the gift of the spirit do not seem to be freely interchangeable. One can, as we have seen, be given a particular trust, such as apostleship, but one is not, in New Testament writings, given the *charis* or *charisma* of trust as a whole, nor is one 'entrusted' with the spirit (though we might hear an implication of entrustedness in the idea that a person is given the power of the spirit).[61] The importance of trust and the importance of the spirit and the gift(s) of the spirit are probably ideas inherited independently by our earliest sources, but there are signs that they are also conceptually interwoven.

The study of the spirit has become a large and complex field in recent years, and scholars of the Hebrew Bible, Judaism, and early Christianity have shown how many and varied understandings are in play, by the beginning of the first millennium CE, of the nature and working of God's spirit, the human spirit, and other spirits.[62] Most of this field lies well beyond our purview, but one widely shared view of the ways in which, in the Hebrew Bible, the spirit comes to human

---

[59] Debates over the relationship between reception of the spirit and baptism in early churches in general need not concern us here, since we can assume that people have normally made a decision to trust God and Christ before they are baptized, and the affirmation of early baptismal formulae (*pisteuo*) does not represent the first moment of trust.

[60] pp. 299–300.

[61] Nor is one said, in New Testament writings, to trust in the spirit, perhaps because the spirit is not sufficiently personified separately from God (though for an argument in the other direction, without discussion of *pistis* language, see e.g. Frey (2014)). But if e.g. God entrusts humanity with Christ, the same can surely be said of the spirit: cf. pp. 305–6.

[62] E.g. Betz (1960), Dunn (1970, 1975, 1998a), 1.115–65, 2, *passim*, Lampe (1977), Schweizer (1978), Davies (1980), Newman (1987), Dreytza (1990), Horn (1992), Fee (1994, 1996), Welker (1994), Levison (1994, 1997, 2009, 2019), Hildebrandt (1995), Turner (1996, 1998), Fatehi (2000), Baumert (2001), Frey (2002), Stanton et al. (2004), Christoph (2005), Strecker (2010), Welker et al. (2010), Frey and Levison (2014).

beings may illuminate the relationship between the gift of the spirit and *pistis* in New Testament writings.

In a recent article Carol Newsom has shown that a pattern identified by Hermann Gunkel and subsequently accepted by many scholars of the Hebrew Bible, though much debated in recent years, is surely right.[63] The spirit that God gives to humanity takes broadly two forms, which Newsom characterizes as 'charismatic *rûah*' and 'life-constitutive *rûah*'. Charismatic *rûah* is that which is described as 'coming upon', 'resting on', or 'rushing on' a person, enabling them to do something (such as to prophesy) which they would not otherwise be able to do, or impelling them to do something extraordinary (e.g. Num. 11.25, Isa. 61.1, Ezek. 11.5). Life-constitutive *rûah* is the force that gives life to inanimate, comatose, or dead bodies, and is always described as placed in or breathed into the person. This is both the breath which gives life to Adam (Gen. 2.7), and the new spirit which Ezekiel (36.26) envisages as put into human beings to renew their relationship with God.

The spirit that is received by humanity in New Testament writings also takes broadly two forms. For Paul, after the Christ event, existence divides sharply into life 'according to the flesh' (Rom. 8.5, cf. Gal. 3.3, 5.16–18), under 'the law of sin and death' (8.2), and life 'according to the spirit' (8.5, cf. Gal. 5.16) or 'in the spirit' (Gal. 5.25), whose concern is 'life and peace [with God]' (Rom. 8.6, cf. 5.1). For those who have put their trust in Christ, in whom Christ is (8.10), are alive in spirit even though their 'body is dead because of sin' (8.10), and they can look forward to eternal life (6.22–3, Gal. 6.8). The faithful have been 'washed...sanctified...justified' in the name of Christ and the spirit of God (1 Cor. 6.11) and they must live as a 'temple of the holy spirit' (6.19). 'The spirit gives life' (2 Cor. 3.6), and is the first instalment of the eternal, heavenly life which God has prepared for the faithful (5.1–5) and the right-standing with God for which they hope (Gal. 5.5).[64] John's Jesus is identified by John the Baptist with the Lamb of God who takes away the world's sin (1.29) and, soon after, as the one who baptizes with the holy spirit (1.33). Those who trust in Jesus are reborn 'from above', of water and spirit (e.g. 3.3, 5) and gain eternal life (3.15, 16). Those who trust in Jesus receive the spirit (7.38–9), and the spirit gives life (6.63, 14.19). Even in Acts, which is dominated by 'charismatic *rûah*', Peter refers to the 'life-giving repentance' (11.18), which leads to the forgiveness of sins and reception of the spirit (2.38).[65]

These passages, diverse though they are in many respects, share the conviction that receiving the spirit, described in various ways, brings a new kind of life to the faithful; a life in opposition to a world of darkness, sin, and death, which is lived

---

[63] Newsom (2020), with a survey of scholarship and discussion in particular of Levison's approach at pp. 104–6; cf. Gunkel (1979).

[64] Making a similar argument, that Paul draws on scripture to portray the spirit as the divine agent of the new creation, see Yates (2008).

[65] Menzies (1994), Turner (1996).

even in this world under the authority of God and Christ, and which looks forward to its fulfilment in eternal life.[66] There is no indication that this life differs in nature from person to person, any more than the spirit which people receive is different from person to person. Nor does any New Testament writer tell us that everyone who belongs to the community of the faithful and receives the spirit has a specific spiritual gift (such as prophecy or healing) as well.[67] The gift of life which people receive when they put their trust in God and Christ is distinctive, universal, and undifferentiated.

The spirit that brings life to the faithful is strongly evocative of 'life-constitutive *rûah*'. To put one's trust in God and Christ is to become part of a new creation and to enter new life under God's power and authority. In addition, those who have put their trust in God and Christ often receive charismatic *rûah*, whose many gifts include prophecy, apostleship, healing, leadership, the gift of tongues and their interpretation, pastoral care, teaching, and knowledge of truth (e.g. Jn 16.12-13, Acts 2.1-21, Rom. 12.6-8, 1 Cor. 4.1-10, 12.6-12, Eph. 4.11).

Unlike the scriptures, however, New Testament writings sometimes describe the reception of what looks like life-constitutive spirit in a way which sounds more like the reception of charismatic spirit. Paul reminds the Thessalonians and the Corinthians that the gospel 'came to them' with a 'demonstration' of spirit and power (1 Thess. 1.5, 1 Cor. 2.4). At Acts 19.6, when the Ephesian followers of John are baptized in the name of Jesus, the holy spirit 'came upon them' (and they spoke in tongues and prophesied). The spirit 'descends' on Jesus at his baptism like a dove (Mk 1.10, Jn 1.32[68]), and the disciples are 'filled with a holy spirit' at Pentecost (Acts 2.4). This, of course, is one reason why, for many commentators, the spirit received by Christ-confessors should always be understood as charismatic spirit, but if we are right that God also gives life-constitutive spirit to those who trust, this crossover in language deserves further investigation. An explanation of it may lie in the nature of the community to which the faithful are called and how it is preached, especially to gentiles.

---

[66] The new life which the faithful receive through the spirit is linked with eschatological hope, which everyone receives through the power of the spirit (Rom. 15.13, Gal. 5.5); with being changed into the image of Christ (2 Cor. 3.18); with being strengthened with power in one's inner self, which everyone can achieve (Eph. 3.16); and with worship, which everyone performs through the spirit (Phil. 3.3).

[67] Turner (1998), 340-7 shows that even in Acts the gift of the spirit is not purely charismatic, since not all community members preach or prophesy, but is also what he calls soteriological (equivalent to what we have called 'life-constitutive'). All community members' everyday activities, he argues, are understood as part of life in the spirit, in terms which put Acts closer to Paul and John than is usually recognized.

[68] Assuming that Mark's model is adoptionist, Jesus presumably receives both life-constitutive and charismatic spirit at 1.10, and the same may be true of the disciples at Acts 2.2-4. It could be true of Jesus at Jn 1.32, but if most commentators are right that John's incarnationalism is not an adoptionistic, Jesus here receives the charismatic gift of his ministry; while at Mt. 3.16 and Lk. 3.22, the gift must be charismatic spirit.

I have argued elsewhere that when Paul describes the new life to which those who trust in God and Christ are called, he describes it in holistic terms as an all-encompassing society.[69] We can see this not least in the remarkable range of imagery which Paul deploys to describe the community of the faithful and his work for it: political, military, legal, economic, domestic, athletic, educational, and philosophical, as well as religious. Scholars have sometimes drawn on these images to argue that early Christianity is modelled, for instance, on a household or a school, but the cumulative effect of Paul's imagery is to portray Christ-confession as an entire way of life in a full-scale, complex society under God's rule. In this society, everyone has something to contribute. Nobody who puts their trust in God and receives the spirit is a passive participant or a spectator. A person's contribution may not be the high-profile work, such as apostleship, which is a charismatic gift of the spirit—it may be something as simple as practising love, or, by one's endurance, acting as an example for others—but everyone contributes something.

This model of Christ-confession, I have suggested, is important to Paul for two reasons. He wants to emphasize to gentile converts, in particular, that putting one's trust in God and Christ is not like adding a new cult to one's portfolio. One does not take part in the Lord's supper as one might take part in the dining society of one cult on one day, and another on another. One does not pray to God when one thinks God might support a particular project, as one might pray to Asclepius for healing and Hermes for help with a new business venture. Trust in God and Christ is a whole-life commitment.[70] The community of those who trust are a society under God's rule and Christ's authority, and, at the end time, this society under God will encompass both earth and heaven. To put it in terms familiar to Jews and godfearers, trusting in God and Christ brings one into the people of God, who (despite the everyday accommodations which must, of course, be made when one lives in this world under worldly powers) live above all as God's people under God's law, in a way which decisively shapes their life and identity.

Paul's letters, in their language and imagery, offer an especially vivid picture of the complexity of life under God's rule and in Christ's hands, but the same vision is detectable elsewhere. Acts, for example, affirms that community members contribute holistically and actively to the new life of the faithful by sharing their property (e.g. 2.44–5, 4.32–3), supporting one another in practical ways (4.34–5, 6.1–3), and meeting and breaking bread together (2.46). Wherever the faithful are

---

[69] Morgan (2020), 169–74.
[70] Morgan (2020), 173–4. Paul could not take for granted that gentiles would understand this, because mainstream cults vary widely in the degree to which they are integrated with worshippers' lives, societies, and sense of identity: some, such as cults of tutelary gods of cities or tribes, define worshippers' identities and shape their lives to a significant degree; some, such as elective cults, might shape an individual's sense of identity to a degree; some, such as prophetic or healing cults, might play a very limited role in worshippers' daily lives or sense of identity.

referred to as children of Abraham, God's household or people (e.g. Acts 3.25, Eph. 2.19-20, Heb. 3.6, 1 Pet. 2.9-10, 3.6), the writer invokes what it means to be part of God's people in all the fullness and complexity of that identity. Paul's followers, meanwhile, pick up his language of the faithful as one body, all of whose members make a contribution to the working of the whole under God and in Christ (Rom. 12.3-8, 1 Cor. 12.12-30), as an image of the church (e.g. Eph. 4.15, 4.25, 5.22-3, 5.29-30, Col. 1.18, 1.24, 2.19, 3.15).

The crossover use of language of the gift of charismatic spirit for the gift of life-giving spirit to all those who trust in God and Christ may, at least in part, be a case of attraction to the paradigmatic stories of the charismatic gift of the spirit to Jesus and the disciples. But it also, I suggest, expresses the conviction of New Testament writers that all those who put their trust in God and Christ and enter new life under God's rule have an active part to play in the society of God's people as they wait for the end time. The faithful are active, like those who have received high-profile charismatic gifts, both within the community, and, by their example, for those outside it. This suggests that we can recognize life-constitutive and charismatic spirit as distinct gifts to Christ-confessors, but also recognize that, in some respects, the two join forces to suffuse every aspect of life under God's kingdom with active work for the service, stewardship, and growth of the kingdom before the end time.

Recognizing that receiving the spirit gives not only charismatic gifts, but also new life to the faithful, further suggests a reason why, for all New Testament writers, in one form or another, trust and the reception of the spirit are closely intertwined. In earlier chapters we have used Doris Brothers' model of trust to illustrate how important it is for people to able to trust if they are to function in everyday life.[71] The world in which we are able to trust and feel trusted is the world which we experience as real, and in which we experience ourselves as real. Those who cannot trust can cease to feel that they are real in the world in which others are living and acting, or that others are real in their world. They may seek refuge in—or find themselves trapped in—dreams or delusions which seem more real than the world around them. They risk losing the ability to interact with others, and they may become prey to anger, insecurity, shame, or depression, with unpredictable consequences for their own lives and those around them.

For Christ-confessors, to put their trust in God and Christ is to affirm the reality of God and the sphere of God's power; to experience themselves as real—living— in that reality, and the rest of the faithful as living and interacting with them in that reality. The sphere of God's power is also the sphere of the spirit, and life under the rule of God is also life in the spirit. The gift of the spirit is the gift of life in relationships of trust with God and Christ and those who confess Christ,

---

[71] E.g. pp. 132, 217-18, 250.

which, all New Testament writers emphasize, constitutes a fullness of life (cf. Col. 2.10) beyond anything that can be experienced in the world ruled over by the deadly powers of the present age. Literally, as Paul might have put it, one cannot trust, or live, in the world of the flesh, as one can trust and live in the world of the spirit. And the life of trust which the faithful live in the spirit, under the rule of God and Christ, is both a foretaste of eschatological life in its own right, and the sign of eternal life which will come in its fullness at the end time.

If trust, however, chronologically and logically, precedes the spirit in the relationship between God, Christ, and the faithful, and trust and the spirit both (distinctly but cooperatively) make possible for the faithful the new life under the rule of God and Christ which is the foretaste of eternal life, we may still wonder what, for the faithful, is the relationship between being entrusted with various forms of activity for God and Christ in this life, and being given the gifts and, in particular, the power of the spirit. This is a pressing question not least in the early twenty-first century, when, in societies which see themselves as committed to democracy and human rights, the power that some people hold over others is constantly open to question and challenge; and when some scholars of Christianity have questioned whether the valorization of the idea that the spirit endows those who are gifted with power—an idea which is deeply rooted in Christian communities—may not constitute a risk to community members as well as a cause for celebration.[72] Power in New Testament writings is another much-discussed theme which lies mainly beyond our scope, but we can make one or two observations about the relationship between power and trust.[73]

As a starting-point, we may note that, in general, gifts and trusts can stand in varying relationships. The modest box of chocolates I give you for your birthday is yours to do what you like with; the gift does not involve any significant trust. The funds which generous parents give to their child to help her buy her first home presumably imply that the parents trust the child to use the money

---

[72] Even where it is recognized, in principle, that all power belongs to God and is enacted by God through human beings (emphasized notably by Dunn (1975), 256). On concerns with claims to power, particularly within modern communities, see e.g. Willems (1967), Dominian (1976), Hart (1978), Wilson and Clow (1981), Deno (2004), Stephenson (2011), Ngunjiri et al. (2012), Ngunjiri and Christo-Baker (2012), Oluwaniji (2012), Espinosa (2014), 361–405, Thornton (2016), ch. 6, Langford (2017), Burchardt (2018), Oom-Dove (2018); see also the wide-ranging collection of Miller et al. (2013) on spirit and power in Pentecostalism, though this does not particularly problematize power. Murray (2012) argues interestingly that charismatic and Pentecostal elements in global Christianities reinforce secular, particularly economic power structures. Studebaker (2008) proposes that more attention should be paid theologically to the authority, rather than the power of the spirit, which would defuse some of the problems which arise within churches when too much value is placed on power. Schnackenburg (1973) notes an evolution within New Testament writings: the gifts of the spirit which in Rom. 12.6–8 and 1 Cor. 12.4–11 are qualities, at Eph. 4.11–12 have become functionaries who are given authority and even power over the 'holy ones'.

[73] On power see e.g. Schweizer (1952), Schürmann (1964), Nolland (1986), Hawthorne (1991), Shelton (1991), Menzies (1993, 1994), Fee (1994), Turner (1996), Savage (1996), Keener (1997), Gräbe (2002a, b), cf. Holmberg (1980) on power and authority in Pauline churches.

responsibly. The gifts of the spirit, which are given to the faithful for the service of God and support of communities of the faithful, imply trust on the part of God and Christ, and, like the home-buying child, the faithful are not free to use them however they like.[74]

The gospels agree that Jesus receives the spirit at his baptism, and thereafter he exercises power over sickness, hostile spirits (in the synoptic gospels), and the natural world.[75] Though the link between the spirit and power is not in doubt, Jesus' power is only twice described explicitly as coming from the spirit: at Matthew 12.28, when Jesus says that 'if it is by the spirit of God that I cast out demons, then the kingdom of God has come upon you', and at Luke 4.18, where he says that the spirit of God has come upon him, and describes the work of the anointed one, in the words of Isaiah, as including giving sight to the blind.[76]

Perhaps surprisingly, in all four gospels, Jesus' acts of power are more often linked explicitly with *pistis/pisteuein* than with the spirit: trust between Jesus and God and between Jesus and other people. Jesus tells the disciples that trust in God gives power over the natural world (e.g. Mt. 21.18–22=Mk 11.22–3, cf. Lk. 17.6). He criticizes them for not having trust, or not enough, when they fail to recognize who he is or to cast out a demon, or are afraid of a storm (e.g. Mt. 8.26=Mk 4.40=Lk. 8.25, Mt. 17.20=Lk. 9.6, Jn. 14.9–12, cf. 14.1). Those who put their trust in Jesus for healing acknowledge his trust and loyalty towards God,[77] and without their own trust (probably in both God and Jesus himself), Jesus' power to act is limited or moot (Mt. 13.58=Mk 6.6). It is also worth noting that when Jesus sends out the twelve, and in Luke the seventy-two, to act in his name (Mt. 10.1=Mk 6.7=Lk. 9.1, cf. Lk. 10.1), including by healing and exorcizing, those who are sent are not said, at this point, to have received the spirit, but they are in a relationship of trust with God and Jesus himself.[78] Their power apparently comes not from the gift of the spirit but from their trust.

Even more surprisingly, given its keen interest in the spirit, a similar pattern is detectable in Acts. At Acts 1.8 Jesus promises the disciples that 'you will receive power when the holy spirit comes on you' (1.8), and, in the early chapters, the apostles perform several deeds of power.[79] These acts, though (which, like acts of power in the gospels, are over demons and forces of nature rather than other

---

[74] So e.g. 1 Cor. 14 seeks to regulate the ways the Corinthians use their gifts of prophecy and tongues; at Acts 8.18–21 the disciples refuse to give Simon Magus the spirit, which he seems to want to misuse.

[75] Hostile spirits are the only beings over which even Jesus exercises power: e.g. Mt. 10.1=Mk 6.7=Lk. 9.1, Lk. 10.19–20.

[76] Also at Acts 10.38.   [77] p. 220.   [78] pp. 215, 218–19, 259–60.

[79] E.g. 4.33, 5.16, 7.33, 8.6–7; Paul performs such a deed at 19.11. At Acts 5.32 the holy spirit is said to be given to those who obey God, so power is enacted by those who subject themselves to God's power.

people[80]), are said to be performed not through the power of the spirit but in the name of Jesus Christ (3.6, 4.10, 16.18 cf. 4.30). The name of Jesus has sometimes been understood as a name of power, of a kind which healers and magic workers use throughout ancient Mediterranean and Near Eastern cultures,[81] but it has rightly been pointed out that this cannot be quite Luke's view.[82] Hans Conzelmann proposes that the name of Jesus represents Jesus himself, while C. K. Barrett argues that, for Luke, the invocation of Jesus' name is an affirmation that the apostles are under Jesus' authority. This suggests that the apostles, in these passages, are not so much using a power which has been given to them, as invoking the relationship of trust in which they stand with Jesus, and using a power which has been entrusted to them within that relationship.

The cautionary tale of Simon Magus (8.4-24) underlines the subordination, for Luke, of power to trust. Simon is an enthusiast for power, and his magic-working in Samaria has earned him the reputation for being the 'power of God' and the nickname 'Great' (v. 10). When Philip travels to Samaria to proclaim the Messiah (v. 5), however, and performs a number of signs (v. 12), Simon is impressed by his power. He affirms his trust in Christ, is baptized, and becomes devoted to Philip (v. 13). When he discovers that the faithful receive the holy spirit through the laying on of hands, he approaches Peter and John (cf. vv. 14-15), asking to receive the spirit for a fee (vv. 18-19). Peter's rebuke is twofold. Simon is catastrophically mistaken in thinking he can buy God's gift (v. 20), and he needs rather to pray for forgiveness, 'for I see that you are full of bitter gall and bound by unrighteousness (*adikia*)' (v. 23). Not only has Simon made a mistake, as any faithful person might, but his desire for power reveals that his *pistis* is not real: he is still under the power of sin.

Given that the connection between the gift of charismatic spirit and acts of power is traditional and undisputed, it is striking that these writers all highlight the relationship between power and trust in God and/or Christ. Recognizing, as all do, the central role of *pisteuein* in the (re)new(ed) divine-human relationship, they seem to want to show not only that power depends on trust indirectly, via the spirit, but that it depends directly on the trust relationship. It is the trust relationship, with all its implications of obedience and service, trustworthiness, self-entrusting, and hope, which must remain at the front and centre of the attitude and actions of everyone who receives and seeks to do the work of the spirit. The story of Simon Magus emphasizes that acts of power can only be performed by

---

[80] The deaths of Ananias and Sapphira are sometimes taken as acts of power over people by Peter (Acts 5.5, 5.10), but (as noted e.g. by Barrett (1994), 267-8) Luke does not say so (cf. 5.4, 9).

[81] For a recent discussion of Christian acts of power as magic-working, from the anthropologically 'outsider' viewpoint, but not from Luke's viewpoint, see Arnal (2018).

[82] E.g. Conzelmann (1987), Barrett (1994), ad Acts 3.6, cf. Dunn (1975), 194-5. Luke's view, of course, is that found all over the ancient world, that acts of God-given power performed by one's own group are quite different from the vulgar magic-working of other peoples, but the relevant point for us is that this is surely his view.

those who authentically put their trust in God and Christ. Trust saves and gives life. The power of the spirit is a sign of God's eschatological kingdom, God's power over the forces of evil and the material world, and the saving power of trust.

In much of Acts, and also in the gospels, the spirit is more closely associated with prophetic speech, preaching, or the direction of those who trust than with acts of power.[83] Jesus begins his ministry by proclaiming the imminence of the kingdom (Mt. 4.17=Mk 1.15), together, in Luke, with his own identity as the anointed one (Lk. 4.18–21). Matthew, Luke, and John all depict Jesus teaching or prophesying more often than performing acts of power.[84] At Pentecost, the gift of the spirit is that of speaking to all those in Jerusalem in their own languages (Acts 2.6–8) followed by Peter's prophetic and protreptic sermon (2.14–36). Throughout the rest of the book (especially from chapter 13 onwards), preaching is the primary focus of the apostles' and others' activity.[85]

Speech, of course, is itself an act, but (despite classical rhetoric's occasional claims to *psychagōgia*[86]) speech in general, including prophetic speech and preaching, does not impose itself on its listeners willy-nilly. The spirit may empower a person to speak, but it does not guarantee the speaker power over his or her audience. Prophetic speech and preaching—as listeners to the scriptural prophets, and ancient speakers and their audiences in general knew well—are at best negotiations between speaker and listener whose outcome cannot be guaranteed. They are acts of persuasion which depend not least on the creation and fortification of trust.[87]

To these observations, we can add what we argued especially in Chapter 4, that for God and Christ to seek to bring or restore humanity to its right relationship with God through the incarnation, crucifixion, and resurrection, is itself an act of trust and entrusting which stands in sharp contrast with the many unambiguous and decisive revelations of divine power in both Jewish and gentile tradition. God trusts and entrusts both Christ and humanity; Christ trusts and entrusts both God and humanity; humanity is invited to trust God and Christ and be entrusted by them. In the Christ event, divine power itself is sublimated to the creation of trust.

---

[83] E.g. Mt. 10.20=Lk. 12.12, in line with its roots in charismatic *rûah*, and also with the fact that the spirit plays the role of overseeing and directing Paul, in particular, which in Paul's own letters is played by Christ (e.g. Acts 8.19, 11.12, 13.2, 13.4, 16.6, 20.22–3, 21.4). In other passages of Acts divine power is enacted by an angel of the Lord: e.g. 5.18–19, 12.7.

[84] The balance is much closer in Mark, which includes relatively little teaching outside the parables.

[85] Early in the synoptic gospels, the spirit drives or leads Jesus into the desert (Mt. 4.1=Mk 1.12=Lk. 4.1). In the second half of Acts, especially, the spirit also tells the apostles where to go (11.12, 13.4, 20.22) or not to go (21.4), prevents them from going where they intended (16.6–7), or physically transports them from one place to another (8.29).

[86] E.g. Pl., *Phdr.* 261a, Xen., *Mem.* 3.10.6, Isoc. 2.49, Lycurg. 33.

[87] The connection is particularly clear to Greek speakers because of the linguistic relationship between *peithein* and *pisteuein*: see e.g. Arist., *Rhet.* 2.1.5 on how the orator establishes himself as trustworthy.

We might think that that if any group of New Testament texts contradicts this view, it is the Pauline corpus. Paul is the writer who most often explicitly connects the spirit with power and affirms that the power of the spirit works through him. Paul, as noted above, reminds both the Thessalonians and the Corinthians that 'his' gospel came to them not only in words but 'with power and the holy spirit' (1 Thess. 1.5), 'with a demonstration of spirit and power' (1 Cor. 2.4). He speaks to the Romans of what Christ accomplished through him to lead the gentiles to obedience, by both word and deed, the power of signs and wonders (Rom. 15.19). 2 Timothy follows Paul, affirming that 'God did not give us a spirit of cowardice, but rather of power and love and self-control' (1.7). No one, moreover, comes closer than Paul to claiming power over other community members, using the ambiguous term *exousia*: 'Even if I should boast a little too much of our authority/power, which the Lord gave for building you up...I shall not be put to shame' (2 Cor. 10.8).

Paul, however, is also the New Testament writer who makes the most use of *pistis* language, and his language of power cannot be heard in isolation from his ubiquitous language of trust, trusting, faithfulness, trustworthiness, and entrustedness. In particular, we saw above that Paul, together with his followers, is the writer who most often refers explicitly to entrustedness, and his references to power are sometimes closely connected with trust and entrustedness. For example, when Paul refers to the power with which his gospel came to the Thessalonians, following his reminder with another allusion to it at 2.1, that allusion is quickly followed by the affirmation that he was 'judged worthy by God to be entrusted with the gospel' (2.4), and that he preached to please God (4.4) in gentleness, not asserting his apostolic authority (2.6), but 'as a nurse cares for her children' (2.7). His power is only power to serve God by using the gift with which he has been entrusted, sharing the gospel and himself (2.8), and caring for others.[88] Galatians 3.5 reminds the Galatians that their power comes from their trust relationship with God and Christ, in which they may be imagined, like Paul himself, as entrusted with the spirit and the 'mighty deeds' which are being worked among them.[89] We can also note that the Corinthian letters, in which Paul most often refers to both his power/ability (*dynamis*) and his power/

---

[88] Cf. Rom. 7.6, where the spirit enables service, and Rom. 1.9, 12.11, where Paul refers to his and the Romans' spirits as serving God, no doubt under the influence of the spirit that has been given to them (cf. 2 Cor. 1.22). There is always an interplay in Paul's rhetoric between service and power, but power is always entrusted to Paul in the service of *pistis*. Rabens (2013), resisting the idea that those who trust are transformed by an infusion of the material spirit, argues that, for Paul, the faithful are enabled by the power of the spirit to make relationships with God, Christ, and fellow-Christians which, in turn, enable ethical living: *'It is primarily through deeper knowledge of, and an intimate relationship with, God, Jesus Christ and with the community of faith that people are transformed and empowered by the spirit for religious-ethical life'* (p. 123: italics original). This well captures the role of the spirit and the power of the spirit, for Paul, following initial trust and enabling further and deeper relationships of trust and life in those relationships.

[89] As does the 'power for salvation' at Rom. 1.16.

authority (*exousia*), are written to try to re-establish his authority when it is being undermined, so we should be wary of assuming that he is equally concerned with power when he does not feel under attack.[90] At 1 Corinthians 5.4, Paul, with the Corinthians in spirit, passes judgment on the man who has committed incest, 'in the name of Lord Jesus' and 'with the power of the Lord Jesus'. Paul's formulation pre-echoes the way in which the apostles in Acts invoke their relationship with Jesus to perform healings: for Paul, here, as for the apostles, it is his relationship of trust with Jesus that is the basis of his authority and allows Jesus to work through him.

It may also be relevant that Paul several times, in slightly different ways, associates the spirit closely with the person of Christ (especially at Rom. 8.9–10, 1 Cor. 6.17, 2 Cor. 3.17, Gal. 4.6, and Phil. 1.19). These passages are much discussed, especially for what they may indicate about Paul's understanding of the nature of the exalted Christ or of the spirit itself, and about Paul's arguable (proto-)Trinitarianism.[91] For our purposes, however, the significant point is that one does not have the spirit without having the closest conceivable relationship with Christ: variously expressed in these passages as having or sharing Christ's spirit (1 Cor. 6.17, Gal. 4.6, Phil. 1.19), and as sharing Christ's relationship with God (Gal. 4.6, cf. 2 Cor. 3.17[92]). Paul's understanding of his relationship with Christ, moreover, as of both Christ's and his own relationship with God, is dominated, as already observed, by the language of service, obedience, trust, and entrustedness. If the nature of the possession of the spirit by the faithful is inseparable from the nature of their relationship with Christ, then it too is dominated by service, obedience, trust, and entrustedness.

We have already discussed the role of entrustedness in the parable of the talents. Matthew's version of the story also has something to say about the relationship between trust and power. The three slaves are initially given or entrusted with (*paradidonai*) their talents in accordance with their perceived powers or abilities

---

[90] Even here, references to power attribute it to God or Christ rather than Paul himself: e.g. 1 Cor. 1.18, 2.4–5, 2 Cor. 10.8, cf. 13.10, Eph. 3.7, Col. 1.29, 2 Tim. 1.7–8.

[91] For a discussion of recent scholarship on the Trinity in Paul, arguing that he does think in Trinitarian terms, see Hill (2015). I am among those who are more sceptical: e.g. Dunn (1998a), 255, Watson (1997), 168, Mitchell and Young (2006), 288, and by omission Wolter (2015a), though undoubtedly the close involvement of God, Christ, and God's spirit is central to Paul's thinking (so e.g. Keck (1986), 363, 373, Fatehi (2000), Eastman (2017)). Schweizer (1969), 433 is surely right, in broad terms, to say that, for Paul, 'the work of God in the Son or the spirit is always to be understood as genuinely God's work, but the question of the way in which God, Lord and spirit are related is not felt to be a problem.' In general, Paul is more interested in what God, Christ, and the spirit do than in framing ontological statements about them. I take it, though, that he understands Christ as imbued to the uttermost with the spirit of God and as living and acting with God, such that God's spirit is, for all practical purposes, Christ's, and Christ acts, as does the spirit, wholly with and for God. On the 'indissoluble unity' of Christ's work and that of the spirit see e.g. Stählin (1973).

[92] Taking 'freedom' at 2 Cor. 3.17 to refer, as at Gal. 4.1–6 (cf. Rom. 6.18), to the freedom from slavery to the 'elemental powers' or to sin which enables one, like Christ, to 'live for God' (cf. Rom. 6.11) as God's child.

(*dynamis*).⁹³ When the master returns, those who have multiplied their talents are commended as *pistos*: 'you have been trustworthy over a little,' the master tells the first slave, 'I will set you over a lot' (25.21, cf. 23). On one level, the master plans to increase the slave's power, but explicitly he is increasing his scope for trustworthiness, and the slave's power, of course, is always subject to his master's. In this story as elsewhere, it is less power that is at issue than trustworthiness and entrustedness.

Early Christians inherit a long tradition that God can empower human beings with God's spirit, and that one of the effects of receiving the spirit can be that a person receives power. New Testament writings, however, usually emphasize that this gift follows trust in God and Christ, is directly dependent on trust, and is an expression of entrustedness by God and Christ, and it is always exercised in service to God. As such, the power of the spirit, like the gift and the gifts of the spirit, can itself be seen as having aspects of a trust: more entrusted to the faithful for use in accordance with divine authority than given to be used as the faithful see fit, and held in trust to be handed back to God at any time. This is not to say that the faithful do not have, or accept, responsibility for how they use their gifts: the texts often attest that they do or show them doing so. But their decisions are made out of God's trust and in trust.

In Chapter 1, we proposed that to trust someone is to put something (or have a disposition such that one could and would put something, if one wanted or needed to) into another person's hands (that is, into her power, responsibility, and/or care), on the basis (such as belief, hope, a wager, or an assumption) that she will respond positively (which might include that she is willing and able to respond and that she is encouraged to do so by one's own trust). Trust may involve reliance, but does not necessarily do so: for instance, when it is therapeutic, or when I trust you to bring a bottle of wine to dinner, but if you don't, I can easily run to the nearby off-licence. Trust is often three-place, but can also be two-place: a relationship which is open-ended and valued in its own right. Because, moreover, trust usually involves one or more positive attitudes towards the other person and a sense of her positive attitude towards oneself, one is liable to feel hurt or betrayed if it fails. This definition fits well with the picture we have outlined of God's trust in the faithful and their entrustedness. God puts the gospel, the growth of God's kingdom in the present time, and the care of God's world and God's people, into the hands of the faithful, in the belief (or, since we have suggested that this is an act of therapeutic trust, the trust) that the faithful will be able and willing to respond, not least in response to God's confidence in them. God's trust is not reliance, since God can always act on God's own behalf, but it is

---

⁹³ *Paradidonai* may bear an implication of entrusting here (and perhaps at Mt. 11.27–Lk. 10.22, Acts 15.26, 15.40), though in the gospels it is usually used of Jesus' being handed over to the authorities.

a risk: an entrusting to the faithful of what is precious to God. The entrusted are quite likely to fail in trustworthiness, perhaps repeatedly (which is the risk they take), and we may imagine that God is grieved by their failure, but God continues to trust and entrust them with God's 'rich trust'. If it is right, as we have suggested, that trust is not only a means to an end, the salvation and eternal life of the faithful, but also good in its own right, then this is another respect in which the divine-human trust relationship is not only three-place, but two-place: an aspect of eternal life already operative in the present time.

Towards an Ethic of Entrustedness

We cannot think about the faithful being entrusted, and what they are entrusted with, without thinking about how they are called to enact this trust before the end time. On one level, we could say that the 'ethic of entrustedness' is simply trustworthiness, which is the appropriate response to being entrusted (at least when one is confident that the truster is not entrusting one with anything destructive or malign). The way that entrustedness and trustworthiness have been portrayed in this chapter, however, suggests that being trustworthy in respect of the people and things with which God and Christ entrust the faithful has more specific content than this. Before we conclude, therefore, it is worth offering some reflections on what an ethic of Christian entrustedness might look like.

We have seen that the faithful are entrusted with the good news about God's kingdom and what God has done and made possible through Christ. Some of Jesus' parables attest to the preciousness of the kingdom, and by extension the news about the kingdom: it is like treasure hidden in a field or the most beautiful imaginable pearl (Mt. 13.44–6). As a trust, the gospel is therefore to be treasured, not taken for granted or treated casually.

The connection between the kingdom and the pearl recalls another Matthaean saying: 'Do not give what is holy to dogs, or throw your pearls before swine, lest they trample them underfoot, and turn and tear you to pieces' (7.6). The meaning of this *logion* is uncertain, and it is one of a cluster of sayings in the Sermon on the Mount, many of which are not closely interconnected.[94] The Sermon as a whole, however, is about discipleship, and its teachings are evidently meant to be as relevant to later Christians as to Jesus' immediate audience. One of the aspects of discipleship with which this section of the discourse is concerned is prophecy and, more broadly, apostolic activity. Listeners are warned to beware of false prophets, who can be recognized because they bear bad fruit (7.15–20), and

---

[94] There is no more indication what this means at G.Th. 93. 'Dogs and swine' probably, for Matthew's first listeners, desecrate what should be honoured, cf. Prov. 23.9. At Mt. 15.26–7 'dogs' are gentiles.

further warned that not everyone who says to Jesus, 'Lord, Lord' will enter the kingdom: not even all those who prophesy, drive out demons, and do mighty deeds in Jesus' name (7.21–3). Listeners are naturally inclined to understand these warnings as referring to other people, not to themselves, but this passage is as much a caution to those who see themselves as faithful followers and apostles of Jesus as a warning about false followers.

It is possible, Matthew 7.21–2 says, to think or claim that one is speaking and acting in Jesus' name, but to bear bad fruit. Looking back to 7.6, one of the ways in which one might bear bad fruit might be by casting one's pearls before swine. This is often taken to mean that 'swine' are not worthy to receive 'pearls' (such as the gospel), but modern readers could equally hear it as saying (without insult to dogs or pigs) that it is foolish to give someone something they are not in a position to appreciate, or wrong to claim to be feeding someone with something which they cannot digest. On such a reading, this saying warns against prophesying or performing great deeds in circumstances in which they are not, or cannot be understood and responded to, or in a way which does not effectively communicate the good news. We can detect the same implication in Matthew 10.16: 'See, I am sending you out like sheep in the midst of wolves: be wise as serpents, and harmless as doves.' Persecution may come to those who are sent out in Jesus' name (cf. 10.17), but they are not encouraged to court it or enable it by not being wise.

Christian apostleship and mission have a long tradition of following Christ by accepting the risks involved in spreading the good news of the kingdom. In light of the idea that the faithful are entrusted with good news which is as precious as a pearl, however, we can hear another implication in these sayings. To prophesy, preach, or act in such a way that one's witness is indigestible to others, or creates incomprehension, anger, or resistance, is not to spread the good news effectively, nor to bear good fruit. Apostleship must be appropriate to its time, place, and audience; wise as a serpent as well as innocent as a dove. It must (as all ancient public speakers knew well) understand its listeners and how they will hear its message, and speak and act in such a way as to connect with them. Those who are entrusted with the gospel must treasure it and handle it with care, not waste it by communicating badly, acting badly, failing to understand those who are listening to it, or failing to understand what its impact or implications may be in a particular setting. Being entrusted with the gospel is therefore a call to emotional intelligence, empathy, cultural sensitivity, and respect for those with whom one is communicating. Not to enact those qualities is to throw away what has been entrusted to one.

Those who trust in God and Christ are likely to agree about the value of the good news that has been entrusted to them, but historically they have tended to disagree about many aspects of its content. Are gentiles called to keep the law of Moses? Are some people predestined not to trust, and so excluded from eternal life? How does Christ save? We have seen that New Testament writings affirm the capacity of human beings, limited and imperfect as they are, even from within the bounds of their existing traditions and circumstances, to recognize in Jesus someone who meets their needs and invites them into a new relationship with God. At the same time, they acknowledge that those who put their trust in Jesus and in God remain limited and imperfect and frequently fail in both trust and understanding.

Ethically, this double affirmation is cause for both confidence and caution. It suggests that the faithful can have some confidence in their mental and moral capacities, together with their experience, in responding to God and Christ and seeking to understand what has been entrusted to them in the Christ event. At the same time, it cautions that later followers of Jesus, like earlier ones, can make mistakes, and their understanding is always imperfect.[95]

The Christ event is not, by its nature, an unambiguous revelation of facts or truths. It is above all an invitation into a life-changing relationship. In everyday life, if we are invited into a relationship of trust with another human being, our response will be based partly on what we see of the other person, and partly on a willingness to take a risk and make a new bond. Within the relationship, we will probably learn more about the other, but our understanding will always be incomplete, and will always be framed by our particular relationship with them. If several people enter a trust relationship with the same person, moreover, they will enter it on the basis of many different viewpoints. Within the relationship, they will probably learn more about the other person through time, but their understanding will also always be framed by the particularities of their relationship. What experience tells us about human relationships is also attested by New Testament writings of relationships with God and Christ. What human beings see of God and Christ at the beginning of the relationship is framed by their existing world-view (hope for the coming of God's rule, hatred of injustice, a desire for healing...) together with their willingness to make a new bond of trust. Within the relationship, they can hope to learn more of God and Christ through time. Meanwhile, others who put their trust in God and Christ will probably see them differently, and, though they too will probably learn more of God and Christ through time, no one can assume that all human understandings of the divine will ever fully converge, at least before the end time. Where trust obtains, however, incomplete understanding need not hamper the relationship or what is possible for those who live in it. They are part of the complexity of persons and personal relationships, and just as we live and thrive with that complexity on the human plane, so the faithful may live and thrive with it in relation to God and Christ.[96]

---

[95] Cf. pp. 351–3.
[96] If we are looking for a basis on which to take a view of others' understanding of God or Christ, we might, for instance, wait to see the fruits of our neighbours' trust (Mt. 7.20, 12.33, cf. Acts 5.38–9), or leave judgment to God (cf. Rom. 12.19).

In Matthew's and Luke's parables of the end time, we saw the importance of the theme of stewardship and care. Until the last day, the faithful are entrusted with care: for God's household and all its members, and for the material wealth of God's creation.[97] Chapter 1 briefly described the ethics of care, including its emphasis that care is situational: what people need and how people can and should act depends on their situation in relation to one another and to wider society. Care and stewardship are similarly situational for the faithful. If there are varieties of gifts, there are also varieties of care. Every person and situation demands a different kind of care, and no one can practise every kind, but everyone can make a contribution.[98] It is vital to discern what kind of care is needed, and how it can be given well to a particular person and in a particular situation. As limited and imperfect human beings, the faithful will not always discern perfectly or give care perfectly. But, as the returning master commends the servants who have made use of his talents not primarily for how much money they have made, but for their trustworthiness, the call to let oneself be entrusted is a call to try to be trustworthy, not a call never to fail.

The parable of the talents suggests, moreover, that the faithful are called not only to care for the resources of God's world, but, like Godself, to be creative with them. To be entrusted with creation is to be trusted not only to preserve it, but to use it and help it to grow and change. The travelling master does not determine how his stewards should use his resources, but he hopes that they will be used. He leaves it open to them to surprise and delight him on his return.[99]

In passages in which Paul commends co-workers to his communities, and in the parable of the Good Samaritan, we see those who have been entrusted entrusting others with the care of an individual or community. Trust is not only to be accepted, but to be passed on. Just as Paul cannot control the behaviour of his co-workers, however, or those to whom they give authority in communities, trusting others means accepting that they may not be carbon copies of oneself in how they understand the gospel, what they preach, or how they act. Trust inescapably involves open-mindedness and tolerance: it recognizes that not everyone understands or fulfils a trust in the same way, or as the truster might hope or expect, or at all, and it trusts nevertheless. If I put my trust in you to save me from falling off a rock-face, I do not quibble about how you do it. If I trust you as my friend, I do not base my trust on an interrogation of your precise understanding

---

[97] Surveying Christian attitudes towards the environment, Shin and Preston (2021) argue that those who see themselves as stewards of creation show significantly more concern for climate change and favour more pro-environmental measures than those who see human beings as exercising dominion over the rest of creation.

[98] Even those who may seem to need care to the point that they cannot actively contribute to the care of others can be understood as contributing in passivity: see the classic account of Vanstone (1982).

[99] Cf. e.g. Wall (2005) arguing from the perspective of theoretical ethics that human moral life and thought should be radically creative.

of friendship. What matters in the relationship is not that everyone involved thinks or acts in the same way, but that everyone seeks to be trusting and trustworthy, as far as they can.

The nature of the ethical ideas which are most often articulated throughout New Testament writings fits well with the theme of entrustedness. These are what are sometimes called 'executive virtues', which tell people not specifically what to do, but generically how to act.[100] There are as many ways, for instance, to act with love, justice, generosity, gratitude, or peace, as there are situations in which to enact them. Executive virtues can also be described as 'therapeutic attitudes': attitudes and/or emotions which people hold in relation to others (divine or human), which also involve actions which either care for others or serve them.[101] In New Testament writings, all executive virtues or therapeutic attitudes are enacted first by God towards humanity, and then by human beings towards God and one another. When they affirm that the faithful are entrusted by God, New Testament writings affirm that God gives the faithful wide discretion in how they act virtuously or therapeutically. God entrusts to the faithful the freedom that God has, in accordance with Godself, to act, together with the responsibility for discerning what constitutes care for others and service to God and to humanity in a given situation.

The dominance of executive ethics and therapeutic attitudes in New Testament writings also underlines that however the faithful act, their actions are ideally an outworking of their relationship with God and Christ, and they are entrusted with freedom and responsibility for their actions as part of their faithfulness and service to God and Christ. The only criterion of 'success' is that the way they act contributes to the work of God and Christ for humanity. The affirmation of 1 Peter 4.19, that 'those who suffer in accordance with God's will hand their souls over to a faithful creator as they do good' can be generalized: all those who seek to do good in any way, at any time, can only do so by handing their souls over to a faithful creator and acting in accordance with God's will.[102]

Roman Faith observed that trust—in striking contrast, for instance, to love, peace, or justice—is never explicitly described by New Testament writers as an ethic or therapeutic attitude that should be practised by community members towards one another simply as community members (or, for that matter, to

---

[100] For discussions of executive virtues see e.g. Kleinig (2020) on loyalty, Sreenivasan (2020), 199–240 on courage. On the prevalence of executive virtues or ethics in ancient popular ethics see Morgan (2007), 180–2.
[101] Morgan (2020), 207–8.
[102] See the discussion of Neugebauer (1970), especially 79–86. The preference in these texts for executive ethics and therapeutic attitudes develops a theme in the scriptures and Jewish tradition (a *locus classicus* being Hos. 6.6), but where the law is not observed, or not uniformly, in early churches, even more weight falls on it than in law-observant communities. Though he does not discuss executive virtues as such, Novick's (2010) discussion of different rabbinic approaches to law-keeping shows how they are informed by what we could call executive virtues.

outsiders).[103] We can now add something to that observation. In practice, trust must be in play among community members in certain contexts. When, for instance, Paul calls himself or other apostles trustworthy, they are trustworthy primarily as 'servants of Christ and stewards of the mysteries of God' (1 Cor. 4.1), but this implies that other community members can trust them, at a minimum, when they exercise their particular ministry. In the case of apostles, that must mean that they can be trusted in other contexts too, since, for Paul, being an apostle also means overseeing and advising communities on their everyday workings and behaviour. The fact that *pistis* is always primarily between God, together with Christ, and human beings, however, highlights that human trustworthiness is always an outworking of that relationship. Human beings are not called to trust each other purely on the basis of their human qualities, nor to seek to be trustworthy to one another on the basis of their human qualities, but always as an expression of their relationship with God.

One implication of this is that we need to add something to the definition of trust we developed in Chapter 1. That definition assumed, with all contemporary philosophy and sociology of trust, that the trustworthiness of another person depends on the other's own ability and will to be trustworthy to the truster. Among the faithful, however, the trustworthiness of another person depends primarily on her will (which may not always be matched by her ability, since human trust in God is imperfect and fragile) to be trustworthy towards God and Christ. From the point of view of the truster, this configuration may have both advantages and disadvantages. It is less optimistic than are most definitions of trust between human beings, which assume that the trusted person has it in his power to be trustworthy. But if the trusted person is among the faithful, this configuration is more optimistic that he *will* be trustworthy if, in a given situation, he can be. Being trustworthy, as and when one can—indeed, practising all ethics as and when one can—is, for the faithful, not simply a choice in particular circumstances, but a requirement of one's relationship with God and Christ. When Paul says, 'While we have the opportunity, let us do good to all, especially to those of the community of trust' (Gal. 6.10),[104] we can hear him not only as commending an ethical practice, but as expressing the ethical imperative which follows from

---

[103] Especially if, as argued, 1 Cor. 12.9 refers to a particular gift such as apostolic trustworthiness, and Gal. 5.22 to ongoing faithfulness to God.

[104] τοὺς οἰκείους τῆς πίστεως. To translate this phrase, with some modern versions of the Bible, as 'members of the household of *the* faith', assumes a more significant evolution in the meaning of *pistis* than is detectable in Paul in general, and also sounds slightly odd, since one cannot be an *oikeios*, for instance, of a set of doctrines, or even the combination of a set of doctrines and an attitude or orientation of the mind and heart. But one can, without difficulty, be an *oikeios* of a community formed by a relationship. To translate this phrase 'fellow members of the relationship [or 'the bond'] of trust' assumes relatively little evolution in the meaning of *pistis* and makes sense in context; if the bond is understood as reified a little further here, we can translate *hē pistis* as 'the community of trust'.

trusting in God and Christ. This should, in principle, make Christ-confessors, if not perfect, at least more than normally willing to be trustworthy.

The commitment of the faithful to respond to the trust of God by being trustworthy to God, and to make this the basis of their relationships with other people, points to another ethical implication of entrustedness. Individuals and communities which seek to be trustworthy towards other human beings because they seek to be trustworthy to God may create a place or space in which those who find it hard to trust can come to trust—in the first place, in that person or group, but potentially also in God and in Christ. Trust in God creates a trustworthiness in the faithful which is not only (they hope) reliable, but universal, and disinterested in the sense that it does not depend on the attitude or circumstances of a potential truster.

Imagine, for instance, that I work in an office notorious for its atmosphere of gossip, bullying, and back-stabbing. Nobody trusts anyone. Everyone is permanently slightly on edge, and people tend to be either aggressive or defensive towards their co-workers. Many of us are working on creative projects, but any kind of exchange of ideas or collaboration is hard to imagine. One colleague, however, has a reputation for being trustworthy.[105] Her trustworthiness is based on her religious convictions, and is unaffected by the behaviour of those around her. Perhaps I might dare to trust her. I might start by taking my coffee break with her and chatting to her. After a while, I risk sharing an idea I have for a new product. She expresses interest and offers some suggestions for improving it. We talk, refine the idea, generate more ideas, pitch one of them successfully to the management. We go on talking. Because we now each have someone we can trust, the working day becomes a little less stressful, more creative, and more enjoyable. We can relax a little more; make a joke; take an interest in one another's hobbies. Perhaps one or two other people drift towards us during the coffee break, intrigued by the sight of trust in operation.

Those whose trust has been damaged (which, to a greater or lesser degree, is most of us) are often wary of trusting people who may have their own agenda: personal reasons to be, or seem trustworthy, or to be trustworthy now without any guarantees for the future. One of the most powerful tools of mission and care with which the faithful are entrusted is what I have just called universal, disinterested trustworthiness: trustworthiness that is not self-interested or limited to particular situations. This kind of trustworthiness creates a space in which trust can take a risk and grow, which is unique and potentially transformative. It can, moreover, change not only the present, but participants' sense of the future: their ability to look forward, hope, and plan, not just for the short but for the longer term. In Chapter 1 we noted a study by Matthew Ratcliffe, Mark Ruddell, and

---

[105] Exploring trustworthiness as a moral quality which encourages trust see Simpson (2012).

Benedict Smith, which argued that victims of trauma suffer from a 'sense of foreshortened future' as a result of their loss of trust in the world.[106] In sharp contrast to this sense of foreshortened future, New Testament texts everywhere attest that trust in God and Christ enables the faithful to look forward, in hope and confidence, as far as human imagination can travel: to the eschatological future, the ultimate rule of God over heaven and earth, and eternal life.

The vision of trust we have sketched begins to point to ways in which entrustedness and trustworthiness may change not only individuals and relationships, but societies. The kind of trustworthiness which arises from accepting one's entrustedness by God has the capacity to attract and retain trust, and relationships of trust based on trustworthiness have the capacity to attract further trust, creating, over time, ever wider and more complex networks of trust. This kind of trustworthiness can be seen, further, as an act of therapeutic trust and entrusting of its own. Those who are trustworthy in human societies because of their acceptance of their entrustedness by God, imitate and act as a sign of the trust and trustworthiness of God and Christ, and become part in God's outreach to the world.

This study has only begun to touch on ecclesiology, but in the idea of an ethic of entrustedness we can begin to see how trust between God, Christ, and the faithful might be enacted in the human sphere, among the faithful as a community and as the faithful reach out to the wider world. The *pistis* relationship has the capacity to shape all other relationships in the human sphere, inviting human beings to relate to one another and the rest of creation with empathy, sensitivity, and respect; to care for one another as they can and as others need; to use own their own gifts and recognize other people's; to entrust others with gifts and responsibilities as they are entrusted themselves; to enjoy and develop their material environment for the benefit of all creation; to recognize the limits of their understanding of the divine–human relationship and its many possible inflections; and to create a space in which every being can trust and flourish.

Conclusion

In Chapter 2 we argued that (specifically for Paul and his followers, but implicitly for all Christ-confessors) God has done a 'new thing', reaching out to humanity in an act of therapeutic trust which seeks to forge a new trust relationship with those who respond. In this, God is faithful to God's past relationship with humanity as a whole, and especially to God's covenants with Israel, and fulfils all God's promises, but the (re)new(ed) relationship God offers is also a new partnership, in

---

[106] pp. 21–2.

which human beings play a new role. This act in itself entrusts human beings: with recognizing God's presence in an atypical Messiah and God's actions through him; with putting their trust in God and in Jesus Christ; and with accepting their part in a new divine–human relationship. Not only trust, but entrustedness stands at the heart of the relationship between God and humanity. In Chapter 4, we saw that, for ex-offenders, being entrusted with new relationships and new roles can form an important part of the restoration of trust which allows them to be rehabilitated and become part of mainstream society. This chapter has focused on the entrustedness of those who have already put their trust in God and Christ, but we can note that God's entrusting of humanity begins even before human beings' response of trust, and is part of the foundation of the relationship as well as part of the relationship itself.

One young offender quoted in Chapter 4 testified to the power of trust, especially therapeutic trust, in making him feel better about himself.[107] Both Brothers' model of how trust develops and the work of McGeer and Pettit, which we described in Chapter 1, also attest to the psychological importance of being trusted and being seen as trustworthy.[108] Being trusted in itself can make people feel trustworthy, and motivate them to be more trustworthy. When we envisage God as reaching out to humanity in trust, therefore, we may envisage God as offering not only a (re)new(ed) relationship of trust, but, just as significantly, a (re)new(ed) trustworthiness; as encouraging humanity to feel capable of being entrusted.

Recognizing and responding to divine trust, however, is demanding, and those who do so are always liable to fail in one way or another. The risk of failure is intrinsic to all trust, especially therapeutic trust, but New Testament writings offer encouragement to those who take the risk. They do not entertain the possibility that a just and loving God would entrust humanity with a trust it could not bear. In the present time, moreover, the faithful have time (though they do not know how much) to make mistakes and learn from them. On the other hand, the logic of Paul's proclamation, in particular (though Paul does not articulate it), leaves open that the God who has acted anew through Christ might choose to do another new thing and invite those who have put their trust in God and Christ to recognize and respond to a new divine initiative. The relationship of trust, which is voluntary on both sides and open to the future, could change. The trusting and entrusted cannot take God's trust for granted.

In almost every chapter so far, we have seen that those who trust in God and Christ are entrusted with the news of what God has done through Christ; with spreading that news; with imitating Christ in their own lives and acting as a model for others; with growing the number of those who trust and entrusting

---

[107] pp. 185–6. [108] pp. 11–12, 19–21.

them in turn with the teaching, inspiration, and responsibilities for action which they have been given; with stewarding God's material world and those who live in it; and, in the process, with becoming more like Christ in their relationship with God and with the world. The God who creates and cares for the world invites those who trust to join with Godself and Christ in caring for creation until the end time. Those who trust have a good deal of discretion as to how they care for creation, but not infinite licence. They cannot, for instance, simply seek to preserve the status quo: they must (in an echo of Gen. 1.28 and 2.15) be creative and work with the world's capacity for creativity and change. They must make allies and share the work with others. Above all, they must not put their interests over those of the whole 'household of God'.

In Chapter 4, a sketch of atonement, beginning from Paul's undisputed letters, which put the restoration of trust at the heart of the restoration of the relationship between God and humanity through the *pistis* of Jesus Christ, saw human beings as entrusted with the memory of Christ's suffering and death, and with trusting in God and Christ despite the enormity of that suffering. God, we argued, trusts Christ to be trusting, trustworthy, and faithful to God, no matter what happens to him. Christ trusts God to work through him, even in his suffering and death. Both God and Christ trust humanity to be able to respond to God's working through Christ, even when it involves Christ's death. Human beings are entrusted, in company with Christ, with taking a journey of death to sin and to the power of both sin and suffering over them, which may look fearfully risky, but which brings them to new life in God's kingdom and under Christ's authority. Those who have undertaken that journey are entrusted even further, with imitating Christ and acting as a model for others to show that those who entrust themselves to God cannot be separated from God or Christ by any physical or metaphysical power. Putting one's trust in God and Christ may bring suffering, even death, in this life, but for those who trust, suffering and death have no more capacity than any other physical or metaphysical power to separate them, as Paul expresses it, from the love of God in Christ Jesus (Rom. 8.39).

The sign of the power of this trust, above all, is the experience of the resurrection, which reveals how trust in God is justified and highlights the continuity between earthly and heavenly life for those who trust and are trusted by God. In the resurrection God entrusts humanity with an experience which testifies to God's ongoing faithfulness and trustworthiness, and by trusting human beings to respond to the experience and pass on the tradition, entrusts to them a role in God's and Christ's ongoing work of bringing humanity to trust. In this process, the resurrection not only entrusts humanity with a revelation about the past and present, but with hope for the future. The divine–human relationship of trust always, in this life, has a future, and, in eternal life, has a future 'always'.

Chapters 5 and 6 argued that, especially for the synoptic gospels, but even, in some respects, for John, those who encounter Jesus in his earthly life are entrusted with recognizing him from within their existing experience, tradition, and culture, whether Jewish or gentile. The invitation to trust in Jesus in his lifetime does not depend on divine self-revelation; on signs, miracles, or acts of power; or even on Jesus' preaching or prophecy. It should be, and, in many stories, is enough for those who trust to encounter a man of God, who is wholly devoted to God and speaks and acts for God. What is more, those who meet Jesus in his earthly life are entrusted with coming to him through themselves: through their own suffering, need, curiosity, or openness. Nor does it matter that their trust is always limited in understanding, imperfect, fragile, and inchoate. The ultimate adequacy of imperfect trust, as those who encounter Jesus exemplify it, confirms God's therapeutic trust in humanity, which, even in its damaged and sinful condition, is entrusted with the life-changing encounter with God in Jesus Christ.

Like human beings who enact therapeutic trust, we may imagine God as hoping that human beings will become more trusting and trustworthy over time.[109] The open-endedness of the future, and the uncertainty of the day and the hour of the end, allows human beings to continue to hope that God is tolerant of their slowness to become fully trusting or trustworthy. But our analysis also suggests that human beings can be optimistic. In themselves, in their experience, their needs, and their openness, in existing tradition and culture, even in their imperfect understanding and vulnerability to fear, doubt, and scepticism, they have all the tools they need for life-giving trust. To be entrusted by God, as a human being in a deeply imperfect world, is in itself a reason to be hopeful and confident in one's trust.

To put it another way, when human beings encounter God in Christ, in his earthly or exalted life, in person, in tradition, or in the community of those who follow Christ, they can trust their impressions, instincts, reason, experience (individual and communal), and traditions, if they invite them to trust in Christ, and in God encountered through Christ. Human beings are imperfect in every way—physically, mentally, morally, imaginatively—and are always liable to mistake much of what they experience or infer from experience. But the human beings to whom God reaches out through Christ in trust are human beings in their imperfect condition. The offer of trust which is entrusted to humanity is one of a process by which human beings may enter and grow in a new kind of life, a new existence, and a new, creative, open-ended relationship with the divine.

Not the smallest part of this relationship is the work it entrusts to humanity to do. This chapter is the culmination of an argument running throughout this study, that the Christian narrative of God as trusting Christ, God and Christ as trusting humanity, and humanity as responding to God and Christ in trust, offers a profoundly optimistic vision of humanity and its capacity, despite all its

---

[109] Cf. pp. 70–2.

limitations and shortcomings, to enter and live in a relationship of right-standing and abundant life with God. Even more: it offers a vision of humanity as invited to share God's optimism for creation, and to join God and Christ in working to substantiate it. To support the work of the faithful for God and Christ, we have proposed that we need an ethic of entrustedness, and have offered a preliminary sketch of one. Accepting one's entrustedness involves accepting both service and partnership with God; both recognition of God's unlimited and awful creativity and recognition of one's own creativity; proclamation of good news which accepts uncertainty about aspects of the proclamation; unconditional trust and faithfulness to God together with close involvement and empathy with one's fellow human beings. It means accepting the pearl of great price and devoting all one's wisdom and all one's innocence to sharing it with the world.

8
'This saying is trustworthy'
Propositional Trust in the Divine-Human Relationship

So far this study has focused on the relationship of trust between God, Christ, and humanity.[1] In Chapter 1, however, we noted that trust—in conjunction, for instance, with knowledge or belief, or in contrast to either—may also act as one of the foundations of the relationship. This chapter turns to 'propositional trust': trust that something is the case. Propositional trust is even more neglected in modern theology than relational trust, but what follows will argue that it has a role to play alongside knowledge and belief as one of the foundations of divine–human trust, and when human beings commit themselves and their future to their trust in God and Christ.[2]

In principle, one could argue that propositional trust could or should take the place of belief or knowledge, and Christians could or should, for example, trust rather than believe that God raised Christ from the dead, or that God, with Christ, made possible the reconciliation of God and humanity through Christ's death. We have seen, however, that, in New Testament writings, relational trust in God and Christ, together with personal knowledge of God and Christ, is sometimes explicitly, and often implicitly based on propositional beliefs. In addition, we have not seen any examples, in New Testament writings, of propositions about God and Christ or their activities which human beings trust, which are not grounded in part in relational trust and/or knowing, and therefore likely, indirectly, in beliefs.[3] We can therefore assume that propositional trust, as understood by New Testament writers, is likely to be rooted at least partly in propositional beliefs, so we will begin by assuming that propositional trust has a role in Christian thinking alongside belief, and also alongside, at least, relational knowing.

This chapter proceeds rather differently from earlier chapters, which are based on close readings of New Testament texts. There are two reasons for this. The

---

[1] The chapter heading quotation is from 1 Tim. 1.15.
[2] It is tempting to describe the account of propositional trust that follows as a 'hermeneutic of trust', but that phrase is already in use with a rather different meaning, in opposition to the hermeneutics of suspicion.
[3] This may seem paradoxical after the previous point, but it reflects the fact that Christian trust and belief do not arise in a vacuum: e.g. resurrection belief has roots in scripture and in Jews' and godfearers' existing trust in God.

great preponderance of trust language in New Testament writings is relational; few passages are explicitly propositional, and we have discussed most of these where we have encountered them.[4] In addition, the idea of propositional trust in itself is less familiar than the idea of relational trust, so one of the aims of this chapter is to investigate it as a concept: to consider what it looks like, how it relates to belief, knowledge, and relational trust, and why it matters.

Propositional Trust

In everyday speech, when we say that we trust that something is the case, we often mean that we hope or assume it is, or wish to be assured it is. 'I trust that you are well' is a (now rather old-fashioned) way of saying, 'I hope you are well'—perhaps with an implication that I have heard nothing to make me doubt it. When my boss says that she trusts that I will arrive on time for our meeting tomorrow, I infer that she expects that I will, and wishes me to assure her that I will.[5] In these cases, 'trust that', is so similar to other attitudes as to be practically indistinguishable from them. In other cases, 'trust that' is resolvable to 'trust in' a person. Saying that I trust that my partner will continue to be faithful to me is tantamount to saying that I trust my partner to continue to be faithful.[6]

Sometimes, however, propositional trust is distinguishable from relational trust and other cognitive or affective attitudes. Every day, for example, thousands of travellers use the elevators at King's Cross underground station in London, trusting that the elevators will not break down and leave them stranded. Cognitively, their trust is less than knowledge that the elevators are in good order, but it could involve the belief, hope, or assumption that they are.[7] Once the travellers are in the elevator, they are also relying on it practically not to fail.[8] But their propositional trust is a little more than this. Whatever their cognitive attitude, when the travellers trust that the elevators are safe, they act on the basis of it, entrusting themselves and their future to the proposition. (Or at least, they are willing to act: on a given day, a traveller could trust propositionally by trusting that the elevators would be safe if he chose to use them.)

---

[4] E.g. pp. 65–6, 117–18, 226–7 n.128.
[5] This could be heard as a coercive form of therapeutic trust, which aims to make someone more trustworthy by articulating the trust that they will be; there is no sign, though, that coercion is an aspect of trust between God, Christ, and the faithful.
[6] Cf. pp. 22–3.
[7] If they are able-bodied, at least, the travellers' trust involves more than an attitude of reliance, because there are also escalators and stairs, so using an elevator is a choice.
[8] They rely on the elevator rather than trust it at this point, because it cannot respond to their attitude to it, but only do what it is programmed to do. The question of trusting in or relying on appliances raises the question what kind of trust one can have in a robot that is programmed to respond, e.g. to the human voice or actions; this is beyond our scope, but on trust in robotics see Coeckelbergh (2012), Kwiatkowska (2017), Nam and Lyons (2021).

As a starting-point, therefore, I suggest, 'trusting that', at its most distinguishable from other attitudes or relationships, means entrusting oneself, or being willing to entrust oneself, to a proposition about which one accepts that one is not certain. As in the case of personal trust, assuming that most people are not self-destructive, the fact that one is willing to entrust oneself to a proposition means that one's attitude to it is likely to be positive (or what one thinks of as a positive attitude[9]). As in the case of personal trust, propositional trust can exist as an attitude even when one is not acting on it, and one can, in principle, act with propositional trust without holding any attitude towards the proposition. Like personal trust, however, propositional trust most characteristically involves both an attitude and an action, or willingness to act.

We have noted that, with the exceptions of Pierangelo Sequeri and Ingolf Dalferth and his collaborators, few contemporary theologians or philosophers of religion writing about faith or belief have had much to say about trust.[10] Both Sequeri and Dalferth, however, focus on the relationship of trust between God and humanity.[11] One of very few scholars who have touched on propositional trust in recent theological or philosophical writing is Robert Audi, who, in his article 'Belief, faith, and acceptance' and the monograph *Rationality and Religious Commitment*, discusses both relational and propositional trust.[12] As we have done, Audi distinguishes between trusting in persons and in propositions, while recognizing that one can 'trust that' something is true of a person in a sense which is equivalent to trusting in that person.[13] Alternatively, one may 'trust that' something is the case in a sense closely connected with what he terms 'propositional faith'. Propositional faith involves a cognitive attitude (which could be belief or something else) 'that' something is the case, together with a positive attitude towards its being the case, and is similar to the first type of 'trust that' which we discussed at the beginning of this section.[14]

Explicit examples of propositional trust are rare in New Testament writings, but we have encountered a few.[15] They fall broadly into four groups. In the Johannine corpus, they nearly always invite Jesus' followers to *pisteuein* that Jesus

---

[9] Though a self-destructive person, presumably, might choose to trust that his parachute is defective, while a sociopath might trust that her actions will hurt others and see this as a positive thing.

[10] pp. 1–2.

[11] As does e.g. Lassak (2010, 2013); Dalferth and Peng-Keller are also interested in 'one-place' trust, or the attitude of general trust towards the world, among human beings: e.g. (2013), 1–11, 212.

[12] Audi (2008, 2011a, cf. 1991, 2011b, 2011c). [13] Audi (2011a), 61, 71–2, 73–4, cf. 54–5.

[14] (2011a), 54–5, 72, 73–4, cf. 54–5; this is similar to the first type of 'trust that' at the top of this section. Non-doxastic propositional faith can be called 'fiducial faith'; this kind of faith can accommodate doubt, and may come close to modern fideism or the 'leap of faith'. Though he does not explain the relationship between this and the traditional 'leap of faith'. Audi (2008), 96–7, (2011), 71, 83; see pp. 1–2. Arguably, rather than believing that something is the case one might, for instance, hope or accept that it is.

[15] As noted at various points, it can be difficult to separate from believing and some passages probably bear an inflection of both, but I have identified *pisteuein* as propositional trust where commitment as well as a cognitive attitude is at stake.

is the Messiah, the Son of God.[16] When, for example, Jesus asks the Twelve, after the 'Bread of life' discourse, whether they want to leave him, as other followers have done, Peter says, 'Master, to whom shall we go? You have the words of eternal life. And we have come to *pisteuein* and know that you are the holy one of God' (6.68–9). Those who *pisteuein* and know that Jesus is the holy one are those who actively follow him, so *pisteuein hoti* is more than propositional belief: it involves self-commitment and is well translated 'trust that'. At 1 John 5.4–5, the one who *pisteuein* that Jesus is the Son of God is the one who is begotten by God and conquers the world, so *pisteuein hoti* involves not only 'believing that', but describes the personal commitment of one who is part of God's family and sides with God and Christ against the world.[17]

In Paul's letters, we saw that instances of propositional trust refer to trust that the resurrection took place or to the eschatological future, when the faithful trust that God will raise the dead (2 Cor. 4.13–14) and that they will live with Christ (Rom. 6.8).[18] In these cases, propositional trust, rooted in belief, hope, and personal trust in God and Christ, commits itself to Christ and entrusts itself and its future to that commitment.[19]

In the pastoral epistles, a *logos* is several times said to be *pistos* (1 Tim. 1.15, 3.1, 4.9, 2 Tim. 2.11, Tit. 1.9, 3.8). At 1 Timothy 1.15, for instance, [Paul] says, 'This saying is *pistos* and worthy of full acceptance: that Christ Jesus came into the world to save sinners.' Accepting this testimony, for Paul and all the faithful, is not only a matter of propositional belief (though it presumes belief), but involves committing themselves to Christ and accepting God's grace and mercy (cf. 1.13, 14, 16) in hope of salvation. The faithful therefore not only believe that this saying is true, but trust that it is true and entrust themselves and their eventual salvation to it, and the saying is not only believable, but (as it is usually translated) trustworthy.[20] Trust in the truth of such sayings is probably based on a complex of trust in the authority of those who handed them down, trust in one's own experience of God, Christ, and other faithful people, and the coherence of one's experience and the teaching with the experience of others and with tradition and

---

[16] Jn 6.69, 8.24, 11.27, 11.42, 13.19, 14.10–11, 16.30, 17.8, 17.21, 20.31; 1 Jn 5.4–5, cf. Jn. 4.21. Contrast the belief (*pisteuein*) of the demons in the Letter of James (2.19) which involves no personal commitment and does not bring one into one's right relationship with God or keep one in it.

[17] John's gospel also offers examples of the kind of propositional trust that is resolvable to trust in a person. Trusting that Jesus is the Son of God is tantamount to trusting in him as Son of God; unsurprisingly, all those in John's gospel who believe and trust that Jesus is the Son of God are also said to trust in him or to trust him as Messiah and Son of God: Morgan (2015a), 425–9.

[18] At Lk. 1.45, Elizabeth praises Mary for believing or trusting (*pisteuein*) that what was spoken to her by the Lord would be fulfilled, referring both to her pregnancy and indirectly to the identity and eschatological triumph of her son (cf. 1.32–3, 35).

[19] We noted above that at 2 Cor. 4.14 Paul expresses the strength of his trust by affirming that he does not only believe but 'knows' that the one who raised Jesus will raise the faithful.

[20] NB when speaking of something or someone as trustworthy in connection with propositional trust, I take 'trustworthy' to mean not 'certain' 'certainly true', or 'reliable' but 'worth taking a risk on' and 'worth entrusting oneself to'.

scripture.[21] If so, then propositional trust here is partly resolvable to relational trust, and is partly based on a mixture of assumption, experience, and trust that scripture and tradition are themselves trustworthy.[22]

Trust and the Challenge of Believing or Knowing

If Sequeri, Dalferth and his collaborators, and Audi are unusual among theologians and philosophers of religion in their interest in trust, they are not entirely alone. In recent years, a handful of other leading philosophers of religion has begun to reflect on trust, in the course of writing about what we can reasonably believe about God. Interest in trust seems to be growing particularly in the context of the modern problematization of the foundations of propositional belief and knowledge of the divine. It is therefore worth sketching—very briefly, and with no aspirations to doing justice to a vast field—some developments in the philosophy of religion and Christian theology which suggest both why trust may be an interesting and topical subject, and where the idea of propositional as well as relational trust has a contribution to make.

Greek philosophers and theologians had been interested in what could be known about the divine, and on what basis one might believe anything about the divine, since long before the emergence of Christianity.[23] Their discussions were typically couched in the language of thinking and knowing: *nomizein, dokein, gignōskein, phronein, doxa*, and *gnōsis*. Platonists, however were unusual in discussing belief using *pistis* and *pisteuein* in their everyday 'belief' register.[24] For very early Christians, as we have seen, the centre of gravity of the divine–human relationship was *pistis* in its common relational sense of trust, trustworthiness, and faithfulness. From the second century, however, Christian philosophers, notably Justin Martyr, Clement of Alexandria, and Origen, influenced by Platonism, increasingly discussed the nature and foundations of belief in God and Christ using *pistis* language. At the same time, they read earlier Christian writings through a Platonist lens, which led them to reinterpret *pistis* and its relatives in early writings as language of belief, rather than trust.[25] By the fourth century, Christian philosophers

---

[21] Cf. pp. 100–8.
[22] The *logoi* in question may be written or oral; the idea that writings become more trustworthy, of course, grows through time, but they are always trustworthy because they are understood as the word of God, so to trust that writings are trustworthy or true is always, for Christians, based ultimately on relational trust in God.
[23] The earliest attestation of the word *theologia* is at Pl., *Rp.* 379a.
[24] I am indebted here to the unpublished essay '*Pistis* and Platonism' by Mark Edwards.
[25] Morgan (2021a), 10–13. The other main reason for increasing Christian interest in belief was disputes among groups of Christ-confessors, e.g. about the nature of Christ, the earliest of which also tended to be couched in the language of thought and knowledge.

writing about *pistis* or *fides* were focusing heavily on its belief aspect, confirming a tendency which continued through the mediaeval and into the modern world.

Modern religious, as well as secular epistemology was given fresh impetus and new directions not least by the work of René Descartes and Immanuel Kant.[26] By asking what human beings can know by reason about the world or about God, they contributed to a world-view in which autonomous human reason seeks objective knowledge which corresponds to physical or metaphysical reality. The nineteenth century saw challenges to this model from diverse viewpoints, from Schleiermacher's argument that religion is rooted in a sense of dependence on God rather than in knowledge of God, to Kierkegaard's claim that 'subjectivity is truth'.[27] The idea, however, that human reason seeks knowledge which corresponds to reality, not least about God, remained dominant into the early twentieth century, fortified by the growth and development of the sciences, which used essentially the same model.

The explosion of debate about the nature and limits of knowledge and reasonable belief, both secular and religious, since the mid-twentieth century has many roots. Empiricism, which dominated early twentieth-century philosophy, was challenged with increasing effectiveness. Modernism, which appealed to reason as a way of analysing the world, even while it worried about its own limitations, and which both valorized and problematized the role of the autonomous subject seeking to understand her world, was confronted from the 1940s by the many forms of postmodernism. Empiricism's recognition that rational people can make conflicting observations about the world, together with post-war social and cultural liberalism and the development of postmodernism, challenged western culture's relatively monolithic world-view and sense of its superiority to other cultures, and fostered cultural and, in some quarters, philosophical relativism.

Two of the major casualties of this period were foundationalism, with its claim that knowledge must rest on justified belief (classically based on experience, self-consciousness, or reason), and correspondence theories of truth, with their claim that true statements must correspond to an external reality.[28] As Stanley J. Grenz and John R. Franke put it, 'In the postmodern context...foundationalism is in dramatic retreat, as its assertions about the objectivity, certainty, and universality of knowledge have come under withering critique. This demise of foundationalism carries fundamental and far-reaching implications for theological method.'[29] In 1999, Bruce Marshall observed that few theologians would self-identify any longer as foundationalists or correspondentists in any traditional sense.[30] Most of the most influential philosophical theologies of the

---

[26] Among many recent surveys see e.g. Byrne (1995), Clements (1995).
[27] Healy and Chervin (2019).
[28] On various forms of foundationalism and justified belief see Audi (2011b), 206–41, 246–67.
[29] Grenz and Franke (2001), 24.   [30] Marshall (1999), 81.

past generation have, in very varied ways, sought alternatives to foundationalism, correspondentism, or both.[31]

Philosophical and theological debates since the mid-twentieth century have been paralleled, and sometimes stimulated, by debates in the philosophy of science about the nature of scientific truth and knowledge, where new arguments about the nature of scientific truth and knowledge have sharpened critiques of correspondentism and foundationalism. Since the ground-breaking work of Karl Popper, Mary Hesse, and Thomas Kuhn, it is no longer normative to see the sciences as demonstrating the nature of reality by observation or by proving reality's correspondence to scientific theories.[32] Scientists are much more widely understood as working within elective paradigms: often metaphorical or imagistic ways of seeing their subject-matter which frame their assumptions, questions, experiments, observations, theories, and proofs.

The later twentieth century saw a wealth of new theories about the nature of religious knowledge or reasonable religious belief. John Hick, for example, argued that Christian doctrine is less indicative than expressive; it does not articulate a metaphysical fact but expresses human attitudes and values.[33] Maurice Wiles understood God as ultimate reality, but the historical actions we attribute to God as symbols and parables of God's purpose rather than statements of objective or verifiable fact.[34] Don Cupitt went further, arguing that all talk of God is a symbolic way of expressing human values.[35]

George Lindbeck divided late twentieth and early twenty-first century theology into three broad schools.[36] The first, most traditional school 'emphasizes the cognitive aspects of religion and stresses the ways in which church doctrines function as informative propositions or truth claims about objective realities'. The second, liberal school 'interprets doctrines as noninformative and nondiscursive symbols of inner feelings, attitudes, or existential orientations'. The third 'attempts to combine these two emphases'.[37] Lindbeck proposes a fourth way which he calls 'cultural-linguistic', which sees religions as analogous to languages and cultures and doctrines as 'communally authoritative rules of discourse, attitude and action' within them, and seeks to describe these rules and how they function within a tradition.[38]

Since the later twentieth century, theologians and philosophers of religion have explored what we can know, truthfully say, or reasonably believe about God and the divine–human relationship from very varied perspectives. Most of these have

---

[31] See notably Phillips (1988), Hector (2011).
[32] Hesse (1955, 1966), Kuhn (1962), Popper (1963, 1973, 1980), Ratzsch (2011), 66–8, cf. Friedman and Carterette (1996), Narmour (2011).
[33] E.g. Hick (2005b), 167–85, (2005a), cf. (1967).
[34] E.g. Wiles (1982), 17–30, (1993), cf. (1977).   [35] E.g. Cupitt (2001).
[36] Lindbeck (2009).   [37] p. 2.
[38] Developing Geertz (1973); cf. especially Phillips (1988, 1993).

in common that they are dissatisfied with traditional theories of truth or knowledge, or think traditional views need new or reworked arguments in their defence. It is in the context of some of these new approaches that some scholars have become interested in trust.[39]

In *Faith and Reason*, Richard Swinburne offers a series of arguments for believing in the Christian understanding of God, in the course of which he points out that we should distinguish between belief, which, in a tradition that reaches back to antiquity, is his main concern, and faith, which is a more complex phenomenon including trust, love, and right action.[40] What Christians can reasonably believe about the God who, through Christ, saves those who believe, is of vital interest to people of faith, but it is not the whole, or even the *sine qua non* of faith.[41] In this context, Swinburne offers a substantial discussion of trust in God as an aspect of the divine–human relationship.[42] He characterizes faith which involves a significant element of trust as 'Lutheran' (as opposed to 'Thomist' faith, which he views as essentially propositional belief).[43] Swinburne understands trust as personal, relational 'trust in the Living God. The person of faith...does not merely believe that there is a God (and believe certain propositions about him), he trusts Him and commits himself to him'.[44] Moving beyond Lutheranism, and drawing on a Pragmatist view of faith indebted to William James, Swinburne also argues that it is possible to act with trust in God without having a firm attitude of belief in God, on the basis that 'religion offers a "vital good" now, and an eternal well-being hereafter', and therefore that it is rational to act, in trust, as though one's religion is true, whether one is sure of it or not.[45] Swinburne does not consider the possibility of propositional trust, but in earlier chapters of this study we have seen abundant parallels for both the personal trust which he characterizes as 'Lutheran' and the idea that one can act with trust without holding firm beliefs about God.[46]

---

[39] In addition to the examples discussed here, recent writing on the rationality of faith occasionally registers consciousness of the relevance of trust by taking faith to involve trust, but without much discussion: e.g. Buchak (2012), 232–3.

[40] Swinburne (2005).

[41] Swinburne notes ((2005), 154–5) that some patristic authors take a significant interest in trust, citing Clement of Alexandria and Cyril of Jerusalem (though for Clement, as for Origen and Augustine, trust is the first step in a relationship which leads to belief and knowledge).

[42] (2005), 142–53.

[43] p. 42. Luther's view that trust was integral to faith caused him to be anathematized by the Council of Trent (*De justificatione*, canon 12), despite the Council's view that trust was one of the steps by which human beings are justified. Later Lutheran theologians subordinated both knowledge and assent to trust (pp. 110–11).

[44] (2005), 142, though recent work in the philosophy of trust has overtaken his definition (pp. 143–4).

[45] pp. 148, 149.

[46] On the basis of this study we can add several further points which Swinburne does not explore, and not all of which he might accept, but none of which is obviously incoherent with his argument: that trust is never, for Christians, only between God and humanity but always between God, Christ, and humanity; that it is two-place as well as three-place; that it looks both back and forward; that it is

We have already mentioned Robert Audi, who explores both relational and propositional trust in the course of his defence of the rationality of religious commitment. For Audi, trust is part of the attitudinal or practical commitment 'faith' (which includes, but is not limited to religious faith): a complex concept with diverse objects (including persons, institutions, and propositions) which may involve a range of attitudes (including belief, hope, loyalty, and acceptance).[47] Trust, Audi argues, is essential to having faith in a person: 'we cannot have faith in a person we do not trust'.[48] It is also part of the attitude of faith: when we have faith, for instance, that God will provide.[49] The kind of trust involved in faith is more than reliance. It may or may not involve belief, but it does involve holding a positive attitude towards, for instance, the person or proposition trusted.[50] Audi's is a study of religious commitment rather than of what we can know or reasonably believe about God, but within that framework he offers novel and nuanced accounts of belief, faith (which he takes as a dimension of religious commitment rather than a synonym for it), and trust, and their complex relationships. For our purposes, it is particularly striking that he understands trust as central to both relational and propositional faith, including faith in God, and as often, but not necessarily, based on belief. On his view, a satisfactory account of religious 'faith', including in its propositional aspects, cannot ignore the centrality of trust.

Some of the philosophical theologians known as 'Reformed epistemologists' are also interested in trust. In his introduction to *Faith and Rationality*, Nicholas Wolterstorff observes that faith is much more than belief or intellectual assent. It is a total stance towards God to which we are called by God, and which includes belief, obedience, hope, fidelity, and trust.[51] Wolterstorff points out that the root meaning of Christian *pistis* is trust. 'Belief,' he suggests, 'is not the organizing center of faith. Trust is that.'[52] Since the nature and rationality of belief is the focus of this volume, Wolterstorff does not pursue his point about trust far, nor does he consider the possibility of propositional as well as relational trust, but his affirmation of the centrality of relational trust in faith, specifically at the roots of Christian tradition, again fits well with the findings of this study.

Some recent studies of religious knowledge also canvass the possibility that trust is part of knowledge of God. Paul Gooch, in his essay 'Faithful knowing', argues (what New Testament commentators, especially on John, have long recognized) that knowledge of God is more like knowledge of one person by another

---

a process as well as an act of commitment; that it may be weaker or stronger and cut with varying degrees of (one-off, intermittent, or persistent) fear, doubt, or scepticism; that human beings not only trust but are entrusted by God and Christ; that God, Christ, and human beings all sometimes act with therapeutic trust; and that trust does not stay between those who trust but is imitable and transmissible.

[47] Audi (2011a), 52–65.　　[48] p. 71, cf. 55.　　[49] pp. 71–2.

[50] pp. 61, 71–2, 83. He proposes (p. 77), that trust tends to diminish or eliminate negative emotions such as fear, which, as we have seen, is not the view of New Testament writings.

[51] Wolterstorff (1983), 10–15.　　[52] p. 11.

than like propositional knowledge. As such, love is intrinsic to it, and so is trust.[53] In *Revitalizing Theological Epistemology*, Steven B. Sherman argues that theological knowledge should be thought of not primarily, as it has been thought of since the Enlightenment, as objective knowledge about God, but as relational knowing, centred on the person and work of Christ.[54] Objective knowledge may be possible for humanity in the eschatological future but, in the meantime, salvation comes through personal knowledge of God and Christ, which comes to humanity as a gift of the spirit and is recognized and enacted in this world in community and in a life of practical perseverance.[55] In the course of this argument, Sherman suggests that not only personal knowing, but trust is central to salvation: the self-revelation of God may be thought of as leading to salvation by means of trust in God and Christ.[56] In addition, he proposes, 'trusting in the kerygma is essentially *trusting that* knowledge of God has been made manifest by God in the Person of Jesus...'.[57] Personal trust is built, not least, on propositional trust that the kerygma reflects what God has revealed through Christ for humanity's salvation.

In the past few years, trust has begun to make its way closer to the centre of the epistemological stage in a series of articles by Daniel Howard-Snyder, Jonathan Kvanvig, and Daniel McKaughan. Kvanvig has argued that faith is not primarily a cognitive state, involving what we think and believe. He is particularly interested in humility as an aspect of faith, but argues that faith also includes trust.[58] Howard-Snyder focuses on the relationship between trust, belief, and other aspects of faith such as resilience, and argues that it is possible to trust in God without holding particular beliefs, or without holding beliefs at all.[59] McKaughan uses the example of St Teresa of Calcutta to argue that one may practise faith by enacting trust and faithfulness over time, even if one feels one cannot feel God's presence or love.[60] All these studies focus on relational trust or faithfulness rather than propositional trust, but some of their arguments are adaptable to propositional trust too. For example, one might think of the faithfulness of St Teresa not only as an act of faithfulness, but as an attitude of trust that God loves her which takes a positive view of God's love, commits to it, and acts on it in the absence of knowledge or belief.[61]

---

[53] Gooch (2012), 21, 23–4.
[54] Sherman (2008), 251–7 and *passim*. *Inter alia* he emphasizes the experiential dimension of knowledge (pp. 262–3).
[55] pp. 255 (the eschatological future), 141–2, 174–7, 183–200, 251–3, 256–60. Insofar as Sherman identifies saving knowledge with *pistis*, however, we have argued above that it does not come through the spirit, as he proposes (pp. 257–8).
[56] Sherman (2008), 172–3, 252.   [57] p. 173, italics mine.
[58] Kvanvig (2018), 24–7, 32–4. Pages 34–6 argue that trust is not necessary for faith, if, for instance, a person of faith relies on God or is obedient to God, relying on the idea that it is adequate for a person of faith to have some aspects of the complex modern understanding of faith, but not all.
[59] E.g. Howard-Snyder (2013, 2016, 2017), and see the discussion of arguments for non-doxastic faith by Eklund (2018).
[60] McKaughan (2017), 23–7.
[61] Kvanvig (2018), 34–6 does not discuss propositional trust, but what he treats as examples of trustless faith can be seen as involving propositional, if not relational trust: e.g. Abraham could have left Ur for Canaan not yet fully trusting in God, but trusting that obeying God was a risk worth taking.

These examples attest to a growing recognition by philosophers of religion and theologians, among whom the possibility, nature, and reasonable grounds of knowledge and belief about God are topics of intensive debate, that (mainly relational, but occasionally also propositional) trust is also a significant part of Christian faith, even central to it; that trust is one of the foundations of human beings' saving commitment to God and Christ, relationship with God and Christ, and affirmations about God and Christ; and that trust therefore deserves more theological discussion.[62] At the same time, most theologians and philosophers of religion continue, in their discussions, to prioritize what can be known or believed about God and on what basis. Other humanities disciplines, since the mid-twentieth century (and, in some cases, much earlier) have moved further from the assumption that the goal of their activity is claims to knowledge or right belief or the correspondence of their conclusions to objective truth.[63] Implicitly, if not often explicitly, these disciplines also rely extensively on propositional trust when making their arguments. They offer food for thought for the theology of trust, so—again very briefly, and with no aspiration to doing justice to the size and complexity of the field—we turn, by way of example, to two of them: the study of history and of music.

The Challenge of Knowing or Believing in Other Humanities Disciplines

Most historians would admit to a fascination with the factuality of the past and its correspondence to historical claims. If the past is another country, it was a real place: people as material as ourselves lived and acted there; things happened and the world changed. Part of the lure of history lies in the desire to encounter and understand people and societies which in some ways were like ours, and in some ways were extraordinarily different, and another part lies in the tension between the reality of the past and the impossibility of fully recapturing it. The challenge of historiography is to do what justice one can to the past, not misunderstanding or oversimplifying it, nor rewriting it for one's own purposes, while recognizing that much of what we would like to know has left no traces; we cannot escape our own concerns and purposes in writing; and what we create is never a transparent

---

[62] From a sociological perspective, Hempel et al. (2012) offer a different critique of belief, finding that strong doctrinal belief commitments among conservative Protestants are negatively related to the propensity to trust other human beings.

[63] So have some scientific disciplines, while many more are increasingly interested in the uncertainties which are embedded in scientific enquiry (see e.g. Palmer and Hardaker (2011), Halpern (2017), De Freitas and Sinclair (2018), and successive Proceedings of the European Conference on Symbolic and Quantitative Approaches to Reasoning with Uncertainty); these too, however, are mainly occupied with problems of knowledge or belief, and I have not yet encountered a discussion of propositional trust.

window on history but, at best, a dialogue between subjects and subjectivities conducted through sources which were rarely created to act as interpreters.[64]

Very few historians claim that that their analyses correspond in any direct or unproblematic way to objective truth. Those in the modern era who have, are regarded by most as having misunderstood mid-nineteenth-century empiricist or 'scientific' history.[65] Empiricist history was a reaction to the historicism of enlightenment historians who, inspired by early modern science, sought to discover the laws which governed human societies, as scientific laws were understood as governing nature. The nineteenth-century reaction against empiricism was led by Wilhelm von Humboldt and Leopold von Ranke, who argued that we do not understand the past by formulating general laws about it. Instead, we should investigate the specificity of the past through empirical examination of the evidence (with special attention to neglected sub-literary sources such as documents and archives).[66] Neither von Humboldt nor von Ranke, however, understood writing history as a straightforward exercise in making truth claims based on the correspondence of their findings to reality. The process of establishing 'how it really [or 'essentially'] was' (arguably better translations of *wie es eigentlich gewesen ist* than the notorious 'what actually happened') was more complex.

Both scholars wrote essays defending their method, but the classic exposition of empiricism is von Humboldt's in his essay 'On the historian's task':

> The historian's task is to present *wie es eigentlich gewesen ist*. The more purely and completely he achieves this, the more perfectly has he solved his problem. A simple presentation is at the same time the primary, indispensable condition of his work and the highest achievement he will be able to attain. Regarded in this way, he seems to be merely receptive and reproductive, not himself active and creative.

---

[64] Capturing this tension see e.g. Novick (1988), 1–18, Rublack (2012), Evans (2018). Among recent discussions in the ethics of historiography see notably Wyschogrod (1998), Gibbs (2000), Marchitello (2001), Carr et al. (2004), Martins (2004), Froeyman (2012, 2016) (arguing that we should consider what a good historian, as well as good history looks like), Hutt (2013) (on the relationship between historical and religious belief); see also notably Hicks and Stapleford (2016) (on ethics in the historiography of science) and Zahl (2018) (on the ethics of retrieving past theological traditions for contemporary purposes).

[65] On the 'myth' of objective history see Novick (1988), 19–108, Clark (2004), 9–28, Katerberg (2010), Kugler (2010); among surveys of ancient and modern philosophies of history see notably Marincola (1997), Burns and Rayment-Pickard (2000), Burrow (2008), and (with a relatively optimistic view of the possibility of determining historical truth, which, however, has been much criticized), Appleby et al. (1994). Some historical scholars of the New Testament continue to articulate what to most historians is a startling positivism: e.g. Crossan (1994), ix–x; for a much more nuanced discussion of the relationship between history and theology, which unfortunately reached me too late to be discussed here, see Heringer (2018), cf. (2014).

[66] Von Humboldt and von Ranke also argued for the intrinsic interest of the past, as opposed to its use as a source of ethical models and maxims.

> An event, however, is only partially visible in the world of the senses; the rest has to be added by intuition, inference, and guesswork. The manifestations of an event are scattered, disjointed, isolated; what it is that gives unity to this patchwork, puts the isolated fragment into its proper perspective, and gives shape to the whole, remains removed from direct observation. For observation can perceive circumstances which either accompany or follow one another, but not their inner causal nexus, on which, after all, their inner truth is solely dependent... Nothing is rarer, therefore, than a narrative which is literally true; nothing is better proof of a sound, well-ordered, and critical intelligence and of a free, objective attitude. Thus historical truth is, as it were, rather like the clouds which take shape for the eye only at a distance. For this reason, the facts of history are in their several connecting circumstances little more than the results of tradition and scholarship which one has agreed to accept as true, because they—being most highly probably in themselves—also fit best into the context of the whole... Thus two methods have to be followed simultaneously in the approach to historical truth; the first is the exact, impartial, critical investigation of events; the second is the connecting of the events explored and the intuitive understanding of them which could not be reached by the first means...
>
> Human judgment cannot perceive the plans of the governance of the world directly but can only divine them in the ideas through which they manifest themselves, and therefore all history is the realization of an idea. In the idea resides both its motivating force and its goal. And thus, merely by steeping oneself in the contemplation of the creative forces one travels along a more correct route to those final causes to which the intellect naturally aspires...[67]

Historical 'truth' turns out to be 'rather like the clouds which take shape for the eye only at a distance'. The elements of the clouds are the evidence (which is 'scattered, disjointed, isolated' and, uninterpreted, tells us little or nothing); past scholarship and tradition which the historian makes a decision to trust because they look plausible; and the historian's own 'intuition, inference and guesswork', which fills in the gaps and connects up all the material according to his sense (and, he hopes that of his readers) of what is plausible and coherent. In Chapter 3, we argued that belief in the resurrection, for Paul and probably for other early Christians, was not a simple claim about the correspondence of preaching to a physical fact, but a more complex combination of the coherence of multiple resurrection experiences (one's own and other people's), trust and belief in Christ-confessing preachers and their words, the coherence of preaching with the scriptures as interpreted by Christ's followers, trust in the trustworthiness of past prophets, and the coherence of all these factors with one's existing commitment

---

[67] 1822, transl. Mink in von Humboldt (1967), 57–8, 71.

to the God of Israel (in the case of Jews) or willingness to commit to God (in the case of gentiles).[68] Von Humboldt's analysis is strikingly similar. He does not add, what many theorists of history have observed since, that even if we thought we had identified some objective historical truth we could not prove it, because we can neither return to the past to check our theory, nor rerun the past like a scientific experiment, but he would surely have agreed.[69]

Von Humboldt's view was developed further in a 1960 essay by Isaiah Berlin on 'The concept of scientific history'. Berlin argues that all historical arguments are based on the coherence of our evidence and interpretations with our intuitions about how societies and people work, rather than on the correspondence of our account to objective truth. He also observes that much of our understanding and evaluation of the past is communal, because it depends on more than any one person can know or think; because it wants to persuade other people of its view; and because our sense of the past is part of our sense of ourselves, which is part of what makes any society work:

> If I am asked what rational grounds I have for supposing that I am not on Mars, or that the Emperor Napoleon existed and was not merely a sun myth, and if in answer to this I try to make explicit the general propositions which entail this conclusion, together with the specific evidence for them, and the evidence for the reliability of this evidence, and the evidence for that evidence in turn, and so on, I shall not get very far. The web is too complex, the elements too many and not, to say the least, easily isolated and tested one by one... The true reason for accepting the propositions that I live on earth, and that an Emperor Napoleon I existed, is that to assert their contradictories is to destroy too much of what we take for granted about the present and the past.[70]

Historians do not tend to talk about propositional trust as an aspect of their methodology, but we can begin to see where it plays a role. When historians draw on their intuitions about how people and societies work, they draw on a range of attitudes which they hold about themselves and their own world (assumptions,

---

[68] On the social and symbolic worlds which construct Jesus' own experience and self-understanding and that of the earliest Christians, see e.g. Kee (1989), 103–6, Theissen (1999), 39. Bauckham (2017), takes issue with modern philosophical epistemology, with its concern for objective truths, arguing that belief in testimony about Jesus, which both historians and theologians need, is based on trust in witnesses to him (pp. 378–88, 479–86), while holding that we are still concerned with the truth about the past; as an argument about the social character of knowledge this has much to commend it, but it underestimates the notoriously variable and unpredictable reliability of memory and testimony (as does Byrskog (2000), though he is slightly more circumspect).

[69] E.g. Berlin (1960), Popper (2002), 96–140; cf. Chartier (1997), 9: 'What are the criteria by which a historical discourse—always a knowledge based on traces and signs—can be held to be a valid and explicative reconstruction... of the past reality it has defined as its object?'

[70] Berlin (1960), 10, cf. Berlin (2013), 80–110.

beliefs, hopes, and so on), on which they are willing to act.[71] Like the elevator-users at King's Cross station, they entrust themselves, in the form of their research and professional reputation, to these attitudes.

As they engage in intersubjective interaction with their sources, historians hold themselves constantly ready to be surprised by how differently people thought, felt, acted, and shaped their societies in different times and places. At the same time, they trust that human beings of the past were similar enough to themselves to have left traces they can interpret.[72] However diverse human languages are (social, cultural, and psychological as well as linguistic), we can communicate.[73] Since we cannot go back in time, we cannot prove this, but historians assume or believe that it is so, and since they act on the assumption and entrust their arguments to it, they also trust that it is so.

Most historical arguments draw on a network of existing interpretations, so to some degree historians also trust that their predecessors and colleagues have done their research responsibly and thought through their arguments carefully.[74] They trust, moreover, that their own readers will trust that they themselves have done their work carefully, whether or not readers know enough about them to trust them personally. Last but not least, historians entrust their interpretations of the past to the future, knowing that they cannot know what impact they will have, or how they will change the way other people think or act, but trusting that they will make a constructive contribution to people's understanding of the past, and so inform, and perhaps even influence the future.

Isaiah Berlin makes a further claim about history-writing in a 1979 essay which has been taken up and applied to theology by Andrew Louth. Berlin argues that most scientists still regard their work as making observations and developing theories which correspond to objective truths, and do not recognize their cultural context or intellectual paradigms as playing any part in their reasoning. He thinks, moreover, that too many scholars in the humanities are still influenced by this way of thinking. He argues that an alternative model is available in the historiography of Giambattista Vico. Vico saw history as seeking to understand not facts or objective truths, but how people see the world. This, Berlin concludes, is

---

[71] These may be positive attitudes, but are not always: a historian might, for instance, share Lord Acton's view that '[p]ower tends to corrupt'.

[72] This falls short of trusting people in the past relationally, since we have no direct relationship with them and are likely to know little about them; the same is true of past scholars and future readers.

[73] This involves what we can call appropriate self-trust (see pp. 359–60), appropriate self-trust which is interactive and intersubjective, and so is formed and informed in part by openness to others, as opposed to mistaken self-trust which e.g. trusts itself to be able, by itself, to assess objectively God's will or the truth about the past.

[74] Making a similar argument for the necessity and role of collegial trust in the sciences see Frost-Arnold (2013).

more like the knowledge we claim of a friend, of his character, of his ways of thought or action, the intuitive sense of the nuances of personality or feeling or ideas which Montaigne describes so well, and which Montesquieu took into account. To [write history like this], one must possess imaginative power of a high degree, such as artists and, in particular, novelists require. And even this will not get us far in grasping ways of life too remote from us and unlike our own. Yet even then we need not despair, for what we are seeking to understand is men—human beings...their works cannot be wholly unintelligible to us, unlike the impenetrable content of non-human nature...[75]

The study of history deals in (our) human perceptions of (others') human perceptions of the world around human beings, and their interactions with it. Human responses to the world are inevitably fragmentary and partial, in both senses of the word, and records of them become increasingly fragmentary over time. We put together our sources to make as coherent a picture as we can, filling in the gaps with our assumptions about how human beings and societies work, while seeking to be open to the possibility that the evidence may challenge our assumptions and cause them to shift. The result is a work of human interaction and imagination as much as observation. It is also a work of trust: that the works of other human beings 'cannot be wholly unintelligible to us', and that our interaction with the past, which is part of our interaction with own world, will be intelligible, perhaps even illuminating, in the future.

Vico thought that the kind of understanding we seek of the past was distinctive to the study of history, but Berlin argues that it applies to all the humanities. Louth uses it in his critique of the application of scientific models of truth to theology in *Discerning the Mystery*.[76] Louth argues against the 'one-sided [quasi-scientific] way that we have come to seek and recognize truth' and proposes that the humanities have their own 'proper engagement with truth'.[77] He argues for attention to theological tradition as an act of reason in its own right and urges us to 'make contact again with an inarticulate living of the mystery...which is the heart of tradition, and from which theology must spring if it is to be faithful to

---

[75] Berlin (2013), 133.

[76] Louth (1983); preceding him see e.g. Baillie (1939), Polanyi (1962), especially 279–86. Humanities scholars sometimes do less than justice to the awareness in the sciences of the role of relational knowing (like that of images and metaphors) in scientific enquiry: see e.g. Polanyi (1962), Polkinghorne (2010), Kayumova et al. (2016) (on the role of relational knowing in scientific education); and occasionally different branches of the sciences do less than justice to each other: so Rizzuto (1979) argues that psychologists must not resort to the model of natural science and the assumptions of correspondence theory, believing that they are dealing with the 'real world of empirical events and regularities' (p. 21).

[77] pp. xi, xiii. We have seen that the ethics of care contributes to the study of interpersonal trust; Dalmiya (2016) explores a 'care-based epistemology' in which what we know is firmly rooted in our relationships, above all relationships of care.

the truth it is seeking to express'.[78] The truth at the heart of theology, Louth argues, following especially the Cappadocian Fathers, 'is not something there to be discovered, but something, or rather someone, to whom we must surrender. The mystery of faith is not ultimately something that invites our questioning, but something that questions us.'[79]

Louth's argument is about truth rather than trust, but trust, both personal and propositional, can be seen as playing a significant role in it.[80] If the truth at the heart of theology is a person to whom we must surrender, that person can only be God. Scripture, reason (not least in the form of theology and philosophy of religion), and tradition all attest that the personal God whom Christians acknowledge (or take for granted, believe, hope, or trust in) is trustworthy. We can therefore speak of ourselves as trusting truth in the person of God. Those who put their trust in a trustworthy God trust that the person of God, unique though God is, cannot be, in Berlin's phrase, wholly unintelligible—personally unknowable—to human persons, just as historians trust that human persons, in different times and places, are not wholly unintelligible to one another.[81] Those who trust in God trust that their own intuitions about persons can help them (however imperfectly) to know God. They trust that they can trust those who report having known God in the past. And—more positively and confidently than most modern historians dare to do—they trust that their trust in God will prove not only intelligible in the future, or even illuminating, but that it will ultimately be vindicated and prove salvific for themselves and others.

If the truth about history is complex and contestable—less a fact to be established than a subject with which we interact to make an argument which may affect the future—that of some other humanities subjects is more elusive still. Musicology offers an intriguing comparison with theology, because some of its central problems are similar, but they are somewhat differently handled.

'Because it is so ubiquitous and universal a phenomenon, whose existence remains unexplained by any apparent practical purpose, and more so because its very nature is elusive, music has been boggling the minds of scholars for well over three thousand years.'[82] In the western world, philosophers and musicologists

---

[78] p. 35. He also cites Gadamer's ((1975), 238) insistence that 'we remain open to the meaning of the other person or text...' and willing to be changed by them. Martin (2017), 109–10 argues similarly for a return to pre-modern understandings of truth and approaches to interpretation.

[79] p. 95.

[80] His vision of truth as something or someone to whom we relate recalls the relational nature of both truth and knowledge in John's gospel.

[81] We noted above that e.g. 'trust that' people in the past were sufficiently like us for us to be able to understand the traces they have left need not resolve to personal trust, given that we do not know these people directly, nor, usually, much about them. The case of God is somewhat different because the faithful may trust that certain things about God are the case, or have the experience of knowing and trusting God relationally, or both.

[82] Serafine (1988), 1, cf. Cardus (1977), Levinson (2011), 267–78 on the nature of music.

have disagreed about the origins and nature of music since classical antiquity.[83] Most Greek philosophers (including Pythagoreans, Platonists, and Stoics) hold that music is metaphysical in origin.[84] The material universe, created by the divine, resonates with the 'harmony of the spheres' which is the (inaudible) expression of its mathematical order.[85] Human beings' capacity to recognize and appreciate music (both audible music and music theory) attests to our intellectual and moral congruity, or potential congruity, with the universe and the divine. For human beings, according to Plato, making music, for instance by singing, restores the soul to 'order and concord with itself' and so to harmony with the divine.[86]

In the modern academy it is normal to assume that music is a physical, rather than metaphysical phenomenon, but there is still little agreement about its origins.[87] Does what we call music exist in the world around us, or is it a creation of the brain, which imposes the impression of pattern, structure, and significance on some of the many noises we hear to help us make sense of them? If the latter, is music distinctively a creation of the human brain, or do some other animals recognize and intentionally make music as human beings do? And why do we perceive some sounds as musical and not others? Many contemporary psychologists of music think it is unlikely that music exists outside the brain, while recognizing that it is a near-universal and powerful human experience that it does.[88]

Every culture we know of has some form of music, and the overwhelming majority of human beings respond to it, often without knowing why. Making and responding to music are both individual and social activities. Music powerfully affects the emotions and perceptions of those who make or respond to it,[89] but why do we respond to it?[90] Two of the theories for which many modern disciplines reach when faced with intractable questions of nature and meaning,

---

[83] Surveying ancient and mediaeval musical metaphysics see Martinelli (2019), 5–39, Katz and HaCohen (2003), 3–20. For discussions of the metaphysics of music that include eastern traditions, see Davies (2001), 254–94, Feagin (2007); for an introduction to key issues in the philosophy of music see Scruton (1997).

[84] Also musical theorists including Nicomachus of Gerasa (C1–2) and Aristides Quintilian in the second century CE (Barker (1984), 399–535).

[85] The phrase 'the harmony [or 'music'] of the spheres' is attributed to Pythagoras: Plin., *HN* 2.3.3, cf. Pl., *Resp.* 617b, Chalcidius (Magee 2016, par. 1.40) on Pl., *Tim.* 35b–36b; Aristotle disagrees (e.g. *De cael.* 290b30–291a25), arguing that while the idea that the heavens resonate is very poetic, it is physically impossible. Stoics followed Pythagoras and Plato in seeing music as divine in origin and able to attune human beings to the virtue of the divine; Epicureans, however, saw music as a phenomenon of the material world with no relationship with ethics (Rispoli (1974), Laurand (2014)).

[86] Pl., *Tim.* 47d, cf. *Symp.*, 187a.

[87] For a modern version of Plato's argument that music brings humanity into harmony with the divine see Moutsopoulos (2008). On mediaeval ideas of music as the fabric of the universe, which are descended from Plato, see Hicks (2017).

[88] These issues are surveyed by Kania (2017); see also Bender (1993), Ockelford (1999), Katz and HaCohen (2003), 3–20, Thomasson (2003), Wolterstorff (1992).

[89] See e.g. Schramm (2005), Garrido and Davidson (2019), Juslin (2019), all of which offer discussions drawing on a wide range of literature.

[90] Harwood (1976) influentially surveys the issues; Harré (2006); Altenmüller et al. (2013) offer an evolutionary perspective.

functionalism and behaviourism, have found little favour in musicology because they produce such obviously simplistic accounts of composition, performance, and listening. Music might, in theory, help people to bond, survive, attract a mate, coordinate their movements, or regulate their society, but no one who has ever made or responded to music thinks that is all it means.[91] Music has often been interpreted as a cultural phenomenon, which finds meaning in specific cultural contexts, but this does not explain the fact that music is highly cross-culturally mobile, and people can respond to music from cultures unfamiliar to them.[92]

Human beings of all cultures find meaning in music, but what music means is notoriously difficult to pin down.[93] What is it 'saying', if anything? Some music is referential (some of the oldest known European songs, for instance, reference birdsong), but most is not, in any simple or detectable way.[94] How and why music stirs the emotions is equally mysterious. Its impact on listeners does not straightforwardly or self-evidently correspond to the emotions of the composer or performer. Sometimes an emotional response is uniform throughout a group of listeners, but sometimes it is very varied, even if those listeners belong to the same social or cultural group. All emotional responses, however, are typically experienced as equally real and regarded by most music lovers as valid.[95] There is no more scholarly consensus around what constitutes understanding music. Two listeners can experience a profound reaction, say, to Beethoven's 'Ode to Joy', while one understands the music's structure, and the other understands only that she likes it.[96] Even the nature of a piece of music is much debated. Every performance of everything any composer writes will be different. Every listener's experience will be unique; yet everyone who writes, performs, or listens to a 'piece of music' has a strong sense that they are sharing something.[97]

Music is everywhere in human societies, extraordinarily powerful, and deeply mysterious. It is easy to see why it has often been seen as divine or metaphysical, and music-talk has some obvious points of comparison with God-talk.[98] Like God, music has never been proven to exist outside human minds, but its existence is a near-universal human intuition. If it does exist independently of human

---

[91] Serafine (1988), 16–17; Forde Thompson (2009), 21–36.
[92] Though there is some debate about this: see the discussion of Higgins (2012).
[93] Scruton (2016), 3.
[94] E.g. the thirteenth-century 'Sumer is icumen in' references the cuckoo. The referentiality of music is discussed e.g. by Bowie (2007), 15–45, who argues that all music conveys meaning but meaning is determined partly by context, so is variable.
[95] Sloboda (1985), 1–2.
[96] These issues are outlined by Levinson (2011), 63–88, and Kania (2017).
[97] Taking various positions on this see e.g. Dodd (2000), Thomasson (2003), Trivedi (2002, 2008).
[98] The theology of music is beyond our scope here, but see e.g. Wilkey (1972), offering prolegomena. In general, theologies of music take the existence of both God and music for granted: among recent writings see e.g. Begbie (1989, 2000, 2014), Brown (2003, 2005), Epstein (2004), Saliers (2007), Zager (2007), Begbie and Guthrie (2011), Charru (2012), Schwöbel (2020), Begbie et al. (2021); see also Watson (1998), 435–7, arguing that no theology of music is possible.

minds, we cannot talk about it outside our experience of it and interaction with it. Like God, music is experienced both individually and socially, and people respond to it individually and in groups. No one who responds to music, any more than anyone who responds to a sense of the divine, thinks that its meaning and significance lie entirely (if at all) in its behavioural or social function. Whatever it is and whatever it means is experienced as inherent in itself and its relationship with those who experience it.

Almost every aspect of our engagement with music involves trust: propositional, relational, or both. When we write, perform, or listen to it we probably simply assume that it exists. When we study it, we do a little more: we trust that it exists and is worth studying. When we make or respond to it we entrust ourselves to it, and we trust that it will not be wholly unintelligible to us. When we study it, we trust that our predecessors in whose footsteps we tread have done their research carefully and responsibly. We trust that anything we say about it will prove intelligible, even illuminating to others in the future.

Contemporary talk about music, however, is notably unlike contemporary talk about God in one respect. Within musicology, the study of whether we can know or reliably believe that music exists is a relatively small field; musicologists spend much more time exploring what it does, how it works, and how people relate to it and, through it, to one another.[99] Beyond the academy, the overwhelming presence of music in human experience and culture is widely accepted, among the unmusical as well as the musical, as a reason to take its existence on trust, and trusting that music exists is not treated, in public discourse, as irrational or outdated. It would be naive to assume that this is because music has little practical power in the material world. It is well recognized as extremely powerful, and used on that basis in contexts from political rallies to religious rituals, and from shopping malls to student bedrooms. In Chapter 1, we noted that all societies make choices about what experiences of themselves and of the world, and what entities, physical and metaphysical, they acknowledge and validate. Music is a striking example of an entity of debatable existence and status which societies around the world at present choose to recognize and validate.

Propositional Trust in the Face of Uncertainty

If the reality of music is not certain, and the reality of the past is certain but inaccessible, all humanities disciplines have in common that they are in dialogue with subjects that are not: not beyond doubt, not literally true (in the case of

---

[99] Arguing for this approach see e.g. Ridley (2003), Bartel (2011); for prioritizing ontology see Kania (2008). Bourbon (2018) argues that philosophical accounts of music should begin not from where it comes from but from how it is experienced.

fiction, for instance), not fixed, not here and now, or not material. The past, the metaphysical, alternative worlds of the imagination, the slipperiness of language, the elusive representationality of art, and the infinite variety of gaps between intention, representation, reception, and understanding, are all staples of their subject-matter.

Humanities disciplines also have in common that they recognize there is always more than one appropriate, interesting, constructive way to discuss any subject, and although there may be agreed to be better and worse (more or less rigorous, satisfying, or fruitful) approaches, there is never only one right one. Moreover, they never forget that the observer's own viewpoint is implicated in her approach. This puts them in a particularly strong position to recognize and make explicit both their own approaches to any subject, and those of others.

The multiplicity of possible worlds, ways of being, and ways of seeing which humanities disciplines study, prise open our imaginations to the possibilities of the world we live and act in. They prompt us to ask, not just 'who are we?' but 'who could we be?', and not just 'how are we?' but 'how could we be? How should we be?' They encourage practitioners not always to start from where we are, in thinking about where we might be, or to accept the material as non-negotiable, but to speculate, dream, and model new possibilities.

One might think that this recognition of plurality would lead either to relativism or to a postmodern refusal to regard any analysis of anything as a basis on which to make any claim or act in any particular way. In practice, even the most committed relativist or postmodernist tends not to behave as if this is the case, if only because he regards his approach as just a little more valid than other people's. (The most rigorous sceptic, notoriously, cannot live his scepticism.[100]) Even as humanities scholars recognize the elusiveness of their subject-matter and the plurality of possible approaches to it, they acknowledge the powerful intuitions underlying it, which range from the reality of the past, the metaphysical, or the moral, to the existence of authorial intention, the meaningfulness of language, or the possibility of communication. They also acknowledge that, however uncertain the status of the worlds we operate in, complex our interactions with them, and debatable our interpretations of them, we do, in fact, act in them all the time, with consequences for the future.

When students of the humanities take views about our subject-matter, therefore, we do so knowing that taking a view is necessary (because intellectual *aporia* prevents further thought and offers no basis for action), but risky (because we cannot prove the rightness of what we say), and that it involves making choices which will affect the future. In this intellectual and ethical sequence of thought

---

[100] Burnyeat (1980); this remains the majority view, though for some arguments against it see Bailey (2002). Kurtén (1994), 112, 118–19, argues that nihilists lack trust, but that one cannot live long as a nihilist.

and action, propositional trust has both a discursive and a protreptic role. We trust that our subject is not wholly unintelligible, to ourselves or others. We trust that our reading of the evidence, combined with our intuitions about the way people and the world work, and the coherence of our arguments, are credible and trustworthy. We trust that our arguments can engage others. And we entrust the future to our views, recognizing that, for all their uncertainty, they may make a difference to it.

Students of many humanities disciplines might acknowledge that they would like to know, or to have sure grounds for right belief, about their subjects: to know the truth about the past, or whether there really is such a thing as goodness, meaning, or music. But in the absence of certainty, they accept propositional trust as a useable tool, and one which has some scope to be tested for its coherence, and also consequentially, on practical and ethical grounds if not grounds of objective truth. They go a little further, and take the view that it is reasonable to trust that subjects with which we do, in practice, interact as human beings, by human means (thought, emotion, action), can be interacted with, tested, and (always provisionally, in the recognition that tomorrow may bring a better interpretation) entrusted with ourselves and our future.

In a world in which knowledge of the divine, or the certainty of right belief about the divine, is notoriously problematic, propositional trust offers, I suggest, a useful addition to our reasoning. This may sound like an argument along Lindbeck's lines, for seeing religion as a cultural-linguistic system whose meaning lies in the sense it makes to users, but it incorporates a sharper sense of jeopardy and a stronger demand for practical, analytical, and argumentative responsibility than that type of model necessarily demands.[101] Whatever we conclude on the basis of our investigation of our subjects, if our investigations have integrity as part of our humanity, then we are liable to commit ourselves and our future, and that of others, to them. When we 'trust that', we must therefore take a high degree of responsibility for the implications of the propositions we trust for ourselves and the world around us.

To put it another way: in the context of this study, propositional trust is important not only when we are seeking to describe the relationship of trust between God, Christ, and humanity, but when we are considering whether our account of this relationship is intelligible; whether it is credible and trustworthy; whether it has the capacity to engage others and inform, even illuminate the world around us; and whether, on that basis, we are willing to commit ourselves and entrust our future to it. Readers will infer from this study so far that I do trust that its subject-matter is intelligible and credible. But what would it take for me to entrust my

---

[101] Above, p. 330; this is not to make a claim about the nature of Lindbeck's commitment to his model, but only to observe that arguments for religions as cultural systems originate as 'outsider' models in anthropology, and do not necessarily demand 'insider' self-commitment.

future, and that of others, to the ideas outlined here, trusting that they have the capacity to engage and even illuminate the world?

The next section offers four test cases. It considers what the idea of propositional trust might have to offer a Christian who holds the view that it is belief in God and Christ that restores one's right-standing with God and ultimately saves; a person who, like many contemporary westerners, has never felt the need of a faith and is what is sometimes called 'unchurched'; a person whose capacity for trust in other people has been damaged; and a person who understands their relationship with God and Christ as one of personal trust.

Four Test Cases for Propositional Trust

The Believer

The rest of this study argues that, in New Testament writings, belief is usually, possibly always one of the foundations of relational trust between God, Christ, and humanity, but seeks to show where and why trust is also vitally important. The more limited question in this section is why someone who believes that it is belief that saves might be persuaded that propositional trust is also important. We can assume that the content of the believer's belief is broadly the same as that of one who trusts (allowing for the variations of belief that exist among Christians who recognize one another's orthodoxy). It is also worth noting that many of those who would affirm that they are saved by believing equate belief with faith and, implicitly if not explicitly, include relational trust in it (and also, for instance, love and obedience to God and Christ).

For such a believer, 'trusting that', even if largely unrecognized, can be seen as already part of 'believing that', 'believing in', and 'trusting 'in'. A believer might say, for example, that God reveals God's saving righteousness through the earthly life, death, resurrection, and exalted life of Jesus Christ. If the believer believes, in traditional terms, that this proclamation is true and an object of knowledge, she must, at a minimum, trust that she is capable of receiving and comprehending divine revelation; that those who have written down and taught the word of God are trustworthy; and that the proclamation about God and Christ is coherent enough with the rest of her understanding of the world to make a world-view she can live with.[102] If, for instance, she understands her faith as a cultural-linguistic construct, then she must trust that she is not speaking an idiolect, but that her

---

[102] We might think that the believer would take some or all of these for granted, rather than actively trust that they are the case. Where cult affiliation and practice are inherited, a great deal typically is taken for granted, but where people are called to worship a new god or make a (re)new(ed) relationship with God, and to enter a new relationship with a new heavenly being such as Christ, I take it that their propositional trust, like their relational trust and belief, is likely to be more intentional.

understanding of her faith is coherent enough with that of others to be part of a shared system of meaning; she must trust that she and others can communicate effectively; and she must trust that this construct coheres well enough with other aspects of her world-view, and yields enough meaning, to be worth committing to.

Many of those who make the strongest case for saving belief, and who most influence those who most strongly affirm that it is belief that makes possible salvation, also argue that saving belief is not fully under human control. Either the capacity for belief is a gift from God, or human belief can only reach so far towards God without God's help.[103] The one who wants to believe must therefore hope, assume, or trust that God will help him to believe, and since this attitude surely involves self-commitment—a willingness to believe if help is given—it must be more than a hope or an assumption. We can therefore say that the one who wants to believe that he will be saved trusts that God will help him, and it is when this trust is vindicated that he is able to believe and to be saved. In this model, as elsewhere in this chapter, propositional trust is a 'bottom-up', human attitude and practice which enables belief. If, alternatively, we take the view of this study that it is not belief on its own that saves, but the commitment of relational trust, propositional trust can be seen as playing the same role in the same narrative, with the addition that belief that one will be saved is accompanied by relational trust in God and Christ.

The Unchurched

Imagine that my friend Tom is not hostile to Christianity, but has little experience of it, does not believe what it teaches, and does not see why he would need or want it.[104] Given that he does not believe, for instance, that it is objectively true that God exists, or that freedom from sin and suffering are possible through trust in God and Christ, might he still be engaged by the idea of trusting that these things are so?[105]

---

[103] E.g. for Augustine *fides* can be a gift of grace (*Gr. et lib. arb.* 17, *Praed. sanct.* 1.12) which will not achieve full understanding until after death (*Ep.* 120.3–4); for Aquinas, belief in revealed truth is 'an act of the intellect assenting to the truth at the command of the will' (*Summa* 2.2 Q. 4 art. 5), but it rests on acceptance or trust in the authority of God as its source and guarantor; for Luther, faith is God's gift that works in human beings to give them a 'living, bold trust in God's grace' (Irmischer (1854), 124–5). Newman (1870), pt 2 ch. 4 appeals to the 'illative sense' which allows human beings to assent to (the truth of) what they cannot know by human reason, while for Rousselot ((1990), 34–5) there is a kind of 'natural knowledge' which enables one to grasp and assent to (the truth of) propositions such as the existence of God which are beyond human reason on its own.

[104] I take this example rather than e.g. that of a convinced atheist because it is a widespread type in modern western Europe from where this is written.

[105] If Tom is to become religiously engaged, of course, he has many options other than Christianity, but the question whether or why one might trust that Christianity is worth trusting in, in comparison with other religious traditions or world-views, is beyond our scope here.

Here again, the 'bottom-up' aspect of propositional trust may play a role. Tom, as a rational twenty-first-century man, dislikes the idea of believing anything on the authority, ultimately, of a being in whose existence he does not believe. But he accepts that we have to make assumptions about the world in order to live in it, including about things we cannot prove, and therefore that we all, in everyday life, 'trust that' certain things are so and entrust our future to them. (He trusts, for instance, that the water in the taps is clean, that most people are fundamentally decent, and that the right man is out there for him somewhere.) He also recognizes that wrongdoing, suffering, and hope are all powerful forces in all human lives. A way of life that offers the possibility of release from the power that his wrongdoings and his suffering have over him, or offers the hope of a more abundant and fulfilling life, has its attractions.

Tom might not be able to believe that God exists or that Christ died for human sins, or to put his trust in a God and a heavenly saviour in whom he does not believe, but he might consider trusting that such a belief and such a relationship could change his life. He might even consider acting on such a trust.[106] This kind of trust would be more than the act of trust, for example, of the novice swimmer who takes her foot off the bottom of the swimming pool before she trusts that she will float, because it involves Tom's taking an attitude to Christian trust and belief, even a positive one, and because it does not automatically involve action.[107] Tom's situation, however, has in common with the novice swimmer's that he might be encouraged in the direction of (in his case) propositional trust by the example and assurance of someone who already trusts. Being a 'bottom-up' form of trust, which makes use, in part, of the testimony of others, together with our intuitions about people and the world and willingness to explore the coherence of our intuitions and experience with those of others, propositional trust is strengthened by interaction with others who trust and appear trustworthy.

Most Christians would regard such an instance of propositional trust as, at best, only a first step in trust or faith, but since we have argued that it is possible to act with trust even when one's attitude of trust is defective, or even nonexistent, and we have also argued for the adequacy of imperfect trust, there is scope to think a little better of it than that. If all trust, as we have argued, and all belief, as many Christians have argued, are incomplete and imperfect in this life, then we must hope that, before the end time, imperfect trust is acceptable to God, and any type of trust that entrusts the future to itself deserves to be treated with respect.

---

[106] This is not the same as non-doxastic trust, cf. p. 22.   [107] Cf. p. 22.

The One whose Trust has been Damaged

In Chapter 4, we noted that the website of the organization Help for Adult Victims of Child Abuse offers advice to victims who want to learn or relearn to trust both themselves and other people.[108] Its webpage on trusting others recognizes the fear that many victims or survivors feel when they contemplate trusting others in general, or trusting them with something specific, such as the history of their abuse. It emphasizes that learning to trust others, like learning to trust oneself, is a major step which takes time and practice. Among its suggestions for practising trust is, 'Take risks: act as though you do trust—be very guarded and then see the result. If you find out you can't trust that individual then you have learnt from the experience...' Advice as specific as this on how to develop greater trust is unusual. Psychological and sociological studies of trust, for instance among victims of trauma or offenders, regularly emphasize the importance of (re-)establishing trust, and the role trustworthy and trusting others can play in the development of trust, but they rarely discuss how a person who struggles to trust can take the first steps. Taking a risk and acting, experimentally, as though one does trust, is a form of acting with trust without the attitude of trust, but there may also be room for propositional trust in the creation or recreation of trust, both between human beings who struggle to trust and between human beings and the divine.

Those whose trust has been damaged, by abuse or any other harmful experience, can suffer acutely from their lack of trust. We have seen how the inability to trust can lead to a sense that one is not real in the world, or that the rest of the world is not real to oneself, and from there to depression, aggression, self-harm, or harm to others.[109] Not all those who have not been able to form trust relationships, or have had their trust betrayed, recognize how damaging their situation is or actively want to (re)learn trust. In Chapter 4, however, we suggested that to someone who does want to (re)learn trust, the possibility of being released from the power of suffering by taking a journey into new life with Christ offers a route.[110]

We can imagine the possibility that such a person, without being able to trust directly in God and Christ, might be willing to trust that release from the power of her suffering is possible, and that the experience and testimony of those who

---

[108] <https://www/havoca.org/survivors/trust/trust-others/>; above, p. 181.   [109] pp. 21–2.
[110] The same route offers freedom from the power of sin, which is not our concern in this section. In practice, the appeal of this route is likely to depend in part on the qualities of those whom the person who struggles to trust encounters, who themselves trust in God and Christ (if these are not obviously trustworthy, or the kind of people the person who is struggling wants to be able to trust, then taking this journey will presumably hold fewer attractions). One of the ways in which those who trust in God and Christ can be seen as entrusted, therefore, is with being the kind of people who enable others to trust.

have found release through Christ is worth taking seriously, and may be worth trusting. She might, further, consider that trusting that release from the power of suffering is possible is an idea to which she might, at some point, be willing to entrust herself and her future. She might even be willing to trust that a tradition which recognizes the damage that is done by the failure of trust, and offers the restoration of trust through a person who is remembered as paradigmatically and transformatively trusting and trustworthy, is worth taking a risk on. On that basis, she might think it worth exploring what Christianity teaches about the release of suffering through Christ. In this, as in Tom's case, propositional trust offers a 'bottom-up', anthropologically grounded route towards relational trust and belief.

The Relational Truster

At the beginning of this chapter, we saw that propositional trust can be synonymous or virtually synonymous with various other attitudes, such as hope or an assumption, and also that it can be resolvable to relational trust, but that it is most distinctive when it leads the truster, on the basis of a positive attitude, to make a commitment and be willing to take action, entrusting the future to his trust. This, I suggest, is where propositional trust adds to the relational trust of the one who trusts in God and Christ.

Relational trust can be a disposition one holds, or a state in which one exists, even when one is not acting with trust: for instance, when one is asleep, or when one is not in communication with a person one trusts.[111] By analogy, a faithful person could, in principle, trust in God and Christ without that trust's involving any particular action or having any particular consequences at a given time. But we have seen in this and previous chapters that the faithful are called not only to have a disposition of trust, but to act on it, and that they are also entrusted with much to do. To act in all the ways in which they are called to act in this world, the faithful must not only trust in God and Christ, but trust that they are called (trusting their experience and that of others, the teaching they have received, their own intuition, and the coherence of all these things), trust that they can fulfil their calling with the help of God and Christ, and be willing to entrust the future to their actions. Propositional trust therefore forms a bridge between relational trust and action; between trusting and taking up that with which one is entrusted; and between trusting and purposefully entrusting the future to that which one trusts.

[111] pp. 23, 311–12.

Propositional Trust and Metaphysical Choices

We have observed, in this chapter and in Chapter 1, that scholars in the humanities make use of a range of assumptions and intuitions about the ways in which people, societies, and the world in general work. What is true of scholars is true of people and societies in general. We navigate our world with the help of many and varied myths, models of reality, and metaphysical assumptions, from the concept of human nature to the conviction of ultimate meaning; from the idea of goodness to the belief that there is a 'theory of everything'; from the hope that everyone can find 'the one' he is meant to be with to the notion that the market has a mind of its own. In any given time and place, some myths, models, and assumptions are widely accepted and little questioned; some are accepted by some and not others, but are not controversial; some are controversial.[112] In the modern western world, for example, it is widely accepted that there are some universal human rights; most people probably do not think that crossing one's fingers brings luck but it is not controversial to do it; but the existence of ultimate meaning is controversial.

Belief and trust in God and Christ have elements of myth, model, and metaphysical assumption, and in the contemporary west they are increasingly controversial. It is in the nature of myths, models, and metaphysical assumptions that one cannot explain or defend them by pointing to their correspondence with reality or objective truth, and in many cases, no one needs to explain or defend them, because they are widely accepted and/or uncontroversial. But where a myth, model, or metaphysical assumption is controversial (as Christianity was in its early years and is in some parts of the world today), it does tend to find itself explaining and defending itself. Propositional trust, I suggest, offers a route of both explanation and defence.

Propositional trust, as we have seen, is typically involved in multiple stages of an argument. We trust that our intuitions and experience of the world around us are trustworthy. We trust that a subject with which we interact is intelligible to us. We trust that others who have experienced or studied our subject have communicated their experience or research carefully and are trustworthy. And we trust that the outcome of our argument is worth committing to for the future, and will be intelligible, and perhaps even illuminating to others.

To say that one trusts in God and Jesus Christ is to say that one trusts that the widespread and powerful human intuition of a personal God (like that of music, or the reality of goodness) is worth taking a risk on, trusting, and acting on. It is to trust that, as we put it in Chapter 2, the power that creates and sustains

---

[112] Arguably some are hangovers from the past with little currency in the present (like what are sometimes called 'dead' metaphors), though one might argue that any myth etc. that is still in circulation probably has currency of some kind.

everything that is, can be interacted with by human beings as a personal being. It is to trust that the life-changing experience of those who have encountered Jesus Christ, in any part of his existence, is also worth trusting, taking a risk on, and acting on.

In trusting God and Christ one trusts that, as persons, God and Christ, in Berlin's phrase, 'cannot be wholly unintelligible'. One trusts that one's own intuitions and experience of God and Christ are trustworthy, and that the intuitions, experience, and communication of others about God and Christ are also worthy of trust. One trusts that trusting in God and Christ is something to which one can commit, and to which one is willing to commit the future.[113]

The person who makes this commitment trusts that—as followers of Christ have experienced and attested; as scripture, interpreted through the encounter with Christ, affirms; as communities of the faithful have discovered through time; and as the coherence of all these things with other aspects of one's world-view confirms[114]—in a new divine initiative of trust, through the person Jesus Christ, new life and a new relationship of trust with God have been made possible for humanity. This new life releases those who trust from the power of both sin and suffering, and has the power to bring the faithful to an abundance of life, peace, and joy beyond human imagination. In the meantime, it brings the faithful new and more life-giving relationships with other human beings and with the cosmos of which they are part.[115]

Those who trust in God and Christ trust that the initiative for this new life comes from somewhere outside material human existence, which so easily gets distracted by everyday life or mired in the damage we receive and the damage we do to others. Human beings encounter it, however, above all in Jesus Christ, in his earthly life and death and in the experienced continuity of his existence and identity beyond death, and, later, in the lives of those who put their trust in Christ. In making possible this new life, Christ both acts for humanity and makes it possible for the faithful, by following him, to act for each other. The faithful, moreover, are entrusted by God and Christ with acting for one another and for the world. When the faithful accept 'this rich trust', and seek to be trustworthy and to foster trust on the basis of their own trust in God and Christ, they trust that their trustworthiness and example may make it possible for others to trust that, in relationship with God and Christ, there is release from the power of sin and suffering and a

---

[113] This is distinct from basic trust as e.g. Dalferth and Peng-Keller (2013) define it (above, pp. 14–15) because their focus is on relational trust. Nor is propositional trust equivalent to foundational belief (cf. pp. 329–30), because foundational beliefs are thought to be true by those who believe them, while propositional trust takes what it trusts as trustworthy, without necessarily claiming it is true.

[114] Other aspects of one's world-view might include, for instance, belief in (or another attitude towards) the reality of the good, or the possibility of new life, salvation, or the triumph of good over evil.

[115] Cf. pp. 89–90.

new abundance of life. By affirming this, those who trust in God and Christ also trust that God and Christ trust them to be able to respond to God and Christ, and to be or become trustworthy when entrusted with work to do in the present time.

As we have repeatedly seen, both relational and propositional trust are risky, not least because they look forward to their vindication and fulfilment in a future about which human beings cannot be certain. But few people live, and no one lives well, entirely without trust, and no one lives without any myths, models, or metaphysical assumptions about the world. There may be many reasons for taking this particular risk. The encounter with God through Christ has proved as life-changing, stimulating, and enriching for many people down the centuries as it did, according to the gospels and other early traditions, for those who encountered Jesus in his earthly life. What those who early encountered God through Christ, and their successors, teach offers a vision of existence as meaningful and hopeful, incorporating the possibility and promise of (re)new(ed) life, salvation, and the prevalence of good over evil. This vision resonates with many people's intuition of the divine, and also with many people's sense of the damaging power of suffering or sin over them. Strong and caring communities have formed around it. It not only offers people someone to trust, but entrusts them with meaningful work to do in and for their world. And, of course, many people are born into the tradition that has formed around this trust and never leave it.[116] Trusters' experiences of the consequences of trust may be very varied, and change throughout life. But where propositional and relational trust, 'trusting that' and 'trusting in', meet, they offer a powerfully integrated vision of the world and humanity within it, which enables those who trust to think, to relate, and to act concertedly and purposefully in relation to the metaphysical, the physical world, and one another.

Propositional Doubt and Scepticism?

Readers may have wondered before now whether propositional doubt and scepticism should not also have played a role in this chapter, especially since we have emphasized elsewhere that relational human trust is always likely to be imperfect and mixed with both. Language of doubt and scepticism (*diakrinein, diakrisis, distazein, dipsychos, ou pisteuein*) is not abundant in New Testament writings,[117] and where it appears, it is usually the opposite of relational trust, suggesting that a person is doubting the trustworthiness of God or Christ.[118] At Matthew 28.17, for

---

[116] This study does not discuss the possibility that it is worth taking the risk of trust because trusting in God or Christ promotes wellbeing or resilience, but the extent to which religion aids wellbeing or resilience is now a large field of study in psychology.
[117] Though Schliesser (2021) investigates it in greater detail.
[118] E.g. Mt. 14.31, 21.21, Mk 11.23, Rom. 14.23, Jas 1.6–8, Jude 22, cf. Jas 4.8.

example, the disciples probably doubt their own worthiness to bow to Jesus, whom they had deserted, or are unsure what the risen Jesus' appearance to them means.[119] When, at Romans 4.20, Paul says that Abraham 'did not doubt God's promise with a lack of trust', Abraham's lack of doubt is based on the personal trust which he has already invested in God.[120] *Ou pisteuein* can refer to not believing something which is not true,[121] or failing to believe something which is true,[122] in which cases it is the opposite of propositional belief rather than propositional trust.[123] In several passages of John's gospel, it refers to someone's not believing something which is true, based on a failure of personal trust in Jesus.[124]

Looking for the opposite or correlate of propositional trust in passages like these, however, is probably to miss the point. We have argued that we make use of propositional trust when we are not certain of what we can believe or know, but are committing ourselves and the future to a conviction. Doubt, scepticism, and even fear are therefore built into propositional trust, and it acknowledges that it is always imperfect. In this light, the argument we have made that imperfect relational trust is nevertheless, in the sight of God and Christ, adequate for receiving righteousness, new life, and, ultimately salvation, extends to propositional trust too. Before the end time, at least, we may never be able to be sure about that to which we entrust the future and ourselves, but New Testament writers would surely have agreed that if we trust the combination of our own experience and that of others, tradition, and interpretation, our propositional trust will be as trustworthy as human trust can be, and adequate in God's sight.

Propositional Trust in the Dialogue between History and Theology in New Testament Studies

We noted in Chapter 1 that the much debated relationship between historical and theological study of the New Testament is not one of the main concerns of this study. Nevertheless, since it seeks to reflect theologically on writings which I have treated historically in a previous book, the question of the relationship between the two arises. Chapter 1 suggested, following, among others, Heikki Räisänen and Gerd Theissen, that both historical and theological study of the New Testament are well seen as forms of dialogue between texts, traditions, experience,

---

[119] p. 107.
[120] τὴν ἐπαγγελίαν τοῦ θεοῦ οὐ διεκρίθη τῇ ἀπιστίᾳ: 4.20 alludes to Gen. 17.17 and looks back to Gen. 15.6.
[121] E.g. Mt. 24.26, Mk 13.21. [122] Lk. 1.20, 22.67, Jn 20.25, 2 Thess. 2.12
[123] Most cases of *ou pisteuein*, though, refer to the failure to trust in God or in Christ: e.g. Mt. 21.25, Mk 11.31, Lk. 8.12, Jn 3.18, 8.45–6, 1 Jn 5.10.
[124] Notably Jn 3.12. At 14.10 the disciples are challenged to believe that Jesus is 'in the Father' on the basis that they do trust in him.

and interpretation.[125] On the basis of what we have argued about propositional trust, we can go a little further.

We have seen that all humanities subjects, including both theology and history, are, in some sense, metaphysical, and in all of them claims to knowledge based on the correspondence of those claims to objective truths are problematic.[126] Rather than trying to establish what we can know or reasonably believe about them, we may do better to think of ourselves as practising propositional trust in our interaction with them, and seeking to come to an interpretation of them that we are willing to trust. When we read New Testament writings, for instance, we are open to the possibility of being surprised by what we read, when they represent persons, ways of thinking, and relationships that are unfamiliar to us, while also trusting that they are not wholly unintelligible to us. We trust that the intuitions and assumptions we bring to them are not misleading; that those who have interpreted them before us did their work responsibly (recognizing that they were probably not always right); and that our own reasoning, as we interact with them, is as good (rigorous, satisfying, productive) as it can be. We trust that whatever conclusions we draw are worth taking a risk on, given that they may change the way people think and act in the future. Rather than asking, what can I know? what is the most certain basis on which I can believe? we do better justice to the writings of the New Testament by asking ourselves, what interpretation am I willing to put my trust in? to what interpretation am I willing to entrust the future?[127]

Thinking in terms of propositional trust offers a different way of 'dissolving the problematic', as Terence Tilley puts it, between theology and history, from those which have been canvassed in recent decades.[128] It recognizes that, as subjects we study, and as myths, models, and metaphysical assumptions that frame our view of the world, history and theology have more in common than is sometimes assumed. It accepts that we cannot make objective truth claims about either, but we can make trust-based claims about both. The difference between them lies not

---

[125] The dialogue could continue, of course, with the whole of the tradition until the present day, but, even though relatively few major figures in the history of the tradition discuss trust at any length, that would make for a much larger book. Since all Christians and students of Christianity agree, however, that New Testament texts are foundational to the tradition in every sense, these texts are, at the least, a natural starting-point for such a dialogue.

[126] Though we have confined ourselves to humanities disciplines here, the same is true of many others, and arguably all.

[127] Though most writing about the bases of faith focuses on what can be known or believed as true, rather than what can be trusted, this chapter's picture of the interplay between multiple bases of propositional trust resonates e.g. with Hooker's argument (*Laws of Ecclesiastical Polity* 5.8.2, with Gibbs (2002)) that faith is based on scripture, reason, and tradition, to which John Wesley (United Methodist Church (2004), 77) adds experience and Macquarrie ((1990), 339–47, with Burge (2021)), the revelation of God's action in nature and culture.

[128] Tilley (2004), 16–18. The most influential discussions of the relationship between history and theology, above all that of Harvey (1966), and recently notably Martin (2017), have been concerned with the relationship between historical and theological knowledge and truth rather than in what is trustworthy.

so much in the epistemological status of the subject-matter, the questions we ask, the status of the claims we make, or even the practical consequences of those claims, as in the communities with which we are consciously in dialogue when we study them, and our own relationship with our claims.

The difference, for instance, between my claiming that Paul, in Romans, understands God's righteousness as a quality of God, and my claiming that God's righteousness is a quality of God, is not fundamentally that the text of Romans is accessible in a way that God is not (the text itself may be relatively unproblematic, but what it means is endlessly debatable), nor that I can make a truth claim about one but not the other, nor that one is a historical and one a theological claim (if one regards Romans as scripture, then a historical claim about it is a type of theological claim), nor that one claim has existential implications which the other does not (because all arguments about all topics have the potential to change the way people think and act). On the argument of this study, the difference does not even lie in the scale of what is at stake, since we have argued that it is not right belief or understanding, historical, theological, or any other kind, that justifies or saves, but personal trust. The difference lies rather in whether I make either claim within the academy or the church, or both, and as an academic or a person of faith, or both. On one model of this relationship, historians and theologians in the academy might use some different methods, find some different questions interesting, have some different conversation partners, and (mostly) accept that disagreements are inevitable, while in churches, there might be a stronger expectation (or assumption, or hope) that historians and theologians should agree on what is interesting, and that historical and theological claims should cohere. On another model, academics might recognize the priority of the needs of their church, and seek to make claims that would be seen as orthodox. My own preference would be to return to the notion of dialogue, and see historians and theologians, equally within the academy, in the *ekklēsia*, and in the wider world, as voices in an ongoing conversation about whom and what we can trust with ourselves, each other, and our future, and how we can act on our trust.

Conclusion

This chapter has argued that, in addition to recognizing and reflecting on the relationship of trust between God, Christ, and humanity, we should pay attention to the role of propositional trust in the relationship. We described 'trusting that' as entrusting oneself, or being willing to entrust oneself to a proposition.

Propositional trust, we argued, can act as a basis for relational trust in God and Christ and relational knowing of God and Christ, which offers an alternative to claims of objective knowledge or reasonable belief. It has a contribution to make to theological epistemology not least at a time when the foundations on which we can know, or believe, anything about the divine or the divine–human relationship have become topics of intensive debate.

Using two other humanities subjects, history and music, as examples, we explored the role of propositional trust in the making of arguments about subjects (including the subjects of humanities disciplines) about which we cannot be certain. We observed that the multiplicity of possible worlds, ways of being, and ways of seeing which these subjects offer, open our imaginations to the possibilities of the world we live and act in: prompting us to ask not only who, or how, we are, but who or how we could or should be. We noted that humanities disciplines recognize that there is always more than one appropriate, interesting, productive way to discuss any subject, and that the student's own viewpoint is always implicated in her approach. When students of the humanities take views about their subject-matter, they therefore do so knowing that taking a view is necessary, but risky, and that it involves making choices which may affect the future.

Propositional trust plays a role both in the construction of arguments about subjects like these, and when we draw conclusions about them. When we have made our argument, we entrust it to the world, trusting that what we say will prove intelligible, even illuminating to others, and that it will make some kind of positive contribution to how people think and act in the future. In doing so, we take a high degree of responsibility for what we trust in, recognizing that it may have an impact on the world around us.

In the context of this study, we argued that propositional trust is involved when we are seeking to describe the relationship of trust between God and humanity, and when we are considering whether our account of the relationship is intelligible—whether it is credible and trustworthy—whether it has the capacity to engage others and inform, even illuminate the world around us—and whether, on that basis, we are willing to commit ourselves, and entrust the future, to it. This led us to ask what it would take for someone to 'trust that' the ideas outlined in previous chapters are worthy of trust. Four test cases were offered—the believer, the unchurched, the person whose trust has been damaged, and the person who trusts relationally in God and Christ—and we considered what the idea of 'trusting that' might offer each of them. In addition, looking back to Chapter 7, we proposed that propositional trust forms a bridge between relational trust and action, and between trusting in God and Christ and taking up that with which one has been entrusted by God and Christ to enact in the world.

Trust in God and Christ is a metaphysical choice, of a kind of which we make many, large and small, throughout our lives. Like all such choices, it is risky, but epistemologically it is no more risky than other such choices, and practically, it may be less risky than many, especially if, as Richard Swinburne argues, trust in God and Christ offers a '"vital good" now, and an eternal well-being hereafter'.[129]

---

[129] Swinburne (2005), 148; above, p. 331.

Finally, we drew on the argument of this chapter to suggest that the difference between historical and theological study of the New Testament lies less in the status of the subject-matter, the way we address it, or the nature of the claims we make about it, than in the context in which we offer our conclusions.

Looking back to earlier chapters, we can see that, though it does not explicitly appear very often in New Testament writings, propositional trust plays a role in a number of aspects of the new relationship of trust between God, Christ, and humanity.[130] When the faithful proclaim that God has acted anew through Christ, revealing God's righteousness to all nations so that all may be justified and ultimately saved, they proclaim something which will only be fully revealed and understood at the end time, so they trust that what they have experienced, heard preached, and learned through new interpretations of the scriptures is coherent and trustworthy, that it is intelligible to them, and that it coheres with their new or existing commitment to God.[131] Similarly, when they proclaim that Christ has been raised and exalted and will come at the end time, they trust that experience, preaching, and interpretation are intelligible, coherent, and trustworthy, and that they can trust that the new heavenly being Christ will prove trustworthy on the 'day of the Lord'.

When the faithful are invited to trust in God and Christ in Christ's death, they trust that God has brought life even out of sin and death, and that by travelling, with Christ, through their own death to the power of sin and suffering, they will come to new life and new hope. When they encounter Jesus in his earthly life, among the leaves of the gospels, they trust, once more, that, though unique, Jesus is not unintelligible to them (and, moreover, that he is intelligible without any special revelation). They trust that, though the evidence for Jesus' earthly life is patchy, sometimes incoherent, and inconsistent, it communicates enough to enable later generations to entrust themselves to him; and that encountering him can be as life-changing for themselves as it is for those who meet him within the gospel stories.

In all these aspects of their trust relationship, the faithful trust that they are able to respond appropriately to God and Christ and, though their trust is always liable to be fragile and imperfect, that God will not ask of them more than they can give, and that even imperfect trust will prove adequate in God's sight. By the same token, they trust that trust is complex and though, ideally, attitude, emotion, action, and relationship hang together, they need not always do so. When one does not feel trust, for instance, it may be enough to act with trust. Last, but not least, the faithful trust their experience and the tradition which tells them that they are entrusted by God and Christ with work for God's creation; and that not only their relationship with God and Christ, but everything they do here and

---

[130] It is also part of trust relationships for Brothers (1995).   [131] pp. 117–18.

now, in this world, bears meaning in light of their trust in God and Christ and their eschatological hope.

It is evident from this summary that propositional trust not only can be seen as central to the divine–human relationship, even essential to it, but that it is anthropologically an optimistic concept. Just as most New Testament writings assume that, however limited human beings are, and however entangled in suffering and sin, they can trust and be made righteous and saved, so they imply that propositional trust is not only necessary but possible. Nor is there any suggestion in New Testament writings that the ability to 'trust that' effectively—trustworthily, salvifically, and with good consequences in the world—is confined to the wise or the learned. Whatever is involved in 'trusting that', it is accessible to every human being at every stage of life from infancy onwards.

Finally, it is worth saying a word here about self-trust, which we have mentioned from time to time throughout these chapters, but not discussed in its own right. Chapters 4 and 5 argued that, for Paul and the gospels, one of the forms of culpable human *apistia/apistein* is the trust that one is in a position to judge for oneself which gods to worship, or how best to worship, for oneself or others, or to judge the status of Jesus in his earthly lifetime or the meaning of what he says and does. This can be seen as an inappropriate and damaging form of self-trust. Chapters 3, 5, and 6, and this chapter, however, argued that, in responding to God and Christ, people can trust, for instance, their experience and that of others, experience of the trustworthiness of the scriptures together with new interpretations of them, and the coherence of their new experiences with their existing commitment to God and/or their understanding of the world. This apparently involves an appropriate and fruitful form of self-trust, so what is the difference?

The difference can be seen, I suggest, in the conviction of Isaiah Berlin that the works of other human beings 'cannot be wholly unintelligible to us', and in Andrew Louth's proposal that the truth at the heart of theology is not 'something there to be discovered' but 'someone to whom we must surrender', and 'not ultimately something that invites our questioning, but something that questions us'.[132] The self-trust which seeks to objectify, interrogate, and draw conclusions about its subject, divine or human, on the basis of its own powers of reason, is limited by the limitations of that relationship and by its own nature, experience, and perspective.[133] The self-trust which recognizes that both the truster and her subject belong to a larger group of human or personal beings, and therefore that they have something in common; which accepts that the subject has its own subjectivity with which the truster must interact to understand it, and therefore that their relationship is properly intersubjective; and which is open to the impact of the

---

[132] Louth (1983), 95, quoted above, pp. 339–40.
[133] Confining discussion here to personal subjects, though one might argue that something analogous would be true of e.g. study of the physical world.

subject on itself and to interacting with it, has a chance to encounter and put its trust in something beyond its individual capacity to know. In other words, appropriate self-trust is not self-trust in a narrow sense, but is better seen as trust in self and subject in relationship, or trust that self and subject in relationship can form the basis of an argument that is worthy of trust.

9
'I trusted, therefore I spoke'
Concluding Reflections

Chapter 1 offered a lengthy outline of Chapters 2 to 7, so we will not offer another chapter summary here, but reflect a little further on some of the proposals made and possibilities raised by these chapters.[1]

We began by noting that, though trust is well recognized as part of the more complex concept and practice of faith, it is little discussed by theologians or philosophers of religion in its own right. This study has sought to show why it might be worth more discussion, taking one of a number of possible approaches by drawing out some of the theological implications of trust language in New Testament writings. The study of God's saving action through Christ, we have argued, is at its heart the study of divine–human trust. Our aim has not been to develop a single, coherent, or systematic account (in either the everyday or the theological sense) of divine–human trust in the New Testament,[2] but we can now see how the outlines of such an account might look.

God, seeking the restoration of trust between humanity and Godself, and, with it, humanity's release from the power of sin and suffering, takes the risk of trusting humanity to respond to a new initiative of trust. God sends God's son into the world, or unites Godself with Jesus of Nazareth, to forge a relationship of trust with those he encounters, and, by his trust and trustworthiness to both God and humanity, to reconcile them. To fulfil this mission in his earthly life, for the synoptic evangelists, Jesus needs only to be recognized by those who encounter him as a man of God, who prophesies, teaches, and performs great deeds by the power of God; for the final redactor of John, however, he needs to be recognized as the Son of God, which is only possible for the elect. Either way, many people do not recognize Jesus, and some seek to end his mission. Jesus allows himself to be arrested, accepting the consequences of his commitment to God, because he trusts God to enact God's plan even if he himself is executed, and because, being the person he is, he cannot be other than trusting and faithful towards God. After his crucifixion, God raises Jesus Christ to life as a sign that trust in God is vindicated, that God continues to seek the trust and salvation of human beings, and that trust between God and humanity is not destroyed by human evil or by death.

---

[1] The chapter heading quotation is from 2 Cor. 4.13. [2] pp. 26–8.

God exalts Christ to heaven, where Christ continues to be trustworthy, to work for trust and reconciliation between God and humanity, and to oversee God's people until the end time. The exalted Christ, moreover, accompanies those who put their trust in him, so that they can go through the 'death' they need to undergo to the power of sin and suffering 'with' him, who has shown that in trust with God there is a quality and abundance of life that outvalues everything else human beings hold dear. Human beings' trust in Christ is focused equally on the exalted Christ as ruler of the faithful, mediator between the faithful and God, and companion as human beings undergo death to the power of sin and suffering; Christ as trusting and trustworthy mediator in his death; Christ in his earthly life as visibly a man trusting and trusted by God; Christ as one who, in every part of his earthly and heavenly life is forgiving of fragile human trust; Christ as the saviour whom the faithful trust will come at the end time; and Christ as the exemplar, by imitating whom the faithful become more like Christ in his relationship with God and with the world.

People can come to trust in God and in Christ at any point in this sequence of events, and ideally continue and grow in trust indefinitely. Divine trust and trustworthiness towards humanity is not a one-off initiative, and human trust in God does not happen all at once or once for all. As is typical, especially where therapeutic trust is involved, trust is a long-term, open-ended, multi-stage relationship, which may encompass many human failures and further divine initiatives. The relationship may be based, on the human side, on very limited understanding of God or Christ, and limited capacity to respond. It is likely to have ups and downs, and it may or may not substantially evolve, but partial and inadequate trust is a good enough starting-point for God, and, before the end, even failures of trust or trustworthiness are not deal-breakers. The God who trusts, entrusts, and invites trust is a God of infinite patience, creativity, and persistence. We can go further, and suggest that trust is salvific and life-changing precisely because human knowledge, reason, and understanding of the divine, together with human trust and trustworthiness, are always imperfect. It is where apprehension and response are inadequate that God's trust in humanity and humanity's in God are most necessary, most appropriate, and hold out the greatest hope.

Running alongside the narrative of what God has done through Christ in the Christ event, we also identified a theme linking Christ with God as creator and the saving activity of both with the restoration of creation as a whole. When trust fails in any part of creation, the whole is put at risk. Only when divine–human trust is restored can creation be whole. The restoration of trust between God, Christ, and humanity is therefore not only humanity's best hope for itself, but also creation's best hope for restoration from its present suffering.

This narrative gives a substantial role to human beings. They are invited not only to trust, but, like Christ, to be entrusted, and to seek to be trustworthy. As individuals or as a group, the faithful are entrusted with sharing God's optimistic perspective on the world, and with joining God in working for the world: with preaching the gospel, creating and sustaining communities, acting as examples, and caring for one another and for creation. Not least importantly, this narrative affirms that trust is not only three-place—a means to the hope of salvation—but also two-place—part, in its own right, of human beings' right relationship with God and Christ. As such, it acts as a foretaste of eternal life or God's kingdom in the present time.

Throughout this study we have made use of writing on trust in moral philosophy and psychology, both of which offer further reasons why trust might stand at the heart of this narrative. Trust (including therapeutic trust) is fundamental where two or more parties are taking a risk on a new or renewed relationship. From a human point of view, no one can commit herself or her future to a new understanding of the world, physical or metaphysical, or to a new earthly or heavenly being without it. Trust is also essential where one person seeks to mediate between others and reconcile them. It is the quality *par excellence* which enables people to restore broken relationships, and to restore the capacity to make relationships when it has been damaged by our own errors or those of others. Where we trust is where we feel most material; where we matter. Trust, moreover, allows persons to work together, to share a perspective and a vision and cooperate to bring it about, or, more broadly, to look together into an open-ended future. We saw in Chapter 1 that philosophers debate the relationship between trust and reliance, and argued that the two are not coextensive. In subsequent chapters we have seen that the faithful can rely on God—to be God, for instance, and to care for creation—but that the *pistis* relationship is about much more than reliance. Though *pistis* is by no means the only attitude and action central to New Testament writers, between them they use it more than any other to capture every dimension of the good news: what God wills, how God acts with and through Christ, how humanity responds, how their relationship is restored, and what is involved in the relationship until the end time.

An integrated narrative like this has a certain appeal, but it also elides some of the assumptions, concerns, focal points, and imaginary of New Testament writings in a way which forfeits some of what makes them rich and thought-provoking. This study has preferred to follow clusters of *pistis* language in New Testament texts and trace the stories and relationships that unfold around them, to create a series of overlapping sketches which do not necessarily cohere at every point. This approach has attractions not only because it invites reflection on the differences between texts, but also because it is not self-evident that what listeners or readers with a confessional interest in these writings most need is a single overarching narrative of trust. When we develop a new trust relationship with another human being, his life story may well play a role in it, but it will not be the only, or necessarily the most important factor. It will also matter to us whether he seems to be interested in us or to care for us; whether we have similar interests and concerns; whether he can help or support us; whether we feel that forging a relationship with him will be enjoyable and life-enhancing. Narrative, moreover, is sometimes less its own *raison d'être* than a memorable way of expressing how relationships and other structures are understood as working, in human societies and the surrounding world.[3] Although, therefore, New Testament writers testify that every aspect of God's relationship with humanity through Christ, and every instantiation of Christ's existence, is significant, we need not take for granted that their significance is tied to their place in a narrative. It may equally be, from a human perspective, that the earthly life, death, resurrection, and exalted life of Christ are significant as different points of connection, at each of which people can engage with God and Christ. As people are attracted to different aspects of one another and form slightly different relationships with one another, one person may be attracted to Christ the teacher; another, by the Christ who offers release from the power of sin; another by the exalted Christ who entrusts them with the gift of healing, and each of these may be enough for the development of trust. Different images of the trust relationship, moreover address different human needs and address people differently at different times. For someone damaged by not being seen, or not being able to make himself seen, by those around him, it may be transformative to hear that everyone is seen and known by God, and can know God in Christ and those who follow him. If we are tempted to be complacent about God's care for us, it may be salutary to hear that God can be relied on to be God, but not always to do what human beings think they want or need.

In the early twenty-first century, trust has become a major issue and a matter of much anxiety and debate. Many of us are preoccupied with questions about who we can trust, or what, and how. Can we trust the government? The internet? Big business? Are we too sceptical, or not sceptical enough, about the integrity of the police or the media? Are our children too trusting, especially when they go online? How do we establish who and what is trustworthy? At the same time, it is well recognized that almost all of us trust, in practice, more people for more things than at any time in human history. We trust—mostly without thinking about it much—people, institutions, and processes to provide us every day with clean water, plentiful food, regular waste disposal, recycling, good schools, Wi-Fi, safe streets, dependable travel, stable currencies, reliable systems for buying and selling, social support, accountable government, competent doctors, effective legal systems, family and friendship groups, and much else. We trust because, as we saw in Chapter 1 and in the last chapter, it is impossible to live without trusting anyone or anything, but how to strike a balance between trusting too much or too easily, and not enough or not readily enough, has become a very difficult question.

---

[3] Lévi-Strauss (1969), especially chs 1–2.

Many contemporary developed societies, in their complexity, their openness to change, their hospitality to multiple perspectives on the world and to diverse myths, models of reality, and metaphysical assumptions, and because those who seek to engage with them do often so from within, and so are part of, and constantly influence, the complexity they are grappling with, are like a vaster, more complex, and more intractable analogue of the humanities disciplines we discussed in the last chapter. In that chapter we argued that those who rely on the intellectual model of the autonomous individual who seeks objective knowledge, or even firm grounds for belief, about such subjects, as a basis for actions or relationships, including relationships of trust, are liable to be frustrated. Objective truths, whether about the physical or metaphysical worlds, the past or the present, have proved hard to establish by such means and, increasingly, scholars across many disciplines are sceptical that this should be their project. But we do have some tools to help us establish who and what we might reasonably trust. We can, for instance, engage intersubjectively with a subject (whether it is music, our local political party, or a website), trusting that it can, in some way, communicate with us, bringing to our interaction with it our own assumptions and attitudes, but also holding ourselves open to being surprised by it. We can seek to interpret what is before us, taking into account existing interpretations, looking for points of coherence between our wider understanding of the world, what our subject represents to us, and what we and others make of it. We can aim to reach an interpretation of it to which, if we cannot be sure it is objectively true, we are willing to entrust ourselves and our future. Up to a point, we can test the trustworthiness of our conclusions. If the water in my tap is drinkable, my surgery goes well, or my friend does not post my confidences online, I can reasonably conclude that my interpretation of the world around me, in relation to these things, is trustworthy.

It is also worth asking, when we are trying to establish to whom or what we are willing to entrust ourselves and our future, how much a given relationship, institution, and so on, matters to us. How much difference would it make if we did not trust it? The world of social media, for example—populated, as it is, with millions of people and organizations with whom we have no direct or close connection—is a sphere which most of us, much of the time, are likely not to have strong grounds for trusting. But, we might argue, if we do not trust social media, nothing catastrophic is likely to happen. The practical truster might simply decide that she need not trust them, or entrust herself or anything that matters to her to them, except, perhaps, insofar as they act as a platform for people with whom or issues with which she has a personal connection.[4]

Reasonable as this may seem, however—especially to anyone born before about 1980—for many people it is not so simple. So many interactions already

---

[4] This also points to the limits of therapeutic trust, which is less likely to work if the truster does not know, or have any connection with the one trusted.

take place via social media that it may be difficult to have a normative social or professional life without trusting them. Because trust itself has a social aspect, moreover, the fact that many people appear to trust social media puts pressure on others to join them, because they seem to testify that they are trustworthy, and, more broadly, because our ability to decide whether anything is trustworthy rests in part on the testimony of others, so there is always an incentive to go with the crowd. In this respect, social media are an example of a much wider phenomenon, that whether or not we are individually inclined to trust the large-scale groups, systems, and organizations with which we are surrounded, it may be difficult not to do so in practice without segregating ourselves from those around us who do trust, in ways which we may not want to do.

Here, though, it is worth bearing in mind what we also saw in the last chapter: that what is trustworthy is always open to debate, that there is almost always more than one model of how the world works available in any context, and that, though trust may be social, almost all societies encompass multiple social groups with slightly, or very, different ways of thinking. There is therefore always scope to appeal to—or create—a different social group or way of thinking. When the boy in the Hans Christian Andersen story insists that the emperor is wearing no clothes, he refuses to go with the crowd, but he locates himself in the wider society of human beings who, through time, have found that the testimony of their own eyes tends to be trustworthy for everyday purposes. When we are considering who and what to trust, and on what grounds, we have more options than we always recognize.

Previous chapters of this study have also suggested that when we are thinking about whom and what to trust, our question need not always be, can the potential subject of my trust prove itself trustworthy to me? We can also ask, as a human being in my place and time, who and what am I entrusted with? What are my powers, responsibilities, or duties of care? For whom and for what am I willing to try to be trustworthy? How can I be trustworthy? What can I do to foster trust in others?[5] Since trust is social, everyone has the opportunity to affect who and what is trustworthy, how, and for what. As when we express and enact trust, when we seek to be trustworthy and to foster trust, there is always scope not only to go with the crowd, but to change its direction of travel. This brings risks of its own—I might be misguided in my ideas, or a sociopath—but it is not obviously more risky than being a passive participant in one's existing culture of trust and mistrust.

Questions such as with whom and what I am entrusted, or for whom and what I will try to be trustworthy, put the focus on my active choices. In the process, they bring to the fore an issue which is also implicit in questions about whom and

---

[5] Cf. O'Neill (2002), 27–31.

what I can trust, but which are more easily missed there. When I ask myself whether I can trust you, I am often asking whether I can trust you for something I want or need, and, normally, I have a good idea what that is. Alternatively, I may be asking whether a relationship of trust with you would enrich my life in a more indefinite sense—but, again, I probably have at least an idea of what might enrich my life. But when I ask with whom or what I am entrusted, or for whom or what I might try to be trustworthy, I am asking about the needs, desires, or the good of other people, of society, or of the world. To answer those questions, I need a bigger vision of what is needed and what is good.

The contemporary world offers many competing visions of what is needed and what is good. We consider them—if at all—very much as we consider other subjects about which we cannot be certain, but to which we might entrust ourselves and our future. This study has sought to demonstrate something of what, in the vision of the New Testament writers, the invitation to trust in, and be trusted by, God and Jesus Christ, has to offer humanity that is needed and is good. In their vision, human beings long for relationships of trust that are productive and enriching; for release from the power of their failures and the suffering which human failures cause; for a different and more abundant life; for relationships of love, peace, justice, joy, and hope; to be trusted and entrusted with work for others and for the world. New Testament writers, and those for whom they write, entrust themselves and their future to God and Jesus Christ, knowing that they cannot be certain that all these things become possible with God and Christ, but trusting that they do. They recognize that people are limited in understanding and prone to make mistakes, but they are convinced that limited and imperfect human beings can come to salvation and more abundant life. They hope, on the largest scale, that ultimately humanity will be restored to all that it was created to be, and, with humanity, creation as a whole. They know that trust is risky, but they also affirm the trustworthiness of experience, testimony, tradition, and interpretation, together with the power of trust to forge and sustain communities and to create trust beyond them. They affirm from experience what moral philosophers and psychologists also affirm, that without trust we cannot live, and where we trust is where we most fully live.

Bibliography

Abegg, Martin G. (2003), *The Concept of Covenant in the Second Temple Period*. Leiden: Brill.
Abraham, William J. (2006), *Crossing the Threshold of Divine Revelation*. Grand Rapids, Mich.: Eerdmans.
Abraham, William J. (2018), *Divine Agency and Divine Action III: Systematic Theology*. Oxford: Oxford University Press.
Achtemeier, Paul J. (1996), *1 Peter*. Minneapolis: Fortress.
Adam, A. K. M. (1995), *Making Sense of New Testament Theology: 'Modern' Problems and Prospects*. Macon: Mercer.
Adams, E. (2007), *The Stars Will Fall from Heaven: Cosmic Catastrophe in the New Testament and its World*. London: T&T Clark.
Adams, Sean A. (2013), *The Genre of Acts and Collective Biography*. Cambridge: Cambridge University Press.
Adams, Sean A. and Domony-Lyttle, Zanne (2019), *Abraham in Jewish and Early Christian Literature*. London: Bloomsbury.
Adamson, Lauren B. and Frick, Janet E. (2003), 'The still face: a history of a shared experimental paradigm', *Infancy* 4: 451–73.
Aland, Kurt (1993), *Synopsis of the Four Gospels: Greek–English Edition of the Synopsis Quattuor Evangeliorum*. Stuttgart: German Bible Society.
Albrektson, Bertil (2003), 'A disputed sense in a covenant context on the interpretation of Genesis 15:6', in A. D. H. Mayes and R. B. Salters eds, *Covenant as Context: Essays in Honour of E. W. Nicholson*. Oxford: Oxford University Press: 1–9.
Aletti, Jean-Noël (2017), *The Birth of the Gospels as Biographies: With Analyses of Two Challenging Pericopae*. Rome: Gregorian and Biblical Press.
Alexander, Loveday (2018), 'A map of understanding: the riskiness of trust in the world of the early Christians', *Journal for the Study of the New Testament* 40: 276–88.
Alexander, Philip S. (1998), 'From Son of Adam to second God: transformations of the biblical Enoch', in Michael E. Stone and Theodore A. Bergren eds, *Biblical Figures Outside the Bible*. Harrisburg, Pa: Trinity International: 87–122.
Alexander, Philip S. (2015), 'Rabbinic biography and the biography of Jesus: a survey of the evidence', in C. M. Tuckett ed., *Synoptic Studies: The Ampleforth Conferences of 1982 and 1983*. London: Bloomsbury: 19–50.
Allen, R. (2009), *The Christ's Faith: A Dogmatic Account*. London: T&T Clark.
Allison, Dale C. Jr (2008), 'The embodiment of God's will: Jesus in Matthew', in Beverly Roberts Gaventa and Richard B. Hays eds, *Seeking the Identity of Jesus: A Pilgrimage*. Grand Rapids, Mich.: Eerdmans: 117–32.
Allison, Dale C. Jr (2010), *Constructing Jesus: Memory, Imagination, and History*. Grand Rapids, Mich.: Baker Academic.
Allison, Dale C. Jr (2021), *The Resurrection of Jesus: Apologetics, Polemics, History*. New York: Bloomsbury.
Alston, William P. (1996), 'Belief, acceptance, and religious faith', in J. Jordan and Daniel Howard-Snyder eds, *Faith, Freedom, and Rationality*. Lanham, Md: Rowman and Littlefield: 3–27.

Alston, William P. (1997), 'Biblical criticism and the resurrection', in Stephen T. Davis, Daniel Kendall, and Gerald O'Collins eds, *The Resurrection: An Interdisciplinary Symposium on the Resurrection of Jesus*. New York: Oxford University Press: 148–83.

Alston, William P. (2007), 'Audi on non-doxastic faith', in Mark Timmons, John Greco, and Alfred Mele eds, *Rationality and the Good: Critical Essays on the Ethics and Epistemology of Robert Audi*. Oxford: Oxford University Press: 123–39.

Altenmüller, Eckart, Schmidt, Sabine, and Zimmermann, Elke eds (2013), *Evolution of Emotional Communication: From Sounds in Nonhuman Mammals to Speech and Music in Man*. Oxford: Oxford University Press.

Amato, Eugenio, Citti, Francesco, and Huelsenbeck, Bart eds (2015), *Law and Ethics in Greek and Roman Declamation: Current Perspectives, Future Directions*. Berlin: De Gruyter.

Ambrus, Grégor (2016), 'In the beginning was the Word: theological reflections on language and technical media in the context of the gospel of John', *Theologica* 6: 135–51.

Amesbury, Richard (2017), 'Fideism', in Edward N. Zalta ed., *The Stanford Encyclopaedia of Philosophy*. Fall 2017 edn. <https://plato-stanford.edu/archives/fall2017/entries/fideism/>.

Anagnostopoulos, Georgios ed. (2018), *Democracy, Justice, and Equality in Ancient Greece: Historical and Philosophical Perspectives*. Cham: Springer.

Anderson, B. W. (1994), *From Creation to New Creation*. Minneapolis: Fortress.

Ando, Clifford (2008), *The Matter of the Gods: Religion and the Roman Empire*. Berkeley: University of California Press.

Ando, Clifford and Rüpke, Jörg (2015), *Public and Private in Ancient Mediterranean Law and Religion*. Berlin: De Gruyter.

Appleby, Joyce, Hunt, Lynn, and Jacob, Margaret (1994), *Telling the Truth about History*. New York: W. W. Norton & Co.

Armstrong, Ruth (2014), 'Trusting the untrustworthy: the theology, practice and implications of faith-based volunteers' work with ex-prisoners', *Studies in Christian Ethics* 27: 299–317.

Arnal, William (2018), 'Textual healing: magic in Mark and Acts', in Jos Verheyden and John S. Kloppenborg eds, *The Gospels and their Stories in Anthropological Perspective*. Leuven: Peeters: 87–124.

Arnold, Clinton E. (1996), 'Returning to the domain of the powers: *stoicheia* as evil spirits in Galatians 4:3, 9', *Novum Testamentum* 38: 55–76.

Arzt-Grabner, Peter (2011), 'Gott als verlässlicher Käufer: einige papyrologische Anmerkungen und bibeltheologische Schlussfolgerungen zum Gottesbild der Paulusbriefe', *New Testament Studies* 57: 392–414.

Ashton, John (2000), *The Religion of Paul the Apostle*. New Haven: Yale University Press.

Ashton, John (2006), 'History and theology in New Testament studies', in Christopher Rowland and Christopher Tuckett eds, *The Nature of New Testament Theology: Essays in Honour of Robert Morgan*. London: John Wiley and Sons:1–17.

Ashton, John (2007), *Understanding the Fourth Gospel*. 2nd edn. Oxford: Oxford University Press.

Ashton, John (2014), *The Gospel of John and Christian Origins*. Minneapolis: Fortress.

Asmussen, Ida Helene (2018), 'Mediation in light of modern identity', in Anna Nylund, Kaijus Ervasti, and Lin Adrian eds, *Nordic Mediation Research*. Cham: Springer: 133–43.

Atran, Scott (2002), *In Gods We Trust: The Evolutionary Landscape of Religion*. Oxford: Oxford University Press, 2005.

Attridge, Harold W. (1989), *The Epistle to the Hebrews*. Philadelphia: Fortress.

Audi, Robert (1991), 'Faith, belief, and rationality', *Philosophical Perspectives* 5: 213–39.

Audi, Robert (2008), 'Belief, faith, and acceptance', *International Journal of the Philosophy of Religion* 63: 87–102.
Audi, Robert (2011a), *Rationality and Religious Commitment*. Oxford: Oxford University Press.
Audi, Robert (2011b), *Epistemology*. 3rd edn. New York: Routledge.
Audi, Robert (2011c), 'The ethics of belief and the morality of action: intellectual responsibility and rational disagreement', *Philosophy* 86: 5–29.
Aulén, Gustaf (1931), *Christus Victor: An Historical Study of the Three Main Types of the Idea of Atonement*. London: SPCK.
Aune, David E. (2002), 'The judgment seat of Christ (2 Cor. 5.10)', in Janice Capel Anderson, Philip Sellew, and Claudia Setzer eds, *Pauline Conversations in Context: Essays in Honor of Calvin J. Roetzel*. London: Bloomsbury: 68–86.
Avalos, Hector, Melcher, Susan J., and Schipper, Jeremy eds (2007), *This Abled Body: Rethinking Disabilities in Biblical Studies*. Atlanta: Society of Biblical Studies.
Bachmann, Michael (2012), 'Paul, Israel and the gentiles: hermeneutical and exegetical notes', in Reimund Bieringer and Didier Pollefeyt eds, *Crosscurrents in Pauline Exegesis and the Study of Jewish-Christian Relations*. London: Bloomsbury: 72–105.
Badenas, Robert (1985), *Christ, the End of the Law: Romans 10.4 in Pauline Perspective*. Sheffield: JSOT Press.
Baier, Annette C. (1986), 'Trust and antitrust', *Ethics* 96: 231–60.
Baier, Annette C. (1995), *Essays on Ethics*. Cambridge, Mass.: Harvard University Press.
Bailey, Alan (2002), *A Life Without Beliefs?* Oxford: Oxford University Press.
Baillie, John (1939), *Our Knowledge of God*. London: Oxford University Press.
Baillie, John (1956), *The Idea of Revelation in Recent Thought*. Oxford: Oxford University Press.
Baker, J. (1987), 'Trust and rationality', *Pacific Philosophical Quarterly* 68: 1–17.
Ball, D. M. (1996), *'I Am' in John's Gospel: Literary Function, Background and Theological Implications*. Sheffield: Sheffield Academic.
Balogh, Amy L. (2018), *Moses Among the Idols: Mediators of the Divine in the Ancient Near East*. Lanham, Md: Fortress Academic.
Bandstra, Andrew J. (1964), *The Law and the Elements of the World: An Exegetical Study in Aspects of Paul's Teaching*. Kampen: J. H. Kok.
Barber, Paul (1988), *Vampires, Burial, and Death: Folklore and Reality*. New Haven: Yale University Press.
Barclay, John M. G. (2010a), '"I will have mercy on whom I have mercy": the golden calf and divine mercy in Romans 9-11 and Second Temple Judaism', *Early Christianity* 1: 82–106.
Barclay, John M. G. (2010b), 'Unnerving grace: approaching Romans 9–11 from The Wisdom of Solomon', in Florian Wilk and J. Ross Wagner eds, *Between Gospel and Election: Explorations in the Interpretation of Romans 9–11*. Tübingen: Mohr Siebeck: 91–110.
Barclay, John M. G. (2014), 'Humanity under faith', in Bruce W. Longenecker and Mikeal C. Parsons eds, *Beyond Bultmann: Reckoning a New Testament Theology*. Waco, Tex.: Baylor University Press: 79–99.
Barclay, John M. G. (2015), *Paul and the Gift*. Grand Rapids, Mich.: Eerdmans.
Barclay, John and Simon Gathercole eds (2008), *Divine and Human Agency in Paul and his Cultural Environment*. New York: T&T Clark.
Barker, Andrew ed. (1984), 'Aristides Quintilian *De Musica*', in *Greek Musical Writings II: Harmonic and Acoustic Theory*. Cambridge: Cambridge University Press: 399–535.

Barker, Margaret (1996), *The Risen Lord: The Jesus of History as the Christ of Faith*, Edinburgh: T&T Clark.
Barker, Paul A. (2004), *The Triumph of Grace in Deuteronomy: Faithless Israel, Faithful Yahweh in Deuteronomy*.Milton Keynes: Paternoster.
Barnett, Paul (1997), *The Second Epistle to the Corinthians*. Grand Rapids, Mich.: Eerdmans.
Barr, James (1961), ' "Faith" and "truth"—an examination of some linguistic arguments', in *The Semantics of Biblical Language*. Oxford: Oxford University Press: 161–205.
Barr, James (1999), *The Concept of Biblical Theology: An Old Testament Perspective*. London: SCM.
Barrett, C. K. (1953), 'New Testament eschatology', *Scottish Journal of Theology* 6: 225–55.
Barrett, C. K. (1956), 'The eschatology of the epistle to the Hebrews', in W. D. Davies and D. Daube eds, *The Background of the New Testament and its Eschatology. Essays in Honour of Charles Harold Dodd*. Cambridge: Cambridge University Press: 363–93.
Barrett, C. K. (1968), *A Commentary on the First Epistle to the Corinthians*. London: A&C Black.
Barrett, C. K. (1973), *A Commentary on the Second Epistle to the Corinthians*. London: A&C Black.
Barrett, C. K. (1978), *The Gospel According to St. John: An Introduction with Commentary and Notes on the Greek Text*. 2nd edn. London: SPCK.
Barrett, C. K. (1991), *A Commentary on the Epistle to the Romans*. 2nd edn. London: A&C Black.
Barrett, C. K. (1994, 1998), *The Acts of the Apostles*. 2 vols. Edinburgh: T&T Clark.
Barrett, C. K. (2002), *Acts of the Apostles: A Shorter Commentary*. London: T&T Clark.
Barrett, C. K. (2003), 'Sectarian diversity at Corinth', in Trevor J. Burke and Keith Elliott eds, *Paul and the Corinthians: Studies on a Community in Conflict. Essays in Honour of Margaret Thrall*. Leiden: Brill: 287–302.
Barry, M. (2000), 'The mentor/monitor debate in criminal justice: what works for offenders', *British Journal of Social Work* 30: 575–95.
Bartel, Christopher (2011), 'Music without metaphysics?,' *British Journal of Aesthetics* 51: 383–98.
Barth, Karl (1932–67), *Church Dogmatics*. 5 vols. London: T&T Clark.
Barth, Karl (1962), *Theology and Church: Shorter Writings 1920–1928*. New York: Harper & Row.
Barth, Karl (1986), *Church Dogmatics III. 1: The Doctrine of Creation, Part I*. Edinburgh: T&T Clark.
Barth, Karl (2011), *The Word of God and Theology*. London: T&T Clark.
Barth, Markus (1974), *Ephesians*. New Haven: Yale University Press.
Barth, Markus and Blanke, Helmut (1994), *Colossians: A New Translation with Introduction and Commentary*. New York: Doubleday.
Bartley, William W. (1962), *The Retreat to Commitment*. New York: Knopf.
Barton, John (1979), 'Natural law and poetic justice in the Old Testament', *Journal of Theological Studies* 30: 1–14.
Barton, John (1994), 'Why Does the Resurrection of Christ Matter?', in Stephen Barton and Graham Stanton eds, *Resurrection: Essays in Honour of Leslie Houlden*. London: SPCK: 108–15.
Barton, John (2003), 'Covenant in Old Testament theology', in A. D. H. Mayes and R. B. Salters eds, *Covenant as Context: Essays in Honour of E. W. Nicholson*. Oxford: Oxford University Press: 23–38.

Barton, Stephen and Stanton, Graham (1994), *Resurrection: Essays in Honour of Leslie Houlden*. London: SPCK.
Bash, Anthony (1997), *Ambassadors for Christ: An Exploration of Ambassadorial Language in the New Testament*. Tübingen: Mohr Siebeck.
Bassler, Jouette M. (1989), 'Mixed signals: Nicodemus in the fourth gospel', *Journal of Biblical Literature* 108: 635–46.
Bassler, Jouette M. (2002), 'Epiphany Christology in the Pastoral letters: another look', in Janice Capel Anderson, Philip Sellew, and Claudia Setzer eds, *Pauline Conversations in Context: Essays in Honor of Calvin J. Roetzel*. London: Bloomsbury: 194–214.
Bates, Matthew W. (2017), *Salvation by Allegiance Alone: Rethinking Faith, Works, and the Gospel of Jesus the King*. Grand Rapids, Mich.: Baker Academic.
Bates, Matthew W. (2018), *Gospel Allegiance*. Grand Rapids, Mich.: Baker Academic.
Bates, Matthew W. (2020), 'The external-relational shift in faith (*pistis*) in New Testament research: Romans 1 as gospel-allegiance test case', *Currents in Biblical Research* 18: 176–202.
Bauckham, Richard (1981), 'The worship of Jesus in apocalyptic Christianity', *New Testament Studies* 27: 322–41.
Bauckham, Richard (1998), *God Crucified: Monotheism and Christology in the New Testament*. Carlisle: Paternoster.
Bauckham, Richard (1999), 'The New Testament teaching on the environment: a response to Ernest Lucas', *Transformation* 16: 99–101.
Bauckham, Richard (2008), *Jesus and the God of Israel: God Crucified and Other Studies on the New Testament's Christology of Divine Identity*. Milton Keynes: Paternoster.
Bauckham, Richard (2012), *Living with Other Creatures: Green Exegesis and Theology*. Bletchley: Paternoster.
Bauckham, Richard (2015), 'The incarnation and the cosmic Christ', in Niels Henrik Gregersen ed., *Incarnation: On the Scope and Depth of Christology*. Minneapolis: Fortress: 25–58.
Bauckham, Richard (2017), *Jesus and the Eyewitnesses: The Gospels as Eyewitness Testimony*. 2nd edn. Grand Rapids, Mich.: Eerdmans.
Bauer, Georg Lorenz (1800–2), *Biblische Theologie des Neuen Testaments*. 4 vols. Leipzig.
Baumert, Norbert (2001), *Charisma-Taufe-Geisttaufe*. 2 vols. Würzburg: Echter.
Baur, Ferdinand Christian (2016), *Lectures on New Testament Theology*. Oxford: Oxford University Press.
Bautsch, Richard J. (2009), *Glory and Power, Ritual and Relationship: The Sinai Covenant in the Postexilic Period*. London: T&T Clark.
Bautsch, Richard J. and Knoppers, Gary N. (2015), *Covenant in the Persian Period: From Genesis to Chronicles*. Winona Lake, Ind.: Eisenbaums.
Baxter, Wayne (2006), 'Healing and the "Son of David": Matthew's warrant', *Novum Testamentum* 48: 36–50.
Baxter, Wayne (2017), *Missing Matthew's Political Messiah: A Closer Look at his Birth and Infancy Narratives*. Philadelphia: Pennsylvania University Press.
Bazzana, Giovanni Battista (2009), 'Early Christian missionaries as physicians healing and its cultural value in the Greco-Roman context', *Novum Testamentum* 51: 232–51.
Beard, M., North, J.,. and Price, S. (1998), *Religions of Rome*. 2 vols. Cambridge: Cambridge University Press.
Beasley-Murray, George Raymons (1999), *John*. 2nd edn. Waco, Tex.: Word Books.
Beaudoin, Jean (2001), 'La participation des laïcs à l'exercise de la charge pastorale d'une paroisse', MA thesis, Laval University.

Beck, B. E. (1981). 'Imitatio Christi and the Lucan Passion Narrative', in William Horbury and Brian McNeil eds, *Suffering and Martyrdom in the New Testament*. Cambridge: Cambridge University Press: 28–47.
Beck, B. E. (1989). *Christian Character in the Gospel of Luke*. London: Epworth.
Beck, David R. (1997), *The Discipleship Paradigm: Readers and Anonymous Characters in the Fourth Gospel*. Leiden: Brill.
Becker, Jurgen (1969), 'Wunder und Christologie', *New Testament Studies* 16: 130–48.
Beckermann, Ansgar (2013), *Glaube*. Berlin: De Gruyter.
Beer, Jennifer E.; Packard, Caroline C.; Stief, Eileen, and Elwood Gates, Elizabeth (2012), *The Mediator's Handbook*. 4th edn rev. expanded. Gabriola: New Society.
Begbie, Jeremy (1989), *Music in God's Purposes*. Edinburgh: Handsel.
Begbie, Jeremy (2000), *Theology, Music, and Time*. Cambridge: Cambridge University Press.
Begbie, Jeremy (2014), *Music, Modernity, and God: Essays in Listening*. Oxford: Oxford University Press.
Begbie, Jeremy, Chua, Daniel K. L., and Rathey, Markus (2021), *Theology, Music, and Modernity: Struggles for Freedom*. Oxford: Oxford University Press.
Begbie, Jeremy and Guthrie, Steven R. (2011), *Resonant Witness: Conversations Between Music and Theology*. Grand Rapids, Mich.: Eerdmans.
Behm, J. and Quell, G. (1964) 'Diatithēmi, diathēkē', in Gerhard Kittel and Gerhard Friedrich eds, *Theological Dictionary of the New Testament* vol. 2. Grand Rapids, Mich.: Eerdmans: 106–34.
Beker, J. Christiaan (1980), *Paul the Apostle: The Triumph of God in Life and Thought*. Philadelphia: Fortress.
Beker, J. Christiaan (1982), *Paul's Apocalyptic Gospel: The Coming Triumph of God*. Philadelphia: Fortress.
Bekken, Per Jarle (2008), 'The controversy on self-testimony according to John 5:31–40, 8:12–20 and Philo, *Legum Allegoriae* III.205-208', in Bengt Holmberg and Mikael Winninge eds, *Identity Formation in the New Testament*. Tübingen: Mohr Siebeck: 19–42.
Bell, Richard H. (2007), *Deliver us from Evil. Interpreting the Redemption from the Power of Satan in New Testament Theology*. Tübingen: Mohr Siebeck.
Bellinger, W. H. Jr. (2015), 'The psalms, covenant, and the Persian period', in Richard J. Bautch and Gary N. Knoppers, *Covenant in the Persian Period: From Genesis to Chronicles*. Philadelphia: Pennsylvania State University Press: 309–21.
Belser, Julia Watts (2015), 'Violence, disability, and the politics of healing: the inaugural Nancy Eiesland endowment lecture', *Journal of Disability and Religion* 19: 177–97.
Belser, Julia Watts and Morrison, Melanie S. (2011), 'What no longer serves us: resisting ableism and anti-Judaism in New Testament healing narratives', *Journal of Feminist Studies in Religion* 27: 153–70.
Bender, John (1993), 'Music and metaphysics', in John Bender and Gene Blocker eds, *Contemporary Philosophy of Art*. Englewood Cliffs, NJ: Prentice Hall: 354–65.
Bennema, Cornelis (2002), *The Power of Saving Wisdom: An Investigation into Spirit and Wisdom in Relation to Soteriology of the Fourth Gospel*. Tübingen: Mohr Siebeck.
Bennema, Cornelis (2009), 'A theory of character in the fourth gospel with reference to ancient and modern literature', *Biblical Interpretation* 17: 375–421.
Bennema, Cornelis (2014) *Encountering Jesus: Character Studies in the Gospel of John*. Milton Keynes: Paternoster.
Ben-Ner, A. and Halldorsson, F. (2010), 'Trusting and trustworthiness: what they are, how to measure them, and what affects them', *Journal of Economic Psychology* 31: 64–79.
Berg, J., Dickhaut, J., and McCabe, K. (1995), 'Trust, reciprocity and social history', *Games and Economic Behaviour*, 10: 122–42.

Berg, Shane (2013), 'Ben Sira, the Genesis creation accounts, and the knowledge of God's will', *Journal of Biblical Literature* 132: 139–57.
Berlin, Isaiah (1960), 'The concept of scientific history', *History and Theory* 1: 1–31.
Berlin, Isaiah (2013), *Against the Current: Essays in the History of Ideas*. 2nd edn. Princeton: Princeton University Press.
Berne, Eric (1961), *Transactional Analysis in Psychotherapy: A Systematic Individual and Social Psychiatry*. New York: Grove Press.
Bersee, Ton (2021), *On the Meaning of 'Miracle' in Christianity: An Evaluation of the Current Miracle Debate and a Proposal of a Balanced Hermeneutical Approach*. Leuven: Peeters,
Bertolet, Timothy (2017), 'Hebrews 5:7 as the cry of the Davidic sufferer', *In Luce Verbi* 51: 1–10.
Bertschmann, Dorothea (2018), 'Is there a kenosis in this text? Rereading Philippians 3:2–11 in the light of the Christ hymn', *Journal of Biblical Literature* 137.1: 235–54.
Berube, Amelinda (2003), 'Tragedy in the gospel of Mark', MA dissertation, McGill University.
Best, Ernest (1972), *A Commentary on the First and Second Epistles to the Thessalonians*. London: A&C Black.
Best, Ernest (1976–7), 'The role of the disciples in Mark', *New Testament Studies* 23: 377–401.
Best, Ernest (1981), *Following Jesus: Discipleship in the Gospel of Mark*. Sheffield: JSOT Press.
Best, Ernest (1988), *Ephesians*. Edinburgh: T&T Clark.
Betsworth, Sharon (2015), *Children in Early Christian Narratives*. London: Bloomsbury.
Betz, H. D. (1967), *Nachfolge und Nachahmung Jesu Christi im Neuen Testament*. Tübingen: Mohr Siebeck.
Betz, H. D. (1979), *Galatians: A Commentary on Paul's Letter to the Churches in Galatia*. Philadelphia: Fortress.
Betz, H. D. (1985), *2 Corinthians 8 and 9: A Commentary on Two Administrative Letters of the Apostle Paul*. Philadelphia: Fortress.
Betz, H. D. (1990), *Hellenismus und Urchristentum*. Tübingen: Mohr Siebeck.
Betz, H. D. (1995), *The Sermon on the Mount, Including the Sermon on the Plain (Matthew 5:3–7.27 and Luke 6:20–49)*. Minneapolis: Fortress.
Betz, Otto (1960), *Offenbarung und Schriftforschung in der Qumransekte*. Tübingen: J. C. B. Mohr (Paul Siebeck).
Bhattacharya, Rajeev, Devinney, Timothy M., and Pillutla, Madan M. (1998), 'A formal model of trust based on outcomes', *Academy of Management Review* 23: 459–72.
Bieringer, Reimund and Pollefeyt, Didier eds (2012), *Crosscurrents in Pauline Exegesis and the Study of Jewish-Christian Relations*. London: Bloomsbury.
Bird, Michael (2012), 'Salvation in Paul's Judaism', in Reimund Bieringer and Didier Pollefeyt eds, *Crosscurrents in Pauline Exegesis and the Study of Jewish-Christian Relations*. London: Bloomsbury: 15–40.
Bird, Michael F. and Willitts, J. eds (2011), *Paul and the Gospels: Christologies, Conflicts and Convergences*. London: T&T Clark.
Blank, David (2009), 'Philodemus on the impossibility of a philosophical rhetoric', in Frédérique Woerther, ed., *Literary and Philosophical Rhetoric in the Greek, Roman, Syriac, and Arabic Worlds*. Hildesheim: Georg Olms: 79–93.
Blanton, Thomas R. (2012), 'Paul's covenantal theology in 2 Corinthians 2.14–7.4', in Reimund Bieringer and Didier Pollefeyt eds, *Crosscurrents in Pauline Exegesis and the Study of Jewish-Christian Relations*. London: Bloomsbury: 61–71.

Blendinger, C., Müller, D. and Bauder, W. (1975), 'Disciple, follow, imitate, after', in Colin Brown ed., *New International Dictionary of New Testament Theology and Exegesis.* Vol. 1: 480–94.

Blenkinsopp, Joseph (2000), *Isaiah 1–39: A New Translation with Introduction and Commentary.* New York: Doubleday.

Blowers, Paul M. (2012), *Drama of the Divine Economy: Creator and Creation in Early Christian Theology and Thought.* Oxford: Oxford University Press.

Blumenthal, David (1987), *God at the Center: Meditations on Jewish Spirituality.* San Francisco: Harper and Row.

Boccaccini, Gabriele (2020), *Paul's Three Paths To Salvation.* Grand Rapids, Mich.: Eerdmans.

Bockmuehl, Markus (1997), *A Commentary on the Epistle to the Philippians.* Black's New Testament Commentaries. London: A&C Black.

Bockmuehl, Markus (2008), 'God's life as a Jew: remembering the Son of God as Son of David', in Beverly Roberts Gaventa and Richard B. Hays eds, *Seeking the Identity of Jesus: A Pilgrimage.* Grand Rapids, Mich.: Eerdmans: 60–78.

Bockmuehl, Markus (2017), 'The personal presence of Jesus in the writings of Paul', *Scottish Journal of Theology*, 70: 39–60.

Bockmuehl, Markus and Stroumsa, Guy (2010), *Paradise in Antiquity: Jewish and Christian Views.* Cambridge: Cambridge University Press.

Boehm, R. A. (2015), *Alexander, "Whose Courage Was Great": Cult, Power, and Commemoration in Classical and Hellenistic Thessaly.* Berkeley: University of California Press.

Boers, Hendrikus (1979), *What is New Testament Theology? The Rise of Criticism and the Problem of a Theology of the New Testament.* Philadelphia: Fortress.

Boers, Hendrikus (1993), 'Polysemy in Paul's use of Christological expressions', in Abraham J. Malherbe and Wayne A. Meeks eds, *The Future of Christology: Essays in Honor of Leander E. Keck.* Minneapolis: Fortress: 91–108.

Boers, Hendrikus (1994), *The Justification of the Gentiles: Paul's Letters to the Galatians and Romans.* Peabody, NY: Hendrickson.

Boers, Hendrikus (2006), *Christ in the Letters of Paul: In Place of a Christology.* Berlin: De Gruyter.

Boismard, É. (1982), 'Rapports entre foi et miracles dans l'Évangile de Jean', *Ephemerides Theologicae Lovanienses* 58: 357–64.

Bolt, P. (2009), 'The faith of Jesus Christ in the synoptic gospels', in Michael F. Bird and Preston M. Sprinkle eds, *The Faith of Jesus Christ: Exegetical, Biblical, and Theological Studies.* Milton Keynes: Paternoster: 209–22.

Bonab, Baghar Ghobary and Kuhsar, Ali Akbar Haddadi (2011), 'Reliance on God as a core construct of Islamic psychology', *Procedia* 30: 216–20.

Bonab, Bagher Ghobary and Namini, Avazeh Sadat Yousefi (2010), 'The relationship between attachment to God and reliance on God', *Procedia Social and Behavioural Sciences* 5: 1098–104.

Bond, Helen (2020), *The First Biography of Jesus: Genre and Meaning in Mark's Gospel.* Grand Rapids, Mich.: Eerdmans.

Botner, Max (2019), *Jesus Christ as the Son of David in the Gospel of Mark.* Cambridge: Cambridge University Press.

Böttrich, Christfried (1997), 'Jesus und der Feigenbaum Km 11:12–14, 20–25 in der Diskussion', *Novum Testamentum* 39: 328–59.

Bourbon, Paskalina (2018), 'Beyond musical metaphysics: a philosophical account of listening to music', *Revista Portuguesa de Filosofia* 74: 1377–98.

Bourgeois, Daniel (2000), 'Théologie de la foi—confiance et modernité', *Pierre d'angle* 6: 199–216.
Bovon, François (2002–12), *A Commentary on the Gospel of Luke.* 3 vols. Minneapolis: Fortress.
Bovon, François (2010), 'First Christology: exaltation and incarnation, or from Easter to Christmas', *Études théologiques et religieuses* 85: 185–295.
Bowie, Andrew (2007), *Music, Philosophy, and Modernity.* Cambridge: Cambridge University Press.
Bowling, Daniel and Hoffman, David (2003), 'Bringing peace into the room: the personal qualities of the mediator and their impact on the mediation', in Daniel Bowling and David Hoffman eds, *Bringing Peace into the Room: How the Personal Qualities of the Mediator Impact the Process of Conflict Resolution.* San Francisco: Jossey-Bass: 13–47.
Boxall, I. (2006), *The Revelation of St. John.* London: A&C Black.
Boyarin, Daniel (1994), *A Radical Jew: Paul and the Politics of Identity.* Berkeley: University of California Press.
Boyce, I., Hunder, G., and Hough, M. (2009), *St Giles Trust Peer Advice Project: An Evaluation.* London: St Giles Trust.
Boyer, P. (1994), *The Naturalness of Religious Ideas.* Berkeley: University of California Press.
Boys-Stones, George (2018), *Platonist Philosophy 80 BC to AD 250: An Introduction and Collection of Sources in Translation.* Cambridge: Cambridge University Press.
Braaten, Laurie (2006), 'All creation groans: Romans 8:22 in light of the biblical sources', *Horizons in Biblical Theology* 28: 131–59.
Brandenburger, Egon (1962), *Adam und Christus: exegetisch-religions-geschichliche Untersuchung zu Röm. 5,12–21 (1 Kor. 15).* Neukirchen: Kreis Moers.
Bratman, Michael (1992), 'Practical reasoning and acceptance in context', *Mind* 101: 1–15.
Brauch, M. T. (2017), 'Perspectives on "God's righteousness" in recent German discussion', in E. P. Sanders, *Paul and Palestinian Judaism.* 40th anniversary edn. Minneapolis: Fortress: 523–42.
Brawley, Robert (2011), 'Homeless in Galilee', *HTS Teologiese Studies/Theological Studies* 67: art. 863.
Bredin, Mark and Bauckham, Richard (2010), *The Ecology of the New Testament: Creation, Re-Creation, and the Environment.* Downers Grove, Ill.: InterVarsity Press.
Bremmer, Jan N. (2019), 'Dying for the community: from Euripides' *Erechtheus* to the gospel of John', in David S. du Toit et al. eds, *Sōtēria: Salvation in Early Christianity and Antiquity: Festschrift in Honour of Cilliers Breytenbach on the Occasion of his 65th Birthday.* Leiden: Brill: 66–85.
Breytenbach, Cilliers (2010), *Grace, Reconciliation, Concord: The Death of Christ in Graeco-Roman Metaphors.* Leiden: Brill.
Breytenbach, Cilliers ed. (2015), *Paul's Graeco-Roman Context.* Leuven: Peeters.
Bridges, Jerry (2016), *Trusting God.* Colorado Springs: NavPress.
Brock, Sebastian (1982), 'Clothing metaphors as a means of theological expression in Syriac tradition', in M. Schmidt and C. Geyer eds, *Typus, Symbol, Allegorie bei den östlichen Vätern und ihren Parallelin im Mittelalter,* Regensburg: Pustet: 11.37.
Brodersen, Kai (2006), *Astrampsychos. Das Pythagoras-Orakel.* Darmstadt: Wissenschaftliche Buchgesellschaft.
Broer, I. (1992), 'Jesus und das Gesetz—Anmerkungen zur Geschichte des Problems und zur Frage der Sündenvergebung durch den historischen Jesus', in I. Broer ed., *Jesus und das jüdische Gesetz.* Stuttgart: Kohlhammer: 61–104.
Brondos, David (2006), *Paul on the Cross.* Minneapolis: Fortress.

Brondos, David (2018), *Jesus' Death in New Testament Thought*. 2 vols. Mexico City: Theological Community of Mexico.
Brothers, Doris (1995), *Falling Backwards: An Exploration of Trust and Self-Experience*. New York: W. W. Norton and Co.
Brothers, Doris (2008), *Toward A Psychology of Uncertainty: Trauma-Centered Psychoanalysis*. New York: Analytic Press.
Brower, Kent (2009), 'Who then is this?—Christological questions in Mark 4:35–5:43.
Brown, Colin ed. (1986), *The New International Dictionary of New Testament Theology*. Rev. edn. Exeter: Paternoster.
Brown, Colin ed. (1998), 'Ernst Lohmeyer's Kyrios Jesus', in Ralph P. Martin and Brian J. Dodd eds, *Where Christology Began: Essays on Philippians 2*. Louisville, |Ky: Westminster John Knox: 6–42.
Brown, David (2020), 'Music, theology, and religious experience', *International Journal for the Study of the Christian Church* 20: 4–7.
Brown, Derek R. (2015), *The God of This Age. Satan in the Churches and Letters of the Apostle Paul*. Tübingen: Mohr Siebeck.
Brown, Frank Burch (2003), *Good Taste, Bad Taste, and Christian Taste: Aesthetics in Religions Life*. Oxford: Oxford University Press.
Brown, Frank Burch (2005), 'Christian music: more than just the words', *Theology Today* 62: 223–9.
Brown, Harold O. J. (1969), 'A theology of trust', *Christianity Today* April 11: 3–5.
Brown, Jeannine K. (2002), *The Disciples in Narrative Perspective: The Portrayal and Function of the Matthaean Disciples*. Atlanta: SBL.
Brown, Raymond E. (1966, 1970), *The Gospel According to John*. 2 vols. New York: Doubleday.
Brown, Raymond E. (1993), *The Birth of the Messiah. A Commentary on the Infancy Narratives in the Gospels of Matthew and Luke*. New updated edn. London: Chapman.
Brown, Raymond E. (1997), *An Introduction to the New Testament*. New York: Doubleday.
Brown, Robert F. (2008), 'Divine omniscience, immutability, aseity, and human free will', *Religious Studies* 27: 285–95.
Brown, Shelby (1991), *Late Carthaginian Child Sacrifice and Sacrificial Monuments in their Mediterranean Context*. Sheffield: Sheffield Academic Press.
Brownlow, S. (1992), 'Seeing is believing: facial appearance, credibility and attitude change', *Journal of Nonverbal Behaviour*, 16: 101–15.
Brownsberger, William L. (2013), *Jesus the Mediator*. Washington DC: Catholic University of America Press.
Bruce, F. F. (1982a), *The Epistle to the Galatians: A Commentary on the Greek Text*. Grand Rapids, Mich.: Eerdmans.
Bruce, F. F. (1982b), *1 & 2 Thessalonians*. Waco, Tex.: Word Books.
Bruce, F. F. (1988), *The Book of Acts*. Rev. edn. Grand Rapids, Mich.: Eerdmans.
Brueggemann, W. (1996), 'The loss and recovery of creation in Old Testament theology', *Theology Today* 53: 177–90.
Bryan, Christopher (2011), *The Resurrection of the Messiah*. Oxford: Oxford University Press.
Bubeck, Diemut Elisabeth (1995), *Care, Gender, and Justice*. Oxford: Oxford University Press.
Buchak, Lara (2012), 'Can it be rational to have faith?', in Jake Chandler and Victoria S. Harrison eds, *Probability in the Philosophy of Religion*. Oxford: Oxford University Press: 225–47.
Buchak, Lara (2017a), 'Reason and faith', in William J. Abraham and Frederick D. Aquino eds, *The Oxford Handbook of the Epistemology of Theology*. Oxford: Oxford University Press: 46–63.

Buchak, Lara (2017b) 'Faith and steadfastness in the face of counter-evidence', *International Journal for Philosophy of Religion* 81: 113–33.
Buchak, Lara (2018), When is faith rational?' in Gideon Rosen, Alex Byrne, Joshua Cohen, Elizabeth Harman, and Seana Shiffrin eds, *Norton Introduction to Philosophy.* 2nd edn. New York: W. W. Norton: 115–29.
Buchanan, George Wesley (2003), 'The covenant in legal context', in Stanley E. Porter and Jaqueline C. R. de Roo eds, *The Concept of the Covenant in the Second Temple.* Leiden: Brill: 27–52.
Büchler, Adolf (1929), *Studies in Sin and Atonement in the Rabbinic Literature of the First Century.* Oxford: Oxford University Press.
Buck, Gillian (2017a), 'the core conditions of peer mentoring', *Criminology and Criminal Justice* 18: 190–206.
Buck, Gillian (2017b), '"I wanted to feel the way they did": mimesis as a situational dynamic of peer mentoring by ex-offenders', *Deviant Behaviour* 38: 1027–41.
Buck, Nicole M. L., Leenaars, Ellie P. E. M., Emmelkamp, Paul M. G., and van Marle, Hjalmar J. C. (2012), 'Explaining the relationship between insecure attachment and partner abuse: the role of personality characteristics', *Journal of Interpersonal Violence* 27: 3149–70.
Buckareff, Andrei (2005), 'How (not) to think about mental action', *Philosophical Explorations* 8: 83–9.
Buckareff, Andrei A. and Nagasawa, Yujin eds (2016), *Alternative Concepts of God.* Oxford: Oxford University Press.
Bühler, Pierre (2010), '"Ist der Glaube und Vertrauen recht, so ist auch Dein Gott recht..." Vertrauen in Gerhard Ebelings Theologie', *Hermeneutische Blätter* 1: 76–86.
Bühner, J.-A. (1977), *Der Gesandte und sein Weg im vierten Evangelium: Die kultur- und religionsgeschichtliche Grundlagen der johanneischen Sendungschristologie sowie ihre traditionsgeschichtliche Entwicklung.* Tübingen: Mohr Siebeck.
Bultmann, Rudolf (1952, 1955), *Theology of the New Testament.* 2 vols. London: SCM.
Bultmann, Rudolf (1958), *Jesus and the Word.* New York: Scribner.
Bultmann, Rudolf (1964), 'Pistis ktl', in Gerhard Kittel and Gerhard Friedrich eds, *Theological Dictionary of the New Testament* vol. 6. Grand Rapids, Mich.: Eerdmans:174–228.
Bultmann, Rudolf (1969), *Faith and Understanding.* Vol. 1. London: SCM.
Bultmann, Rudolf (1971), *The Gospel of John: A Commentary.* Oxford: Blackwell.
Bultmann, Rudolf (1997), *What is Theology?* Minneapolis: Fortress.
Bultmann, Rudolf (2007), *Theology of the New Testament.* Waco, Tex.: Baylor University Press.
Bultmann, Rudolf and Lührmann, D, (1974), 'Phaneros etc.', in Gerhard Kittel and Gerhard Friedrich eds, *Theological Dictionary of the New Testament* vol. 9. Grand Rapids, Mich.: Eerdmans: 1–11.
Burch, Ernest W. (1931), 'Tragic action in the second gospel: a study in the narrative of Mark', *Journal of Religion* 11: 346–58.
Burchardt, Marian (2018), 'Saved from hegemonic masculinity? Charismatic Christianity and men's responsibilities in South Africa', *Current Sociology* 66: 110–27.
Burge, Stephen R. (2021), 'Revelation and reason: theological epistemology in John Macquarrie's thought', *Journal of Anglican Studies* 19: 84–97.
Burkert, Walter (1966), 'Greek tragedy an sacrificial ritual', *Greek, Roman, and Byzantine Studies* 7: 87–121.
Burkert, Walter (2005), 'Signs, commands and knowledge: ancient divination between enigma and epiphany', in S. I. Johnston and P. Struck eds, *Mantikē: Studies in Ancient Divination.* Leiden: Brill: 29–49.

Burnett, Fred W. (1993), 'Characterization and reader construction of characters in the gospels', *Semeia* 63: 3–78.
Burns, Elizabeth (2009), 'Must theists believe in a personal God'? *Think* 8: 77–86.
Burns, Robert M. and Rayment-Pickard, Hugh eds (2000), *Philosophies of History from Enlightenment to Modernity*. Oxford: Blackwell.
Burnyeat, M. (1980), 'Can the Sceptic Live his Scepticism?', in M. Schofield, M. Burnyeat, and J. Barnes eds, *Doubt and Dogmatism: Studies in Hellenistic Epistemology*. Oxford: Oxford University Press: 20–53.
Burridge, Richard A. (2000), 'Gospel genre, Christological controversy and the absence of Rabbinic biography: some implications of the biographical hypothesis', in David G. Horrell and Christopher M. Tuckett eds, *Christology, Controversy and Community: New Testament Essays in Honour of David R. Catchpole*. Leiden: Brill: 137–56.
Burridge, Richard A. (2007), *Imitating Jesus: An Inclusive Approach to New Testament Ethics*. Grand Rapids, Mich.: Eerdmans.
Burridge, Richard A. (2018), *What Are the Gospels? A Comparison with Graeco-Roman Biography*. 25th anniversary edition. Waco, Tex.: Baylor University Press.
Burridge, Richard A. (2020), 'The gospels and ancient biography: 25 years on, 1993-2018', in Robert Matthew Calhoun, David P. Moessner, and Tobias Nicklas eds, *Modern and Ancient Literary Criticism of the Gospels: Continuing the Debate on Gospel Genre(s)*. Tübingen: Mohr Siebeck: 9–56.
Burrow, John (2008), *A History of Histories*. London: Penguin.
Burt, Robert (2012), *In the Whirlwind: God and Humanity in Conflict*. Cambridge, Mass.: Harvard University Press.
Burton, Ernest DeWitt (1921), *A Critical and Exegetical Commentary on the Epistle to the Galatians*. Edinburgh: T&T Clark.
Büssing, Arndt, Recchia, Daniela Rodrigues, and Baumann, Klaus (2015), 'Reliance on God's help scale as a measure of religious trust—a summary of findings', *Religions* 6: 1358–67.
Buttrick, George Arthur ed. (1962), *The Interpreter's Dictionary of the Bible: An Illustrated Encyclopedia*, I. New York: Abingdon.
Byrne, Brendan, SJ (1979), *Sons of God—Seed of Abraham*. Rome: Biblical Institute Press.
Byrne, Brendan, SJ (1996), *Romans*. Collegeville, Minn.: Liturgical Press.
Byrne, Brendan, SJ (1997), 'Christ's pre-existence in Pauline soteriology', *Theological Studies* 58: 308–30.
Byrne, Peter (1995), 'Philosophy: introduction', in Peter Byrne and J. L. Houlden eds, *Companion Encyclopedia of Theology*. London: Routledge: 337–42.
Byrskog, Samuel (2000), *Story as History—History as Story: The Gospel Tradition in the Context of Ancient Oral History*. Tübingen: Mohr Siebeck.
Byrskog, Samuel (2014), 'The message of Jesus', in Bruce W. Longenecker and Mikeal C. Parsons eds, *Beyond Bultmann: Reckoning a New Testament Theology*. Waco, Tex.: Baylor University Press: 3–22.
Caginalp, Gunduz (2002), 'Does the market have a mind of its own, and does it get carried away with excess cash?' *The Journal of Psychology and Financial Markets* 3: 72–5.
Caird, George with Hurst, L. D. (1994), *New Testament Theology*. Oxford: Oxford University Press.
Calderone, Salvatore (1968), *Pistis-Fides: Ricerche di Storia e Diritto Internazionale nell'Antichità*. Messina: Università degli studi.
Calhoun, Robert Matthew, Moessner, David P., and Nicklas, Tobias eds (2020), *Modern and Ancient Literary Criticism of the Gospels: Continuing the Debate on Gospel Genre(s)*. Tübingen: Mohr Siebeck.

Campbell, Douglas A. (1992), *The Rhetoric of Righteousness in Romans 3.21-6*. Sheffield: Sheffield University Press.
Campbell, Douglas A. (2009), *The Deliverance of God: An Apocalyptic Rereading of Justification in Paul*. Grand Rapids, Mich.: Eerdmans.
Campbell, Douglas A. (2012), 'Beyond justification in Paul: the thesis of the deliverance of God', *Scottish Journal of Theology* 65: 90-104.
Campbell, William S. (2012), 'Covenantal theology and participation in Christ: Pauline perspectives on transformation', in Reimund Bieringer and Didier Pollefeyt eds, *Crosscurrents in Pauline Exegesis and the Study of Jewish-Christian Relations*. London: Bloomsbury: 41-60.
Caneva, Stefano G. ed. (2020), *The Materiality of Hellenistic Ruler Cults*. Liège: Presses Universitaires de Liège.
Cantarella, Eve (2016), 'Women and patriarchy in Roman law', in Paul J. du Plessis, Clifford Ando, and Kaius Tuori, *The Oxford Handbook of Roman Law and Society*. Oxford: Oxford University Press: 419-31.
Cantwell-Smith, Wilfred (1979), *Faith and Belief*. Princeton: Princeton University Press.
Cara, Robert J. (2017), *Cracking the Foundation of the New Perspective on Paul. Covenantal Nomism Versus Reformed Covenantal Theology*. Fearn: Mentor.
Cardus, Sir Neville (1977), *What is Music?* London: White Lion Publishers.
Carlson Brown, Joanne, (1992), 'Divine child abuse?', *Daughters of Sarah* 18: 24-8.
Carlson Brown, Joanne and Bohn, Carole R. eds (1989), *Christianity, Patriarchy, and Abuse: A Feminist Critique*. New York: Continuum.
Carnley, Peter (1987), *The Structure of Resurrection Belief*. Oxford: Oxford University Press.
Carr, David, Flynn, Thomas R., and Makkreel, Rudolf A. eds (2004), *The Ethics of History*. Evanston, Ill.: Northwestern University Press.
Carroll, John T. (1979), *When Prophecy Failed: Reactions and Responses to Failure in the Old Testament Prophetic Traditions*. London: SCM.
Carroll, John T. (1995), 'Sickness and healing in the New Testament gospels', *Interpretation* 49: 130-42.
Carroll, John T. (2003), 'Welcoming grace, costly commitment: an approach to the gospel of Luke', *Interpretation* 57: 16-23.
Carroll, John T. (2012), *Luke: A Commentary*. Louisville, Ky: Westminster John Knox.
Carson, D. A. (1991), *The Gospel According to John*. Grand Rapids, Mich.: Eerdmans.
Carson, D. A., O'Brien, P. T., and Seifrid, Mark A. (2004), *Justification and Variegated Nomism—Volume 2: The Paradoxes of Paul*. Grand Rapids, Mich.: Baker Academic.
Carter, Warren (2004), *Matthew: Storyteller, Interpreter, Evangelist*. Rev. edn. Ada, Mich.: Baker Academic.
Casquillo Fumenal, Ángel Luis (2008), 'Muerte, despedazamiento y apoteosis de Rómulo: un studio sobre la realidad histórica del primer rey de Roma', *Espacio, Tiempo y Forma serie 2: Historia Antigua* 21: 123-84.
Castleden, Rodney (1990), *Minoans: Life in Bronze Age Crete*. London: Routledge.
Chaniotis, Angelos (2003), 'The divinity of the Hellenistic rulers', in A. Erskine ed., *A Companion to the Hellenistic World*. Oxford: Blackwell: 431-45.
Charles, R. H. (1975), *A Critical and Exegetical Commentary on the Revelation of St. John*. Edinburgh: T&T Clark.
Charlesworth, James H. (1992), 'Forgiveness (Early Judaism)', in David Noel Freedman ed., *Anchor Bible Dictionary*. 5 vols. New York: Doubleday and Co.
Charlesworth, James H. ed. (2006), *Jesus and Archaeology*. Grand Rapids, Mich.: Eerdmans.
Charlesworth, James H., Elledge. C. D., Crenshaw, James L., Boers, Henrikus, and Waite, Willis W. (2006), *Resurrection: The Origin and Future of a Biblical Doctrine*. NY: T&T Clark International.

Charru, P. (2012), 'At the intersection of theology and music', *Laval théologique et philosophique* 68: 311–18.
Chartier, Roger (1997), *On the Edge of the Cliff: History, Language, and Practices*. Baltimore: Johns Hopkins University Press.
Chester, Andrew (2007), *Messiah and Exaltation: Jewish Messianic and Visionary Traditions and New Testament Christology*. Tübingen: Mohr Siebeck.
Chignell, Andrew (2013), 'Prolegomena to any future non-doxastic religion', *Religious Studies* 49: 195–207.
Childs, Brevard S. (1992), *Biblical Theology of the Old and New Testaments: Theological Reflection on the Hebrew Bible*. Minneapolis: Fortress.
Chow, J. K. (1992), *Patronage and Power: A Study of Social Networks in Corinth*. Sheffield: Sheffield Academic.
Christiansen, Ellen Juhl (1995), *The Covenant in Judaism and Paul: A Study of Ritual Boundaries as Identity Markers*. Leiden: Brill.
Christofferson, O. (1990), *The Earnest Expectation of the Creature: The Flood Tradition as Matrix of Romans 8.18–27*. Stockholm: Almquist and Wiksell.
Christoph, Monika (2005), *Pneuma und das neue Sein der Glaubenden: Studien zur Semantik und Pragmatik der Rede von Pneuma in Röm 8*. Frankfurt: Lang.
Chronis, Harry L. (1982), 'The torn veil: cultus and Christology in Mark 15:37–9', *Journal of Biblical Literature* 101: 97–114.
Clark, Elizabeth A. (2004), *History, Theory, Text: Historians and the Linguistic Turn*. Cambridge, Mass.: Harvard University Press.
Clark, Patricia (2014), 'Reversing the ethical perspective: what the allegorical interpretation of the Good Samaritan parable can still teach us', *Theology Today* 7: 300–9.
Cleland, Liza, Davies, Glenys, and Llewelyn-Jones, Lloyd (2007), *Greek and Roman Dress from A to Z*. London: Routledge.
Clements, Keith (1995), 'Theology now', in Peter Byrne and J. L. Houlden eds, *Companion Encyclopedia of Theology*. London: Routledge: 272–90.
Coeckelbergh, Mark (2012), 'Can we trust robots?', *Ethics and Information Technology* 14: 53–60.
Collier, Andrew (2003), *On Christian Belief: A Defence of a Cognitive Conception of Religious Belief in a Christian Concept*. London: Routledge.
Collins, Adela Yarbro (1979), *The Apocalpyse*. Dublin: Veritas.
Collins, Adela Yarbro (1990), *Is Mark's Gospel A Life of Jesus? The Question of Genre*. Milwaukee: Marquette University Press.
Collins, Adela Yarbro (1993), 'The empty tomb in the gospel according to Mark', in Eleonore Stump and Thomas P. Flint eds, *Hermes and Athena: Biblical Exegesis and Philosophical Theology*. Notre Dame, Ind.: University of Notre Dame Press: 107–37.
Collins, Adela Yarbro (1995), 'Genre and the gospels', *Journal of Religion* 75: 239–46.
Collins, Adela Yarbro (2007), *Mark: A Commentary*. Minneapolis: Fortress.
Collins, Adela Yarbro (2019), 'The metaphorical use of ἱλαστήριον in Romans 3:25', in David S. du Toit et al eds, *Sōtēria: Salvation in Early Christianity and Antiquity. Feschrift in Honour of Cilliers Breytenbach on the Occasion of his 65th Birthday*. Leiden: Brill: 273–86.
Collins, Adela Yarbro and Collins, John (2008), *King and Messiah as Son of God: Divine, Human, and Angelic Messianic Figures in Biblical and Related Literature*. Grand Rapids, Mich.: Eerdmans.
Collins, John J. (1988), 'Messianism in the Maccabean period', in Jacob Neusner, William Scott Green, and Ernest S. Frerichs eds, *Judaisms and their Messiahs at the Turn of the Christian Era*. Cambridge: Cambridge University Press: 97–110.

Collins, John J. (1993), 'The *Son of God* text from Qumran', in Martinus C. de Boer ed., *From Jesus to John: Essays on Jesus and New Testament Christology in Honour of Marinus de Jonge*. London: Bloomsbury: 65–82.
Collins, John J. (2016), *The Apocalyptic Imagination: An Introduction to Jewish Apocalyptic Literature*. 3rd edn. Grand Rapids, Mich.: Eerdmans.
Collins, John N. (2014), *Diakonia Studies: Critical Issues in Ministry*. Oxford: Oxford University Press.
Collins, Raymond F. (1995), 'From John to the beloved disciple: an essay on Johannine characters', *Interpretation* 49: 359–69.
Collins, Raymond F. (1999), *First Corinthians*. Collegeville, Minn.: Liturgical Press.
Colson, John R. (2017), 'Jesus and the spirit in Paul's theology: the earthly Jesus', *Catholic Biblical Quarterly* 79: 77–96.
Comrie, B. and Thompson, S. (2007), 'Lexical nominalization', in T. Shopen ed., *Language Typology and Syntactic Description*. 2nd edn. Vol. 3. Cambridge: Cambridge University Press: 334–81.
Congar, Yves (1969), *Faith and Spiritual Life*. London: Darton, Longman & Todd.
Connolly, Joy (2007), *The State of Speech: Rhetoric and Political Thought in Ancient Rome*. Princeton: Princeton University Press.
Conzelmann, Hans (1969), *An Outline of the Theology of the New Testament*. London: SCM.
Conzelmann, Hans (1975), *1 Corinthians*. Philadelphia: Fortress.
Conzelmann, Hans (1987), *Acts of the Apostles*. Minneapolis: Fortress.
Coogan, Jeremiah (2021), 'Gospel as recipe book', *Early Christianity* 12: 1–21.
Cook, John Grainger (2017), 'Resurrection in paganism and the question of an empty tomb in 1 Corinthians 15', *New Testament Studies* 63: 56–75.
Cook, John Grainger (2019), *Crucifixion in the Ancient Mediterranean World*. 2nd extended edn. Tübingen: Mohr Siebeck.
Cooke, G. (1961), 'The Israelite king as son of God', *Zeitschrift für die Alttestamentliche Wissenschaft*, 73: 202–25.
Cotesta, Vittorio (2015), *Kings into Gods: How Prostration Shaped Eurasian Civilizations*. Leiden: Brill.
Cotter, Wendy (1999), *Miracles in Graeco-Roman Antiquity: A Sourcebook for the Study of New Testament Miracle Stories*. London: Taylor and Francis.
Coulson, John R. (2016), *The Righteous Judgment of God: Aspects of Judgment in Paul's Letters*. Eugene, Ore.: Wipf and Stock.
Coventry, John (1968), *The Theology of Faith*. Cork: Mercier Press.
Cox, R. (2007), *By the Same Word: Creation and Salvation in Hellenistic Judaism and Early Christianity*. Berlin: De Gruyter.
Craffert, Pieter F. (2011), 'I "witnessed the raising of the dead": resurrection accounts in a neuroanthropological perspective', *Neotestamentica* 45: 1–28.
Cranfield, C. E. B. (1962), '*Metron pisteōs* in Romans xii.3', *New Testament Studies* 8: 345–51.
Cranfield, C. E. B. (1975, 1979), *A Critical and Exegetical Commentary on the Epistle to the Romans*. 2 vols. 6th edn. Edinburgh: T&T Clark.
Cranfield, C. E. B. (1991), '"The works of the law" in the epistle to the Romans', *Journal for the Study of the New Testament* 43: 89–101.
Crawford, Nathan (2013), *Theology as Improvisation: A Study in the Musical Nature of Theological Thinking*. Leiden: Brill.
Creaney, Sean (2020), 'Children's voices—are we listening? Progressing peer mentoring in the youth justice system', *Child Care in Practice* 26: 22–37.

Crisp, Oliver D., D'Costa, Gavin, Davies, Mervyn, and Hampson, Peter eds (2012), *Theology and Philosophy: Faith and Reason*. London: T&T Clark.
Crossan, John Dominic (1994), *Jesus: A Revolutionary Biography*. New York: HarperSanFrancisco.
Cullmann, Oscar (1967), *Salvation in History*. London: SCM.
Culpepper, R. Alan (1983), *Anatomy of the Fourth Gospel: A Study in Literary Design*. Philadelphia: Fortress Press.
Cuneo, Terence (2017), 'Aligning with lives of faith', *International Journal of Philosophy of Religion* 81: 83–97.
Cupitt, Don (2001), *Taking Leave of God*. London: SCM.
Currie, Bruno (2005), *Pindar and the Cult of Heroes*. Oxford: Oxford University Press.
Czajkowski, Kimberley (2017), *Localized Law: The Babatha and Salome Komaise Archives*. Oxford: Oxford University Press.
Dahl, Nils Alstrup (1991), *Jesus the Christ: The Historical Origins of Christological Doctrine*. Minneapolis: Fortress.
Dalferth, Ingolf U. (1992), 'Über Einheit und Vielfalt des christlichen Glaubens: Eine Problemskizze', in Wilfried Härle and Reiner Preul eds, *Glaube*. Marburg: N. G. Elwert: 99–137.
Dalferth, Ingolf U. (2006), *Becoming Present: An Inquiry into the Christian Sense of the Presence of God*. Leuven: Peeters.
Dalferth, Ingolf U. (2010), 'Vertrauen ist menschlich', *Hermeutische Blätter* 1/2: 142–57.
Dalferth, Ingolf U. (2016), *Radical Theology: An Essay on Faith and Theology in the Twenty-First Century*. Minneapolis: Fortress.
Dalferth, Ingolf U. and Peng-Keller, Simon (2012a), *Kommunikation des Vertrauens*. Leipzig: Evangelische Verlagsanstalt.
Dalferth, Ingolf U. and Peng-Keller, Simon (2012b), *Gottvertrauen: Die ökumenische Diskussion um die fiducia*. Freiburg: i. Br.
Dalferth, Ingolf U. and Peng-Keller, Simon (2013), *Grundvertrauen: Hermeneutik eines Grenzphänoms*. Leipzig: Evangelische Verlagsanstalt.
Dalmiya, Vrinda (2016), *Care-Knowing*. Oxford: Oxford University Press.
Dalton, Anne Marie and Simmons, Henry C. (2010), *Ecotheology and the Practice of Hope*. Albany, NY: State University of New York Press.
Danker, Frederick W. (1982), *Benefactor: Epigraphic Study of a Graeco-Roman and New Testament Semantic Field*. St Louis: Clayton.
Darr, John A. (1992), *On Character Building: The Reader and the Rhetoric of Characterization in Luke-Acts*. Louisville, Ky: Westminster John Knox.
Darwall, Stephen (2017), 'Trust as a second-personal attitude (of the heart)', in Paul Faulkner and Thomas W. Simpson eds, *The Philosophy of Trust*. Oxford: Oxford University Press: 35–50.
Dasgupta, Partha (1999), 'Economic progress and the idea of social capital', in P. Dasgupta and I. Serageldin eds. (1999), *Social Capital: A Multifaceted Perspective*. Washington, DC: The World Bank: 325–424.
Daube, David (1972), 'Responsibilities of master and disciples in the gospels', *New Testament Studies* 19: 1–15.
Davies, Stephen (2001), *Musical Works and Performances: A Philosophical Exploration*. Oxford: Oxford University Press.
Davies, William D. *Paul and Rabbinic Judaism: Some Rabbinic Elements in Pauline Theology*. 4th edn. Philadelphia: Fortress, 1980.
Davies, W. D. and Allison, Dale (1988–2004), *The Gospel According to Saint Matthew*. 3 vols. London: Bloomsbury.

Davies, W. D., Meyer, P. D., Aune D. E. (1981), 'Review of H. D. Betz, *Galatians*', *Religious Studies Review* 7: 310–28.
Davis, P. G. (1994), 'Divine agents, mediators, and New Testament Christology', *Journal of Theological Studies* 45: 479–503.
Davis, Stephen T. (2006), *Christian Philosophical Theology*. New York: Oxford University Press.
Davis, Stephen T., Kendall, Daniel, and O'Collins, Gerald (2002), *The Incarnation*. Oxford: Oxford University Press.
Day, J. (2007), 'Rhetoric and ethics from the sophists to Aristotle', in I. Worthington ed., *A Companion to Greek Rhetoric*. Oxford: Blackwell: 378–92.
D'Costa, Gavin (2017), 'Supersessionism: harsh, mild, or gone for good?', *European Judaism: A Journal for the New Europe* 50: 99–107.
Deaver, Katie M. (2017), 'Gentle strength: reclaiming atonement theory for survivors of abuse', Ph.D. dissertation, Lutheran School of Theology, Chicago.
De Boer, M. C. (2007), 'The meaning of the phrase *ta stoicheia tou kosmou* in Galatians', *New Testament Studies* 53: 2-4-24.
De Boer, M. C. (2011), *Galatians: A Commentary*. Louisville, Ky: Westminster John Knox Press.
De Boer, W. P. (1962), *The Imitation of Paul*. Kampen: Kok.
De Freitas, Elizabeth and Sinclair, Nathalie (2018), 'The quantum mind: alternative ways of reasoning with uncertainty', *Canadian Journal of Science, Mathematics and Technology* 18: 271–83.
Deichgräber, Reinhard (1967), *Gotteshymnus und Christushymnus in der frühen Christenheit: Untersuchungen zu Form, Sprache und Stil der frühchristlichen Hymnen*. Göttingen: Vandenhoeck & Ruprecht.
Deidun, T. J. (1981), *New Covenant Morality in Paul*. Rome: Biblical Institute.
De Jong, Janneke (2016), 'Emperor meets gods: divine discourse in Greek papyri from Roman Egypt', *Collegium* 20: 22–55.
De Jonge, Marinus (1971), *Nicodemus and Jesus: Some Observations on Misunderstanding and Understanding in the Fourth Gospel*. Manchester: John Rylands Library.
De Jonge, Marinus (1977), *Jesus: Stranger from Heaven and Son of God. Jesus Christ and the Christians in Johannine Perspective*. Atlanta: SBL.
De Jonge, Marinus (1988), *Christology in Context: The Earliest Christian Response to Jesus*. Philadelphia: Westminster Press.
De Jonge, Marinus (1993), 'The Christological significance of Jesus' preaching of the kingdom of God', in Abraham J. Malherbe and Wayne A. Meeks eds, *The Future of Christology: Essays in Honor of Leander E. Keck*. Minneapolis: Fortress: 3–17.
De Jonge, Marinus (1998), *God's Final Envoy: Early Christology and Jesus' Own View of his Mission*. Grand Rapids, Mich.: Eerdmans.
De Jonge, Marinus (2000), 'Christology, controversy and community in the Gospel of John', in David G. Horrell and Christopher M. Tuckett eds, *Christology, Controversy and Community: New Testament Essays in Honour of David R. Catchpole*. Leiden: Brill: 209–30.
De Lange, F (2014), 'The Heidelberg Catechism: elements for a theology of care', *Acta Theologica* 2014 suppl. 20: 156–73.
Dell, Katharine J. (2003), 'Covenant and creation in relationship', in A. D. H. Mayes and R. B. Salters eds, *Covenant as Context: Essays in Honour of E. W. Nicholson*. Oxford: Oxford University Press: 111–33.
Dell, Katharine J. (2010), *Ethical and Unethical in the Old Testament: God and Humans in Dialogue*. London: T&T Clark.

De Lubac, Henri (1996), *Theology in History*. San Francisco: Ignatius Press.
Deno, Vivian (2004), 'God, authority, and the home: gender, race, and U.S. Pentecostals, 1900-1926', *Journal of Women's History* 16: 83-105.
Dentale, Francesco, Vecchione, Michele, Shariff, Azim, Verrastro, Valeria, Petruccelli, Irene, Diotaiuti, Pierluigi, Petruccelli, Filippo, and Barbaranelli, Claudio (2018), 'Only believers rely on God? A new measure to investigate Catholic faith automatic associations and their relationship with psychological well-being', *Psychology of Religion and Spirituality* 10: 185-94.
Denzinger, Heinrich, Hünermann, P., Hoping, H., Fastiggi, R. L., and Nash, A. E. eds (2012), *Compendium of Creeds, Definitions, and Declarations on Matters of Faith and Morals*. 43rd edn. San Francisco: Ignatius Press.
DeSilva, David (2009), 'On the sidelines of the *pistis Christou* debate: the view from Revelation', in M. Bird and P. Sprinkle eds. (2010), *The Faith of Jesus Christ: Exegetical, Biblical, and Theological Studies*. Milton Keynes: Paternoster: 259-74.
DeVille, Christophe (2017), *Accroître sa foie en Dieu*. Olonzac: Editions l'Oasis.
De Villiers, P. G. R. (2000), 'Pagan oracles and Jewish apocalypses in Graeco-Roman times', *Acta Patristica et Byzantina* 11: 47-73.
Dibelius, Martin and Conzelmann, Hans (1972), *The Pastoral Epistles*. Philadelphia: Fortress.
Diehl, Judith A. (2011), 'What is a "gospel"? Recent studies in the gospel genre', *Currents in Biblical Research* 9: 171-99.
Dietrich, J. (2014), 'Friendship with God: Old Testament an Ancient Near Eastern Perspectives', *Scandinavian Journal of the Old Testament* 28: 157-71.
Dille, Sarah J. (2004), *Mixing Metaphors: God as Mother and Father in Deutero-Isaiah*. London: T&T Clark.
Dinkler, Michal Beth (2017), 'Building character on the road to Emmaus: Lucan characterization in contemporary literary perspective', *Journal of Biblical Literature* 136: 687-706.
Dinkler, Michal Beth (2020), 'What is a genre? Contemporary genre theory and the gospels', in Robert Matthew Calhoun, David P. Moessner, and Tobias Nicklas eds, *Modern and Ancient Literary Criticism of the Gospels: Continuing the Debate on Gospel Genre(s)*. Tübingen: Mohr Siebeck: 77-96.
Dodd, C. H. (1932), *The Epistle of Paul to the Romans*. London: Hodder and Stoughton.
Dodd, C. H. (1952), *According to the Scriptures: The Substructure of New Testament Theology*. London: Nisbet.
Dodd, C. H. (1962), 'Une parabole cachée dans le quatrième évangile', *Revue d'histoire de de philosophie religieuses* 42: 107-15.
Dodd, Julian (2000), 'Musical works as eternal types', *British Journal of Aesthetics* 40: 424-40.
Doeve. J. W. (1953), 'Some notes with reference to *ta logia tou theou* in Romans 3.2', in J. N. Sevenster and W. C. van Unnik eds, *Studia Paulina in honorem Johannis De Zwaan*. Haarlem: Bohn: 111-23.
Dognin, Paul-Dominique (2005), 'La Foi du Christ dans la théologie de Saint Paul', *Revue des sciences philosophiques et théologiques* 89: 713-28.
Domenicucci, Jacopo and Holton, Richard (2017), 'Trust as a two-place relation', in Paul Faulkner and Thomas W. Simpson eds, *The Philosophy of Trust*. Oxford: Oxford University Press: 149-60.
Dominian, J. (1976), 'A psychological evaluation of the Pentecostal movement', *The Expository Times* 87: 292-7.

Donahue, John R. (1983), *The Theology and Setting of Discipleship in the Gospel of Mark*. Milwaukee: Marquette University Press.
Donahue, John R. (1989), 'The changing shape of New Testament theology', *Theological Studies* 50: 314–36.
Donahue, John R. (1996), 'The literary turn and New Testament theology: detour or new direction?', *The Journal of Religion* 76: 250–75.
Donahue, John R., S. and Harrington, Daniel J., SJ (2002), *The Gospel of Mark*. Collegeville, Minn.: Liturgical Press.
Donaldson, Terence L. (2006), 'Jewish Christianity, Israel's stumbling and the *Sonderweg* reading of Paul', *Journal for the Study of the New Testament* 29: 27–54.
Donfried, Karl P. (2002a), 'Justification and last judgment in Paul (for Gunther Bornkamm on his 70th birthday)', in *Paul, Thessalonica, and Early Christianity*. Grand Rapids, Mich.: Eerdmans: 253–78.
Donfried, Karl P. (2002b), 'Justification and last judgment in Paul—twenty-five years later', in *Paul Thessalonica, and Early Christianity*. Grand Rapids, Mich.: Eerdmans: 279–92.
Doole, J. Andrew (2017), 'Jesus "at home": did Jesus have a house in Capernaum?' *Protokolle zur Bibel* 26: 36–64.
Dormandy, Katherine (2020a), 'Epistemic self-trust: it's personal', *Episteme* (no issue number): 1–16.
Dormandy, Katherine ed. (2020b), *Trust In Epistemology*. London: Routledge.
Dougherty, T. (2014), 'Faith, trust, and testimony. An evidentialist account', in Laura Frances Callaghan and Timothy O'Connor eds, *Religious Faith and Intellectual Virtue*. Oxford: Oxford University Press: 97–123.
Downing, F. Gerald (2015), 'Contemporary analogies to the gospels and Acts: "genres" or "motifs"?', in C. M. Tuckett ed., *Synoptic Studies: The Ampleforth Conferences of 1982 and 1983*. London: Bloomsbury: 51–66.
Downs, David J. and Lappenga, Benjamin J. (2019), *The Faithfulness of the Risen Christ:* Pistis *and the Exalted Lord in the Pauline Letters*. Waco, Tex.: Baylor University Press.
Draycott, Jane (2015), 'Reconstructing the lived experience of disability in antiquity: a case study from Roman Egyt', *Greece and Rome* 62: 189–205.
Drewermann, Eugen (2020), *Vertrauen kann man nur auf Gott*. Publik-Forum Edition.
Dreytza, Manfred (1990), *Der theologische Gebrauch von Ruaḥ im Alten Testament: Eine ort- und satzsemantische Studie*. Giessen: Brunnen.
Driediger-Murphy, Lindsay G. (2019), *Roman Republican Augury: Freedom and Control*. Oxford: Oxford University Press.
Driediger-Murphy, Lindsay and Eidinow, Esther eds (2019), *Ancient Divination and Experience*. Oxford: Oxford University Press.
Driediger-Murphy, Lindsay and Gayle, Lindsay (2019), *Ancient Divination and Experience*. Oxford: Oxford University Press.
Duff, T. E. (1999), *Plutarch's Lives: Exploring Virtue and Vice*. Oxford: Oxford University Press.
Dulles, Avery (1983), *Models of Revelation*. Dublin: Gill and Macmillan.
Dulles, Avery (1994), *The Assurance of Things Hoped For: A Theology of Christian Faith*. Oxford: Oxford University Press.
Dumbrell, W. J. (1984), *Covenant and Creation*. Nashville: Thomas Nelson.
Dunn, James D. G. (1970), *Baptism in the Holy Spirit: A Re-Examination of the New Testament Teaching on the Gift of the Spirit in Relation to Pentecostalism Today*. London: SCM.
Dunn, James D. G. (1975), *Jesus and the Spirit: A Study of the Religious and Charismatic Experience of Jesus and the First Christians as Reflected in the New Testament*. London: SCM.

Dunn, James D. G. (1977), *Unity and Diversity in the New Testament: An Inquiry into the Character of Earliest Christianity*. London: SCM.
Dunn, James D. G. (1988, 1991), *Romans*. 2 vols. Dallas: Word Books.
Dunn, James D. G. (1989), *Christology in the Making: A New Testament Inquiry into the Origins of the Doctrine of the Incarnation*. 2nd edn. London: SCM.
Dunn, James D. G. (1993a), *The Epistle to the Galatians*. Peabody, NY: Hendrickson.
Dunn, James D. G. (1993b), 'Christology as an aspect of theology', in Abraham J. Malherbe and Wayne A. Meeks eds, *The Future of Christology: Essays in Honor of Leander E. Keck*. Minneapolis: Fortress: 202–12.
Dunn, James D. G. (1998a), *The Christ and the Spirit: Collected Essays of James D. G. Dunn, Volume 1: Christology*. Grand Rapids, Mich.: Eerdmans.
Dunn, James D. G. (1998b), *The Theology of Paul the Apostle*. Edinburgh: T&T Clark.
Dunn, James D. G. (2003a), *1 Corinthians*. London: Continuum.
Dunn, James D. G. (2003b), 'Did Paul have a covenant theology?' in Stanley E. Porter and Jaqueline C. R. de Roo eds, *The Concept of Covenant in the Second Temple Period*. Leiden: Brill: 287–310.
Dunn, James D. G. (2008), 'New Testament theology', in Judith M. Lieu and J. W. Rogerson eds, *The Oxford Handbook of Biblical Studies*. Oxford: Oxford University Press: 698–714.
Dunn, James D. G. (2009), *New Testament Theology: An Introduction*. Nashville: Abingdon.
Dunn, James D. G. and McKnight, Scot (2005), *The Historical Jesus in Recent Research*. Winona Lake, Ind.: Eisenbrauns.
Duyndam, Joachim (2004), 'Hermeutics of imitation: a philosophical approach to sainthood and exemplariness', in Marcel Poorthuis and Joshua Schwartz eds, *Saints and Role Models in Judaism and Christianity*. Leiden: Brill: 7–23.
Easter, Matthew C. (2010), 'The *pistis Christou* debate: main arguments and responses in summary', *Currents in biblical research* 9: 33–47.
Eastman, Susan Grove (2010a), 'Israel and the God of mercy: a re-reading of Galatians 6.16 and Romans 9–11', *New Testament Studies* 56: 367–95.
Eastman, Susan Grove (2010b), 'Israel and divine mercy in Galatians and Romans', in Florian Wilk and J. Ross Wagner eds, *Between Gospel and Election: Explorations in the Interpretation of Romans 9–11*. Tübingen: Mohr Siebeck: 147–70.
Eastman, Susan Grove (2013), 'The shadow-side of intersubjective identity: sin in Paul's letter to the Romans', *European Journal for Philosophy of Religion* 5: 125–44.
Eastman, Susan Grove (2017), *Paul and the Person: Reframing Paul's Anthropology*. Grand Rapids, Mich.: Eerdmans.
Eastman, Susan Grove (2018), 'Knowing and being known: interpersonal cognition and the knowledge of God in Paul's letters', in Andrew Torrance ed., *Knowing Creation*. Nashville: Zondervan: 155–69.
Ebeling, Gerhard (1955), 'The meaning of biblical theology', *JTS* 6: 210–25.
Ebeling, Gerhard (1963), *Word and Faith*. London: SCM.
Ebert, Andreas, Kolb, Meike, Heller, Jörg, Edel, Marc-Andreas, Roser, Patrik, and Brüne, Martin (2013), 'Modulation of interpersonal trust in borderline personality disorder by intranasal oxytocin and childhood trauma', *Social Neuroscience* 8: 305–13.
Edwards, J. Christopher (2012), *The Ransom Logion in Mark and Matthew: Its Reception and its Significance for the Study of the Gospels*. Tübingen: Mohr Siebeck.
Edwards, James R. (2015), *The Gospel According to Luke*. Grand Rapids, Mich.: Eerdmans.
Edwards, Mark (2006), 'Gospel and genre: some reservations', in Brian McGing and Judith Mossman eds, *Limits of Ancient Biography*. Swansea: Classical Press of Wales: 51–75.
Edwards, Mark (unpublished), '*Pistis* and Platonism'.

Eiesland, Nancy L. (1994), *The Disabled God: Towards a Liberatory Theology of Disability.* Nashville: Abingdon.
Eklund, Dan-Johan Sebastian (2014), 'Is non-evidential believing possible?' John Bishop on passionally caused beliefs', *Religious Studies* 50: 309–20.
Eklund, Dan-Johan Sebastian (2018), 'The cognitive aspect of Christian faith and non-doxastic propositional attitudes', *Neue Zeitschrift für systematische Theologie und Religionsphilosophie* 60: 386–405.
Elgvin, Torleif (1994), 'The Genesis section of 4Q422 (4QparaGenExod)', *Dead Sea Discoveries* 1: 180–96.
Elliott, John H. (2000), *1 Peter: A New Translation with Introduction and Commentary.* New York: Doubleday.
Elliott, Matthew (2005), *Faithful Feelings: Emotion in the New Testament.* Leicester: InterVarsity.
Engberg-Pedersen, Troels ed. (2001), *Paul Beyond the Judaism/Hellenism Divide.* Louisville, Ky: Westminster John Knox.
Engster, Daniel (2007), *The Heart of Justice: Care Ethics and Political Theory.* Oxford: Oxford University Press.
Epstein, Heidi (2004), *Melting the Venusberg: A Feminist Theology of Music.* New York: Continuum.
Erikson, E. (1959), *Identity and the Life-Cycle.* New York: Norton.
Erzberger, Johanna (2011), *Kain, Abel und Israel: die Rezeption von Gen 4,1–16 in rabbinischen Midraschim.* Stuttgart: W. Kohlhammer.
Esler, Philip F. (2005), *New Testament Theology: Communion and Community.* London: SPCK.
Espinosa, Gastón (2014), *Latino Pentecostals in America: Faith and Politics in Action.* Cambridge, Mass.: Harvard University Press.
Estes, Daniel J. (2010), 'What makes the strange woman of Proverbs 1–9 strange?', in Katharine Dell ed., *Ethical and Unethical in the Old Testament: God and Humans in Dialogue.* London: T&T Clark.
Evans, Craig A. (1993), *Paul and the Scriptures of God.* London: Bloomsbury.
Evans, Craig A. (2001), *Mark 8:27–16:20.* Grand Rapids, Mich.: Zondervan.
Evans, Craig A. (2006), 'Assessing progress in the third quest for the historical Jesus', *Journal for the Study of the Historical Jesus* 4: 35–54.
Evans, Craig A. and Licona, Michael R. (2017), *Why are there Differences in the Gospels? What we can Learn from Ancient Biography.* New York: Oxford University Press.
Evans, C. F. (1970), *Resurrection and the New Testament.* London: SCM.
Evans, Donald (1980), *Faith, Authenticity and Morality.* Edinburgh: Handsel.
Evans, James H. (2012), *We Have Been Believers: An African-American Systematic Theology.* 2nd edn. Minneapolis: Fortress.
Evans, Richard J. (2018), *In Defence of History.* 2nd edn. London: Granta.
Eve, Eric (2002), *The Jewish Context of Jesus' Miracles.* Sheffield: Sheffield Academic Press.
Exum, J. Cheryl (1992), *Tragedy and Biblical Narrative: Arrows of the Almighty.* New York: Cambridge University Press.
Farenga, Vincent (2006), *Citizen and Self in Ancient Greece: Individuals Performing Justice and the Law.* Cambridge: Cambridge University Press.
Fatehi, Mehrdad (2000), *The Spirit's Relation to the Risen Lord in Paul: An Examination of Its Christological Implications.* Tübingen: Mohr Siebeck.
Faulkner, P. (2007), 'A Genealogy of Trust', *Episteme* 4: 305–21.
Faulkner, P. (2011), *Knowledge on Trust.* Oxford: Oxford University Press.

Faulkner, P. (2015), 'The attitude of trust is basic', *Analysis* 75: 424–9.
Faulkner, P. (2017), 'The problem of trust', in Paul Faulkner and Thomas Simpson eds, *The Philosophy of Trust*. Oxford: Oxford University Press: 109–27.
Faulkner, Paul and Simpson, Thomas (2017), *The Philosophy of Trust*. Oxford: Oxford University Press.
Fea, John, Green, Jay, and Miller, Eric eds (2010), *Confessing History: Explorations in Christian Faith and The Historian's Vocation*. Notre Dame, Ind.: University of Notre Dame Press.
Feagin, Susan L. ed. (2007), *Special Issue on Global Theories of the Arts and Aesthetics. Journal of Aesthetics and Art Criticism* 65.
Fee, Gordon D. (1994), *God's Empowering Presence: The Holy Spirit in the Letters of Paul*. Peabody, NY: Hendrickson.
Fee, Gordon D. (1995), *Paul's Letter to the Philippians*. Grand Rapids, Mich.: Eerdmans.
Fee, Gordon D. (1996), *Paul, the Spirit, and the People of God*. London: Hodder and Stoughton.
Fee, Gordon D. (2009), *The First and Second Letters to the Thessalonians*. Grand Rapids, Mich.: Eerdmans.
Fehribach, Adeline (1998), *The Women in the Life of the Bridegroom: A Feminist Historical-Literary Analysis of the Female Characters in the Fourth Gospel*. Collegeville, Minn.: Liturgical Press.
Feldmeier, Reinhard and Spieckermann, Hermann (2011), *Der Gott der Lebendigen: Eine biblische Gotteslehre*. Tübingen: Mohr Siebeck.
Fewster, Gregory P. (2015), 'The Philippians "Christ hymn": trends in critical scholarship', *Currents in Biblical Research* 13: 191–206.
Finger, Reta Halteman (1988), 'How can Jesus save women? Three theories on Christ's atonement', *Daughters of Sarah* 14: 14–18.
Fiore, Benjamin (2007), *The Pastoral Epistles: First Timothy, Second Timothy, Titus*. Collegeville, Minn.: Liturgical Press.
Fitzmyer, Joseph A. (1981, 1985), *The Gospel According to Luke*. 2 vols. New York: Doubleday.
Fitzmyer, Joseph A. (1993a), *Romans: A New Translation with Introduction and Commentary*. The Anchor Bible. New York: Doubleday.
Fitzmyer, Joseph A. (1993b), 'The Christology of the epistle to the Romans', in Abraham J. Malherbe and Wayne A. Meeks eds, *The Future of Christology: Essays in Honor of Leander E. Keck*. Minneapolis: Fortress: 81–90.
Fitzmyer, Joseph A. (1997), *The Acts of the Apostles*. New York: Doubleday.
Fitzmyer, Joseph A. (2000), *The Letter to Philemon*. New York: Doubleday.
Fitzmyer, Joseph A. (2008), *First Corinthians: A New Translation with Introduction and Commentary*. New Haven: Yale University Press.
Flebbe, Jochen (2008), *Solus Deus: Untersuchungen zur Rede von Gott im Brief des paulus an die Römer*. Berlin: De Gruyter.
Fleddermann, Harry (1979), 'The flight of a naked young man (Mark 14: 51–52), *Catholic Biblical Quarterly* 41: 412–18.
Fletcher, George P. (1993), *Loyalty: An Essay on the Morality of Relationships*. Oxford: Oxford University Press.
Fletcher-Louis, Crispin (1997), 'The high priest as divine mediator in the Hebrew Bible: Dan. 7:13 as a test case', *Society of Biblical Literature Seminar Papers* 36: 161–93.
Fletcher-Louis, Crispin (1999), 'The worship of divine humanity as God's image and the worship of Jesus', in Carey C. Newman et al. eds, *The Jewish Roots of Christological Monotheism*. Leiden: Brill: 112–28.

Florkowski, Joseph (1971), *La Théologie de la foi chez Bultmann*. Paris: Éditions du Cerf.
Forbes, Chris (2001), 'Paul's principalities and powers: demythologizing apocalyptic?', *Journal for the Study of the New Testament* 82: 61–88.
Forbis, Elizabeth (1996), *Municipal Virtues in the Roman Empire: The Evidence of Italian Honorary Inscriptions*. Stuttgart and Leipzig: B. G. Teubner.
Ford, David F. (2013), 'Meeting Nicodemus: a case study in daring theological interpretation', *Scottish Journal of Theology* 66: 1–17.
Fortenbaugh, W. (2002), *Aristotle on Emotion: A Contribution to Philosophical Psychology, Rhetoric, Poetics, Politics, and Ethics*. 2nd edn. London: Duckworth.
Fossum, Jarl E. (1995), *The Image of the Invisible God: Essays on the Influence of Jewish Mysticism on Early Christology*. Göttingen: Vandenhoeck & Ruprecht.
Fowl, Stephen E. (1990), *The Story of Christ in the Ethics of Paul: An Analysis of the Function of the Hymnic Material in the Pauline Corpus*. Sheffield: JSOT Press.
Fowl, Stephen E. (2005), *Philippians*. Grand Rapids, Mich.: Eerdmans.
Fraenkel, Edward (1916), 'Zur Geschichte des Wortes *fides*', *Rheinisches Museum* NS 71: 187–99.
France, R. T. (1982), 'The worship of Jesus—a neglected factor in Christological debate?', *Vox Evangelica* 12: 19–33.
Franck, Raphael and Iannaccone, Laurence R. (2014), 'Religious decline in the 20th century West: testing alternative explanations', *Public Choice* 159: 385–414.
Franke, William (2012), 'Gospel as personal knowing: theological reflections on not just a literary genre', *Theology Today* 68: 413–23.
Frede, Dorothea and Laks, André eds (2002), *Traditions of Theology: Studies in Hellenistic Theology, its Background and Aftermath*. Leiden: Brill.
Fredriksen, Paula (2010), 'Judaising the nations', *New Testament Studies* 56: 232–52.
Fredriksen, Paula (2014), 'Paul's letter to the Romans, the ten commandments, and pagan justification by faith', *Journal of Biblical Literature* 133: 801–7.
Freed, Edwin D. (1967), 'The Son of Man in the fourth gospel', *Journal of Biblical Literature* 86: 402–9.
Freedman, David Noel and Miano, David (2003), *The Concept of Covenant in the Second Temple Period*. Leiden: Brill.
Frei, Hans W. (2013), *The Identity of Jesus Christ: The Hermeneutical Bases of Dogmatic Theology*. Rev. edn. Philadelphia: Fortress.
Frein, Brigid Curtin (2008), 'Genre and point of view in Luke's gospel', *Biblical Theology Bulletin* 38: 4–13.
Fretheim, Terence E. (2005), *God and World in the Old Testament: A Relational Theology of Creation*. Nashville: Abingdon.
Frey, Jörg (2002), 'Flesh and Spirit in the Palestinian Jewish Sapiential Tradition and in the Qumran Texts: An Inquiry into the Background of Pauline Usage', in C. Hempel, A. Lange, and H. Lichtenberger eds, *The Wisdom Texts from Qumran and the Development of Sapiential Thought*. Leuven: Leuven University Press: 367–404.
Frey, Jörg (2011), 'Continuity and discontinuity between "Jesus" and "Christ": the possibilities of an implicit Christology', *Revista Catalana de Teologia* 36: 69–98.
Frey, Jörg (2014), 'Johannine Christology and eschatology', in Bruce W. Longenecker and Mikeal C. Parsons eds, *Beyond Bultmann: Reckoning a New Testament Theology*. Waco, Tex.: Baylor University Press: 101–32.
Frey, Jörg (2018), *The Glory of the Crucified One: Christology and Theology in the Gospel of John*. Waco, Tex.: Baylor University Press.
Frey, Jörg and Levison, John eds (2014), *The Holy Spirit, Inspiration, and the Cultures of Antiquity: Multidisciplinary Perspectives*. Berlin: De Gruyter.

Frey, Jörg, Schliesser, Benjamin, and Ueberschaer, Nadine (2017), *Glaube: Das Verständnis des Glaubens im frühen Christentum und in seiner jüdischen und hellenistisch-römischen Umwelt*. Tübingen: Mohr Siebeck.
Freyburger, Gérard (2007), *Fides: Étude sémantique et religieuse depuis les origines Jusqu'à l'époque Augustéenne*. 2nd edn. Paris: Société d'Édition Les Belles Lettres.
Fried, Lisbeth S. (2002), 'Cyrus the Messiah? The historical background to Isaiah 45:1', *Harvard Theological Review* 95: 373–93.
Friedman, Morton P. and Carterette, Edward C. eds (1996), *Cognitive Ecology*. San Diego: Academic Press.
Friedrich, G. (1982), 'Glaube und Verkündigung bei Paulus', in F. Hahn and H. Klein eds. (1982), *Glaube im Neuen Testament: Studien zu Ehren von Hermann Binder anlässlich seines 70. Geburtstags*. Neukirchen-Vluyn: Neukirchener Verlag: 93–113.
Froeyman, Anton (2012), 'Virtues of historiography', *Journal of the Philosophy of History* 6: 415–31.
Froeyman, Anton (2016), *History, Ethics, and the Recognition of the Other: A Levinasian View on the Writing of History*. New York: Routledge.
Frost-Arnold, Karen (2013), 'Moral trust and scientific collaboration', *Studies in History and Philosophy of Science* 44: 301–10.
Frost-Arnold, Karen (2014a), 'The cognitive attitude of rational trust', *Synthese* 191: 1957–74.
Frost-Arnold, Karen (2014b), 'Trustworthiness and truth: the epistemic pitfalls of internet accountability', *Episteme* 11: 63–81.
Frost-Arnold, Karen (2016), 'Social media, trust, and the epistemology of prejudice', *Social Epistemology* 30: 513–31.
Fuchs, Ernst (1964), *Studies of the Historical Jesus*. London: SCM.
Fuertes, M., Lopes dos Santos, P., Beeghly, M., and Tronick, E. (2006), 'More than maternal sensitivity shapes attachment: infant coping and temperament', *Annals of the New York Academy of Sciences* 1094: 292–6.
Fuertes, M., Lopes dos Santos, P., Beeghly, M., and Tronick, E. (2009), 'Infant coping and material interactive behavior predict attachment in a Portuguese sample of healthy preterm infants', *European Psychologist* 14: 320–31.
Fukuyama, Francis (1995), *Trust: The Social Virtues and the Creation of Prosperity*. New York: Simon and Schuster.
Fuller, Lon L. (2006), *The Morality of Law*. Rev. edn. Delhi: Universal Law.
Fumanal, Ángel Luis Casquillo (2008), 'Muerte, dispedazamiento y apotheosis de Rómulo: un studio sobre la realidad hisórica del primer rey de Roma', *Espacio, Tiempo y Forma, serie II, Historia Antigua* 21: 123–84.
Funda, Otokar A. (2012), *Das Entstehen des christichen Glaubens*. Prague: Verlag Karolinum.
Furnish, Victor Paul (1968), *Theology and Ethics in Paul*. Nashville: Abingdon Press.
Furnish, Victor Paul (1984), *II Corinthians*. Garden City, NY: Doubleday.
Furnish, Victor Paul (1993), '"He gave himself (was given) up . . .": Paul's use of a Christological assertion', in Abraham J. Malherbe and Wayne A. Meeks eds, *The Future of Christology: Essays in Honor of Leander E. Keck*. Minneapolis: Fortress: 109–21.
Gadamer, Hans-Georg (1975), *Truth and Method*. New York: Seabury Press.
Gallagher, Michael Paul S.J. (2008), 'Truth and trust: Pierangelo Sequeri's theology of faith', *Irish Theological Quarterly* 73: 3–31.
Gargarin, Michael (2002), *Antiphon the Athenian: Law and Justice in the Age of the Sophists*. Dallas: University of Texas Press.
Garland, David E. (2003), *1 Corinthians*. Nashville: Broadman & Holman.

Garland, Robert (1995), *The Eye of the Beholder: Deformity and Disability in the Graeco-Roman World*. Leiden: Brill.
Garrido, Sandra and Davidson, Jane W. (2019), *Music, Nostalgia and Memory: Historical and Psychological Perspectives*. Cham: Palgrave Macmillan.
Gathercole, Simon J. (2002), *Where is Boasting? Early Jewish Soteriology and Paul's Response in Romans 1–5*. Grand Rapids, Mich.: Eerdmans.
Gathercole, Simon J. (2006a), *The Pre-existent Son: Recovering the Christologies of Matthew, Mark, and Luke*. Grand Rapids, Mich.: Eerdmans.
Gathercole, Simon J. (2006b), 'The doctrine of justification in Paul and beyond: some proposals', in Bruce L. McCormack ed., *Justification in Perspective: Historical Developments and Contemporary Challenges*. Grand Rapids, Mich.: Baker Academic: 219–41.
Gathercole, Simon J. (2014), *The Gospel of Thomas: Introduction and Commentary*. Boston: Brill.
Gathercole, Simon J. (2015), *Defending Substitution: An Essay on Atonement in Paul*. Grand Rapids, Mich.: Baker Academic.
Gathercole, Simon J. (2018), 'The historical and human existence of Jesus in Paul's letters', *Journal for the Study of the Historical Jesus* 16: 183–212.
Gaventa, Beverly Roberts (2004), 'The cosmic power of sin in Paul's letter to the Romans: towards a widescreen edition', *Interpretation* 58: 229–40.
Gaventa, Beverly Roberts (2010), 'On the calling-into-being of Israel: Romans 9.6–29', in Florian Wilk and J. Ross Wagner eds, *Between Gospel and Election: Explorations in the Interpretation of Romans 9–11*. Tübingen: Mohr Siebeck: 255–70.
Gaventa, Beverly Roberts ed. (2013), *Apocalyptic Paul: Cosmos and Anthropos in Romans 5–8*. Waco, Tex.: Baylor University Press.
Gaventa, Beverly Roberts and Hays, Richard B. eds (2008), *Seeking the Identity of Jesus: A Pilgrimage*. Grand Rapids, Mich.: Eerdmans.
Gaventa, Beverly Roberts and Hays, Richard B. (2008), 'Seeking the identity of Jesus', in Beverly Roberts Gaventa and Richard B. Hays eds, *Seeking the Identity of Jesus: A Pilgrimage*. Grand Rapids, Mich.: Eerdmans: 1–24.
Gayer, Asaf (2015), 'The centrality of prayer and stability of trust: an analysis of the Hymn of the Maskil in 1QS IX, 25b-XI, 15a', in Stefan C. Reif ed., *Ancient Jewish Prayers and Emotions: Emotions Associated with Jewish Prayer in and around the Second Temple Period*. Berlin: De Gruyter: 317–33.
Gaziaux, E. (1995), *Morale de la foi et moral autonome: confrontation entre P. Delhaye et. J. Fuchs*. Leuven: Peeters.
Geertz, Clifford (1973), *The Interpretation of Cultures: Selected Essays*. New York: Basic Books.
Gelpi, Donald L., SJ (2009), *Encountering Jesus Christ: Rethinking Christological Faith and Commitment*. Milwaukee: Marquette University Press.
Geneva Cannon, Katie, Emilie M. Townes, and Angela D. Sims eds, *Womanist Theological Ethics*. Louisville, Ky: Westminster John Knox.
Gerhardsson, Birger (1994), 'Mighty acts and rule of heaven: "God is with us"', in T. E. Schmidt and M. Silva eds, *To Tell the Mystery: Essays on New Testament Eschatology in Honor of Robert H. Gundry*. London: Bloomsbury: 34–48.
Gerhart, E. V. et al. (1863), *The Heidelberg Catechism, in German, Latin, and English: With an Historical Introduction*. New York: Scribner.
Giambrone, Anthony (2019), 'Schweitzer, Lagrange, and the German roots of historical Jesus research', *Journal for the Study of the Historical Jesus* 1–2: 121–44.
Gibbs, Lee W. (2002), 'Richard Hooker's via media doctrine of scripture and tradition', *Harvard Theological Review* 95: 227–35.

Gibbs, Robert (2000), *Why Ethics? Signs of Responsibilities*. Princeton: Princeton University Press.
Gill, Anthony and Lundsgaarde, Erik (2004), 'State welfare spending and religiosity', *Rationality and Society* 16: 399–436.
Gilligan, Carol (1982), *In A Different Voice: Psychological Theory and Women's Development*. Cambridge, Mass.: Harvard University Press.
Glassman, Lindsay W. (2018), '"You help them out and God gets the glory": social class and inequality in a fundamentalist Christian church', *Social Inclusion* 6: 127–39.
Gnilka, Joachim (1971), *The Epistle to the Philippians*. London: Sheed and Ward.
Gnilka, Joachim (1994), *Theologie des Neuen Testaments*. Freiburg: Herder.
Godfrey, J. J. (2012), *Trust of People, Words and God: A Route for Philosophy of Religion*. Notre Dame, Ind.: Notre Dame University Press.
Golding, Joshua (1990), 'Toward a pragmatic conception of religious faith', *Faith and Philosophy* 7: 486–503.
Gooch, Paul W. (2012), 'Faithful knowing', in Paul Moser and Michael McFall eds, *The Wisdom of the Christian Faith*. Cambridge/New York: Cambridge University Press: 19–38.
Goodman, Martin (2010), 'Paradise, gardens, and the afterlife in the first century CE', in Markus Bockmuehl and Guy Stroumsa eds, *Paradise in Antiquity: Jewish and Christian Views*. Cambridge: Cambridge University Press: 57–63.
Goppelt, Leonhard (1981), *Theology of the New Testament*. 2 vols. Grand Rapids, Mich.: Eerdmans.
Gowler, David B. (1991), *Host, Guest, Enemy, and Friend. Portraits of the Pharisees in Luke and Acts*. New York: Peter Lang.
Grabbe, Lester L. (2003), 'Did all Jews think alike? 'Covenant' in Philo and Josephus in the context of Second Temple Judaic religion', in Stanley E. Porter and Jacqueline C. R. de Roo eds, *The Concept of the Covenant in the Second Temple Period*. Leiden: Brill: 251–66.
Gräbe, P. J. (2002a), *The Power of God in Paul's Letters*. Tübingen: Mohr Siebeck.
Gräbe, P. J. (2002b) 'The Pentecostal discovery of the New Testament theme of God's power and its relevance to the African context', *Pneuma* 24: 225–42.
Grabiner, Steven (2015), *Revelation's Hymns: Commentary on the Cosmic Conflict*. London: Bloomsbury.
Grässer, E. (1965), *Der Glaube im Hebräerbrief*. Marburg: NG Elwert Verlag.
Gratton, Carolyn (1982), *Trusting: Theory and Practice*, NY: Crossroad.
Grayston, K. (1984), 'The translation of Matthew 28.17', *Journal for the Study of the New Testament* 21: 105–9.
Green, Joel B. (1997), *The Gospel of Luke*. Grand Rapids, Mich.: Eerdmans.
Greenberg, Gillian (2004), *Indications of the Faith of the Translator in the Peshitta to the 'Servant Songs' of Deutero-Isaiah*. Leiden: Brill.
Gregersen, Niels Henrik ed. (2001), 'The cross of Christ in an evolutionary world', *Dialog* 40: 192–207.
Gregersen, Niels Henrik (2015), *Incarnation: On the Scope and Depth of Christology*. Minneapolis: Fortress.
Grenz, Stanley J. and Franke, John R. (2001), *Beyond Foundationalism: Shaping Theology in a Postmodern Context*. Louisville, Ky: Westminster John Knox.
Grey, Jacqueline N. (2018), 'Isaiah's vision of Yahweh and ethical replication', *Old Testament Essays* 3: 591–612.
Grieb, A. Katherine (2010), 'Paul's theological preoccupation in Romans 9–11', in Florian Wilk and J. Ross Wagner eds, *Between Gospel and Election: Explorations in the Interpretation of Romans 9–11*. Tübingen: Mohr Siebeck: 391–400.

Grieb, A. Katherine (2012), 'The righteousness of God in Romans', in Jerry L. Sumney ed., *Reading Paul's Letter to the Romans*. Atlanta: Society of Biblical Literature: 65–78.
Grindheim, Sigurd (2011), *God's Equal: What Can We Know about Jesus' Self-Understanding?* London: Bloomsbury.
Grindheim, Sigurd (2012), *Christology in the Synoptic Gospels*. London: T&T Clark.
Grindheim, Sigurd (2016), 'Faith in Jesus: the historical Jesus and the object of faith', *Biblica* 97: 79–100.
Grindheim, Sigurd (2017), 'A theology of glory: Paul's use of doxa terminology in Romans', *Journal of Biblical Literature* 136: 451–65.
Grundmann, W. (1965), 'Matth. XI 27 und die johanneischen "der Vater-der-Son"-Stellen', *New Testament Studies* 12: 42–9.
Grypeou, Emmanouela and Spurling, Helen (2013), *The Book of Genesis in Late Antiquity: Encounters Between Jewish and Christian Exegesis*. Leiden: Brill.
Guasto, Gianni (2014), 'Trauma and the loss of basic trust', *International Forum of Psychoanalysis* 23: 44–9.
Gudmundsdottir, Arnfridur (2010), *Meeting God on the Cross: The Cross, and the Feminist Critique*. New York: Oxford University Press.
Gunkel, Hermann (1979), *The Influence of the Holy Spirit: The Popular View of the Apostolic Age and the Teaching of the Apostle Paul*. Philadelphia: Fortress.
Gunnlaugur A. Jonsson (1988), *The Image of God: Genesis 1:26–28 in a Century of Old Testament Research*. Stockholm: Almquist & Wiksell International.
Gunton, Colin (1995), *A Brief Theology of Revelation: The 1993 Warfield Lectures*. Edinburgh: T&T Clark.
Gupta, Nijay K. (2020), *Paul and the Language of Faith*. Grand Rapids, Mich.: Eerdmans.
Gutierrez, Gustavo (1973), *A Theology of Liberation: History, Politics, and Salvation*. Maryknoll: Orbis Books.
Haacker, Klaus (1999), *Der Brief des Paulus an die Römer*. Leipzig: Evang. Verl-Anst.
Habermann, Jürgen (1990), *Präexistenzaussagen im Neuen Testament*. Frankfurt: Peter Lang.
Haenchen, Ernst (1971), *The Acts of the Apostles: A Commentary*. Philadelphia: Westminster Press.
Haenchen, Ernst (1984), *A Commentary on the Gospel of John*. Philadelphia: Fortress.
Hafemann, Scott J. (2019), *Paul: Servant of the New Covenant*. Tübingen: Mohr Siebeck.
Hafizi, Sina, Rosmarin, David H., and Koenig, Harold G. (2014), 'Brief trust/mistrust in God scale: psychometric properties of the Farsi version in Muslims', *Mental Health, Religion and Culture* 17: 415–20.
Hahn, F. (1963), *Christologische Hoheitstitel*. Göttingen: Vandenhoeck and Ruprecht.
Hahne, Harry Alan (2006), *The Corruption and Redemption of Creation: Nature in Romans 8.19–22 and Jewish Apocalyptic Literature*. London: T&T Clark.
Haight, Roger, SJ (1994), 'Jesus and salvation: an essay in interpretation', *Theological Studies* 55: 225–51.
Haight, Roger, SJ (2005), *The Future of Christology*. New York: Continuum.
Halbwachs, Verena (2016), 'Women as legal actors', in Paul J. du Plessis, Clifford Ando, and Kaius Tuori eds, *The Oxford Handbook of Roman Law and Society*. Oxford: Oxford University Press: 443–56.
Hales, B. D. (2012), *Christ's Unique Place as the Mediator*. Chessington: Bible and Gospel Trust.
Halpern, Joseph Y. (2017), *Reasoning About Uncertainty*. Cambridge, Mass.: MIT Press.
Hamerton-Kelly, R. G. (1973), *Pre-existence, Wisdom, and the Son of Man: A Study of the Idea of Pre-existence in the New Testament*. Cambridge: Cambridge University Press.

Hamm, D. (1990), 'Faith in the epistle to the Hebrews: the Jesus factor', *CBQ* 52: 270-91.
Hankel, Benjamin (2015), 'Mitigating risk and facilitating access to capabilities: the role of affect in the design of an ICT-tool for queer youth in Asia', *Emotion, Space and Society* 18: 35-43.
Hansen, G. Walter (1994), *Galatians*. Downers Grove, Ill.: InterVarsity.
Hansen, G. Walter (2009), *The Letter to the Philippians*. Grand Rapids, Mich.: Eerdmans.
Hanson, James (1998), 'The disciples in Mark's gospel: beyond the pastoral/polemical debate', *Horizons in Biblical Theology* 20: 128-55.
Hardin, Russell (2002), *Trust and Trustworthiness*. New York: Russell Sage Foundation.
Hardin, Russell (2006), *Trust*. Oxford: Polity.
Härle, Wilfried and Preul, Reiner eds (1992), *Glaube*. Marburg: N. G. Elwert.
Harré, Rom (2006), 'Universals and the psychology of music: an exemplar for cultural studies', in Carlos Kölbl, Jürgen Straub, Doris Weidemann, and Barbara Zielke eds, *Pursuit of Meaning: Advances in Cultural and Cross-Cultural Psychology*. Steinfurt: Transcript Verlag: 153-62.
Harrington, Daniel J., SJ (1991), *The Gospel of Matthew*. Collegeville, Minn.: Liturgical Press.
Harrington, Wilfred J., OP (1993), *Revelation*. Collegeville, Minn.: Liturgical Press.
Harris, E. M. (2015), 'Towards a typology of Greek regulations about religious matters', *Kernos* 28: 53-83.
Harris, Paul L. and Koenig, Melissa A. (2006), 'Trust in testimony: how children learn about science and religion', *Child Development* 77: 505-24.
Harrison, James R. (2003), *Paul's Language of Grace in its Graeco-Roman Context*. Tübingen: Mohr Siebeck.
Harrison, James R. (2013), 'Augustan Rome and the body of Christ: a comparison of the social vision of the *Res gestae* and Paul's letter to the Romans', *Harvard Theological Review* 106: 1-36.
Härry, Thomas (2011), *Voll Vertrauen: Erfahren, wie Gott mich trägt*. Wuppertal-Elberfeld: SCM R. Brockhaus.
Hart, Hendrik (1994), 'Faith as trust and belief as intellectual credulity: a response to William Sweet. *Philosophy, Theology* 8: 251-6.
Hart, Larry (1978), 'Problems of authority in Pentecostalism', *Review and Expositor* 75: 249-66.
Hartin, Patrick J. (2003), *James*. Collegeville, Minn.: Liturgical Press.
Harvey, A. E. (1976), *Jesus on Trial*. London: SPCK.
Harvey, A. E. (1987), 'Christ as agent', in L. D. Hurst and N. T. Wright eds, *The Glory of Christ in the New Testament: Studies in Christology in Memory of George Bradford Caird*. Oxford: Oxford University Press: 239-50.
Harvey, Van A. (1966), *The Historian and the Believer*. Philadelphia: Westminster.
Harwood, Dane L. (1976), 'Universals in music: a perspective from cognitive psychology', *Ethnomusicology* 20: 521-33.
Hatina, Thomas R. (2013), *New Testament Theology and its Quest for Relevance: Ancient Texts and Modern Readers*. London: T&T Clark.
Haught, John F. (1993), *Mystery and Promise: A Theology of Revelation*. Collegeville, Minn.: Liturgical Press.
Hauken, Tor (1998), *Petition and Response: An Epigraphic Study of Petitions to Roman Emperors 181-249*. Bergen: Norwegian Institute at Athens.
Hauser, Alan J. (1982), 'Genesis 2-3: The theme of intimacy and alienation', in Alan J. Hauser, David M. Gunn, and David J. A. Clines eds, *Art and Meaning: Rhetoric in Biblical Literature*. London: T&T Clark: 20-36.
Hawley, Katherine (2012), *Trust: A Very Short Introduction*. Oxford: Oxford University Press.

Hawthorne, Gerald F. (1983), *Philippians*. Waco, Tex.: Word Books.
Hawthorne, Gerald F. (1991), *The Presence and the Power: The Significance of the Holy Spirit in the Life and Ministry of Jesus*. Dallas: Word Publishing.
Hayes, Christine (2002), *Gentile Impurities and Jewish Identities: Intermarriage and Conversion from the Bible to the Talmud*. New York: Oxford University Press.
Hayes, Christine (2015) *What is Divine about Divine Law? Early Perspectives*. Princeton: Princeton University Press.
Hays, Richard B. (1989), *Echoes of Scripture in the Letters of Paul*. New Haven: Yale University Press.
Hays, Richard B. (1993), 'Christ prays the psalms: Paul's use of an early Christian exegetical convention', in Abraham J. Malherbe and Wayne A. Meeks eds, *The Future of Christology: Essays in Honor of Leander E. Keck*. Minneapolis: Fortress: 122–36.
Hays, Richard B. (1997a), *First Corinthians*. Louisville, Ky: John Knox.
Hays, Richard B. (1997b), '*Pistis* and Pauline Christology: what is at stake?', in E. E. Johnson and D. M. Hay eds, *Pauline Theology IV: Looking Back, Pressing On*. Atlanta: Scholars Press: 35–60.
Hays, Richard B. (2002), *The Faith of Jesus Christ: The Narrative Substructure of Galatians 3:1–4:11*. 2nd edn. Grand Rapids, Mich.: Eerdmans.
Hays, Richard B. (2014a), 'Humanity prior to the revelation of faith', in Bruce W. Longenecker and Mikeal C. Parsons eds, *Beyond Bultmann: Reckoning a New Testament Theology*. Waco, Tex.: Baylor University Press: 61–77.
Hays, Richard B. (2014b), *Reading Backwards: Figural Christology and the Fourfold Gospel Witness*. Waco, Tex.: Baylor University Press.
Healy, Michael J. and Chervin, Ronda de Sola (2019), 'Interpreting Kierkegaard's notion that "Truth is subjectivity"', *Quaestiones Disputatae* 9: 31–42.
Hector, Kevin W. (2011), *Theology without Metaphysics: God, Language, and the Spirit of Recognition*. Cambridge: Cambridge University Press.
Hegermann, Harald (1990), '*Diathēkē*', in H. Balz and G. Schneider eds, *Exegetical Dictionary of the New Testament* 1. Grand Rapids, Mich.: Eerdmans: 301.
Heilig, Christoph et al. eds (2017), *God and the Faithfulness of Paul*. Minneapolis: Fortress.
Held, H. J. (1963), 'Matthew as interpreter of the miracle stories', in G. Bornkamm, G. Barth, and H. J. Held, *Tradition and Intepretation in Matthew*. London: SCM: 165–299.
Held, Virginia, ed. (1995), *Justice and Care: Essential Readings in Feminist Ethics*. Boulder, Colo.: Westview.
Held, Virginia (2006), *The Ethics of Care*. Oxford: Oxford University Press.
Held, Virginia (2015), 'Care and justice, still', in Daniel Engster and Maurice Hamington eds, *Care Ethics and Political Theory*. Oxford: Oxford University Press: 19–34.
Helm, Paul (2000), *Faith with Reason*. Oxford: Oxford University Press.
Helm, Paul (2002), 'The perfect trustworthiness of God', in Paul Helm and Carl R. Trueman eds, *The Trustworthiness of God: Perspectives on the Nature of Scripture*. Grand Rapids, Mich.: Eerdmans: 237–52.
Helm, Paul and Trueman, Carl R. eds (2002), *The Trustworthiness of God: Perspectives on the Nature of Scripture*. Grand Rapids, Mich.: Eerdmans.
Hempel, Lynn M., Matthews, Todd, and Bartkowski, John (2012), 'Trust in a "fallen world": the case of Protestant theological conservatism', *Journal for the Scientific Study of Religion* 51: 522–41.
Henderson, Suzanne Watts (2006), *Christology and Discipleship in the Gospel of Mark*. Cambridge: Cambridge University Press.
Hengel, Martin (1977), *The Son of God*. London: SCM.

Hengel, Martin (1981), *The Atonement: The Origins of the Doctrine in the New Testament.* London: SCM.
Heringer, Seth (2014), 'Forgetting the power of leaven: the historical method in recent New Testament theology', *Scottish Journal of Theology* 67: 85–104.
Heringer, Seth (2018), *Uniting History and Theology: A Theological Critique of the Historical Method.* Lanham, Md: Lexington/Fortress.
Herrman, Margaret S. ed. (2006), *The Blackwell Handbook of Mediation: Bridging Theory, Research, and Practice.* Oxford: Blackwell.
Hesse, Mary (1955), *Science and the Human Imagination.* New York: Philosophical Library.
Hesse, Mary (1966) *Models and Analogies in Science.* Notre Dame, Ind.: Notre Dame University Press.
Hibbard, J. Todd (2015), 'Breaking an eternal covenant: Isaiah 24:5 and Persian-period discourse about the covenant', in Richard J. Bautch and Gary N. Knoppers eds, *Covenant in the Persian Period: From Genesis to Chronicles.* Philadelphia: Pennsylvania State University Press: 195–209.
Hick, John (1967), *Faith and Knowledge.* 2nd edn. London: Macmillan.
Hick, John ed. (2005a), *The Myth of God Incarnate.* 2nd edn. London: SCM.
Hick, John (2005b), *The Metaphor of God Incarnate*, 2nd edn. London SCM.
Hicks, Andrew (2017), *Composing the World: Harmony in the Mediaeval Platonic Cosmos.* New York: Oxford University Press.
Hicks, Daniel J. and Stapleford, Thomas A. (2016), 'The virtues of scientific practice: MacIntyre, virtue ethics, and the historiography of science', *Isis* 107: 449–72.
Hieronymi, Pamela (2008), 'The reasons of trust', *Australasian Journal of Philosophy* 86: 213–36.
Higbie, C. (2003), *The Lindian Chronicle and the Greek Creation of their Past.* Oxford: Oxford University Press.
Higgins, Kathleen M. (2012), 'Biology and culture in music emotions', *Emotion Review* 4: 273–82.
Hildebrandt, Wilf (1995), *An Old Testament Theology of the Spirit of God.* Peabody, NY: Hendrickson.
Hill, Wesley (2015), *Paul and The Trinity: Persons, Relations, and the Pauline Letters.* Grand Rapids: Eerdmans.
Hinchman, Edward S. (2017), 'On the risks of resting assured', in Paul Faulkner and Thomas Simpson eds, *The Philosophy of Trust.* Oxford: Oxford University Press: 51–69.
Hofbeck, Sebald (1966), *Semeion: Der Begriff des "Zeichens" im Johannesevangelium unter Berücksichtigung seiner Vorgeschichte.* Münsterschwarzach: Münsterschwarzacher Studien.
Hofius, Otfried (1980), 'Erwägungen zur Gestalt und Herkunft des paulinischen Versöhnungsgedankens', *Zeitschrift für Theologie und Kirche* 77: 186–99.
Holden, Terence (2016), 'Honneth, Kojeve and Levinas on intersubjectivity and history', *Continental Philosophy Review* 49: 349–69.
Holleman, Joost (1995), *Resurrection and Parousia: A Tradition-Historical Study of Paul's Eschatology in 1 Cor. 15.20–23.* Leiden: Brill.
Holleman, Joost (2014), *Resurrection and Parousia: A Traditio-Historical Study of Paul's Eschatology in 1 Corinthians 15.* Leiden: Brill.
Hollis, M. (1998), *Trust Within Reason.* Cambridge: Cambridge University Press.
Holloway, Paul A. (2017), *Philippians: A Commentary.* Minneapolis: Fortress.
Holmberg, Bengt (1980), *Paul and Power: The Structure of Authority in the Primitive Church as Reflected in the Pauline Epistles.* Philadelphia: Fortress.
Holton, Richard (1994), 'Deciding to trust, coming to believe', *Australasian Journal of Philosophy* 72: 63–76.

Holtz, Gudrun (2018), 'Paul, the law, and Judaism: Stoification of the Jewish approach to the law in Paul's letter to the Romans', *Zeitschrift für neutestamentliche Wissenschaft* 109: 185–221.
Holtzen, William Curtis (2019), *The God Who Trusts: A Relational Theology of Divine Faith, Hope, and Love*. Downers Grove, Ill.: InterVarsity.
Hook, Joshua N., Van Tongeren, Daryl R., Davis, Don E., Hill, Peter C., Lewis Hall, M. Elizabeth, McKaughan, Daniel J., and Howard-Snyder, Daniel (2021), 'Trust in God: an evaluative review of the literature and research proposal', *Mental Health, Religion and Culture* <https://doi.org.10.108013674676.2021.1939291>: 1–19.
Hooker, Morna D. (1959), *Jesus and the Servant*. London: SPCK.
Hooker, Morna D. (1967), *The Son of Man in Mark: A Study of the Background of the Term 'Son of Man' and its Use in St. Mark's Gospel*. London: SPCK.
Hooker, Morna D. (1979), *Pauline Pieces*. Eugene, Ore.: Wipf and Stock.
Hooker, Morna D. (1989), '*Pistis Christou*', *New Testament Studies* 35: 321–42.
Hooker, Morna D. (1990), *From Adam to Christ: Essays on Paul*. Cambridge: Cambridge University Press.
Hooker, Morna D. (1991), *The Gospel According to St Mark*. London: A&C Black.
Hooker, Morna D. (1994), *Not Ashamed of the Gospel: New Testament Interpretations of the Death of Christ*. Carlisle: Paternoster.
Hooker, Morna D. (1996), 'A partner in the gospel: Paul's understanding of his ministry', in Eugene H. Lovering Jr and Jerry L. Sumney eds, *Theology and Ethics in Paul and his Interpreters*. Nashville: Abingdon: 83–100.
Hooker, Morna D. (2003), 'From God's faithfulness to ours: another look at 2 Corinthians 1:17–24', in Trevor J. Burke and Keith Elliott eds, *Paul and the Corinthians: Studies on a Community in Conflict. Essays in Honour of Margaret Thrall*. Leiden: Brill: 233–9.
Hooker, Morna D. (2006), 'The nature of New Testament theology', in Christopher Rowland and Christopher Tuckett eds, *The Nature of New Testament Theology: Essays in Honour of Robert Morgan*. London: John Wiley & Sons: 75–108.
Hooker, Morna D. (2013), 'Conformity to Christ', *Theology*, 116: 83–92.
Hopkins, Julie (1994), *Towards A Feminist Christology: Jesus of Nazareth, European Women, and the Christological Crisis*. Grand Rapids, Mich.: Eerdmans.
Horbury, William (1998), *Jewish Messianism and the Cult of Christ*. London: SCM.
Horbury, William (2003), *Messianism among Jews and Christians*. London: T&T Clark.
Horbury, William (2005a), 'Jewish Messianism and early Christology', in Richard N. Longenecker ed., *Contours of Christology in the New Testament*. Grand Rapids, Mich.: Eerdmans: 3–24.
Horbury, William (2005b), '"Gospel" in Herodian Judaea', in Markus Bockmuehl and Donald A. Hagner eds, *The Written Gospel*. Cambridge: Cambridge University Press: 7–30.
Horbury, William (2016), *Messianism among Jews and Christians: Biblical and Historical Studies*. London: Bloomsbury.
Horn, Friedrich Wilhelm (1992), *Das Angeld des Geistes: Studien zur paulinischen Pneumatologie*. Göttingen: Vandenhoeck & Ruprecht.
Horn, Friedrich Wilhelm (2018), *Glaube*. Tübingen: Mohr Siebeck.
Horney, Karen (1950), *Neurosis and Human Growth*. New York: W. W. Norton and Co.
Horrell, David G. (2010), 'A new perspective on Paul? Rereading Paul in a time of ecological crisis', *Journal for the Study of the New Testament* 33: 3–30.
Horrell, David G. (2016), *Solidarity and Difference: A Contemporary Reading of Paul's Ethics*. 2nd edn. London: Bloomsbury.
Horrell, David G. and Tuckett, Christopher M. eds (2000), *Christology, Controversy and Community: New Testament Essays in Honour of David R. Catchpole*. Leiden: Brill.

Horsburgh, H. J. N. (1960), 'The ethics of trust', *Philosophical Quarterly* 10: 343–54.
Horton, Fred L. Jr (1976), *The Melchizedek Tradition: A Critical Examination of the Sources to the Fifth Century A.D. and in the Epistle to the Hebrews*. Cambridge: Cambridge University Press.
Houts, Margo G. (1992), 'Atonement and abuse: an alternative view', *Daughters of Sarah* 18: 29–32.
Howard-Snyder, Daniel (2013), 'Propositional faith: what it is and what it is not', *American Philosophical Quarterly* 50: 357–72.
Howard-Snyder, Daniel (2016), 'Does faith entail belief?' *Faith and Philosophy* 33: 142–62.
Howard-Snyder, Daniel (2017), 'Markan faith', *International Journal of the Philosophy of Religion* 81: 31–60.
Howard-Snyder, Daniel (2018), '*Pistis, fides* and propositional belief', *Religious Studies* 54: 585–92.
Howard-Snyder, Daniel (2019), 'Three arguments to think that faith does *not* entail belief', *Pacific Philosophical Quarterly* 100: 114–28.
Hubbard, Benjamin Jerome (1974), 'The Matthaean redaction of a primitive apostolic commissioning: an exegesis of Matthew 28:16-20', PhD thesis, University of Iowa.
Hubbard, Moyer V. (2002), *New Creation in Paul's Letters and Thought*. Cambridge: Cambridge University Press.
Hughes, Aaron W. (2012), *Abrahamic Religions: On the Uses and Abuses of History*. Oxford: Oxford University Press.
Hull, John Martin (2002), *In the Beginning There Was Darkness: A Blind Person's Conversations with the Bible*. Harrisburg: Trinity Press International.
Hull, John Martin (2015), 'Through the many to the one: diverse human worlds and the path to human understanding', *Journal of Disability and Religion* 19: 198–208.
Hultgren, Arland J. (1987), *Christ and his Benefits: Christology and Redemption in the New Testament*. Philadelphia: Fortress.
Hunt, Steven A., Tolmie, Francis, and Zimmermann, Ruben eds (2013), *Character Studies in the Fourth Gospel: Narrative Approaches to Seventy Figures in John*. Tübingen: Mohr Siebeck.
Hunziker, Andreas and Peng-Keller, Simon (2009), 'Gott vertrauen—was heist das', *Reformatio* 58: 264071.
Hunziker, Andreas and Peng-Keller, Simon (2010), 'Vertrauensprobleme, Vertrauensformen und Vertrauensforschung', *Hermeneutische Blätter* 1/2: 5–21.
Hurst, L. D. (1987), 'The Christology of Hebrews 1 and 2', in L. D. Hurst and N. T. Wright eds, *The Glory of Christ in the New Testament: Studies in Memory of George Bradford Caird*. Oxford: Oxford University Press: 151–64.
Hurtado, Larry (1988), *One God, One Lord: Early Christian Devotion and Ancient Jewish Monotheism*. London: SCM.
Hurtado, Larry (2003), *Lord Jesus Christ: Devotion to Jesus in Earliest Christianity*. Grand Rapids, Mich.: Eerdmans.
Hurtado, Larry (2004), 'Jesus' death as paradigmatic in the New Testament', *Scottish Journal of Theology* 57: 413–33.
Hurtado, Larry (2011), *Who Is This Son of Man? The Latest Scholarship on a Puzzling Expression of the Historical Jesus*. London: Bloomsbury.
Hutt, Curtis (2013), *John Dewey and the Ethics of Historical Belief: Religion and the Representation of the Past*. Albany, NY: State University of New York Press.
Hylen, Susan (2009), *Imperfect Believers: Ambiguous Characters in the Gospel of John*. Louisville, Ky: Westminster John Knox.

Ibn Pekuda, B. (1996), *Duties of the Heart*. Northvale, NJ: Jason Aronson.
Irmischer, Johan K. ed. (1854), *Dr Martin Luther's vermischte deutsche Schriften*. Vol. 63. Erlangen: Heyder and Zimmer.
Jacob, Haley Goranson (2018), *Conformed to the Image of his Son: Reconsidering Paul's Theology of Glory*. Downers Grove, Ill.: InterVarsity.
Jansen, John Frederick (1980), *The Resurrection of Jesus Christ in New Testament Theology*. Philadelphia: Westminster.
Jeanrond, Werner G. (1988), *Text and Interpretation as Categories of Theological Thinking*. London: Gill and Macmillan.
Jegen, Carol Frances (1989), *Restoring our Friendship with God: The Mystery of Redemption from Suffering and Sin*. Wilmington: Michael Glazier Inc.
Jensen, Alexander S. (2004), *John's Gospel as Witness: The Development of the Early Christian Language of Faith*. Aldershot: Ashgate.
Jeremias, Joachim (1971), *New Testament Theology*. Vol. 1. Translated by John Bowden. Chatham: W. & J. Mackay and Co. Ltd.
Jewett, Robert (2007), *Romans: A Commentary*. Minneapolis: Fortress.
Jim, T. S. F. (2017), 'Private participation in ruler cults: dedications to Philip Sōtēr and other Hellenistic kings', *The Classical Quarterly* 67: 429–43.
Jim, T. S. F. (2021), *Saviour Gods and Sōtēria In Ancient Greece*. Oxford: Oxford University Press.
Johansson, Daniel (2011), '"Who can forgive but God alone?" Human and Angelic Agents, and divine forgiveness in early Judaism', *Journal for the Study of the New Testament* 33: 351–74.
Johnson, Elizabeth A. C.S.J. (2009), 'Deep Christology: ecological soundings', in Ellen M. Leonard and Kate Merriman eds, *From Logos to Christos: Essays in Christology in Honor of Joanne McWilliam*. Waterloo: Wilfred Laurier University Press: 163–80.
Johnson, Luke Timothy (1991), *The Gospel of Luke*. Collegeville, Minn.: Liturgical Press.
Johnson, Luke Timothy (1992), *The Acts of the Apostles*. Collegeville, Minn.: Liturgical Press.
Johnson, Luke Timothy (1995), *The Letter of James: A New Translation with Introduction and Commentary*. New York: Doubleday.
Johnson, Luke Timothy (2001), *The First and Second Letters to Timothy: A New Translation with Introduction and Commentary*. New York: Doubleday.
Johnson, Luke Timothy (2013), *Contested Issues in Christian Origins and the New Testament: Collected Essays*. Leiden: Brill.
Johnson, Luke Timothy (2014), 'The rise of Church order', in Bruce W. Longenecker and Mikeal C. Parsons eds, *Beyond Bultmann: Reckoning a New Testament Theology*. Waco, Tex.: Baylor University Press: 155–72.
Johnson, Nathan C. (2017), 'Rendering David a servant in *Psalm of Solomon* 17.21', *Journal for the Study of the Pseudepigrapha* 26: 235–50.
Johnston, Sarah Iles (2017), 'Many (un)happy returns: ancient Greek concepts of a return from death and their later counterparts', in Frederick S. Tappenden and Carly Daniel-Hughes eds, *Coming Back to Life: The Permeability of Past and Present, Mortality and Immortality, Death and Life in the Ancient Mediterranean*. Montreal: McGill University Press: 17–36.
Johnston, S. I. and Struck, P. eds (2005), *Mantikē: Studies in Ancient Divination*. Leiden: Brill.
Jones, Karen (1996), 'Trust as an affective attitude', *Ethics* 107: 4–25.
Jones, Karen (2017), '"But I was counting on you!"', in Paul Faulkner and Thomas Simpson eds, *The Philosophy of Trust*. Oxford: Oxford University Press: 90–107.

Joosten, Jan (2019), 'Covenant', in Pamela Barmash ed., *The Oxford Handbook of Biblical Law*. Oxford: Oxford University Press: 7-18.
Jordan, J. and Howard-Snyder, Daniel eds (1996), *Faith, Freedom, and Rationality*. Lanham, Md: Rowman and Littlefield.
Juslin, Patrik N. (2019), *Musical Emotions Explained: Unlocking the Secrets of Musical Affect*. Oxford: Oxford University Press.
Kania, Andrew (2008), 'Piece for the end of time: in defence of musical ontology', *British Journal of Aesthetics* 48: 65-79.
Kania, Andrew (2017), 'The Philosophy of Music', in Edward N. Zalta ed., *The Stanford Encyclopedia of Philosophy*. Fall 2017 edn. <https://plato.stanford.edu/archives/fall2017/entries/music/>.
Käsemann, Ernst (1945), 'Die evangelische Kirche im deutschen Zusammenbruch: Vortrag vor evang. Akademikern Gelsenkirchen am 4.12.1945, unpublished.
Käsemann, Ernst (1950), 'Kritische Analyse von Phil. 2.5-11', *Zeitschrift für Theologie und Kirche* 47: 313-60
Käsemann, Ernst (1957), 'Neutestamentliche Fragen von heute', *Zeitschrift für Theologie und Kirche* 54: 1-21.
Käsemann, Ernst (1962), 'Zum Thema der urchristlichen Apokalyptik', *Zeitschrift für Theologie und Kirche* 59: 257-84.
Käsemann, Ernst (1964), *Essays on New Testament Themes*. London: SCM.
Käsemann, Ernst (1969), *New Testament Questions of Today*. London: SCM.
Käsemann, Ernst (1971a), *Perspectives on Paul*. London: SCM.
Käsemann, Ernst (1971b), 'Some thoughts on the theme "the doctrine of reconciliation in the New Testament"', in James A. Robinson ed., *The Future of our Religious Past: Essays in Honour of Rudolf Bultmann*. London: SCM: 49-64.
Käsemann, Ernst (1972), *The Problem of a New Testament Theology*. Cambridge: Cambridge University Press.
Käsemann, Ernst 1980), *Commentary on Romans*. Grand Rapids, Mich.: Eerdmans.
Käsemann, Ernst (1984), *The Wandering People of God*. 2nd edn. Minneapolis: Augsburg Publishing House.
Katerberg, William (2010), 'The "objectivity question" and the historian's vocation', in John Fea, Jay Green, and Eric Miller eds, *Confessing History: Explorations in Christian Faith and the Historian's Vocation*. Notre Dame, Ind.: Notre Dame University Press: 101-27.
Katz, Neil H. (2006), 'Enhancing mediator artistry: multiple frames, spirit, and reflection in action', in Margaret S. Herrman ed., *The Blackwell Handbook of Mediation: Bridging Theory, Research, and Practice*. Oxford: Blackwell: 374-83.
Katz, Ruth and HaCohen, Ruth (2003), *Tuning the Mind: Connecting Aesthetics to Cognitive Science*. New Brunswick, NJ: Transaction.
Kay, James F. (1994), *Christus Praesens: A Reconsideration of Rudolf Bultmann's Christology*. Grand Rapids, Mich.: Eerdmans.
Kayumova, Shakhnoza, Tippins, Deborah , Ritchie, Stephen M., and Tobin, Kenneth (2016), 'Toward re-thinking science education in terms of affective practices: reflections from the field', *Cultural Studies of Science Education* 11: 567-75.
Keck, Leander E. (1986), 'Towards the renewal of New Testament Christology', *New Testament Studies* 32: 362-77.
Keck, Leander E. (1993), 'Toward the renewal of New Testament Christology', in Martinus C. de Boer ed., *From Jesus to John: Essays on Jesus and New Testament Christology in Honour of Marinus de Jonge*. London: Bloomsbury: 321-40.
Keck, Leander E. (1996), 'Rethinking New Testament ethics', *Journal of Biblical Literature* 115: 3-16.

Keck, Leander E. (2005), *Romans*. Nashville: Abingdon.
Keck, Leander E. (2015a), *Christ's First Theologian: The Shape of Paul's Thought*. Waco, Tex.: Baylor University Press.
Keck, Leander E. (2015b), *Why Christ Matters: Towards a New Testament Christology*. Waco, Tex.: Baylor University Press.
Keck, L. E. and Martyn, J. L. (1968), *Studies in Luke-Acts*. London: SPCK.
Kee, Howard Clark (1989), *Knowing the Truth: A Sociological Approach to New Testament Interpretation*. Minneapolis: Augsburg Fortress.
Keener, Craig S. (1997), *The Spirit in the Gospels and Acts: Divine Purity and Power*. Peabody, NY: Hendrickson.
Keener, Craig S. (2005), *1-2 Corinthians*. Cambridge: Cambridge University Press.
Keener, Craig S. (2009), *The Historical Jesus of the Gospels*. Grand Rapids, Mich.: Eerdmans.
Keener, Craig and Wright, Edward T. eds (2016), *Biographies and Jesus: What Does it Mean for the Gospels to be Biographies?* Lexington, Mass.: Emeth.
Keesmaat, Sylvia C. (1999), *Paul and his Story: (Re)interpreting the Exodus Tradition*. Sheffield: Sheffield Academic.
Kelber, Werner H. (2020), 'On "mastering the genre"', in Robert Matthew Calhoun, David P. Moessner, and Tobias Nicklas eds, *Modern and Ancient Literary Criticism of the Gospels: Continuing the Debate on Gospel Genre(s)*. Tübingen: Mohr Siebeck: 57-76.
Kelly, Henry Ansgar (2014), 'Adam citings before the intrusion of Satan: recontextualizing Paul's theology of sin and death', *Biblical Theology Bulletin* 44: 13-28.
Kelman, Harold C. (2008), 'Reconciliation from a social-psychological perspective', in Arie Nadler, Thomas E. Malloy, and Jeffrey D. Fisher eds, *The Social Psychology of Intergroup Reconciliation*. Oxford/New York: Oxford University Press: 15-32.
Kennedy, George A. (1984), *New Testament Interpretation through Rhetorical Criticism*. Chapel Hill, NC: University of North Carolina Press.
Kennedy, George A. (1994), *A New History of Classical Rhetoric*. Princeton: Princeton University Press.
Kertelge, Karl (1967), *'Rechtfergigung' bei Paulus: Studien zur Struktur und zum Bedeutungsgehalt des paulinischen Rechtfertigungsbegriffs*. Münster: Aschendorff.
Keshgegian, Flora A. (2000), *Redeeming Memories: A Theology of Healing and Transformation*. Nashville: Abingdon.
Kholod, Maxim M. (2016), 'The cults of Alexander the Great in the Greek cities of Asia Minor', *Klio* 98_ 495-525.
Kimelman, Reuven (1996), 'The seduction of Eve and the exegetical politics of gender', *Biblical Interpretation* 4: 1-39.
Kingsbury, Jack (1981), *Jesus Christ in Matthew, Mark, and Luke*. Philadelphia: Fortress Press.
Kingsbury, Jack (1989), *Conflict in Mark: Jesus, Authorities, Disciples*. Minneapolis: Fortress.
Kirkpatrick, Kate (2016), 'Analytic theology and the phenomenology of faith', *Journal of Analytic Theology* 4: 222-33.
Kittay, Eva Feder (2020), *Love's Labors: Essays on Women, Equality, and Dependency*. 2nd edn. Oxford: Abingdon.
Kittel, Gerhard et al. (1964), '*Eikōn*', in Gerhard Kittel and Gerhard Friedrich eds, *Theological Dictionary of the New Testament* vol. 2. Grand Rapids, Mich.: Eerdmans: 381-97.
Klauser, T. (1950), 'Akklamation', Realenzyklopädie für Antike und Christentum 1: 213-33.
Kleinig, John (2020), "Loyalty", in Edward N. Zalta ed., *The Stanford Encyclopedia of Philosophy*. Fall 2020 edn. <https://plato.stanford.edu/archives/win2020/entries/loyalty/>.

Koch, Christoph (2008), *Vertrag, Treueid und Bund: Studien zur Rezeption des altorientalischen Vertragsrechts im Deuteronomium und zur Ausbildung der Bundestheologie im Alten Testament*. Berlin: De Gruyter.
Koehn, Daryl (1998), *Rethinking Feminist Ethics: Care, Trust and Empathy*. London: Routledge.
Koester, Craig (1989), 'Hearing, seeing, and believing in the gospel of John', *Biblica* 70: 327–48.
Koester, Craig (2001), *Hebrews: A New Translation with Introduction and Commentary*. New York: Doubleday.
Koester, Craig (2003), *Symbolism in the Fourth Gospel: Meaning, Mystery, Community*. 2nd edn. Minneapolis: Augsburg Fortress.
Koester, Craig (2008), *The Resurrection of Jesus in the Gospel of John*. Tübingen: Mohr Siebeck.
Koester, Craig ed. (2018), *Portraits of Jesus in the Gospel of John*. London: Bloomsbury.
Kohn, M. (2008), *Trust: Self-Interest and the Common Good*. Oxford: Oxford University Press.
Kok, Kobus (2010), 'As the Father has sent me, I send you: towards a missional-incarnational ethos in John 4', in Ruben Zimmermann and Jan G. van der Watt eds, *Moral Language in the New Testament: The Interrelatedness of Language and Ethics in Early Christian Writings*. Tübingen: Mohr Siebeck: 168–93.
Konstan, David (2018), 'Trusting in Jesus', *Journal for the Study of the New Testament* 40: 247–54.
Krause, N. (2004), 'Assessing the relationships among prayer expectancies, race and self-esteem in late life', *Journal for the Scientific Study of Religion* 43: 395–408.
Krause, N. (2015a), 'Trust in God and psychological distress: exploring variations by religious affiliation', *Mental Health, Religion and Culture* 18: 235–45.
Krause, N. (2015b), 'Trust in God, forgiveness by God, and death anxiety', *OMEGA—Journal of Death and Dying* 72: 20–41.
Krause, N. and Hayward, R. D. (2015), 'Assessing whether trust offsets the effects of financial strain on health and well-being', *International Journal for the Psychology of Religion* 25: 307–22.
Krause, N., Chatters, L. M., Meltzer, T., and Morgan, D. L. (2000), 'Using focus groups to explore the nature of prayer in late life', *Journal of Aging Studies* 14: 191–212.
Krauter, Stefan (2020), 'Adam und Romulus. Lateinische Dichtung in der Paulusexegese', *Zeitschrift für neutestamentliche Wissenschaft* 111: 227–50.
Krumrei, E. J., Pirutinsky, S., and Rosmarin. D. H. (2013), 'Jewish spirituality, depression, and health: an empirical test of a conceptual framework', *International Journal of Behavioral Medicine* 20: 327–36.
Kruse, Colin G. (2015), *2 Corinthians: An Introduction and Commentary*. 2nd edn. Nottingham: Inter-Varsity Press.
Kugler, Chris (2016), '*Pistis Christou*: the current state of play and key arguments', *Currents in Biblical Research* 14: 244–55.
Kugler, Michael (2010), 'Enlightenment history, objectivity, and the moral imagination', in John Fea, Jay Green, and Eric Miller eds, *Confessing History: Explorations in Christian Faith and the Historian's Vocation*. Notre Dame, Ind.: Notre Dame University Press: 128–52.
Kuhn, Thomas S. (1962), *The Structure of Scientific Revolutions*. Chicago: University of Chicago Press.
Kunath, F, (2016), *Die Präexistenz Jesu im Johannesevangelium*. Berlin: De Gruyter.
Küng, Hans (1980), *Does God Exist? An Answer For Today*. Eugene, Ore.: Wipf and Stock.

Kupp, David D. (1996), *Matthew's Emmanuel: Divine Presence and God's People in the First Gospel*. Cambridge: Cambridge University Press.
Kurtén, Tage (1994), 'Basic trust—the hidden presence of God', *Theologica* 48: 110–24.
Kuschel, Karl-Josef (1992), *Born Before All Time? The Dispute over Christ's Origin*. London: SCM.
Kvanvig, Jonathan (2016), 'The idea of faith as trust: lessons in noncognitivist approaches to faith', in Michael Bergmann and Jeffrey Brower eds, *Reason and Faith: Themes from Richard Swinburne*. Oxford: Oxford University Press: 4–25.
Kvanvig, Jonathan (2018), *Faith and Humility*. Oxford: Oxford University Press.
Kwiatkowska, Marta (2017), 'Cognitive reasoning and trust in human-robot interactions' *Theory and Applications of Models of Computation* 03/21: 3–11.
Laes, Christian (2014), *Bepurkt? Gehandicapten in het Romeinse rijk*. Leuven: Davisfonds.
Laes, Christian, Goodey, C. F., and Rose, M. L. eds (2013), *Disabilities in Roman Antiquity: Disparate Bodies a capite ad calcem*. Leiden: Brill.
Lambrecht, Jan (1999), *Second Corinthians*. Collegeville, Minn.: Liturgical Press.
Lamont, John (2009), 'A conception of faith in the Greek Fathers', in Oliver D. Crisp and Michael C. Rea eds, *Analytic Theology: New Essays in the Philosophy of Theology*. Oxford: Oxford University Press: 87–116.
Lampe, G. W. H. (1977), *God as Spirit*. Oxford: Oxford University Press.
Lampe, G. W. H. (1981). 'Martyrdom and inspiration', in William Horbury and Brian McNeil eds, *Suffering and Martyrdom in the New Testament*. Cambridge: Cambridge University Press: 118–35.
Landau, Mark J., Khenfer, Jamel, Keefer, Lucas A., Swanson, Trevor J., and Kay, Aaron C (2018), 'When and why does belief in a controlling God strengthen goal commitment?' *Journal of Experimental Social Psychology* 75: 71–82.
Lang, Friedrich (1986), *Die Briefe an die Korinther*. Göttingen: Vandenhoeck & Ruprecht.
Langford, Joy (2017), 'Feminism and leadership in the Pentecostal movement', *Feminist Theology* 26: 69–79.
Langlands, Rebecca (2018), *Exemplary Ethics in Ancient Rome*. Cambridge: Cambridge University Press.
Langton, D. R. (2005–6), 'The myth of the "traditional view of Paul" and the role of the apostle in modern Jewish–Christian polemics', *Journal for the Study of the New Testament* 28: 69–104.
Larkins, Cath and Wainwright, John (2014), *'Just Putting Me on the Right Track': Young People's Perspectives on What Helps Them Stop Offending*. Preston: University of Central Lancashire Press.
Larsen, Brian (2018), *Archetypes and the Fourth Gospel: Literature and Theology in Conversation*. London: Bloomsbury.
Lassak, Andrea (2010), 'Welchen Sinn es hat, vom Vertrauen in Gott zu reden', *Hermeneutische Blätter* 1/2: 109–18.
Lassak, Andrea (2013), 'Grenzphänomene des Vertrauens: Theologische Erörterungen zum Verhältnis von Grund- und Gottvertrauen', *Hermeneutische Blätter* 1/2: 113–21.
Lassak, Andrea (2015), *Grundloses Vertrauen: Eine theologische Studie zum Verhältnis von Grund- und Gottvertrauen*. Tübingen: Mohr Siebeck.
Laurand, Valery (2014), 'Les Effets éthiques de la musique: la lecture problématique de Diogène de Babylone par Philodème de Gadara', *Méthexis* 27: 197–214.
Lawrence, Louise J. (2014), *Sense and Stigma in the Gospels: Depictions of Sensory-Disabled Characters*. Oxford: Oxford University Press.
Lawrence, R. T. (1997), 'Measuring the image of God: the God image inventory and the God image scales', *Journal of Psychology and Theology* 25: 214–26.

Lebens, Samuel (2017), 'The life of faith as a work of art: a rabbinic theology of faith', *International Journal for the Philosophy of Religion* 81: 61–81.
Lee, Dorothy (1994), *The Symbolic Narratives of the Fourth Gospel: The Interplay of Form and Meaning*. Sheffield: Sheffield Academic Press.
Lee, Dorothy (2002), *Flesh and Glory: Symbolism, Gender, and Theology in the Gospel of John*. New York: Crossroad.
Lee, Dorothy (2018), 'Symbolism and "signs" in the fourth gospel', in Judith M. Lieu and Martinus C. de Boer eds, *The Oxford Handbook of Johannine Studies*. Oxford: Oxford University Press: 259–73.
Lee, San Mok (2019), 'Christ's *pistis* vs. Caesar's *fides*: *Pistis Christou* in Galatians and the Roman imperial cult', *The Expository Times* 130: 243–55.
Leonhardt, Jutta (2001), *Jewish Worship in Philo of Alexandria*. Tübingen: Mohr Siebeck.
Leroy, Herbert (1974), *Zur Vergebung der Sünden*. Stuttgart: KBW Verlag.
Letteny, M. D. and Larsen, M. D. C. (2019), 'Christians and the codex: generic materiality and early gospel traditions', *Journal of Early Christian Studies* 27: 383–415.
Levenson, Jon D. (1993), *The Death and Resurrection of the Beloved Son: The Transformation of Child Sacrifice in Judaism and Christianity*. New Haven: Yale University Press.
Levenson, Jon D. (2012), *Inheriting Abraham: The Legacy of the Patriarch in Judaism, Christianity and Islam*. Princeton: Princeton University Press.
Levering, Matthew (2011), *Predestination*. Oxford: Oxford University Press.
Levin, Y. (2006), 'Jesus, "son of God" and "son of David": The "adoption" of Jesus into the Davidic line', *Journal for the Study of the New Testament*, 28: 415–42.
Levinson, Bernard M. (2008), *Legal Revision and Religious Renewal in Ancient Israel*. Cambridge: Cambridge University Press.
Levinson, Jerrold (2011), *Music, Art, and Metaphysics: Essays in Philosophical Aesthetics*. Oxford: Oxford University Press.
Levison, John R. (1988), *Portraits of Adam in Early Judaism: From Sirach to 2 Baruch*. London: Hart.
Levison, John R. (1994), 'The debut of the divine Spirit in Josephus's *Antiquities*', *Harvard Theological Review* 87: 123–138.
Levison, John R. (1997), *The Spirit in First-Century Judaism*. Leiden: Brill.
Levison, John R. (2009), *Filled with the Spirit*. Grand Rapids, Mich.: Eerdmans.
Levison, John R. (2019), *The Holy Spirit Before Christianity*. Waco, Tex.: Baylor University Press.
Lévi-Strauss, Claude (1969), *The Raw and the Cooked*. London: Pimlico.
Lewicki, Roy J., McAllister, Daniel J., and Bies, Robert J. (1998), 'Trust and distrust: new relationships and realities', *Academy of Management Review* 22: 438–58.
Lewicki, Roy J., Tomlinson, Edward C., and Gillespie, Nicole (2006), 'Models of interpersonal trust development: theoretical approaches, empirical evidence, and future directions', *Journal of Management* 32: 991–1022.
Lewis, John G. (2005), *Looking for Life: The Role of 'Theo-Ethical Reasoning' in Paul's Religion*. London: T&T Clark.
Lietzmann, Hans (1932), *An die Galater*. Tübingen: J. C. B. Mohr.
Lietzmann, Hans (1949), *An die Korinther I-II*. Tübingen: J. C. B. Mohr.
Lieu, Judith (2015), *Marcion and the Making of a Heretic: God and Scripture in the Second Century*. Cambridge: Cambridge University Press.
Lieu, Judith (2018), 'Faith and the fourth gospel: a conversation with Teresa Morgan', *Journal for the Study of the New Testament* 40: 289–98.
Lightfoot, J. B. (1921), *Saint Paul's Epistle to the Galatians: A Revised Text with Introduction, Notes, and Dissertations*. London: Macmillan and Co.

Lightstone, Jack N. (2006), *The Commerce of the Sacred*. New York: Columbia University Press.
Lincoln, Andrew T. (1990), *Ephesians*. Dallas: Word Books.
Lincoln, Andrew T. (2000), *Truth on Trial: The Lawsuit Motif in the Fourth Gospel*. Peabody, NY: Hendrickson.
Lincoln, Andrew T. (2005), *The Gospel According to John*. Peabody, NY: Hendrickson.
Lincoln, Andrew (2013), *Born of a Virgin? Reconceiving Jesus in the Bible, Tradition, and Theology*. London: SPCK.
Lindbeck, George A. (2009), *The Nature of Doctrine: Religion and Theology in a Postliberal Age*. 25th anniversary edn. Louisville, Ky: Westminster John Knox.
Lindemann, Andreas (2000), *Der erste Korintherbrief*. Tübingen: Mohr Siebeck.
Lloyd-Jones, H. (1983), *The Justice of Zeus* 2nd edn. Berkeley: University of California Press.
Löfstedt, T. (2010), 'Paul, sin and Satan: the root of evil according to Romans', *Svensk Exegetisk Årsbok* 75: 109–34.
Løgstrup, Knud Ejler (1997), *The Ethical Demand*. Rev. edn. Notre Dame, Ind.: University of Notre Dame Press.
Lohmeyer, Ernst (1928), *Kyrios Jesus: Eine Untersuchung zu Phil. 2.5–11*. Heidelberg: Carl Winters.
Lohmeyer, Ernst (1937), *Das Evangelium des Markus*. Göttingen: Vandenhoeck & Ruprecht.
Lohse, Eduard (1971), *Colossians and Philemon*. Philadelphia: Fortress.
Longenecker, Bruce W. (1998), *The Triumph of Abraham's God: The Transformation of Identity in Galatians*. Edinburgh: T&T Clark.
Longenecker, Bruce W (2007), 'On Israel's God and God's Israel: assessing supersessionism in Paul', *Journal of Theological Studies* 58: 26–44.
Longenecker, Bruce W. and Parsons, Mikeal C. eds (2014), *Beyond Bultmann: Reckoning a New Testament Theology*. Waco, Tex.: Baylor University Press.
Longenecker, Richard N. (1970), *The Christology of Early Jewish Christianity*. London: SCM.
Longenecker, Richard N. (1990), *Galatians*. Dallas: Word Books.
Longenecker, Richard N. ed. (2005a), *Contours of Christology in the New Testament*. Grand Rapids, Mich.: Eerdmans.
Longenecker, Richard N. (2005b), 'Christological materials in the early Christian communities', in Richard N. Longenecker ed., *Contours of Christology in the New Testament*. Grand Rapids, Mich.: Eerdmans: 47–76.
Longenecker, Richard N. (2015), *Paul: Apostle of Liberty*. 2nd edn. Grand Rapids, Mich.: Eerdmans.
López, Elisa Estévez (2009), 'Transformative spirituality and mission as healing and reconciliation', *International Review of Mission* 98: 283–301.
Lorberbaum, Yair (2015), *In God's Image: Myth, Theology, and Law in Classical Judaism*. New York: Cambridge University Press.
Louth, Andrew (1983), *Discerning the Mystery: An Essay on the Nature of Theology*. Oxford: Oxford University Press.
Lozano, Ray M. (2019), *The Proskynesis of Jesus in the New Testament: A Study on the Significance of Jesus as an Object of 'Proskuneo' in the New Testament Writings*. New York: Bloomsbury.
Lüdemann, Gerd (1984), *Paul: Apostle to the Gentiles. Studies in Chronology*. London: SCM.
Lührmann, Dieter (1992a), *Galatians*. Minneapolis: Fortress.
Lührmann, Dieter (1992b), 'Glaube, Bekenntnis, Erfahrung', in Wilfried Härle and Reiner Preul eds, *Glaube*. Marburg: N. G. Elwert: 12–36.
Lührmann, Dieter (1993), 'Bornkamm's response to Keck revisited', in Abraham J. Malherbe and Wayne A. Meeks eds, *The Future of Christology: Essays in Honor of Leander E. Keck*. Minneapolis: Fortress: 66–78.

Luz, Ulrich (1995), 'The disciples in the gospel according to Matthew', in Graham N. Stanton ed., *The Interpretation of Matthew*. Edinburgh: T&T Clark.
Luz, Ulrich (2001–2007), *Matthew*. 3 vols. Minneapolis: Fortress.
Luz, Ulrich (2014), *Theologische Hermeneutik des Neuen Testaments*. Neukirchen: Neukirchener Verlag.
Macaskill, Grant (2010), 'Paradise in the New Testament', in Markus Bockmuehl and Guy Stroumsa eds, *Paradise in Antiquity: Jewish and Christian Views*. Cambridge: Cambridge University Press: 64–81.
McCarthy, Denis J. (1963), *Treaty and Covenant*. Rome: Pontifico Istituto Biblico.
McCraw, Benjamin W. (2015), 'Faith and trust', *International Journal of the Philosophy of Religion* 77: 141–58.
McCuistion, Paul R., Warner, Colin, and Viljoen, François P. (2014), 'The influence of Greek drama on Matthew's gospel', *HTS Teologiese Studies* 70: art. 2024.
MacDonald, Margaret Y. (2000), *Colossians and Ephesians*. Collegeville, Minn.: Liturgical Press.
McDonough, Sean M. (2009), *Christ as Creator: Origins of a New Testament Doctrine*. Oxford: Oxford University Press.
McDowell, Catherine (2015), *The Image of God in the Garden of Eden*. Philadelphia: Pennsylvania State University Press.
McFadden, Kevin W. (2015), 'Does *pistis* mean faith[fulness] in Paul?', *Tyndale Bulletin* 66: 251–70.
McGeer, Victoria and Pettit, Philip (2017), 'The empowering theory of trust', in Paul Faulkner and Thomas W. Simpson eds, *The Philosophy of Trust*. Oxford: Oxford University Press: 14–34.
McGrath, Alister E. (2011), *Luther's Theology of the Cross: Martin Luther's Theological Breakthrough*. Chichester: Wiley-Blackwell.
McGrath, B. (1952), '"Syn" words in Saint Paul', *Catholic Biblical Quarterly*, 14: 219–26.
McGraw, Claire (2019), 'The imperial cult and the individual: the negotiation of Augustus' private worship during his lifetime at Rome', Ph.D. dissertation, University of Missouria-Columbia.
MacGregor, Kirk R. (2020), *A Historical and Theological Investigation of John's Gospel*. Charm: Palgrave Macmillan.
McIntyre, John (1992), *The Shape of Soteriology*. Edinburgh: T&T Clark.
McIntyre, John (1998), *The Shape of Christology: Studies in the Doctrine of the Person of Christ*. Edinburgh: T&T Clark.
McKaughan, Daniel (2013), 'Authentic faith and acknowledged risk: dissolving the problem of faith and reason', *Religious Studies* 49: 101–24.
McKaughan, Daniel (2016), 'Action-centered faith, doubt, and rationality', *Journal of Philosophical Research* 41: 71–90.
McKaughan, Daniel (2017), 'On the value of faith and faithfulness', *International Journal for Philosophy of Religion* 81: 7–29.
McKaughan, Daniel (2018a), 'Cognitive opacity and the analysis of faith: acts of faith interiorized through a glass only darkly', *Religious Studies* 54: 576–85.
McKaughan, Daniel (2018b), 'Faith through the dark of night: what perseverance amidst doubt can teach us about the nature and value of religious faith', *Faith and Philosophy* 35: 195–218.
McKaughan, Daniel and Howard-Snyder, Daniel (2021), 'Theorizing about faith and faithfulness with Jonathan Kvanvig' *Religious Studies* first view 1–21.
McKenna, P. P. OP (1914), *The Theology of Faith*. Dublin: Browne and Nolan, Ltd.

Mackey, James P. (1975), 'The theology of faith: a bibliographical survey', *Horizons* 2: 207–37.
Mackey, James P. (2006), *Christianity and Creation: The Essence of the Christian Faith and its Future among Religions: A Systematic Theology*. New York: Continuum.
Mackey, James P. (2008), *Jesus of Nazareth: The Life, the Faith, and the Future of the Prophet*. Blackrock: The Columba Press.
McKnight, D. Harrison, Cummings, Larry L., and Chervany, Norman L. (1998), 'Initial trust formation in new organizational relationships', *Academy of Management Review* 23: 473–90.
Macquarrie, John (1960), *The Scope of Demythologizing: Bultmann and his Critics*. London: SCM.
McWhirter, Jocelyn (2006), *The Bridegroom Messiah and the People of God: Marriage in the Fourth Gospel*. Cambridge: Cambridge University Press.
Magee, John ed. (2016), *Chalcidius on Plato's Timaeus*. Cambridge, Mass.: Harvard University Press.
Magonet, Jonathan (1984), 'Abraham and God', *Judaism* 33: 160–70.
Maier, Harry O. (2018), *New Testament Christianity in the Roman World*. New York: Oxford University Press.
Malbon, Elizabeth Struthers (2000), *In the Company of Jesus. Characters in Mark's Gospel*. Louisville, Ky: Westminster John Knox.
Malbon, Elizabeth Struthers (2009), *Mark's Jesus: Characterization as Narrative Christology*. Waco, Tex.: Baylor University Press.
Malcolm, Finlay (2018), 'Can fictionalists have faith?' *Religious Studies* 54: 215–32.
Malevez, L. (1969), *Pour une théologie de la foi*. Bruges: Desclée de Brouwer.
Malherbe, Abraham J. (2000), *The Letters to the Thessalonians: A New Translation with Introduction and Commentary*. New York: Doubleday.
Malherbe, Abraham J. and Meeks, Wayne A. eds (1993), *The Future of Christology: Essays in Honor of Leander E. Keck*. Minneapolis: Fortress.
Mannering, Helenka (2020), 'A rapprochement between feminist ethics of care and contemporary theology', *Religions* 11: 185–97.
Mansfield, George (1849), *A Picture of Grace; or, The True Friend: A Scripture Narrative [the Parable of the Good Samaritan in St. Luke's Gospel] Illustrative of Gospel Truth*. Trowbridge: Lond. & co.
Marchitello, Howard (2001), *What Happens to History: The Renewal of Ethics in Contemporary Thought*. New York: Routledge.
Marcus, Joel (2000–9), *Mark: A New Translation with Introduction and Commentary*. 2 vols. New York: Doubleday.
Marincola, John (1997), *Authority and Tradition in Ancient Historiography*. Cambridge: Cambridge University Press.
Marohl, Matthew J. (2008), *Faithfulness and the Purpose of Hebrews: A Social Identity Approach*. Cambridge: James Clarke & Co.
Marshall, Bruce (2000), *Trinity and Truth*. Cambridge: Cambridge University Press.
Marshall, I. Howard (1978), *The Gospel of Luke: A Commentary on the Greek Text*. Exeter: Paternoster.
Marshall, I. Howard (2002), '"Sins" and "sin"', *Bibliotheca Sacra* 159: 3–20.
Marshall, I Howard and Peterson, David (1998), *Witness to the Gospel: The Theology of Acts*. Grand Rapids, Mich.: Eerdmans.
Marshall, I. Howard and Towner, Philip H. (1999), *The Pastoral Epistles*. Edinburgh: T&T Clark.

Martin, Dale B. (2017), *Biblical Truths: The Meaning of Scripture in the Twenty-first Century*. New Haven: Yale University Press.
Martin, Francis with Smith, Evan (2006), *Acts*. Downers Grove, Ill.: InterVarsity.
Martin, J. (2020), *Trust God's Plan: Finding Faith in Difficult Times*. No publisher.
Martin, Neil (2018), 'Returning to the *stoicheia tou kosmou*: enslavement to the physical elements in Galatians 4.3 and 9?' *Journal for the Study of the New Testament* 40: 434–52.
Martin, Ralph P. (1967), *Carmen Christi: Philippians 2.5–11 in Recent Interpretation and in the Setting of Early Christian Worship*. Cambridge: Cambridge University Press.
Martin, Ralph P. (1981), *Reconciliation: A Study of Paul's Theology*. London: Marshall, Morgan and Scott.
Martin, Ralph P. (1986), *2 Corinthians*. Waco, Tex.: Word Books.
Martin, Ralph P. (2014), *2 Corinthians*. 2nd edn. Grand Rapids, Mich.: Zondervan.
Martin, Ralph P. and Dodd, Brian J. eds (1998), *Where Christology Began: Essays on Philippians 2*. Louisville, Ky: Westminster John Knox.
Martinelli, Riccardo (2019), *Philosophy of Music: A History*. Berlin: De Gruyter.
Martins, F. (2004), 'Historiografia, biografia e ética', *Análise Social* 39: 391–408.
Martyn, J. Louis (1979), *The Gospel of John in Christian History: Essays for Interpreters*. New York: Paulist Press.
Martyn, J. Louis (1985), 'Apocalyptic antinomies in Paul's letter to the Galatians', *New Testament Studies*, 31: 410–24.
Martyn, J. Louis (1993), 'Covenant, Christ, and church in Galatians', in Abraham J Malherbe and Wayne A. Meeks eds, *The Future of Christology: Essays in Honor of Leander E. Keck*. Minneapolis: Fortress: 137–51.
Martyn, J Louis (1997a), *Galatians: A New Translation with Introduction and Commentary*. New York: Doubleday.
Martyn, J. Louis (1997b), *Theological Issues in the Letters of Paul*. Edinburgh: T&T Clark.
Martyn, J. Louis (1998), *Galatians*. New York: Doubleday.
Martyn, J. Louis (2000), 'The apocalyptic gospel in Galatians', *Interpretation: A Journal of Bible and Theology*, 54: 246–66.
Martyn, J. Louis (2003), *History and Theology in the Fourth Gospel*. 3rd edn. Louisville, Ky: Westminster John Knox.
Marxsen, Willi (1993), *New Testament Foundations for Christian Ethics*. Edinburgh: T&T Clark.
Mason, Steven D. (2007), 'Another flood? Genesis 9 and Isaiah's broken eternal covenant', *Journal for the Study of the Old Testament* 32: 177–98.
Massinell, Georges OFM (2015), 'Christ and the law in Romans 10:4', *Catholic Biblical Quarterly* 77: 707–26.
Masters, R. (1986), 'The biology of social participation', in M. Gruter and R. Masters eds, 'Ostracism: a social and biological phenomenon', *Ethnology and Sociobiology*, 7(3/4) (Special issue) 231–47: 234.
Matera, Frank J. (1987), *What Are They Saying About Mark?* New York: Paulist Press.
Matera, Frank J. (1992), *Galatians*. Collegeville, Minn.: The Liturgical Press.
Matera, Frank J. (1999), *New Testament Christology*. Louisville, Ky: Westminster John Knox.
Matera, Frank J. (2005), 'New Testament theology: history, method, and identity', *Catholic Biblical Quarterly* 67: 1–21.
Matera, Frank J. (2006), 'Christ in the theologies of Paul and John: a study in the diverse unity of New Testament theology', *Theological Studies* 67: 237–56.
Matera, Frank J. (2007), *New Testament Theology: Exploring Diversity and Unity*, Louisville, Ky: Westminster John Knox.

Matlock, R. Barry (1996), *Unveiling the Apocalyptic Paul: Paul's Interpreters and the Rhetoric of Criticism.* Sheffield: Sheffield Academic Press.
Matlock, R. Barry (1998), 'Sins of the flesh and suspicious minds: Dunn's new theology of Paul', *Journal for the Study of the New Testament* 72: 67-90.
Mattson, Witney I., Ekas, Naomi V., Lambert, Brittany, Tronick, Ed, Lester, Barry M., and Messinger, Daniel S. (2012), 'Emotional expression and heart rate in high-risk infants during the face-to-face/still face', *Infant Behavior and Development* 36: 776-85.
Mayer, R., Davis, J. and Schoorman, F. (1995), 'An integrative model of organizational trust', *Academy of Management Review*, 20: 709-34.
Mayes, Andrew (1973), 'The nature of sin and its origin in the Old Testament', *Irish Theological Quarterly* 40: 250-63.
Meeks, Wayne A. (1986), *The Moral World of the First Christians.* Philadelphia: Westminster.
Meeks, Wayne A. (1990), 'On trusting an unpredictable God: a hermeneutical meditation on Romans 9-11', in John T. Carroll, Charles H. Cosgrove, and E. Elizabeth Johnson eds, *Faith and History: Essays in Honor of Paul W. Meyer.* Atlanta: Scholars Press: 105-24.
Meeks, Wayne A. (1993), *The Origins of Christian Morality: The First Two Centuries.* New Haven: Yale University Press.
Melcher, Sarah J., Parsons, Mikael C., and Yong, Amos eds (2017), *The Bible and Disability: A Commentary.* Waco, Tex.: Baylor University Press.
Menken, Maarten J. J. (2015), 'Review of Anthony M. Moore, *Signs of Salvation*', *Novum Testamentum* 57: 330-2.
Menzies, Robert P. (1993), 'Spirit and power in Luke-Acts: a response to Max Turner', *Journal for the Study of the New Testament* 15: 11-20.
Menzies, Robert P. (1994), *Empowered for Witness: The Spirit in Luke-Acts.* Sheffield: Sheffield Academic Press.
Mercier, Hugo (2020), *Not Born Yesterday: The Science of Who We Trust and What We Believe.* Princeton: Princeton University Press.
Merk, Otto (1972), *Biblische Theologie des Neuen Testaments in ihrer Anfangszeit.* Bonn: Elwert.
Meyer, P. (2002), 'Ethnic solidarity as risk avoidance: an evolutionary view', in F. Salter ed., *Risky Transactions: Trust, Kinship and Ethnicity.* New York: Berghahn: 219-42.
Meyers, Eric M. ed. (1999), *Galilee through the Centuries: Confluence of Cultures.* Winona Lake, Ind.: Eisenbaums.
Michaelis, W. (1964), '*mimeomai*', in Gerhard Kittel and Gerhard Friedrich eds, *Theological Dictionary of the New Testament* vol. 4. Grand Rapids, Mich.: Eerdmans: 659-74.
Michel, Otto (1995), 'The conclusion of Matthew's gospel', in Graham N. Stanton ed., *The Interpretation of Matthew.* Edinburgh: T&T Clark.
Michon, Cyrille (2017), 'Believing God: an account of faith as personal trust', *Religious Studies* 53: 387-401.
Middleton, Paul (2006), *Radical Martyrdom and Cosmic Conflict in Early Christianity.* London: T&T Clark.
Mikkelson, B. (2006), 'Just dying to get out', <http://www.snopes.com/horros/gruesome/buried/asp>.
Millar, Fergus (1992), *The Emperor in the Roman World.* 2nd edn. London: Duckworth.
Millar, J. Gary (2002), '"A faithful God who does no wrong": history, theology, and reliability in Deuteronomy', in Paul Helm and Carl R. Trueman eds, *The Trustworthiness of God: Perspectives on the Nature of Scripture.* Grand Rapids, Mich.: Eerdmans: 3-17.
Miller, David (2017), 'Justice', in Edward N. Zalta ed., *The Stanford Encyclopedia of Philosophy.* Fall 2017 edn. <https://plato.stanford.edu/archives/fall2017/entries/justice/>.
Miller, Donald E., Sargeant, Kimon H., and Flory, Richard (2013), *Spirit and Power: The Growth and Global Impact of Pentecostalism.* Oxford: Oxford University Press.

Miller, P. D. (1995), 'Creation and covenant', in S. J. Kraftchick ed., *Biblical Theology: Problems and Perspectives*. Nashville: Abingdon: 155–68.
Miller, Susan (2004), *Woman in Mark's Gospel*. London: T&T Clark.
Miller, Susan (2012), '"I came that they may have life, and have it abundantly" (John 10:10): an ecological reading of John's gospel', *Expository Times* 124: 64–71.
Miller, William R. and Thoresen, Karl E. (2003), 'Spirituality, religion, and health: an emerging research field', *American Psychologist* 58: 24–35.
Minear, Paul S. (1994), *Christians and the New Creation: Genesis Motifs in the New Testament*. Louisville, Ky: Westminster John Knox.
Mitchell, Alan C. (2007), *Hebrews*. Collegeville, Minn.: Liturgical Press.
Mitchell, Margaret M. and Young, Frances M. eds (2006), *The Cambridge History of Christianity. Volume 1: Origins to Constantine*. Cambridge: Cambridge University Press.
Mitchell, Stephen (1993), *Anatolia: Land, Men, and Gods in Asia Minor*. Oxford: Oxford University Press.
Moberly, E. W. L. (2000), *The Bible, Theology, and Faith*. Cambridge: Cambridge University Press.
Moloney, Francis J. SDB (1994), 'The faith of Martha and Mary: a narrative approach to John 11,17–40', *Biblica* 75: 471–93.
Moloney, Francis J. SDB (1998), *The Gospel of John*. Collegeville, Minn.: Liturgical Press.
Moloney, Francis J. SDB (2003), 'Can everyone be wrong? A reading of John 11.1–12.8', *New Testament Studies* 49: 505–27.
Monserrat, J.-L. Roura (2016), *La Conception paulinienne de la foie en Romains 4*. Paris: Éditions du Cerf.
Montemaggi, Francesca E. (2017), 'Belief, trust and relationality: a Simmelian approach for the study of faith', *Religion* 47: 147–60.
Moo, Douglas J. (1987), 'Paul and the law in the last ten years', *Scottish Journal of Theology* 40: 287–307.
Moo, Douglas J. (2000), *The Epistle to the Romans*. Grand Rapids, Mich.: Eerdmans.
Moo, Jonathan (2008), 'Romans 8.19–22 and Isaiah's cosmic covenant', *New Testament Studies* 54: 74–89.
Moore, Anthony M. (2013), *Signs of Salvation: The Theme of Creation in John's Gospel*. Cambridge: James Clarke.
Moore, Margaret (1999), 'The ethics of care and justice', *Women and Politics* 20: 1–16.
Morales, Jorge, Bax, Axel, and Firestone, Chaz (2020), 'Sustained representation of perspectival shape', *Proceedings of the National Academy of Sciences of the United States of America* 117: 14873–82.
Morgan, Robert C. (1973), *The Nature of New Testament Theology: The Contribution of William Wrede and Adolf Schlatter*. London: SCM.
Morgan, Robert C. (1998), 'Incarnation, myth, and theology: Ernst Käsemann's interpretation of Philippians 2.5–11', in Ralph P. Martin and Brian J. Dodd eds, *Where Christology Began: Essays on Philippians 2*. Louisville, Ky: Westminster John Knox: 43–73.
Morgan, Robert C. (2003), 'Historical and canonical aspects of New Testament theology', *Biblical Interpretation* 11: 629–39.
Morgan, Robert C. (2008), 'Biblical theology since Bultmann', *The Expository Times* 119: 472–80.
Morgan, Robert C. (2016), 'New Testament theology as implicit theological interpretation of Christian scripture', *Interpretation: A Journal of Bible and Theology* 70: 383–98.
Morgan, Robert C. (2018), 'Two types of critical theological interpretation', *Journal for the Study of the New Testament* 41: 204–22.

Morgan, Teresa (2007), *Popular Morality in the Early Roman Empire*. Cambridge: Cambridge University Press.
Morgan, Teresa (2013), 'Divine-human relations in the Aesopic corpus', *Journal of Ancient History* 1: 3-26
Morgan, Teresa (2015a), *Roman Faith and Christian Faith: Pistis and Fides in the Early Roman Empire and Early Churches*. Oxford: Oxford University Press.
Morgan, Teresa (2015b), 'Not the whole story? Moralizing biography and *imitatio Christi*', in Rhiannon Ash, Judith Mossman, and Frances Titchener eds, *Fame and Infamy: Essays for Christopher Pelling in Greek and Roman Biography and History*. Oxford: Oxford University Press: 378-402.
Morgan, Teresa (2015c), 'To err is human, to correct divine: a recessive gene in ancient Mediterranean and Near Eastern religiosity?', in J. Barton and P. Groves eds, *The New Testament and the Church: Essays in Honour of John Muddiman*. London: Bloomsbury: 64-77.
Morgan, Teresa (2020), *Being 'in Christ' in the Letters of Paul: Saved through Christ and in his Hands*. Tübingen: Mohr Siebeck.
Morgan, Teresa (2021a) 'Two aspects of early Christian faith', in Charlotte Methuen, Alec Ryrie, and Andrew Spicer eds, *Inspiration and Institution in Christian History*. Cambridge: Cambridge University Press: 6-31.
Morgan, Teresa (2021b), 'Origen's Celsus and imperial Greek religiosity', in James Carleton Paget and Simon Gathercole eds, *Celsus in his World*. Cambridge: Cambridge University Press: 149-77.
Morgan, Teresa (forthcoming), *The Invention of Faith*.
Morris, Michael (2016), 'Deuteronomy in the Matthean and Lucan temptation in light of early Jewish antinomian tradition', *Catholic Biblical Quarterly* 78: 290-301.
Morris, Thomas V. ed. (1988), *Philosophy and the Christian Faith*. Notre Dame, Ind.: University of Notre Dame Press.
Morrison, Glenn (2017), 'A theology of feasting: encountering the kingdom of God', *Irish Theological Quarterly* 82: 128-47.
Moser, P. (2010), *The Evidence for God: Religious Knowledge Re-examined*. New York: Cambridge University Press.
Moser, Paul and McFall, Michael eds (2012), *The Wisdom of the Christian Faith*. Cambridge: Cambridge University Press.
Moss, Candida (2010), 'The man with the flow of power: porous bodies in Mark 5:25-34', *Journal of Biblical Literature* 129: 507-19.
Mossman, Judith M. (1988), 'Tragedy and epic in Plutarch's *Alexander*', *Journal of Hellenic Studies* 108: 83-93.
Moule, C. F. D. (1956), *The Sacrifice of Christ*. London: Hodder and Stoughton.
Moule, C. F. D. (1977), *The Origin of Christology*. Cambridge: Cambridge University Press.
Moule, C. F. D. (1978), *The Holy Spirit*. London: Mowbray.
Moule, C. F. D. (1981), *Birth of the New Testament*. 3rd edn. London: A&C Black.
Moule, C. F. D. (1982), *Essays in New Testament Interpretation*. Cambridge: Cambridge University Press.
Moule, C. F. D. (1998), *Forgiveness and Reconciliation: Biblical and Theological Essays*. London: SPCK.
Mouroux, Jean (1959), *I Believe: The Personal Structure of Faith*. London: G. Chapman.
Moutsopoulos, Evanghélos (2008), 'Métaphysique et musique', *Les Études philosophiques* 87: 473-85.
Moxnes, Halvor (1980), *Theology in Conflict: Studies in Paul's Understanding of God in Romans*. Leiden: Brill.

Muddiman, John (2001), *A Commentary on The Epistle to the Ephesians.* London: Continuum.
Müller, Christian (1964), *Gottes Gerechtigkeit und Gottes Volk: eine Untersuchung zu Römer 9–11.* Göttingen: Vandenhoeck & Ruprecht.
Murphy-O'Connor, Jerome (1976), 'Christological anthropology in Phil. 2.6–11', *Révue Biblique* 83: 25–50.
Murphy-O'Connor, Jerome (2009), *Keys to First Corinthians: Revisiting the Major Issues.* Oxford: Oxford University Press.
Murphy-O'Connor, Jerome (2010), *Keys to Second Corinthians: Revisiting the Major Issues.* Oxford: Oxford University Press.
Murray, Kyle (2012), 'Christian "renewalism" and the production of global free market hegemony', *International Politics* 49: 260–76.
Murray, Robert (1992), *The Cosmic Covenant.* London: Sheed and Ward.
Muyskens, James L. (1979), *The Sufficiency of Hope: The Conceptual Foundations of Religion.* Philadelphia: Temple University Press.
Myers, Tobias (2019), *Homer's Divine Audience: The Iliad's Reception on Mount Olympus.* Oxford: Oxford University Press.
Nadler, Arie and Shnabel, Nurit (2008), 'Instrumental and socioemotional paths to intergroup reconciliation and the needs-based model of socioemotional reconciliation', in Arie Nadler, Thomas E. Malloy, and Jeffrey D. Fisher eds, *The Social Psychology of Intergroup Reconciliation.* Oxford: Oxford University Press: 37–56.
Nagasawa, Yujin (2017), *Global Philosophy of Religion and its Challenges.* Oxford: Oxford University Press.
Nagel, Thomas (1979), *Mortal Questions.* New York: Cambridge University Press.
Naiden, F. S. (2007), 'The fallacy of the willing victim', *Journal of Hellenic Studies* 127: 61–73.
Nam, Chang S. and Lyons, Joseph B. (2021), *Trust in Human-Robot Interaction.* London: Academic Press.
Narmour, Eugene (2011), 'Our varying histories and future potential: models and maps in science, the humanities, and in music theory', *Music Perception: An Interdisciplinary Journal* 29: 1–21.
Nel, Marius J. (2017), 'The conceptualisation of sin in the Gospel of Matthew', *In die Skriflig/In Luce Verbi* 51: 1–8.
Nelson, Janet L. (1990), 'The problematic in the private', *Social History* 15: 355–64.
Neugebauer, Fritz (1961), *In Christus: Eine Untersuchung zum paulinischen Glaubensverständnis.* Göttingen: Vandenhoeck & Ruprecht.
Neugebauer, Fritz (1970), 'Zur Deutung und Bedeutung des 1. Petrusbriefes', *New Testament Studies* 26: 61–86.
Neusner, Jacob (1984), *In Search of Talmudic Biography: The Problem of the Attributed Saying.* Chico, Calif.: Scholars Press.
Neusner, Jacob (1988a), *Why No Gospels in Talmudic Judaism?* Chico, Calif.: Scholars Press.
Neusner, Jacob (1988b), *The Incarnation of God: The Character of Divinity in Formative Judaism.* Philadelphia: Fortress.
Neusner, Jacob, Green, W. S., and Frerichs, Ernest eds (1987), *Judaisms and their Messiahs at the Turn of the Christian Era.* Cambridge: Cambridge University Press.
Newman, Carey C. (1992), *Paul's Glory-Christology: Tradition and Rhetoric.* Leiden: Brill.
Newman, Carey C. (1996), 'Election and predestination in Ephesians 1:4–6a: an exegetical-theological study of the historical, Christological realization of God's purpose', *Review and Expositor* 93: 237–47.
Newman, Carey C., Davila, James R., and Lewis, Gladys S. eds (1999), *The Jewish Roots of Christological Monotheism.* Leiden: Brill.

Newman, John Henry (1870), *An Essay in Aid of A Grammar of Assent*. New York: Catholic Publication Society.
Newman, Louis (1998), *Past Imperatives: Studies in the History and Theory of Jewish Ethics*. Albany, NY: State University of New York Press.
Newman, Paul W. (1987), *A Spirit Christology: Recovering the Biblical Paradigm of Christian Faith*. Lanham, Md: University Press of America.
Newsom, Carol A. (2020), 'In search of cultural models for divine spirit and human bodies', *Vetus Testamentum* 70: 104–23.
Neyrey, Jerome H. SJ (2007), *The Gospel of John*. Cambridge: Cambridge University Press.
Ngunjiri, Faith Wambura and Christo-Baker, E. Ann (2012), 'Breaking the stained glass ceiling: African women's leadership in religious organizations', *The Journal of Pan African Studies* 5: 1–4.
Ngunjiri, Faith Wambura, Gramby-Sobukwe, Faith, and Williams-Gegner, Kimberly (2012), 'Tempered radicals: black women's leadership in the church and commmunity', *The Journal of Pan African Studies* 5: 84–109.
Nichols, James H. (2014), *"Georgias" and "Phaedrus": Rhetoric, Philosophy, and Politics*. Ithaca, NY: Cornell University Press.
Nicholson, E. W. (1986), *God and his People: Covenant and Theology in the Old Testament*. Oxford: Oxford University Press.
Niebuhr, H. Richard (1941), *The Meaning of Revelation*. New York: Macmillan.
Niebuhr, H. Richard (1989), *Faith on Earth: An Inquiry into the Structure of Human Faith*. New Haven: Yale University Press.
Niehoff, Maren (2003), 'Circumcision as a marker of identity: Philo, Origen and the rabbis on Gen. 17:1–14', *Jewish Studies Quarterly* 10: 89–123.
Niezwiedzki, Tomasz (2016), *Joseph's Two Garments: The Reception of Joseph in Targum Neofiti*. Leiden: Brill.
Noddings, Nel (1984), *Caring: A Feminist Approach to Ethics and Moral Education*. Berkeley: University of California Press.
Noffke, Eric (2007), 'Man of glory or first sinner? Adam in the book of Sirach', *Zeitschrift für die alttestamentliche Wissenschaft* 119: 618–24.
Nolland, John (1986) 'Grace as power', *Novum Testamentum* 28: 26–31.
Nolland, John (1989), *Luke 1–9.20*. Dallas: Word Books.
Nordmann, Alfred (2012), 'Another parting of the ways: intersubjectivity and the objectivity of science', *Studies in the History and Philosophy of Science* 43: 38–46.
Nörr, D. (1989), *Aspekte des römischen Völkerrechts: Die Bronzetafel von Alcáantara*. Munich: Verlag der Bayerischen Akademie der Wissenschaften.
Novenson, Matthew V. (2012), *Christ among the Messiahs: Christ Language in Paul and Messiah Language in Ancient Judaism*. Oxford: Oxford University Press.
Novick, Peter (1988), *That Noble Dream: The 'Objectivity' Question and the American Historical Profession*. Cambridge: Cambridge University Press.
Novick, Tzvi (2010), *What is Good, and What God Demands: Normative Structures in Tannaitic Literature*. Leiden: Brill.
Oakes, Peter (2018), '*Pistis* as a relational way of life in Galatians', *Journal for the Study of the New Testament* 40: 255–75.
Oakeshott, Philip (2015), *Jesus on Stage: John's Gospel and Greek Tragedy*. Bloomington, Ind.: AuthorHouse.
Obatusin, Oluwasegun and Ritter-Williams, Debbie (2019), 'A phenomenological study of employer perspectives on hiring ex-offenders', *Cogent Social Sciences* 5: 1571730.
O'Brien, Peter Thomas (1991), *The Epistle to the Philippians: A Commentary on the Greek Text*. Grand Rapids, Mich.: Eerdmans.

O'Brien Wicker. K. (1978), '*Mulierum virtutes (Moralia* 242e-263c)', in H. D. Betz ed., *Plutarch's Ethical Writing and Early Christian Literature.* Leiden: Brill: 106–34.

Ockelford, Adam (1999), *The Cognition of Order in Music: A Metacognitive Study.* London: Centre for Advanced Studies in Music Education.

O'Collins, Gerald (2016), *Revelation: Towards a Christian Interpretation of God's Self-Revelation in Jesus Christ.* Oxford: Oxford University Press.

O'Collins, Gerald and Kendall, Daniel (1992), 'The faith of Jesus', *Theological Studies* 53: 403–23.

Oepke, A. (1964), '*Epistatēs*', in Gerhard Kittel and Gerhard Friedrich eds, *Theological Dictionary of the New Testament* vol. 2. Grand Rapids, Mich.: Eerdmans: 622–3.

Olivares, Carlos (2015), 'The term *oligopistos* (little faith) in Matthew's gospel: narrative and thematic connections', *Colloquium* 47: 274–91.

Ollenburger, Ben C. (1986), 'What Krister Stendahl "meant"—a normative critique of "descriptive biblical theology"', *Horizons in Biblical Theology* 8: 61–98.

Olson, Paul J. and Beckwith, David (2008), 'Any given Sunday: weekly church attendance in a Midwestern city', *Journal for the Scientific Study of Religion* 47: 443–61.

Oluwaniyi, Oluwatoyin O. (2012), 'No more glass ceiling? Negotiating women's leadership role in eternal sacred order of Cherubim and Seraphim', *Journal of Pan African Studies* 5: 128–49.

O'Neal, Gary E. (2013), 'Bringing many sons to glory: the *archēgos* motif in the Letter to the Hebrews', Ph.D. dissertation, Mid-America Baptist Theological Seminary.

O'Neill, Onora (2002), *A Question of Trust.* Cambridge: Cambridge University Press.

Onians, R. B. (1954), *The Origins of European Thought about the Body, the Mind, the Soul, the World, Time, and Fate.* Cambridge: Cambridge University Press.

Oom-Dove, Sherrema A. (2018), 'Revivalist women's submission: women's spiritual authority, biblical feminism and cosmofeminism', *Women's Studies International Forum* 67: 118–27.

Orr, Peter (2018), *Exalted Above the Heavens: The Risen and Ascended Christ.* Nottingham: Apollos.

Ostenfeld, Erik Nils (2018), *Ancient Greek Psychology and the Modern Mind-Body Debate.* 2nd edn. Baden-Baden: Academia.

Oswalt, John N. (1998), *The Book of Isaiah: Chapters 40–66.* Grand Rapids, Mich.: Eerdmans.

Outka, Paul (1972), *Agapē: An Ethical Analysis.* New Haven: Yale University Press.

Pace, Michael (2017), 'The strength of faith and trust', *International Journal for Philosophy of Religion* 81: 135–50.

Pace, Michael (2020), 'Trusting in order to inspire trustworthiness', *Synthese* 198: 11897–11923.

Pace, Michael and McKaughan, Daniel J. (2020), 'Judaeo-Christian faith as trust and loyalty', *Religious Studies*: 56: 1–31.

Painter, John (2000), *1, 2, and 3 John.* Collegeville, Minn.: Liturgical Press.

Palmer, T. N. and Hardaker, P. J. eds (2011), *Handling Uncertainty in Science.* London: The Royal Society.

Pannenberg, Wolfhart, Rendtorff, Rolf, Rendtorff, Trutz, and Wilckens, Ulrich (1969), *Revelation as History.* New York: Macmillan.

Parker, Robert (2004), 'What are sacred laws?' in E. Harris and L. Rubinstein eds, *The Law and the Courts in Ancient Greece.* London: Duckbacks: 57–70.

Parker, Robert (2011), *On Greek Religion.* Ithaca, NY: Cornell University Press.

Patterson, Cynthia (1985), '"Not worth the rearing": the causes of infant exposure in ancient Greece', *Transactions of the American Philological Association* 115: 103–23.

Patterson, William (2016), 'The problem of evil and liberal theologies', *Essays in the Philosophy of Humanism* 24: 187–205.
Paul, Gregory (2009), 'The chronic dependence of popular religiosity upon dysfunctional psychosociological conditions', *Evolutionary Psychology* 7: 398–441.
Pawar, Sheela (2016), *Trusting Others, Trusting God: Concepts of Belief, Faith and Rationality*. Abingdon: Routledge.
Pelikan, Jaroslav (1971), *Historical Theology: Continuity and Change in Christian Doctrine*. London: Hutchinson.
Pelkmans, Mathijs (2013), *Ethnographies of Doubt: Faith and Uncertainty in Contemporary Societies*. London: I. B. Tauris & Co.
Pelling, Christopher (1988), 'Aspects of Plutarch's characterization', *Illinois Classical Studies* 13: 257–74.
Pelling, Christopher (1995), 'The moralism of Plutarch's *Lives*', in Doreen C. Innes, H. Hine, and Christopher Pelling eds, *Ethics and Rhetoric: Classical Essays for Donald Russell on his Seventy-Fifth Birthday*. Oxford: Oxford University Press: 205–20.
Peng-Keller, Simon and Hunziker, Andreas (2011), 'Gott vertrauen', *Unimagazin* 20: 40–1.
Pennington, Jonathan T. (2012), *Reading the Gospels Wisely: A Narrative and Theological Introduction*. Grand Rapids, Mich.: Baker Academic.
Peppard, M. (2011), *The Son of God in the Roman World*. Oxford: Oxford University Press.
Perdue, Leo G., Morgan, Robert, and Sommer, Benjamin D. (2009), *Biblical Theology: Introducing the Conversation*. Nashville: Abingdon.
Pervo, Richard I. (2009), *Acts: A Commentary*. Minneapolis: Fortress.
Petridou, Georgia (2016), *Divine Epiphany in Greek Literature and Culture*. Oxford: Oxford University Press.
Petrovic, Andrej and Petrovic, Ivana (2016), *Inner Purity and Pollution*. Oxford: Oxford University Press.
Petrucci, Federico M. (2017), *Plato on Virtue in the Menexenus*. Cambridge: Cambridge University Press.
Phillips, D. Z. (1988), *Faith after Foundationalism*. London: Routledge.
Phillips, D. Z. (1995), *After Foundationalism: Critiques and Alternatives*. Boulder, Colo.: Westview.
Phillips, D. Z. (2002), 'On trusting intellectuals on trust', *Philosophical Investigations* 25: 33–53.
Pickett, Raymond (2005), 'Following Jesus in Galilee: resurrection as empowerment in the gospel of Mark', *Currents in Theology and Mission* 32: 434–44.
Pinnock, Clark, Rice, Richard, Sanders, John, Hasker, William, and Basinger, David (1994), *The Openness of God: A Biblical Challenge to the Traditional Understanding of God*. Downers Grove, Ill.: InterVarsity.
Pirutinsky, Steven and Rosmarin, David (2020), 'My God, why have you abandoned me? Sexual abuse and attitudes towards God among Orthodox Jews', *Mental Health, Religion and Culture* 23: 579–90.
Pitre, Brant James (2005), *Jesus, the Tribulation, and the End of Exile: Restoration Eschatology and the Origin of the Atonement*. Tübingen: Mohr Siebeck.
Pitre, Brant James (2019), *Paul, a New Covenant Jew: Rethinking Pauline Theology*. Grand Rapids, Mich.: Eerdmans.
Pitre, Brant James, Barber, Michael Patrick, and Kincaid, John A. eds (2019), *Paul, a New Covenant Jew: Rethinking Pauline Theology*. Grand Rapids, Mich.: Eerdmans.
Pitts, Andrew W. (2020), 'The Fowler fallacy: biography, history, and the genre of Luke-Acts', *Journal of Biblical Literature* 139: 341–59.

Plantinga, Alvin (1983), 'Reason and belief in God', in Alvin Plantinga and Nicholas Wolterstorff eds, *Faith and Rationality: Reason and Belief in God*. Notre Dame, Ind.: University of Notre Dame Press: 16-93.

Plantinga, Alvin and Wolterstorff, Nicholas eds (1983), *Faith and Rationality: Reason and Belief in God*. Notre Dame, Ind.: University of Notre Dame Press.

Platt, Verity (2011), *Facing the Gods: Epiphany and Representation in Graeco-Roman Art, Literature and Religion*. Cambridge: Cambridge University Press.

Plevan, William (2009), 'Meet the new Paul, same as the old Paul', *CrossCurrents* 59: 217-28.

Plisch, U.-K. (1999), 'Probleme und Lösungen: Bemerkungen zu einer Neuübersetzung des Thomasevangeliums (NHC 11,2)', in S. Emmel et al. eds, *Ägypten und Nubien in spätantiker und christlicher Zeit: Akten des 6. Internationalen Koptologenkongressen in Münster 20.-26 Juli 1996*. Wiesbaden: Reichert: II.523-8.

Plummer, Alfred (1989), *The Gospel According to S. Luke*. London: Bloomsbury.

Pojman, L. (1986), 'Faith without belief?', *Faith and Philosophy* 3: 157-76.

Polanyi, Michael (1962), *Personal Knowledge: Towards a Post-Critical Philosophy*. London: Routledge and Keegan Paul.

Polaski, Donald C. (1998), 'Reflections on a Mosaic covenant: the eternal covenant (Isaiah 24.5) and intertextuality', *Journal for the Study of the Old Testament* 77: 55-73.

Polish, David (1985), 'Covenant—Jewish universalism and particularism', *Judaism* 34: 284-300.

Polkinghorne, John (2000), *Faith, Science, and Understanding*. New Haven: Yale University Press.

Polkinghorne, John ed. (2010), *The Trinity and an Entangled World: Relationality in Physical Science and Theology*. Grand Rapids, Mich.: Eerdmans.

Poorthuis, Marcel and Schwartz, Joshua eds (2004), *Saints and Role Models in Judaism and Christianity*. Leiden: Brill.

Pope, Michael (2018), 'Peircean faith: perception, trust, and religious belief in the conduct of life', *Transactions of the Charles S. Peirce Society* 54: 457-79.

Popper, Karl (1963), *Conjectures and Refutations: The Growth of Scientific Knowledge*. London: Routledge.

Popper, Karl (1973), *Objective Knowledge: An Evolutionary Approach*. Oxford: Oxford University Press.

Popper, Karl (1980), *The Logic of Scientific Discovery*. London: Hutchinson.

Popper, Karl (2002), *The Poverty of Historicism*. 2nd edn. London: Routledge.

Porter, Stanley E. (2003), 'The concept of covenant in Paul', in Stanley E. Porter and Jaqueline C. R. de Roo eds, *The Concept of Covenant in the Second Temple Period*. Leiden: Brill: 269-86.

Porter, Stanley E. ed. (2006), *Paul and his Theology*. Leiden: Brill.

Porter, Stanley E. ed. (2008), *Paul: Jew, Greek, and Roman*. Leiden: Brill.

Porter, Stanley E. and de Roo, Jacqueline C. R. eds (2003), *The Concept of Covenant in the Second Temple Period*. Leiden: Brill.

Porter, Stanley E. and Stanley, Christopher D. (2008), *As it is Written: Studying Paul's Use of Scripture*. Leiden: Brill.

Porterfield, Amanda (2005), *Healing in the History of Christianity*. Oxford: Oxford University Press.

Porúbčan, Štefan (1963), *Sin in the Old Testament: A Soteriological Study*. Rome: Herder.

Pratt Morris-Chapman, Daniel (2007), *Nonfoundationalism Considered as a Handmaiden for Theology*. Burbage: William Wathes and Sons.

Price, S. R. F. (1984), *Rituals and Power: The Roman Imperial Cult in Asia Minor*. Cambridge: Cambridge University Press.

Putnam, Robert D. (2000), *Bowling Alone: The Collapse and Revival of American Community*. New York: Simon and Schuster.
Putthoff, Tyson L. (2020), *Gods and Humans in the Ancient Near East*. Cambridge: Cambridge University Press.
Quell, G. (1964), '*Dikē* etc.', in Gerhard Kittel and Gerhard Friedrich eds, *Theological Dictionary of the New Testament* vol. 2. Grand Rapids, Mich.: Eerdmans: 174–8.
Rabens, Volker (2013), *The Holy Spirit and Ethics in Paul: Transformation and Empowering for Religious-Ethical Life*. 2nd edn. Tübingen: Mohr Siebeck.
Rabie-Boshoff, Annelien C. and Buitendag, Johan (2020), 'Jesus: divine relationality and suffering creation', *HTS Teologiese Studies* 76: art. 6128.
Räisänen, Heikki (1985), 'Galatians 2.16 and Paul's break with Judaism', *New Testament Studies* 31: 543–53.
Räisänen, Heikki (1987), 'Paul's conversion and the development of his view of the law', *New Testament Studies* 33: 404–19.
Räisänen, Heikki (2000), *Beyond New Testament Theology: A Story and a Programme*. 2nd edn. London: SCM.
Ratcliffe, Matthew, Ruddell, Mark, and Smith, Benedict (2014), 'What is a "sense of foreshortened future"? A phenomenological study of trauma, trust, and time', *Frontiers in Psychology* 5: art. 1026.
Rath, Beth A. (2017), 'Christ's faith, doubt, and the cry of dereliction', *International Journal for Philosophy of Religion* 81: 161–9.
Ratzsch, Del (2011), 'Science and religion', in Thomas P. Flint and Michael C. Rea eds, *The Oxford Handbook of Philosophical Theology*. Oxford: Oxford University Press: 54–78.
Rayburn, Robert Gibson II (2019), *'Yesterday, Today and Forever': The Narrative World of [Ps.] 94 (Ps. 95) as a Hermeneutical Key to Hebrews*. Berlin: Peter Lang.
Remus, Harold (1983), *Pagan–Christian Conflict over Miracle in the Second Century*. Cambridge, Mass.: Philadelphia Patristic Foundation.
Renberg, Gil. H. (2016), *Where Dreams May Come: Incubation Sanctuaries in the Greco-Roman World*. Leiden: Brill.
Rendtorff, R. (1989), 'Covenant as a structuring concept in Genesis and Exodus', *Journal of Biblical Literature* 108: 385–93.
Rendtorff, R. (1993), 'Where were you when I laid the foundation of the earth?" Creation and salvation history', in *Canon and Theology: Overtures to an Old Testament Theology*. Minneapolis: Fortress: 102–17.
Rengstorf, Karl Heinrich (1964), 'Apostolos', in Gerhard Kittel and Gerhard Friedrich eds, *Theological Dictionary of the New Testament* vol. 1. Grand Rapids, Mich.: Eerdmans: 407–46.
Reumann, John Henry Paul (1999), 'Justification and justice in the New Testament', *Horizons in Biblical Theology* 2: 26–45.
Reumann, John Henry Paul (2008), *Philippians: A New Translation with Introduction and Commentary*. New Haven: Yale University Press.
Reynolds, Benjamin E., Lugioyo, Brian, and Vanhoozer, Kevin J. eds (2014), *Reconsidering the Relationship between Biblical and Systematic Theology in the New Testament: Essays by Theologians and New Testament Scholars*. Tübingen: Mohr Siebeck.
Reynolds, Scott (2016), *The Messiah and Eschatology in the Psalms of Solomon*. Langley: Trinity Western University Press.
Reynolds, Thomas E. (2012), 'Theology and disability: changing the conversation', *Journal of Religion, Disability and Health* 16: 33–48.
Rhee, Victor (2001), *Faith in Hebrews: Analysis within the Context of Christology, Eschatology, and Ethics*. New York: Peter Lang.

Rice, Richard (1985), *God's Foreknowledge and Man's Free Will*. Minneapolis: Bethany House.
Rice, R. L. H., McKaughan, D., and Howard-Snyder, D. (2017), 'Approaches to faith', editorial preface, *International Journal for Philosophy of Religion* 81: 1–6.
Richard, Earl (1995), *First and Second Thessalonians*. Collegeville, Minn.: Liturgical Press.
Richardson, Christopher A. (2012), *Pioneer and Perfecter of Faith: Jesus' Faith as the Climax of Israel's History in the Letter to the Hebrews*. Tübingen: Mohr Siebeck.
Riches, John (1994), 'A future for New Testament theology?', *Literature and Theology* 8: 343–53.
Riches, John (2010), 'Review article: seeking the identity of Jesus', *Journal for the Study of the New Testament* 32: 347–62.
Ricoeur, Paul (1965), *History and Truth*. Chicago: Chicago University Press.
Ricoeur, Paul (2004), *Memory, History, Forgetting*. Chicago/London: University of Chicago Press.
Ricotta, Daniela (2007), *Il Logos, in verità, è amore: introduzione filosofica alla teologia di Pierangelo Sequeri*. Milan: Ancora.
Ridley, Aaron (2003), 'Against musical ontology', *Journal of Philosophy* 100: 203–20.
Riesner, Rainer (2003), 'Back to the historical Jesus through Paul and his school (the Ransom Logion—Mark 10.45; Matthew 20.28), *Journal for the Study of the Historical Jesus* 1: 171–99.
Rispoli, Gioia Maria (1974), 'Filodemo sulla musica', *Cronache Ercolensi* 4: 57–87.
Rissler, James D. (2006), 'Open theism: does God risk or hope?' *Religious Studies* 42: 63–74.
Rivkin, Ellis (1984), *What Crucified Jesus? Messianism, Pharisaism, and the Development of Christianity*. Nashville: Abingdon.
Rizzuto, Ana-María (1970), 'Critique of the contemporary literature in the scientific study of religion', paper read at the annual meeting of the Society for the Scientific Study of Religion, New York.
Rizzuto, Ana-María (1979), *The Birth of the Living God: A Psychoanalytic Study*. Chicago: University of Chicago Press.
Rizzuto, Ana-María (1982), 'The father and child's representation of God: a developmental approach', in S. Cath, A. Gurwitt, and J. Ross eds, *Father and Child: Developmental and Clinical Perspectives*. Boston: Little, Brown: 357–81.
Rizzuto, Ana-María (2001), 'Religious development beyond the modern paradigm discussion: the psychoanalytic point of view', *International Journal for the Psychology of Religion* 11: 201–14.
Robertson, Archibald and Plummer, Alfred (1912), *The First Epistle of Saint Paul to the Corinthians*. Edinburgh: T&T Clark.
Robertson, Jon M. (2007), *Christ as Mediator: A Study of the Theologies of Eusebius of Caesarea, Marcellus of Ancyra, and Athanasius of Alexandria*. New York: Oxford University Press.
Roetzel, Calvin J. (1972), *Judgement in the Community: A Study of the Relationship between Ecclesiology and Eschatology in Paul*. Leiden: Brill.
Rohrbacher, David (2010), 'Physiognomics in imperial Latin biography', *Classical Antiquity* 29: 92–116.
Roller, Matthew (2018), *Models from the Past in Roman Culture: A World of Exempla*. Cambridge: Cambridge University Press.
Rose, D. (2011), *The Moral Foundations of Economic Behavior*. Oxford: Oxford University Press.
Rose, Herbert Jennings and Scheid, John (2014), 'Romulus and Remus', in Simon Hornblower, Antony Spawforth, and Esther Eidinow eds, *The Oxford Companion to Classical Civilization*. 2nd edn. Oxford: Oxford University Press.

Rose, Martha L. (2003), *The Staff of Oedipus: Transforming Disability in Ancient Greece*. Ann Arbor: University of Michigan Press.
Rosmarin, David H., Pargament, Kenneth I., and Mahoney, Annette (2009), 'The role of religiousness in anxiety, depression, and happiness in a Jewish community sample: a preliminary investigation', *Mental Health, Religion and Culture* 12: 97–113.
Rosmarin, David H., Pirutinsky, S., and Pargament (2011), 'A brief measure of core religious beliefs for use in psychiatric settings', *International Journal of Psychiatry in Medicine* 41: 253–61.
Rosmarin, David H., Pirutinsky, Steven, Pargament, Kenneth I., and Krumrei, Elizabeth J. (2009), 'Are religious beliefs relevant to mental health among Jews?', *Psychology of Religion and Spirituality* 3: 180–90.
Rosner, Brian S. (1994), *Paul, Scripture, and Ethics: A Study of 1 Corinthians 5–7*. Leiden: Brill.
Rosner, Brian S. (2017), *Known by God: A Biblical Theology of Personal Identity*. Grand Rapids, Mich.: Zondervan.
Roth, Dieter (2014), 'What *en tō kosmō* are the *stoicheia tou kosmou*?' *HTS Teologiese Studies* 70: art. 2676.
Rouché, Charlotte (1984), 'Acclamations in the later Roman empire: new evidence for Aphrodisias', *Journal of Roman Studies* 74: 181–99.
Rousseau, D. M., Sitkin, S. B., Burt, R. S., and Camerer, C. (1998), 'Not so different after all: a cross-discipline view of trust', *Academy of Management Review* 23: 393–404.
Rousselot, Pierre(1990), *The Eyes of Faith*. New York: Fordham University Press.
Rowe, C. Kavin (2006), *Early Narrative Christology: The Lord in the Gospel of Luke*. Berlin: De Gruyter.
Rowland, Christopher (1985), *Christian Origins: An Account of the Setting and Character of the Most Important Messianic Sect of Judaism*. London: SPCK.
Rowland, Christopher and Tuckett, Christopher eds (2006), *The Nature of New Testament Theology: Essays in Honour of Robert Morgan*. Oxford: Blackwell.
Rublak, Ulinka (2012), 'The status of historical knowledge', in Ulinka Rublack ed., *A Concise Companion to History*. Oxford: Oxford University Press: 57–80.
Ruddick, S. (2002), 'An appreciation of *Love's Labor*', *Hypatia* 17: 214–24.
Rundin, John S. (2004), 'Pozo Moro, child sacrifice, and the Greek legendary tradition', *Journal of Biblical Literature* 123: 425–47.
Rüpke, Jörg (2014), *From Jupiter to Christ: On the History of Religion in the Roman Imperial Period*. Oxford: Oxford University Press.
Russell, Amy (2015), *The Politics of Public Space in Republican Rome*. Cambridge: Cambridge University Press.
Rutgers, L. V., van der Horst, P. W., Havelaar, H. W., and Teugel, L. eds (1999), *The Use of Sacred Books in the Ancient World*. Leuven: Peeters.
Ruthven, J. (2000). 'The "Imitation of Christ" in Christian Tradition: Its Missing Charismatic Emphasis', *Journal of Pentecostal Theology*, 8: 60–78.
Ryan, Eugene E. (2003), 'Aristotle's rhetoric and ethics and the ethos of society', *Greek, Roman, and Byzantine Studies* 13: 291–308.
St-Pierre, Céline (2001), 'Religion, sécularité, foi chrétienne chez les 20-30 ans', Ph.D. dissertation, Montreal University.
Salier, W. (2009), 'The obedient son: the "faithfulness" of Christ in the fourth gospel', in Michael F. Bird and Preston M. Sprinkle eds, *The Faith of Jesus Christ: Exegetical, Biblical, and Theological Studies*. Milton Keynes: Paternoster: 223–38.
Saliers, Don (2007), *Music and Theology*. Nashville: Abingdon.
Saller, Richard P. (1982), *Personal Patronage in the Early Empire*. Cambridge: Cambridge University Press.

Sanders, E. P. (1983), *Paul, the Law, and the Jewish People*. London: SCM.
Sanders, E. P. (1992), *Judaism: Practice and Belief 63 BCE–66 CE*. London: SCM.
Sanders, E. P. (2017), *Paul and Palestinian Judaism*. 40th anniversary edn. Minneapolis: Fortress.
Sandnes, Karl Olav (1991), *Paul—One of the Prophets? A Contribution to the Apostle's Self-Understanding*. Tübingen: Mohr Siebeck.
Sang, Barry R. (2007), 'A nexus of care: process theology and care ethics', *Process Studies* 36: 229–44.
Sauter, Gerhard and Barton, John eds (2000), *Revelation and Story: Narrative Theology and the Centrality of Story*. Aldershot: Ashgate.
Savage, Timothy B. (1996), *Power Through Weakness: Paul's Understanding of the Christian Ministry in 2 Corinthians*. Cambridge: Cambridge University Press.
Sawyer, John F. A. (2018), *Isaiah Through the Centuries*. Hoboken: Wiley Blackwell.
Scanlon, T. M. (1998), *What We Owe To Each Other*. Cambridge, Mass.: Harvard University Press.
Schaeder, H. H., (1967), '*Nazarēnos, Nazōraios*', in Gerhard Kittel and Gerhard Friedrich eds, *Theological Dictionary of the New Testament* vol. 4. Grand Rapids, Mich.: Eerdmans: 874–9.
Schaefer, Jame (2005), 'Valuing earth intrinsically and instrumentally: a theological framework for environmental ethics', *Theological Studies* 66: 783–814.
Schaper, Joachim (2010), 'The Messiah in the garden: John 19.38-41, (royal) gardens, and messianic concepts', in Markus Bockmuehl and Guy G. Stroumsa eds, *Paradise in Antiquity: Jewish and Christian Views*. Cambridge: Cambridge University Press: 17–27.
Schellenberg, J. L. (2005), *Prolegomena to a Philosophy of Religion*. Ithaca, NY: Cornell University Press.
Schellenberg, J. L. (2013), *Evolutionary Religion*. Oxford: Oxford University Press.
Schenk, Wolfgang (1984), *Die Philipperbriefe des Paulus: Kommentar*. Stuttgart: W. Kohlhammer.
Schertz, M. H. (1994), 'God's cross and women's questions: a biblical perspective on the atonement', *Mennonite Quarterly Review* 68: 194–208.
Schillebeeckx, Edward (1979), *Jesus: An Experiment in Christology*. London: Collins.
Schillebeeckx, Edward and van Iersel, Bas eds (1973), *Truth and Certainty*. London: Burns and Oates.
Schliesser, Benjamin (2007), *Abraham's Faith in Romans 4: Paul's Concept of Faith in Light of the History of Reception in Genesis 15:6*. Tübingen: Mohr Siebeck.
Schliesser, Benjamin (2012), '"Abraham did not 'doubt' in unbelief" (Rom. 4:20): faith, doubt, and dispute in Paul's letter to the Romans', *Journal of Theological Studies* 63: 492–522.
Schliesser, Benjamin (2021), *Zweifel: Phänomene des Zweifels und der Zweiseeligkeit im frühen Christentum*. Tübingen: Mohr Siebeck.
Schmid, H. H. (1984), 'Creation, righteousness, and salvation: "Creation theology" as the broad horizon of biblical theology', in B. W. Anderson ed., *Creation in the Old Testament*. London: SCM.
Schmidt, Peter (1993), *How to Read the Gospels: Historicity and Truth in the Gospels and Acts*. London: St Pauls.
Schmiedel, Ulrich (2014), 'Vertrauen Verstanden? Zur Vertrauenstrilogie von Ingolf U. Dalferth und Simon Peng-Keller', *Neue Zeitschrift für systematische Theologie und Religionsphilosophie* 56: 379–92.
Schnabel, Eckhard J. (2017), 'Knowing the divine and divine knowledge in Greco-Roman religion', *Tyndale Bulletin* 68: 287–312.

Schnackenburg, Rudolf (1968-72), *The Gospel According to St John*. 3 vols. London: Burns and Oates.
Schnackenburg, Rudolf (1973), 'Christus, Geist und Gemeinde', in Barnabas Lindars and Stephen S. Smalley eds, *Christ and the Spirit in the New Testament: Studies in Honour of C. F. D. Moule*. Cambridge: Cambridge University Press: 279-96.
Schneider, Gerhard (1992), *Jesusüberlieferung und Christologie*. Leiden: Brill.
Schnelle, Udo (1998), *The History and Theology of the New Testament Writings*. London: SCM.
Schnelle, Udo (2009a), *Theology of the New Testament*. Grand Rapids, Mich.: Baker Academic.
Schnelle, Udo ed. (2009b), *The Letter to the Romans*. Leuven: Peeters.
Schnelle, Udo (2018), 'The person of Jesus Christ in the gospel of John', in Judith M. Lieu and Martinus C. de Boer eds, *The Oxford Handbook of Johannine Studies*. Oxford: Oxford University Press: 311-29.
Schniewind, Julius and Friedrich, Gerhard (1964), '*Epangelō* etc.', in Gerhard Kittel and Gerhard Friedrich eds, *Theological Dictionary of the New Testament* vol. 2. Grand Rapids, Mich.: Eerdmans: 576-86.
Schofer, Jonathan Wyn (2005), *The Making of a Sage: A Study in Rabbinic Ethics*. Madison: University of Wisconsin Press.
Schofer, Jonathan Wyn (2010), *Confronting Vulnerability: The Body and the Divine in Rabbinic Ethics*. Chicago: Chicago University Press.
Schofield, M. (1991), *The Stoic Idea of the City*. Cambridge: Cambridge University Press.
Schottroff, L. (1970), *Der glaubende und die feindliche Welt: Beobachtungen zum gnostischen Dualismus und seiner Bedeutung für Paulus und das Johannesevangelium*. Neukirchen-Vluyn: Neukirchener Verlag.
Schrage, Wolfgang (1991, 2001), *Der Erst Brief an die Korinther*. Zurich: Benziger.
Schramm, Holger (2005), *Mood Management durch Musik: Die altägliche Nutzung von Musik zur Regulierung von Stimmungen*. Cologne: Herbert von Halem.
Schreber, Daniel Paul (1973), *Denkwürdigkeiten eines Neuvenkranken*. Berlin: Samuel Weber.
Schreiber, Johannes (1967), *Theologie des Vertrauens: Eine redaktionsgeschichtliche Untersuchung des Markusevangeliums*. Hamburg: Furche.
Schröter, Jens (1993), *Der versöhnte Versöhner: Paulus als unentbehrlicher Mittler im Heilsvorgang zwischen Gott und Gemeinde nach 2 Kor 2,14-7,4*. Tübingen: Franke.
Schröter, Jens (2013), *From Jesus to the New Testament: Early Christian Theology and the Origin of the New Testament Canon*. Waco, Tex.: Baylor University Press.
Schüle, Andreas (2015), 'The "eternal covenant" in the priestly Pentateuch and the major prophets', in Richard J. Bautch and Gary N. Knoppers, *Covenant in the Persian Period: From Genesis to Chronicles*. Philadelphia: Pennsylvania State University Press: 41-58.
Schürer, Emil, Vermes, G., and Millar, Fergus (1973-87), *The History of the Jewish People in the Age of Jesus Christ (173 B.C.—A.D. 135)*. Rev. edn. 3 vols. Edinburgh: T&T Clark.
Schürmann, Heinz (1964), 'Der "Bericht vom Anfang": Ein Rekonstruktionsversuch auf Grund vom Lk. 4.14-16', *Studia Evangelica* 2: 242-58.
Schüssler Fiorenza, Elisabeth (1999), *Rhetoric and Ethics: The Politics of Biblical Studies*. Minneapolis: Fortress.
Schütz, John Howard (1975), *Paul and the Anatomy of Apostolic Authority*. Cambridge: Cambridge University Press.
Schweizer, Eduard (1952), 'The Spirit of power: the uniformity and diversity of the concept of the Holy Spirit in the New Testament', *Interpretation* 6: 259-78.
Schweizer, Eduard (1969), '*Pneuma* in the New Testament', in Gerhard Friedrich and Gerhard Kittel eds, *Theological Dictionary of the New Testament* vol. 6. Grand Rapids, Mich.: Eerdmans: 398-455.

Schweizer, Eduard (1978), *The Holy Spirit*. London: SCM.
Schwitzgebel, Eric (2019), 'Belief', in Edward N. Zalta ed., *The Stanford Encyclopaedia of Philosophy*. Fall 2019 edn. <https://plato.stanford.edu/archives/fall2019/entries/belief>.
Schwöbel, Christoph (2020), 'Mutual resonances: remarks on the relationship between music and theology', *International Journal for the Study of the Christian Church* 1: 8–22.
Scruton, Roger (1997), *The Aesthetics of Music*. New York: Oxford University Press.
Scruton, Roger (2016), *Understanding Music: Philosophy and Interpretation*. London: Bloomsbury.
Scully, Diana (1988), 'Convicted rapists' perceptions of self and victim: role taking and emotions', *Gender and Society* 2: 200–213.
Segal, Alan (1977), *Two Powers in Heaven: Early Rabbinic Reports about Christianity and Gnosticism*. Leiden: Brill.
Seifrid, Mark A. (2000), 'The "new perspective on Paul" and its problems', *Themelios* 25: 4–18.
Seifrid, Mark A. (2009), 'The faith of Christ', in Michael F. Bird and Preston M. Sprinkle eds, *The Faith of Jesus Christ: Exegetical, Biblical, and Theological Studies*. Milton Keynes: Paternoster: 129–46.
Seifrid, Mark A. (2014), *The Second Letter to the Corinthians*. The Pillar New Testament Commentary. Grand Rapids, Mich.: Eerdmans.
Seils, Martin (1996), *Glaube*. Gütersloh: Gütersloher Verlagshaus.
Seldon, A. (2009), *Trust: How We Lost It and How To Get It Back*. London: Biteback.
Senior, Donald C., CP and Harrington, Daniel J., SJ (2003), *1 Peter, Jude and 2 Peter*. Collegeville, Minn.: Liturgical Press.
Sequeri, Pierangelo (1993), *Estetica e teologica: l'indicibile emozione del Sacro. R. Otto, A. Schönberg, M. Heidegger*. Milan: Glossa.
Sequeri, Pierangelo (1996), *Il Dio affidabile: saggio di teologia fondamentale*. Brescia: Queriniana.
Sequeri, Pierangelo (2002), *L'idea della fede: trattato di teologia fondamentale*. Milan: Glossa.
Sequeri, Pierangelo (2007), *Teología fundamental: la idea de la fe*. Salamanca: Ediciones Sígueme.
Serafine, Mary Louise (1988), *Music as Cognition: The Development of Thought in Sound*. New York: Columbia University Press.
Sering, Richard E. (2000), 'Reclamation through trust: a program for ex-offenders', *Christian Century* 6 Dec.: 1263–4.
Sessions, William Ladd (1994), *The Concept of Faith: A Philosophical Investigation*. Ithaca, NY: Cornell Univeristy Press.
Sevenhuijsen, Selma (1998), *Citizenship and the Ethics of Care: Feminist Considerations on Justice, Morality, and Politics*. London: Routledge.
Shapira, Haim (2015), *"For the Judgment is God's": Human Judgment and Divine Justice in the Hebrew Bible and in Jewish Tradition*. Cambridge: Cambridge University Press.
Shaw, David A. (2013), 'Apocalyptic and covenant: perspectives on Paul or antimonies at war?', *Journal for the Study of the New Testament* 36: 155–71.
Shelton, J. B. (1991), *Mighty in Word and Deed: The Role of the Holy Spirit in Luke-Acts*. Peabody, NY: Hendrickson.
Sheppard, B. and Sherman, D. (1998), 'The grammars of trust: a model and general implications', *Academy of Management Review*, 23: 422–37.
Sherman, Steven B. (2008), *Revitalizing Theological Epistemology: Holistic Evangelical Approaches to the Knowledge of God*. Cambridge: James Clarke and Co.
Sherwin, Byron L. (2009), *Faith Finding Meaning: A Theology of Judaism*. Oxford: Oxford University Press.

Shin, Faith and Preston, Jesse L. (2021), 'Green as the gospel: the power of stewardship messages to improve climate change attitudes', *Psychology of Religion and Spirituality* 13: 437–47.
Shin, Sookgoo (2019), *Ethics in the Gospel of John: Discipleship as Moral Progress*. Leiden: Brill.
Shively, Elizabeth (2020), 'A critique of Richard Burridge's genre theory: from a one-dimensional to a multi-dimensional approach to gospel genre', in Robert Matthew Calhoun, David P. Moessner, and Tobias Nicklas eds, *Modern and Ancient Literary Criticism of the Gospels: Continuing the Debate on Gospel Genre(s)*. Tübingen: Mohr Siebeck: 97–112.
Sieber, Peter (1971), *Mit Christus leben: eine Studie zur paulinischen Auferstehungshoffnung*. Zurich: Theologischer Verlag.
Siker, Jeffrey (2020), *Sin in the New Testament*. New York: Oxford University Press.
Siliezar, Carlos Raúl Sosa (2015), *Creation Imagery in the Gospel of John*. London: Bloomsbury.
Simpson, Thomas W. (2012), 'What is trust?' *Pacific Philosophical Quarterly* 93: 550–69.
Simpson, Thomas W. (2013), 'Trustworthiness and moral character', *Ethical Theory and Moral Practice* 16: 543–57.
Skinner, C. W. ed. (2013), *Characters and Characterization in the Gospel of John*. London: Bloomsbury.
Skinner, John (1930), *A Critical and Exegetical Commentary on Genesis*. 2nd edn. Edinburgh: T&T Clark.
Sloboda, John A. (1985), *The Musical Mind: The Cognitive Psychology of Music*. Oxford: Oxford University Press.
Slote, Michael (2007), *The Ethics of Care and Empathy*. London: Routledge.
Slusser, Michael (1983), 'Primitive Christian soteriological themes', *Theological Studies* 44: 555–69.
Smalley, Stephen S. (2007), *1, 2, 3 John*. Rev edn. Nashville: Thomas Nelson.
Smart, Ninian (1996), *Dimensions of the Sacred: An Anatomy of the World's Beliefs*. London: HarperCollins.
Smit, Peter-Ben (2015), 'The end of early Christian adoptionism? A note on the invention of adoptionism, its sources, and its current demise', *International Journal of Philosophy and Theology* 76: 177–99.
Smith, Justin Marc (2015), *Why bios? On the Relationship between Gospel Genre and Implied Audience*. London: Bloomsbury.
Smith, Mark S. (2002), *The Early History of God: Yahweh and the Other Deities in Ancient Israel*. New York: Harper and Row.
Smith, Warren (1988), 'The disguises of the gods in *The Iliad*', *Numen* 35: 161–78.
Solberg, Mary M. (1997), *Compelling Knowledge: A Feminist Proposal for an Epistemology of the Cross*. New York: State University of New York Press.
Sorensen, E. (2002), *Possession and Exorcism in the New Testament and Early Christianity*. Tübingen: Mohr Siebeck.
Soulen, R. Kendall (1996), *The God of Israel and Christian Theology*. Minneapolis: Fortress.
Speaks, Jeff (2018), *The Greatest Possible Being*. Oxford: Oxford University Press.
Spencer, F. Scott (2005), '"Follow me": the imperious call of Jesus in the synoptic gospels', *Interpretation* 59: 142–53.
Spina, Frank Anthony (2005), *The Faith of the Outsider: Exclusion and Inclusion in the Biblical Story*. Grand Rapids, Mich.: Eerdmans.
Sreenivasan, Gopal (2020), *Emotion and Virtue*. Princeton: Princeton University Press.

Stack, Judith V. (2020), *Metaphor and the Portrayal of the Cause(s) of Sin and Evil in the Gospel of Matthew*. Leiden: Brill.
Stager, Lawrence and Wolff, Samuel R. (1984), 'Child sacrifice in Carthage: religious rite or population control?', *Journal of Biblical Archeological Review* 10: 31–46.
Stählin, G. (1973), '*Τὸ πνεῦμα Ἰησοῦ* (Apostelgeschichte 16:7)', in Barnabas Lindars and Stephen S. Smalley eds, *Christ and the Spirit in the New Testament: Studies in Honour of C. F. D. Moule*. Cambridge: Cambridge University Press: 229–52.
Staley, Jeffrey L. (1991), 'Stumbling in the dark, reaching for the light: reading character in John 5 and 9', *Semeia* 53: 55–80.
Stanley, Christopher D. (2012), *Paul and Scripture: Continuing the Conversation*. Atlanta: Society of Biblical Literature.
Stanton, Graham (1995), *Gospel Truth? New Light on Jesus and the Gospels*. London: HarperCollins.
Stanton, Graham (2002), *The Gospels and Jesus*. 2nd edn. Oxford: Oxford University Press.
Stanton, G., Longenecker, B. W., and Barton, S. C. eds (2004), *The Holy Spirit and Christian Origins: Essays in Honor of James D. G. Dunn*. Grand Rapids, Mich.: Eerdmans.
Stendahl, Krister (1962), 'Biblical theology, contemporary', *The Interpreter's Dictionary of the Bible*. Vol. 1. Nashville: Abingdon: 418–32.
Stendahl, Krister (1984), *Meanings: The Bible as Document and as Guide*. Philadelphia: Fortress.
Stephenson, Lisa P. (2011), 'Prophesying women and ruling men: women's religious authority in North American Pentecostalism', *Religions* 2: 410–26.
Sterling, Gregory E. (1992), *Historiography and Self-Definition: Josephus, Luke-Acts, and Apologetic Historiography*. Leiden: Brill.
Sterling, Gregory E. (2012), '"The image of God": becoming like God in Philo, Paul, and early Christianity', in Susan E. Myers ed., *Portraits of Jesus: Studies in Christology*. Tübingen: Mohr Siebeck: 157–73.
Stowers, S. K. (1989), '*Ek pisteōs* and *dia tēs pisteōs* in Romans 3:30', *Journal of Biblical Literature* 108: 665–74.
Stowers, S. K. (1994), *A Rereading of Romans: Justice, Jews, and Gentiles*. New Haven: Yale University Press.
Strange, James F. (1979), 'Archaeology and the religion of Judaism in Palestine', in Wolfgang Haase ed., *Aufstieg und Niedergang der römischen Welt* 19/1. Berlin: De Gruyter: 646–85.
Strange, James F. (2019), 'Archaeology of the gospels', in David K. Pettegrew, William R. Caraher, and Thomas W. Davis eds, *The Oxford Handbook of Early Christian Archaeology*. Oxford: Oxford University Press.
Strauss Clay, Jenny (2019), 'Hide and go seek: Hermes in Homer', in John F. Miller and Jenny Strauss Clay eds, *Tracking Hermes, Pursuing Mercury*. Oxford: Oxford University Press: 67–77.
Strawbridge, Jennifer (2015), *The Pauline Effect*. Berlin: De Gruyter.
Strawn, Brent and Bowen, Nancy P. eds (2003), *God So Near: Essays on Old Testament Theology in Honor of Patrick D. Miller*. Winona Lake, Ind.: Eisenbrauns.
Strecker, Georg ed. (1975), *Das Problem der Theologie des Neuen Testaments*. Darmstadt: WBG.
Strecker, Georg (1996), *The Johannine Letters*. Minneapolis: Fortress.
Strecker, Georg (2000), *Theology of the New Testament*. Berlin: De Gruyter.
Strecker, Georg (2010), 'Zugänge zum Unzugänglichen: "Geist" als Thema neutestamentlicher Wissenschaft', *Zeitschrift für Neues Testament* 25: 3–20.
Streufert, Mary J. (2006), 'Reclaiming Schleiermacher for twenty-first century atonement theory: the human and the divine in feminist Christology', *Feminist Theology* 15: 98–120.

Strotmann, Angelika (1991), *"Mein Vater bist Du" (Sir. 51.10): Zur Bedeutung der Vaterschaft Gottes in kanonischen und nichtkanonischen fruhjüdischen Schriften*. Frankfurt: Knecht.
Studebaker, John A. Jr. (2008), *The Lord is the Spirit: The Authority of the Holy Spirit in Contemporary Theology and Church Practice*. Eugene, Ore.: Pickwick Publications.
Stuhlmacher, Peter (1965), *Gerechtigkeit Gottes bei Paulus*. Göttingen: Vandenhoeck & Ruprecht.
Stuhlmacher, Peter (1979), 'The gospel of reconciliation in Christ: basic features and issues of a biblical theology of the New Testament', *Horizons in Biblical Theology* 1: 161–90.
Stuhlmacher, Peter (1983), 'Sühne oder Versöhnung?', in Ulrich Luz and Hans Weder eds, *Die Mitte des Neuen Testaments: Einheit und Vielfalt neutestamentlicher Theologie. Festschrift für Eduard Schweizer zum siebzigsten Geburtstag*. Göttingen: Vandenhoeck and Ruprecht: 291–316.
Stuhlmacher, Peter (1986), *Reconciliation, Law, and Righteousness: Essays in Biblical Theology*. Philadelphia: Fortress.
Stuhlmacher, Peter (1995), *How to do Biblical Theology*. Allison Park, Pa: Pickwick.
Stuhlmacher, Peter (2006), *Biblical Theology of the New Testament*. Grand Rapids, Mich.: Eerdmans.
Stump, Eleonore (2010), *Wandering in Darkness: Narrative and the Problem of Suffering*. Oxford: Oxford University Press.
Stump, Eleonore (2018), *Atonement*. Oxford: Oxford University Press.
Surlis, Paul ed. (1972), *Faith: Its Nature and Meaning*. Dublin: Gill and Macmillan.
Swinburne, Richard (2005), *Faith and Reason*. 2nd edn. Oxford: Oxford University Press.
Swinburne, Richard (2008), *Christian Philosophy in a Modern World*. Frankfurt: Ontos-Verlag.
Talbert, Charles H. (1993), '"And the word became flesh": when?', in Abraham J. Malherbe and Wayne A. Meeks eds, *The Future of Christology: Essays in Honor of Leander E. Keck*. Minneapolis: Fortress: 43–52.
Talbert, Charles H. (2007), *Ephesians and Colossians*. Grand Rapids, Mich.: Baker Academic.
Talbert, Charles H. (2011), *The Development of Christology during the First Hundred Years: And Other Essays on Early Christian Christology*. Leiden: Brill.
Tallent, Daniel (2012), '"Until God shall visit the earth": the role of covenant theology in the Qumran movement', MA thesis, University of Missouri.
Tannehill, Robert (1967), *Dying and Rising with Christ: A Study in Pauline Theology*. Berlin: Töpelmann.
Tannehill, Robert (1977), 'The disciples in Mark: the function of a narrative role', *Journal of Religion* 57: 386–405.
Tappenden, Frederick S. and Daniel-Hughes, Carly eds (2017), *Coming Back to Life: The Permeability of Past and Present Mortality and Immortality, Death and Life in the Ancient Mediterranean*. Montreal: McGill University Press.
Tasker, David (2004), *Ancient Near Eastern Literature and the Hebrew Scriptures about the Fatherhood of God*. New York: P. Lang.
Taylor, Joan (2018), *What Did Jesus Look Like?* London: Bloomsbury.
Taylor, Mark (2014), *1 Corinthians: An Exegetical and Theological Exposition of Holy Scripture*. Nashville: B&H Publishing.
Taylor, Vincent (1946), *Forgiveness and Reconciliation: A Study in New Testament Theology*. 2nd edn. London: Macmillan.
Taylor, Vincent (1952), *The Gospel According to St Mark: The Greek Text with Introduction, Notes, and Indexes*. London: Macmillan.

Taylor, Vincent (1958), *The Atonement in New Testament Teaching.* 3rd edn. London: Epworth.
Tenkorang, Eric Y., Owusu, Adobea Y., and Kundhi, Gubhinder (2018), 'Help-seeking behavior of female victims of intimate partner violence in Ghana: the role of trust and perceived risk of injury', *Journal of Family Violence* 33: 341–53.
Tennant, F. R. (1989), 'Faith', in T. Penelhum ed., *Faith.* New York: MacMillan Publishing.
Theissen, Gerd (1985), *Biblical Faith: An Evolutionary Approach.* Philadelphia: Fortress.
Theissen, Gerd (1999), *A Theory of Primitive Christian Religion.* London: SCM.
Theissen, Gerd (2014), *Polyphones Verstehen: Entwürfe zur Bibelhermeneutik.* Berlin: LIT.
Theissen, Gerd and Merz, Annette (1998), *The Historical Jesus: A Comprehensive Guide.* London: SCM.
Thielman, Frank (1989), *From Plight to Solution: A Jewish Framework for Understanding Paul's View of the Law in Galatians and Romans.* Leiden: Brill.
Thielman, Frank (2010), *Ephesians.* Grand Rapids, Mich.: Baker Academic.
Thistleton, Anthony C. (2000), *The First Epistle to the Corinthians: A Commentary on the Greek Text.* Grand Rapids, Mich.: Eerdmans.
Thom, Johann (2012), 'Kosmiese mag in Pseudo-Aristotles *De mundo*, en die Nuwe Testament', *HTS Teologiese Studies* 68: art. 1102.
Thomas, Heath (2009), *'Until He Looks Down and Sees': The Message and Meaning of the Book of Lamentations.* Cambridge: Grove.
Thomasson, Amie (2003), 'The ontology of art', in Peter Kivy ed., *The Blackwell Guide to Aesthetics.* Oxford: Blackwell: 78–92.
Thompson, Christopher (2017), 'Trust without reliance', *Ethical Theory and Moral Practice* 20: 643–55.
Thompson, Marianne Meye (2008), 'Word of God, Messiah of Israel, Savior of the world: learning the identity of Jesus from the Gospel of John', in Beverly Roberts Gaventa and Richard B. Hays eds, *Seeking the Identity of Jesus: A Pilgrimage.* Grand Rapids, Mich.: Eerdmans: 166–79.
Thompson, Thomas L. (2001), 'The messiah epithet in the Hebrew Bible', *Scandinavian Journal of the Old Testament* 15: 57–82.
Thompson, William Forde (2009), *Music, Thought, and Feeling: Understanding the Psychology of Music.* Oxford: Oxford University Press.
Thoneman, Peter (2020), *An Ancient Dream Manual: Artemidorus' The Interpretation of Dreams.* Oxford: Oxford University Press.
Thornton, Brendan Jamal (2016), *Negotiating Respect, Pentecostalism, Masculinity, and the Politics of Spiritual Authority in the Dominican Republic.* Gainesville, Fla: University Press of Florida.
Thrall, Margaret E. (1982), 'Salvation proclaimed: V. 2 Corinthians 5.18-21: reconciliation with God', *Expository Times* 93: 227–32.
Thrall, Margaret E. (1994, 2000), *A Critical and Exegetical Commentary on the Second Epistle to the Corinthians.* 2 vols. Edinburgh: T&T Clark.
Thurston, Bonnie Bowman and Ryan, Judith (2005), *Philippians and Philemon.* Collegeville, Minn.: Liturgical Press.
Tigchelaar, Eibert J. C. (2014), 'Historical origins of the early Christian concept of the Holy Spirit', in Jörg Frey and John Levison eds, *The Holy Spirit, Inspiration, and the Cultures of Antiquity: Multidisicplinary Perspectives.* Berlin: De Gruyter: 167–240.
Tilley, Terrence W. (2004), *History, Theology, and Faith: Dissolving the Modern Problematic.* Maryknoll, NY: Orbis Books.
Tillich, Paul (1957), *The Dynamics of Faith.* New York: Harper and Row.
Tilling, Chris (2012), *Paul's Divine Christology.* Tübingen: Mohr Siebeck.

Tillotson, Nicole, Short, Monica, Ollerton, Janice, Hearn, Cassandra, and Sawatzky, Bonita (2017), 'Faith matters: from a disability lens', *Journal of Disability and Religion* 21: 319–37.
Tirres, Christopher D. (2014), *The Aesthetics and Ethics of Faith: A Dialogue between Liberationist and Pragmatic Thought*. Oxford/New York: Oxford University Press.
Tonstad, S. (2006), *Saving God's Reputation: The Theological Function of Pistis Iesou in the Cosmic Narratives of Revelation*. London: T&T Clark.
Torrance, Andrew B. and McCall, Thomas H. (2018), *Knowing Creation: Perspectives from Theology, Philosophy, and Science*. Grand Rapids, Mich.: Zondervan.
Torrance, Thomas F. (1980), *The Ground and Grammar of Theology*. Charlottesville, Va: University Press of Virginia.
Towner, Philip H. (2006), *The Letters to Timothy and Titus*. Grand Rapids, Mich.: Eerdmans.
Tracey, Elizabeth B. (2015), *See Me! Hear Me! Divine/Human Relational Dialogue in Genesis*. Leuven: Peeters.
Trebilco, Paul R. (1991), *Jewish Communities in Asia Minor*. Cambridge: Cambridge University Press.
Tremlin, T. (2006), *Minds and Gods: The Cognitive Foundations of Religion*. Oxford: Oxford University Press.
Trigo, Tomas (2013), *En los brazos del Padre: Confianza en Dios*. Casablanca: Editorial Casablanca.
Trivedi, Saam (2002), 'Against musical works as eternal types', *British Journal of Aesthetics* 42: 73–82.
Trivedi, Saam (2008), 'Music and metaphysics', *Metaphilosophy* 39: 124–43.
Tronick, Edward Z. (2003), ' "Of course all relationships are unique": how co-creative processes generate unique mother–infant and patient–therapist relationships and change other relationships', *Psychoanalytic Inquiry* 23: 473–91.
Tronick, E., Adamson, L. B., Als, H., and Brazelton, T. B. (April 1975), 'Infant emotions in normal and perturbated interactions', paper presented at the biennial meeting of the Society for Research in Child Development. Denver, Colo.
Tronick, E., Als, H., Adamson, L., Wise, S., and Brazelton, T. B. (1978), 'The infant's response to entrapment between contradictory messages in face-to-face interaction', *Journal of the American Academy of Child Psychiatry* 17: 1–13.
Tuckett, Christopher M. ed. (1984), *Synoptic Studies: The Ampleforth Conferences of 1982 and 1983*. Sheffield: Sheffield Academic Press.
Tuckett, Christopher M. (2001), *Christology and the New Testament: Jesus and his Earliest Followers*. Edinburgh: Edinburgh University Press.
Tuggy, Dale (2016), 'Jesus as an exemplar of faith in the New Testament', *International Journal for the Philosophy of Religion* 81: 171–91.
Tuori, Kaius (2016), *The Emperor of Law: The Emergence of Roman Imperial Adjudication*. Oxford: Oxford University Press.
Tuori, Kaius and Nissin, Laura eds (2015), *Public and Private in the Roman House and Society*. Portsmouth: Journal of Roman Archaeology.
Turner, Max (1996), *Power from on High: The Spirit in Israel's Restoration and Witness in Luke-Acts*. Sheffield: Sheffield Academic Press.
Turner, Max (1998), 'The "Spirit of prophecy" as the power of Israel's restoration and witness', in I. Howard Marshall and David Peterson eds, *Witness to the Gospel: The Theology of Acts*. Grand Rapids, Mich.: Eerdmans: 327–48.
Turner, Max (2011), 'Levison's *Filled with the Spirit*: a brief appreciation and response', *Journal of Pentecostal Theology* 20: 193–200.

Twelftree, Graham H. (1993), *Jesus the Exorcist*. Tübingen: Mohr Siebeck.
Twelftree, Graham H. (1999), *Jesus the Miracle Worker: A Historical and Theological Study*. Downers Grove, Ill.: IVP Academic.
Ulrichs, Karl Friedrich (2007), *Christusglaube*. Tübingen: Mohr Siebeck.
United Methodist Church (2004), *The Book of Discipline of the United Methodist Church*. Nashville: Abingdon
United Nations (1999), 'Istanbul Protocol: Manual on the effective investigation and documentation of torture and other cruel, inhuman, or degrading treatment or punishment'. Geneva: Office of the United Nations High Commissioner for Human Rights.
Vainio, Olli-Pekka (2010), *Beyond Fideism: Negotiable Religious Identities*. Farnham: Ashgate.
Valentin, Réka-Ibolya (2016), 'Perspectives on immortality and eternal life in the Book of Wisdom and the gospel of John: a conceptual analysis based on metaphorical structuring', Ph.D. thesis, Radboud University.
Vallotton, Pierre (1963), *Le Christ et la foi: étude de théologie biblique*. Geneva: Labor et Fides.
Van Beeck, Frans Jozef, SJ (1979), *Christ Proclaimed: Christology as Rhetoric*. New York: Paulist Press.
Van Belle, Gilbert; Van der Watt, Jan G; and Maritz, P. eds (2005), *Theology and Christology in the Fourth Gospel: Essays by the Members of the SNTS Johannine Writings Seminar*. Leuven: Peeters.
VandenBerg, Mary (2007), 'Redemptive suffering: Christ's alone', *Scottish Journal of Theology* 60: 394–411.
Van der Bergh, Ronald H. (2012), 'The reception of Matthew 27:19B (Pilate's wife's dream) in the early Church', *Journal of Early Christian History* 2: 70–85.
Van der Horst, Pieter W. (1999), '*Sortes*: sacred books as instant oracles in late antiquity', in L. V. Rutgers, P. W. van der Horst, H. W. Havelaar, and L. Teugel eds, *The Use of Sacred Books in the Ancient World*. Leuven: Peeters: 143–73.
Van der Horst, Pieter W. (2000), 'Ancient Jewish bibliomancy', *Journal of Greco-Roman Christianity and Judaism* 1: 9–17.
VanderKam, James C. (1995), *Enoch: A Man for All Generations*. Columbia: University of South Carolina Press.
Van der Loos, H. (1965), *The Miracles of Jesus*. Brill: Academic Publishers.
Van der Watt, Jan G. ed. (2005), *Salvation in the New Testament: Perspectives on Soteriology*. Leiden: Brill.
Van Dyk, Leanne, (1996), 'Do theories of atonement foster abuse?', *Dialog* 35: 21–5.
Van Hoof, L. (2010), *Plutarch's Practical Ethics: The Social Dynamics of Philosophy*. Oxford: Oxford University Press.
Vanhoye, Albert (1999), '*Pistis Christou*: faith in Christ or the "trustworthiness" of Christ: on the problem of alternative interpretations in the Pauline epistles', *Biblica* 80: 1–21.
Van Inwagen, Peter (1995), *God, Knowledge and Mystery: Essays in Philosophical Theology*. Ithaca, NY: Cornell University Press.
Van Kooten, George H. (2003), *Cosmic Christology in Paul and the Pauline School: Colossians and Ephesians in the Context of Graeco-Roman Cosmology, with a New Synopsis of the Greek Texts*. Tübingen: Mohr Siebeck.
Van Kooten, George H. (2005), *The Creation of Heaven and Earth: Re-Interpretation of Genesis I in the Context of Judaism, Ancient Philosophy, Christianity, and Modern Physics*. Leiden: Brill.
Vanstone, W. H. (1982), *The Stature of Waiting*. London: Darton, Longman and Todd.
Van Tongeren, Daryl R., DeWall, C. Nathan, Chen, Zhansheng, Sibley, Chris G., and Bulbulia, Joseph (2020), 'Religious residue: cross-cultural evidence that religious

psychology and behavior persist following deidentification', *Journal of Personality and Social Psychology* 120: 1-20.
Vearncombe, Erin Kathleen (2013), 'Cloaks, conflict, and Mark 14.51-52', *Catholic Biblical Quarterly* 75: 683-703.
Vearncombe, Erin Kathleen (2014), 'What would Jesus wear? Dress in the synoptic gospels', Ph.D. dissertation, University of Toronto.
Veres, Otniel L. (2008), 'A study of the "I am" phrases in John's gospel', *Perichoresis* 6: 109-25.
Verheyden, Joseph and Kloppenborg, John S. (2018), *The Gospels and their Stories in Anthropological Perspective*. Tübingen: Mohr Siebeck.
Veyne, Paul ed. (1987), *A History of Private Life from Pagan Rome to Byzantium*. Cambridge, Mass.: Harvard University Press.
Via, Dan O. (1975), *Kerygma and Comedy in the New Testament: A Structuralist Approach to Hermeneutic*. Philadelphia: Fortress.
Via, Dan O. (2002), *What is New Testament Theology?* Minneapolis: Fortress.
Vincent, Marvin Richardson (1897), *A Critical and Exegetical Commentary on the Epistles to the Philippians and to Philemon*. New York: C. Scribner's Sons.
Vines, Michael E. (2002), *The Problem of Markan Genre: The Gospel of Mark and the Jewish Novel*. Atlanta: Society of Biblical Literature.
Volf, Judith M. Gundry (1990), *Paul and Perseverance: Staying in and Falling away*. Tübingen: Mohr Siebeck.
Von Balthasar, Hans (1968), *La Foi du Christ: cinq approches christologiques*. Auber: Éditions Montaigne.
Von Dobbeler, Axel von (1987), *Glaube als Teilhabe: historische und semantische Grundlagen der paulinischen Theologie und Ekklesiologie des Glaubens*. Tübingen: Mohr Siebeck.
Von Dobbeler, Axel von (1987), *Glaube als Teilhabe: historische und semantische Grundlagen der paulinischen Theologie und Ekklesiologie des Glaubens*. Tübingen: Mohr Siebeck.
Von Humboldt, Alexander (1967), 'On the historian's task', transl. Louis O. Mink in *History and Theory* 6: 57-71.
Von Sass, Hartmut (2011), '*Assensus fiduciae*: Glaube als Vertrauen bei Rudolf Bultmann', *Kerygma und Dogma* 57: 243-68.
Von Wahlde, Urban C. (2010), *The Gospel and the Letters of John. Vol. 3: Commentary on the Three Johannine Letters*. Grand Rapids, Mich.: Eerdmans.
Vorster, W. S. (1983), 'Kerygma/history and the gospel genre', *New Testament Studies* 29: 87-95.
Wabgou, Michel (2005), 'L'Ecclésiologie de communion revue et pratiquée dans une eglise locale: pour une réorganisation du diocese de Dapaong', Ph.D. thesis, University of Montreal.
Wagner, J. Ross (2011), 'Baptism "into Christ Jesus" and the question of universalism in Paul', *Horizons in Biblical Theology* 33: 45-61.
Wagner, J. Ross (2014), 'Is God the father of Jews only, or also of gentiles? The peculiar shape of Paul's "universalism", in Felix Albrecht and Reinhard Feldmeier eds, *The Divine Father: Religious and Philosophical Concepts of Divine Parenthood in Antiquity*. Leiden: Brill: 233-54.
Wall, John (2005), *Moral Creativity: Paul Ricoeur and the Poetics of Possibility*. Oxford: Oxford University Press.
Walsh, Carey and Elliott, Mark W. eds (2016), *Biblical Theology: Past, Present, and Future*. Eugene, Ore.: Cascade.

Walton, Steve (2015), 'What are the gospels? Richard Burridge's impact on scholarly understanding of the genre of the gospels', *Currents in Biblical Research* 14: 81–93.
Wanamaker, C. A. (1987), 'Philippians 2.6-11: Son of God or Adamic Christology?' *New Testament Studies* 33: 179–93.
Wanamaker, C. A. (1990), *The Epistles to the Thessalonians*. New International Greek Testament Commentary. Grand Rapids, Mich.: Eerdmans.
Wang, X. (2002), 'Kith-and-kin rationality in risky choices: theoretical modelling and cross-cultural empirical testing', in F. Salter ed., *Risky Transactions: Trust, Kinship and Ethnicity*. New York: Berghahn: 47–70.
Ward, Keith (1994), *Religion and Revelation*. Oxford: Oxford University Press.
Ware, James P. (2011), 'Law, Christ, and covenant: Paul's theology of the law in Romans 3:19-20', *Journal of Theological Studies* 62: 513–40.
Warren, M. J. (2018), '"When the Christ Appears, Will He Do More Signs Than This Man Has Done?" (Jn 7.31): Signs and the Messiah in the Gospel of John', in B. Reynolds and G. Boccaccini eds, *Reading the Gospel of John's Christology as a Form of Jewish Messianism: Royal, Prophetic, and Divine Messiahs, Ancient Judaism, and Early Christianity*. Leiden: Brill: 229–47.
Watson, Francis (1987), 'Is John's Christology adoptionist?' in L. D. Hurst and N. T. Wright eds, *The Glory of Christ in the New Testament: Studies in Christology in Memory of George Caird*. Oxford: Oxford University Press: 113–24.
Watson, Francis (1997), *Text and Truth: Redefining Biblical Theology*. Edinburgh: T&T Clark.
Watson, Francis (1998), 'Theology and music', *Scottish Journal of Theology* 51: 435–63.
Watson, Francis (2007), *Paul, Judaism, and the Gentiles: Beyond the New Perspective*. Rev. edn. Grand Rapids, Mich.: Eerdmans.
Watson, Francis (2008), 'Veritas Christi: how to get from the Jesus of history to the Christ of faith without losing one's way', in Beverly Roberts Gaventa and Richard B. Hays eds, *Seeking the Identity of Jesus: A Pilgrimage*. Grand Rapids, Mich.: Eerdmans: 96–114.
Way, David V. (1991), *The Lordship of Christ: Ernst Käsemann's Interpretation of Paul's Theology*. Oxford: Oxford University Press.
Weaver, B. (2015), *Offending and Desistence: The Importance of Social Relations*. London: Routledge.
Weaver, J. Denny (2001), *The Nonviolent Atonement*. Grand Rapids, Mich.: Eerdmans.
Weaver, Jason G. (2013), 'Paul's call to imitation: the rhetorical function of the theme of imitation in its epistolary context', Ph.D. dissertation, Catholic University of America.
Weber, Günther (1998), *I Believe, I Doubt: Notes on Christian Experience*. London: SCM.
Wedderburn, A. J. M. (1999), *Beyond Resurrection*. London: SCM.
Wedderburn, A. J. M. (2013), *The Death of Jesus: Some Reflections on Jesus-Traditions and Paul*. Tübingen: Mohr Siebeck.
Weinberg, M. K., and Tronick, E. Z. (1996), 'Infant affective reactions to the resumption of maternal interaction after the still-face', *Child Development* 67: 905–14.
Weinfeld, Moshe (1972), *Deuteronomy and the Deuteronomic School*. Oxford: Oxford University Press.
Welch, John and Rennaker, Jacob (2019), 'Paul and the covenant', in Pamela Barmash ed., *The Oxford Handbook of Biblical Law*. Oxford: Oxford University Press: 437–50.
Welker, Michael (1994), *God the Spirit*. Minneapolis: Fortress.
Welker, Michael, Rudolf Weth, Martin Ebner, et al. (2010), *Heiliger Geist. Jahrbuch für Biblische Theologie 24*. Neukirchen-Vluyn: Neukirchener Verlag.
Wells, Kyle B. (2015), *Grace and Agency in Paul and Second Temple Judaism: Interpreting the Transformation of the Heart*. Leiden: Brill.

Wendt, Heidi (2016), *At the Temple Gates: The Religion of Freelance Experts in the Early Roman Empire*. Oxford: Oxford University Press.
Wenham, Gordon J. (1987), *Genesis 1–15*. Nashville: Thomas Nelson.
Wessels, G. F. (1992), 'The call to responsible freedom in Paul's persuasive strategy, Galatians 5:13–6:10', *Neotestamentica* 26: 461–74.
Westerholm, Stephen (2004), *Perspectives Old and New on Paul: The 'Lutheran' Paul and his critics*. Grand Rapids, Mich.: Eerdmans.
Westermann, Claus (1966, 1976, 1982), *Genesis*. 3 vols. Neukirchen-Vleyn: Neukirchener Verlag des Erziehungsvereins.
Wettstein, J. J., Strecker, Georg, and Schnelle, Udo eds (1996–), *Neuer Wettstein: Texte zum Neuen Testament aus Griechtentum und Hellenismus*. Berlin: De Gruyter.
Wettstein, Howard (2012), *The Significance of Religious Experience*. Oxford: Oxford University Press.
Whitmarsh, Tim (2015), *Battling the Gods: Atheism in the Ancient World*. New York: Alfred A. Knopf.
Whittle, Sarah (2015), *Covenant Renewal and the Consecration of the Gentiles in Romans*. Cambridge: Cambridge University Press.
Wigg-Stevenson, Natalie (2014), *Ethnographic Theology: An Inquiry into the Production of Theological Knowledge*. New York: Palgrave Macmillan.
Wilckens, Ulrich (1978), *Resurrection: Biblical Testimony to the Resurrection: An Historical Examination and Explanation*. Atlanta: John Knox.
Wiles, Maurice (1975), *Faith, Doubt and Theology*. London: Westfield College.
Wiles, Maurice (1977), 'Myth in theology', in John Hick ed., *The Myth of God Incarnate*. London: SCM: 148–66.
Wiles, Maurice (1982), *Faith and the Mystery of God*. London: SCM.
Wiles, Maurice (1993), 'Can we still do Christology?' in Abraham J. Malherbe and Wayne A. Meeks eds, *The Future of Christology: Essays in Honor of Leander E. Keck*. Minneapolis: Fortress: 229–38.
Wilk, Florian and Wagner, J. Ross eds (2010), *Between Gospel and Election: Explorations in the Interpretation of Romans 9–11*. Tübingen: Mohr Siebeck.
Wilkey, Jay W. (1972), 'Prolegomena to a theology of music', *Review and Expositor* 69: 507–17.
Willems, Emilio (1967), 'Validation of authority in Pentecostal sects of Chile and Brazil', *Journal for the Scientific Study of Religion* 6: 253–8.
Williams, Bernard (1981), *Moral Luck*, Cambridge: Cambridge University Press.
Williams, Catrin (2018), 'Faith, eternal life, and the spirit in the gospel of John', in Judith M. Lieu and Martinus C. de Boer eds, *The Oxford Handbook of Johannine Studies*. Oxford: Oxford University Press: 347–62.
Williams, Drake (2002), '"Let God be proved true": Paul's view of scripture and the faithfulness of God', in Paul Helm and Carl R. Trueman eds, *The Trustworthiness of God: Perspectives on the Nature of Scripture*. Grand Rapids, Mich.: Eerdmans: 96–117.
Williams, Guy (2009), *The Spirit World in the Letters of Paul: A Critical Examination of the Role of Spiritual Beings in the Authentic Pauline Epistles*. Göttingen: Vandenhoeck and Ruprecht.
Williams, J. F. (1994), *Other Followers of Jesus: Minor Characters as Major Figures in Mark's Gospel*. Sheffield: Sheffield Academic Press.
Williams, Rowan (2007), *Tokens of Trust: An Introduction to Christian Belief.* Norwich: Canterbury.
Williams, Sam K. (1980), 'The "righteousness of God" in Romans', *Journal of Biblical Literature* 99: 241–90.

Williams, Sam K. (1997), *Galatians*. Philadelphia: Fortress.
Wilson, John and Clow, Harvey K. (1981), 'Themes of power and control in a Pentecostal assembly', *Journal for the Scientific Study of Religion* 20: 241–50.
Wilson, Robert McLachlan (2005), *A Critical and Exegetical Commentary on Colossians and Philemon*. London: T&T Clark.
Witherington, Ben, III (1998), *The Many Faces of the Christ: The Christologies of the New Testament and Beyond*. New York: Crossroad.
Witmer, Amanda (2012), *Jesus, the Galilean Exorcist: His Exorcisms in Social and Political Context*. London: T&T Clark.
Wolter, Michael (2014, 2019), *Der Briefe an die Römer*. 2 vols. Neukirchen-Vluyn: Neukirchener Theologie Patmos.
Wolter, Michael (2015a), *Paul: An Outline of his Theology*. Transl. Robert L. Brawley. Waco, Tex.: Baylor University Press.
Wolter, Michael (2015b), '"Spirit" and "letter" in the New Testament', in Paul S. Fiddes and Günter Bader eds, *The Spirit and the Letter: A Tradition and a Reversal*. London: Bloomsbury: 31–46.
Wolter, Michael (2016), *The Gospel According to Luke. Volume 1 (Luke 1–9.50)*. Waco, Tex.: Baylor UP.
Wolter, Michael (2018), 'Ein exegetischer und theologischer Blick auf Röm 11.25-32', *New Testament Studies* 64: 123–42.
Wolterstorff, Nicholas P. (1964), 'Faith and philosophy', in Alvin Plantinga ed., *Faith and Philosophy: Philosophical Studies in Religion and Ethics*. Grand Rapids, Mich.: Eerdmans: 3–36.
Wolterstorff, Nicholas P. (1983), 'Introduction', in Alvin Plantinga and Nicholas Wolterstorff eds, *Faith and Rationality: Reason and Belief in God*. Notre Dame: University of Notre Dame Press: 1–15.
Woodington, J. David (2020), *The Dubious Disciples*. Berlin: De Gruyter.
Woyke, Johannes (2008), 'Nochmals zu den "schwachen und unfähigen Elementen" (Gal. 4.9): Paulus, Philo und die *stoicheia tou kosmou*', *New Testament Studies* 54: 221–34.
Wrede, William (1907), *Paul* Transl. Edward Lummis. London: Philip Green.
Wright, N. T. (2009), *Justification: God's Plan and Paul's Vision*. Downers Grove, Ill.: IVP Academic.
Wright, N. T. (2013), *Paul and the Faithfulness of God*. London: SPCK.
Wyschogrod, Edith (1998), *An Ethics of Remembering: History, Heterology, and the Nameless Others*. Chicago: University of Chicago Press.
Wyschogrod, Michael (1996), *The Body of Faith: God and the People of Israel*. Northvale, NJ: Jason Aronson.
Yates, John W. (2008), *The Spirit and Creation in Paul*. Tübingen: Mohr Siebeck.
Yinger, Kent L. (2011), *The New Perspective on Paul: An Introduction*. Eugene, Ore.: Wipf and Stock.
Yong, Amos (2009), 'Many tongues, many senses: Pentecost, the body politic, and the redemption of dis/ability', *Pneuma* 31: 167–88.
Young, David C. (2005), '*Mens sana in corpore sano*? Body and mind in ancient Greece', *International Journal of the History of Sport* 22: 22–41.
Zager, Daniel ed. (2007), *Music and Theology: Essays in Honor of Robin A. Leaver*. Lanham, Md: Scarecrow.
Zagzebski, Linda T. (2012), *Epistemic Authority: A Theory of Trust, Authority, and Autonomy in Belief*. Oxford: Oxford University Press.
Zahl, Simeon (2018), 'Tradition and its "use": the ethics of theological retrieval', *Scottish Journal of Theology* 71: 308–23.

Zakowitch, Yair (1984), '[Tragedy] and [comedy] in the Bible', *Semeia* 32: 107–14.
Zangenberg, Jürgen, Attridge, Harold W., and Martin, Dale B. eds (2007), *Religion, Ethnicity, and Identity in Ancient Galilee: A Region in Transition.* Tübingen: Mohr Siebeck.
Zeller, Dieter (1990), *Charis bei Philon und Paulus.* Stuttgart: Katholisches Bibelwerk.
Zeller, Dieter (2001), 'New Testament Christology in its Hellenistic reception', *New Testament Studies* 46: 312–33.
Ziegert, Carsten (2019), 'Glauben und Vertrauen im Alten Testament. Eine kognitiv-linguistische Untersuchung', *Zeitschrift für die alttestamentliche Wissenschaft* 131: 607–24.
Ziesler, J. A. (1972), *The Meaning of Righteousness in Paul: A Linguistic and Theological Enquiry.* Cambridge: Cambridge University Press.
Zwiep, Arie W. (2010), *Christ, The Spirit, and the Community of God.* Tübingen: Mohr Siebeck.

Index of Biblical Passages Cited

For the benefit of digital users, indexed terms that span two pages (e.g., 52–53) may, on occasion, appear on only one of those pages.

Genesis
  1 81, 81n.199
  1–2 64n.134
  1–3 81–3, 224
  1.1 81
  1.3 81, 165n.103
  1.4 81
  1.5 81
  1.22 81
  1.26 81, 81n.200
  1.28 81–2, 320–1
  1.28–29 81
  1.28–30 82
  1.29 81–2
  2–3 80n.198, 81n.202, 82, 229
  2.2 81
  2.4 81
  2.4–3.23 81n.199
  2.7 226, 301
  2.8 81–2
  2.9 81
  2.15 81–3, 320–1
  2.15–17 82
  2.16–17 82–3
  2.17 82–3
  2.17–18 81–2
  2.18 81–2
  2.18–24 81–2
  2.24 81–2
  2.26 226
  3 145, 147n.28
  3.1 82–3
  3.1–7 81
  3.3 82–3
  3.5 83, 83n.209
  3.11–24 81–2
  3.12 83
  3.14–24 81–2
  3.16–19 83n.212
  3.17 225–6
  3.17–19 225–6
  3.19 226
  4 145, 147n.28
  4.3–4 81–2
  4.4–5 145
  4.5 145
  4.7 145
  5.21–4 100n.13, 122
  5.24 142–3
  7.4 227n.131
  9 89–90
  9.9 53–4
  11.5–6 47–8
  12 76–7
  12.1 52n.69, 53–4
  12.2 76–7
  12.3 55n.90
  12.7 55n.90, 55n.91, 76–7
  13.3–4 76–7
  13.14–16 76–7
  13.17 76–7
  14 76–7
  14.17–20 161n.84
  14.18–20 160–1
  15 198–9
  15.2 76–7
  15.2–5 55n.90
  15.5 76–7
  15.6 52n.69, 55–6, 69, 75–7, 77n.190, 80–1, 354n.120
  15.8 76–7
  17 69
  17.1 69
  17.2 53–4
  17.5 57n.99
  17.10 69
  17.10–11 57
  17.5 69
  17.8 69
  17.17 354n.120
  17.17–18 69
  18.1–16 237n.172

Genesis (cont.)
  18.18 55n.90
  18.25 64n.134
  25.8 100n.16
Exodus
  2.1-10 273n.102
  2.24 78n.192
  4.1 78-9
  4.1-5 213n.75
  4.5 52n.70, 202, 241n.189
  4.8-9 52n.70, 78-9
  4.31 78-9
  6.7 52n.69
  9.16 164n.99
  9.33 227n.131
  14.31 52n.70, 78-9, 202, 213n.75, 241n.189
  16.3 241n.189
  16.10 47n.51, 206n.50
  17.2 241n.189
  19.9 52n.70, 78-9, 213n.75
  20.5 200n.13
  20.8 52-3
  24.16 47n.51
  32-34 60n.113
  32.1 241n.189
  32.13 78n.192
  33.11 54n.78
  33.19 47-8
  33.22 50
  34.6 164n.97
Leviticus
  26.14-33 200n.13
Numbers
  6.25-26 129n.130
  11.25 301
  12.7 161, 298
  12.7 LXX 298
  14.11 213n.75
  14.18 164n.97
  20.1-12 142n.3
  21.5-9 62
  35.55 105n.39
Deuteronomy
  1.37-38 142n.3
  6.3 76
  6.4 76
  6.16 206n.49
  7.9 78-9, 202
  7.9 LXX 41n.19
  8.10-20 52-3
  9.27 78n.192
  11.17 227n.131
  18.15 213

  28.15-68 200n.13
  29.1 58n.103
  30 76
  30.11-14 69, 76
  30.14 48
  30.15 76
  32 58n.105
  32.4 76, 202
  32.20 129n.130
Joshua
  23.13 LXX 105n.39
  24.25 58n.103
Judges
  13.3-5 273n.102
1 Samuel
  1.19-12.1 273n.102
  1.20 273
  3.1 273
2 Samuel
  22.11 227n.131
1 Kings
  3.5 164n.97
  10.1-5 274n.108
  17.17-24 99n.10
  19.19-21 215n.82
1 Reigns LXX
  2.35 298
2 Kings
  2.11 142-3
  4.32-37 99n.10
  11.17 58n.103
  13.21 99n.10
  23.2-3 58n.103
4 Reigns LXX
  2.11 100
2 Chronicles
  20.7 54n.78
  21.15 200n.13
  21.18-19 200n.13
Nehemiah
  9.8 76n.186
Job
  15.8 165n.101
  37.6 227n.131
  38.8 227n.131
  38.11 227n.131
Psalms
  4.8 228n.132
  14.7 46n.48
  16.8-11 76

INDEX OF BIBLICAL PASSAGES CITED 439

16.8–11 (15.8–11 LXX) 176n.149
16.10 103n.28
18 84–5
18.1 84–5
18.8 84–5
18.8 LXX 46n.48
20.1 46n.48
22 262–3
22.1 (21.1 LXX) 262
22.1–3 262
22.5–6 262
22.9 (21.9 LXX) 262–3, 262n.59
22.23 46n.48
23.1–4 204n.40
24.6 46n.48
32 LXX 84
32.4 202
32.4 LXX 46n.48, 84
32.5–7 LXX 84
32.8–9 LXX 84
32.13 LXX 84
32.15 LXX 84
32.18–20 LXX 84
33.7 227n.131
34.8 280
44.4 46n.48
45 87n.230
46.7 46n.48
46.11 46n.48
47.4 46n.48
51.6 LXX 45n.39
53.6 46n.48
59.13 46n.48
65.7 227n.131
75.9 46n.48
76.6 46n.48
77.15 46n.48
77.22 46n.48
78.5 46n.48
78.21 46n.48
78.71 46n.48
79.7 46n.48
81.1 46n.48
81.4 46n.48
82.6 205n.44
84.8 46n.48
85.1 46n.48
86.15 64n.134
87.2 46n.48
88.29 204n.40, 213n.77
88.31–38 LXX 44
88.33–35 (32–34) 58n.103
88.38 LXX 46–7
89.9 227n.131
89.38 41n.19
94.7 46n.48
99.4 46n.48
95.5 64n.134
101.26–28 87
103.3 200n.13
103.8 164n.97
103.17 164n.97
104.9 227n.131
105.6 46n.48
105.8–11 LXX 78n.192
105.10 46n.48
105.12 202
105.42 78n.192
105.23 46n.48
106.1 64n.134
107.23–30 212–13
107.29 227n.131
109.4 LXX 160–1
109.4 LXX 160–1, 161n.84
110.1 76
110.3–6 202
110.7 213n.77
110.7 LXX 46n.48
114.1 46n.48
114.7 46n.48
115 LXX 125
115.1 LXX 124n.115, 286n.17
115.4 125
115.6 125
115.7 125
115.8 125
116.10–15 (115.1–6) 176n.149
116.11 45n.39
118.18 LXX 128n.126
118.66 LXX 46n.48, 213n.77
132.2 46n.48
132.5 46n.48
135.3 64n.134
136.5–9 64n.134
139.1 72
145.15–16 225n.123
145.17 64n.134
146.5 46n.48
147.5 64n.134
147.9 225n.123
147.19 46n.48
145.8 164n.97
148.1–6 64n.134
148.8 227n.131

Proverbs
3.3 85n.219
3.5 85n.219
3.24 228n.132

Proverbs (cont.)
  3.34 147n.27
  8.29 227n.131
  12.22 46n.48, 76n.186
  14.5 201n.19
  14.25 201n.19
  15.27-28 46n.48, 76n.186
  15.27a 46n.48, 76n.186
  16.20 85n.219
  21.1 64n.133
  23.9 312n.94
  29.25 85n.219
  30.4 227n.131

Isaiah
  1-39 52n.69
  2-3 44
  2.8 148n.29
  2.20 148n.29
  6.3 47n.51
  6.9-10 209n.62
  7.14 273n.102
  7.16 274-5
  8.4 274-5
  9.2-3 274-5
  9.5 273n.102
  9.6 274-5
  24 89-90
  24-27 89-90
  24.5 60n.114, 89-90
  24.5-6 60n.114
  25.1 46-7
  26.19 231n.145
  27.9 49-50
  28.16 113
  29.18-19 231n.145
  35.5-6 231n.145
  40.11 204n.40
  40.13 165n.101
  41.8 54n.78, 57n.96
  42.6 44, 44n.37, 46-7
  42.21 46-7
  43.19 61-2
  45 46n.46
  45.8 46-7
  45.8-18 64n.134
  46.10 64n.134
  48.22 LXX 298
  49.1 285
  49.6 44
  49.7 41n.19, 46-7, 202, 204n.40
  49.9-10 204n.40
  51.2 57n.96
  53.1 LXX 105
  53.4-12 105
  53.5 105n.38
  53.11 232n.149
  53.12g LXX 105n.36
  54.4-5 233n.152
  55.1-3 LXX 213n.77
  58.6 207n.52
  60.6 274n.108
  61.1 301
  61.1-2 207n.52
  62.4-7 233n.152

Jeremiah
  1.3 72
  1.50 285
  2.2 233n.152
  3.14 233n.152
  5.22 227n.131
  10.13 227n.131
  23.18 165n.101
  30.22 52n.69
  31.31 52-3
  31.31-34 58n.103
  31.32 233n.152
  32.18-19 164n.97

Ezekiel
  11.5 301
  11.23 226n.126
  16.13-15 233n.152
  16.32 233n.152
  16.59-63 58n.103
  28.44 105n.39
  34 230n.137
  36.26 301

Daniel
  3.1-30 179n.161
  4.35 64n.134
  9.4 164n.97
  11.31 148n.29

Hosea
  2.6-7 233n.152
  2.14-16 233n.152
  2.18-25 58n.103
  2.19-20 233n.152
  5.9 79n.195
  6.6 316n.102
  6.7 81n.199

Joel
  2.13 164n.97
  3.1-5 76

Jonah
  4.2 164n.97

Micah
  3.4 129n.130

INDEX OF BIBLICAL PASSAGES CITED

6.8 52–3
7.20 46n.48, 78n.192

Nahum
  1.3 164n.97
  1.7 64n.134

Habakkuk
  2.4 42–3, 75–6, 146, 146n.22, 232n.149

Zechariah
  14.4 226n.126

Wisdom of Solomon
  1.2 46n.48, 85n.219
  3.1 85n.219, 218n.91
  3.8 46n.48
  3.8–9 202
  9.13 165n.101
  9.16–17 208n.58
  10.5 85n.219
  10.7 85n.219
  12.2 46n.48, 85n.219
  14.11 148n.29
  16.24–25 85n.219
  16.26 213n.77

Sirach (Ecclesiasticus)
  1.4 84n.214
  1.14 84n.214
  2.6 46–7, 85n.219
  2.8 85n.219
  2.10 46–7, 85n.219
  2.13 85n.219
  11.21 202
  15.14 84–5
  15.15 84n.216
  15.17 84–5
  15.20 84–5
  17.10 81n.199
  32.24 85n.219
  44.19–20 76n.186
  45.4 76n.186
  46.15 76n.186
  46.15 LXX 298

1 Maccabees
  2.52 76n.186
  14.41 LXX 298

3 Maccabees
  2.10 54

Matthew
  1.2 78n.192
  1.17 78n.192
  1.20 275–6
  1.20–21 275
  1.22–23 274
  1.23 128–9, 214, 214n.79, 275

2.2 274–5
2.11 274–5
2.13–15 275n.109
2.15 274
2.18 274
2.21 200n.12
3.4 269n.90
3.9 78n.192
3.16 302n.68
3.16–17 225–6
3.17 238
4.1 258–9, 308n.85
4.1–7 265n.68
4.6–7 220n.100
4.7 206n.49
4.17 207, 219n.96, 308
4.18–20 215
4.21 215n.82
4.21–22 215
4.23–25 203n.33, 208n.60
4.23–5.1 256n.33
4.24 247n.2
5.6 230n.140
5.10 230n.140
5.17 48n.57, 213n.76
5.20 230n.140
6.10 254–5
6.11 254–5, 256n.34
6.15 254–5
6.19–21 254–5, 256n.34
6.25 254–5
6.25–34 225–6
6.30 201n.25, 225–6, 254–5
6.30–31 201
6.31 72
6.33 225–6, 230n.140
7.6 313
7.9–10 256n.34
7.20 314n.96
7.21–22 313
7.22–23 207
7.23 216n.85
7.28 208–9
7.29 225–6
8.5 190–1, 248
8.5–7 260–1
8.5–13 198–9, 219–20, 247–8
8.6 230
8.8 230, 230n.138
8.8–9 220
8.10 78n.194, 201n.21, 220, 248, 250n.11, 252–3, 260–1
8.11 78n.192, 115–16, 200, 221
8.11–12 225n.122, 252–3

Matthew (*cont.*)
  8.12 252–3
  8.15 252–3
  8.16 203n.33
  8.23–27 212–13, 227–8
  8.25 230, 231n.141
  8.26 201n.24, 212–13, 217, 227–8, 306
  8.27 227–8
  8.29 217n.86, 258–9
  9.1–8 190–1, 247–8
  9.2 143–4, 190–1, 201, 201n.21, 247n.2, 248
  9.2–6 200
  9.6–7 190–1
  9.9 215, 260–1
  9.10 260–1
  9.11–13 260–1
  9.13 265n.68
  9.18–26 247–8
  9.20 269n.90
  9.20–22 247–8
  9.21 201n.21, 248n.4
  9.21–22 264n.65
  9.22 200n.12, 247n.2
  9.27 201n.21, 230n.137, 249
  9.27–31 247–8
  9.28 230, 280
  9.34 211–12
  9.35–6 203n.33
  9.36 208n.60, 256n.33
  9.37 197–8
  10.1 271–2, 292, 306, 306n.75
  10.1–16 207
  10.1–36 264
  10.2–4 271–2
  10.5 271–2
  10.16 313
  10.17 313
  10.20 308n.83
  10.22 200n.12
  10.24 219n.98
  10.30 72
  10.40–42 292
  11.3 198–9
  11.4 197–8
  11.15 209n.61
  11.18–19 264
  11.21–24 198n.9
  11.27 236n.166, 258–9, 311n.93
  12.1–32 200n.16
  12.9–13 248n.3
  12.10 271n.94
  12.23 238n.179
  12.24 211–12
  12.24–30 264n.65
  12.26 211–12
  12.28 197–8, 306
  12.31–32 264n.65
  12.33 314n.96
  12.36 244–5
  12.39 198n.9, 204, 220n.100
  12.39–42 200
  12.42 260–1
  12.46–50 270n.91
  12.48–50 256n.34
  13.9 209n.61
  13.10–17 209
  13.11 198n.9
  13.24 295n.51
  13.30 292n.40
  13.31 295n.51
  13.31–32 197–8
  13.43 209n.61
  13.44–46 256n.34, 312
  13.54–58 220n.100
  13.55 244n.191
  13.58 190n.195, 244, 267–8, 306
  14.13 255–6, 353n.118
  14.14–15 256n.33
  14.15 271–2
  14.22–33 227–8
  14.24–25 259–60
  14.26 227–8, 259–60
  14.27 227–8, 259–60
  14.28 230, 259–60
  14.30 200n.12, 230, 259–60
  14.31 217, 259–60
  14.33 227–8
  14.34–36 203n.33
  14.35 247n.2
  15.1–20 264
  15.21–28 190–1, 198–9, 247–8, 260–1
  15.22 198–9, 230
  15.22–25 230n.137, 249
  15.23 249, 271–2
  15.25 230
  15.26–27 312n.94
  15.26–8 271
  15.27 249–50
  15.28 201n.21, 260–1
  16.2–3 207
  16.4 204, 220n.100
  16.8 217
  16.15–16 201n.17
  16.17 238n.174
  16.19 261n.54
  16.21 234
  16.22 271–2
  16.24 219n.98, 222
  16.25 200n.12, 218
  17.2 269n.90

INDEX OF BIBLICAL PASSAGES CITED   443

17.3–4 78n.194
17.5 211n.69, 238
17.14–18 221, 265–6
17.14–21 190–1
17.15 230, 231n.142
17.16 271–2
17.17 221, 265–6
17.20 189n.190, 190n.194, 201n.24, 217, 221, 259n.48, 298–9, 306
17.22 189n.190
17.23 234
17.27 227n.130
18.6 197n.8, 264–5, 265nn.70,71
18.6–9 264
18.15–20 260–1
18.17 260–1
18.18 261n.54
18.19–20 128–9
18.20 214, 214n.79
19.13 271–2
19.16–19 210n.65
19.16–20 78n.194
19.16–22 256n.35
19.24 264n.65
19.25 271–2
19.29 256n.34
20.18–19 234
20.21 144n.15, 271–2
20.23 219n.98
20.24 271–2
20.25–8 219n.98
20.26 154n.61
20.28 234
20.30 198–9, 249n.9
20.31 249
20.34 252–3
21.11 207
21.18–22 306
21.20–2 201n.24
21.18–22 221, 227–8
21.21 228, 298–9, 353n.118
21.21–22 39n.6, 190, 221
21.22 228
21.23–27 207n.55, 264
21.25 354n.123
21.28–32 220n.100
21.32 225n.122, 230n.140
21.33–46 294–5
22.1–14 115–16
22.6–7 147n.27
22.13 260–1
22.23–33 220n.100
22.32 78n.192
22.34 210n.65
23.1–36 264

23.3 210n.67, 264
23.3–4 264
23.5 269n.90
23.6–12 264
23.13 230n.140, 264
23.13–15 264
23.23 225n.122, 230n.140, 264
23.23–30 264
23.28 225n.122
23.30–36 264
23.37 264
23.38 230n.140
24.1–36 207
24.3 204n.35
24.13 200n.12
24.22 200n.12
24.23–24 110n.65
24.23–26 207
24.26 354n.121
24.30 217n.88
24.34 253n.22
24.45–51 110–11, 147, 200, 292–3
24.49 292–3
24.50–51 293–4
24.51 225n.122
25.1–13 294n.48
25.10 293–4
25.13 110
25.14–30 7n.32, 110, 200, 293–4
25.21 267
25.23 267
25.26 267
25.26–30 230n.140
25.30 267
25.31–32 234
26.8–9 271–2
26.22 271–2
26.24 217n.88, 267n.80
26.28 234
26.29 115–16
26.33 271–2
26.39 154n.61, 188–9, 222, 261
26.51 271–2
26.64 234, 238n.176
26.69–75 271–2
26.73 269n.88
26.75 213–14
27.11 144n.15
27.19 238n.174, 270n.92
27.37 144n.15
27.42 199–200
27.43 188–9, 220n.100, 222, 262–3, 262n.59
27.45 273n.104
27.46 261–3
27.50 262–3

444 INDEX OF BIBLICAL PASSAGES CITED

Matthew (*cont.*)
  27.51–52 273n.104
  27.51–53 262–3, 273n.104
  27.56 271–2
  27.57–61 271–2
  28.1 271–2
  28.3 269n.90
  28.5 108n.55
  28.10 108n.55
  28.13–15 108–9
  28.16–20 107
  28.17 107, 107n.50, 353–4
  28.18 234
  28.18-19 107
  28.20 107, 214n.79

Mark
  1.1 238
  1.6 269n.90
  1.10 302, 302n.68
  1.10–11 225–6, 274
  1.11 238, 238n.175
  1.12 308n.85
  1.15 200n.13, 201nn.21,23,26, 207, 219n.96, 268, 308
  1.16–18 215
  1.19–20 215
  1.20 215n.82
  1.20–26 201n.24
  1.21 208–9
  1.22 238n.178
  1.23 252n.17
  1.24 217n.86, 258–9
  1.27 238n.178
  1.31 252–3
  1.32 203n.33, 247n.2
  1.35–38 256n.33
  1.38 207
  1.39 208n.60
  1.45–2.2 256n.33
  2.1–12 190–1, 247–8
  2.4 249n.9
  2.5 143–4, 190–1, 201, 247n.2, 248
  2.5–11 200
  2.11 190–1
  2.14 215
  3.1 271n.94
  3.1–5 247n.2
  3.8–10 203n.33
  3.13–15 292
  3.13–19a 207
  3.16–19 271–2
  3.22 211–12
  3.22–27 264n.67
  3.23 211–12

3.28–30 264n.65
3.31–5 269n.90
3.33–5 256n.34
4.9 209n.61
4.10–12 209
4.11–12 198n.9
4.12 209n.62
4.14 292n.40
4.23 209n.61
4.26–29 291–2
4.31 197–8
4.35–41 227–8
4.38 231n.141
4.40 201n.25, 217, 227–8, 259, 306
4.41 227–8
5.7 217n.86, 252n.17, 258–9
5.18–20 252–3
5.21–43 247–8
5.22–3 200
5.23 251
5.25–34 247–8
5.27 249–50, 269n.90
5.30 271n.94
5.33 250
5.34 200n.12, 201n.21, 247nn.1,2
5.35–42 200
5.25–26 248–9
6.1–6 220n.100
6.3 244n.191, 267–8
6.4 207
6.5a 268n.83
6.5b 268n.83
6.5–6 267–8
6.6 190n.195, 244, 306
6.7 271–2, 306, 306n.75
6.15 207
6.32–33 256–7
6.34 208n.60, 256n.33
6.41 295n.51
6.45–52 227–8
6.50 227–8
6.52 260n.50
6.53–56 203n.33
6.55 247n.2
7.1–23 264
7.24–30 190–1, 198–9, 247–8
7.27–29 271
7.28 249–50
8.6 6.41 295n.51
8.12 198n.9, 204, 220n.100
8.22 247n.2
8.29 198–9, 238n.177
8.31 234
8.34 219n.98

INDEX OF BIBLICAL PASSAGES CITED 445

8.35 200n.12, 218
9.2–3 226–7
9.3 269n.90
9.4 226–7
9.4–5 78n.194
9.7 211n.69, 226–7, 238
9.9 227n.128
9.14–27 221
9.14–29 190–1
9.16–27 265–6
9.17 230, 231n.141
9.19 221, 259, 265–6
9.24 221, 266n.74
9.29 190n.194
9.31 234
9.41 292
9.42 197n.8, 265n.70
10.17 216n.85
10.17–22 256n.35
10.18 64n.134
10.25 264n.65
10.29–30 256n.34
10.33–34 234
10.45 234
10.46–48 249n.9
10.46–52 247–8
10.48 249
10.52 250n.11, 252–3
11.12–14 227–8
11.20–24 221
11.20–26 227–8
11.22 39n.5, 298–9
11.23 298–9, 314n.96
10.26 200n.12
10.37 144n.15
10.39 219n.98
10.42–45 219n.98
10.43 154n.61
10.45 135n.159
10.52 200n.12
11.10 144n.15
11.22 259
11.22–23 306
11.22–24 190
11.27–33 207n.55
11.31 314n.96
12.1–12 294–5
12.18–27 220n.100
12.26 78n.192, 78n.194
12.28–34 210n.65
13.1–27 207
13.13 110, 200n.12
13.21 314n.96
13.21–22 110n.65, 197n.8

13.26 217n.88
13.30 253n.22
14.21 267n.80
14.24 234
14.36 154n.61, 188–9, 222, 261
14.51–52 270n.92
14.62 217n.88, 234
14.72 213–14
15.2 144n.15
15.26 144n.15
15.32 199–200
15.33 273n.104
15.34 261–3
15.38 273n.104
15.40 271–2
15.43–16.1 271–2
16.1 271–2
16.5 269n.90
16.7 201n.24
16.8 271–2
16.11 266n.76
16.14 266n.76
16.16 201n.21, 266n.76

Luke
1.1 103n.29
1.12–13 275–6
1.18–20 238n.173
1.20 207n.54, 275–6, 354n.122
1.30 275–6
1.31–33 274
1.38 275–6
1.45 207n.54, 275–6, 327n.18
1.46–55 78n.192
1.48 275
1.50 78n.192
1.51 147n.27
1.54–55 274
1.68–79 78n.192
1.72–3 78n.192
2.1–10 273
2.8–14 224
2.9–10 275–6
2.10–18 275
2.15 275
2.25–32 274
2.30 197–9, 275
2.34 275
2.36 275
2.37 275
2.38 275
2.40 269
2.41–50 275n.109
2.41–52 273n.103
2.46 270n.91

Luke (cont.)
  2.46–7 273n.103
  2.47 273n.103
  2.49 238n.175, 273n.103
  3.6 217n.88
  3.8 78n.192
  3.21–22 225–6
  3.22 238, 238n.175, 302n.68
  3.23 275
  3.38 85n.218
  4.1 308n.84
  4.1–4 265n.68
  4.1–13 258–9
  4.9–12 220n.100, 265n.68
  4.12 206n.49
  4.16–30 207
  4.18 294
  4.18–21 308
  4.22 244n.191
  4.31–2 238n.178
  4.31–6 216–17
  4.32 208–9
  4.34 216–17, 217n.86, 252n.17, 258–9
  4.36 238n.178
  4.39 252–3
  4.40 203n.33, 247n.2
  4.40–44 208n.60
  4.43 207
  5.1–11 215–17
  5.3 216–17
  5.4 216–17
  5.5 216–17, 231
  5.8 216–17
  5.9 216–17
  5.10 130, 216–17
  5.11 216–17
  5.17–26 190–1, 247–8
  5.19 249n.9
  5.20 143–4, 190–1, 201, 248
  5.20–24 200
  5.24–50 191
  5.27–8 215
  5.32 232–3
  6.6 271n.94
  6.6–10 248n.3
  6.12–16 207
  6.13 271–2, 292
  6.14–16 271–2
  6.16 203n.33
  6.40 219n.98
  6.43–44 264n.66
  7.1–10 191, 198–9, 219–20, 247–8
  7.6 231
  7.6–8 220
  7.9 220, 252–3

  7.12–13 271n.94
  7.16 207
  7.22 197–8
  7.36–50 247–8
  7.38 249n.9
  7.48 251
  7.50 200n.12, 251
  8.1–3 271–2
  8.2–3 252–3
  8.6 230n.138
  8.8 209n.61
  8.9–10 209
  8.10 198n.9
  8.12 200n.12, 206n.48, 354n.123
  8.19–21 270n.91
  8.21 256n.34
  8.22–5 227–8
  8.24 231n.141
  8.25 201n.25, 217, 227–8, 306
  8.28 217n.86, 252n.17, 258–9
  8.38–39 252–3
  8.40–42 200
  8.40–56 247–8
  8.43–48 247–8
  8.44 249–50, 269n.90
  8.45 231, 271n.94
  8.47 250
  8.48 200n.12, 247n.2
  8.49–55 200
  8.50 247n.2
  9.1 271–2, 292, 306, 306n.75
  9.6 306
  9.8 207
  9.20 198–9, 238n.177
  9.22 234
  9.23 219n.98
  9.24 200n.12
  9.29 269n.90
  9.30–33 78n.194
  9.33 231
  9.35 211n.69, 238
  9.36 217n.88
  9.37–42 221
  9.37–43 191
  9.38 231n.142
  9.38–42 265–6
  9.41 221, 265–6
  9.44 234
  9.49 231
  9.54 292
  9.59–60 264n.65
  10.1 306
  10.1–9 292
  10.1–12 271–2
  10.2 197–8, 208n.60

INDEX OF BIBLICAL PASSAGES CITED 447

10.12–15 198n.9, 264
10.16 292
10.17–20 271–2
10.19–20 306n.75
10.22 236n.166, 258–9, 311n.93
10.25 232n.151
10.25–28 210n.65
10.39–42 271–2
11.2 254–5
11.3 254–5, 256n.34
11.5 211–12
11.11–12 256n.34
11.14 238n.178
11.15 264n.67
11.16 204
11.17–23 264n.67
11.18 211–12
11.20 197–8
11.29 198n.9, 204
11.37–44 264
11.42 264
12.7 72
12.10 264n.65
12.16 254–5
12.22 254–5, 308n.83
12.22–23 232n.151
12.28 254–5
12.28–29 201, 201n.25
12.29 220n.100
12.29–30 72
12.32–38 294n.48
12.33 254–5, 256n.34
12.41–46 110–11, 200–1
12.41–48 292–3
12.42 110–11
12.45 292–3
12.46 301
12.54–56 207
13.10–17 248n.3
13.11–12 271n.94
13.16 78n.192
13.19–21 197–8
13.23 200n.12
13.25–28 207
13.28 78n.192
13.28–29 252–3
13.29 200
13.33 117, 207
14.13 39n.6
14.15–24 115–16
14.35 209n.61
16.10–12 201n.23, 294
16.19–31 78n.192
16.23 39n.6
16.31 78n.194

17.5 259n.48
17.6 217, 221, 298–9, 306
17.11–19 247–9
17.12–13 249n.9
17.15–19 253n.21
17.16 249n.9
17.19 200n.12
17.21 197–8
17.33 218
18.1–8 201n.23, 247–8
18.3–5 249
18.8 251n.14
18.9–14 264–5, 265n.71
18.11–27 201
18.18 232n.151
18.18–23 256n.35
18.26 200n.12
18.29 256n.34
18.30 232n.151
18.32 147n.27
18.32–33 234
18.35–43 247–8, 251n.14
18.37–39 249n.9
18.42 200n.12, 201n.21
18.43 252–3
19.2–10 256n.35
19.9 78n.192
19.10 200n.12
19.11–27 110, 293–4
19.17 267
19.22 267
19.25 200n.12
19.38 144n.15
20.1–8 207n.55
20.9–19 294–5
20.27–40 220n.100
20.37 78n.192, 78n.194
20.46 269n.90
21.1–28 207
21.7 204n.35
21.19 110
21.27 217n.88
21.32 253n.22
22.4 222
22.19–20 234
22.22 267n.80
22.25–27 219n.98
22.31–34 260
22.32 188–9, 260
22.33 231
22.34 260
22.42 154n.61, 188–9, 261
22.43b 102–3
22.61 213–14
22.67 197n.8, 354n.122

448 INDEX OF BIBLICAL PASSAGES CITED

Luke (cont.)
  22.67-68 238n.175
  22.69 217n.88
  23.3 144n.15
  23.8 204
  23.35 200n.12
  23.38 144n.15
  23.44 273n.104
  23.50-24.1 271-2
  24.4 269n.90
  24.6-8 213-14
  24.7 103
  24.10 271-2
  24.11 265-6
  24.19 207
  24.25-27 101n.18, 207n.54
  24.25-28 103
  24.26-27 135
  24.27 78n.194, 271-2
  24.36-43 103
  24.39 103
  24.40 103
  24.41 103, 265-6
  24.42-43 103
  24.44 78n.194, 103, 213-14
  24.44-45 135
  24.44-46 101n.18, 103
  24.44-47 103
  24.46 234
  24.47 234
John
  1 219n.96
  1.1-2 85-6
  1.1-3 24n.134, 85-6, 107n.48, 136-7
  1.1-14 235
  1.3 226
  1.3-4 226-7
  1.4 235-6
  1.6-7 218n.95
  1.7 218n.95
  1.9 86, 226-7
  1.10 200n.16
  1.12 86, 136-7, 200, 208n.56, 216n.83, 235-6
  1.13 218
  1.14 200n.16, 213n.76, 214n.79
  1.18 217n.88, 258-9
  1.26 226
  1.29 200, 217n.88, 235n.160, 301
  1.32 211n.69, 302, 302n.68
  1.32-33 225-6
  1.33 238, 238n.175
  1.34 215, 235-6
  1.35-51 215
  1.36 215, 235n.160

1.36-37 218n.95
1.37 204n.41
1.38 215
1.41 198-9, 215, 218n.95
1.42 215
1.43 215
1.45-46 215
1.45 78n.194
1.47 215
1.48 215
1.49 215, 235-6
1.49-50 201n.22, 235-6
1.50 204n.41, 209-10, 215, 217n.88
1.51 217n.88, 235n.161
2.1-11 201n.17
2.2 213-14
2.3-5 271-2
2.11 203, 209-10
2.14 208
2.19 208
2.21 208
2.22 208, 209n.64
2.23 203, 208n.56, 256n.33
2.23-25 204, 206n.48
2.24 282-3
3.1-2 256n.33
3.1-21 209-10, 213, 256-7
3.2 204, 256-7
3.3 1.13 218, 301
3.4 208
3.4-9 271-2
3.5 301
3.11 217n.88, 257n.40
3.12 201n.21, 208, 213, 264n.62, 265-6, 354n.124
3.14 106n.47, 208, 235n.161
3.15 208, 301
3.15-16 204n.41, 256-7
3.16 24n.134, 86, 198-200, 208, 301
3.17 200n.12
3.17-18 204n.41, 265
3.18 208n.56, 235-6, 256-7, 264-5, 264n.62, 354n.123
3.21 256-7
3.32 217n.88
3.34 209-10
4.4-42 257-8
4.9 257-8
4.10-14 256n.34
4.11 257-8
4.13-15 209-10
4.14 86, 218
4.17-18 271
4.19 207, 257-8

INDEX OF BIBLICAL PASSAGES CITED 449

4.21 327n.16
4.26 235n.162
4.29 209–10, 257–8
4.34 222–3
4.36 200
4.39 209–10, 257–8
4.42 218n.95
4.44 207
4.45 256n.33
4.46–54 190–1, 198–9, 247–8
4.47–49 271
4.48 204, 264, 264n.62
4.50 187n.184, 201n.21
4.53 86
5.1–9 248n.3
5.6 271
5.17 222n.111
5.19 217n.88, 222n.111
5.19–20 222n.110
5.21 86, 200
5.24 197–8, 200n.15, 201
5.25 235–6, 236n.163
5.27 235n.161
5.30 222–3
5.31 209–10
5.31–32 211n.69
5.31–40 211n.72
5.31–67 222n.111
5.34 200n.12
5.38 206n.48, 264n.62, 267n.81
5.45–46 78n.194
5.46 213
5.46–47 78n.194
5.47 264n.62
6.1–5 255–6
6.2 256n.33
6.7 271–2
6.9 271–2
6.15 256n.32
6.16–21 227–8
6.19 227–8
6.21 227–8
6.25 201n.19
6.26 235n.161, 257–8
6.26–27 256n.33
6.27 256n.34
6.27–29 218
6.27–40 201n.19
6.29 257–8
6.30 257–8
6.34 257–8
6.35 86, 200, 236n.165
6.37–38 222n.111
6.39 106n.47

6.40 106n.47
6.44 106n.47
6.46 217n.88, 222–3
6.47–48 201n.21
6.53 235n.161
6.54 106n.47
6.56 222n.111
6.63 301
6.64 264n.62, 266–7
6.65 266–7
6.68 86, 209–10, 218n.95
6.68–69 218
6.69 20, 66n.144, 198–9, 327n.16
7.1–9 270n.93
7.3–4 271–2
7.16 209–10, 222–3
7.31 203
7.37–38 256n.34
7.37–39 201n.23
7.38 86
7.38–39 301
7.42 230n.137
7.46 238n.178
7.50 209–10, 256–7
8.2–11 224
8.12 86, 86n.225, 209–10, 235
8.12–20 206n.46, 211n.72
8.14 209–10
8.24 106n.47, 201n.21, 236n.165, 327n.16
8.28 106n.47, 222n.111, 235n.161
8.31–59 78n.192
8.38 217n.88
8.45–46 264, 264n.62, 354n.123
8.49 222–3
8.50 222n.111
8.57 217n.88
8.58 240n.187
8.59 240n.187
9 200n.13
9.1–7 268
9.2–3 144n.13
9.15 258
9.17 258
9.18 248n.3
9.25 258
9.30 204
9.33 258
9.35 235, 248n.3, 258
9.35–37 235n.161
9.35–38 268
9.36 248n.3
9.36–38 235
9.38 248n.3
9.39 200, 235

450 INDEX OF BIBLICAL PASSAGES CITED

John (*cont.*)
  10 256–7
  10.9 86, 200n.12, 204n.41
  10.11 86
  10.14–15 72
  10.20 211–12
  10.22 204–5
  10.22–39 204–6
  10.24–25 204n.37, 209–10
  10.25 204–5
  10.25–26 264n.62
  10.25–28 204–5
  10.26 204–5, 209–10, 256–7, 264
  10.26–27 204–5
  10.26–28 200
  10.27 201n.19
  10.27–28 204–5
  10.28 86
  10.29–30 205
  10.30 222–3, 240n.187
  10.31 240n.187
  10.33 205, 240n.187
  10.36 205n.44, 235–6
  10.36–37 235–6
  10.37–38 205
  10.38 189n.192
  10.41 205–6
  10.42 205–6
  11 226–7
  11.1–44 190–1
  11.4 226–7
  11.12 190n.193, 200n.12
  11.17–44 271–2
  11.21 251
  11.21–22 226
  11.25 86, 218
  11.25–26 200, 226, 236n.165
  11.25–27 187n.184, 235–6, 241n.188
  11.26 204n.41, 226–7, 280n.116
  11.26–27 201n.22
  11.27 226–7, 235–6, 280n.116, 327n.16
  11.39 226
  11.40 217n.88, 226–7
  11.42 226–7, 327n.16
  11.44 226
  12.1–8 271–2
  12.10b–11 203
  12.16 213–14
  12.20–22 271–2
  12.25 86, 219n.98
  12.26–27 154n.61
  12.27 222, 222n.111, 261n.55
  12.28 211n.69
  12.28–29 238
  12.32 106n.47, 197–8

  12.34–36 235n.161
  12.37–40 209n.62
  12.37–41 235n.162
  12.39 264, 264n.62
  12.44 222n.110
  12.44–47 204n.41
  12.47 200n.12
  12.48 244–5
  12.49 222n.111
  13.16 219n.98
  13.19 188–9, 209n.64, 327n.16
  13.25 271–2
  13.27 267n.80
  13.31–32 222–3
  14.1 80, 188–90, 222–3, 306
  14.1–2 235–6
  14.1–3 200, 201n.23, 204n.41
  14.1–4 110n.66
  14.3 197–8
  14.6 86
  14.8 265–6
  14.9 211n.72
  14.9–10 214, 235–6, 242–3, 258n.44
  14.9–12 306
  14.10 264n.62, 265–6
  14.10–11 222–3, 327n.16
  14.10–12 188–90
  14.12 189n.192
  14.14 256n.34
  14.15–17 208
  14.16–17 299–300
  14.19 188–9, 301
  14.29 209n.64
  15.4–5 86
  15.15 259n.47
  15.18–21 219n.98
  15.18–25 208
  15.19 88n.231
  16.8–9 265
  16.9 188–9, 264–5
  16.12–13 302
  16.12–15 208
  16.16–24 208
  16.19 264n.62
  16.24 213–14
  16.25 208
  16.27 188–90
  16.28 222n.111
  16.30 188–90, 222n.110, 327n.16
  16.32 260n.52
  17 224–5
  17.2–3 86
  17.4 222–3
  17.5 224–5
  17.8 188–90, 213n.76, 222n.110, 327n.16

17.20-21 188-9
17.21 222-3, 222n.111
17.25 222n.111
18 225n.120
18.10 271-2
18.33 144n.15
19 225n.120
19.7 235-6
19.14 144n.15
19.19-21 144n.15
19.30 225n.120
19.38-42 271-2
19.39 209-10, 256-7
20.14-15 215n.82
20.14-17 105
20.17 105-6
20.19-23 105-6
20.20 105-6
20.24-29 105-7
20.25 264n.62, 265-6, 271-2, 354n.122
20.27 105-7, 265-6, 266n.78
20.27-29 203
20.28 218n.95, 236n.165
20.29 106-7, 196n.1, 217n.88, 265-6, 266n.78
20.31 106n.47, 235-6, 236n.164, 327n.16

Acts
  1.3 103n.29
  1.5 299-300
  1.8 130, 306-7
  1.24 72
  2.1-21 302
  2.2-4 302n.68
  2.4 302
  2.6-8 308
  2.14-36 76, 203, 308
  2.17 76
  2.21 76
  2.22 232
  2.22-24 203
  2.22-40 265n.69
  2.23 64n.134, 72
  2.23-24 100
  2.25-28 76
  2.30-32 103n.28
  2.32 100
  2.33-36 234
  2.34-35 76
  2.36 76
  2.38 72, 129-30, 234, 301
  2.42-47 297
  2.44 101n.19, 110-11
  2.44-45 303-4
  2.46 303-4
  3.6 129-30, 307n.82

3.11-26 265n.69
3.13 232
3.14 232
3.15 232
3.16 129-30, 220n.101, 232
3.18-24 76n.185
3.19 110-11
3.21 110-11
3.22 78n.194
3.25 303-4
4.4 110-11
4.7 129-30
4.9-12 232
4.10 129-30, 232
4.17-18 129-30
4.30 129-30
4.32 110-11
4.32-33 303-4
4.32-35 297
4.33 306n.79
4.34-35 303-4
5.1-11 297
5.4 307n.80
5.5 307n.80
5.9 307n.80
5.10 307n.80
5.12-14 203n.33
5.12-15 207n.54
5.14 110-11
5.16 4.33 306n.79
5.18-19 308n.83
5.26-33 101
5.28 129-30
5.29-32 232
5.30 101, 101n.18
5.31 232
5.32 101, 306n.79
5.38-39 314n.96
5.39 101n.19
5.40 129-30
6.1-3 303-4
6.1-4 110-11
6.1-7 297
6.6 296n.52
6.7 110-11
7.2-53 232
7.33 306n.79
7.37 78n.194
7.38 43n.33
7.51-53 265n.69
7.52 232
8.4-24 307
8.5 307
8.6-7 306n.79
8.10 307

452 INDEX OF BIBLICAL PASSAGES CITED

Acts (*cont.*)
8.12 130n.135, 307
8.13 307
8.14–15 307
8.14–17 299–300, 299n.56
8.16 129–30
8.18–19 307
8.18–21 306n.74
8.18–25 297
8.19 308n.83
8.20 65–6, 307
8.23 307
8.29 308n.85
8.37–38 265n.69
9.3–6 130
9.4 265n.69
9.15–16 130n.135
9.27–28 129–30
9.42 203n.33
10.13 129–30, 129n.133
10.36 101
10.38 101, 306n.76
10.39–41 101
10.41 101
10.42 234
10.43 101, 103n.28, 129–30
10.48 129–30
11.12 308nn.83,85
11.18 301
11.21 207n.54
12.7 308n.83
13.2 130n.134, 308n.83
13.4 130n.134, 308nn.83,85
13.12 207n.54
13.16–39 265n.69
13.26 110–11
13.27 101
13.28 101
13.30–31 101
13.39 78n.194, 101n.19, 110–11
13.47 44n.36
13.48 101n.19
14.3 10.13 129–30, 129n.133
14.8–13 237n.172
14.15 237n.172
14.22–23 110–11
14.23 295–6, 296n.52
15.6–29 297
15.7 44n.36, 207n.54
15.7–8 299–300
15.9 44n.36
15.10 44n.36
15.11 44n.36
15.26 130n.135, 311n.93

15.40 311n.93
16.5 110–11
16.6 130n.134, 308n.83
16.6–7 308n.85
16.10 130n.134
16.15 110–11
16.20 68
16.25–31 203n.33
16.25–34 68
16.31 68
16.34 68, 295n.51
17 89
17.10–12 207n.54
17.11–12 111n.68
17.20 101n.18
17.22–31 88–9
17.23–24 88–9
17.27 88–9
17.29 65–6
17.30 88–9, 234, 265n.69
17.30–31 88–9, 101n.18, 110–11
17.31 244–5
17.32 99n.11
17.34 88–9, 101n.19, 110–11
18.8 129n.133
18.9 129n.133
19.1–6 299–300
19.6 302
19.2 201n.24
19.5 129–30
19.11–20 129–30, 306n.79
19.17 130n.135
20.17–38 283n.6
20.22 130n.134, 308n.85
20.22–23 308n.83
20.23 130n.134
20.28 283n.6
20.32 295–6
21.4 308nn.83,85
21.13 130n.135
22.1–21 104n.32
22.6–10 130
22.16 129–30
24.25 110–11
26.2–20 104n.32
26.9 130n.135
26.13–18 130
26.18 130
26.22–23 78n.194
27.23 129n.133
27.25 39n.4
28.23 78n.194

Romans
1 42n.24

INDEX OF BIBLICAL PASSAGES CITED

1–2 50
1–4 60n.113
1.1 179n.162
1.4 116n.88
1.5 27n.148, 146n.21, 153–4, 284
1.7 73n.173, 126–7, 284n.9
1.8–10 125n.118
1.9 309n.88
1.12 153–4, 290n.35
1.16 42–3, 146, 309n.89
1.16–17 42–3, 146
1.16–18 165
1.17 42–3, 63–4, 164
1.18 147, 153
1.18–23 88–9
1.19–20 147
1.20–21 88–9
1.21 88–9, 147
1.21–23 151
1.22 147, 149
1.23 147
1.24 147n.26
1.24–31 147
1.25 151n.47
1.26 147n.26
1.26–27 88–9
1.28 88–9
1.30 88–9, 147, 150n.42
1.31 88–9
1.32 147
2 43n.31
2–4 57–8
2.1 147–8, 153–4
2.1–2 149n.37
2.5 57–8, 64–5, 147–8, 166
2.7 115–16, 169
2.8 147–8
2.10 42–3, 69n.153
2.10–11 43
2.12 44n.34, 57–8
2.13 57–8
2.18 147–8
2.20 147–9
2.21–25 57–8
2.25 57–8
2.27 54–5, 57–8
2.29 44n.34, 54–5, 57–8, 147–8
3 43, 47–8, 189–90
3–4 54–5
3.1–3 43–4
3.1–9 43n.31
3.2 43, 47–8, 155n.63, 283n.7, 289
3.2–4 47–8
3.3 45, 50, 71, 148, 153–4

3.3–4 44n.35, 64n.133
3.4 45, 151n.47
3.7 45
3.9 44, 149, 183n.172
3.9–10 47–9, 153–4
3.10–12 44
3.17 69n.153
3.19–20 149n.37
3.20 48n.54, 54–5, 57–8
3.21 45–6, 63–4, 76, 154, 164–5
3.21–22 42–4, 142n.1
3.21–26 45–6, 58–9, 76, 153–4, 157–8
3.22 42–3, 134n.153, 154, 157
3.22–23 153–4
3.22–24 284n.9
3.23 44, 112
3.24 42–8, 91, 134n.153, 143n.8, 154, 164–5
3.24–25 76–7
3.25 45–6, 143n.8
3.26 45–6, 73n.173, 88–9, 110, 112, 154–6
3.28 46n.45
3.29 57–8
3.30 46n.45, 76, 155n.63
3.31 47n.51
4 57–8
4.3 57
4.4 57–8
4.5 57–8
4.5–8 77
4.9 57, 77
4.10–11 57
4.13 55n.90, 57–8, 77
4.14 57, 77
4.14–15 57, 57n.99
4.15 57–8
4.16 77
4.17–22 57
4.19–21 59n.109
4.20 77, 298–9, 353–4
4.23–24 57n.97
4.24 57, 153
5.1 153, 284n.9, 301
5.1–2 112
5.1–5 112, 301
5.2 112, 153, 284n.9
5.3–5 62–3, 112
5.6 156, 164–5
5.6–7 154n.61, 155n.63
5.8 73n.173
5.9 112, 153
5.10 153
5.14 146n.21
5.15 73n.173, 146n.21, 155n.65, 284n.9
5.15–21 83n.210

454 INDEX OF BIBLICAL PASSAGES CITED

Romans (*cont.*)
5.16 146n.21
5.19 146n.21
5.20 47–8, 54–5, 57–8
5.21 112, 183n.172
6.1–14 173n.135
6.2 69, 170–1
6.3 171n.130
6.4 169–71
6.5 169–71
6.6 66n.144, 169–70, 183n.172
6.7 183n.172
6.8 115–17, 169–71, 327
6.9 183n.172
6.10–11 136
6.11 59–60, 169, 171, 310n.92
6.17 291n.38
6.18 310n.92
6.19 301
6.22–23 74, 301
6.23 75n.179, 115–16, 125n.117, 169
7.6 309n.88
7.14 150
7.14–24 150
7.15 150
7.19 150
7.23 150
7.24–25 150
8 89–90
8.2 301
8.4 59n.112
8.5 301
8.6 301
8.9–10 310
8.10 301
8.11–13 49
8.13 69
8.17 169–70
8.18 166
8.21 116n.89
8.22 89–90
8.24–25 74n.176
8.28 178n.160
8.29 64n.134
8.29–30 115–16, 169–70
8.30 74n.177
8.32 110n.66, 115–16
8.34 124–5
8.37–39 64n.134
8.38 120n.104
8.39 73n.173, 128–9, 321
9 50, 164n.99
9–10 57–8
9–11 47–50, 54–5, 58n.105, 60n.113, 75n.179, 148

9.3 128–9
9.4 58n.104
9.4–5 43n.33, 47n.51
9.6 47–8
9.7–8 47–8
9.8 47–8, 47n.51
9.11 47–8, 74n.177
9.13 69n.153
9.14 27n.147, 64n.133, 73n.173, 164n.99
9.14–15 47–8
9.14–16 63–4
9.15 50, 78n.194
9.16 47–8, 74n.177
9.17 47–8, 64n.134, 164n.99
9.18 47–8
9.19 74n.177, 164n.99
9.22–23 47–8
9.23 116n.89, 164n.99
9.24 74n.177, 164n.99
9.30–32 48n.54
9.31 47–8, 48n.54, 148
9.31–32 58n.102
9.32 44n.34, 47–8, 48n.54, 148
9.32–33 48n.54
10.1 47–8, 125n.118
10.2 48, 148n.34, 149–50
10.3–4 48n.54
10.4 46n.45, 48, 59n.112, 126–7, 148, 213n.76
10.5–13 78n.194
10.6–11 48n.54
10.8 48, 76
10.8–10 48
10.8–11 148
10.9 5n.23, 47n.51
10.12 47n.51
10.14 148
10.17 48, 148
10.19 49
11 49, 95–6, 148
11.1 27n.147, 49, 64n.133, 73n.173, 149
11.2 49, 72
11.2–8 74n.177
11.3 49
11.5 49
11.11 47n.51, 49
11.14 49
11.17 44n.34
11.17–18 49
11.17–24 170–1, 170n.124
11.20 148, 170–1
11.23 170–1
11.25 49–50
11.25–26 61, 75n.179
11.26 49–50, 72
11.26b–27 59n.111

INDEX OF BIBLICAL PASSAGES CITED

11.27 49–50, 58n.104
11.28 49–50
11.29 299n.56
11.31 73n.173
11.32 50
11.34 165, 167n.112
11.36 64n.134, 155n.63
12.1 136n.160
12.3 288–9
12.3–8 303–4
12.6 288–9
12.6–8 59–60, 177n.154, 288–9, 302, 305n.72
12.9 69n.153
12.11 309n.88
12.19 69n.153, 314n.96
13.8–10 69n.153
13.9 73n.173
13.11 75n.179
13.11–14 115–16
13.12 120n.104
14 49
14.1 49, 126–7
14.3 126–7
14.7–8 74n.176
14.15 69n.153
14.18 49
14.19 69n.153
14.23 353n.118
15.1–3 177n.153
15.7 127–8, 136
15.8 56n.94
15.13 302n.66
15.19 165n.104, 309
15.33 69n.153
16.5 69n.153
16.8–9 69n.153
16.12 69n.153
16.20 120n.104
16.26 146n.21

1 Corinthians
1.1–2 74n.177
1.2 128–9, 129n.130
1.3 98, 284n.9
1.6 66n.144
1.7 64–5, 110, 166
1.8 111, 166
1.8–9 62, 69
1.10–17 167n.112
1.17 130n.134
1.18 75n.179, 148, 175–6, 194n.201, 310n.90
1.18–23 148
1.18–2.10 194n.201
1.19 148, 169n.119
1.20 148
1.21 148, 148n.35, 151, 175–6

1.22–3 148, 151
1.23 151
1.24 148n.35, 148n.36
1.26 74n.177
1.30 143n.8, 175–6
2.4 66n.144, 130n.134, 165–6, 194n.201, 302, 309
2.4–5 310n.90
2.7 116n.89, 165–6, 194n.201
2.8 194n.201
2.9 69n.153, 165–6
2.9–10 194n.201
2.10 165–6, 194n.201
2.11 66n.144
2.12 165–6
2.16 167n.112
3.5 129
3.5–9 286–7
3.6 74
3.6–7 171n.128
3.9 286
3.11 127–9
3.13 166n.106
3.16 289
3.23 175–6
4.1 284–5, 284n.13, 316–17
4.1–2 42–3, 115, 175–6, 284–5
4.1–10 302
4.2 115
4.3–5 175–6
4.5 72, 166
4.6 115, 175–6, 175n.145
4.6–13 115
4.7 175–6
4.9 65–6
4.9–10 175–6
4.9–13 136n.160, 164n.97
4.10 115
4.10–13 115
4.12 115
4.13 69n.153
4.14 69n.153
4.16 62n.126
4.16–17 115, 175–6
4.17 69n.153, 286–7
4.18 175n.145
4.19 175n.145
4.21 69n.153
5.2 74, 175n.145
5.4 309–10
5.5 75n.179, 120n.104
6.6 106n.44
6.11 301
6.17 310
6.19 69, 289, 301

456 INDEX OF BIBLICAL PASSAGES CITED

1 Corinthians (*cont.*)
 6.19–20 128n.128
 7.5 119n.96, 120n.104
 7.12–15 152n.50
 7.15 69n.153
 7.17 74n.177
 7.17–24 49n.61
 7.21 74n.177
 7.22 179n.162
 7.26 65–6
 7.36 65–6
 7.40 65–6
 8 49
 8.1 175n.145
 8.3 69n.153
 8.9 49, 284n.9
 9.1 105n.39
 9.2 128n.127
 9.4 74
 9.4–5 93–4
 9.13 165n.101
 9.14 284n.12, 284n.13
 9.16 284–5, 284n.12
 9.17 43n.33, 284–5, 284nn.12,13
 10.1–13 79n.195
 10.4 62
 10.7 49n.60
 10.9 62
 10.13 62
 10.14 49n.60
 10.20 120n.104
 10.31–11.2 176–7
 11.1 136n.160, 176–7, 243, 286–7
 11.2 176–7
 11.12 155n.63
 11.24 58n.103
 11.25 58n.104
 12 288–9
 12.3 165–6
 12.4 165–6
 12.4–11 305n.72
 12.6–12 302
 12.7 64–5, 288–9
 12.8–10 59–60, 177
 12.9 27–8, 201n.20, 287–8, 299–300, 299n.55, 317n.103
 12.12–30 303–4
 12.27 280–1
 12.28–31 177n.154
 13.2 59n.112, 298–9
 13.4 175n.145
 14 306n.74
 14.1 69n.153, 165–6
 14.1–2 177n.154

14.6 165–6
14.15 128n.128
14.22–24 152n.50
14.25 128n.128, 152n.50, 165–6
14.26 165–6
14.30 165–6
14.37 66n.143
15 103, 111, 224
15.1–2 110–11, 112n.75
15.2–4 118–19
15.3 64–5, 104
15.3–4 105, 155n.65
15.3–8 103–5
15.4 64–5, 176n.149
15.5–8 64–5, 165n.102
15.8 128n.127
15.10 104
15.11 65–6, 97n.1, 103–4
15.19 74n.176
15.20 115–16
15.21 104, 155n.65
15.22 81n.200, 85n.218, 104
15.23 101n.18, 110
15.24 118–19
15.24–28 64n.134, 75n.179, 118–19
15.25 127
15.27 118–19
15.28 118–19
15.35–54 169n.118
15.36 74n.177
15.50 169
15.52–54 115–16
15.52–57 115–16, 121
15.57 115–16, 169
15.58 69n.153, 74n.176
16.7 130n.134, 135n.155
16.11 69n.153
16.13 110–11
16.24 69n.153

2 Corinthians
 1.2 127–8, 284n.9
 1.18 41, 46, 80
 1.20 56n.94
 1.22 52n.72, 309n.88
 1.24 153n.52
 2.4 69n.153
 2.8 69n.153
 2.10 128–9, 129n.130
 2.11 120n.104
 2.14 165, 167n.112
 2.15 75n.179, 169
 3 54–5
 3.2 290
 3.5–16 57–8

INDEX OF BIBLICAL PASSAGES CITED

3.6 58n.104, 301
3.7–8 54–5
3.7–18 54–5, 55n.86
3.9–10 54–5
3.10 31–2, 56–8, 80, 126–7
3.14 54–5, 58n.104
3.14–16 54–5
3.16 54–5
3.17 310n.92
3.17–18 54–5, 299n.55, 310
3.18 116n.89, 165n.103, 302n.66
4.3 169
4.4 116n.89, 146n.21
4.6 66n.144, 116n.89, 165n.103
4.8–9 62–3
4.10 69, 165, 289n.34
4.10–14 124
4.11 165
4.12 284n.10
4.13 27–8, 153n.52, 176n.149, 287–8, 299–300, 361n.1
4.13–14 117, 169, 286, 327
4.14 62–3, 66n.144, 115–18, 327n.19
4.17 116n.89
5.1–5 301
5.2 75n.179
5.5 52n.72
5.8 115–16, 153n.52
5.17 59–60, 62n.121, 69, 169
5.18 125n.117
5.21 156, 284n.9
6.4 74
6.6 69n.153
6.14–15 152–3
7.1 69n.153
8.7 77n.190
8.7–8 69n.153
8.9 115–16
8.21 128–9, 129n.130
8.24 69n.153
10.4 120n.104
10.7 66n.144
10.8 309, 310n.90
10.15 77n.190, 110, 286–7
11.6 165n.103
12.1 64–5
12.2 105n.39
12.3 128n.127
12.4 64–5
12.8 64–5
12.7 70, 105n.39, 120n.104
12.7–10 62–3, 62n.123, 70, 105n.39
12.9 70
12.10 70

12.12 165n.104
12.15 69n.153
12.19 69n.153
12.20 175n.145
13.2–5 128n.128, 284n.10, 289n.34
13.3 289
13.4 136
13.5 77n.190, 289
13.7–9 125n.117
13.11 69n.153
13.13 127–8

Galatians
1.3 127–8, 284n.9
1.4 143n.8
1.6 74n.177
1.6–9 151, 167n.112
1.10 179n.162
1.12 165n.102
1.13–14 48n.53
1.13–16 44n.38
1.14 149–51
1.15 41
1.15–16 49, 165, 284n.11, 285
1.19 218n.91
1.23 165n.102, 289n.33
1.24 128n.128
2 157, 189–90
2–3 58n.102, 153n.51
2.2–10 48n.55
2.7 43n.33
2.7–9 283–4
2.15–20 55–9, 157
2.15–21 153n.53
2.16 64–5, 110, 134n.153, 154–6, 170–1
2.16–20 133n.152
2.17 134n.153, 284n.9
2.19 77, 169–71
2.19–20 59–60, 170–1
2.20 59–60, 61n.117, 64–5, 69–70, 134n.153, 154n.61, 170–1, 284n.9, 289n.34
2.21 170–1, 284n.9
3 50, 55–6
3.2 151, 201n.24, 299–300
3.2–5 55n.86
3.3 301
3.5 309–10
3.5–6 77
3.6 54–6
3.7 77
3.8 55n.90, 56n.94, 77n.189
3.9 77n.189
3.10 54–5
3.11 42–3, 42n.24
3.13 54–5, 143n.8, 299–300

458 INDEX OF BIBLICAL PASSAGES CITED

Galatians (*cont.*)
  3.13–14 155–6
  3.14 77, 77n.189, 299–300
  3.15 55n.88, 58n.104
  3.16 55–6, 55n.91, 58n.104, 77, 77n.189
  3.17 54–6, 55n.88, 58n.104, 77
  3.18 55–6, 77
  3.19 54–6, 58n.102, 77, 126–7
  3.21 77
  3.22 54–6, 77
  3.23 164–5
  3.23–26 153n.51
  3.25 55–6
  3.26 115–16
  3.26–4.7 53n.74
  3.28 49n.61
  3.29 77
  4.1–6 310n.92
  4.1–7 115–16, 169
  4.1–11 153n.51
  4.3 153n.51
  4.5 143n.8, 153n.51
  4.4 58n.102, 165
  4.6 310
  4.7 294n.47
  4.9 54n.82, 72, 153n.51, 165
  4.14 165
  4.24 58n.104
  4.24–26 57n.95
  5.4 128–9
  5.5 74n.176, 301, 302n.66
  5.13 74n.177
  5.13–14 69n.153
  5.14 59n.112
  5.16 301
  5.16–18 301
  5.19 49n.60, 149n.39
  5.21 169
  5.22 27–8, 69, 69n.153, 74, 201n.20, 287–8, 299–300, 317n.103
  5.25 301
  6.8 75n.179, 115–16, 171n.128, 301
  6.10 317–18

Ephesians
  1.1 88
  1.3–6 87, 137n.163
  1.4–15 88n.231
  1.5 88
  1.7 88
  1.12 88
  1.13 88, 159n.78, 201n.24, 299–300
  1.14 88
  1.15 159n.78
  1.18–19 115–16

  1.18–22 120n.98
  2.2 120n.104
  2.5 125n.120
  2.8 159
  2.13 159
  2.16 159
  2.19–20 303–4
  3.16 302n.66
  4.5 159, 287
  4.11 177n.154
  4.11–12 305n.72
  4.11–13 159
  4.15 303–4
  4.25 303–4
  5.1–2 177n.150
  5.5 115–16
  5.22–23 303–4
  5.29–30 303–4
  6.11 119
  6.13–17 119
  6.21–2 287

Philippians
  1.1 127–8, 179n.162
  1.1 284n.9
  1.3 62–3
  1.3–4 125n.118
  1.6 66n.144, 69, 74n.177
  1.9 125n.118
  1.11 284n.9
  1.12–14 62–3
  1.16 69n.153
  1.19 310
  1.20 128n.128
  1.21–3 168n.115
  1.23 115–16
  1.25 157n.71
  1.27 88n.232
  1.28 169
  1.28–9 74n.177
  1.29 136–7, 157n.71
  2.5 149–50
  2.5–11 177
  2.6–7 154n.61
  2.6–11 88n.232
  2.7–11 137n.163
  2.12 69n.153
  2.13 74n.177, 289
  2.17 88n.232
  2.25–30 287n.22
  3 157
  3.3 302n.66
  3.3–4 66n.144
  3.6 48n.53
  3.7–11 153n.53, 157

INDEX OF BIBLICAL PASSAGES CITED

3.8 165n.102
3.9 149–50, 154, 155n.63, 157n.71, 165n.102
3.9–11 157
3.10 169–70
3.12 130n.134, 157n.71
3.12–14 74n.176
3.14 74n.177, 93–4
3.14–15 165
3.15 165
3.17 62n.126
3.20 75n.179
3.20–21 128n.125
3.21 115–16, 169–70
3.22 75n.179
4.1 69n.153, 128–9
4.1–9 129
4.4 128–9
4.5 128–9
4.6 128–9
4.7 128–9

Colossians
1.2 136
1.3 120n.98
1.4 136
1.7 136, 287n.22
1.10 120n.98
1.11 120n.98
1.12 136
1.13 120n.98
1.15–16 136
1.15–20 136, 137n.163
1.18 303–4
1.19–20 159
1.20 136
1.21 68n.149, 136
1.21–23 159n.79
1.22 136
1.23 136
1.24 303–4
1.24–25 124n.116
1.26–28 115–16
1.28 136
2.7 171n.128
2.10 304–5
2.12 67–8
2.18 132n.145
2.19 303–4
3.2 66n.142
3.4 115–16, 121
3.15 303–4
4.7–9 287n.22

1 Thessalonians
1.1 127–8, 284n.9
1.2 125n.118
1.3 70–1, 136n.162
1.3–4 69n.153
1.4 74n.177
1.5 165–6, 165n.104, 298–9, 302, 309
1.6 62n.126, 136n.160, 174–5, 178–9, 290
1.6a 136n.162
1.6–8 179n.161
1.6b–7 136n.162
1.7 290
1.8 290
1.8–10 112n.75
1.9 5n.23, 41, 54n.82, 151n.47
1.10 64–5, 80, 109–10
1.23 74
2.2 147n.27
2.4 43n.33, 109, 155n.64, 298–9
2.8 69n.153
2.12 116n.89
2.13 128n.128
2.14 174–5, 290
2.18 120n.104
3.1–8 286–7
3.2–3 74, 77n.190
3.5 119
3.5–6 77n.190
3.6 69n.153
3.10 77n.190, 110, 125n.118, 129, 174–5
3.11 130n.134, 135n.156
3.12 110, 127–9, 136
3.13 174–5
4.7 74n.177
4.9 69n.153
4.13–14 74n.176
4.14 117–18
4.16–17 115–16, 168n.115
5.8 69n.153, 119
5.10 115–16
5.13 69n.153
5.19–20 177n.154
5.20–21 27n.148
5.23–24 62
5.24 39n.1

2 Thessalonians
1.3 109–10
1.4 111
1.4–7 115
1.11–12 115
2.9 119–20
2.10–11 119–20
2.12 119–20, 354n.122
2.15 119–20
3.3 109n.61, 128n.125
3.7–9 177n.150

460 INDEX OF BIBLICAL PASSAGES CITED

1 Timothy
  1.2 289n.33
  1.12 210n.66, 285n.15
  1.13 149–50, 327–8
  1.14 327–8
  1.15 290–1, 324n.1, 327–8
  1.16 327–8
  1.18 295–6, 296n.52
  2.4 159
  2.5–6 159
  2.7 159
  3.1 210n.66, 290–1
  3.9 111
  4.1 289n.33
  4.8 290–1
  4.9 210n.66, 290–1
  5.8 152n.49, 289n.33
  5.22 296n.52

2 Timothy
  1.5 160
  1.7 309
  1.7–8 310n.90
  1.8 160, 170n.120
  1.9 160
  1.10 160, 285n.16
  1.12 285n.15, 285n.16
  1.12–13 151n.45
  1.14 282n.1, 295–6
  2.2 295–6
  2.3 170n.120
  2.11 170n.120, 210n.66, 290–1, 327–8
  2.11–13 125
  2.12 115–16
  2.12b–13 125
  2.13 80, 125
  2.19 72
  3.2 147n.27
  3.8–9 78n.194
  3.10 160
  3.10–14 115
  3.10–16 160
  3.14 160, 290–1
  3.14–15 110n.64, 160
  3.15 290–1
  4.5 296n.52
  4.7 115
  4.8 115

Titus
  1.1 88
  1.2 88
  1.4 88
  1.9 110n.64, 327–8
  1.15 152n.49
  2.13–14 120n.98
  3.8 210n.66, 290–1, 327–8

Philemon
  1 69n.153
  3 127–8
  5 69n.153
  7 69n.153
  9 69n.153
  16 69n.153

Hebrews
  1.1 148n.34
  1.2 124
  1.3 87, 113n.78
  1.10 113
  1.10–12 87, 137n.163
  2.2 87
  2.3 87
  2.3–4 87
  2.8 120n.104
  2.10 87
  2.13 87
  2.14 87, 120n.104
  2.15 87
  2.17 124, 160–1
  2.17–18 161
  3.1–2 124, 161
  3.2 237n.172, 298
  3.2–5 78–9
  3.5–6 161
  3.6 154n.61, 303–4
  3.8 152n.49
  3.11 78–9
  3.12 78–9, 124, 152n.49
  3.14 113n.78
  4.1 124
  4.2–3 67n.147
  4.11 124
  4.13 72
  4.14 124
  4.15 124
  4.16 124
  5.12 43n.33
  6.1 67n.147
  7.22 67n.147
  8.6 67n.147
  8.8–10 67n.147
  9.15 67n.147
  10.16–17 67
  10.18–19 67
  10.23 67, 67n.146
  10.25 67
  10.30–31 67

INDEX OF BIBLICAL PASSAGES CITED   461

10.32–38 79
10.35 79
10.38 42n.24, 79
10.38–11.39 92n.244
10.39 79
11.1 1n.1, 27n.145, 113–14
11.4 79, 92n.246
11.4–40 79
11.5 79
11.6 39n.6, 108n.54
11.7 79
11.11 78
11.8 79
11.8–12 78
11.13 80
11.23 79
11.24–25 79
11.29 79
11.31 79
11.33–35 79
11.35–7 92n.246
11.35–38 79
11.40 80
12.1 79
12.1–2 80
12.1–3 177n.155
12.2 67n.147
12.22–24 121
12.24 67n.147
12.28 115–16
13.7 67n.147
13.8 139–40, 278–9

James
 1.2–3 111
 1.3 111–12
 1.6–8 39n.8, 353n.118
 2.14–26 111–12
 2.19 5n.23, 108n.54, 327n.16
 2.23 54n.78, 77n.190
 4.6 147n.27
 4.7 120n.104
 4.8 39n.8, 353n.118
 5.7–8 111–12
 5.7–11 111–12
 5.10 111–12
 5.11 111–12
 5.13–15 190n.195
 5.17–18 111–12
 5.18 111–12

1 Peter
 1.1 68n.149
 1.3 121n.106
 1.3–9 107–8

1.4–5 115–16
1.5 62n.122, 115–16
1.5–7 111
1.7 115–16
1.8 115–16
1.10 108n.54
1.12 108n.54
1.20–21 68
1.21 121n.106
2.4–5 154n.61
2.7 152n.49
2.9–10 303–4
2.21 177n.150
2.22–25 105n.38
2.23 121n.106
2.23–24 177n.150
3.6 303–4
3.18 105n.38
4.7 88
4.11 43n.33
4.13 88
4.13–14 295–6
4.17–18 295–6
4.19 88, 121, 295–6, 316
4.19b 121n.106
5.4 88
5.5 147n.27
5.6–8 120n.98
5.7 121n.106
5.8–9 62n.122
5.8–11 115
5.9 115, 120n.98
5.10 120n.98
5.12 287n.22

2 Peter
 120n.104

1 John
 1.1 86, 86n.227
 1.1–2 67, 85–6, 137n.163
 1.1–3 85
 1.1–4 86
 1.2 86
 1.3 67, 86, 123–4
 1.6–8 123–4
 1.7 67, 86
 1.9 67, 67n.146, 86, 123–4, 126n.121
 2.1 123–4
 2.1–2 123–4
 2.4 123–4
 2.4–6 123–4
 3.23 48n.56, 121
 4.1 27n.148, 121
 5.1 121

462 INDEX OF BIBLICAL PASSAGES CITED

1 John (*cont.*)
    5.4–5 120, 326–7, 327n.16
    5.10 68n.151, 121, 354n.123
    5.13 48n.56

2 John
    6–7
    97

3 John
    120n.99
    122–3
    5 289n.30

Jude
    2–3 110n.64
    3 290n.36
    20–1 110
    22 353n.118

Revelation
    1.5 67n.146, 120, 126, 222n.112
    2–3 222n.112
    2.2 120
    2.10 111, 120
    2.13 120
    2.19 111, 120

3.8 120
3.14 126, 222n.112
13.10 111
14.1–5 120
14.2 222n.112
14.4 120, 126
14.6–12 126
14.7 126
14.8 126
14.11 126
14.12 111, 126
15.3 78n.194
19.11 120, 222n.112
20.4 120
21.1–4 88n.233, 115–16
21.1–5 89
21.1–8 121
21.5 115–16, 126
21.6–8 126
21.8 115–16, 148n.29, 152n.49
22.6 126
22.9 126
22.18–19 126
22.20 126

Index of Subjects

For the benefit of digital users, indexed terms that span two pages (e.g., 52–53) may, on occasion, appear on only one of those pages.

Abraham, as model of trust 57, 76–9
    covenant with 51–2
    God's promise to 47–8, 50, 53n.74, 55–7, 63n.129, 73–4, 275
    trust of 51–2, 54n.78, 55–6, 76–7, 79–81, 168n.113, 298–9, 353–4
abuse, trust following 181, 186–8, 191–2, 349–50
    see also 'Daphne and Delius'
Adam and Eve 52–3, 81–5, 146n.21, 195n.202, 224–6, 229, 301
anthropology, optimistic 38, 322–3, 359
anti–ableist reading 35–6, 250–4, 279
apistein 103, 146, 160, 263–4, 359
apistia, apistos 143–53, 153n.52, 164n.99, 169, 171, 181, 191–3, 206, 232–3, 263–8, cf. 266–7, 359
    of followers of Jesus Christ 215, 217, 259, 267
    of Israelites 44n.34, 78n.194, 170–1
apocalyptic 166, 280–1
Audi, Robert 15, 326, 328, 332

Baier, Annette 10–12, 16, 82
beliefs, basic and non–basic 64–5, 93–4, 99, cf. 327–8
    see also 'resurrection belief'
belief, among Christian Platonists 329
    relation to Christian commitment 5–6, 5n.23, 218–19
Berlin, Isaiah 337–40, 359–60
body of Christ, corporate identity as 280–1, 288–9
breastplate of trust 119–20
Breytenbach, Cilliers 127
Brothers, Doris 19–21, 83–4, 93, 216–18, 250, 304

calls of disciples, relation to trust 215–19
care, of God or Christ for creation 32–3, 35, 38, 44, 52–3, 64n.131, 70, 74, 81–90, 131, 133–5, 138–9, 141, 158, 173, 194–5, 198–9, 201–2, 224–9, 281, 320–1, 363–4
    ethics of, see 'ethics of care'
    of creation by the faithful, see 'stewardship'

coherence, as criterion for belief or trust 33, cf. 37–8, 93, 102–3, 105, 108, 112n.75, 233nn.153,154, 233, 327–8, 336–7, 339, 344–5, 346–7, 348, 350, 352
contract, relation to trust 11–12, 23, 52n.71, 57–8, 294–5
correspondence, as basis for belief or knowledge 28–9, 329–30, 334–8, 342, 351, 355–6
cosmic conflict 118–21, 166, 218–19
    See also 'devil', 'evil', 'Satan'
covenant and creation, Hebrew Bible 89–90
    as socio–legal instrument 51–4
    relation to *pistis* 45–64
creation, hope for 32–3, 89–90, 93, 245–6, 319, 362, 367
    see also 'care, of God or Christ for creation'
creator, Christ as, with God 32–3, 85–90, 136–7, 224–9
cry of dereliction 261–3

Dalferth, Ingolf 1–2, 14–15, 326
Daphne and Delius 181–8, 191–3, cf. 280
death, models for significance of 142–3
Dell, Katherine 89–90
devil 115, 120n.98, 206n.48, 211–12, 220n.100, 258–9
    see also 'cosmic conflict', 'evil', 'Satan'
disobedience 50, 80n.198, 83, 146n.21, 147–8
    see also *apistia*
dokein 4–5, 65–6, 328–9
doubt 8, 13–16, 15n.86, 22, 25, 39n.8, 70–1, 83, 93–4, 101–4, 107, 114, 131–2, 140, 199–200, 221, 227–8, 238n.173, 259–60, 263, 278, 322, 326n.14, 343–4, 353–4

ecclesiology 133, 221–2, 319
encheiristic meaning of *en* + dative, see 'in Christ's hands'
encheirizein 282n.2, 295–8
endurance 62–3, 79, 88, 110–12

464 INDEX OF SUBJECTS

entrustedness, cascade of 287, 292, 295, cf. 296
  ethic of 312
  in scriptures 297–8
  of apostles 203, cf. 292, 296
  of Christians 289–92, 296–7, 313–20, 349n.110
  of community members with specific roles 283n.6, 287–9, cf. 292–4, 295–6, 316–17
  of Israel 47n.51, 48n.54, 289, 296
  of Paul 283–7, 296
  of Paul's co-workers 287, 296
  of slaves in parables 292–5
  with responsibility 297
eschatology 32–3, 35, 36, 36–7, 56–7, 59nn.111,112, 59, 88, 91, 104, 109–18, 133, 166, 193–4, 197–8, 201–2, 223, 228n.132, 229–30, 234, 244–6, 278, 282, 285, 291, 294, 304–5, 318–19, 321, 327, 332–3, 358–9
ethical, divine-human trust as 17, 38, 69, 92, 133, 201n.20, 312–19, 344–5, 362
ethics of care 16, 82–3, 295n.50, 315, 339n.77
evil 115, 118–20, 120n.98, 126, 128n.125, 147n.27, 150n.43, 158, 173, 182–4, 186–8, 193, 204, 223–6, 241–2, 252–5, 254n.26, 256n.36, 268, 307–8, 352n.114, 353, 361–2
  See also 'cosmic conflict', 'devil', 'Satan'
executive virtues 316
exemplar(s) of trust 4n.19, 62–3, 75–80, 172–3, 243, 270
  Jesus as 173n.135, 174–80, 192–3, 219–23, 228, 271, 279–80, 361–2
  John the Baptist as 215
  Paul as 62–3
  see also 'Abraham', 'imitation'
ex-offenders, rehabilitated through trust 184–6, 193

faith, scope of, compared with trust 1–2
faithfulness, of Christ to both God and humanity 153–62 and *passim*
  of God 31, 38–50, 55–7, 62, 64–5, 67, 73–4, 78–9, 89–92, 198
  of Israel 43–4, 58n.103, 60, 71, 78–9, 92, 124, 148, 153–4, 202
  See also 'mediator, Christ as'
fear (negatively marked) 8, 22, 25, 37, 93–4, 108n.55, 131–2, 140, 181, 199, 212–13, 250, 254–7, 259–60, 262–3, 278, 322, 349, 354
fideism 1n.3, 114n.81, 163, 326n.14
fides, range of meaning in Latin 4
foundationalism 329–30

genre of gospels 268–9
Gethsemane, trust in 36, 188–9, 261–3, 279–80

gift(s) of the spirit 9, 27–8, 36, 59–60, 74, 102–3, 118, 165–6, 177, 187–8, 286–8, 298–312, 315, 319, 332–3, 347
Godfrey, Joseph J. 13–14, 83n.212, 258n.42
golden ages 31–2, 59–60, 91
glory, hope of 43, 54–5, 87–8, 93, 104, 112–13, 115–16, 153, 166, 169, 226
grace 1, 1n.5, 2n.7, 14–15, 34, 44–6, 49, 52n.71, 55n.89, 58–9, 70, 87–9, 91, 96, 104, 108, 112, 124, 127–31, 133, 153, 155n.65, 156, 160, 163–5, 169–71, 173, 180, 187–8, 243, 284–5, 288–91, 295, 297–9, 299n.55, 327–8, 347

healings, role of trust in 251–5
history, empiricist or 'scientific' 335–8
  role of propositional trust in 338–9
  study of in relation to theology 26–31, 78–80
hoi pisteuontes, hoi pistoi, meaning 97
hope 2–3, 5–8, 13, 18, 21–3, 31–4, 38, 46–7, 49–50, 52–3, 62–3, 65–72, 74–5, 84, 86–7, 89–96, 102–3, 110–19, 131–2, 138, 144–5, 153–5, 159, 166–7, 169, 182, 185–7, 189–90, 192–3, 198, 245–6, 248, 251, 255, 257n.41, 262–3, 268, 277, 279, 281, 292, 295–7, 301, 302n.66, 307–8, 314–16, 318–19, 321–2, 325, 327–8, 332, 347–8, 353, 358–9, 362–3, 367
  See also 'eschatology'
Howard-Snyder, Daniel 333
humanities, knowledge, belief, and trust in 343–5

identity of Jesus Christ in pre-existence, earthly life, death, risen and exalted life 25, 33, 98, 104–7, 109, 139–40, 162–3, 168, 171–2, 245–6, 258–9, 279–80
imitation, of Christ 33, 37, 74, 120, 135–9, 154n.61, 174–80, 188, 190–3, 219n.98, 221–3, 244, 247, 282, 298–9, 319–21, 361–2
  of Paul 115, 175–7, 243, 286–7
  outlies modern typologies of imitation 178–9
  see also 'exemplar(s)'
imperfect trust, adequacy of 35–6, 38, 70–1, 95–6, 163–4, 190, 197n.6, 201–2, 234, 241, 244–6, 251–2, 254, 258–63, 265–6, 278–9, 300, 313–15, 317–18, 321–2, 348, 353–4, 358–9, 362, 367
'in Christ's hands', meaning of *en Christō* 131–2
intersubjectivity 29–30, 216, 234n.155, 334–5, 338, 340, 359–60, 365

justification by faith 163, 280–1

knowledge, divine 29, 32, 38, 64, 71–2, 74n.177, 92–4, 100, 140–1, 154–5, 203–5, 209–10, 215, 218–19, 236n.166, 271, 282n.2, 363–4

INDEX OF SUBJECTS

knowledge of Christ 124, 157, 159, 205, 208, 216–19, 236n.166, 258–9, 285n.16, 327, 356–7
  of God 52–3, 88–9, 95–6, 147–9, 153n.51, 154–5, 164–7, 175–6, 206n.48, 236n.166, 239n.180, 314, 324, 328–34, 345, 354, 356–7, 362–4
  in Greek philosophy 328–9
  in modern philosophy and philosophy of religion 329–31, 334
  in philosophy of science 330

Lazarus, raising of 190–1, 226–7
Lindbeck, George 330, 345
Løgstrup, Knut Eijer 13, 132n.144
Louth, Andrew 338–40, 359–60
love 2n.6, 6–7, 13, 15–16, 29n.157, 31–2, 49, 52n.71, 54n.79, 58–9, 62–3, 69–72, 73n.173, 75n.180, 76, 84, 87, 91, cf. 99, cf. 101–2, 107–8, 110–12, 115, 118–19, 120n.98, 121, 127–9, 134–5, 136n.162, 144–5, 152, 157–8, 160, 164–6, 169, 172, 174n.137, 178n.160, 180, 182, 216n.85, 222–3, 226–7, 248–9, 251, 262n.59, 275n.109, 277, 287–8, 291, 295, 297, 303, 309, 316–17, 321, 331–3, 346, 367
loyal protest, tradition of 27n.147, 64n.133
loyalty 4, 7n.33, 51, 154n.61, 159n.76, 160–1, 175–6, 219n.97, 220, 306, 332
Luther 20, 163, 239n.182, 331

McKaughan, Daniel 15–16, 179n.164, 333
mediator, Christ as 25n.139, 33–4, 37, 61n.119, 98–9, 123–7, 134, 137–8, 143–4, 143n.10, 153n.52, 156n.70, 158–62, 167–8, 173, 180, 189n.189, 192, 194, 196–7, 202, 244, 361–2
  of the covenant 56n.93, 78n.193
  others as 185–6, 202, 243–4, 292, 296, 363
  others, in imitation of Christ 190–1, 271–2, 282
  Paul as 284n.10
messianic age 59–60
messianic titles 229–31, 235–6
Moo, Douglas 89–90
Moses, as paradigm of trust 54n.78, 78–9, 80n.198, 161, 213, 298
music, comparison with theology 342–3
  debates about nature and knowability 340–2
  trust in relation to 343

narrative, in relation to trust 276–7
new creation 45–6, 49–50, 53n.73, 53n.74, 56–7, 58n.103, 59–60, 60n.113, 67, 69, 88n.233, 91–2, 114, 126–7, 133, 143, 145, 161–2, 169, 194–5, 301–2
Newsom, Carol 301

'new thing', God as doing 31–2, 61–2, 95, 196, 243, 319–20
New Testament theology 26–7
nomizein 4n.19, 65–6, 328–9

obedience 36, 58–9, 70, 73n.172, 74n.174, 75, 113n.76, 125, 132, 136, 146n.21, 149–50, 153–5, 158n.73, 160–1, 177, 188–9, 222–3, 233–4, 242–3, 261, 265n.68, 275–6, 279, 281, 284, 297–9, 307–10, 332, 346
oligopistos 201, 212–13, 215, 221, 225–8, 254–5, 259–60, 266n.79
ou pisteuein, see *apistein*

Pace, Michael 12, 15–16
parables of the end time 110–11, 267, 292–5, 310–11, 315
paradidonai 8, 105n.36, 147n.26, 156n.66, 282n.2, 291n.38, 310–11
paratithenai 8, 282n.2, 285n.16, 295–8
parousia, see 'eschatology'
passion narrative, trust in 34, 188–90, 222, 279–80
patience 111–12, 115, 120n.98, 160, 362
perseverance 115, 125, 159n.79, 172, 256–7
phronein 4, 65–6, 328–9
pistis, as fruit of the spirit 27–8, 69, 287–8, 300
  as gift of the spirit 9, 27–8, 36, 59–60, 102–3, 118, 165–6, 177, 187–8, 201n.20, 224–5, 286–8, 298–304, 308, 311, 315, 317n.103, 319, 332–3
  measure of 288–9
  prevalence of in NT 6–7
pistis lexicon, meaning 4, 106–7, 158–9
pistis Christology 98
pistis Christou, pistis Iēsou 55n.86, 126, 154–5, 156n.69, 157–9
pistologists 15
pistos ho logos ('the saying is trustworthy') 1n.1, 125, 210, 290–1, 327–8
power, consequence of *pistis* 78n.193, 298–9, 306–11
  modern concerns with 305
  of spirit, relation to trust 299–300, 311
pre-election 35, cf. 47–8, 85, 86n.224, 88, 120, 126, 187n.184, 205n.42, 206, 235–6, 240–2, 245, 257n.37, 278n.115, 285n.14, 299–300, 361–2
pre-existence of Christ 32–3, 37, 85–7, 88n.232, 89–90, 89n.237, 136–7, 160–2, 168, cf. 196–7, 224, 235–6
promises of God 1–2, 31, 39–65, 67, 73–4, 76–80, 88, 91–5, 113–14, 124, 126–7, 213–14, 273–6, 353–4

INDEX OF SUBJECTS

prophecy, of Jesus, relation to *pistis* 35, 207–8, cf. 210–11, 212, 219
scriptural, as basis for *pistis* 105, 108
prophet, Jesus recognizable in his lifetime as 35, 232–3, 242–3, 361–2
propositional doubt 353–4
propositional scepticism 353–4
propositional trust 36–7, 65–6, 117–18, 227n.129, 324–60 *passim*, 345
  as defence of metaphysical assumptions 351–3
  attitude and action in 326
  definition 325–6
  in history 337–8
  in humanities disciplines 343–6
  in music 343
  in New Testament writings 326–8
  relation to belief and knowledge for Christians 324, 345, cf. 355n.127
  relation to personal trust for Christians 350

Räisänen, Heikki 27, 354–5
reconciliation 34, 49, 86–7, 127, 136, 143–4, 146n.19, 149n.37, 153–63, 168, 171, 187–8, 192, 202, 260–1, 284n.10, 324, 361–3
  see also 'mediation'
resurrection of Jesus as sign 163, cf. 164–7, 321
resurrection belief, complex basis of 99–109
reliability 17, 25, 35, 40n.10, 52n.69, 58n.103, 62n.123, 72–6, 94, 101–2, 114, 140–1, 210–11, 281, 318, 327n.20, 337, 343, 364
reliance, on God 32, 54n.80, 72–4, 92
  on unreliable people 181, 264
  relation to trust 10–13, 14n.73, 24, 41n.18, 72–4, 239n.182, 311–12, 325, 332, 363–4
  see also 'self-trust'
revelation 104, 164–8, 191–2, 237–41, 245, 314
rhetoric and trust 210
risk, in humanities subjects 344–5, 357
  relation to divine–human trust 23–5, 31–3, 38, 41, 50–2, 68–74, 77n.188, 78n.191, 82–4, 86, 92–4, 109, 111–12, 116–19, 123–4, 131–2, 134–5, 140–1, 153–4, 163, 171, 173, 180, 184, 216–17, 254–5, 281–3, 304–5, 311–12, 318–21, 327n.20, 333n.61, 349–53, 355, 361–2
  relation to trust in general 12, 15–16, 22–3, 37, 50–1, 184–6, 216–17, 263, 304, 314, 318–19, 349, 353, 363, 366–7
  see also 'therapeutic trust'
Rizzuto, Ana-Maria 19n.112, 277–8, 339n.76

Satan 75n.179, 119–20, 120n.104, 133, 150n.43, 166, 206n.49, 211–12, 224, 232–3, 267n.80
  see also 'cosmic conflict', 'devil', 'evil'
scepticism 8, 13–14, 22, 25, 37, 93–4, 105–6, 114, 140, 150n.43, 199, 204n.37, 206, 213, 215–17, 220n.100, 233, 244n.191, 257–9, 263, 275–6, 322, 331n.46, 344, 353–4, 364–5
scriptures, Jewish, as source of New Testament ideas about *pistis* 35, 38–40, 46–7, 75–80, 91–2, 136–7, 158–9, 181, 193, 196–7, 202, 212–14, 227–8, 273, 290–1, 297–8, 340, 358
  interpretation of, as basis for *pistis* 33, 64–5, 103, 105, 108, 135, 146, 160, 164–5, 208–10, 212–14, cf. 233, 264–5, 296, 327–8, 336–7, 352
seeing and being seen, as basis for trust 216
self-trust, negative 148–51, 169, 175–6, 184, 191–2, 204, 206, cf. 206n.47, 211–12, 214, 218–19, 220n.100, cf. 233–4, 241–2, 264–5, 338n.73, 359–60, 365
  positive 181, 261–3, 322, 359–60
Sequeri, Pierangelo 1–2, 17, 80n.198, 140, 167n.111, 326, 328
service to God or Christ 44, cf. 47–8, 70–2, 74, 125, 128–9, 132–4, 139–40, 149–50, 175–6, 178–9, 196, 200n.16, 219n.99, 232, 261, 264–5, cf. 267, 275n.109, 279, 284–5, 289n.29, 292–4, 297, 304–10, 316–17, 322–3
Sherman, Steven B. 332–3
shield of trust 119–20
sign, Christ's death as 172–3
  entrustedness of faithful as 319
  see also, 'resurrection as sign'
signs of Jesus, relation to trust 203–6, 212
spirit, charismatic or life-giving 300–1
  connection with prophecy and preaching 308
  evil or unclean 6n.24, 190–1, 216–19, 252–3, 258–9
  faithful can entrust experience of 112
  relationship of charismatic and life-giving in Christian communities 301–5
  relation to *pistis* 27–8, 36, 52n.72, cf. 65n.137, 102–3, 109, 112, 117, 124, 151, 165–6, 187–8, 201–3, 218n.94, 264n.65, 286, 295–6, 298–312
  role in this study 27–8
  trustworthiness and 27n.148
  working through the faithful 128–9
Stendahl, Krister 28–9
stewardship 36, 82–3, 110–11, 115, 117, 139, 175–6, 243, 284–7, 294, 297, 304, 315–17, 320–1

INDEX OF SUBJECTS

suffering 33–4, 142–95 *passim*
  natural 254n.26
supersessionism 61–2
'surpassed', of covenant and law 31–2, 52n.71, 54–8, 91–2, 95–6, 126–7
Swinburne, Richard 15, 331, 357–8

teaching, relation to trust 208–11
telos of law, Christ as 48–9, 126–7
theology, study of in relation to history, *see* 'history'
therapeutic attitudes 316
therapeutic trust 12–14, 23–4, 32, 36–8, 69n.156, 71–2, 92, 140–1, 156, 185–6, 189n.191, 193–4, 221–2, 240n.184, 281, 283, 284n.8, 285, 294–5, 298, 311–12, 319–22, 325n.5, 331n.41, 363, 365n.4
Thomas, doubt of 105–7, 265–6
train journey, as image of atonement 172–3, 177–8, 194
trust, analogy between human and divine–human 25
  as 'bottom-up' attitude 94–5, 347–50
  attitude and action, not always co-existent 4–5, 13–14, 22, 23n.129, 70–1, 111–12, 163–4, 260–1, 263, 293, 316–17, 348–50, 358–9
  growth in 38, 71, 92, 110, 117, 208–9, 213–14, 362
  one-place 10n.44, 22n.126

  propositional, *see* 'Propositional trust'
  relational, definition 311–12, 317–18
  role-specific in Christian communities 283–5, 287–9
  three-place 10–12, 32, 38, 75, 80, 86, 93–4, 217–18, 311–12, 362–3
  two-place 11–13, 32, 38, 80, 83–4, 86, 93–4, 217–18, 311–12, 362–3
  see also 'propositional trust', 'self-trust'
trustworthiness, of God, sometimes distinguishable from 'faithfulness' 39n.8
  of the faithful, *see* 'exemplar, Paul as' 'imitation of Christ', 'imitation of Paul', 'mediator, others, in imitation of Christ' 'mediator, Paul as'
  of writings, *see* 'scriptures', '*pistos ho logos*'
  see also 'faithfulness'
truth, of God 1–2, 17, 41, 45–7, 63n.129, 114, 159, 339–40

Von Humboldt, Wilhelm 335–7

'with Christ', dying and living 168–73, 180, 192
witness, as basis of belief or trust 17, 45, 66n.144, 84–6, 90–1, 100–3, 115, 120, 126, 129–30, 206n.47, 218n.95, 222n.112, 232, 256n.33, 295–6, 299–300, 313, 337
Wolterstorff, Nicholas 15, 332
words, as basis of trust 210–11

The manufacturer's authorised representative in the EU for product safety is
Oxford University Press España S.A. of el Parque Empresarial San Fernando de
Henares, Avenida de Castilla, 2 – 28830 Madrid (www.oup.es/en or product.
safety@oup.com). OUP España S.A. also acts as importer into Spain of products
made by the manufacturer.

www.ingramcontent.com/pod-product-compliance
Lightning Source LLC
Chambersburg PA
CBHW071846290825
31867CB00003B/275